AF599058

# The Treasury of Precious Instructions: Essential Teachings of the Eight Practice Lineages of Tibet

## Volume 16: Mahāsiddha Practice

## The Tsadra Foundation Series

*published by Snow Lion, an imprint of Shambhala Publications*

Tsadra Foundation is a U.S.-based nonprofit organization that contributes to the ongoing development of wisdom and compassion in Western minds by advancing the combined study and practice of Tibetan Buddhism.

Taking its inspiration from the nineteenth-century nonsectarian Tibetan Buddhist scholar and meditation master Jamgön Kongtrul Lodrö Taye, Tsadra Foundation is named after his hermitage in eastern Tibet, Tsadra Rinchen Drak. The Foundation's various program areas reflect his values of excellence in both scholarship and contemplative practice, and the recognition of their mutual complementarity.

Tsadra Foundation envisions a flourishing community of Western contemplatives and scholar-practitioners who are fully trained in the traditions of Tibetan Buddhism. It is our conviction that, grounded in wisdom and compassion, these individuals will actively enrich the world through their openness and excellence.

This publication is a part of Tsadra Foundation's Translation Program, which aims to make authentic and authoritative texts from the Tibetan traditions available in English. The Foundation is honored to present the work of its fellows and grantees, individuals of confirmed contemplative and intellectual integrity; however, their views do not necessarily reflect those of the Foundation.

Tsadra Foundation is delighted to collaborate with Shambhala Publications in making these important texts available in the English language.

# Mahāsiddha Practice

*From Mitrayogin and Other Masters*

The Treasury of Precious Instructions:
Essential Teachings of the Eight Practice
Lineages of Tibet
Volume 16

Compiled by Jamgön Kongtrul Lodrö Taye

TRANSLATED BY
*the Padmakara Translation Group*

Snow Lion

Snow Lion
An imprint of Shambhala Publications, Inc.
2129 13th Street
Boulder, Colorado 80302
www.shambhala.com



Cover art: Detail from thangka "The Kadampa Practice Lineage of Tibetan Buddhism." Collection Eric Colombel. Photo: Rafael Ortet, 2018. © Eric Colombel, New York.



9 8 7 6 5 4 3 2 1

First Edition
Printed in the United States of America

♾ This edition is printed on acid-free paper that meets the American National Standards Institute z39.48 Standard.
♻ Shambhala Publications makes every effort to print on recycled paper. For more information please visit www.shambhala.com.
Snow Lion is distributed worldwide by Penguin Random House, Inc., and its subsidiaries.

LIBRARY OF CONGRESS CATALOGING-IN-PUBLICATION DATA
Names: Kong-sprul Blo-gros-mtha'-yas, 1813–1899, author. | Comité de traduction Padmakara, translator.
Title: Mahāsiddha practice: from Mitrayogin and other masters. Volume 16 / compiled by Jamgön Kongtrul Lodrö Taye; translated by Padmakara Translation Group.
Description: Boulder: Shambhala, 2021. | Series: The Treasury of Precious Instructions: Essential Teachings of the Eight Practice Lineages of Tibet; volume 16 | Includes bibliographical references and index.
Identifiers: LCCN 2020033958 | ISBN 9781611808933 (hardback)
Subjects: LCSH: Spiritual life—Tantric Buddhism. | Tantric Buddhism—Tibet Region—Doctrines. | Tantric Buddhism—India—Doctrines. | Mitrayogi—Teachings. | Siddhas.
Classification: LCC BQ8939.5 .K66 2021 | DDC 294.3/923—dc23
LC record available at https://lccn.loc.gov/2020033958

# Contents

# Foreword

In his vast work *The Treasury of Precious Instructions* (*gDams ngag rin po che'i mdzod*), Jamgön Kongtrul Lodrö Taye, that most eminent of Tibetan Buddhist masters, collected together all the empowerments, instructions, and practices of the eight great chariots of the practice lineages. Not only that, but he himself received the complete transmissions for all the practices, accomplished them including the retreats, and preserved them in his own mind stream. He then passed on the transmissions to his own students and all who requested them.

*The Treasury of Precious Instructions* exemplifies how Jamgön Kongtrul Lodrö Taye's whole life was dedicated to teaching and spreading the dharma, whether it be sutra or mantra, *kama* or *terma*, old or new translation school, free of sectarian bias. Without his supreme efforts, many traditions of Tibetan Buddhism would have been lost.

The teachings of the Buddha have now spread throughout the Western world, and there is a growing need for major texts to be translated into English so that Western dharma students and scholars have access to these essential teachings. I was, therefore, delighted to hear that having successfully published a translation in ten volumes of Jamgön Kongtrul Lodrö Taye's *Treasury of Knowledge* (*Shes bya kun khyab mdzod*), the Tsadra Foundation has embarked on a second major project, the translation of *The Treasury of Precious Instructions*, and I would like to express my gratitude to them.

May their work be of benefit to countless sentient beings.

His Holiness the Seventeenth Karmapa, Ogyen Trinley Dorje
Bodhgaya
February 21, 2016

# Series Introduction

The *Treasury of Precious Instructions* (*gDams ngag rin po che'i mdzod*) is the fourth of the five great treasuries compiled or composed by Jamgön Kongtrul Lodrö Taye (1813–1900), also known as Karma Ngawang Yönten Gyatso, among many other names. Kongtrul was one of the greatest Buddhist masters of Tibet. His accomplishments were so vast and varied that it is impossible to do them justice here. The reader is referred to an excellent short biography in the introduction to the first translated volume of another of his great works, *The Treasury of Knowledge*, or the lengthy *Autobiography of Jamgön Kongtrul*. Even if his achievements had consisted solely of his literary output represented in these five treasuries, it would be difficult to comprehend his level of scholarship.

Unlike *The Treasury of Knowledge*, which is Kongtrul's own composition, his other four treasuries may be considered anthologies. Kongtrul's stated mission was to collect and preserve without bias the teachings and practices of all the lineages of Tibetan Buddhism, particularly those that were in danger of disappearing. The English publication of *The Treasury of Knowledge* in ten volumes and the forthcoming translations of this *Treasury of Precious Instructions* in some eighteen volumes can attest to the success of his endeavor, perhaps even beyond what he had imagined.

*The Treasury of Precious Instructions* is, in some ways, the epitome of Kongtrul's intention. He first conceived of the project around 1870, as always in close consultation with his spiritual friend and mentor Jamyang Khyentse Wangpo (1820–1892). The two of them, along with other great masters, such as Chokgyur Dechen Lingpa, Mipam Gyatso, and Ponlop Loter Wangpo, were active in an eclectic trend in which the preservation of the texts of Tibetan Buddhism was paramount.[1] It was with Khyentse's encouragement and collaboration that Kongtrul had created *The Treasury of Knowledge*—his incredible summation of all that was to be known—and compiled the anthologies of *The Treasury of Kagyu Mantra* and *The Treasury of Precious Hidden Teachings*. This next treasury expanded the scope by aiming to collect in one place the most important instructions of *all* the main practice lineages.

Kongtrul employed a scheme for organizing the vast array of teachings that flourished, or floundered, in Tibet during his time into the Eight Great Chariots of the practice lineages (*sgrub brgyud shing rta chen po brgyad*), or eight lineages that are vehicles of attainment. He based this on a much earlier text by Sherap Özer (Skt. Prajñārasmi, 1518–1584).[2] The structure and contents of that early text indicate that the seeds of the so-called nonsectarian movement (*ris med*) of the nineteenth century in eastern Tibet had already been planted and just needed cultivation. The organizing principle of the scheme was to trace the lineages of the instructions for religious practice that had come into Tibet from India. This boiled down to eight "charioteers"—individuals who could be identified as the conduits between India and Tibet and who were therefore the sources of the practice lineages, all equally valid in terms of origin and comparable in terms of practice. This scheme of eight practice lineages became a kind of paradigm for the nonsectarian approach championed by Kongtrul and his colleagues.[3]

*The Treasury of Precious Instructions* implements this scheme in a tangible way by collecting the crucial texts and organizing them around those eight lineages. These may be summarized as follows:

1. The Nyingma tradition derives from the transmissions of Padmasambhava and Vimalamitra during the eighth century, along with the former's illustrious twenty-five disciples (*rje 'bangs nyer lnga*) headed by the sovereign Trisong Detsen.
2. The Kadam tradition derives from Atiśa (982–1054) and his Tibetan disciples headed by Dromtön Gyalwai Jungne (1004–1063).
3. The Sakya tradition, emphasizing the system known as the "Path with Its Result," derives from Virūpa, Dombhi Heruka, and other mahāsiddhas, and passes through Gayadhara and his Tibetan disciple Drokmi Lotsāwa Śākya Yeshe (992–1072).
4. The Marpa Kagyu tradition derives from the Indian masters Saraha, Tilopa, Nāropa, and Maitrīpa as well as the Tibetan Marpa Chökyi Lodrö (1000?–1081?).
5. The Shangpa Kagyu tradition derives from the ḍākinī Niguma

and her Tibetan disciple Khyungpo Naljor Tsultrim Gönpo of Shang.

6. Pacification and Severance derive from Padampa Sangye (d. 1117) and his Tibetan successor, Machik Lapkyi Drönma (ca. 1055–1143).
7. The Six-Branch Yoga of the *Kālacakra Tantra* derives from Somanātha and his Tibetan disciple Gyijo Lotsāwa Dawai Özer during the eleventh century and was maintained preeminently through the lineages associated with Zhalu and Jonang.
8. The Ritual Service and Attainment of the Three Vajras derives from the revelations of the deity Vajrayoginī, compiled by the Tibetan master Orgyenpa Rinchen Pal (1230–1309) during his travels in Oḍḍiyāna.

The very structure of *The Treasury* thus stands as a statement of the nonsectarian approach. With all these teachings gathered together and set side by side—and each one authenticated by its identification with a direct lineage traced back to the source of Buddhism (India)—maintaining a sectarian attitude would be next to impossible. Or at least that must have been Kongtrul's hope. In explaining his purpose for the collection, he states:

> Generally speaking, in each of the eight great mainstream lineages of accomplishment there exists such a profound and vast range of authentic sources from the sutra and tantra traditions, and such limitless cycles of scriptures and pith instructions, that no one could compile everything.[4]

Nevertheless, he made a good start in *The Treasury of Precious Instructions*, which he kept expanding over the years until at least 1887. The woodblocks for the original printing—carved at Palpung Monastery, where Kongtrul resided in his nearby retreat center—took up ten volumes. An edition of this is currently available in twelve volumes as the Kundeling printing, published in 1971–1972.[5] With the addition of several missing texts, an expanded and altered version was published in eighteen volumes in 1979–1981 by Dilgo Khyentse Rinpoche. Finally, in 1999 the most complete version became available in the edition published by Shechen Monastery, which is the basis for the current translations.[6] The structure of this enhanced edition, of course, still centers on the eight lineages, as follows:

1. Nyingma ("Ancient Tradition"), volumes 1 and 2;
2. Kadampa ("Transmitted Precepts and Instructions Lineage"), volumes 3 and 4;
3. Sakya, or Lamdre ("Path with Its Result"), volumes 5 and 6;
4. Marpa Kagyu ("Precept Lineage of Marpa"), volumes 7 through 10;
5. Shangpa Kagyu ("Precept Lineage of Shang"), volumes 11 and 12;
6. Zhije ("Pacification"), volume 13, and Chöd ("Severance"), volume 14;
7. Jordruk ("Six Yogas [of Kalāchakra]"), volume 15; and
8. Dorje Sumgyi Nyendrup ("Approach and Accomplishment of Three Vajras," also called after its founder "Orgyenpa"), volume 15.

Volumes 16 and 17 are devoted to various other cycles of instruction. Volume 18 mainly consists of the *One Hundred and Eight Teaching Manuals of Jonang*, a prototype and inspiration for Kongtrul's eclectic anthology, and also includes his catalog to the whole *Treasury*.

# Translator's Introduction

*Mahāsiddha Practice*, the sixteenth volume of *The Treasury of Precious Instructions*, contains works that could not be included among those of the eight major schools presented in the earlier volumes—hence their designation as "miscellaneous instructions" (*khrid sna tshogs*). This should not, however, be taken to suggest that they are texts of minor interest, or that they consist of a variety of texts having little in common with one another, or even that they have nothing to do with the eight schools. Indeed, the first text in this volume has everything to do with them: it is a ritual honoring the teachers of all eight lineages, which makes its inclusion at the beginning of this volume entirely appropriate. As for the other texts, they are all concerned with the Indian mahāsiddhas, either conjointly or individually, and two-thirds of the volume is devoted to the works of one mahāsiddha in particular: Mitrayogin, whose profound teachings on introducing the nature of the mind can hardly be considered of minor interest even if they are comparatively less well known.

*Mahāsiddha* means literally "great accomplished being" and in this context refers generally to exceptional tantric practitioners who had gained the highest accomplishment, the realization of the nonconceptual wisdom of Mahāmudrā, the Great Seal. Many of them expressed their attainments in songs of realization, or dohās, examples of which are given in the empowerment in chapter 2. The lives of eighty-four Indian mahāsiddhas were celebrated by Abhayadatta in his *Caturaśītisiddhapravṛtti* in the late eleventh or early twelfth century. This work clearly describes the extent to which some of these dedicated tantrikas eschewed the conventions of the day to seek spiritual advancement in charnel grounds, brothels, and similar supposedly undesirable surroundings. Others followed more conventional lifestyles but used their environments or particular trades to achieve an inner transformation of their minds.

Some of the Indian mahāsiddhas such as Padmasambhava, Nāropa, and Āryadeva were of vital importance in transmitting the Vajrayāna teachings to Tibetan masters who subsequently passed them down through the lineages of the eight major schools, and their teachings are included in the corresponding volumes of *The Treasury of Precious Instructions*. Other great siddhas, like Shāntideva, famous for his composition of *The Way of the Bodhisattva* (*Bodhicaryāvatāra*), and Nāgārjuna, author of the *Root Verses of the Middle Way* (*Mūlamadhyamakakārikā*) and other important treatises, are revered by all schools.

Apart from the first text, which is absent from the Palpung edition and appears to have been inserted into the Shechen edition, the works in this volume can be divided into two principal groups. The first of these consists of four texts featuring the eighty-four mahāsiddhas: an empowerment ritual for conferring the mahāsiddhas' blessings, a sādhana including detailed offering and praise sections, a guru yoga practice that can be adapted to any mahāsiddha of one's own choosing, and finally a series of teachings given by some of these mahāsiddhas to a yakṣhinī in a charnel ground.

The eighty-four mahāsiddhas were not, of course, the only highly realized tantric practitioners in India. Included in the guru yoga in chapter 4 are two sixteenth-century siddhas, Shāntigupta and his disciple Buddhagupta, who visited Tibet and taught Tāranātha. And the second main group of texts, occupying almost two-thirds of this volume, have their origin in the teachings of another mahāsiddha, Mitrayogin (also known as Jagatamitrānanda or Ajitamitrayogin), who lived from the mid-twelfth to the early thirteenth century—rather too late to be included in Abhayadatta's *Lives*. He was one of the few siddhas, as distinct from paṇḍitas, who actually visited Tibet, where he was known as Mitrajoki. The esteem in which he was held by his contemporaries is reflected in one of the texts in this volume where he is referred to as "the eighty-fifth lord of yogis." Kongtrul himself clearly regarded Mitrayogin highly. In the first text in this volume, the eight principal teachers of the Eight Great Chariots are visualized on an eight-petaled lotus, with Guru Padmasambhava in the center of the lotus and the other seven disposed around him: it is Mitrayogin whom Kongtrul asks us to visualize on the unoccupied eighth petal.

Details of Mitrayogin's life and activities emerge as we read through these texts, including an account of his twenty wondrous deeds, which is also to be found in *The Blue Annals*.[1] His tantric teacher is said to have been

Lālitavajra, whose own guru, Tilopa, had such an important influence on the teachings of the Kagyupas.

Aside from Mitrayogin's twenty wondrous deeds, three events in his life are of particular interest to readers of this volume. First, though not necessarily in chronological terms, is the period of practice he undertook in a charnel ground, during which he concentrated on the sādhanas of six tantric deities—Mañjushrī, Avalokiteshvara, Vajrapāṇi, Amitāyus, Tārā, and the Yellow Jambhala—and subsequently received instructions from them in a vision. The empowerment and authorization rituals for these deities, along with the instructions related to their sādhanas, make up the first group of texts in this volume associated with Mitrayogin. However, the only sādhana texts included here are those of Avalokiteshvara and of the protector of these teachings, Draklha Gönpo. All these instructions that Mitrayogin received were kept extremely secret and only transmitted, orally, to one disciple at a time. They were eventually written down, principally by the fourteenth-century Tibetan master Öpak Dorje. Although Mitrayogin visited Tibet, he does not appear to have introduced these teachings to Tibetan masters himself. Precisely when they entered Tibet is not clear, as little seems to be known of the masters in this particular lineage. Mitrayogin's disciple Shrīputra transmitted the teachings to Drakpa Rinchen. The colophon of the text in chapter 12 suggests that it was at this point they were translated, without specifying whether into Tibetan or a different Indian language, and the fact that Drakpa Rinchen (*grags pa rin chen*) is a Tibetan name does not necessarily mean that he was actually a Tibetan, for the other name with which he appears in these texts is Girti Ratna—a Tibetanized spelling of the Indian name Kīrtiratna.[2] Drakpa Rinchen transmitted them to Buddhashrī (another Indian, presumably—the same Buddhashrī with whom Tropu Lotsawa studied in Nepal?). He in turn gave them to the Tibetan Öpak Dorje, who, as has been mentioned, was the first to write them down.

The instructions in these texts include both the generation and perfection stages (*bskyed rim* and *rdzogs rim*, also called the development and completion phases). The former relates to the visualization of the deity and recitation of the corresponding mantra. The latter, in this tradition, includes the practices of sustained calm or calm abiding (*zhi gnas*; Skt. *shamatha*), profound insight (*lhag mthong*; Skt. *vipashyana*), illusory body (*sgyu lus*), dream (*rmi lam*), luminosity (*'od gsal*), the intermediate state (*bar do*), and transference (*'pho ba*). Only the instructions on Avalokiteshvara contain all seven of these.

A second event in Mitrayogin's life, highlighted in the last group of texts, was his vision of Avalokiteshvara (after twelve years practicing his sādhana), in which he received the Mahāmudrā mind teaching *Resting in the Nature of Mind*, a twenty-five-verse poem that introduces the awareness-emptiness nature of the mind and allows gnosis or primordial wisdom (*ye shes*) to blossom. This poem is complemented by a detailed commentary, a text correlating the verses with scriptural sources, a series of notes showing how to put the poem into practice, a guide on how to teach it, a song of experience based on the poem, and a prayer to the lineage masters who transmitted it. The root verses of *Resting in the Nature of Mind* are grouped in the Tibetan *pecha* with a number of other "mind teachings," which in this translation are placed after the series of texts directly concerned with *Resting in the Nature of Mind*. These other teachings comprise a short work on an introduction to the nature of the mind, three sets of three pith instruction introducing the three buddha bodies, and a poem in thirty verses in which Mitrayogin expresses the realization he experienced when he heard *Resting in the Nature of Mind*, followed by an explanation of the latter by Mitrayogin's disciple Jampa Pal. The volume concludes with a pith instruction by Mitrayogin called *Three Quintessential Points* and three texts associated with it: a lineage prayer, a method for putting the instruction into practice, and a recitation text for use in daily practice.

The third important event as far as we are concerned, and of particular significance with respect to his Tibetan heritage and the lineage of *Resting in the Nature of Mind* and other mind teachings, was Mitrayogin's meeting with the Tibetan translator Tropu Lotsawa Jampa Pal (1172?–1236?). Tropu Lotsawa met the great siddha while studying in Nepal with Buddhashrī. Deeply impressed by Mitrayogin, he could not imagine himself returning home without inviting the Indian to visit Tibet. So important was this for him that, unable to accept Mitrayogin's repeated refusals, he attempted suicide, and it was only then that the great siddha finally agreed to join him on his return journey, as is related in chapter 26. Mitrayogin stayed in Tibet for a year and a half, teaching and translating. Before leaving Tibet, he consecrated the land on which Tropu Monastery would be built and a giant statue of the buddha Maitreya erected. Tropu Monastery thus became a center from which his mind teachings spread throughout Tibet, passed down by such realized lineage masters as the omniscient Butön Rinchen Drup (1290–1364).[3]

As with the other volumes in *The Treasury of Precious Instructions*, the texts in this sixteenth volume fall into three general categories: source texts, empowerments, and instructions and practice texts. However, this arrangement is not strictly adhered to, and for the seven empowerments in Mitrayogin's lineage, there are only two corresponding sādhanas, the practices of the other five deities being described in instruction manuals but without recited sādhana texts.

## Acknowledgments

The texts in this volume were translated by Stephen Gethin of the Padmakara Translation Group at the invitation of Eric Colombel and Tsadra Foundation, who have generously and patiently funded this project and many others over the past years. The translation would have been impossible without the help of the lamas who answered numerous questions on difficult points: Jigme Khyentse Rinpoche, Pema Wangyal Rinpoche, Alak Zenkar Rinpoche, Ringu Tulku, Taklung Matrul Rinpoche, Dagpo Rinpoche and Matthieu Ricard, and Khenpo Sönam Tsewang. I am also indebted to my colleagues Drupgyu Anthony Chapman, Elizabeth Callahan, Sarah Harding, Wulstan Fletcher, Helena Blankleder, John Canti, and Greg Seton for their support and help with researching related material. Finally, thanks are due to Nikko Odiseos, Anna Wolcott Johnson, Tracy Davis, and the Shambhala team, whose encouragement and expertise have shaped this book.

# Technical Note

The texts in this volume have not, for the most part, been integrated into the mainstream of the Eight Great Chariots, and they are generally less well known and little commented upon. The resulting paucity of other related texts to refer to has made their translation all the more difficult. We have done our best to seek advice from learned lamas on difficult points, but there remain certain passages whose interpretation remains speculative, particularly those that concern the various teachings on the perfection stage (*rdzogs rim*) and the uncommented quotations from the tantras in chapter 27, expressed in code that only the oral tradition can properly decipher.

This translation was made primarily from volume 16 of the Shechen edition (DNZ) of the *The Treasury of Precious Instructions*. Constant reference was made to volume 11 of the Kundeling printing (DNZ-K) of the Palpung woodblocks, which contains the same texts in the same order, with the exception of the first text, a ritual for venerating the teachers who embody the Eight Great Chariots of the practice lineage. A number of orthographic differences appear in the Shechen edition, and we have generally relied on the Kundeling printing to resolve ambiguities. As we were in the process of completing the translation, we came across an additional printing, clearly made from the same woodblocks, in volume 209 of the 221-volume *Collection of Texts from Dzongsar Lama Lakhang in Derge* (DzLL). It appears to be the only volume from *The Treasury of Precious Instructions* in this collection, which consists for the most part of handwritten *ume* folios. The order of the texts differs slightly from DNZ and DNZ-K. It has not been possible to ascertain when it was printed, but despite the rather dark appearance of the scanned pages, the lettering is often clearer than some of the fainter impressions in the Kundeling printing; it proved useful in confirming our reading of the latter and solving a few questions, notably a missing word indicated by a blank space in the Shechen edition and some faint and indistinguishable marks in the Kundeling printing (which would lead one to suspect that it was printed earlier than the latter and that the woodblock had, in the meanwhile, been damaged). Wherever possible, other source texts have been referred to, and in some cases relied upon, in the translator's quest for accuracy. Numbers in curly brackets { } embedded in the translations indicate the arabic page numbers in the Shechen edition.

A number of texts, or groups of texts, listed in Jamgön Kongtrul's catalog do not appear in the available editions. These have been included in the listed contents of *The Treasury of Precious Instructions* on the Tsadra Foundation website, where they are numbered according to their order in the catalog. In this book, the chapters have been numbered according to their sequence in the Shechen edition, without taking account of these missing texts, resulting in different numberings from the website. An exception, however, has been made for the texts included with the root text of *Resting in the Nature of Mind*: these have been placed in separate chapters at the end of the group of chapters devoted to *Rest in the Nature of Mind* and its associated texts in part 5.

The structural outlines (*sa bcad*) in some of the texts contain inconsistencies, possibly as a result of scribal errors. It proved necessary to edit some of the section headings, using common sense.

The use of square brackets [ ] to signal words that were added by the translator has been restricted mainly to those cases where the Tibetan might be open to different interpretations; the inserted words do not necessarily represent the only interpretation possible. A number of prayers that were sufficiently well known (at least in Kongtrul's time) to be referred to simply by their opening words have been provided in full in the appendix. A few other prayers have been completed in the text, with the added lines enclosed in square brackets. Marginal notes in the Tibetan text are set in small type and enclosed in parentheses.

Romanized Sanskrit words and names have been rendered with the traditional diacritics, with the following modifications: *ṛi*, *ch*, *sh*, and *ṣh* in place of *ṛ*, *c*, *ś*, and *ṣ*. However, standard diacritics have been retained for mantras and text titles. Tibetan and Sanskrit terms that now appear in the Merriam-Webster dictionary have been treated as English words (e.g., lama, chakra, mandala).

Seed syllables (*oṁ*, *āḥ*, *hūṁ*, *hrīḥ*, etc.) are all indicated in lowercase with the exception of the basic vowel *a* (ཨ) which has been capitalized (*A*) in order to prevent any possible confusion with the Tibetan *a chung* (འ) and the English indefinite article.

## PART ONE

# The Eight Great Chariots of the Practice Lineage

This section contains a single text, a sādhana, written by Jamgön Kongtrul himself, venerating the teachers of the Eight Great Chariots. It appears in the first volume of the 2002 Shechen edition of his *Treasury of Extensive Teachings* (*rGya chen bka' mdzod*) and the second volume of the 1975–1976 Paro edition, but not in the Kundeling printing of the Palpung edition of *The Treasury of Precious Instructions*, nor does Kongtrul appear to mention it in his catalog. The colophon suggests that it was extracted from the (or a?) *Treasury of Instructions* (referred to simply as *gdams mdzod*, presumably a contraction for the sake of meter of *gdams ngag rin po che'i mdzod*), yet it is absent from the Palpung (Kundeling) edition of *The Treasury of Precious Instructions*. Did it form part of Kongtrul's original *Treasury of Precious Instructions* and was it subsequently included in the *Treasury of Extensive Teachings* before being returned to the first collection? Its source is all the more mysterious for the fact that in all these editions, the colophon mentions the person who sponsored the printing, which would lead one to imagine that it might have been a stand-alone text at some point or was sponsored separately from the rest of the collection. Whatever the case, its inclusion in the Shechen edition immediately after the last of the fifteen volumes devoted to the eight principal lineages of Tibetan Buddhism could not be more appropriate. Far from being a "miscellaneous instruction" without any properly defined place in the other parts of the collection, it appears to have been inserted here as Kongtrul's concluding homage to the masters of the lineages represented in the preceding volumes. This homage takes the form of a ritual of venerating the teacher (*bla ma mchod pa*), a genre based on the guru yoga or lama sādhana with expanded offering and praise and supplication sections. Kongtrul adapted a ritual veneration of the teacher written five centuries earlier by the Jonang translator Lodrö Palzang.* In the sādhana, the principal masters of the eight lineages are grouped around the central figure of Guru Padmasambhava as described in the visualization section, which is followed by a long and detailed offering section and lineage prayer.

*Jonang Lotsawa blo gros dpal bzang, 1299–1353/4.

# 1. The Source of All Blessings, Accomplishments, and Qualities

*A Ritual for Venerating the Teachers Who Embody the Eight Great Chariots of the Practice Lineage*[1]

{2}

*namo guru buddhaya*
More highly praised than all the merit
Of venerating the buddhas of the ten directions
For kalpas as numerous as the atoms in the universe
Is the act of anointing a pore of one's teacher's body with a drop of sesame oil.
Bowing down to the root and lineage teachers,
Who join us in a single life to the level of the three bodies,
I will arrange the sequence of practices for accumulating merit in relation to them,
Based on the words of the holy beings of the past.

Here is an all-inclusive method for venerating and praying to the teachers of the Eight Great Chariots of the practice lineage, which are famed throughout the Land of Snows. In general, for venerating the teacher, there are two universal methods in the Sutra and Mantra traditions, and there are ritual sequences exclusive to the Mantra Vehicle. {3} The following is an arrangement according to the general way of practicing, common to Sutra and Mantra. There are three sections: (1) preliminaries; (2) main practice; and (3) conclusion.

## I. Preliminaries

### A. Preparations

In the middle of a pleasing shrine room that has been cleaned and beautifully decorated with whatever ornaments are available, carefully set out representations of the body, speech, and mind of the Three Jewels and whatever statues, paintings, or bas-relief images you may have of the lineage teachers described here. Before these, in the middle of an elevated, broad altar covered with fine cloth, place a precious mandala, sprinkle it with perfumed water, and on it draw with colored powder an eight-petaled lotus, with its center. On that arrange piles of grain. Alternatively, if you do not have any colored powder, arrange a single pile of flowers in the middle and around it eight piles, {4} and place them on the altar.

For the offerings, you should set out as many offerings as you possibly can—a hundred, for example. If there are many sets of the two water bowls and five outer offerings, set them out in rows arranged concentrically.[2]

At the very least, it is indispensable to make nine sets of offerings, so prepare eight sets in the eight directions and one row in front. Set up pictures or carved images of the five sense offerings, the [eight] auspicious articles and [eight] auspicious emblems, the seven precious substances, and so on, as convenient. In front place an offering mandala and a round offering torma, together with all kinds of delicious food. Assemble musical instruments, offering grains, and so on.

### B. Preliminaries to the Ritual

Driven by disenchantment with cyclic existence and determination to be free, never part from one-pointed devotion to the Three Jewels embodied in the teacher or from the thought of bodhichitta, with compassion for all sentient beings. In that state, say the refuge prayer three, seven, or more times:

> I and all beings, as numerous as space is vast, take refuge in the sublime, glorious teachers—our gracious root and lineage teachers,
> Who are the very embodiments of all the body, speech, mind, qualities, and activities of all the tathāgatas of the ten directions and the three times,

The sources of the eighty-four thousand sections of the dharma, {5}
The lords of the whole sangha of noble beings.
We take refuge in the Buddha.
We take refuge in the dharma.
We take refuge in the sangha.

In the Buddha, the dharma, and the supreme assembly
We take refuge until enlightenment is reached.
Through the merit of practicing generosity and the like,
May we attain buddhahood for the benefit of beings.

Meditate on the four boundless attitudes.

## Dispelling Obstacle Makers

In an instant, I take on the form of the glorious heruka, the Great Blazing One.
Listen to me, all you hosts of obstacle makers
Dwelling in body, speech, or mind—
Gods, demigods, guhyakas, kataputanas, or whatever.
I, the Glorious Vajra Strength,
Will create the protection circle:
With my body of blazing vajras
I will break apart all those born in the three bodies.[3]
Anyone who disobeys me
Will face nothing but complete destruction. {6}

[Banish them] with the four-*hūṁ* mantra[4] and the fearful sound of the cymbals.

From the emanation and reabsorption of multicolored rays of light
All directions become a tent of blazing vajras,
With, outside, a blazing mass of wisdom fire,
A solid protection circle.
*oṁ vajra cakra rakṣa bhrūṁ hūṁ*

With this, meditate on the special protection circle.[5]

## Blessing the Place and Offerings

Cleanse the place and offerings with the *amṛta* mantra and purify them with the *svabhāva* mantra.

> From the state of emptiness, and from the syllable *bhrūṁ*, the shrine room becomes a multistory measureless palace made of precious materials, perfect and complete with all the attributes. In the middle of it, from the syllable *oṁ* there arise vast, broad containers made of precious substances, in which *hūṁ* syllables melt and become the offerings, made from celestial substances: drinking water, water for bathing the feet, flowers, incense, lamps, scented water, delicacies, and music; the five sense offerings; the seven attributes of royalty; the auspicious articles and emblems; the supreme drink and the sixteen vajra consorts, and so forth—clouds of outer, inner, and secret offerings whose nature is wisdom, taking the form of enjoyable offerings filling the furthest reaches of space and manifesting uninterruptedly until the end of time.
>
> *oṁ sarva bid pūra pūra sura sura āwartaya hūṁ svāhā* {7}
>
> *oṁ vajra argham āḥ hūṁ* . . . and so on, to . . . *oṁ vajra śabda āḥ hūṁ*

Say the *Cloud of Offerings* dhāraṇī and the mantras for blessing the musical instruments.

### II. Main Practice

Begin by visualizing the support for accumulation.

> *oṁ svabhāva śuddāḥ sarvadharmāḥ svabhāva śuddho 'haṃ*
> Dualistic appearances dissolve into the expanse of emptiness.
> From the state of radiant light, the union display manifests:
> The outer container is a perfectly pure buddha field.
> The golden ground, which gives when stepped on and springs
> back when the foot is lifted,
> Is checkered with beryl.

There are mountains of precious substances, with jeweled rock overhangs to give shelter,
Flowing rivers of nectar, endowed with the eight qualities of purity,
Groves of wish-fulfilling trees, multicolored lotuses,
And beautiful manifested birds and deer moving to and fro.
Flowers rain down; the air is full of rays and circles of rainbow light.
On this wondrously arrayed ground, surpassing the imagination,
Is the measureless palace of great liberation, complete with all the attributes,
The displayed dwelling of the sugatas, transcending the three worlds,
The ornament of enlightenment and gateway to perfect liberation—
Boundless and vast as space.
In its center, upon a lion throne, lotus, sun, and moon, one on top of the other,
Is the embodiment of all the buddhas, Padmasambhava. {8}
He is white, tinged with red, smiling peacefully, and wearing the three dharma robes.
On his head is the beautiful paṇḍita's hat, symbolizing the three scriptural collections.
His right hand holds a vajra, his left a skull cup.
He is seated with his two legs crossed, in an expanse of rays of rainbow light.

Above his head are Glorious Vajrasattva,
Vajradhara—the sixth buddha, lord of all the buddha families—
And the primordial protector, Changeless Light,
Seated one above the other. All around
Are the teachers of the mind lineage of the conquerors, the symbol lineage of the vidyādharas,
The hearing lineage of ordinary beings, the lineage of predestined treasure finders, and the rest,
Surrounded by the many assemblies of power-wielding vidyādharas
Of the three yogas and eight classes of accomplishment.

In front of him and to the right, on a mandala of lotus and moon,
Is Jamyang Khyentse Wangpo, holder of the seven transmissions.
He is reddish brown, smiling wrathfully, and of dignified demeanor.
His hands in the gestures of supreme gift and meditation hold vajra and bell
And the stems of utpala flowers, embellished with sword and book.
He is wearing the paṇḍita's hat and the three dharma robes
And is seated with his two legs in the vajra posture.

To the left, in the middle of a seat of white lotus and moon, {9}
Is the charioteer of the five treasuries of the oral and treasure transmissions,
Mañjushrī the Lord of Speech in person, Yönten Gyatso.
He is brilliant white, old in appearance, and sitting erect,
With his two hands crossed at his heart, holding vajra and bell.
His body is beautifully adorned with the paṇḍita's hat and the three dharma robes,
And he is seated, immovable, with his two legs in the vajra posture.

Outside them, at the different compass points, are seats of lotus and moon, and upon them:
In the east, the glorious Lord Atisha,
Brilliant white, wearing the paṇḍita's hat and the three dharma robes.
He displays the gesture of teaching the dharma and is seated cross-legged.
Above his head are the assembled masters of the lineages of the profound view,
Of the extensive activity, and of the practice and blessings.
And he is surrounded by an entourage of Khutsön, Ngok Lekpai Sherap, and Dromtön, the three brothers,[6]
And the *geshe*s of the Kadampa tradition and the assembled masters of the Ancient and New schools.

In the southeast is he who is filled with great love, Sakyapa,
Bald and old-looking, in the attire of a celibate upāsaka.

His two hands in the gestures of supreme giving and teaching the dharma each hold a white lotus.
He is seated in the posture of royal ease. {10}
Above his head are Birvapa and the four translators
And the assembled siddhas of the Path and Result lineage,
And he is surrounded by an entourage of the seven successive Jamyangs
And the holders of the Ngor, Dzong, and Tsarpa teachings.

In the south is Lord Marpa the Translator,
Dark red, with an intense expression, in the white attire of a mantra adept.
He displays the gestures of touching the earth and meditative equipoise, the latter holding a skull cup filled with nectar.
He is seated in the posture of royal ease, with above his head Tilopa,
Nāropa, Maitrīpa, and the masters of the the four doctrinal lineages,
And he is surrounded by an entourage of the four great pillars and Gampopa
And countless siddhas of the four great and eight lesser schools [of the Kagyu tradition].

In the southwest is Lord Khyungpo [Neljor], holder of the five culminant practices,
Wearing the paṇḍita's hat and dressed in the three dharma robes.
He displays the gestures of touching the earth and resting at ease and is seated in the posture of royal ease.
Above his head are the two wisdom ḍākinīs,
The four sublime ones, and the hundred fifty learned and accomplished beings.
He is surrounded by an entourage of the earlier and later successions of jewels
And the assembly of siddhas of the long and short lineages.

In the west is the Indian Jetsun Padampa,
Who is as dark as a rain cloud and is wearing a woolen gown.

He touches the earth and holds a casket of good fortune at his heart. {11}
On his left is Machik Lapdrön, white tinged with red, in ḍākinī's attire,
Her two hands holding ḍāmaru and bell, her two feet performing a dance.
Above his head are his yidam deities, the twelve sugatas,
The thirty-six celestial masters, the fifty siddhas, and the rest.
He is surrounded by an entourage of the masters of the initial, middle, and final transmissions
And the sixteen close spiritual children of the Severance tradition, and so on.

In the northwest is Kunpang Tukje Tsöndru,
Dressed in monk's robes, in constrained physical attitude,[7]
Sitting straight with yogic gaze and legs crossed in vajra posture.
Above his head are the thirty-two Rikden kings,
The greater and lesser Kālachakrapāda, and the assembled masters of accomplishment.
He is surrounded by an entourage of Ra Chörap, Dro Sherap Drak, Tsami Sangye Drak, and the teachers
Of the seventeen main lineage traditions.

In the north is the learned and accomplished Orgyen Rinchen Pal,
Who is heavily built and thoroughly awe inspiring,
Dressed in monk's clothes, touching the earth, and sitting cross-legged.
Above his head are the five classes of wisdom ḍākinīs,
The four learned and accomplished teachers, and so on. {12}
He is surrounded by an entourage of the four supreme incomparable sons
At the head of the host of great beings who have come to successively hold the lineage.

In the northeast is the great siddha Mitrayogin,
In yogi's attire, with a wooden mandala set out in front of him.
In his two hands he holds a hand drum and a skull cup filled with nectar.

Above his head are noble Avalokiteshvara,
Ekajaṭī, and the assembly of accomplished yogis.
He is surrounded by an entourage of the assembled learned and accomplished ones
Of India and Tibet: Shrīputra, Tropu Lotsawa, and others.

Outside all these masters are the Six Ornaments, the Four Great Ones, the Two Marvelous Ones,
The Six Gatekeepers, the Eighty-Two Great Siddhas, and so on—
The assemblies of scholar-siddhas of India and Tibet.
On the right are the buddhas of the three times and the yidam deities,
On the left are the sangha of ḍākas and yoginīs.
Behind is the dharma of transmission and realization, in the form of volumes of the scriptures.
In front are the dharmapālas with an ocean of loyal protectors.
They are all shining with blessings and compassion
In an expanse of masses of rays and circles of rainbow light,
Lovingly considering their faithful disciples,
And present from the beginning as the vajra body, speech, and mind. {13}
From them light streams forth,
Inviting with yearning devotion the mandalas of teachers
In the sky in front.
*vajra samājaḥ.*

Although it is sufficient to simply visualize the support for accumulation, to make it easier for them to appear to beginners' minds, here is the invitation of the wisdom deity.

Three refuges, filling all directions and time, together with your attendants,
Consider us defiled beings with knowledge and love,
And from infinite buddha fields, through unobstructed miraculous displays,
We pray, come to this place and take your seats in the midst of ocean-like clouds of offerings.
Supreme beings, you who possess the eye of nondual gnosis,

Although in the body of truth there is no coming or going,
We pray you, through great compassion, manifest in the form body
And come as the object of offering for those who have faith.
*ratna guru saparivāra vajra samājaḥ*

Sprinkling drinking water:

Excellent protectors, you who have come for the welfare of beings,
Accept this, my offering of drinking water,
And until we have finished venerating you,
Be seated comfortably on a pleasing throne.
*oṁ pravara satkara arghaṃ pratitccha svāhā*

The request to remain:

As we offer you this blissful, spacious [throne]—
An eight-petaled lotus, together with its pistil cup,
Equal in size to the whole billionfold universe— {14}
Pray be seated on it comfortably.
*oṁ padma āsana stvaṃ*

If you wish to make the bathing offering here, collect the bathing materials and make the offerings of bathing, of drying the body, and of raiment in the general fashion. These offerings do not, however, appear in most ritual texts.

Next, begin the practices of accumulation and purification with an homage:

To the peerless teachers, precious buddhas,
Blessed with the body, speech, and mind
Of all the sugatas of the three times and their heirs,
To those immensely kind beings we submit obeisance.

Through their kindness
Great bliss arises in an instant:
To the teachers whose bodies are like precious jewels,
At the lotus feet of those vajra holders, we bow down.

They are treasures of all good qualities:
Simply thinking of their names

Relieves our troubled minds.
To the glorious teachers we pay homage.

Those in whom stainless qualities have fully bloomed
Are the crown ornaments of all beings,
Precious sources of all one could need or want.
To these revered teachers we pay homage.

The light of their realization of what to adopt and avoid
Clears away the gloom of all beings' ignorance. {15}
To these sublime and spotless suns,
To these revered teachers, we pay homage.

The cooling rays of their merit and wisdom
Make the garden of benefit and happiness blossom.
To these sublime and purest moons,
To these revered teachers, we pay homage.

The sublime nectarous medicine of their sacred teachings
Rids us of the illness of defilements and suffering.
To these sublime and skilled physicians of beings,
To these revered teachers, we pay homage.

They are great vessels of means and wisdom
Carrying us across the ocean of existence and peace.
To these sublime and powerful guides of beings,
To these revered teachers, we pay homage.

Protecting us from every kind of harm,
They bring us infinite benefit.
To these loving protectors, the only friends of beings,
To these revered teachers, we pay homage.

Truth body teacher, unfabricated, unelaborated,
Enjoyment body teacher, great bliss, lord of dharma,
Manifestation body teacher, born from a lotus—
To the vajra holder, embodiment of the three bodies, we pay homage.

Display of the union of the spontaneously present nature, uncompounded radiant light,
And the unfabricated primordial purity,
To the teachers of the manifold lineages—those of mind, symbol,
Hearing, treasure, and the rest—we pay homage. {16}

Having trained their minds through the paths of the three kinds of beings,
They set infinite sentient beings in happiness.
To the teachers of the Kadampa lineage,
Glorious Jowo Atisha and the others, we pay homage.

With the pith instructions of the hearing lineage on the three appearances and the three continua,
They dissolved the four pulsations into the central channel and gained the supreme accomplishment.
To the teachers of the lineage of Path and Result,
Lord Virūpa and the others, we pay homage.

When the conditions of energy and mind coincided in the vajra body,
They realized the wisdom of the four joys, the dance of bliss and emptiness,
The union clear light, free of coming and going.
To the teachers of Marpa's doctrinal lineage we pay homage.

Training their minds with the profound practices of the illusory body and dream,
They attained mastery in the union Great Seal.
To the teachers of the Shangpa Kagyu lineage,
The scholar-siddha Khyungpo Neljor and the others, we pay homage.

Training their minds through the path of the connection of means and wisdom,
They realized outer and inner unfavorable conditions as the great body of truth.
To the teachers of the Pacification lineage,
The venerable Indian Padampa and the others, we pay homage.

Training their minds in the meaning of there being nothing to purify,
Through the conduct of even taste, they directly cut through whatever arises. {17}
To the teachers of the Severance tradition,
Machik Lapdrön and the others, we pay homage.

With the vajra yoga comprising threefold motionlessness,
They realized the ten signs of purity of energy and mind.
To those who trained in the path of avadhūtī and dwell in the state of clear light,
To the teachers of the lineage of the Six Applications, we pay homage.

From their training their beings with the vajra point of the body,
Through the vajra point of speech, the energies and mind entered the central channel,
And with the vajra point of the mind they accomplished the wisdom body.
To the teachers of the lineage of approach and accomplishment we pay homage.

Training their beings in the meaning, beyond bondage and liberation,
They realized the innate state of clear light, free of coming and going.
To the teachers of the lineage of *Resting*,
Venerable Mitrayogin and the others, we pay homage.

To him who held all the blessings of the Eight Great Chariots of the practice lineage
And the words and meanings of their instructions,
Elucidating once more the precious teachings in their entirety—
To Jamyang Khyentse Wangpo we pay homage.

To him who propagated the entire transmissions of explanation and composition,
The gem-like, nonsectarian treasure of the profound instructions of the oral and treasure lineages,

To the omniscient dharma lord, champion of the Five Treasuries, {18}
To the lord of speech, Yönten Gyatso, we pay homage.

Cloud of the wheel of inexhaustible ornaments, the three secrets
Of the primordial buddha, lord of all the buddha families,
Magical net of emanations responding to the aspirations of beings—
To the root and lineage teachers we pay homage.

To the unsurpassable Teacher, precious Buddha;
The unsurpassable protection, precious dharma;
The unsurpassable guides, precious sangha—
To the Three Jewels, our refuge, we pay homage.

To those who are perfectly described in the six classes of tantra
Of Kriya, Charya, Yoga, Creation, Completion, and Great Perfection,
Raining down accomplishments, appearing in peaceful and wrathful forms—
To the hosts of yidam deities we pay homage.

To those who, from the supreme and indestructible sacred places,
Through compassion endowed with preternatural knowledge and miraculous power,
Unforgettingly care for practitioners like their own children—
To the host of ḍākinīs of the three places we pay homage.

To the lords of magical emanation and preternatural knowledge,
Keeping watch and perfectly guarding
The treasure store of the precious teachings—
To the adamantine dharma protectors we pay homage. {19}

To those who, through their ocean-vast accumulation of merit from former generosity,
Won longevity, riches, and power in abundance
And rain down wealth upon practitioners—
To the yakṣhas and treasure guardians we pay homage.

To all those worthy of homage
We bow down with bodies
Numerous as the atoms in the universe.
Constantly and with the greatest faith, we pay homage.
*oṁ guru sarva tathāgata kāya vāka citta praṇamena bhandhanaṃ ka ro mi*

All this comprises the homage. Next, for the offerings and praise there are four sections: outer, inner, secret, and ultimate. First, the outer, material offerings:

All kinds of flowers, real and imagined,
Mandaravas, utpalas, water lilies, and others,
Beautifully colored, perfectly shaped, and sweetly scented,
We offer to the host of glorious teachers, our supreme refuge.
*oṁ ratna guru saparivāra vajra puṣpe pūja megha samudra sapharaṇa samaye hūṁ*

All kinds of incense, real and imagined,
With fine ingredients, smelling sweetly fragrant,
Aloe, the finest sandalwood, and others,
We offer to the host of glorious teachers, our supreme refuge.
*oṁ ratna guru saparivāra vajra dhūpe pūja megha samudra sapharaṇa samaye hūṁ*

All forms of light, real and imagined,
Shining splendidly, clearing away the darkness, lighting everything, {20}
The light of lamps, the sun and moon, the body's light, and others,
We offer to the host of glorious teachers, our supreme refuge.
*oṁ ratna guru saparivāra vajra āloke pūja megha samudra sapharaṇa samaye hūṁ*

All sublime perfumes, real and imagined,
Sweet scents that feel blissful when applied,
Camphor, musk, and other satisfying scents,
We offer to the host of glorious teachers, our supreme refuge.
*oṁ ratna guru saparivāra vajra gandhe pūja megha samudra sapharaṇa samaye hūṁ*

All kinds of food, real and imagined,
Attractive, nutritious, and delicious to taste,
Scented rice and sugar, berry juice, and other treats,
We offer to the host of glorious teachers, our supreme refuge.
*oṁ ratna guru saparivāra vajra naividye pūja megha samudra sapharaṇa samaye hūṁ*

All musical instruments, real and imagined,
Deeply inspiring, melodious to the ear,
Drums, conches, cymbals, and lutes,
We offer to the host of glorious teachers, our supreme refuge.
*oṁ ratna guru saparivāra vajra śabda pūja megha samudra sapharaṇa samaye hūṁ*

These offerings are followed by a praise:

Wholly rid of every kind of fault,
Possessed of every excellent quality,
Sources of all benefit and happiness, glory and prosperity,
Glorious teachers, to you we give praise.

In order to mature and liberate beings,
You manifest in the form of guides,
Embodiments of all the buddhas of the three times. {21}
Glorious teachers, to you we pay homage.

Your bodies transcend flesh and bone,
Bodies that are wisdom manifesting as form—
Seen with the eye of faith, they are sublime.
Lords of enlightened body, to you we bow.

Spontaneously and effortlessly,
With the sixty expressive qualities of speech
You teach all subjects, profound and vast.
Lords of enlightened speech, to you we bow.

Although free of the elaborations of knowing and something to be known,
Your minds illuminate the mandala of knowledge.
Manifold treasures of the compassionate powers of retention and eloquence,
Lords of enlightened mind, to you we bow.

Were all beings to relate just a few of your qualities
For kalpas long, they would never be finished,
So endless are your vision, clairvoyance, miraculous powers, and the rest.
Lords of enlightened qualities, to you we bow.

If seeing you, hearing you, thinking of you brings benefit,
No need to mention being freed by following you.
You act spontaneously, unceasingly.
Lords of enlightened activity, to you we bow.

Making offerings that have no owner:

In a pure buddha field, where glory and riches abound,
We offer to the teachers all the perfect buddha fields
Filled with buddhas and bodhisattvas
With infinite retinues, qualities, and activities. {22}

On the vast and solid mandala of the four elements,
We offer to the teachers the perfect universe,
Beautifully laid out and adorned with Mount Meru, the continents, and surrounding ocean,
Filled and heaped up with the glory of everything animate and inanimate.

The clear sky enriched with the sun and moon and stars,
Beautified with rainbows, mists, and clouds,
Accommodating everything, more lustrous than any jewel—
We offer to the teachers the perfect realm of space.

Precious mountains, source of everything desired,
Forested slopes of blossoming medicinal plants, snow mountains, and others,
Perfectly shaped, massive abodes for beings—
We offer to the teachers all perfect mountains.

Clear streams flowing in waves,
Lakes and pools filled with water having the eight perfect qualities,
Pleasing, free of cloudiness, quenching every thirst—
We offer to the teachers all perfect and abundant waters.

Woodlands, plains, and valleys, where life is easy and there are no distractions,[8]
Mansions with encircling moats, estates, and so on,
Filled with riches that give pleasure and delight— {23}
We offer to the teachers all perfect dwelling places.

Pearls and crystals, conches, silver and gold,
All sorts of precious materials fulfilling all desires,
And all the best medicines, potent in the curing of disease—
Saffron, *giwang*,[9] and sandalwood, white or red—we offer.

Tasty and nutritious sustenance as well,
Cereals, grass, vegetables, and other crops,
In short, all the riches and prosperity worth offering in the world
We take in our imagination and offer to the peerless teachers.

Lords of the three worlds, Brahmā, Indra,
Rulers like the universal king and nāga lords,
Queens and royal heirs, and others with extensive power—
We offer all the marvelous rulers of beings.

Well-bred, wealthy ministers and householders,
Their sons and daughters singing lovely songs,
Handsome, soft-spoken, upright, and well attired—
We offer to the teachers all kinds of fine people.

Poised on hillsides, snow lions and buffaloes,
Roaming through the valleys, antelope and deer,
Strong and healthy, steady in their gait— {24}
We offer to the teachers beautiful wild animals.

Forested hills echo to mynahs' and cuckoos' calls;
Swans and cranes adorn the land,
With beautiful songs and plumage and dancing ways—
We offer to the teachers all kinds of lovely birds.

In short, the offerings and beings that dwell
In all the lovely places in the world—
All those that are owned and have no owner
We take in our imagination and offer to the teachers, dharma lords.

All that is perfect in samsara and beyond
Arises from the sacred dharma,
And that in turn has come from you.
Source of benefit and happiness, to you we give praise.

With omniscience of the nature and multitude of things,
You eliminated obscurations related to defilements and knowledge
And thus became the chief of humankind.
Perfect buddha, to you we give praise.

Sublime dharma realized in your mind,
Transmitted dharma taught as its compatible cause—
Supreme avenue to complete freedom,
Precious sacred dharma, to you we give praise.

You who have realized the natural clear light
And are free of all dualistic thought— {25}
Sublime field for gaining merit,
Chief of supreme assemblies, to you we give praise.

Rid of all the fetters of desire,
You observed the three trainings without stain.

Chief of monks who wear the saffron robes,
Supreme son of the Shākyas, to you we give praise.

With the sublime thought of emptiness and compassion
You strove to benefit others all together.
Father of bodhisattvas, the buddhas' heirs,
Loving warrior, to you we give praise.

By training on the path of empowerment and liberation,
You mastered the yogas of the two phases.
Lord of all awareness holders,
Buddha Vajradhara, to you we give praise.

Begin the offering of the body and offerings manifested by the mind with an elaborate or condensed mandala offering, as appropriate, reciting the traditional lines and making the offering as many times as possible.

In order to venerate the Three Jewels and to benefit beings
We make a perfect offering of our merit, wealth, and our own bodies
To you, Supreme Being, considering ourselves as your servants.
Whatever your instructions, we will fulfill them all.

On the vast and spotless ground of beryl,
We offer a sublimely beautiful measureless palace,
With walls, domes, and lattices of gold and silver, {26}
Held up by jeweled columns, and of vast extent;

Decorated on top with canopies, victory banners, parasols, and the like,
The walls adorned with drapery of fluttering strips of silk,
The floors magnificent with cushioned thrones and seats—
In this we offer every perfect bed and necessity for sleep.

Saffron-colored dharma robes, the victory banners of liberation,
Broad spreads of five-colored cloth, light and soft,
Fine and fragrant cotton from Benares, and the like—
All kinds of perfect raiment we offer to the teachers.

The crown ornaments of the five families, silken headdresses,
Pearl necklaces, and strings of gems,
Jeweled ornaments, golden bracelets, and the like—
All perfect adornments we offer to the teachers.

Riches produced from the glory of many merits,
The precious wheel, jewel, queen, and minister,
The elephant, supreme horse, and general—
All the precious attributes of royalty we offer to the teachers.

Riches that fulfill all one's needs,
Groves, swords, mansions, bedding,
Divine garments, snakeskins, and shoes— {27}
All the seven semiprecious articles we offer to the teachers.

Riches that bring happiness and virtue to all beings,
Eternal knots, wheels, lotuses, victory banners,
Parasols, vases, white conches, and golden fish—
All the eight auspicious symbols we offer to the teachers.

In short, we offer bountiful cows, wish-fulfilling trees,
Spontaneous harvests, wish-fulfilling gems,
The elixir of immortality, food with a hundred tastes, and the like—
All the most perfect and abundant riches we offer to the teachers.

Through the union of emptiness and compassion
You attained sublime nirvana,
Dwelling in neither extreme—existence or peace.
To you, supreme refuge, we give homage and praise.

Completing the ten transcendent perfections,
You mastered the channels and winds in the twenty-four places
And thus brought to a halt the twelve links.
To you who completed the ten levels we give praise.

Not existent, not nonexistent,
Neither both nor neither

Is the expanse of reality, pure and without taint.
Unelaborated body of truth, to you we give praise.

Radiant and glorious with the major and minor marks,
You eternally teach the dharma of the Supreme Vehicle
To beings to be trained in pure buddha fields. {28}
Body of perfect enjoyment, Great Bliss, to you we give praise.

Through boundless buddha manifestations
To match the attitudes of different kinds of beings,
You content all beings with benefit and happiness.
Body of manifestation, skilled in means, to you we give praise.

For all the form body's diverse manifestations,
Its nature never changes.
It is the wondrous, inexpressible state of union.
Body of the essential nature, to you we give praise.

With the eight consciousnesses transformed
And all defilements and obscurations eliminated,
You are totally free of the five aggregates.
Lord of primordial wisdom, to you we give praise.

Possessing in your mind the four perfect knowledges,
With the ten strengths you overcome the hordes of demons
And with the four fearlessnesses you teach the dharma.
Sovereign of qualities, to you we give praise.

In your conduct, realization, wisdom,
And activities, you have eighteen buddha qualities
That are not shared with others.
Incomparable holy being, to you we give praise.

After this offering and praise, proceed to the inner offerings:

All sublime forms of different shapes and colors worth offering {29}
In the countless worlds in the ten directions,

Mentally emanated as goddesses of most exquisite form,
We offer to the lords' unobscured vajra eyes.
*oṁ ratna guru saparivāra rupa kāma guṇa pūja āḥ hūṁ*

All sublime sounds worth offering, embraced and not embraced
[by consciousness]
In the countless worlds in the ten directions,
Mentally emanated as goddesses of most exquisite sound,
We offer to the lords' unobscured vajra ears.
*oṁ ratna guru saparivāra śabda kāma guṇa pūja āḥ hūṁ*

All sublime scents blended together
In the countless worlds in the ten directions,
Mentally emanated as goddesses of most exquisite fragrance,
We offer to the lords' unobscured vajra noses.
*oṁ ratna guru saparivāra gandhe kāma guṇa pūja āḥ hūṁ*

All sublime-tasting offerings of food and drink
In the countless worlds in the ten directions,
Mentally emanated as goddesses of most exquisite taste,
We offer to the lords' unobscured vajra tongues.
*oṁ ratna guru saparivāra rasa kāma guṇa pūja āḥ hūṁ*

All sublime physical feelings, related to sentient beings or
otherwise,
In the countless worlds in the ten directions,
Mentally emanated as goddesses of the most exquisite touch,
We offer to the lords' unobscured vajra bodies.
*oṁ ratna guru saparivāra sparśe kāma guṇa pūja āḥ hūṁ*

Drafts that make one drunk with untainted bliss,
The five fleshes that give one strength,
The five nectars, treasures of immortality— {30}
All sublime secret substances we offer to the teachers.
*guhya pūja āḥ hūṁ*

From union with the four mudrās,
The experience of the sublime, unchanging coemergent bliss

Develops the untainted aggregates, constituents, and
 senses-and-fields.
This, the great, most secret offering, we offer to the teachers.
*anurakto pūja āḥ hūṁ*

To you who possess the vajras of body, speech, and mind,
The true union of means and wisdom
In which bliss and emptiness are inseparable—
Glorious protectors of beings, to you we pay homage.

The aggregates of your body are the five buddhas;
The elements are the five mothers, female buddhas;
Their union is the coemergent vajra body.
Glorious protectors of beings, to you we pay homage.

Your sense organs are the male bodhisattvas;
The six sense objects are the assembly of female bodhisattvas;
Their union is the coemergent vajra body.
Glorious protectors of beings, to you we pay homage.

Your limbs are the wrathful conquerors;
Your activities are the ten female wrathful deities;
Their union is the coemergent vajra body.
Glorious protectors of beings, to you we pay homage.

The constituents of your body are ḍākas;
The stationary channels are the assemblies of ḍākinīs;
Their union is the coemergent vajra body.
Glorious protectors of beings, to you we pay homage.

The major winds are the five fathers;
The elements are the five mothers; {31}
Their union is the coemergent vajra speech.
Glorious protectors of beings, to you we pay homage.

Your mind is the nature of primordial wisdom;
The object that appears to it is the expanse of reality;

Their union is the coemergent vajra mind.
Glorious protectors of beings, to you we give praise.

The secret offering and praise:

Enchantingly beautiful, adorned with the major and minor marks,
And blue in color is she who makes the vina sound,
And hosts of many lovely maidens just like her.
With many such pleasing offerings, delightedly we venerate.
*oṁ vīni vajrini āḥ hūṁ*

Enchantingly beautiful, adorned with the major and minor marks,
And yellow in color is she who makes the flute resound,
And hosts of many lovely maidens just like her.
With many such pleasing offerings, delightedly we venerate.
*oṁ vaṃse vajrini āḥ hūṁ*

Enchantingly beautiful, adorned with the major and minor marks,
And blue in color is she who makes the clay drum sound,
And hosts of many lovely maidens just like her.
With many such pleasing offerings, delightedly we venerate.
*oṁ muraje vajrini āḥ hūṁ*

Enchantingly beautiful, adorned with the major and minor marks,
And red in color is she who makes the round drum sound,
And hosts of many lovely maidens just like her.
With many such pleasing offerings, delightedly we venerate.
*oṁ mṛtaṃgi vajrini āḥ hūṁ*

Enchantingly beautiful, adorned with the major and minor marks,
And red in color is she who displays the gesture of explanation,
And hosts of many lovely maidens just like her.
With many such pleasing offerings, delightedly we venerate.
*oṁ hasya vajrini āḥ hūṁ*

Enchantingly beautiful, adorned with the major and minor marks,
And blue in color is she who displays the gesture of grace, {32}

And hosts of many lovely maidens just like her.
With many such pleasing offerings, delightedly we venerate.
*oṁ lāsya vajrini āḥ hūṁ*

Enchantingly beautiful, adorned with the major and minor marks,
And green in color is she who sings the sweetest songs,
And hosts of many lovely maidens just like her.
With many such pleasing offerings, delightedly we venerate.
*oṁ girti vajrini āḥ hūṁ*

Enchantingly beautiful, adorned with the major and minor marks,
And yellow in color is she who performs a beautiful dance,
And hosts of many lovely maidens just like her.
With many such pleasing offerings, delightedly we venerate.
*oṁ nṛti vajrini āḥ hūṁ*

Enchantingly beautiful, adorned with the major and minor marks,
And white in color is she who holds a vase of flowers,
And hosts of many lovely maidens just like her.
With many such pleasing offerings, delightedly we venerate.
*oṁ vajra puṣpe vajrini āḥ hūṁ*

Enchantingly beautiful, adorned with the major and minor marks,
And blue in color is she who holds a censer of incense,
And hosts of many lovely maidens just like her.
With many such pleasing offerings, delightedly we venerate.
*oṁ vajra dhūpe vajrini āḥ hūṁ*

Enchantingly beautiful, adorned with the major and minor marks,
And red in color is she who holds a brightly shining lamp,
And hosts of many lovely maidens just like her.
With many such pleasing offerings, delightedly we venerate.
*oṁ vajra āloke vajrini āḥ hūṁ*

Enchantingly beautiful, adorned with the major and minor marks,
And green in color is she who holds a vessel of scented water,
And hosts of many lovely maidens just like her.
With many such pleasing offerings, delightedly we venerate.
*oṁ vajra gandhe pūja āḥ hūṁ*

On the spotless ground of the essence of the sugatas
Soaked with the pure water of the two bodhichittas
And strewn with the flower petals of the ten virtuous deeds,
We offer thick clouds of incense, the purity of the three vows.

Rows of the precious lamps of preternatural vision and
knowledge, {33}
The sublime scent of the four pure states filling all the air,
The delicious festive food of the nine absorptions piled up,
We offer with the sweet music of explanation, debate, and
composition.

A mandala of four elements—the two stages of liberation,[10]
Decorated with the mountain and continents—the thirty-seven
elements for enlightenment,
The brightly shining sun and moon of emptiness and compassion,
We offer, surrounded by the ring of the two accumulations.

The open treasure vase of the ten powers (over life and so on),
The growing spontaneous crop of the five paths and ten levels,
The heavily laden great wish-fulfilling tree of the ten transcendent
perfections,
We offer, with the bountiful cow of the four ways of gathering
disciples.

Flowing robes and dangling ornaments—memory, eloquence, and
the major and minor marks;
The five pleasures displayed—the untainted aggregates;
The sublime and precious royal attributes—the seven noble riches,
We offer with the auspicious articles, the eight perfect freedoms.

Hoisting the victory banner of the ten strengths topped with the
four buddha bodies,
Twirling the precious white parasol of the four fearlessnesses,
Raising the multicolored standard of the eighteen distinctive
qualities,
And wafting the fan of the powers of perceptual limitlessness and
domination, we offer. {34}

The dancing ḍākas of the sixteen joys,
Resplendent with the two phases, the glory of the secret mantras,
We offer with beautiful wisdom consorts, the sixteen emptinesses,
Perfectly endowed with many expressions of bliss-emptiness.

We offer the universal monarch of the supreme accomplishment,
Adorned with the ornaments of the eight great siddhis,
Lord of the glory of the eight qualities of mastery,
Surrounded by the excellent retinue of the four activities.

And all the qualities, as well, of elimination and realization
Of the ground, path, and result of the three vehicles
We take and manifest with devoted minds
And offer to the teachers, the dharma kings.

Your body has no hollow, empty space,
And neither has it flesh or bones or blood.
To you who reveal your body
Like a rainbow in the sky we bow.

Your body has no sickness or uncleanliness;
Thirst and hunger do not occur.
And yet, to engage with the world,
You display worldly deeds. To you we bow.

Like the moon's reflection, you cannot be grasped.
Nowhere do you dwell in any phenomenon.
Free of pride, you do not abide. {35}
To you who are beyond concepts we give homage and praise.

You do not go, you do not stay, nor likewise sleep.
In all your conduct
You settle constantly in evenness.
To you who are beyond concepts we give homage and praise.

With the illusion-like concentration
You manifest great miracles
While evenly remaining in undiversified absorption.
To you who are beyond concepts we give homage and praise.

Totally liberated from the three worlds,
You are equal to space,
Untainted by desires.
To you who are beyond concepts we give homage and praise.

You do not take the support of aggregates
Or constituents or senses-and-fields
And are freed from all mistaken ways.
To you who are beyond concepts we give homage and praise.

Without discursive and conceptual thoughts,
Your mind does not dwell anywhere.
Your mind is inconceivable.
To you who are beyond concepts we give homage and praise.

Just as space has no fixed place,
Has no elaboration, nor any fear,
Your mind is equal to the sky.
To you who are beyond concepts we give homage and praise.

The ultimate offering and praise:

The view of all beings as being like the moon's reflection, {36}
The correct hearing of sounds as like an echo,
The mind seen as like a desert mirage,
And thus food and drink as like the sky;
Smells smelled as like a flower growing in space,
The mind pervading all like the sun and moon,
Correct abiding like the highest mount,
Things dreamed, like maidens in a dream,
Conventions expressed like illusions that trick the eye,
Coemergent bliss arising, likewise
The inconceivable mind, devoid of the nature of existence,
Arising constantly—this, the supreme path of the sugatas, we offer.

The meaning of the natural state, profound, peaceful, unelaborate,
Is both appearance and emptiness and neither.
Wonder! You hold the view free of thinking, "This is it."
Display of coemergent great bliss, to you we bow.

The inexpressible, inconceivable nature
Is the experience of bliss, bliss-emptiness devoid of grasping.
Wonder! You stay in relaxed meditation, free of effort.
Display of coemergent great bliss, to you we bow. {37}

The radiant nature free of the activity of avoidance or adoption
Is pure and free from the adventitious stains of dualistic beliefs.
Wonder! You hold the fruit, the spontaneously present nature.
Display of coemergent great bliss, to you we bow.

Next, for the remaining sections, begin, if you wish, by reciting three times the general confession, "Teacher, great vajra holder . . ."

From time without beginning,
Under the influence of karma and defilements,
We have, with body, speech, and mind,
Committed deeds of evil nature
And transgressed the three vows:
Deeply regretting all these faults,
In the presence of those who are worthy of veneration,
We confess them, determined not to repeat them in the future.

We rejoice in the marvelous activities of the teachers
And in all the virtuous deeds
Of the buddhas, bodhisattvas, solitary realizers,
Arhats, and ordinary beings.

In order that all beings be matured and liberated,
We exhort the teachers and buddhas
To turn the wheel of dharma,
The profound and extensive teachings.

Folding our hands, we pray to them
To not pass into nirvana, but remain forever,
For as long as there are sentient beings in existence,
And to work for the benefit of all beings. {38}

Until we reach the heart of enlightenment,
We will take refuge, constantly and with respect,

In the sublime teachers, the Buddha,
The dharma, and the noble sangha.

In order to attain perfect enlightenment
For the benefit of all sentient beings,
We will arouse the mind intent on enlightenment
And will follow the ways of the bodhisattvas.

Through the merit of this virtuous deed
And other virtues all added together,
May we soon attain perfect buddhahood
For the benefit of all sentient beings.

As did the buddhas and bodhisattvas,
So too will we, following them,
Fully dedicate all the merit
Of this and other virtuous deeds.

If you wish to repeat your vows, take the twenty-eight sacred commitments with "*oṁ* Lord of yogis . . ."[11] and the vows of the five families with "Just like all the buddhas, past, present, and to come . . . ."[12] To resume these, repeat three times:

Just as the buddhas and bodhisattvas of the past
And the ocean-like assemblies of vidyādharas and ḍākinīs
Kept the supreme inner, outer, and secret commitments
And an infinite ocean of vows, {39}
So too will we, having entered the great path,
Henceforth keep these vows to benefit all beings.

Next, recite whichever prayers you can of the lineage prayers in the empowerments and instructions of each of the Eight Great Chariots of the practice lineage and the hagiographic prayers of the principal lineages. If you do not know them or do not have time, say the following condensed prayer:

To the buddhas and bodhisattvas of all the directions and times,
Who manifest in similar form to bring benefit
For us, the beings of the decadent age who are without protector—
To the teachers, true buddhas, we pray.

To Samantabhadra, Vajrasattva, Garap Dorje, Shrī Simha,
Padmākara and the twenty-five disciples—king and subjects,
So, Zur, Nub, and Nyak, the one hundred treasure revealers, and
the others—
To the vidyādharas of the Ancient Translations we pray.

To glorious Dīpaṃkara, and Khutsön, Ngok Lekpai Sherap, and
Dromtön,
The three brothers, and Tsongkhapa, Mañjushrī in person,
To the spiritual friends who hold
The Old and New Kadampa traditions we pray.

To the glorious protectors of the dharma, the five forefathers of
the Sakya,
Ngorchen, Dzongpa, and the Tsarchen father and sons,
And the other scholar-siddhas who came successively to hold their
lineage— {40}
To the lineage masters of the Path and Result we pray.

To the great Vajradhara, Tilopa, Nāropa,
Marpa, Milarepa, venerable Gampopa,
And the countless siddhas of the four great and eight lesser schools—
To the masters of the Dakpo Kagyu lineage we pray.

To the wisdom ḍākinīs, to Khyungpo Neljor and the others
In the two lineage strings of seven jewels,
And to Tangtong Gyalpo and others in the recent lineage—
To the successors of the Shangpa Kagyu lineage we pray.

To Padampa Sangye and Machik Lapdrön,
Ma Chökyi Sherap, Sochung Gendun Bar, Kam Yeshe Gyaltsen,
and the four authorized adepts,
The recipients of the initial, middle, and final transmissions, and
the rest—
To the masters of the Pacification and Severance lineages we pray.

To the Rikden kings and the Greater and Lesser Kālachakrapāda,
Ra Chörap, Dro Sherap Drak, Tsami Sangye Drak, Rangjung
Dorje and Dolpopa,

And the eminent scholar Butön, the principal masters and disciples—
To the masters of the lineage of the six applications we pray.

To the vajra queens and the scholar-siddha Orgyenpa,
Rangjung Dorje, Kharchuwa, Putrapa,
Neringpa, and the other masters of the lineage
Of approach and accomplishment of the six yogas we pray.

To Lord Avalokiteshvara, Mitrayogin,
Shrīputra, Drakpa Rinchen, {41}
Jampa Pal, and other masters of the aural lineage of the six instructions
And the lineage of *Resting* we pray.

To Tsembupa and Bodong Jikdrel Chenpo,
Rongtön Chenpo, Drölwai Gönpo,[13] and others;
To the holders of the lineages
Of common, extraordinary, and unexcelled instructions we pray.

To him who, by dint of previous training, possessed the full force
  of the two kinds of knowledge,
Who held the seven marvelous great transmissions,
Unsurpassed lord of dharma who trained the beings of the
  degenerate age,
To Jamyang Khyentse Wangpo we pray.

To him who, with the knowledge and realization acquired by
  habituation through many previous lives,
Drew the chariot of the five marvelous great treasuries
And rekindled the embers of the entire doctrine,
To Lodrö Taye we pray.

From the palace of the Highest Realm, the expanse of reality,
You show us directly that our own minds are the body of truth.
Essence of all the buddhas of the three times,
Root teachers, to you we pray.

To the Precious Jewels, rare and supreme, the buddhas and
  bodhisattvas;
To the mandala of yidam deities, to the ḍākas and ḍākinīs; {42}

To those with eyes of wisdom who protect and guard the teachings
We pray, bestow on us your blessings.

The following is an arrangement of the writings of the omniscient Longchen Rapjam, which are full of blessings:

Alas, alack! Wretched beings like ourselves
Have long been oppressed by karma and defilements.
Stretch forth your hand of compassion
And guide us this very day, we pray.

Though from the very beginning we are buddhas,
Because of ignorance we wander here in existence,
Exhausted from circling deludedly as in a dream.
Be our refuge and protector here.

For us and all the infinite beings there are
It is hard to cross the endless ocean of samsara.
With the unexcelled great ship of wisdom,
Carry us across the waters of suffering.

Were our tendencies, grown habitual over ages long, to take form
They would be a towering mountain of dualistic deluded perceptions.
Use the adamantine wisdom of supreme liberation
To destroy it all this very instant.

In the dark and dense obscurity of ignorance
It is hard to discern things far away; there is no end in sight. {43}
With the rays of primordial wisdom, we pray,
Rid us of this blackness that obscures the essence of clear light.

Whatever efforts we make, they lead to defilements and suffering.
Help us to turn this mind of ours completely away
From meaningless worldly activities
And to pass our days and nights in dharma.

Our improper mental activities are like ripples on water,
All kinds of conceptual thoughts chasing after the five sense objects.
Bring all the eight consciousnesses, habitual tendencies, and the ground of all
To peace in the expanse of reality.

Conceptual habitual tendencies lead to mental defilements in the desire realm,
Clarity in the form realm, and absence of thought in the formless realm—
Please purify these mental processes of existence
That follow our habitual tendencies.

Help us turn away from our base habits and devotion to our own welfare
And our interest in gaining peace for ourselves alone;
Help us set out on the path of the supreme teachings, outer, inner, and secret,
And accomplish others' good on a vast scale.

Completely purifying the deeds, defilements, and habitual tendencies {44}
Of all beings on mistaken, wrong, or lower paths,
Help us all without exception to proceed together
To the city of liberation, according to our deepest wishes.

Though we have been immersed in the muddy ocean of obscuration
For ages long, with no beginning or end,
It is impossible to gain freedom by our own means.
You whose love is so great, draw us out, we pray.

From the mind's defilements, so powerful and hard to bear,
There come the torments of existence, with much suffering.
From the fearful consequences of our overwhelming carelessness and laziness
Give us sure protection, this very day.

Make us truly realize, from the heart, that essenceless phenomena
Are impermanent, unreliable, deceptive illusions,
And help us to pass every moment of the day and night
With disenchantment and determination to be free.

In pleasant locations, high on lonely mountainsides,
Help us to accomplish our potential, preternatural powers, and concentration,
And in this very life to reach the expanse of great bliss,
In which the two goals are spontaneously accomplished.

Help us to practice alone with persistent diligence, {45}
Not distracted for an instant by the affairs of this life,
To follow the beings of the past and perfect what they did,
And to constantly serve our teachers, we pray.

May we never break our commitments and vows,
And realize without mistake the view, meditation, conduct, and result.
Never moving, day or night, from the state of radiant light,
Help us to accomplish both our own and others' goals.

May we perfect the purity of phenomenal existence in the approach and accomplishment,
And from the ḍākinīs and loyal protectors gathered around like clouds
May the two kinds of accomplishment fall on us like rain,
And may we accomplish the four activities.

May pure perception and devotion arise impartially.
May there be no interruption in our love and compassion.
May the qualities of the view, meditation, experience, and realization blaze forth.
Help us accomplish beings' benefit impartially, we pray.

As a result of this, our excellent virtuous aspiration,
May all beings without exception be fully liberated together,
And grant that in this very life we may reach
The realm of Samantabhadra, spontaneously accomplished great bliss.

After praying in this manner with intense devotion and longing, say the following prayer for the general fulfillment of wishes:

Essence of all the body, speech, mind, qualities, and activities of all the tathāgatas in the ten directions and three times, {46}
Mandalas without exception of the glorious teachers, lords of dharma,
And hosts of yidam deities, buddhas, noble bodhisattvas, listeners, and solitary realizers, and ḍākas, yoginīs, ḍākinīs, and dharma protectors, all without any exception, listen to us sentient beings.
Sublime glorious protectors, possessed of omniscient wisdom,
Loving tenderness and compassion,
And inconceivable activities,
Grant the blessing that what we pray for here
Be unfailingly fulfilled at this very moment!

Grant that the precious teaching of the Buddha, rare and supreme—
The Vinaya, Sutra, Abhidharma, and Vidyādhara collections—
May flourish and spread in all directions
And long endure without decline.

In particular, may the traditions of the great chariots of the practice lineage
That join us to buddhahood in one lifetime
Spread everywhere, endure, and never wane,
And may we practice them properly.

May outer and inner obstacles to accomplishment be removed. {47}
May we naturally come by places, companions, and everyday necessities favorable to the dharma.
Grant that all the activities of demons be eliminated and that we do not give up our diligence,
So that we may accomplish the result of the practice.

Wherever the Buddha's doctrine is present
Grant that human and animal epidemics be halted, that livestock and crops thrive,

That troubled times are resolved and ages of warfare fade away,
And that happiness reigns throughout the land.

Strengthen the lives and dominion of kings who preserve the dharma,
And grant that all the people too abide by the precepts of the ten virtuous deeds,
That they are friendly with each other and enjoy every joy and happiness,
As in the time of the universal monarch Ngalenu.

Grant that all the aspirations of the supreme charioteers,
Guides and lamps of the doctrine of the buddhas who came in the past,
May be completely fulfilled, rejoicing all,
And that they may care for us with compassion.

Grant that we may please all our masters and teachers,
Who have been the most kind to us, more so than our parents in this life;
That their lives, merit, and wisdom may increase;
And that all their wishes may be accomplished.

Grant that all of us gathered here with our teachers and benefactors {48}
May cut the stream of wrong thoughts and grow in devotion and wisdom.
May we live in harmony and happiness and accomplish our wishes in accord with the dharma,
And may we obtain all the accomplishments without exception.

Grant that in this way we may invoke the promises of the Three Jewels
With our pure altruistic intentions
And that all these prayers for the benefit of the doctrine and beings
Be fulfilled, unfailingly and without hindrance.

All the merit that there is in this we offer
To our root teachers, the buddhas and bodhisattvas,
Praying that the teachers' lives and activities may thereby flourish
And achieve great benefit for the doctrine and beings.

Grant that we too, forever in our series of lives,
May be of good family and clear-minded and gain higher rebirth and power.
May we meet the holy teachers who teach the dharma without mistake,
And may we attain the sublime jewel of the twofold fulfillment of our goals.

Bless us that in everything we do, without exception,
We may honor the Three Jewels and benefit sentient beings.
And having made the conquerors glad, may we swiftly
Attain the level of the buddhas, protectors of beings.

This prayer has been taken from the writings of the great Katok Rikzin, {49} with a few additions.

## III. Conclusion

Perform the seven branches again with the following condensed prayer:

To all the sublime teachers and those worthy of homage
We bow down with bodies numerous as the atoms in the universe,
Our mouths praising them with expressions of their qualities
And our minds paying homage with respect and altruistic intent.

Our bodies, wealth, and accumulated merit
And all the glory and riches in this world and beyond
We manifest mentally as ocean-like clouds of outer and inner offerings
And offer to the hosts of glorious teachers, worthy of veneration.

Since time without beginning, under the influence of defilements,
We have used our body, speech, and mind to commit harmful deeds, both naturally negative and those that violate edicts.

All these, and those we ordered or wholeheartedly approved,
We remorsefully regret and now confess, determined not to commit them henceforth.

We rejoice with joyful hearts
At the lives of the supreme beings and their heirs
And at all the virtuous deeds of body, speech, and mind
That all beings have done, will do, and are doing now.

To bring benefit and virtue to all beings, {50}
We pray to the kings of dharma and their heirs
To turn continuously the wheel of dharma,
The profound and extensive teachings that benefit according to need.

Although the body of truth does not arise or perish,
We pray that your form body may not depart to benefit other realms:
With compassion for the helpless beings of this degenerate age,
May you not pass into nirvana but remain for ages long.

So that all beings may attain unsurpassable enlightenment,
We take refuge constantly in you, the supreme refuge.
Henceforth we will adopt the vows and commitments,
Common and extraordinary, and accomplish them properly.

By the force of the merit we have gathered in the three times,
May all beings be released from the fetters of existence.
Guided by sublime and glorious teachers,
May they obtain the supreme accomplishment of omniscience.

A prayer for the forgiveness of mistakes:

Whatever mistakes we have unknowingly made
Out of ignorance and carelessness,
We confess in your presence, you who are possessed of love.
Please forgive them, you who are compassionate.

Receiving the empowerments: {51}

> Teachers, Three Jewels, buddhas and bodhisattvas,
> Think of us, your faithful children, with compassion.
> Bestow on us the four empowerments, mature the four streams of being,
> And bless us to attain the level of the four bodies.

Recite this three times.

As a result of this prayer, all the hosts of deities present above the head of the main deity and all around him in the cardinal directions dissolve in stages into light and are absorbed into him. The three centers of the main deity, who is the essential embodiment of all the sources of refuge, are marked with [the syllables that represent] the essential nature of the body, speech, and mind of all the buddhas: a white *oṁ* in the crown center, a red *āḥ* in the throat, and a blue *hūṁ* in the heart.

From *oṁ* in the teacher's crown center white rays of light stream forth and dissolve into our own crown center. With this, we receive the vase empowerment, the stains of our bodies are purified, we are empowered to practice the generation stage as the path, and we gain the fortune to attain the manifestation body as the result.

From *āḥ* in the throat red rays of light stream forth and dissolve into our throat center. With this, we receive the secret empowerment, the stains of our speech are purified, we are empowered to practice the channels and winds as the path, {52} and we gain the fortune to attain the enjoyment body as the result.

From *hūṁ* in the heart center blue rays of light stream forth and dissolve into our heart center. With this, we receive the wisdom empowerment, the stains of our minds are purified, we are empowered to practice the essential drops as the path, and we gain the fortune to attain the body of truth as the result.

Again, from the three centers white, red, and blue rays of light stream forth and dissolve into our own three centers. We obtain the fourth empowerment, the stains shared by our three doors are purified, we are empowered to practice union as the path, and we gain the fortune to attain the body of the essential nature as the result.

The dissolution into oneself:

> Supreme refuge, you who completely benefit beings,
> Although in the body of truth you never change,
> Give rise to the form body in our bodies
> And bless us with your great love.

The teacher comes onto the crown of our head and, melting into light, dissolves into our heart. Thus the body, speech, and mind of the teacher, the buddhas, and the bodhisattvas become indivisible from our own body, speech, and mind.

Dedication:

> In all our lives, life after life,
> May we be of good family, clear-minded, and free of pride. {53}
> May we have great compassion and devotion to the teacher.
> May we keep the commitments with the glorious teacher.
>
> Regarding the lifestyles of our glorious teachers
> May we never give rise to wrong view, even for an instant.
> Through our devotion in seeing everything they do as perfect,
> May the teachers' blessings infuse our minds.
>
> In all our lives, may we never separate from authentic teachers
> And always enjoy the glory of the teachings.
> Having perfected all the qualities of the levels and paths,
> May we swiftly attain the level of Vajradhara.

As well as these, say any other prayers you know: prayers common to all traditions such as the *Prayer of Good Conduct*,[14] and excellent prayers of aspiration related to the uncommon Mantra Vehicle such as the *Summary of the Fifty Verses on the Teacher*.[15]

Prayer for auspiciousness:

Like the wish-fulfilling jewel on the top of the victory banner,
You are the crown ornament of the supreme deity,
Bestowing on practitioners the supreme accomplishment.
Sublime, peerless teacher, make all auspicious!

Beginning with this prayer, recite at length a series of verses to promote virtue and excellence, while playing music and throwing down a rain of flowers.

Inconceivable are the marvelous life stories
Of each of the learned and accomplished beings,
Principal teachers of the chariots that are the eight great practice
lineages. {54}
The benefits of venerating and praying to them defy description.

As a result of this mountainlike merit,
May all beings never be parted from the sublime protectors,
May their attainments in accord with the dharma be effortlessly and
spontaneously accomplished,
And may they reach the great kingdom of the buddhas, their teachers.

In accordance with the wishes of a few spiritual friends, I acquired the good fortune of collecting in the vase of my faithful mind and heart the river of nectar of the complete oral instructions of the system of teachings of the Eight Great Chariots, principally from the supreme incarnation of Yangön Jedrung, Trinle Jampa Jungne, holder of the royal lineage of accomplishment of Taklung Martang in the extraordinary mandala that is the seat of the peerless precious Kagyu. I, Lodrö Taye, who, in this age of degeneration, merely have the appearance of a monk, based this ritual on the veneration of the teacher, full of blessings, composed by the lord of siddhas, the translator Lodrö Pal,[16] completing it from other suitable sources. I wrote it at Palpung in the upper retreat center, Kunzang Dechen Ösel Ling, the sacred place Shri Devikotri, Tsadra Rinchen Drak. May virtue and excellence increase.

*oṁ svasti siddhi*
Nurtured by the explanation and practice of the transmission and
realization of the Muni's doctrine,

The ten great pillars that hold up the exegetical lineage
And the Eight Great Chariots that draw the practice lineage
Are the glorious protectors of the doctrine in the Land of Snows.

The complete system of teachings of all of them,
Together with explanations of maturation and liberation, is like a jewel in the ocean; {55}
It has been preserved by the force of the intentions, aspirations, and diligence
Of the two Jamgön lamas, sun and moon.[17]

To Jamgön Lodrö Taye's ritual
Of the Veneration of the Teachers Who Embody the Eight Practice Lineages
The dharma lord Khenchen Tashi Özer[18] added a supplement.
This ritual, which is easy for fortunate practitioners to implement,
Has been extracted from the treasury of instructions.
It was printed by the sublime Chöying Tashi,
Retired khenpo and vajra master who holds the three trainings.

Through the great waves of virtue acquired by this
May mother beings pervading space enter the door of the definitive secret essence,
And, swiftly completing the qualities of the levels and paths,
May they become Vajradhara in this life.

These verses of aspiration were written as a printing colophon by the vagabond Karma Tashi Chöpel,[19] who has the greatest respect for the tradition of the eight practice lineages.
*suṣre yobha vatu*
*sarvadā maṅgalaṃ*

## PART TWO

# The Eighty-Four Mahāsiddhas

This section contains four texts that can be loosely classified as an empowerment, a sādhana, a guru yoga practice, and a series of instructions on the perfection stage (*rdzogs rim*). The first two feature all eighty-four mahāsiddhas. The guru yoga practice may be adapted to any one of a selection of mahāsiddhas, including two sixteenth-century siddhas who were Tāranātha's lineage teachers. The fourth text, *A Precious Necklace*, comprises a series of profound instructions given by some twenty of the eighty-four mahāsiddhas, accompanied by two ḍākinīs, to a yakṣhiṇī (a female spirit) living in a charnel ground.

It should be noted that the names of the mahāsiddhas vary between different texts and even within the same text. To maintain consistency and avoid confusion, we have chosen one version of each mahāsiddha's name and employed it throughout.

# 2. The Stream of Accomplishment

*A Method for Combining the Blessings of the Teacher Vajradhara and the Eighty-Four Siddhas*[1]

The second text in this volume, with which the corresponding volume in the Kundeling edition begins, is a ritual for transmitting the blessings of the eighty-four siddhas. Jamgön Kongtrul based it on the tradition that came down from Jonang Jetsun Kunga Drölchok and Tarānātha, which, he states in the catalog, can be considered authentic; and he received specific authorization to write it from Jamyang Khyentse Wangpo, according to the advice he had received in a vision from the mahāsiddha Lvavapa.* It begins with a Vajradhara empowerment, followed by a section in which the disciple is required to visualize each of the eighty-four siddhas in order to receive their blessings. An unusual feature of the empowerment is the manner in which the fourth empowerment is bestowed, introducing the disciple to the nature of the mind using the words of each of the siddhas quoted from their songs of realization (dohā), at the same time giving the oral transmission (*lung*) of each of these short verses. These songs are mostly drawn from Vīraprabhāsvara's *Essence of the Eighty-Four Siddhas' Realization.*† The ritual ends with a section invoking the blessings of the protector of the Vajrayāna teachings.

*See Catalog, p. 108.

†*Caturaśītisiddhasambodhihṛdaya*, *Grub thob brgyad cu rtsa bzhi'i rtogs pa'i snying po*, Dg.T. rgyud 'grel, *zhi* (Toh. 2292).

{58}

*namo guru vajradharaya*
I bow to the teacher and the lords of yogis
Who have successfully attained the great kingdom
Of the union Vajradhara and who, through skill in means,
Work to liberate numerous beings.

Here I shall show
How to obtain in a single session
The stream of all their blessings and wisdom,
As authorized by my lord, the vajra holder.[2]

The method for invoking the individual blessings of the eighty-four great siddhas, together with the opening sections and [one for] the guardian of the teachings, that came down from the tradition of Āchārya Vīraprabhāsvara appears to be well known. Here, however, I have arranged a concise practice that includes them all together.

In general, since this is an empowerment of male and female vajra wisdom deities, the person giving the empowerment obviously needs to be someone who is able to transfer the ultimate wisdom of realization to the mind streams of the disciples by their inwardly encountering their true nature, the Great Seal, the teacher's bliss-emptiness nature. As for the disciples, it is important that they should either have the fortune, through a combination of devotion and concentration, to be able to dissolve and absorb the wisdom in the teacher's mind, or at least they should definitely be able to maintain one-pointed concentration on the object, with intense faith and devotion. For anyone else, since this empowerment does not contain a lot of empowerment sections as in other, elaborate empowerments with different articles, mantras, and concentrations, it will be hard to really receive the empowerment simply by requesting it and being present.

The time for giving the empowerment should be a favorable day such as the tenth or twenty-fifth day of the month, when the right outer and inner conditions coincide and the auspicious connections between master and disciples, place, and time come together. {59}

The method for the blessing ritual comprises three stages: preparation, main practice, and conclusion.

First, the preparation. Clean the hall in which the ritual is to be performed, set up images, and in the middle place a clean shrine. On it draw a square mandala, with a blue circle in the middle, surrounded by the eight petals of a lotus, and outside it, arranged concentrically, a sixteen-petaled lotus, and further out again three twenty-petaled lotuses—all drawn with beautiful colored sand. The directional sectors of the square should bear the corresponding colors. In the middle arrange a heap of flowers or an image of Vajradhara. On the western side arrange the principal ritual vase[3] with its neck decorated with a ribbon, a skull cup containing wine mixed with the three sweet ingredients, and a miniature of the wisdom consort. Around all this, place the two water offerings and the five sense offerings. If the ritual is connected with the authorization ritual for the yidam deity Achala, place in front and to the right a mandala with an eight-petaled lotus, with a sun throne in the middle and on it a blue heap. In front and to the left, for the dharma protectors place a mandala and, on a tripod over it, a black triangular torma or a heart-shaped *paltor*[4] adorned with a four-petaled lotus and a silken canopy. In front, set out abundant offerings for the feast offering. In front of the master, place a vajra, a bell, and the "inner offering."[5]

Second, the main practice. It is not necessary to go through a detailed ritual for the front visualization, sādhana ceremony,[6] and so forth. {60} After first blessing the inner offering and the place and materials, begin with the refuge and bodhichitta and go through the self-visualization, recitation, and dissolution and reemergence of any suitable Unexcelled Yoga Tantra deity such as Chakrasaṃvara, Hevajra, or Vajravarāhī. Then, for the feast offering, sprinkle all the assembled food and drink that constitutes the samaya ingredients with the nectar of the inner offering. Cleanse them with *oṁ sumbhani* and purify them with *oṁ svabhāva*:

> The feast-offering ingredients become emptiness, devoid of concepts.
> From that state of emptiness, under the feast-offering ingredients, there appears a syllable *yaṃ*, from which manifests the wind. From the syllable *raṃ*, there manifests the mandala of fire. On top of it is the letter *A*, from which appears a vast, open wisdom kapāla. Inside it, the five fleshes and the five nectars melt into the five wisdoms, from which the feast-offering ingredients arise as a great ocean of untainted wisdom nectar.

Say *oṁ āḥ hūṁ ha hoḥ hrīḥ* three times.

*namo* The vast wheel of the feast offering, skillful means and
wisdom inseparable,
Is sealed with the perfectly pure nature, unborn,
With perfectly pure attributes, the vowels and consonants,
And the perfectly pure essence, the five fleshes and five nectars.
This I offer to the root and lineage teachers, the root of
blessings—
*gaṇacakra pūja megha samudra sapharaṇa samaye hūṁ*

Repeat these lines with the following adaptations:

*namo* The vast wheel of the feast offering, skillful means and wisdom inseparable . . .
. . . the five fleshes and five nectars.
This I offer to the host of yidam deities, the root of accomplishments . . .

*namo* The vast wheel of the feast offering, skillful means and wisdom inseparable . . .
. . . the five fleshes and five nectars.
This I offer to the ḍākinīs and the hosts of protectors and guardians of the teachings, the root of activities . . .

*namo* The vast wheel of the feast offering, skillful means and wisdom inseparable . . .
. . . the five fleshes and five nectars.
This I offer to my fellow practitioners, vajra brothers and sisters, the root of the samaya . . .

After this, invoke the descent of blessings:

In the expanse of reality, the great palace of absence of thought,
bliss, and clarity,
Lord, great Vajradhara, protector of beings,
Principal refuge, appearing to itself,
Kind father, root teacher,
Gather with your manifestations like clouds in the sky.
Come here and accept this feast offering.

Bless this practice place,
Infuse this feast torma with potent essence, {61}
And bestow on us practitioners assembled here
The supreme and common accomplishments.
*oṁ mahā guru caturā śīti siddhi labdha jñāna āveśaya a ā*

You who took birth in the central land of Magadha
For the benefit of mother beings,
Hosts of accomplished masters of yoga,
Gather with your manifestations like clouds in the sky.
Come here and accept this feast offering.
Bless this practice place,
Infuse this feast torma with potent essence,
And bestow on us practitioners assembled here
The supreme and common accomplishments.
*oṁ mahā guru caturā śīti siddhi labdha jñāna āveśaya a ā*

You who took birth in the east of India,
For the benefit of mother beings . . . and so on, repeating as above.

You who took birth in the south of India,
For the benefit of mother beings . . . and so on.

You who took birth in the west of India,
For the benefit of mother beings . . . and so on.

You who took birth in the north of India,
For the benefit of mother beings . . . and so on.

You who took birth in the royal caste, the brahmin caste, the merchant caste,
As noble citizens, or of common caste—
Lords, hosts of accomplished masters of yoga . . . and so on.

Fathers, infinite lords of yoga,
Mothers, your secret consorts,
And sisters, bestowing the experiences of the four joys—all of you
Gather with your manifestations like clouds in the sky . . . and so on.

Eighty yogis who have attained realization and liberation,
And four yoginīs who have attained realization and liberation—
Hosts of the eighty-four siddhas,
Gather with your manifestations like clouds in the sky . . . and so on.

In the densely arrayed buddha field free of fear,
In the midst of hundreds of thousands of dakas and ḍākinīs,
Lord Achala, deity of adamantine ferocity,
Bhagavān Heruka,
Gather with your manifestations like clouds in the sky . . . and so on, to
*guru deva ḍākinī jñāna āveśaya a ā*

In the delightful unexcelled buddha field of the unwavering state,
The pure celestial land of bliss and emptiness,
Mother creator of the bliss that delights the buddhas,
Vajravarāhī, queen of the ḍākinīs,
Gather with your manifestations like clouds in the sky . . . and so on.

In the eight great charnel grounds,
The realm of activities where the whole host of demons is subdued, {62}
Glorious protectors and your consorts and retinue
Who vanquish obstacle makers and fulfill all wishes,
Gather with your manifestations like clouds in the sky . . . and so on.

Hosts of teachers, yidams, and ḍākinīs,
With the tasseled crowns of your family swinging to and fro,
Silk ribbons fluttering,
Your numerous ornaments tinkling,
A multitude of musical instruments resounding,
Moving here and there with songs and dances,
Your hundreds of thousands of retinues whirling round,
Illusory self-appearance, nakedly vivid;
Unfixated awareness, clear and radiant;
Evanescent in the inexpressible expanse,

Dancing in great bliss,
In order to bless us, come, I pray,
Bestow your blessings on this sublime place.
Grant us the supreme accomplishment.
Dispel obstacles due to spirits that obstruct and lead us astray.
Mingle with us in the state where there are no dualistic concepts
with regard to the three spheres.
*guru deva ḍākinī jñāna āveśaya a ā*

Consider that as a result of this invitation, the teacher Vajradhara and the host of eighty-four siddhas instantly arrive from the celestial land, the Unexcelled, and actually take their places in the mandala in front, as perfectly manifest as they were in the historical accounts. Next, the shrine master should take in their left hand a skull cup filled with nectar and cover it with their right hand in the trident gesture.

Look at the perfect ingredients here.
May there be no doubt among those who are assembled:
Consider that brahmins, dogs, and outcastes
Are of the same nature, and enjoy!
*a ho mahā sukhaṃ*

Go around the assembly, beginning with the lord of the assembly. They take it, saying:

The dharma of the sugatas is priceless,
Free of attachment and other stains,
Free of subject-object duality.
To the ultimate nature we pay homage.
*a ho mahā sukhaṃ*

Then, offer the first part of the feast:

This deliciously prepared food offering,
Bewitching with its hundred tastes,
I offer with faith to the teacher and host of deities:
May all these beings have the fortune to enjoy the food of
concentration.

*oṁ mahā guru siddhi labadha buddha bodhisattva vīra ḍākinī sapari vāri bhyaḥ*
*namaḥ sarva tathāgate bhyoḥ viśva mukhe bhyaḥ sarvathā khaṃ udgate sapharaṇa imaṃ gagana khaṃ ghṛhaṇe dam balindaye svāhā* {63}

Or add *oṁ akāro* seven times while offering to the teacher and siddhas and their retinue, and *oṁ canda mahā roṣana hūṁ phaṭ* adding the *akāro* mantra three times for Achala, and *oṁ śrī mahākālaya śāsana* . . . and so on, to . . . *māraya hūṁ phaṭ* for Mahākāla and the host of dharma protectors.
With

*oṁ āḥ hūṁ ha hoḥ hrīḥ*
*phem vajra aralli hoḥ*
*jaḥ hūṁ baṃ hoḥ*
*vajra ḍākinī samaya stvaṃ dri śya hoḥ*
*oṁ kha kha* and so on

as for the general torma offering to the ḍākinīs, make the offering to the other guests. Holding up the inner offering, offer it by saying:

*oṁ* I offer.
The supreme samaya of all the buddhas,
Which utterly transcends inferior objects
And is the ground of all accomplishments,
I offer with this sublime nectar.
Dispel all the stains of obscurations,
Free us definitively from all ordinary thoughts,
And be pleased with this offering of great bliss,
The unsurpassed bodhichitta.

As occurs in the oral tradition of the lineage, properly take the blessings in the manner of a self-empowerment, as in the ritual described below.

Next, summon any suitable disciples, whose mind streams have been matured with the four empowerments of an appropriate Unexcelled Yoga Tantra deity. Ritually cleanse them outside and banish obstacles. Have them sit down inside and proceed with the distribution and gathering of flowers.

Beings who have been our mothers are as numerous as space is infinite. Since time without beginning they have been drowning in cyclic existence, the ocean of suffering. We must set them all in perfect freedom and lasting happiness, true and perfect buddhahood, whose nature is the four bodies and five wisdoms, the state of union, the great Vajradhara. To that end, thinking, "I will properly receive the profound blessings of the eighty-four lords of accomplishment of India and put into practice the instructions on the different stages," please arouse the mind intent on supreme enlightenment and, reminding yourselves of the correct conduct to be adopted when receiving the teachings, listen properly.

The teachings we will listen to are those of the perfect Buddha, who was skilled in means and possessed of great compassion. {64} He taught an inconceivable number of ways to access the dharma to match the different natures, faculties, and aspirations of the infinite beings to be trained. Of all these teachings the highest is the Great Vehicle, which is superior to lower vehicles on account of its greatness in seven respects.[7] The Great Vehicle has two aspects, general and particular, which are distinguished in terms of the way in which it makes the cause or the result the path. Of these two aspects, we are concerned here with the one that makes the result the path—the Secret Mantra Vajrayāna.

The root of the path of the Great Vehicle depends on following a spiritual teacher. In the *Verses That Summarize the Perfection of Wisdom* it is said:

> Excellent disciples who have devotion to the teacher
> Should rely wholly on learned teachers.
> Why? Because the qualities of learning come from them.[8]

In particular, all true realization of the Vajrayāna path arises solely from making the teacher's blessings the path. The *Hevajra Tantra* states:

> It cannot be expressed by anyone else; it is innate,
> Not to be found in any way.
> It is to be known from following a teacher constantly and
> skillfully
> And from one's own merit.[9]

And in another tantra[10] we find:

If one makes offerings with a mind full of faith
To the teacher, that ocean of good qualities,
One will swiftly obtain all the accomplishments,
Common and supreme.

There are many other quotations that show this. Even in the case of a fortunate person with the very highest faculties, who is instantly liberated by the power of the blessings, this happens through the coming together of the teacher's compassion and the disciple's devotion, as is illustrated in numerous stories of the great siddhas of the past in India and Tibet, most of whom attained liberation through signs and mental transmission. In this case, we are relying on the eighty-four mahāsiddhas of India, and although this is not an actual specific maturing empowerment serving as an entrance to the Vajrayāna, it is an opportunity for performing, by means of the four empowerments, a blessing ritual that is complete in its intention and extremely simple.

It is impossible to imagine or describe the [lives of the] mighty yogis who, on account of the extraordinary strength of our compassionate Teacher's[11] spiritual intent and prayers of aspiration, {65} have appeared and attained accomplishment through the Vajrayāna path, which is but rarely taught by other buddhas. Suffice it to say that after the perfect Buddha had passed into nirvana, the three well-known councils took place, at which the listeners' piṭakas were compiled, and subsequently, at the same time that the Great Vehicle piṭakas were beginning to be propagated, the great brahmin, the master Saraha, appeared. From that time on, and up to the time of the Six Learned Gatekeepers, there came masters who followed the path of the Great Yoga in the Vajrayāna and thereby attained accomplishment, appearing in a single gaṇachakra gathering. Here in Tibet there are many inauthentic and unreliable stories and other sources concerning them, but this tradition of the scholar Vīraprabhāsvara was well known in India throughout the ages and can be considered authentic. This is testified by an emanation of the mahāsiddha Kṛiṣhṇāchāri, Jetsun Kunga Drölchok, and his reincarnation, the omniscient Tāranātha, who both remembered their previous lives, and by the writings of genuine learned and accomplished beings in India, which accept this tradition as being authentic. The stories connected with it can be briefly related as follows.

In the west of India, in a district of Saurashṭa called Kantamara, there lived a devout king named Kuñji, who governed his kingdom in accord with the dharma. One day, his mother fell ill and was on the point of death. The king lovingly said to his mother, "Mother, it seems you do not have long to live. In order to help you in your future lives, I will make offerings to the sangha of monks, to the brahmins, and to the temples and make gifts to charity. Please tell me what you wish me to do."

His mother replied: "There is no need to do other virtuous acts for me. But do invite the eighty-four accomplished yogis and yoginīs to {66} a feast offering and pray to them for my sake." So saying, she passed away.

At this, the king thought to himself: "Ordinary people nowadays cannot see those siddhas of the past. How can I invite them? On the other hand, it would be wrong to ignore my mother's dying wish. Those great siddhas are the embodiments of compassion, so I will pray to them." As he prayed to them one-pointedly, the wisdom ḍākinīs Kokali and Dharmavishva appeared to him in person and said: "We will help you. Invite the siddhas and set up a hall for the feast offering." Thereupon, the king erected an immense assembly hall, while the two ḍākinīs, using their magical powers, traveled instantaneously to each of the siddhas' sacred abodes to deliver the invitation. Lūyipa arrived first, followed in succession by the other eighty-three siddhas, who arrived forthwith and took their seats.

The king set out an abundant feast offering, and they remained assembled at the feast for a long time. At the end, despite the king's entreaties that the siddhas stay longer so that he could venerate them, they did not accept. Each siddha sang a vajra song of spiritual realization (*dohā*) and then vanished without trace. The king had an image of each of the siddhas made, and in front of these he wrote down their respective songs of realization and venerated them.

At that time, a scholar named Vīraprabhāsvara, traveling far to the east, heard that the eighty-four siddhas had appeared in person to King Kuñji to be venerated by him. He hastened to reach Kantamara but found, on arriving there, that the siddhas had left seven days earlier. Vowing fervently to stay there and wait, he began praying. A week passed, and the two ḍākinīs appeared to him in person. They bestowed on him the transmission of the songs of realization and instructions such as *A Precious Necklace*,[12] along with the stories of the mahāsiddhas. By practicing these teachings, {67} Vīraprabhāsvara acquired extraordinary realization and became a great siddha himself. He also wrote a compilation of the various dohās. These he transmitted to the brahmin scholar Kamala, who taught them to the hermit siddha Jamaripa, and he in turn taught them to a scholar from Magadha, Abhayadatta. The latter composed commentaries on the dohās, along with the mahāsiddhas' life stories.[13] All these were collected together by that same scholar and his disciple, the translator from Minyak, Möndrup Sherap, and translated here in Tibet. These teachings were further taught and studied, and they thus became established and propagated throughout Tibet. Both the dohās and the stories of the mahāsiddhas have been established as authentic by all the learned compilers of the Tengyur in the past, and they have been indisputably included in all versions of the Tengyur in Ü and Tsang, so they can be considered reliable.

To continue the uncorrupted tradition of this lineage of blessings, first, the four empowerments of the root teacher will be given as an introduction, so to receive that, I request you to offer a mandala.

In this way, invite the disciples to make the mandala offering:

Next, do the following visualization.

The mandala in front is the boundlessly vast realm of a perfect buddha, in which is your root teacher. This wondrously arrayed, endless realm is filled with self-appearing clouds of offerings. In the center, on a lion throne, lotus, sun, and moon, is your noble root teacher in the form of Vajradhara, the essential embodiment of all the buddhas of the three

> times. He is blue in color, like a heap of sapphires, shining with rays of light. He is extremely peaceful, with the major and minor marks clear and complete. His two hands hold a vajra and bell crossed at the level of his heart center, and he is seated with his legs in vajra posture, in blissful union with his own manifestation, the supreme wisdom consort. He is adorned with the silk garments and jewel ornaments. The mere thought of him has the power to give rise to the wisdom of great bliss. This great being is present as the embodiment of all the three roots. In his presence, offer the mandala, imagining that you are offering your body, possessions, and merit accumulated in the three times {68} in the form of a mandala of the universe and its inhabitants, the support and the supported.
>
> The ground is purified with scented water . . . and so on.[14]

Now, consider your body—the aggregates that result from the ripening of your karma—and imagine that the top of your head is sliced off [to form a skull cup], into which the whole of the rest of your body is put. As I say *oṁ āḥ hūṁ*, it melts completely into wisdom nectar, which is white with a red luster and endowed with a hundred tastes. Consider that the teacher drinks it, drawing it up through his vajra tongue, which is in the form of tube-like rays of light. Repeat after me:

> This deliciously prepared food offering,
> Bewitching with its hundred tastes,
> I offer with faith to the glorious teacher.
> May all these beings have the fortune to enjoy the food of concentration.

*oṁ āḥ hūṁ guru ganacakra sapari vāre bhyaḥ idaṃ baling grihaṇanantu mama sarva siddhimem prayaccha*

Next, consider that you emanate bodies numerous as the atoms in the universe and pay homage, touching your head at the teacher's feet, repeating after him, with folded hands:

> Through your kindness
> Great bliss arises in an instant:

Teacher, your body is like a precious jewel.
Vajra holder, at your lotus feet I bow.

Paying homage like this, consider that as the result of your intense, fervent prayer of aspiration and devotion, your root teacher, the great Vajradhara, takes a precious vase filled with wisdom nectar and empowers you on your head.

With this, actually place the vase on the disciples' heads. With

The great vajra empowerment
Is saluted by everyone in the three worlds.
It is given from the three centers
Corresponding to the three secrets of all the buddhas.
As from the moment of your birth . . .[15]

and so on, with the mantra, give the empowerment water from the vase.

Consider that, as a result of this empowerment, your whole body is filled with the stream of water. The impurities of your body are purified. You receive the vase empowerment. You are empowered to practice the generation stage as the path, and the extraordinary potential to attain the result, the manifestation body, is established within you. {69}

Again,

The sound of joy of the teacher Vajradhara in union with his own manifestation, the consort Vajragarvā, and the rays of light from his heart invite all the buddhas from the ten directions, who enter his mouth and, as a result of their affection, dissolve. The white and red bodhichitta descend from the secret space as nectar. Consider that it is of one taste with the nectar in the skull cup. By tasting it on your tongue, you receive the secret empowerment.

With this, give the inner offering present in the skull into the disciples' cupped left hands:

> Just as the buddhas of the past
> Empowered their children, the bodhisattvas,
> Likewise, with this stream of bodhichitta,
> You are this day empowered.
> *oṁ āḥ hūṁ*

The disciples should say *a ho mahā sukhaṃ* and taste it.

> Consider that in this way, the bodhichitta passes through your throat. It reaches all the stationary channels and fills them, giving rise to the wisdom of great bliss. The impurities of your speech are purified. You receive the secret empowerment. You are empowered to practice the path of skillful means, relying on your own body, and the extraordinary potential to accomplish the result, vajra speech, the body of perfect enjoyment, is established within you.

Again,

> Consider that from the teacher's heart center a wisdom consort, of perfect form and youthfulness, appears and confers on you the accomplishment of mudrā.
> The goddess who bestows joy, who bestows the state [of great bliss],
> The lady of beauty in different forms—
> Take her, take her, great hero,
> Take her and always venerate her.

With this, show the image of the consort.

> Visualizing yourselves as Vajradhara, enter into union with this consort that I am now showing you, who is by nature Vajragarvā, maintaining the three perceptions beginning with blessing the secret space.[16]
>
> As a result, the bodhichitta flows into the four centers, {70} and you experience the four joys in descending and ascending order. Through this, remain in meditative equipoise in natural awareness, the inexpressible bliss-emptiness.

Consider that with this you receive the wisdom empowerment.

The impurities of the mind are purified. You are empowered to practice the path of the wisdom consort, relying on another's body, and the potential to accomplish the result, the vajra mind, the body of truth, is established within you.

The illustrative wisdom experienced in this way during the third empowerment is the nature of awareness, the ultimate way things are. Its essence is uncompounded; it is present as the vital force of the whole of samsara and nirvana. Recognizing it correctly as one's own nature purifies the stains of adventitious habitual tendencies and leads to realization of the resultant divestment.[17] Considering that you have been introduced to your own awareness, seen nakedly, the truth body of all the buddhas, please settle in meditative equipoise, adopting the correct physical posture and the right gaze, with your minds in the uncontrived state of awareness, bliss-emptiness, untainted by the proliferation and dissolution of conceptual thoughts related to the past, present, and future.

This primordial wisdom is extremely subtle,
Adamantine, like the midst of space,
Free of defilement, ultimate, the state of peace;
You are your own father.[18]

Consider that with this the impurities of your body, speech, and mind are purified. You have received the fourth empowerment. You are empowered to practice the path of the Great Seal, and the extraordinary potential to attain the result, adamantine primordial wisdom, the body of the essential nature, is established within you.

Finally, consider that as a result of your fervent devotion, the root teacher, the great Vajradhara, looking pleased and loving, melts into a mass of light, the nature of great bliss. It dissolves through the crown of your head, and you settle in the baseless state of the great spontaneous presence, the teacher's mind and your mind inseparable. Consider that the blessings of the teacher's body, speech, and mind have entered you.

Play music to accompany the descent of blessings.

The stages of the general entrance empowerment have now been properly completed. Next, to receive the blessings of the eighty-four siddhas all together, consider the following. {71}

The support for the visualization, the mandala in front, is a vast, boundless pure wisdom buddha field, surrounded outside by an impenetrable protection circle. At its heart is the measureless palace of a manifested charnel ground, extraordinary in its layout, decorated with infinite divine offerings. Inside it, in the center, is a seat consisting of a lion throne, lotus, sun, and moon, on which is your root teacher, Vajradhara. Starting from in front of him, and in successive order clockwise, are eight lords of the siddhas:

On an antelope-skin[19] seat is the great accomplished master Lūyipa, dressed in the attire of a powerful Indian āchārya. His body is light blue in color, and he has a slightly emaciated appearance. His hair is partly tied in a topknot, and he is wearing a cotton dhoti. In front of him is a meal of heaped-up fish entrails, which he appears to be taking with his hand and eating. He is seated with his legs half-crossed.

On a jeweled throne is the great siddha Līlapa, dressed in royal attire, his complexion white tinged with red. He is adorned with silken garments and all the ornaments—crown, necklace, and so forth.

On an antelope-skin seat is the revered great lord of yogins, Birvapa or Virūpa. He is dark brown, short and fat, with a large belly. His shortish, curly hair is decorated with a garland of flowers. He is looking with his eyes gazing fixedly. His right hand is raised to the sky in the threatening gesture; his left hand holds a decorative horn cup filled with nectar. He is wearing a triangular hemp skirt and sitting with his legs in the posture of royal ease. To his left is a yoginī from the ḍākinīs' realm, appearing as a maiden, holding a vase of nectar and offering it to him.

Ḍombi Heruka is white in color, tinged with red, and adorned with the six bone ornaments. He is further ornamented with snakes whose touch is poisonous {72} and holds a whip in the form of a snake, venomous to behold. His head is hooded by seven snakes with noxious breath. He is riding a fearful tigress. On his left thigh is his secret consort, a lower-caste yoginī, who is so beautiful one can never tire of looking at her. She bears the marks of a padminī consort. She is embracing him and delighting with him in the supreme bliss.

On an antelope-skin seat is Shavaripa, who is black in color. He stares with protruding eyes. In his right hand he holds an arrow, in his left a bamboo bow. On the ends of the bow are attached the front and rear parts of a boar. He is wearing a lower garment made up of rows of peacock feathers, and he is adorned with all kinds of flowers and fruits. On his right and left he is accompanied by two wisdom consorts who have the same ornaments and attire as himself and are holding quivers.

On a deerskin seat is glorious Saraha, white in color tinged with red. His hair is uncut, and he wears a brahmin's thread. He is dressed in red cotton shorts. He holds his two hands in the gesture of straightening an arrow, symbolizing that he teaches the coemergent wisdom of thatness without mistake, directly. On his left he is accompanied by a yoginī from the buddha fields, in the guise of a huntress.

Kaṅkālapāda is azure blue in color, with uncut hair. He is seated with his hands in the gesture of meditation and has no ornaments. In front of him lies the skeleton, stripped of flesh, of a woman.

The great Mīnapa is azure blue in color, naked and unadorned, his hair in disarray. His two hands perform a dance. He is emerging from the middle of the cut-open abdomen of a great fish (*mīna* in Sanskrit), standing up with his two feet in a dance posture.

In a circle outside them are sixteen siddhas, in successive order clockwise: {73}

Shrī Gorakṣha[20] is white-fleshed, with a fixed gaze. His ears are adorned with black bone earrings[21] and his throat with a horn trumpet. His body is naked[22] or he is wearing a chakrakanta cloth, with wheel-like motifs, and he is resting his chin on a meditation stick, sitting cross-legged. Close by, he is surrounded by a herd of cows.

Chauraṅgi has his long hair tied up in a small topknot. His body is azure blue, and he is wearing a cotton dhoti. His hands are in the gesture of meditation, and he sits cross-legged, leaning against a tree.

Vīnapa is white tinged with red, wearing the attire of a king, with silken garments and a turban, and he is adorned with numerous jeweled ornaments. He is seated on a jewel throne, concentrating one-pointedly on the sound of a three-stringed vina[23] that he is playing with his two hands.

Ratnākarashānti is light blue and looks slightly old. He is wearing the three dharma robes and the paṇḍita's hat. With his right hand in the teaching gesture and his left holding a book, he is turning the wheel of the profound and extensive dharma. He is sitting on a monk's mat.

Tantipa is azure blue in color and of a very mature age. His drooping beard and mustache and his hair are all as white as jasmine. He is wearing a cotton dhoti and working hard at a loom, indicating symbolically that he abides in the certainty of the dharma.

Chamaripa is azure blue in color and wearing a cotton dhoti. His two hands are engaged in the work of a shoemaker, indicating by relative symbols the meaning of the natural state of mind.

Khaḍgapa is azure blue in color and wears cotton shorts. In his right hand he holds the sword of accomplishment, blazing with wisdom fire. He is flying through the sky. His locks are tied in a topknot.

The glorious protector of beings noble Nāgārjuna is azure blue in color, {74} as bright as a precious jewel and utterly beautiful and free of blemish. Adorned with the major and minor marks, he holds his two hands at his heart in the gesture of teaching the dharma. He is dressed in the three dharma robes and seated cross-legged in the vajra posture. The supreme kings of the nāgas, taking the form of snakes to venerate and honor him, are offering him the shade of their hoods and providing a backrest for him to lean against.

Kṛiṣhṇāchāri is black in color. With his right hand he is playing a hand drum; in his left, at his heart center, he holds a skull cup full of nectar. In the crook of his arm he holds a khātvāṇga trident. On his body he is wearing the six bone ornaments and a tiger-skin skirt. He is sitting with his legs half-crossed on top of a seat or mount of the terrifying form of Pishvarūpinī, the queen of the rākṣhasa ogres. Sometimes he displays various kinds of miraculous powers such as riding on a huge revived corpse garlanded with flowers. In the sky above him seven parasols turn without anyone holding them, and seven hand drums resound without anyone playing them. Sometimes he magically multiplies the seven parasols and seven hand drums a hundredfold. He constantly gathers around him a circle of infinite male and female practitioners—siddhas and vidyādharas—both visible and invisible.

Āryadeva is azure blue and has the appearance of a monk, with the three dharma robes. He is seated on a monk's mat with his legs crossed. In his hand he holds the large leaf of a karnari tree.

Thaganapa has bluish flesh and is seated on an animal skin leaning against a tree, sitting comfortably with his hand on the ground.

The glorious Nāropa is dark maroon in color and overwhelmingly resplendent. His hair is tied up in a topknot, {75} and his body is adorned with the six bone ornaments and so forth. He wears silk shorts or a tiger-skin skirt. In his hands he holds the hands and feet of his human-skin upper garment, stretching them on either side. Alternatively, he is stretching the human skin with his right hand and holding a skull cup full of nectar with his left. He stands with his feet in the dancing posture, or with one leg extended and the other folded. In front of him is his secret consort, a dakinī in the form of a human woman of perfect beauty, making an offering of nectar.

Shyalipa is azure blue and dressed in cotton shorts. He is carrying a jackal's corpse on his shoulder.

Tilopa's flesh is dark blue, and his hair is tied up in a topknot. He is wearing cotton shorts and has the appearance of a sesame grinder. In front of him is his secret consort, a yoginī from a buddha field in the form of a female sesame vendor, hard at work in the sesame trade, symbolizing the introduction to the wisdom of the natural state being inherently present within oneself.[24]

Chatrapa is white in color, tinged with red, dressed in monk's attire, carrying a load of books on his back and holding a small book in his hand.

Bhadrapa's flesh is white tinged with red, and he is handsome, in the full bloom of youth. His hair is combed and tied in a topknot. He is adorned with the brahmin's thread and different jewel ornaments such as earrings. He holds his hands in the gesture of meditation, and he is sitting cross-legged on an antelope-skin mat. In front of him is some pork and a jar of liquor.

In another circle outside them are twenty siddhas, in successive order clockwise:

Dhukhandi is azure blue in color, with uncut hair. He has the appearance of a sewer, stitching together rags from refuse heaps, symbolizing that all phenomena are gathered together in ultimate reality. He is seated on an animal skin with his right leg stretched out in front and his left leg drawn in. {76}

Āyogipāda is light blue in color, with his hair partly tied up in a topknot. He has the appearance of being asleep, lying on his side.

Kalapa is white in color, tinged with red, and so handsome one can never tire of looking at him. He has his hair in a small topknot. His two hands are in the meditation gesture, and he is sitting cross-legged.

Dhombipa[25] is azure blue in color and wears a cotton dhoti. He is kneeling. In front is a stream, in which he is washing a variety of dirty clothes, symbolizing cleansing the mind of impurities. He is accompanied by his wisdom consort on his left.

Kaṅkana is a radiant white tinged with red, dressed as a king, adorned with silks and jewel ornaments. He is looking fixedly at a precious jeweled bracelet on his right arm shining with light. He is seated with his feet in the posture of royal ease on a jeweled throne and satin cushion. He is surrounded by his queens, ministers, and subjects. From the sky above him, gods and goddesses are making offerings to him.

Kambala is white in color, tinged with red, with the attributes of a monk, and wears a rough woolen garment. With his hands in the meditation gesture, he is absorbed in concentration.

Ḍiṅgipa is wearing a cotton dhoti and has his hair tied up in a topknot. With his two hands he is filling a pot with rice and husking it with a wooden pestle, rinsing away the chaff with water. This symbolizes his extracting the essential meaning. He is kneeling. Next to him, his excellent secret consort is pouring a stream of water.

Bhandhepa is attired as a king. His body is radiant white tinged with red. He is dressed in silk robes and a turban and adorned with various jewel ornaments. He is seated in the posture of royal ease on a jeweled throne and satin cushion.

Tandhepa is azure blue in color, dressed as an ordinary Indian, with a cotton dhoti and turban. His two hands hold Indian-style dice, {77} and he is playing on a gameboard.

Kukkuripa is flesh-colored with a bluish tinge. He has his hair tied up in a topknot and is adorned with bone ornaments. He wears a cotton dhoti. His left hand holds a kapāla filled with nectar. His right hand holds Vajrayoginī on his lap, in the form of a young dog, in whom he takes delight.

Kujipa[26] is azure blue in color and attired as a yogi, wearing cotton shorts. He has a tumor on his neck. In front of him is the master Nāgārjuna, whom he is serving respectfully.

Dhamapa is bluish white and in the attire of a brahmin, with his hair knot, brahmin's sacred thread, and small water pot. He has a cotton dhoti. In his hand he holds a book, and around him are numerous volumes of the scriptures.

Mahila is well built in body and limb, with folds in his flesh. His appearance is of one who rivals others with his physical strength.

Achinta is wearing a cotton dhoti. He has the appearance of a woodcutter, holding a bundle of wood and an ax, to symbolize cutting the net of delusion.

Babhahi has the attributes of a ruler. He is white in color, tinged with red. Apart from a lower garment, he has no other clothes but is adorned with a crown and jeweled bangles on his arms and legs. On his left he is being embraced by his consort, of astounding and perfect beauty, manifesting the delightful enjoyment of unchanging great bliss. He is seated on a jeweled throne.

Nalina is white in color, tinged with red, and has the attributes of a brahmin. He is cutting the stem of a lotus flower and its root, in the middle of a lake.

Shāntideva is white in color, tinged with red, with healthy features. He is attired as a monk, wearing the dharma robes, and sitting cross-legged on a mat. He appears to be rising higher and higher into the air, from the midst of a great assembly of monks, as he fearlessly teaches *The Way of the Bodhisattva (Bodhicaryāvatāra)*.

The dharma king Indrabhūti is a beautiful white color, tinged with red. He is attired as a great universal monarch {78} and is seated on a jeweled throne and satin cushion. He is surrounded by the riches of the Lord of the Three Worlds. Vajrayoginī, taking the form of five hundred astoundingly beautiful and perfect maidens, is continuously venerating him with offerings of song, dance, music, and caresses. He is delighting in these and a feast of pleasures of the five senses as he undertakes the great practice with conceptual elaborations of taking pleasure as the path.

Mekopa's body is white tinged with red, and his hair is tied up in a topknot. He has the appearance of an ordinary layman, wearing a short-sleeved garment. With his two hands he is at work making fried pastries. In front of him are displayed a variety of pastries. His beautiful wisdom consort is doing the work of cooking them.

Togchepa is dark blue in color, with his hair tied up in a topknot, and he is wearing a cotton dhoti. In his two hands he holds a mattock, with which he is tilling the hard earth of a barren field, symbolizing the need to break in one's own rigid mind.

In another circle outside them are twenty siddhas, in successive order clockwise:

Kamparipa is dark blue in color and wears a hemp dhoti. His hair is tied up in a topknot. His two hands hold a hammer and tongs, and he is hard at work in his trade as a blacksmith, symbolizing training and purifying the three poisons as the body of truth.

Jālandhara is white in color, tinged with red. His hair is in a topknot, and he is wearing bone ornaments and a red dhoṭi. With one leg tucked back over his shoulder, he stands on the other leg, or is kneeling. His two hands are opposed in the vajra uṣhnīṣha mudra, binding the crown. On his left, his wisdom consort, in the attire of a yoginī, is bowing down to him.

Rāhula is azure blue and somewhat elderly. His hair is uncut, and he holds his two hands in the meditation gesture. He is sitting with his two legs crossed on an antelope-skin mat. {79}

Dharmapa is azure blue, of a very mature age, and has the attributes of a monk. He is holding a volume of the scriptures in his hand and sitting with his feet in the bodhisattva posture on a monk's mat.

Dhokaripa is dark maroon in color and has the appearance of a beggar. In his two hands he holds a stick from which, tied with a rope, hangs a large pot of food in a bundle called a jola. He is holding it up in the manner of a beggar begging for alms.

Medhina is azure blue in color and has the appearance of a plowman. His hair is slightly tied up, and he is wearing a cotton dhoti. He is yoking a pair of oxen to plow the field, symbolizing his understanding of the dharma.

Saṅkaja is white in color, tinged with red, and youthful in appearance, with the attributes of a brahmin. He is standing in the dancing posture, worshipping the shrine of noble Avalokiteshvara on the edge of a lotus pool.

Ghaṇḍhapa is flesh colored with a light-blue tinge. He is semiwrathful. His hair is tied up in a topknot, and he is adorned with the six bone ornaments. He wears a tiger-skin skirt. His two hands hold a vajra and bell, embracing his consort. His consort, in the form of Vajrayoginī, holds a curved knife and skull cup, wears the five symbolic ornaments, and is extremely beautiful. They are delighting in the bliss of union. With his right leg extended and the left bent, they are rising high into the sky.

Yogipa has the appearance of a yogi. He is azure blue and naked. He is holding a mendicant's staff, has his belongings tied to the end of a stick carried over his shoulder, and is holding a skull cup.

Chaluki has the attributes of a yogi. He is lying asleep on a thick cushion called a laṭi. In front of him is a discarded meditation stick. On his left he is accompanied by his wisdom consort.

Gorura is azure blue in color, his lower body clothed in leaves. His hair is uncut. {80} He has the appearance of a hunter, setting traps to catch different kinds of birds.

Luchika is white in color and has the attributes of a brahmin. He is plucking out his hair and whiskers with tweezers.

Naguṇa has the appearance of a layman. He is white in color, tinged with red. He is leaning back on a couch and eating some food.

Jayānanti has the attributes of a celibate brahmin master and teacher. He is wearing a cotton dhoti and seated on an antelope-skin mat. In his hands he holds a pair of small cymbals which he is striking, as he offers a variety of tormas. In front of him, all kinds of birds have gathered. He is surrounded by a retinue of different men and women playing music—beating clay drums, blowing wind instruments, and so forth.

Pachari has the appearance of a shaven-headed yogi. He is sitting in front of a tree and has no clothes apart from a triangular skirt. He has made a fire in front of him and is frying pastries, while eating a piece of pastry himself. In front, Avalokiteshvara has manifested and is teaching the dharma.

Champaka is white in color, tinged with red, in the full bloom of youth. He is wearing a short-sleeved silk robe and is adorned with jewels. In his hand he holds a garland of flowers. All around are groves of champac trees, with their branches growing in round clusters, dark-green leaves and pale golden flowers. He is sitting on a jeweled satin throne in the midst of such a grove.

Bhikṣhana is azure blue in color. In one hand he holds a gourd, and with the other hand one of his own teeth, which he is offering to a peaceful red wisdom ḍākinī with bone ornaments in the sky in front, who is teaching him the dharma.

Dhilipa is wearing a cotton turban and upper and lower garments. In front of him are set out for sale numerous large pots of sesame oil {81} and a variety of foods.

Kumbharipa has the appearance of a potter and is turning a potter's wheel, making earthenware. He is accompanied by a wisdom consort at his side.

Charpaṭipa is white in color, tinged with red. He is wearing a garment called a mekhali, with a hole for the head and neck, and right and left halves front and back, tied with a belt. In his two hands he holds a container of elixir and a vase filled with alchemical essence, whose contents he is sprinkling with a leafy twig, thus instantly setting infinite men and women to the great objective.

Outside them are twenty more siddhas, disposed clockwise starting from the front:

The great lady of yogis Maṇibhadrā is an astoundingly beautiful and perfect young woman in the full bloom of youth, adorned with all kinds of ornaments. She is flying through the sky, looking at a broken water pot on the ground below.

The yoginī Mekhali is white in color, tinged with red, a beautiful young woman in the full bloom of youth. Her hair is loose and she is naked, wearing bone ornaments. She holds a vajra khāṭvāṇga in the crook of her arm. From her mouth she has drawn the sword of wisdom, which she is holding in her right hand. Her left hand holds a skull cup full of nectar. She is standing with her two feet in the dance posture, one leg extended, the other drawn in.

The yoginī Kanakhalā is white in color, tinged with red, naked, in the full bloom of youth, and adorned with bone ornaments. In her right hand she holds the sharp sword of wisdom; in her left, she holds her own decapitated head, as if it were a chopped-off sow's head. She is dancing in the sky with one leg extended and the other drawn in, in the dancing posture.

Kalakala is dark blue and naked. He is absorbed in concentration in the middle of a fearful charnel ground. {82} In the air in front of him is a siddha wearing bone ornaments, who is teaching the dharma.

Kandhalipa is light blue in color and wears a cotton dhoti. His two hands are holding a needle and thread and a patchwork blanket, which he is sewing. He is seated on an animal hide.

Dhahulipa is azure blue in color and has his hair partially tied up in a topknot. He is wearing a cotton dhoti. On his left is his wisdom consort bowing to him. He is making[27] a length of twisted grass rope.

Udhilipa has a reddish-brown appearance and a fine beard. He has the attributes of a layman, with his short-sleeved garment, cotton turban, and so forth. He is adorned with precious ornaments and is sitting on a fine seat. He is looking at the sky, in which there appear five-colored clouds shaped like elephants, horses, birds, and other creatures. Some swans are flying through the sky. In front of him is a yogi holding some leaves and teaching the dharma.

Kapālapa has the appearance of a yogi and is dark blue in color. Apart from a dhoti, he is naked and is adorned with bone ornaments. In front of him lies the corpse of his wife, whose skull he has cut off and is holding in his hand.

Kiravalapa is reddish-brown, with a slightly wrathful look and a fine beard. He is wearing a crown whose five tips (one in the middle and four in the four directions) are topped with jewels. From the precious gold rings in his hair arrangement called the dāka's crown, silken ribbons flutter behind his right and left ears. In his right hand he holds a sword, in his left a shield. He is seated in the posture of royal ease on a jeweled throne.

Sakarapa has the attributes of a fully ordained monk. He is wearing the three dharma robes. In front of him stands noble Avalokiteshvara, whom he is venerating. {83}

Sarvabhakṣhapa is azure blue in color and of low-caste appearance, wearing a cotton dhoti. His hair is tied up. In front of him is a vessel with a variety of foods inside, which he is eating with relish.

Ṇāgabodhi is flesh colored with a light-blue hue and has the appearance of a fully ordained monk. His two hands are held in the meditation gesture, and he is seated on a monk's mat, absorbed in concentration.

Dārikapa is azure blue in color, holding in his two hands a vajra and bell, and flying and soaring through the sky to the accompaniment of rainbow lights. He is attended by the most excellent of women, of inconceivable and perfect form and youth, as he travels to a celestial land.

Putalipa has the attributes of a yogi, with his hair uncut, and is wearing a meditation belt and shorts. He is seated on an antelope-skin mat. He is looking fixedly at a picture painted on cloth of glorious Hevajra, displayed in front of him.

Panahapa is white with a pale-blue tinge, wearing a cotton dhoti and turban. His two hands rest on his hips. His chin is bearded. He is running to the musical sounds of the many tinklers and other ornaments attached to the tops of shoes. This symbolizes the need to be diligent in proceeding speedily to the level of great bliss.

Kokilapa has the attributes of a king. He is white in color, tinged with red, and adorned with brocade garments and precious ornaments. He is seated on a jeweled throne. All around him is a pleasure grove full of fruit trees, in which the most beautiful young maidens are singing and dancing and fanning and bathing him. From the trees come the sweet calls of many black cuckoos.

Anonga is white in color, tinged with red, and so handsome that one cannot take one's eyes off him. He is sitting cross-legged in a grass hut, absorbed in concentration, with one hand in the meditation gesture and the other touching the earth. {84}

The great lady of yogis Lakṣhmīnkarā is white in color, tinged with red, in the full bloom of youth, with an utterly blissful expression. She is the very height of beauty. She is naked, with fully developed breasts and bhaga. She has a semiwrathful appearance. In her right hand she brandishes a vajra curved knife, in her left a skull cup full of blood. She holds a khātvāṇga in the crook of her arm and is adorned with bone ornaments. She is sitting in the posture of royal ease, with one leg stretched out and the other drawn in.

Samudrapa is white in color, tinged with red, and has the attributes of a seafarer, with a dyed robe and a turban. He is sitting with his legs half crossed in the middle of a perfectly built ocean-going ship filled with precious jewels. He is surrounded by many attendants. In the sky above him is the long-haired, naked siddha Achinta, teaching the dharma.

Vyālipa is white in color, tinged with red, and shines with rays of light colored like jewels. He has the attributes of a brahmin, with the brahmin's sacred white thread tied over his shoulder, and wears a cotton dhoti. In his two hand he holds a vessel of elixir. Next to him is a basin of alchemical essence and piles of iron that he is transforming into gold. With him, on his left are his wife, son, and daughter-in-law. In front is a supreme horse, a creature that possesses knowledge of all things, adorned with ornaments.

Visualize all of them shining in a hundred directions with the brilliant light of the coemergent, unchanging wisdom of great bliss. Their bodies are radiant and unbearably bright, like the heart of the sun. Their voices spontaneously proclaim the teachings of the Great Vehicle, the secret mantras. Their minds dwell constantly in meditation on the great union of bliss and emptiness, the Great Seal, profundity and clarity inseparable. In their deeds they display all kinds of unpredictable activities, with magical manifestations that are hard for one to imagine. Bringing phenomenal existence under their power, they overwhelm the three worlds. Infinite gods and goddesses venerate them with ocean-like clouds of offerings. {85}

In their presence, consider your body—the aggregates that result from the ripening of your karma—and imagine that the top of your head is sliced off [to form a skull cup], into which the whole of the rest of your body is put. As I say *oṁ āḥ hūṁ,* it melts completely into wisdom nectar, white with a red luster and endowed with a hundred tastes. The teacher and male and female siddhas drink the nectar, drawing it up through their vajra tongues, which are in the form of tube-like rays of light. As you imagine this, repeat after me:

This deliciously prepared food offering,
Bewitching with its hundred tastes,
I offer with faith to the glorious teacher.
May all these beings have the fortune to enjoy the food of concentration.

*oṁ āḥ hūṁ guru caturā śīti mahā yogeśvara sapari vare bhyaḥ idaṃ baling griṇśanantu mama sarva siddhimem prayaccha*

Next, consider that you emanate bodies numerous as the atoms in the universe and pay homage, touching your head at the feet of the teacher and the male and female mahāsiddhas, and repeat with folded hands:

Through their kindness, great bliss
Arises in an instant.
At the feet of the jewel-like teacher
And of the eighty great siddhas I bow.

Consider that, as a result of your paying homage and praying like this with intense devotion, from the foreheads of the teacher and the eighty-four siddhas, lords of yogis, there flows a stream of white semen bodhichitta,[28] associated with the *kyangma* channel on the left and having the nature of the blessings of the body. It dissolves into your forehead.

The impurities of your body are purified. You receive the vase empowerment, and the blessings of the vajra body enter you.

From their throat centers, there flows a stream of red blood bodhichitta,[29] associated with the *roma* channel on the right and having the nature of the blessings of speech. It dissolves into your throat.

The impurities of your speech are purified. You receive the secret empowerment, and the blessings of the vajra speech enter you. {86}

From between their eyebrows there comes a stream of bodhichitta, a mixture of semen and blood, associated with the central channel and constituting the blessings of mind. It dissolves between your eyebrows.

The impurities of your mind are purified. You receive the wisdom empowerment, and the blessings of the vajra mind enter you.

With these three empowerments you are empowered to practice the three corresponding paths as indicated earlier.[30]

Now, to receive the fourth empowerment, that of the vajra gnosis, without moving from the correct physical posture and the right gaze, please settle in meditation for a moment in the state of intrinsic awareness, the inexpressible bliss-emptiness, unspoiled by the proliferation of conceptual thoughts related to the past, present, and future.

In this regard, as an introduction to the meaning of the natural state, consider that the teacher, in the form of the eighty-four male and female yogis beginning with the mahāsiddha Lūyipa, successively gives you instruction by means of the vajra songs or dohās in which they expressed their own realization.

If you know the melodies, employ them. If not, voice these songs with sweet words, spoken unhurriedly and clearly.

When honey is placed on a wild dog's nose, it does not choose but
eats up everything.
So too, when those with little fortune and intelligence receive the
highest teachings, they are consumed by fire.
Those with good fortune who have realized the unborn
nature destroy conceptual thoughts simply by encountering
appearances,
Like the drunk elephant Rapten[31] whose sword-tipped trunk
annihilates the enemy troops. [Lūyipa][32]

In the jungle of the four boundless attitudes,
The king of yogis is like a lion,
Its head adorned with a mane of five turquoise locks—
The five buddha families arising as the signs of the practice.
With its ten claws, the lion
Rips an elephant's flesh from the bones;
With the ten perfections, the yogi
Rips away their opposites, conceptual thoughts.
With such realization was Līlapa freed. [Līlapa]

Rest in your own natural state—not thought, not known, no
self—
Coemergent with the state of the Great Seal.[33]
Not a nihilist nothing, it is experienced and knows itself.
Not an eternalist something, it is union, without grasping.
[Virūpa] {87}

Like the alchemist's elixir
That turns iron into gold,
The precious empowerment is able to transform
Defilements into nondual gnosis. [Ḍombipa]

In the forest of ignorance
There roamed the deer of subject-object dualism.
Drawing the bow of means and wisdom,
I shot the single arrow of the essential meaning,
And death ensued—the death of all conceptual thought.
I ate the flesh as nonduality.

I savored its taste as great bliss
And obtained the result—the Great Seal. [Shavaripa]

Behold, my friends, the coemergent state
Is not to be found elsewhere but in the holy teacher's words.
When you realize the essence of that ultimate nature,
The mind will never die; the body will not disintegrate. [Saraha]

In the emptiness of space,
When one and other are abandoned,
The self-appearing queen of gnosis takes form,
Beyond compare, beyond all designation. [Kaṅkālapāda]

A fisherman who held on to his hook
Was swept into the sea by karma's force
But kept alive inside a giant fish,
Wherein he practiced Mahādeva's words.
Earth and rock could not support his weight,
So excellent was he they called Fish Man or Mīnapa. [Mīnapa]

When one's potential—highest, least, or in between—
Is reinforced by circumstance, the unobstructed power of deeds
Will lead to the result—a wondrous thing, indeed.
With bodhichitta I served Chauraṅgi;
Because of that, the seed of enlightenment was sown.
Achinta showed me the nectar of deathlessness,
And I, Gorakṣha, beheld the nondual ultimate reality.
So marvel at me, the cowherd king of the three worlds!
[Gorakṣha]

For ages in this world without beginning,
The tree of ignorance had taken root,
And watered by conditioning,
Its boughs—existence—grew and spread.
But I, Chauraṅgi, swung my ax—
And with my holy teacher's words
And wisdom gained by threefold means,
I felled that mighty tree of ignorance! [Chauraṅgi]

With perseverance and devotion, I distinguished {88}
The sound of my habitual errors
And then enjoyed the unarisen sound of the unborn.
Thus did I, Vīnapa, realize no-self. [Vīnapa]

Like little boys who, nurtured by their mothers,
Grow into able-bodied men,
Small-minded folk are counseled by their teachers
And led in stages to the Great Vehicle.
Like the doctor's medicine that cures
Those with wind or bile or phlegm disease,
The teacher's guidance and advice at once burn up
The "I" and the belief in "I." [Ratnākarashānti]

The weavers of the world
Weave together all their threads,
While I, listening to my teacher's words,
Weave together all phenomena.
Emptiness is my loom, the five wisdoms my threads;
The pith instructions are my heddle,
And wisdom the shuttle that I use to weave
The body of truth, the nonduality of expanse and awareness.
[Tantipa]

This leather of attributes and conceptual thoughts
I soak in emptiness and compassion,
And using the thread of freedom from the eight concerns,
I sew it with the awl of wisdom and experience.
Spontaneously creating the shoe of the body of truth,
I am Chamaripa, the supreme cobbler. [Chamaripa]

However constantly an unarmed warrior
Does battle with his enemies,
He will be overpowered by suffering.[34]
But with the sword of deathless wisdom
The enemies of the three worlds were vanquished,
And Khaḍgapa enjoys the greatest happiness. [Khaḍgapa]

Those who are not realized should not act as if they are:
They'd be like common subjects trying to seize the throne.
Realized beings should never follow ordinary ways:
They'd be like elephants mired in a swamp. [Nāgārjuna]

Without four wheels, a car will never get one anywhere:
Without a teacher, efforts on the paramita path will never bring supreme accomplishment.
A vulture, fully fledged, on outstretched wings can soar across the sky:
Yogis blessed with fortune absorb the teachings that empower and thus gain happiness. [Kṛiṣhṇāchāri]

The buddhas of the three times are of a single essence.
That essence, when realized, is the nature of your own mind.
If you wish for realization, settle in the unfabricated nature. {89}
Once you are used to that, you will truly be a yogi. [Āryadeva]

Like someone with water in their ear
Using water to blow it out again,
Get used to the lie—the falsehood of appearance and existence—
And then you'll come to see the truth. [Thaganapa]

Like the universal monarch and his armies
Ruling over the entire world,
The yogi who discovers the taste of the innate
Dominates samsara and knows great bliss. [Nāropa]

Well-trained artists draw and paint
Pictures that strike terror in one's heart.
But look at what it is that frightens you:
It's just an image, there's nothing real there! [Shyalipa]

Birds that dwell on Meru's heights
Look as if they're made of gold.
The wise who realize the unborn
Forsake materiality and gain great bliss. [Tilopa]

Everything that yogis see they see as an instruction;
Realization that it is unborn is their greatest teacher.
They'll never taste the fruits of deeds, both good and bad,
That come from immature beings' dualistic thoughts. [Chatrapa]

Through the realization of emptiness, delusion is purified.
Through meditation on love, conduct is perfected.
Through meditation on the absence of two in diversity,
The result is the one taste, the common ground. [Bhadrapa]

Meditating on the Great Seal—the union
Of the relative, the generation stage,
And the ultimate, the perfection stage—
I saw the wisdom of the three bodies, the result. [Dhukhandi]

With the instructions of my holy teacher
I meditated on a drop on the tip of my nose,
And with mind fixed firmly on that upper door,
I saw a billion worlds within a mustard seed. [Āyogipāda]

Since time without beginning these beings have been deluded,
And so it is the whole world called me mad.
The nectarous medicine of my teacher's words
Consumed in an instant the sickness of delusion. [Kalapa]

However long one tries to wash out stains,
There is no making charcoal's nature white.
To cleanse the stains that cover emptiness—already pure—
The teacher's counsel is the best of washermen. {90} [Dhombipa]

The wish-fulfilling gem of realization
Glows with the luster of experience,
Powerful activity fulfilling every need.
It is the prize of those with even taste. [Kaṅkana]

I wonder at the ocean, deep and vast and filled with jewels,
And the nāga kings who revel in all that wealth.

I wonder at the sights and sounds that are primordially the body of truth,
And those with realization reveling in its wealth. [Kambala]

A horse, an elephant, the ocean illustrate the highest bliss.
Monkeys, children, water-drawings illustrate realization.
A river, the sun, and medicine illustrate indivisibility.
A topknot, an eye, and a wheel symbolize the result attained. [Ḍiṅgipa]

Absence of attachment is the highest love.
Compassion is to know just how things are.
Bliss completely free of taint is joy.
Impartiality is basic harmony—one taste. [Bhandhepa]

All kinds of memories and conscious thoughts
Come to an end in the space of thoughtlessness;
And likewise all things that appear and exist
Come to an end in the space of emptiness. [Tandhepa]

"Buddha, dharma, . . ." such thoughts do not benefit—
Wishes and efforts cannot lead to buddhahood.
The glory of experience comes from the teacher's blessings:
It's there inside you, lucky one, but you can't see it. [Kukkuripa]

Under the spotlight of the teacher's words,
One fails to find extremes like "is" and "isn't."
Finding nothing is itself an extreme;
To realize that is the ultimate goal. [Kujipa]

The poison of dualism and ignorance
Constantly afflicts the rational.
The blessings of the teacher's word
Remove the poison of delusion in the world. [Dhamapa]

The mountain of one's ignorance and pride
Conceals the wishing gem of realization,

Whose powerful activity fulfills one's every need.
It is the prize of those with even taste. [Mahila]

In the nonconceptual Great Seal,
Empty all your deluded thoughts.
With the light of gnosis and awareness,
See everything that appears as the Great Seal. [Achinta]

Like the king of swans,
Which separates milk from water, {91}
The holy teacher's words
Distill the nectarous bodhichitta.[35]

Bliss! Bliss! Immaterial bliss!
Devoid of clinging, immaterial bliss!
Bliss—every thought recognized as bliss!
Bliss—the secret of nothing to be attained. [Babhahi]

In the petaled lotus of the crown,
The motile seed leads to joy.
In the heart and throat, supreme joy,
And then the unsurpassed coemergent and special joys.[36] [Nalina]

Until one is realized, one loves to experience different tastes,
And that's the great distinction between samsara and
buddhahood.
But once realization is attained, samsara and nirvana are great bliss,
Like a precious jewel shining in the ocean's depths. [Shāntideva]

If one does not have the blessings at the crucial time,
Outer and inner conduct will not lead to enlightenment.
There is no difference between joyous bliss and the buddhas;
When one abandons clinging, supreme experience will naturally
arise. [Indrabhūti]

The teachers say, "First realize the nature of your mind.
After that, make no distinctions in any way:

Get used to nonduality and stay in charnel grounds.
When you've realized sameness, lead a madman's way of life."
[Mekopa]

The source of all happiness and pain is mind,
So use the teachings to excavate the mountain of the mind.
However much one toils to dig away a mountain made of earth,
The great bliss of the natural state will never be attained.

Wake up the "ordinary" mind in the center of your heart;
When the six senses are purified, the flow of great bliss never stops.
There's no point in analysis; it's all a source of suffering.
Whether you are meditating or not, rest in the natural state.
[Togchepa]

My body is a blacksmith's forge,[37]
My thoughts and concepts burning coals;
The right- and left-hand veins are bellows,
Blowing the central, wisdom, vein ablaze
To forge the ultimate body of truth
By hammering out defiling thoughts.
I am Kamparipa, the smith
Who realized this and thus was freed. [Kamparipa]

In order that I bless myself
I will bind in the right, left, and central veins
All the thoughts and concepts of the triple world
Related to my body, speech, and mind. [Jālandhara] {92}

The planet Rāhu outside
Eclipses the light of the moon,
And the two are no longer there.
The Rāhu of space and awareness
Eclipses the lunar circle of relative phenomena,
And duality disappears.[38] [Rāhula]

Pour the oil of the awakening mind
Into the lamp of the phenomenal world,
And light the wick of the six consciousnesses
With the flame of nondual gnosis,
To banish the darkness of deluded thought. [Dharmapa]

In the bowl that is the expanse of reality
Place the ingredients—awareness, the body of truth.
A fortunate practitioner, with awareness,
Realizes the fruit of expanse and awareness inseparable. [Dhokaripa]

With the wisdom of the natural state, awareness,
And the skillful means of training in experience,
From the pure ground of the natural way things are
The spontaneous result of great bliss is realized. [Medhina]

To one without a teacher and with no realization
The wishing gem and a cheap trinket look the same.
But under a teacher's guidance, once realization is gained,
They are as different as the light of sun and moon and a firefly's glow. [Saṅkaja]

In order to bring blessings on oneself,
One binds the right, left, and central veins.
In order to give rise to realization,
The wise attend to teacher, mind, and appearances. [Ghaṇḍhapa]

It is by training the ordinary mind,
Which is as bright and subtle as the tip of a flame,
That all things, the animate and inanimate,
Dissolve into the expanse of reality. [Yogipa]

When one has meditated for great lengths of time
On the holy teacher's words of advice,
One by one, earth and the other elements dissolve,
And thence one's own perceptions transform into the Great Seal. [Chaluki]

All outer and inner phenomena are gathered in the mind,
And mind itself is clarity. When this is realized,
The four modes of conduct are realized as the body of truth.
Such realization is perfect buddhahood. [Gorura]

One who, since beginningless time,
Was drifting in samsara's sea,
So hard to cross, today is saved
By that great ship, the holy guide. [Luchika]

Stabilize experiences, which are like waves,
And then proceed with conduct, step by step.
With the advice the holy teacher gives,
Desire and hatred will naturally subside. [Naguṇa] {93}

The concentration that knows primordial wisdom
Dwells on the natural state from the very beginning.[39]
To realize this, as it is, is certainty.
Concepts and memories are not that state. [Jayānanti]

Not looking anywhere, look at the center:
Supreme joy, absence of joy, great bliss!
If one examines the secret power of mantra,
It is subsumed in the yogi's buddha nature. [Pachari]

Like the clear light of means and wisdom,
The stream of the teacher's blessings permeates all.
On the wish-fulfilling tree of the innate,
The radiant fruits of the three bodies are complete. [Champaka]

Following the path of the union Great Bliss
To the sacred land of highest enlightenment, so difficult to reach,
The supreme lord of yogis, free of partiality,
Attains realization through the teacher's kindness and advice.
[Bhikṣhana]

From the very beginning, I am enlightened:
Because of my realization, everything is ultimate reality.

With the innate [wisdom] received through empowerment
I affix the seal of the unborn, Vajradhara.[40] [Dhilipa]

The self-perpetuating wheel of deeds
Produced the manifold drama of the world.
The fire of primordial wisdom and awareness
Has consumed all delusion and impurity. [Kumbharipa]

The supreme commitment of all the buddhas,
Realized by oneself, is nothing other than
Realization of the natural state, the nature of mind,
And with it the vision of all the buddhas. [Charpaṭipa]

As long as one is not realized,
All kinds of thoughts chase after sounds.
When one has realized the nature of thatness,
All that appears is by nature thatness. [Maṇibhadrā]

Everything, without, within, is gathered in the mind,
And when it is free of clinging, all is of even taste.
To be without effort is the highest meditation.
Nondual great bliss is perfect buddhahood. [Mekhali]

Donning the [bodhisattva's] great armor,
With jewel-like determination
One sets sail in the boat of one's mind
And is certain to enter a human corpse. [Kanakhalā][41]

In the pure firmament of the expanse of reality
The thunder of the unborn resounds:
All the world's delusory phenomena
Are beautified by the result—the gnosis of the three bodies.
[Kalakala] {94}

With the needle of the sacred guide
And the thread of compassion,
I sewed the yogi's marvelous cloth,
Clothing all the beings in the three worlds. [Kandhalipa]

The precious treasure of union awareness,
The state of nonduality, is not something that can be sought.
Give up activity, and in that state of mind,
Settling there, you will find bliss. [Dhahulipa]

Following thoughts, one is deluded.
Make not following them a habit, and do not give it up.
Dwelling nowhere, gather in all movements:
You will not find anything by looking elsewhere. [Udhilipa]

Nondual Vajradhara, the nature of all things;
These ornaments and skull, which are momentary;
And the delusion of grasping at an "I" too—
One will never find them by looking for them. [Kapālapa]

Until one gains realization, one is fettered by concepts of self and others.
When realization is achieved, self and others no longer exist.
So-called buddha is one's own intellectual label.
Without elaboration or contrivance, settle the mind in its own state. [Kiravalapa]

On the people tormented by suffering
A rain of all good things was showered down.
In the sacred land of suchness,
On fortunate male and female vidyādharas
Who have coerced the nāga king of awareness,
A rain of secret mantra awareness is showered down.[42] [Sakarapa]

For one who has no realization, different flavors are quite distinct.
When one is realized, flavors are in essence no different.
So too, when one is not realized, samsara and nirvana appear to be distinct.
For one who realizes thatness, samsara is buddhahood, great bliss. [Sarvabhakṣhapa]

If one lives on the earth, everything is good fortune.
If one reaches the depths of the sea, one is never poor.

If one brandishes a sword, one has great wealth.
If one comes to those without partiality, one meets with friends.
[Nāgabodhi]

Great bliss is present in us, but we do not know that; it is hidden by delusion.
Those who wish for bliss and clarity must gather merit and wisdom.
Those who fail to accumulate these two may live a hundred lives of toil,
But, lacking a great teacher, they will never realize great bliss.
[Dārikapa]

All is the nature of sugata;
Give up wrong paths based on intellect {95}
And strive on the essential path:
There is no doubt you will get the essential fruit.
Those who take empowerment from a holy teacher
Are entirely pervaded by the flavor
Of the coemergent wisdom,
Affixing the seal of the unborn, Vajradhara. [Putalipa]

In reflecting on the essence, the meaning of the natural state,
What you reflect on is what you will realize.
That is all there is to it,
And all you wish for will come effortlessly. [Pahanapa]

To give up activity is the pith instruction.
To be without hope is realization.
Bliss without substantiality is meditation.
Nothing to accomplish is the supreme result. [Kokilapa]

All samsara is hollow, essenceless,[43]
Yet, poisoned by ignorance, attachment, and pride,
We cling to this body like a rainbow
And believe that we are happy.
Once our poisoning by attachment is cured,
Samsara is itself the body of truth. [Anonga]

First, the wise develop realization,
Then they meditate, undistracted from the actual way things are.
After that, as their experience grows,
They should engage in conduct gradually. [Lakṣhmīnkarā]

One who has realized the unborn but has no experience
Is like an ogress with a baby in her arms.
One whose experience is not related to the actual way things are
Is like an elephant mired in a swamp. [Samudrapa]

To see the holy teacher is to see thatness.
To meditate on the sky's expanse is the highest solitude.
To fully realize the nature of phenomena is to be free of conflict.
To drink the milk of space is to find your sustenance. [Vyālipa]

Consider that you have been given each of these instructions. Again, think that you are requesting blessings, and consider that as a result of your intense devotion, the teacher and all the eighty-four siddhas, the lords of yogis, gradually melt into a mass of light and dissolve into you. All the blessings of their body, speech, and mind are transferred into your mind as if imprinted on it.

With this, place a few grains from the colored sand mandala on the disciples' heads and ring the bell. As you do so, say: {96}

All you hosts of male and female siddhas who appeared in India,
 every one of you without exception, grant your blessings.
And in particular, all you eighty-four great lords of yogis, Lūyipa
 and the others, grant your blessings on these vajra disciples.
Bless their bodies with the vajra body.
Bless their speech with the vajra speech.
Bless their minds with the vajra mind.
Bless them with the wheel of the ornaments of inexhaustible
 qualities.
Bless them with the four activities.
Bless them with the inconceivable secret.
Bless them this very moment.
Bless them quickly.

> Bless them in this very session.
> *jaḥ hūṁ baṃ hoḥ*

> With this, consider that the obscurations preventing the transformation of the three doors are purified, you receive the four empowerments, and the blessings of the vajra gnosis enter you.
>
> You have now received the blessings of the eighty-four great siddhas all together.

At this point, it is customary to give the authorization empowerment of Achala by way of introducing the disciples to a yidam deity, but there is no fault in omitting it. However, if you wish to do so, give it here. For this, you may use whichever tradition is convenient, but the usual practice is to give the empowerment from Dorje Denpa's six yidam deities.[44]

At the end, bestow the blessings of the attendant dharma protector. For this you can simply use the concise daily practice of the Protector with the Curved Knife (Gönpo Triguk), but you may also do so according to the customary practice with the four-armed Gönpo found in the Drukpa Kagyu texts, as follows:

> Next, to receive the blessings of the Glorious Wisdom Lord, the protector of the Vajrayāna teachings who attends the mahāsiddhas, concentrate on the following. This mandala in front, which is the basis of appearance, is a boundlessly vast buddha field, the Unexcelled Display of the Great Secret, completely surrounded by a protection circle. Inside it, in the center of a terrifying charnel ground, on a throne of lotus, sun, and the corpses of liberated enemies and obstacle makers, is the Great Glorious Wisdom Protector (Mahākāla), his color as black as the clouds and darkness at the end of the kalpa. Short and corpulent, with his belly hanging down and thick limbs, he has a single wrathful face and four arms. He rolls his three eyes, {97} which are round and red, like sparks of fire. His mustache, eyebrows, and beard are orange, emitting a fiery light. Of his four hands, the first on the right displays the gesture of supreme giving, and the second holds a blazing fiery sword. The first left hand holds a skull cup full of blood, while the second brandishes a trident draped with silks

and a small hand drum. He has a crown of five dried-out human skulls topped with a black vajra. He is wearing a long necklace of fifty freshly severed heads dripping blood, and he is adorned with venomous snakes and bone ornaments. His lower garment is a fresh tiger skin. He sits with his two legs in different postures of royal ease, with one leg stretched out and the other bent. He manifests in the middle of a fiercely blazing mass of wisdom fire in the form of the utterly terrifying, great glorious heruka, the sovereign of the wrathful ones. All the haughty spirits of the three worlds bow down to him. In his presence, consider your body, the aggregates that result from the ripening of your karma, and imagine that the top of your head is sliced off [to form a skull cup], into which the whole of the rest of your body is put. As I say *oṁ āḥ hūṁ*, it melts completely into wisdom nectar, which is white with a red luster and endowed with a hundred tastes. Consider that Mahākāla drinks it, drawing it up through his vajra tongue, which is in the form of tube-like rays of light. Repeat after me:

> This deliciously prepared food offering,
> Bewitching with its hundred tastes,
> I offer with faith to venerable Mahākāla.
> May all these beings have the fortune to enjoy the food of concentration.
>
> *oṁ āḥ hūṁ śrī mahākāla ganacakra sapari vāre bhyaḥ idaṃ baling grihaṇanantu mama sarva siddhimem prayaccha*

For the homage:

> You who have attained a wealth of magical powers and knowledge,
> Who perfectly guard the treasury of the precious teachings
> According to the command of the buddhas—
> To the supreme vajra dharma protector we pay homage.

And:

Consider that, as the result of your paying homage and praying

> like this with intense devotion, from the forehead of the Glorious Wisdom Protector . . . and so on, up to . . . settle in meditation for a moment in the state of intrinsic awareness, the inexpressible bliss-emptiness, unspoiled by the proliferation of conceptual thoughts related to the past, present, and future,

following the same sequence as above.[45]

> Now, consider that from your having prayed with intense devotion and longing, the Glorious Wisdom Protector melts completely into a mass of light, which dissolves into you, so that you acquire all the blessings of the body, speech, mind, qualities, and activities.

Place the torma representing the mandala on the disciples' heads and say:

> Glorious Vajra Mahākāla and your retinue, {98} do not transgress your respective commitments with the great Vajradhara and other buddhas and with the glorious and sacred root and lineage teachers.
>
> Preserve the Buddha's teachings and foster beings' happiness.
>
> Especially, from now on until they attain perfect buddhahood, protect these vajra disciples from all adverse conditions and obstacles.
>
> Remove everything that is unfavorable and bring about all favorable conditions.
>
> Perform the activities of eradicating all evil enemies and obstacle makers who harm and endanger the Buddha's doctrine in general and these vidyādharas in particular. In short, fulfill the wishes of those who practice this vidyādhara path and bestow all the common and extraordinary accomplishments without exception.

Recite the essence mantra and the root mantra *śā sa na*, and so on, and say:

> *jaḥ hūṁ baṃ hoḥ*

> This completes the series of blessings of the eighty-four siddhas

> of India, along with the supporting elements, which you have been properly offered, free of the faults of omissions, additions, or errors, and in accordance with the views and teachings of the Indian siddhas and their intended meaning, established by the most learned scholars and holy accomplished beings. So now, thinking that you will keep all the root and branch commitments without deteriorating them, repeat after me:
>
> > Whatever the lord commands . . .[46]
>
> Offer the mandala by way of giving thanks,

and so on.

> Again, as you offer to the teacher inseparable from the deity your body, possessions, and virtue accumulated in the past, present, and future, think, "Please use every last part of it," and repeat after me: {99}
>
> > From now on, . . .[47]
>
> Please now dedicate the merit of all this together for the benefit of sentient beings as numerous as the sky is vast.

Conclude by reciting:

> By this merit . . .[48]

After that, the master, with the symbolic gestures of offering and accepting, enjoys the gaṇachakra ingredients in the manner of an inner fire offering. Plant a light on the remainders and cleanse and purify them.

> From the state of emptiness appears a letter *A*, from which there manifests a vast and spacious wisdom kapāla, in which the remainders torma becomes a great ocean of nectar, excellent and vast.
> *oṁ āḥ hūṁ ha hoḥ hrīḥ*

Say the *akaro* mantra three times.

> This is given to the host of wild *jungpo* spirits who dwell outside before the gate and are not allowed to see the samaya rituals. May they come to possess the fortune of practicing the yoga of the supreme secret in the Vajrayāna.
> *oṁ ucchiṣṭa baliṅgta bhakśasi svāhā.*

Send it outside. Then add this vajra song, ringing the bell:

*kolla i renṭha*[49] *a bolla*
*mumma ṇire ka kako la*
*ghaṇa kripita ho vajja i*
*karuṇi ki a i ṇarolā*
*tā hiṃvala khājja ī*
*gāḍmaṃ aṇā vajja a i*
*haleka liñca rapa ṇi a i*
*dudhura vajji a i*
*ca usama kaccha raṃ sahil*
*kasura la i a i*
*mala inddhana sāliṃjaḥ*
*tahi bharu kha i a i*
*phreṃ khaṇa kheṭa karanta*
*śurdha aśurdhaṇaṇ mani a i*
*ni raṃ ru aṃ gaṃ caḍavi*
*ha hi jaṃ sarāva vāṇi a i*
*mala acakuntu ruva a i*
*ḍiṇa ḍima tahina vajja a i*

Alternatively, you may add it at the end after going straight through the concluding sections. Besides this, sing whatever vajra songs are appropriate. Rest in meditation on the bliss-emptiness of union with the mudrā, real or imagined. If the self-visualization is Chakrasaṃvara, go through the individual concluding stages beginning with donning armor and securing the directions. Recite the general prayers of aspiration of the great secret and in particular, "By venerating the vīras without duality . . ." and so on, along with extensive prayers for auspiciousness, to make the light of fortune and excellence shine far and wide.

Through the blessings of the great vajra primordial wisdom,
May inconceivable fortunate beings attain realization and liberation at the same time, {100}
And without separating from the supreme siddhas,
May they become the lords of all that lives.

This way [of conferring blessings] is not something I thought up and invented for convenience and ease of implementation. Rather, I was fortunate enough to receive the specific approval of my lord Jamyang Khyentse Wangpo, who is inseparable from the great charioteers of India, to make this arrangement in accord with the instructions he received in a pure wisdom vision from the mahāsiddha Lvavapa (Kambala)—the one who wears a woolen cloak. Accordingly, I, Karma Ngawang Yönten Gyatso, took as a basis the tradition and practices of the first and second Jonang Jetsuns, uncorrupted by the stains of compounded confusion, and made this clear arrangement in the dharma college of Tashi Lhatse at Dzongsar.

May virtue and excellence increase.

# 3. The Source of Accomplishments

*An Offering and Prayer Ritual to the Eighty-Four Mahāsiddhas of India*[1]

THIS IS a long offering and prayer ritual to the eighty-four mahāsiddhas, centered around Vajradhara. Jamgön Kongtrul compiled it from a number of different sources, arranging it on the lines of a ritual of venerating the teacher (*bla ma mchod pa*), with the detailed offering section characteristic of this genre. The praise includes an optional section containing verses in praise of each of the eighty-four mahāsiddhas. In many cases, the first two lines of these verses provide extremely condensed accounts of the respective siddhas' lives.*

{102}
*namo guru yogeshvaraya*
By following the path of the unsurpassable mantras as instructed,
They attained the union state beyond training in one body, one life:
At the lotus feet of the yogis and yoginīs who attained supreme
  accomplishment
Respectfully I bow down: bless my stream of being.

Simply hearing their names brings great benefit,
So if we venerate and pray to them with faith,

*See Abhayadatta, *Buddha's Lions: The Lives of the Eighty-Four Siddhas*, trans. James B. Robinson (Berkeley, CA: Dharma Publishing, 1979), and Keith Dowman, *Masters of Mahamudra: Songs and Histories of the Eighty-Four Buddhist Siddhas* (Albany: State University of New York Press, 1985).

They will free us from the bonds of existence and peace and effortlessly
bestow the two accomplishments.
Rid of all doubt, I will here explain this point.

The way to perform a detailed accumulation of merit, making offerings and praying to the eighty-four mahāsiddhas according to the tradition of Āchārya Vīraprabhāsvara, comprises a practice in three sections, similar to the general sections for a veneration of the teacher described by Jetsun Tāranātha: the preparation, which consists of setting out the ritual articles and offerings; the main practice, comprising the stages for accumulating merit; and the conclusion, in which one receives the blessings, dissolves the visualization, and so on.

First, the preparation. In a quiet, pleasant location, clean the venue and decorate it with whatever you can collect in the way of canopies, victory banners, and so forth. In a central position, put up a painting of the hundred siddhas. In front of it, set up an altar covered with a cloth, and in the middle of it arrange a tripod or a high table on which you should place the mandala. In front, set out a hundred or so each of the two water offerings and, if you have them, of flowers, incense, lamps, scented water, {103} and food offerings. If you do not have so many, arrange three sets of offerings or just a single set. If they are available, set out two- or three-dimensional images representing the offerings such as forms, sounds, smells, flavors, and physical sensations; the auspicious objects and symbols; the seven attributes of royalty; the sixteen offering goddesses; and so on. If you don't have these, they can be visualized. Gather the inner offering—a skull cup of nectar—and whatever offerings you can for the feast offering.

In front of you prepare the finest precious mandala, clean grains for the piles, a conch filled with pure ablution water, the ingredients from a cow[2] and scented water, the offering mandala, vajra and bell, and the different musical instruments.

Second, the main practice. First of all, maintaining the pride of yourself as the postmeditational deity, bless the place and offerings. Cleanse and purify them with

*oṁ vajra amṛta kuṇḍalī hana hana hūṁ phaṭ*
*oṁ svabhāva śuddāḥ sarvadharmāḥ svabhāva śuddho 'haṃ*
From the state of emptiness the place appears as the syllable

*bhrūṁ*, from which there manifests a multistory measureless palace made of precious materials, complete with all the attributes.

In its center is the syllable *oṁ*, from which vast and spacious containers made of precious materials appear. {104} Inside them, from the melting of *hūṁ* syllables, there appear offerings made from celestial substances: drinking water, water for the feet, flowers, incense, lamps, scented water, food offerings, musical instruments, and so forth—excellent, meritorious offerings filling the whole of space.

*oṁ vajra arghaṃ svāhā*
*oṁ vajra pādyaṃ svāhā*
*oṁ vajra puṣpe āḥ hūṁ*
*oṁ vajra dhūpe āḥ hūṁ*
*oṁ vajra āloke āḥ hūṁ*
*oṁ vajra gandhe āḥ hūṁ*
*oṁ vajra naividye āḥ hūṁ*
*oṁ vajra śabda āḥ hūṁ*

In this way, playing music, bless the offerings.[3]

Recite condensed or detailed verses of refuge and bodhichitta as appropriate, in the usual manner, or in short, say three times:

> In the Buddha, the dharma, and the supreme assembly . . .[4]

Meditate on the four boundless attitudes with:

> May all beings come to possess happiness and the causes of happiness . . .[5]

> In an instant, there appear, present in the sky in front, the teacher Vajradhara and the assembly of male and female siddhas.

Bless the water with *oṁ vajra udake hūṁ svāhā*. Take the little conch with *oṁ hrīḥ svāhā*. Rinse their mouth with *oṁ vaṃ svāhā*. Washing the head and face, recite:

As from the moment of your birth . . .[6]
*oṁ sarva tathāgata abhiṣekata samaya śrī ye hūṁ*

Touching the three centers, say: *oṁ āḥ hūṁ.* Place a flower on the seat and say: *oṁ tiṣṭha vajra āsana hūṁ oṁ vajra vava nava naya svāhā.*

Put a flower behind the ear and say: *oṁ vajra amṛta kuṇḍali rakṣa maṃ sarva vighnān bhyaḥ.*

Blessing the scented water: *oṁ vajra udake hūṁ svāhā.*

Blessing the flowers: say three or seven times: *oṁ namo bhagavate puṣpa ketu rājāya tathāgatāya arhate samyaksambuddhaya tadyaṭhā oṁ puṣpe puṣpe mahāpuṣpe supuṣpe puṣpe saṃbhave buṣpotbhave puṣpa girṇe svāhā.*

Blessing the ingredients from a cow and so on: *oṁ gomaye svāhā.*

Cleansing away obstacle makers: *oṁ vajra sattva vighnanu sāraya hūṁ phaṭ.*

Designing the mandala:

*oṁ vajra rekhe svāhā*
Generosity in adding cow's dung and urine,
Discipline in cleaning,
Patience in removing insects,
Diligence in the endeavor one applies,
Concentration as one thinks of these, {105}
Wisdom in very clear visualization—
These are the six transcendent perfections
That make the Capable One's mandala the perfect deed.
By such physical deeds
One's body will become like gold.
One will be completely free from all disease.
One will be superior to gods and humans,
Be resplendent as the moon,
Have perfect and abundant riches and gold,
And be born in the supreme house
Of a royal family and of the Buddha.

After this, to make the design, say: *oṁ vajra rekhe sarva buddha adhiṣṭhāntu svāhā.* Rinse the mandala with the water: *oṁ vaṃ svāhā.* Wipe the mandala with: *oṁ candra arka vimale svāhā.* Strew it with flowers and recite the hundred syllables: *oṁ vajra sattva samaya . . . .*

Then dispose the twenty-three piles in order. Begin by placing one pile in the center, as you say: *oṁ haṃ sumeru namaḥ.*

In the east: *yaṃ videhadvīpa namaḥ.*
In the south: *ri jambudvīpa namaḥ.*
In the west: *laṃ godanīdvīpa namaḥ.*
In the north: *vaṃ kurudvīpa namaḥ.*
In the east, on the right and left: *yaḥ yaḥ upadvīpa namaḥ.*
In the south, to the right and left: *raḥ raḥ upadvīpa namaḥ.*
In the west, to the right and left: *laḥ laḥ upadvīpa namaḥ.*
In the north, to the right and left: *vaḥ vaḥ upadvīpa namaḥ.*
In the northwest: *laḥ tu radga ratnāya namaḥ.*
In the southwest: *raḥ hasti ratnāya namaḥ.*
In the southeast: *yaḥ gaja ratnāya namaḥ.*
In the northeast: *vaḥ stī ratnāya namaḥ.*
In the center, to the east: *yaḥ gaḍga ratnāya namaḥ.*
In the center, to the south: *raḥ maṇi ratnāya namaḥ.*
In the center, to the north: *vaḥ nidhi ratnāya namaḥ.*
In the center to the west: *laḥ cakra ratnāya namaḥ.*
In the east: *oṁ aṃ candra.*
In the west: *oṁ āḥ sūrya.*

> *oṁ oṁ* The boundless riches of realms, worldly and beyond the world, whose nature is infinite clouds of offerings like those that Samantabhadra magically manifested—*namaḥ*
> The accumulations of virtue that I and others have gathered with our body, speech, and mind in the three times,
> This excellent mandala of the most perfect riches,
> I pledge and offer to the host of glorious teachers. {106}
> Accept it out of compassion and grant your blessings.

Reciting this, place the mandala in the middle of the altar.

The visualization of the support:

> This mandala is a pure wisdom buddha field of full dimensions and extent, perfect in its adornments and layout, surrounded by an impenetrable outer protection circle. In its center is the measureless palace of great liberation, whose specific materials and architecture are to be marveled and wondered at. It is decorated

with infinite charnel ground attributes and celestial offerings. In its center is a great lion throne, with cushions of lotus, sun, and moon. And in all the directions around it are visualized the particular thrones appropriate to each of the siddhas.

Inviting the fields of merit:

*oṁ* All-pervading lord, the very nature of all things,
Without location, free of coming and going, like the sky,
Although you are not characterized by coming and staying,
Glorious Heruka, you who delight in great bliss,
Hosts of male and female siddhas, sovereign yogis and yoginīs,
With the teachers, yidam deities, and ḍākinīs,
As I pray to you now with faith,
Appear here through the power of nonconceptual compassion.
Supreme beings, you who have the eye of nondual wisdom,
Though in the body of truth there is no departing or arriving,
Please manifest out of compassion in the form body:
Come, I pray, as the objects of veneration by the faithful.
*oṁ guru vajradhara sarva yogeśvara deva ḍākinī ehaye hi vajra samājaḥ*

With this, consider that the fields of merit come like gathering clouds and take their places on their respective seats.

Upon the central throne is my root teacher in the form of the all-pervading lord, the great Vajradhara, blue in color, with one face and two hands crossed at his heart level, holding vajra and bell and embracing his wisdom consort, who is his own manifestation. He is seated with his legs crossed in the vajra posture and is adorned with all the silks and jewel ornaments. {107} He has all the major and minor marks complete and is smiling, naturally joyful. His body radiates infinite lights and rays of light.

In all the directions around him, headed by the great accomplished master Lūyipa, are the eighty mahāsiddhas and the four sister ḍākinīs.

All of them are dazzlingly brilliant like the heart of the sun, shining in a hundred directions with the light of the wisdom of coemergent great bliss. They look extremely courageous, with their yogic gaze that overawes the three worlds. Their voices constantly intone the indestructible vajra sounds of the secret mantras. Their minds never waver from meditation in the state of the Great Seal, nondual gnosis. The display of their spontaneous, uninterrupted activities is inexhaustible. Venerated and praised by infinite ḍākas and ḍākinīs, they are joyfully considering the rulers of the three worlds honoring them.

As well as them, there are present the lineage teachers, the hosts of deities of the yidam mandalas, the buddhas and bodhisattvas, the noble listeners and solitary realizers, and all the dharma protectors and guardians.

Noble lords, you who have come for the sake of beings,
Accept the drinking water I offer,
And until I have finished venerating you,
Please stay happily on these pleasing thrones.

With *oṁ pravara sarkara argham̩ pratīccha svāhā* offer the drinking water, and with *oṁ padma āsana stvaṃ* consider that they take their seats.

Paying homage:

Through your kindness
Great bliss arises in an instant:
Teachers, your bodies are like precious jewels;
Vajra holders, at your lotus feet I bow.

You are treasures of all good qualities: {108}
Just thinking of your names
Brings peace to our troubled minds.
To the glorious teachers I pay homage.

Replete with immaculate qualities,
You are the crown ornaments of all beings,
Precious sources fulfilling all needs and desires.
At the feet of the teachers I pay homage.

Sublime and stainless suns,
You dispel the darkness of all beings' ignorance

With the light of realization of what to adopt and avoid.
At the feet of the teachers I pay homage.

Sublime and perfectly pure moons,
You make the garden of benefit and happiness blossom
With the cooling rays of merit and wisdom.
At the feet of the teachers I pay homage.

Most skillful of doctors for beings,
You cure the ailments of defilements and suffering
With the supreme ambrosial medicine of the sacred teachings.
At the feet of the teachers I pay homage.

Mighty pilots of all that lives,
You ferry beings across the ocean of existence and peace
In the great ship of means and wisdom.
At the feet of the teachers I pay homage.

Sole loving protectors of beings,
You protect everyone from harm
And benefit all on an infinite scale.
At the feet of the teachers I pay homage.

Through the union of emptiness and compassion
You do not dwell in the extremes of existence or peace.
You who have attained supreme nirvana,
To you, lords of refuge, I bow down in homage.

By completing the ten transcendent perfections
And mastering the channels corresponding to the twenty-four
[sacred lands] and the winds,
You have blocked the twelve links
And thus reached the end of the ten levels—to you I bow.

Not existent, not nonexistent, not both,
Nor yet neither—
Perfectly pure, untainted expanse of reality,
Body of truth free of elaboration, to you I bow.

Shining with the glory of the major and minor marks,
You constantly teach the dharma of the Supreme Vehicle
To disciples in pure buddha fields.
Great bliss, body of perfect enjoyment, to you I bow.

Through infinite buddha manifestations
In accordance with the attitudes of different disciples, {109}
You satisfy all beings with benefit and happiness.
Body of manifestation, skilled in means, to you I bow.

The manifestations of the body of form are of all kinds,
Yet their nature is unchanging.
It is the true state of union, wondrous and inexpressible:
Body of the essential nature, to you I bow.

By transforming the eight consciousnesses
And eliminating all defilements and obscurations
You are completely freed from the five aggregates.
Lords of the five kinds of gnosis, to you I bow.

You whose minds possess the four perfect knowledges
Have conquered the armies of demons with the ten strengths
And teach the dharma by means of the four fearlessnesses.
Possessors of all good qualities, to you I bow.

In your conduct, realization, gnosis, and activities
You possess the eighteen qualities of a buddha
That are not shared with others.
Peerless holy beings, to you I bow.

To the great Vajradhara, Lūyipa, Līlapa,
Virūpa, Ḍombipa, Shavaripa,
Saraha, Kangkālipāda,
Mīnapa, and Gorakṣha I pay homage.

To Chauraṅgi, Vīnapa, and Ratnakarashānti,[7]
Tantipa,[8] Chamaripa, and Khaḍgapa,

Nāgārjuna, Kṛiṣhṇāchāri,[9] and Āryadeva,
Thaganapa, and Nāropa I pay homage.

To Shyalipa,[10] Tilopa, Chatrapa, and Bhadrapa,
Dhukhandi, Āyogipāda, and Kalapa,
Dhombipa,[11] Kaṅkana, and Kambala,
Ḍiṅgipa,[12] and Bhandhepa I pay homage.

To Tandhepa, Kukkuripa, and Kujipa,[13]
Dhamapa, Mahila,[14] Achinta,
Babhahi, Nalina, Shāntideva,[15]
And Indrabhūti I pay homage.

To Mekopa, Togchepa,[16] Kamparipa,
Jālandhara,[17] Rāhula, Dharmapa,
Dhokaripa, Medhina, Saṅkaja,[18]
And Ghaṇḍhapa I pay homage.

To Yogipa, Chaliki,[19] Gorura,
Luchika, Jayānanti, Naguṇa,[20]
Pachari, Champaka, Bhikṣhana,
Dhilipa,[21] and Kumbharipa I pay homage.

To Charpaṭipa,[22] Maṇibhadrā,
Mekhali, Kanakhalā,
Kalakala, Kandhalipa,
Dhahulipa, and Udhilipa[23] I pay homage.

To Kapālapa, Kiravalapa,[24]
Sakarapa, Sarvabhakṣhapa,
Nāgabodhi, the great Dārikapa,
And Putalipa[25] I pay homage. {110}

To Pahanapa,[26] Kokilapa,[27]
Anonga,[28] Lakṣhmīnkarā,
Samudrapa, and Vyālipa—
To all these eighty-four great siddhas I pay homage.

Guided by the supreme deities and siddhas,
You awakened the supreme potential and beheld the truth of
ultimate reality.
On the path beyond training you attained the sublime body of
union.
To the lords of yogis I pay homage.

To the root and lineage teachers, hosts of yidam deities,
Buddhas, bodhisattvas, ḍākinīs, and dharma protectors,
Manifesting forms as numerous as the atoms in the entire universe,
With great respect of body, speech, and mind I pay homage.

To make the offerings, begin with the two water offerings and five sense offerings.

Untainted, pure, and pleasing substance of the gods,
The ornament of vajra drinking water, endowed with eight qualities—
As I offer it with the utmost faith in mind,
I pray, accept it joyfully, as you please.
*oṁ āḥ hri pravara sarkaraṃ arghaṃ pratīccha svāhā*

Untainted, pure, and pleasing substances of the gods,
Scented waters that remove the dirt from your lotus feet,
As I offer them with the utmost faith in mind,
I pray, accept them joyfully, as you please.
*oṁ āḥ hri pravara sarkaraṃ pādyaṃ pratīccha svāhā*

All kinds of flowers, real and imagined by the mind,
Māndāravas, utpalas, kumuda lilies, and the like,
Of lovely colors, perfect shape, and sweet and satisfying scent—
These I offer to the teacher, the siddhas, and assembly of the
mandala.
*oṁ guru vajradhara sarva yogeśvara deva ḍākinī saparivāra vajra
puṣpe praticcha svāhā*

All kinds of incense, real and imagined by the mind,
Aloe, snakeheart sandalwood, and the like,

Of good ingredients, and the sweetest smell—
These I offer to the teacher, the siddhas, and assembly of the mandala.
*oṁ guru vajradhara sarva yogeśvara deva ḍākinī saparivāra vajra dhūpe praticcha svāhā*

All kinds of lights, real and imagined by the mind,
Lamps, the sun and moon, physical radiance, and the like,
Dispelling darkness, radiant with the light of accomplishment—
These I offer to the teacher, the siddhas, and assembly of the mandala.
*oṁ guru vajradhara sarva yogeśvara deva ḍākinī saparivāra vajra āloke praticcha svāhā* {111}

All kinds of perfumes, real and imagined by the mind,
Camphor, musk, and other ingredients sweet to smell,
All the finest fragrances, unguents blissful to the touch—
These I offer to the teacher, the siddhas, and assembly of the mandala.
*oṁ guru vajradhara sarva yogeśvara deva ḍākinī saparivāra vajra gandhe praticcha svāhā*

All kinds of delicacies, real and imagined by the mind,
Scented rice and sugar, berry juice, and other treats,
Beautifully colored, blissfully flavored, and nutritious—
These I offer to the teacher, the siddhas, and assembly of the mandala.
*oṁ guru vajradhara sarva yogeśvara deva ḍākinī saparivāra vajra naividye praticcha svāhā*

All kinds of musical instruments, real and imagined by the mind,
Drums and conches, cymbals, lutes, and the like,
Profoundly inspiring and pleasantly melodious—
These I offer to the teacher, the siddhas, and assembly of the mandala.
*oṁ guru vajradhara sarva yogeśvara deva ḍākinī saparivāra vajra śabda praticcha svāhā*

Next, to make the offering of the mandala, as if holding the outer universe in your hands, perform a detailed offering such as the mandala with thirty-seven piles, or a condensed one, as many times as you can. And:

The supreme mountain, the golden mountain ranges, hundred seas of enjoyment, and outer mountain ring,
And the continents, all adorned with all the riches of gods and humankind,
And embellished with goddesses bestowing untainted bliss, of beautiful form and perfect limbs,
I dedicate as the perfect buddha field of all the buddhas.

The utterly vast and solid mandala of the four elements,
Adorned in perfect layout by Mount Meru, the continents, mountain ring, and oceans,
Completely filled with the glory of all worlds and beings—
With this perfect and abundant offering of the universe, I venerate the teachers.

This beautiful place that is the universe,
And all the beings and offerings contained therein—
All that is owned or has no owner
I mentally take and offer to the mandala of the teachers.

Use the same mantra as before, with *ratna maṇḍala pūja megha samudra sapharaṇa samaye hūṁ*.

On the vast and spotless beryl ground,
With walls of gold and silver, domes and latticework,
Held up by jeweled pillars, and of vast dimensions,
The supreme and lovely measureless palace I offer.

Adorned on top with canopies, victory banners, parasols, and the like,
Its sides decorated with curtains of gently waving silks, {112}
Its floors magnificently laid out with thrones and cushions,
All these perfect palatial furnishings I offer.

Saffron dharma robes—the victory banner of liberation—
Rainbow-colored cloth that is fine and light and soft,
Sweetly scented Benares cloth of finest stuff,
And every other kind of excellent raiment I offer to the teachers.

The crown of the five families, the silken headdress,
Long necklaces of pearls, strings of jewel beads,
Golden bracelets set with precious jewels,
And every other kind of splendid ornament I offer to the teachers.

Items fashioned from the wealth of abundant merit—
The precious wheel, jewel, queen, and minister,
Elephant, supreme horse, and general—
All these precious attributes of royalty I offer to the teachers.

Articles that fulfill one's daily needs—
Woodlands, swords, mansions, bedclothes,
Divine garments, snakeskin, and shoes—
All these seven semiprecious articles I offer to the teachers.

Things creating happiness and virtue for all beings—
Durva grass, vilva fruit, bezoar, and curds,
Mirrors, vermilion, white mustard, and conches spiraling right—
These eight auspicious objects I offer to the teachers.

Created from the major marks of those with the eight kinds of merit[29]—
The eternal knot, wheel, lotus, victory banner,
Parasol, excellent vase, white conch, and golden fish—
These eight auspicious symbols I offer to the teachers.

The bountiful cow, the wish-fulfilling tree,
The spontaneous harvest, and the wish-fulfilling gem,
The nectar of immortality, nutritious, tasty foods, and the like—
All perfect and abundant things to be enjoyed I offer to the teachers.

In order to venerate the Three Jewels and benefit beings,
My merit, possessions, and bodies
I offer entirely for the service of you, sublime beings,
And I will do whatever you command.

The inner offering, the five offerings pleasing to the senses:

In all the worlds in the immensity of the ten directions,
All sublime forms worth offering, the finest in color and shape, {113}
I mentally manifest as goddesses of exquisite form
And offer to the refuge lords' unobscured vajra eyes.

Use the same mantra as before, with *rūpa kāma guṇa pūja āḥ hūṁ.*

In all the worlds in the immensity of the ten directions,
All sublime sounds worth offering, of animate and inanimate origin,
I mentally manifest as goddesses of exquisite sound
And offer to the refuge lords' unobscured vajra ears.
*. . . śabda kāma guṇa pūja āḥ hūṁ.*

In all the worlds in the immensity of the ten directions,
All sublime fragrances worth offering, natural and prepared,
I mentally manifest as goddesses of exquisite smell
And offer to the refuge lords' unobscured vajra noses.
*. . . gandhe kāma guṇa pūja āḥ hūṁ.*

In all the worlds in the immensity of the ten directions,
All sublime flavors worth offering, delicious food and drink,
I mentally manifest as goddesses of exquisite taste
And offer to the refuge lords' unobscured vajra tongues.
*. . . rasa kāma guṇa pūja āḥ hūṁ.*

In all the worlds in the immensity of the ten directions,
All sublime sensations worth offering, produced by beings and not so produced,

I mentally manifest as goddesses of exquisite touch
And offer to the refuge lords' unobscured vajra bodies.
. . . *sparṣe kāma guṇa pūja āḥ hūṁ.*

*oṁ āḥ hūṁ*
The food of the five nectars—
The supreme nature of all accomplishments;
The food of the five meats—
The principal samaya of all the buddhas;
The sublime and flawless drink of peace—
The five intoxicating liquors (mead, sugarcane beer,
Grain beer, fruit wine, and processed alcohol)—
All these, which have the nature of wisdom, I offer.

Use the same mantra as before, with *pañca amṛta . . .*

The secret offering, the offering of the sixteen offering goddesses:

Radiating the perfect illusory enjoyment of supreme bliss,
Those who play a vina, flute, round drum, and kettledrum;
The ladies of laughter, charm, song, and dance;
Of flowers, incense, lamps, and perfume;
Of form, taste, touch, and the expanse of reality—
These are the sixteen goddesses who have perfected the aspect of joy.
With these vajra consorts who delight in joy
May you vajra herukas be pleased.

Through the blessings of the vajras in the lotuses,
The great unchanging bliss of union is achieved.
The melting bliss, by nature pure appearance,
Fills the whole of the three worlds,
Delighting you with the secret offering.

At the end of the mantra, add *anurakto mahāsukha . . .*

The offering of thatness: {114}

Beings are viewed as like the moon's reflection in water.
Sounds are heard authentically, resembling echoes.

The mind is seen as like a mirage in the desert.
Thus the nature of food and drink is like space;
Fragrances are smelled as if they were flowers in the sky.
The mind pervades everything like the sun and moon.
This authentic mode of being is like the supreme mountain.
It is how a young girl's dream is dreamed.
Conventional designations are uttered like magical illusions or visual tricks.
Thus does coemergent bliss arise,
And likewise the mind—inconceivable, free of the nature of existence—
Arises constantly. These, the sublime ways of the sugatas, I offer.

Next, recite any suitable authentic praises composed by the teachers of India and Tibet, and, as a general praise:

Your pure bodies are free of defects and dysfunction.
Your perfect melodious speech embraces every topic of knowledge.
Your minds know the truth of the profound and extensive teachings:
Hosts of teachers, embodiments of the three vajras, to you I give praise.

Wholly rid of every kind of fault,
Possessed of every excellent quality,
Sources of all benefit and happiness, glory and prosperity—
Glorious teachers, to you I give praise.

In order to mature and liberate beings,
You manifest in the form of guides,
Embodiments of all the buddhas of the three times.
Glorious teachers, to you I give praise.

Your bodies transcend flesh and bone,
Bodies that are wisdom manifesting as form.
Seen with the eye of faith, they are sublime.
Lords of enlightened body, to you I give praise.

Spontaneously and effortlessly,
With the sixty expressive qualities of speech
You teach all subjects, profound and vast.
Lords of enlightened speech, to you I give praise.

Although free of the elaborations of knowing and something to be known,
Your minds illuminate the mandala of knowledge.
Manifold treasures of the compassionate powers of retention and eloquence,
Lords of enlightened mind, to you I give praise.

Were all beings to relate just a few of your qualities {115}
For kalpas long, they would never be finished,
So endless are your vision, clairvoyance, miraculous powers, and the rest.
Lords of enlightened qualities, to you I give praise.

If seeing you, hearing you, thinking of you brings benefit,
No need to mention being freed[30] by following you.
You act spontaneously, unceasingly.
Lords of enlightened activity, to you I give praise.

Bliss and emptiness being inseparable,
You personify the union of means and wisdom.
You who possess the adamantine body, speech, and mind,
Glorious protectors of beings, to you I give praise.

The aggregates of your bodies are the five male buddhas,
The elements are the five female buddhas,
And their union is the coemergent vajra body.
Glorious protectors of beings, to you I give praise.

Your sense organs are the male bodhisattvas,
Their six objects are the female bodhisattvas,
And their union is the coemergent vajra body.
Glorious protectors of beings, to you I give praise.

Your limbs are the wrathful kings,
Your ten activities are the wrathful queens,
And their union is the coemergent vajra body.
Glorious protectors of beings, to you I give praise.

The constituents of your body are ḍākas,
The stationary channels are the hosts of ḍākinīs,
And their union is the coemergent vajra body.
Glorious protectors of beings, to you I give praise.

The major winds are the five fathers,
The five elements are the mothers,
And their union is the coemergent vajra speech.
Glorious protectors of beings, to you I give praise.

Your mind is the nature of primordial wisdom,
The objects that appear are the expanse of reality,
And their union is the coemergent vajra mind.
Glorious protectors of beings, to you I give praise.

This praise on its own is sufficient, but if you wish to do a slightly more detailed praise, you may also recite the following:

Enlightened state of all phenomena in the expanse of reality,
Union of bliss and emptiness, glory of existence and peace,
All-pervading lord of the hundred families, lord of the mandala,
To Vajradhara, homage and praise!

Abandoning your kingdom, on the banks of the Ganges
You lived by eating fish guts.
You who attained supreme accomplishment,
Lūyipa, lord of yogis, at your feet I bow.

Charmed by the five pleasures of royal life,
Through concentration with one-pointed mindfulness
You attained supreme accomplishment.
Līlapa, lord of yogis, at your feet I bow. {116}

By practicing Vajravarāhī, you were blessed by her in person
And displayed many wondrous miraculous powers.
You who attained supreme accomplishment,
Virūpa, lord of yogis, at your feet I bow.

Accomplishing Hevajra,
You rode a tiger and engaged in yogic conduct.
You who attained supreme accomplishment,
Ḍombipa, lord of yogis, at your feet I bow.

Guided by Avalokiteshvara,
In the wisdom body you benefited beings.
You who attained supreme accomplishment,
Shavaripa, lord of yogis, at your feet I bow.

Born in a brahmin family, you cut through dualistic thought
And realized the ultimate Great Seal.
You who attained supreme accomplishment,
Saraha, lord of yogis, at your feet I bow.

The thought of your ordinary wife
You dissolved into the radiant expanse of bliss and emptiness.
You who attained supreme accomplishment,
Kaṅkālapāda, lord of yogis, at your feet I bow.

In the belly of a fish you gained the highest mundane level
And successively completed the qualities of the levels and paths.
You who attained supreme accomplishment,
Mīnapa, lord of yogis, at your feet I bow.

While living as a cowherd, you were liberated by the instructions,
And you set a million beings in lasting happiness.
You who attained supreme accomplishment,
Gorakṣha, lord of yogis, at your feet I bow.

Through the instructions on no-thought
Your amputated limbs grew back on their own.

You who attained supreme accomplishment,
Chauraṅgi, lord of yogis, at your feet I bow.

From the sound of the vina you practiced concentration
And established in dharma the cities of Ghahuri.
You who attained supreme accomplishment,
Vīnapa, lord of yogis, at your feet I bow.

With your learning and accomplishment you preserved the
Buddha's doctrine,
And with your student's instructions you saw the truth.
You who attained supreme accomplishment,
Shāntipa, lord of yogis, at your feet I bow.

An old weaver in the body of a youth,
You brought the citizens of Sandhonāgara to the celestial lands.
You who attained supreme accomplishment,
Tantipa, lord of yogis, at your feet I bow.

As a shoemaker you trained your mind, and on a single seat
You purified all stains and realized the true condition of things.
You who attained supreme accomplishment,
Chamaripa, lord of yogis, at your feet I bow.

Attaining the common siddhi of the sword,
You cleansed your three doors of the stains of delusion.
You who attained supreme accomplishment,
Khaḍgapa, lord of yogis, at your feet I bow.

Observing the deeds of a second Buddha, {117}
You founded the tradition of the Great Charioteer.
You who attained supreme accomplishment,
Noble Nāgārjuna, lord of yogis, at your feet I bow.

With three thousand disciples you practiced yogic discipline
And attained true enlightenment in the intermediate state.
You who attained supreme accomplishment,
Kāṇḥapa,[31] lord of yogis, at your feet I bow.

Born miraculously, unstained by a womb,
You conquered the enemy of defilement and saw ultimate reality.
You who attained supreme accomplishment,
Āryadeva, lord of yogis, at your feet I bow.

As an antidote to lying, you meditated on lies
And thus realized phenomenal existence to be itself a lie.
You who attained supreme accomplishment,
Thaganapa, lord of yogis, at your feet I bow.

A paṇḍita perfectly learned in the five sciences,
You underwent twelve major ordeals.
You who attained supreme accomplishment,
Nāropa, lord of yogis, at your feet I bow.

All sounds subsided into the howl of the wolf
And were liberated by themselves in fearlessness: experiences and realization arose.
You who attained supreme accomplishment,
Shyalipa, lord of yogis, at your feet I bow.

Blessed by the lineage of the four precepts,
You were taken as a disciple by Vajradhara.
You who attained supreme accomplishment,
Tilopa, lord of yogis, at your feet I bow.

Meditating on uniting emptiness and compassion,
You departed to a celestial land with five hundred followers.
You who attained supreme accomplishment,
Chatrapa, lord of yogis, at your feet I bow.

Understanding the meaning of the symbols of view, meditation, and conduct,
You saw that phenomenal existence is a delusory facade.
You who attained supreme accomplishment,
Bhadrapa, lord of yogis, at your feet I bow.

You patched together rags from rubbish heaps
And realized the inseparability of deity and mantra as the body of truth.
You who attained supreme accomplishment,
Dhukhandi, lord of yogis, at your feet I bow.

Achieving clear visualization of the thousand worlds on the tip of your nose, your upper door,
You dissolved conceptual beliefs into the state of ultimate reality.
You who attained supreme accomplishment,
Āyogipāda, lord of yogis, at your feet I bow.

Of handsome body, you trained in the generation and perfection phases
And engaged in spontaneous, free conduct.
You who attained supreme accomplishment,
Kalapa, lord of yogis, at your feet I bow.

By washing with water and concentration together,
You completely purified the two obscurations.
You who attained supreme accomplishment,
Dhombipa,[32] lord of yogis, at your feet I bow.

Having concentrated on your bracelet, after five hundred years {118}
You attained the celestial land with your ministers and people.
You who attained supreme accomplishment,
Kaṅkana, lord of yogis, at your feet I bow.

Through the instructions of your mother your mind was liberated.
You subdued many witches and wore a woolen cloak.
You who attained supreme accomplishment,
Kambala, lord of yogis, at your feet I bow.

By threshing rice, you purified the concept of karma
And attained the celestial land with seven hundred followers.
You who attained supreme accomplishment,
Ḍiṅgipa, lord of yogis, at your feet I bow.

Practicing the view, meditation, and conduct of the four
boundless attitudes,
You departed to a celestial land with four hundred followers.
You who attained supreme accomplishment,
Bhandhepa, lord of yogis, at your feet I bow.

You used the analogy of losing all your wealth gambling,
And the concepts of the three worlds were consumed in the
expanse of reality.[33]
You who attained supreme accomplishment,
Tandhepa, lord of yogis, at your feet I bow.

Possessed of preternatural powers and venerated by the gods,
You followed a ḍākinī who had taken the form of a puppy.
You who attained supreme accomplishment,
Kukkuripa, lord of yogis, at your feet I bow.

By eliminating the two conceptual extremes
Of your tumor existing and not existing, you realized the state
beyond extremes.
You who attained supreme accomplishment,
Kujipa, lord of yogis, at your feet I bow.

After diligently retaining what you had studied,
You gave rise to realization of the many teachings as one taste.
You who attained supreme accomplishment,
Dharmapa, lord of yogis, at your feet I bow.

The pride you had in your immense strength
You conquered with the instructions on the power of
insubstantiality.
You who attained supreme accomplishment,
Mahila, lord of yogis, at your feet I bow.

All your thoughts of longing for wealth
You dissolved into the thoughtless state of the sky.
You who attained supreme accomplishment,
Achinta, lord of yogis, at your feet I bow.

Through the yoga of the channels, winds, and drops
You savored the taste of unchanging great bliss.
You who attained supreme accomplishment,
Babhahi, lord of yogis, at your feet I bow.

Making your living from lotus roots, you completed the path of melting bliss
And purified the stains of delusion.
You who attained supreme accomplishment,
Nalina, lord of yogis, at your feet I bow.

Leading the lifestyle of an idle loafer,[34]
You taught the *Bodhicaryāvatāra* and rose into the sky.
You who attained supreme accomplishment,
Shāntideva, lord of yogis, at your feet I bow.

For you, with your court of five hundred queens,
Sense pleasures are not to be rejected but are ornaments of ultimate reality. {119}
You who attained supreme accomplishment,
Indrabhūti, lord of yogis, at your feet I bow.

Realizing the meaning of the natural state, you roamed the charnel grounds,
Acting like a madman, with fearsome gaze.
You who attained supreme accomplishment,
Mekopa, lord of yogis, at your feet I bow.

With the mattock of awareness
You continuously dug the mountain of the mind.
You who attained supreme accomplishment,
Togchepa,[35] lord of yogis, at your feet I bow.

You used the blacksmith's craft to purify
The concepts and defilements in your mind.
You who attained supreme accomplishment,
Kamparipa, lord of yogis, at your feet I bow.

Matured and liberated by a wisdom ḍākinī,
You were the guide of all the supreme siddhas.
You who attained supreme accomplishment,
Jālandhara, lord of yogis, at your feet I bow.

With the rogue planet[36] of nondual realization
You eclipsed the moon of dualistic beliefs.
You who attained supreme accomplishment,
Rāhula, lord of yogis, at your feet I bow.

As a scholar, you spent most of your life teaching,
But in old age you meditated, and wisdom arose.
You who attained supreme accomplishment,
Dharmapa, lord of yogis, at your feet I bow.

Carrying the bowl of emptiness, you always begged for alms
And garnered thus the fruit, great bliss.
You who attained supreme accomplishment,
Dhokaripa, lord of yogis, at your feet I bow.

Through farmer's work, you purified conceptual thoughts;
Rising into the sky, you liberated many beings.
You who attained supreme accomplishment,
Medhina, lord of yogis, at your feet I bow.

Born from a lotus, you received instruction from a noble one,
And by meditating for seven days you were released from bondage.
You who attained supreme accomplishment,
Saṅkaja, lord of yogis, at your feet I bow.

Through the path of the consort, you accomplished great bliss
And arose in the body of Chakrasaṃvara.
You who attained supreme accomplishment,
Ghaṇḍhapa, lord of yogis, at your feet I bow.

Practicing sādhana in the twenty-four sacred places,
In twelve years you purified all stains.

You who attained supreme accomplishment,
Yogipa, lord of yogis, at your feet I bow.

Gathering phenomenal existence into your body, speech, and mind,
You guided the right and left channels into the central one.
You who attained supreme accomplishment,
Chaluki, lord of yogis, at your feet I bow.

By purifying all sounds as the songs of birds,
You realized ultimate reality—sound and emptiness inseparable.
You who attained supreme accomplishment,
Gorura, lord of yogis, at your feet I bow. {120}

Turning your mind from samsara, you trained in the two stages
And saw existence and peace as the great sameness.
You who attained supreme accomplishment,
Luchika, lord of yogis, at your feet I bow.

As you slept, you meditated on the union of appearance and emptiness.
Released from the bonds of delusion, you departed to a celestial land.
You who attained supreme accomplishment,
Naguṇa, lord of yogis, at your feet I bow.

With torma offerings, you made all the birds content.
In secret you were diligent in the inner yoga.
You who attained supreme accomplishment,
Jayānanti, lord of yogis, at your feet I bow.

Though poor, you offered pastries
To the Ārya's manifestation, and so he guided you.
You who attained supreme accomplishment,
Pachari, lord of yogis, at your feet I bow.

By taking the thought of a flower as the path
You freed all phenomena in the state of sameness.

You who attained supreme accomplishment,
Champaka, lord of yogis, at your feet I bow.

By offering your teeth to a wisdom ḍākinī,
You were freed by her instructions on the union of appearance and emptiness.
You who attained supreme accomplishment,
Bhikṣhana, lord of yogis, at your feet I bow.

Relying on the glory of your wealth as an oil merchant,
You gained realization of the self-liberation of attributes.
You who attained supreme accomplishment,
Dhilipa, lord of yogis, at your feet I bow.

As a potter, you integrated the concepts of your work
Inseparably with the wisdom beyond concepts.
You who attained supreme accomplishment,
Kumbharipa, lord of yogis, at your feet I bow.

By accomplishing the extraction of essence
You introduced many people instantly to the great goal.
You who attained supreme accomplishment,
Charpaṭipa, lord of yogis, at your feet I bow.

With your mind matured by a siddha's instructions,
You broke your pitcher and were naturally freed.
You who attained supreme accomplishment,
Maṇibhadrā, queen of yogis, at your feet I bow.

Daughter of a householder, liberated by the instructions,
You cut off your head and had it restored again.
You who attained supreme accomplishment,
Mekhali, queen of yogis, at your feet I bow.

Guided by Kṛiṣhṇāchāri, you offered your teacher
The symbol of your having cut through elaborations.
You who attained supreme accomplishment,
Kanakhalā, queen of yogis, at your feet I bow.

As you lost the concept of sound in the expanse of the sky,
Appearances and sound arose as the Great Seal.
You who attained supreme accomplishment,
Kalakala, lord of yogis, at your feet I bow.

Sewing things together on the outer and inner levels,
You realized the union of emptiness and compassion. {121}
You who attained supreme accomplishment,
Kandhalipa, lord of yogis, at your feet I bow.

From the grass rope of imputed and dependent realities
You attained siddhi and realized the nondual nature.
You who attained supreme accomplishment,
Dhahulipa, lord of yogis, at your feet I bow.

Seeking special medicines in the twenty-four sacred places,
You gained the miraculous ability to fly through the sky.
You who attained supreme accomplishment,
Udhilipa, lord of yogis, at your feet I bow.

From your wife's skull you made a cup,
And from your sons' bones, the six ornaments.
You who attained supreme accomplishment,
Kapālapa, lord of yogis, at your feet I bow.

Making use of the disposition of your kingdom and army,
You refined your realization of the path.
You who attained supreme accomplishment,
Kiravalapa, lord of yogis, at your feet I bow.

Empowered by the Noble One, liberated by his instructions,
You protected those in trouble with a rain of all that they
desired.
You who attained supreme accomplishment,
Sakarapa, lord of yogis, at your feet I bow.

Phenomenal existence you ate as food and drink,
And even the sun and moon ran off in fright.

You who attained supreme accomplishment,
Sarvabhakṣhapa, lord of yogis, at your feet I bow.

Ever dwelling on Mount Shrī Parvata,
You bestow on beings the eight great siddhis.
You who attained supreme accomplishment,
Nāgabodhi, lord of yogis, at your feet I bow.

Pursuing your teacher, you gave up your kingdom
And worked as a prostitute's servant.
You who attained supreme accomplishment,
Dārikapa, lord of yogis, at your feet I bow.

Achieving concentration with a painting of Hevajra,
You reversed the positions of deity and demon.
You who attained supreme accomplishment,
Putalipa, lord of yogis, at your feet I bow.

Running along to the sound of your boots, you were freed
By instructions for taking attachment as the path.
You who attained supreme accomplishment,
Panahapa, lord of yogis, at your feet I bow.

In a grove, you relied on the sound of the cuckoo's song,
And all thoughts arose as the great primal wisdom.
You who attained supreme accomplishment,
Kokilapa, lord of yogis, at your feet I bow.

Vain and proud of your handsome looks,
You took as the path the self-liberation of the six consciousnesses.
You who attained supreme accomplishment,
Anonga, lord of yogis, at your feet I bow.

Born in the family of a great king, you trained on the supreme path
By renouncing the world and behaving like a lunatic. {122}
You who attained supreme accomplishment,
Lakṣhmīnkarā, queen of yogis, at your feet I bow.

With the four boundless attitudes outwardly and inwardly the
four joys,
You destroyed the delusion of the eight ordinary preoccupations.[37]
You who attained supreme accomplishment,
Samudrapa, lord of yogis, at your feet I bow.

Making use of an elixir of mercury,
You and your companions attained immortality.
You who attained supreme accomplishment,
Vyālipa, lord of yogis, at your feet I bow.

By the power of this offering of devotion and praise,
May the stains of my deeds and habitual tendencies be purified,
And may liberation and wisdom simultaneously grow.
Supreme siddhas, may I become the same as you!

Next, to pray[38] to the mahāsiddhas, use here any suitable prayers to the individual mahāsiddhas or general prayers that occur elsewhere. Recite the verses from the homage section above,[39] "To the great Vajradhara, Lūyipa, Līlapa . . . ," adapting the end of the quatrain: "Mīnapa, and Gorakṣha I pray," and adding at the end the following single quatrain:

Grant the blessings that I may train
In love and compassion impartially
And truly realize the ultimate, coemergent gnosis,
Just as did the great accomplished yogis.

At this point you may add a prayer for calling the lama from afar (*bla ma rgyang 'bod*), in a detailed or condensed version, as you like. After that, go through the remaining branches, beginning with confession.

Since time without beginning, under the influence of defilements,
I have physically, verbally, and mentally committed negative
deeds, both naturally negative and in violation of edicts;
I have incited others to do them, and I have rejoiced at such deeds.
All these I acknowledge and confess, with a mind full of remorse
and determination to refrain in the future.

In particular, due to my lack of diligence regarding the view and conduct
Of the Vajrayāna, I have been unable to practice it as I should.
Indulging in doubts and distinctions, I have unconsciously deteriorated the commitments
And deviated from the secret mantras: such deeds I confess from the depth of my heart.

With delighted mind I rejoice
In the lives and examples of the supreme beings and their heirs
And in all the virtuous deeds as well that all beings have done,
Will do, and are performing now, with their bodies, speech, and minds. {123}

Great waves of virtue cannot approach the merit
Of the smallest good deed connected with the mantras.
I rejoice even more, therefore, in the wondrous virtue
Related to the Great Secret.

In order to benefit all beings and incite them to virtue,
I request the kings of dharma and their heirs
To continuously turn the wheel of dharma,
The profound and extensive teachings that train according to need.

Swiftly cut the long stream of the unbearable cycle of delusion that is existence,
And make the melodious vajra sound
That brings lasting happiness to living beings who have been our mothers
Resound impartially throughout all space and time.

Though for the body of truth there is no coming into being and perishing,
I beseech you not to depart in your form body to benefit other buddha fields
But, out of compassion for the protectorless beings in the age of degeneration,
To remain for a long time without passing into nirvana.

Protectors of beings living in this world
Who do not have the fortune to follow you in wonderful celestial lands,
Manifest as masters teaching the Vajrayāna
And constantly remain as long as the Buddha's doctrine endures.

In order that all beings attain unsurpassed enlightenment,
I will always take refuge in you, the supreme refuge,
And henceforth I will take and properly practice
The common and extraordinary commitments and vows.

By the power of tainted and untainted virtue, epitomized by this prayer,
May every being be freed from all the fetters of existence,
And, guided by the host of accomplished teachers,
May they complete the supreme path beyond training in one lifetime.

Through all my practice of virtue in the three times,
May all beings, who are as limitless as space,
Become vessels for the unsurpassed Vajrayāna
And swiftly attain the level of Samantabhadra Vajradhara.

Next, perform the feast offering. Set out whatever food and drink you have that are suitable as samaya ingredients and sprinkle them with the nectar of the inner offering. Cleanse them with *oṁ sumbhani* . . . and purify them with *oṁ svabhāva* . . . .

The feast-offering ingredients become emptiness, devoid of concepts. From that state of emptiness, under the feast-offering ingredients, there appears a syllable *yaṃ*, from which manifests the wind. {124} From the syllable *raṃ*, there manifests the mandala of fire. On top of it is the letter *A*, from which appears a vast, open wisdom kapāla. Inside it, the five fleshes and the five nectars melt into the five wisdoms, from which the feast-offering ingredients arise as a great ocean of untainted wisdom nectar.

Say *oṁ āḥ hūṁ ha hoḥ hrīḥ* three times.

*namo* The vast wheel of the feast offering, skillful means and wisdom inseparable,
Is sealed with the perfectly pure nature, unborn,
With perfectly pure attributes, the vowels and consonants,
And the perfectly pure essence, the five fleshes and five nectars.
This I offer to the root and lineage teachers, the root of blessings—
*gaṇacakra pūja megha samudra sapharaṇa samaye hūṁ*

Repeat these lines with the following adaptations:

*namo* The vast wheel of the feast offering, skillful means and wisdom inseparable . . .
. . . the five fleshes and five nectars.
This I offer to the hosts of yidam deities, the root of accomplishments—
*gaṇachakra* . . .

*namo* The vast wheel of the feast offering . . .
This I offer to the ḍākinīs and the hosts of protectors and guardians of the teachings, the root of activities . . .

*namo* . . .
This I offer to our fellow practitioners, vajra brothers and sisters, who are the root of the samaya . . .

After this, invoke the descent of blessings:

In the expanse of reality, the great palace of absence of thought, bliss and clarity,
Lord, great Vajradhara, protector of beings,
Principal refuge, appearing to itself,
Kind father, root teacher,
Gather with your manifestations like clouds in the sky.
Come here and accept this feast offering.
Bless this practice place,
Infuse this feast torma with potent essence,

And bestow on us practitioners assembled here
The supreme and common accomplishments.
*oṁ mahā guru caturā śīti siddhi labdha jñāna āveśaya a ā*

You who took birth in the central land of Magadha
For the benefit of mother beings,
Hosts of accomplished masters of yoga,
Gather with your manifestations like clouds in the sky.
Come here and accept this feast offering.
Bless this practice place,
Infuse this feast torma with potent essence,
And bestow on us practitioners assembled here
The supreme and common accomplishments.
*oṁ mahā guru catura shiti siddhi labdha jñana abeshaya a a*

You who took birth in the east of India,
For the benefit of mother beings . . . and so on, repeating as above.

You who took birth in the south of India,
For the benefit of mother beings . . . and so on.

You who took birth in the west of India,
For the benefit of mother beings . . . and so on. {125}

You who took birth in the north of India,
For the benefit of mother beings . . . and so on.

You who took birth in the royal caste, the brahmin caste, the merchant caste,
As noble citizens, or of common caste—
Lords, hosts of accomplished masters of yoga . . . and so on.

Fathers, infinite lords of yoga,
Mothers, your secret consorts,
And sisters, bestowing the experiences of the four joys—all of you
Gather with your manifestations like clouds in the sky . . . and so on.

Eighty yogis who have attained realization and liberation,
And four yoginīs who have attained realization and liberation—
Hosts of the eighty-four siddhas,
Gather with your manifestations like clouds in the sky . . .
and so on.

In the densely arrayed buddha field free of fear,
In the midst of hundreds of thousands of dakas and ḍākinīs,
Buddha of the five families, all-pervading lord of the mandala,
Bhagavān Heruka,
Gather with your manifestations like clouds in the sky . . .
and so on, to
*guru deva ḍākinī jñāna āveśaya a ā*

In the delightful unexcelled buddha field of the unwavering state,
The pure celestial realm of bliss and emptiness,
Mother creator of the bliss that delights the buddhas,
Vajravarāhī, queen of the ḍākinīs,
Gather with your manifestations like clouds in the sky . . .
and so on.

In the eight great charnel grounds,
The realm of activities where the whole host of demons is subdued,
Glorious protectors and your consorts and retinue,
Who vanquish obstacle makers and fulfill all wishes,
Gather with your manifestations like clouds in the sky . . .
and so on.

Hosts of teachers, yidams, and ḍākinīs,
With the tasseled crowns of your family swinging to and fro,
Silk ribbons fluttering,
Your numerous ornaments tinkling,
A multitude of musical instruments resounding,
Moving here and there with songs and dances,
Your hundreds of thousands of retinues whirling around,
Illusory self-appearance, nakedly vivid,
Unfixated awareness, clear and radiant,

Evanescent in the inexpressible expanse,
Dancing in great bliss,
In order to bless us, come, I pray,
Bestow your blessings on this sublime place.
Grant us the supreme accomplishment.
Dispel obstacles due to spirits that obstruct and lead us astray.
Mingle with us in the state where there are no dualistic concepts
  with regard to the three spheres. {126}
*guru deva ḍākinī jñāna āveśaya a ā*

As you recite this, make the invocation to the music of the ḍāmaru, bell, and suchlike at the end of each verse. Next, the shrine master should take in their left hand a skull cup filled with nectar and cover it with their right hand in the trident gesture.

Look at the perfect ingredients here.
May there be no doubt among those who are assembled:
Consider that brahmins, dogs, and outcastes
Are of the same nature, and enjoy!
*a ho mahā sukhaṃ*

Go around the assembly, beginning with the central figure. They take it, saying:

The dharma of the sugatas is priceless,
Free of attachment and other stains,
Free of subject-object duality.
To the ultimate nature we pay homage.
*a ho mahā sukhaṃ*

Then, offer the first part of the feast:

This deliciously prepared food offering,
Bewitching with its hundred tastes,
I offer with faith to the teacher and host of deities.
May these beings have the fortune to enjoy the food of
  concentration.

*oṁ mahā guru vajradhara caturā śīti siddhi labdha buddha bodhi-*
*sattva vīra ḍākinī sapari vāri bhyaḥ*
*namaḥ sarva tathāgate bhyo viśva mukhe bhyaḥ sarvathā khaṃ*
*udgate sapharaṇa imaṃ gagana khaṃ ghṛhane daṃ balinta svāhā*

Or add *oṁ akāro* seven times while offering to the teacher and siddhas and their retinue; *oṁ śrī heruka vajra yoginī sapari vāra akāro* . . . and so on three times for the yidam deity, and *oṁ śrī mahākālaya śāsana* . . . and so on, up to . . . *māraya hūṁ phaṭ* for Mahākāla and the host of dharma protectors. With

*oṁ āḥ hūṁ ha hoḥ hrīḥ*
*phem vajra aralli hoḥ*
*jaḥ hūṁ baṃ hoḥ*
*vajra ḍākinī samaya stvaṃ dri śya hoḥ*
*oṁ kha kha* and so on

as for the general torma offering to the ḍākinīs, make the offering to the other guests. Holding up the inner offering, offer it by saying:

*oṁ* I offer.
The supreme samaya of all the buddhas,
Which utterly transcends inferior objects
And is the ground of all accomplishments,
I offer with this sublime nectar.
Dispel all the stains of obscurations,
Free us definitively from all ordinary thoughts,
And be pleased with this offering of great bliss,
The unsurpassed bodhichitta. {127}

Enjoy the feast offering in the manner of an inner fire offering. Plant a light on the remainders that have been collected, and cleanse and purify them.

From the state of emptiness appears a letter *A*, from which manifests a vast and spacious wisdom kapāla, in which the remainders torma becomes a great ocean of nectar, excellent and vast.
*oṁ āḥ hūṁ ha hoḥ hrīḥ*

Say the *akaro* mantra three times.

> It is given to the host of wild *jungpo* spirits abiding at the outer gate, who are not allowed to see the samaya rituals. May they come to possess the fortune to practice the yoga of the supreme secret in the Vajrayāna.
> *oṁ ucchiṣṭa baliṅgta bhakśayi svāhā*

Take the torma outside and set the boundary with wrathful mantras and so on. Then sing the vajra song:

> *kolla i reṭṭha a bolla*
> *mammu ṇiri kakkola*
> *ghaṇa kripita ho vajja i*
> *karuṇiki a a ṇirolā*
> *tāhiṃ vala khājja ī*
> *gāḍāṁ ma aṇā vijja a i*
> *hale kaliñca rapani a i*
> *dudhura vajji a i*
> *ca upama kaccha ri sahil*
> *kapura la sa i a i*
> *mala inddhana sālijaḥ*
> *tahiṃ bhatu kha i a i*
> *phreṃ khaṇa kheṭa karante*
> *śuddha aśurdhaṇaṇ mana a i*
> *ni raṃ ru aṃ ga caḍavi*
> *ha hi jaṃ parāva sāṇi a i*
> *mala acakuntu ruva a i*
> *ḍiṇa ḍima tahina vajja a i*

This song can be sung here or, alternatively, you may add it at the end after completing all the sections according to the general liturgy. Besides this, sing whatever vajra songs are appropriate. Meditate on the bliss-emptiness of union with the mudrā, real or imagined. Then pray for the fulfillment of your wishes:

> Lords of accomplishment, you who embody all the buddhas and their heirs,

Protectors of beings, I request and pray to you.
Bring about the spread, through listening, reflection, and practice,
Of the sacred dharma, the Buddha's teaching, source of benefit
  and happiness.

Ensure that the pilots to liberation, the spiritual friends who hold
  the teachings,
Remain in good health and that their activities develop fully,
So that beings who are always suffering
Are brought to the happiness of liberation.

Enable all those who are diligent in practicing the sacred dharma
To perfect the profound path through devotion to the teacher {128}
And, by completing elimination and realization, to attain the level
  of the teacher,
Bringing boundless benefit to others.

Grant that in the meantime, until we achieve that level,
The supreme teachers may constantly care for us;
May we serve them with our bodies, possessions, and virtue,
And may we receive their compassionate blessings.

May the supreme siddhas' bodies and our bodies
Become inseparable and be blessed as the adamantine body.
May whatever the lords of yogis have taught
And our own speech become inseparable as the vajra speech.
May we hold the entire treasury of the secret of their minds
And receive the blessing of their minds and ours mingling
  inseparably.
May we receive the teachers' blessings to accomplish all virtuous
  deeds
And become equal to them in enlightened activities.

Next, to receive the path empowerment, first pray intently with any prayers you know, and give rise to intense devotion by reciting this prayer in particular, from the Indian oral tradition, as many times as you can:

To the eighty-four great siddhas

I pay homage and pray from the depths of my heart.
You know all my happiness and suffering;
I have no other refuge than you.

As a result of praying like this, from the foreheads of the teacher and siddhas, the lords of yogis, comes a stream of white bodhichitta essence—the blessings of the enlightened body, connected with the left *kyangma* channel. It dissolves into my own forehead, purifying the stains of the body, and I receive the vase empowerment; the blessings of the adamantine body enter me.

From their throats comes a stream of red bodhichitta essence—the blessings of the enlightened speech, connected with the right *roma* channel. It dissolves into my own throat, purifying the stains of speech, and I receive the secret empowerment; the blessings of the adamantine speech enter me.

From between their eyebrows comes a mixture of white and red bodhichitta[40]—the blessings of the enlightened mind, connected with the central channel. It dissolves between my own eyebrows, purifying the stains of mind, and I receive the wisdom empowerment; the blessings of the adamantine mind enter me. {129}

Then the male and female mahāsiddhas, with one voice, bestow the pointing-out instruction:

This primordial wisdom is extremely subtle,
Adamantine, like the midst of space,
Free of defilement, ultimate, the state of peace;
You are your own father.
Fundamentally uncontrived, spontaneously present from the very beginning,
When ordinary persons establish this great natural way,
They will behold in the vast expanse of space, free of birth and death,
The unchanging body that is the body of truth.
Having received this, expressed in vajra words,
Relax and remain for a little in the state beyond thought,
Letting go in the state that is uncontrived, fresh, self-arising, vivid,

Spontaneously present, and devoid of effort.

Refreshing your memory with these words, rest for a little while in meditation.

By this means, the most subtle stains of the three doors are
purified,
I receive the fourth empowerment,
And the blessings of adamantine gnosis enter my stream of being.

Confession of errors:

All the faults and things I have done wrong
On account of ignorance and carelessness
I confess in your presence, you who are possessed of love.
Please forgive them, you who are compassionate.

Recite the hundred-syllable mantra three times. Again, give rise to intense devotion:

Supreme refuge, you who perfectly benefit beings,
Although there is nothing that changes in the body of truth,
I pray to you to stir from it in the form body
And, out of great love, to bless my body.

As a result of this prayer, all the deities of the retinue dissolve into the mandala of teachers. All the male and female siddhas dissolve into the central figure of the mandala, Vajradhara. Vajradhara himself completely melts into a mass of light and dissolves into me, so that all the blessings of enlightened body, speech, and mind are transferred in their entirety into my stream of being, as if imprinted on it.

Considering this, preserve the state of your own true nature, the ultimate reality.

A prayer of aspiration:

In all my successive lives,
May I be of good family, clear minded, and free of pride.
May I have great compassion and firm devotion to the teacher
And observe the commitments of the Vajrayāna.

May I always hold the vajra, bell, and so forth, {130}
Realize the meaning of the profound and extensive teachings,
Always eat the five fleshes and five nectars,
And ultimately have the good fortune to accomplish great bliss.

May the ḍākinīs of the three places keep the promises they made
In the presence of the sugatas and bestow the supreme siddhis;
May I take the commitments and always keep them
And in this very life attain the three kinds of accomplishment.

And:

By venerating the vīras without duality, in this life
May I put an end to my obscurations and achieve the
accomplishment of the mudrā.
In all my lives may I be born in the midst of a world of
accomplished beings
Who have attained the highest bliss.

May those who enjoy the sacred pledges, symbols, and sensual
enjoyments
On the twelve [levels]—Domain, Inner Domain, and the rest[41]—
Think of me as their child and purify my obscurations,
Setting me on the level of supreme bliss.

Always bowing at the feet of the teachers,
May I become the servant of the vajra queen,
And, constantly enjoying the feast of the queen's essence,
May I venerate and revel in her secret lotus.

May I have the vision of the twenty-four
Dākas and ḍākinīs and attain their nature,

And may I become like a jewel, providing for the spiritual needs
Of beings deprived of the supreme bliss.

May these manifold merits
Be the ground on which, for myself and others, the highest virtue grows.
May I become a sovereign elucidating thatness, overcoming confusion,
And bestowing fearlessness on beings.

Transcending all ordinary concepts,
I fully dedicate the virtue I have accumulated
To the nonconceptual absorption of [mastery of the] vowels and consonants,
The untainted expanse of the wheel of great bliss.

By this merit of mine, again and again in my different lives
May I forever accomplish the benefit of beings and fearlessly delight in the ultimate teachings.
May the light rays from the principal deity fill space and bestow empowerment,
And may the three worlds revel in the Diamond [Vehicle] and together attain its level. {131}

Having cleared away the whole city of concepts and bewilderment, may the buddhas—the herukas, surrounded by the wheel of ḍākinīs—
Who are the source of the highest gnosis and grant us the supreme city of liberation,
Completely fulfill the hopes that beings entertain,
And may we constantly experience the glory and wealth of the most loving noble ones.

With this, make extraordinary aspirations on a vast scale. Then recite prayers for auspiciousness. Begin by reciting "Like the wish-fulfilling jewel on the top of the victory banner . . . ,"[42] "Possessed of all perfection . . . ," and other prayers taken from the scriptures, one after the other. At the end say, "May the morning be blessed . . . ,"[43] and so on, and

Glorious teacher, grant this today.
Buddhas, grant this today.

And likewise, add the same ending to

Sacred teachings . . .
Sangha assemblies . . .
Forefathers and ancestors . . .
Sovereigns and rulers . . .
Protectors of the world . . .
Virtuous protectors, grant this today.

As you do this, throw flowers, to the soft and melodious strains of musical instruments.

The mass of merit gained from venerating
A vajra master who teaches the secret mantras is boundless.
Such veneration, specifically praised in all the tantras,
Is clearly expressed here—the wise should thus rejoice!

If with heartfelt devotion one venerates and prays,
There is no doubt one will be blessed.
So fortunate beings who have entered the Vajrayāna
Must be diligent in this, the best of all dharma practices.

By this merit may I and all beings
Instantly cleanse our beginningless delusion.
May the sun of coemergent gnosis rise from within,
And may we be inseparable from the supreme siddhas.

At the request of the omniscient precious teacher Jamyang Khyentse Wangpo, and in consideration of its being a good occasion for making connections and accumulating merit, I, the beggar Karma Ngawang Yönten Gyatso Trinle Kunkhyap Palzangpo, wrote this in the dharma college of Tashi Lhatse at Dzongsar, splicing together mostly compositions such as offering liturgies and the blessed writings of the holy beings of the past.

May virtue and excellence increase.

# 4. Collecting the Essence Drops of Accomplishment

*A Universally Applicable Guru Yoga on the Supreme Siddhas, according to the Indian Tradition*[1]

THE FIRST HALF of this text comprises an arrangement by Jamgön Kongtrul of a guru yoga practice in which one visualizes the mahāsiddha Saraha, venerates him with offerings and praise, pays homage to him, and recites his mantra. This ritual can be adapted to any other mahāsiddha whom one might wish to invoke simply by substituting the visualization, homage, and mantra sections with the appropriate "modules," which are supplied for some twenty mahāsiddhas in the second half of the text. The last two of these mahāsiddhas, Shāntigupta and Buddhagupta, were alive during the sixteenth century and therefore do not feature in Vīraprabhāsvara's list of eighty-four siddhas. Their inclusion here undoubtedly provides the clue to Kongtrul's certainty in attributing this guru yoga to Tāranātha, for Tāranātha received numerous instructions from Buddhagupta during the siddha's visit to Tibet and described him in his biography.* Buddhagupta's own teacher was Shāntigupta.

{134}

*namo guru mahāsiddha labedha bhya*

On the basis of thought, they attained no-thought,
And from within no-thought, their gnosis dawned.

*Tāranātha's remarkable description of this master can be found on the Treasury of Lives website at https://treasuryoflives.org/biographies/view/Buddhagupta-natha/6412.

To the vajra holder, who is inseparable from
Those supreme beings who attained the union state, I bow.

I will write a profound method for receiving the blessings
That come from the succession of teachers,
In accordance with the oral instructions of the lineage siddhas
And uncorrupted by the stains of deluded thoughts.

The cult of the eighty-four most important siddhas founded by Āchārya Vīraprabhāsvara follows the tradition of oral instructions from the great siddhas of the past, Āchārya Paramāshvapāda and the glorious heruka of the age of strife, Shāntigupta. If you wish to practice a guru yoga that can be applied to any of these great siddhas, you should proceed as follows.

In an isolated place, assemble the requisites for a mandala and set out suitable offerings (outer, inner, and secret) if you have them. Begin in the general fashion by taking refuge, arousing bodhichitta, and meditating on the four boundless attitudes.

Wipe clean the mandala plate, cleansing it of impurities as you say *oṁ vajra bhūmi svāhā*, and sprinkling it with scented water and the ingredients from a cow[2] as you say *oṁ vajra rekhe hūṁ svāhā.* With your right hand, place a heap of fresh flowers in the middle, saying *hūṁ sumeru madhyema.*

Then place a heap to the east, saying, *ya sūrva videhadvīpa*; place a heap to the south, with *ra jambudvīpa dakṣiṇaḥ*; place one to the west with *va godanīya vaścamadvīpa*, and one to the north with *la uttarakurudvīpa.* {135}

Next place heaps to the right and left of the eastern heap with *yaṃ yaḥ dehaśca videha*; to the right and left of the southern heap with *raṃ raḥ camaraśca apacamaraḥ*; to the right and left of the western heap with *vaṃ vaḥ śaṣśaca uttara mattriṇaḥ*; and to the right and left of the northern heap with *laṃ laḥ kuravaṣca koravā.* After that, place a heap to the east of the eastern pile and one to the west of the western pile, saying as you do so *candra sūrya bhūṣita.* Then pray:

> This supreme mountain made of different precious
>   substances,
> Adorned with eight turrets,
> And having four continents and the subcontinents
> I offer and pray you to accept.

As you say this, scatter flowers, then place the mandala on the shrine in front.

In the middle of the mandala is a pure wisdom buddha field of full dimensions and extent, perfect in its adornments and layout, surrounded by an impenetrable outer protection circle. In its center is a measureless palace of perfect materials and architecture, decorated with infinite charnel ground attributes and celestial offerings. In the center of the palace, seated upon an antelope skin, is the lord of accomplished beings, glorious Saraha, inseparable from my root teacher.

He is white in color, tinged with red, and has the appearance of a brahmin. He has avoided becoming old and senile and remains eternally youthful. His hair is uncut, and he is wearing red cotton shorts. His two hands display the gesture of straightening an arrow, symbolizing the fundamental mode of existence. {136} He is sitting with his legs half-crossed. On his left he is accompanied by his spiritual consort, a wisdom yoginī in the guise of a huntress. Shining in a hundred directions with the radiance of the gnosis of coemergent great bliss, they are as dazzlingly brilliant as the very heart of the sun. With a gaze that overawes the three worlds, he has an appearance of intense spiritual power.

His mind constantly rests in meditation in the state of nondual gnosis, the Great Seal, the body of truth.

He endlessly manifests a display of spontaneous, uninterrupted activities.

Resplendent, he is venerated by infinite ḍākas and ḍākinīs and honored by the rulers of the three worlds.

In his crown center is the syllable *oṁ*, in his throat center the syllable *āḥ*, and in his heart center the syllable *hūṁ*.

The meditation deity and wisdom deity are inseparable from the beginning.

He is the embodiment of all one's present teachers and
lineage teachers,
The embodiment of all the infinite peaceful and wrathful
yidam deities,
The embodiment of the Buddha, Dharma, and Sangha,

The embodiment of all the ḍākinīs and dharma protectors
and guardians,
The all-pervading lord of the world and its inhabitants,
The glorious protector of samsara and nirvana,
The great, universal embodiment, in person, of all sources of
refuge.

*oṁ āḥ* At the lotus feet of the supreme glorious vajra teacher who reveals the true gnosis I submit obeisance *hūṁ*
*adhya siddhā māṃ*

Saying this three times, make prostrations.

Through your kindness
Great bliss arises in an instant:
Teacher whose body is like a precious jewel,
Saraha the Archer, at your lotus feet I bow down.

To the teacher, who is all the buddhas come in person,
Clouds of offerings, presented in reality and manifested in the
imagination,
And my three doors, possessions, and sources of good
I respectfully offer and request you to accept.

Since time without beginning, under the sway of defilements,
I have accumulated evil deeds, obscurations, faults, and downfalls.
All these, with intense remorse, I confess from the depths of my
heart.
Purify them and bestow the accomplishment of purity. {137}

With great joy, I rejoice
In all the merit accumulated,
Tainted and untainted,
By ordinary and noble beings and the buddhas and their heirs.

I exhort you to teach unceasingly
The ways to practice the dharma, profound and extensive,

And especially the unsurpassed Supreme Vehicle,
In accord with the characters, faculties, and aspirations of beings.

Until the wheel of samsara has been destroyed,
Moved by compassion
May you not enter the expanse of peace
But stay here steadfast and forever, I pray.

By the merit of this, representing all merit, past, present, and future,
May I swiftly attain supreme enlightenment
And free beings, as numberless as the sky is vast,
From the ocean of existence.

Perform these branches as many times as you can and offer the common mandala in the usual way, either detailed or condensed, many times. After that, make the inner mandala offering. As you set out the piles, consider that:

In an instant the sharp sword of gnosis appears in my hand,
And with it I cut my own body into pieces and present them as a mandala.
*hūṁ mastaka sumeru yavā mavāda videhaḥ*
*rahi nipāda jambudvīpa*
*va paści madvīpa hina hasta*
*la vāma hasta kuru uttara*
*śūtra kusuma candra sūrya bhūṣri taṃ*

Offer the mandala, saying:

*idaṃ guru ratna ātmanaṃ kāya maṇḍala niryata yāmi*

Again,

Into the skull cup severed from my own body (the aggregates of my ripened karma)
Are inserted all my remaining aggregates,

And with the three syllables, they are purified,
Transformed, and magnified, melting into an ocean of nectar.

Say *oṁ āḥ hūṁ ha ho hrīḥ* three times. Consider that:

[The teacher] drinks it through his tongue—a vajra-shaped tube of light.

Then:

This deliciously prepared food offering,
Bewitching with its hundred tastes,
I offer with faith to the glorious teacher.
May all these beings have the fortune to enjoy the food of concentration.
*oṁ āḥ śrī māna sadguru mahā siddhi māna saraha sapari vāre bhyaḥ*
*idam bali gaṇacakra mahā pūja khā hi*
*sarva siddhi mem prayacchantu*

At this point, the original text[3] states that one should make whatever outer and inner offerings one has, {138} so if you wish to make detailed offerings, use any suitable verses from an offering liturgy. Otherwise, continue as follows, making the offerings with *puṣpe* and so on:[4]

With the flower of authentic joy
The vajra sun is drawn into the lotus
And offered to the sovereign of the flower,
The supreme nature of the three vajras.

Conceptual thoughts, not being objects of the sense consciousnesses,
Are burned up by the blazing mystic heat in the navel:
The smell of incense as they burn
I offer to the vajra mind.

The pure light of shining lamps,
The brilliant rays of light of the mantra

Arising from the syllable *hūṁ*,
Is offered to the vajra mind.

The state of resting in the expanse of great bliss
Is anointed with the awakening of bodhichitta
And with thatness:
That perfume is offered to the vajra mind.

The enjoyment of everything here
Is the true display of the senses.
All these are the vajra mind,
Offered as the offering of food.

With the mind focused on the vajra cessation,
The sweet melody of indestructible sound,
The cuckoo's call of one's own experience,
I make the offering of the vajra mind.

To offer the nectar of the inner offering:

*oṁ āḥ hūṁ*
The food of the five nectars,
The supreme nature of all accomplishments;
The food of the five meats,
The principal samaya of all the buddhas;
The sublime and flawless drink of peace,
The five intoxicating liquors (mead, sugarcane beer,
Grain beer, fruit wine, and processed alcohol)—
All these, which have the nature of wisdom, I offer.

Considering that you are offering authentic wisdom consorts, make the secret offering:

These goddesses, great mudrās,
Who confer infinite bliss,
Born from the five families, I offer:
May I perfect the yogic practice of awareness.

The sum of all the bliss of gods and humans
Could never equal just a sixteenth part
Of a vajra holder's unsurpassed bliss,
Which I now offer.

For the praise, recite any specific prayers of praise that you know for the relevant mahāsiddha, and as a general prayer recite the following:

The meaning of the natural state, profound, peaceful, unelaborate,
Is both appearance and emptiness and neither.
Wonder! You hold the view free of thinking "This is it." {139}
Display of coemergent great bliss, to you we bow.

The inexpressible, inconceivable nature
Is the experience of bliss, bliss-emptiness devoid of grasping.
Wonder! You stay in relaxed meditation, free of effort.
Display of coemergent great bliss, to you we bow.

The radiant nature free of the activity of avoidance or adoption
Is pure and free from the adventitious stains of dualistic beliefs.
Wonder! You hold the fruit, the spontaneously present nature.
Display of coemergent great bliss, to you we bow.

Again, the original text states that one should perform the seven branches, so you may insert detailed or condensed versions as appropriate. Otherwise simply continue with this:

*oṁ āḥ* I submit obeisance at the lotus feet of the supreme glorious vajra teacher, who reveals true gnosis.
*hūṁ* Until I reach the heart of enlightenment,
I pay homage to the teacher, the Buddha.
I pay homage to the protector, the dharma.
I pay homage to the venerable sangha.
To all the buddhas, worthy of homage,
To the teachings given by the victorious ones,
And to the sangha possessed of excellent discipline—
To the Three Jewels I go for refuge.
All the negative deeds without exception

That I have committed, induced others to do, and rejoiced in—
I confess each one in the presence of those who destroy all faults,
And I take the vow not to commit them again.
I truly rejoice in all the virtue performed
By the listeners, solitary realizers,
Unsurpassed buddhas, and bodhisattvas,
And I dedicate it all to enlightenment.
In the Three Jewels, the precious buddhas and the others,
I take refuge by every means.
I arouse the mind set on supreme enlightenment,
And likewise I will follow the unsurpassed path.
As a result of all the virtue that I have performed in the three times,
May beings as infinite as space
Become vessels for the unsurpassed Vajrayāna
And may they all swiftly attain the level of Vajradhara.

Next, pray fervently with whichever words are appropriate, either:

*ātmanaṃ sukha duḥkhate me jñāne sukha kiduḥkha tomathi* {140}
*nasthi saraha namo stuti*

or, in English translation:

You know all my joys and sorrows.
In joy or pain, I have no one but you.
To you, Saraha, I bow down in homage.

And:

*guru śaranaṃ gacchami*

Repeat this many times. Recite the name mantra as many times as you can:

*oṁ āḥ mahāsiddha labdha saraha pāda hūṁ hūṁ*

At the end, consider that:

In the body of the teacher, the lord of yogis who has gained accomplishment,
I visualize the three channels and five chakras.
The male essence associated with the *kyangma* on the left side,
The nectar of the blessings of the body in the form of white light,
Issues from between the teacher's eyebrows and dissolves into my own forehead.
The obscurations of the body are purified, and I receive the vase empowerment.
The female essence associated with the *roma* on the right side,
The nectar of the speech in the form of red light,
Issues from the throat center and dissolves into my own throat.
The obscurations of speech are purified, and I receive the secret empowerment.
The blessings of mind in the form of the dark essence associated with the central channel,
Nectar in the form of deep-blue light,
Issues from the heart center and dissolves into my own heart.
The obscurations of mind are purified, and I gain the gnosis of the wisdom empowerment.
The teacher melts into light and dissolves into me.
I rest in the nondual state beyond thought and word.
The most subtle obscurations of the three doors are purified, and I receive the word empowerment.
The teacher and my own mind are mingled indistinguishably.

Now settle in meditative equipoise in your true nature, the natural state beyond thought. Arising from that state, say extraordinary prayers of dedication and aspiration, beginning with:

Wonderful! Excellent! By the merit of this and all virtue, past, present, and future,
May we and all the infinite beings who have been our mothers
Always be guided by the supreme accomplished beings
And swiftly attain the accomplishment of the Great Seal.

May our heads be crowned by the teacher,
Our hands hold the vajra and bell,

> Our voices recite the kingly secret mantras,
> And our minds meditate on the union state.

Conclude beautifully with prayers for auspiciousness.

The ritual procedure for other siddhas is similar. At the stage of the visualization, begin the above visualization and continue, for example, with: {141}

> . . . seated upon an antelope skin is the glorious protector noble Nāgārjuna, inseparable from my root teacher. He is azure blue in color, as radiant as a jewel, free of blemish, and adorned with the major and minor marks. His two hands are held at his heart in the gesture of teaching the dharma. He is dressed in the three dharma robes and seated cross-legged in the vajra posture. Shaṃkha and other supreme kings of the nāgas, taking the form of snakes, are offering him the shade of their hoods and providing a backrest for him to lean against. His mind constantly rests in meditation in the state of nondual gnosis, the Great Seal, the body of truth.

From here on, continue as above until the last line of the praise, where you should say:

> Nāgārjuna, at your lotus feet I bow down.

For the name mantra, in place of Saraha, you should say Nāgārjuna. The rest is the same as above.

The same principle applies for Shavaripa:

> . . . the lord of accomplished beings, the glorious Great Hermit, inseparable from my root teacher. He is black in color, symbolizing the unchanging ultimate reality. His long hair is tied up on his head, held with a bamboo stem. He stares with protruding, bloodshot eyes. In his two hands he holds an arrow and a bamboo bow, on the ends of which are attached the front and rear halves of a wild boar. He is adorned with a skirt made up of rows of peacock feathers, and with all kinds of flower and fruit ornaments. He is seated in the posture of royal ease, with a dignified

> air. On his right and left he is accompanied by two wisdom consorts who have the same ornaments and attire as himself and are holding quivers. Shining in a hundred directions with the radiance of the gnosis of coemergent great bliss . . .

The rest is as the same as above, except for

> Lord of the Mountains, at your lotus feet we bow down

and *śavari pāda* in the name mantra. For the praise, if you wish, you can recite the great praise of Shavaripa composed by Vanaratna.[5]

Likewise, for the mahāsiddha Kāṇḥapa:[6]

> . . . the master of accomplished beings, lord of yogic practitioners, the great Kāṇḥapa, inseparable from my root teacher. He is black in color, looking brave, attractive, and calmly poised. With his right hand he is playing a hand drum; in his left he holds a skull cup full of nectar, with a vajra khātvāṇga rising from the crook of his arm. {142} His hair is tied up in a topknot, and his body is ornamented with the six ornaments made from human bones. He is wearing a tiger-skin skirt. He is sitting in the posture of royal ease on top of a seat or mount of the terrifying form of Pishvarūpinī, the queen of the rākṣhasīs. From time to time, he displays various kinds of miraculous powers such as riding on a revived corpse adorned with garlands of flowers. In the sky above him seven parasols turn without anyone holding them, and seven hand drums sound spontaneously without anyone playing them. Sometimes he magically multiplies the seven parasols and seven hand drums a hundredfold. He manifests in the middle of countless male and female yogis—siddhas and vidyādharas—a visible following of seven hundred, an invisible following of seven hundred, and so on. Shining in a hundred directions with the radiance of the gnosis of coemergent great bliss . . .

The rest is the same as above, with the following adaptations:

> Lord of Practitioners, at your lotus feet we bow down

and *cāryavajra* or *kāṇḥacārya pāda* in the name mantra.

> [For Virūpa:] . . . the lord of accomplished beings, the great Virūpa, inseparable from my root teacher. He is dark brown, short and fat, with a large belly. His uncut hair is decorated with a garland of flowers. He is devoid of any other ornaments. His right hand is raised in the threatening gesture, tethering and subduing the sun. His left hand rests on his hip holding a decorative drinking horn filled with liquor. He is wearing a hemp loincloth and sitting in the posture of royal ease. To his left is his spiritual consort, holding a bowl of liquor and bowing down to him. Shining in a hundred directions with the radiance of the gnosis of coemergent great bliss . . .

The rest is the same as above, with the following adaptations:

> Virūpa, to you in homage we bow

and *virūpāda*.

> [For Ḍombi Heruka:] . . . the lord of accomplished beings, Ḍombi Heruka, inseparable from my root teacher. He is white in color, tinged with red, with his hair in a topknot, and bedecked with the six bone ornaments. He is adorned with terrifying snakes, poisonous to the touch, and holds a whip in the form of a snake, venomous to behold. {143} His head is hooded by seven snakes with noxious breath. He is mounted on a fearful man-eating tigress. On his left thigh is his secret consort, a lower-caste yoginī, who is naked and possesses all the marks of a padminī consort. They are in close embrace, delighting in the bliss of their union. Shining in a hundred directions with the radiance of the gnosis of coemergent great bliss . . .

The rest is the same as above, with the following adaptations:

> Ḍombipa, to you in homage we bow

and *ḍombi heruka pāda*.

> [For Lūyipa:] . . . the lord of accomplished beings, the great Lūhipa,[7] inseparable from my root teacher. His body is azure blue in color, and he looks emaciated. His hair is partly tied in a topknot, and he is wearing a cotton dhoti. In front of him is a meal of heaped-up fish entrails, which he is picking at and appearing to eat. He is seated with his legs half-crossed. Shining in a hundred directions with the radiance of the gnosis of coemergent great bliss . . .

The rest is the same as above, with the following adaptations:

> Lūhipa, to you in homage we bow

and *lūhi pāda.*

> [For Gorakṣha:] . . . the lord of accomplished beings, Gorakṣhanātha, inseparable from my root teacher. He is light blue in color, with a shiny complexion. He has a protruding nose and is smiling. His beard and hair are yellowish green. His gaze is fixed in a stare. He is wearing black bone earrings, a siṅganāda horn trumpet round his neck, and on his body a chakrakanta cloth, with wheel-like motifs. He is resting his chin on a meditation stick, sitting straight with his legs crossed. In his hands in the gesture of meditation he holds a gourd. Seeing him instantly brings delight and utterly destroys ordinary perceptions. Shining in a hundred directions with the radiance of the gnosis of coemergent great bliss . . .

The rest is the same as above, with the following adaptations:

> Gorakṣha, to you respectfully we bow

and *gorakṣhanātha pāda.*

> [For Tantipa:] . . . the great master of accomplished beings, Tantipa, inseparable from my root teacher. His body is azure blue, and he is of an advanced age, with drooping beard, mustache, and

> hair all completely white. He is wearing a cotton loincloth and working hard at a loom. {144} Shining in a hundred directions with the radiance of the gnosis of coemergent great bliss . . .

The rest is the same as above, with the following adaptations:

> Tantipa, to you respectfully we bow

and *tantika pāda.*

> [For Ghaṇḍhapa:] . . . the lord of accomplished beings, Ghaṇḍhapa, inseparable from my root teacher. He is light blue in color. His hair is tied up in a topknot, and he is draped with the six bone ornaments and a tiger-skin skirt. His two hands hold a vajra and bell, embracing his consort: she has all the marks of a padminī consort, in the form of Vajrayoginī, radiant white and entrancingly beautiful. They are delighting in the bliss of union. He is standing with his right leg extended . . .
>
> Bell-ringer Ghaṇḍhapa, to you in homage we bow

and *vajra ghaṇḍa pāda.*

> [For Jālandhara:] . . . the great lord of accomplished beings, Jālandhara, inseparable from my root teacher. He is white in color, tinged with red. His hair is dressed in a topknot, and he is wearing bone ornaments and a red dhoti. With one leg tucked back over his shoulder, he stands on the other leg. His two hands are opposed in the vajra uṣhnīṣha mudra, binding the crown. On his left, his wisdom consort, in the attire of a yoginī, is bowing down to him . . .
>
> Jālandhara, to you respectfully we bow

and *jālandhara pāda.*

> [For Kukkuripa:] . . . the great master of accomplished beings, Kukkuripa, inseparable from my root teacher. He is azure blue in color, wears bone ornaments, and has his hair tied up in a top-

knot. Sitting with his legs half-crossed, he holds a skull cup. On his lap he holds Vajrayoginī, in the form of a young dog, in whom he takes delight . . .

Kukkuripa, to you in homage we bow

and *kukkuri pāda.*

> [For Lvavapa:] . . . the great master of accomplished beings, Lvavapa,[8] inseparable from my root teacher. He is white in color, tinged with red, attired as a monk, and wearing a garment sewn together from a hundred pieces of rough wool. His two hands are in the meditation gesture, and he is seated cross-legged. Pretending to be fast asleep, he is settling in meditation on inconceivable luminosity. . . . {145}
>
> Lvavapa, to you in homage we bow.

and *kambala pāda.*

> [For Indrabhūti:] . . . and celestial offerings. In the center of the palace is the great master of accomplished beings Indrabhūti [inseparable from my root teacher]. Being the sovereign of humankind, he is attired as a universal monarch, resplendent and beautiful, white in color, tinged with red, with an attractive expression. He is adorned with silks and jewels and is comfortably seated on a lofty, broad jeweled throne, perfectly disposed. He is surrounded by five hundred queens bearing all the marks of the most precious ladies and is constantly and passionately delighting in all the pleasures of the senses . . .
>
> Indrabhūti, to you we pay homage

and *śrī narandra bhūti pāda.*

> [For Padmākara:] . . . the great master of accomplished beings, Glorious Great Bliss, Padmākara, inseparable from my root teacher. He has a white complexion, tinged with red. His face is round and full, his eyes and lips like lotuses in full bloom. His forehead is ornamented with the figure of a blossoming lotus marked with a vajra. Every part of his body is adorned with

exclusively virtuous marks—lotuses, utpalas, hooks, lassos, and the like. He wears a kāṇṭaka crown[9] and is dressed in the three dharma robes on top of the secret undergarment. In his right hand he holds up a five-pronged vajra at the level of his heart, and in his left hand, resting on his hip, he holds a kapāla full of nectar. A vajra khātvāṅga is tucked into the crook of his left arm. He sits with his legs crossed in the vajra posture and is accompanied on his right and left by sixteen-year-old maidens bearing all the marks of padminīs. Shining in a hundred directions with the radiance of the gnosis of coemergent great bliss. . . .

Padmākara, to you in homage we bow.

and *śrī mahāsukha padma vajra pāda.*

[For Kṛiṣhṇavirūpa:] . . . the great master of accomplished beings Kṛiṣhṇavirūpa, inseparable from my root teacher. On his head he wears the blue Vajra Skull crown, which confers blessings through any connection with it. {146} He is drinking from a decorative drinking horn full of nectar, which he holds in his right hand. His left hand rests on his knee. In front of him is a kapāla filled with mahābala. His hair is uncut; he is seated on an animal skin and wearing a loincloth. He wears no other ornaments and has the appearance of an elegant yogi. To his left is his spiritual consort, with her hands folded. Shining in a hundred directions with the radiance of the gnosis of coemergent great bliss . . .

Kṛiṣhṇavirūpa, to you we bow

and *kṛṣṇa virū pāda.*

[For Tillipa:] . . . In the center of the palace is the lord of accomplished beings, the great Tillipa,[10] inseparable from my root teacher. He is dark blue in color, with his hair tied up in a topknot. He is wearing cotton shorts and is levitating to the height of a person. He has the appearance of a sesame grinder. In front of him in the air is his spiritual consort, in the form of a female sesame vendor, hard at work in the sesame trade, symbolically showing how the coemergent gnosis arises with skillful means.

> Shining in a hundred directions with the radiance of the gnosis of coemergent great bliss . . .
>
> Tillipa, to you we pay homage

and *tilliku pāda hūṁ hūṁ.*

> [For Nāropa:] . . . the great master of accomplished beings, glorious Nāropa, inseparable from my root teacher. He is dark maroon in color, dazzlingly resplendent. His locks are tied up in a topknot, and his body is adorned with the six bone ornaments. He wears silk shorts. As an upper garment, he is wearing a freshly flayed human skin, dripping blood, the hands and feet of which he holds in his hands, stretching them to either side. He stands in the dancing posture, with one leg extended and the other bent. Shining in a hundred directions with the radiance of the gnosis of coemergent great bliss . . .
>
> Nāropa, at your feet we bow

and *nāro pāda.*

> [For Ratnākarashānti:] . . . In the center of the palace is the great master of accomplished beings Ratnākarashānti,[11] inseparable from my root teacher. He is light blue in color and takes the form of a sthavira, a great vajra holder of rather mature years. He is wearing the three dharma robes and the paṇḍita's hat. {147} With his two hands in the gesture of teaching the dharma, he holds a book written on palm leaves. He is sitting on a mat with his legs crossed in the vajra posture . . .
>
> Shāntipa, to you we pay homage

and *ratnākaraśāntipā.*

> [For Shāntigupta:] . . . In the center of the palace is the great master of accomplished beings Shrī Satvanāthashāntigupta, inseparable from my root teacher. He is dark maroon in color and adorned with a few jewel and bone ornaments. Fully fleshed and resplendent, he has the appearance of a calmly poised yogi. His hair is uncut, and he wears a triangular cotton loincloth. He

> is sitting in the style [of Maitreya] on a jeweled throne covered with an animal skin, with both feet [flat on the ground]. His two hands are held at the level of his heart in the gesture of teaching the dharma. Shining in a hundred directions with the radiance of the gnosis of coemergent great bliss . . .
>
> Shāntigupta, to you we pay homage

and *śrī satvanāthaśāntigupta hūṁ hūṁ*.

> [For Buddhagupta:] . . . on an animal-skin seat is the great master Shrī Buddhagupta, inseparable from my root teacher. He takes the form of a yogi, with a white complexion tinged with red. He is physically large and dignified, inspiring clear faith. The sight of him immediately makes one's hairs stand on end, and he has a fearful presence. His long hair is tied in a topknot, from the top of which a few locks of hair are hanging down his back. He is wearing a head wrapping of freshly bloomed yellow flowers. He has avoided becoming old and senile and remains youthful and elegant. He wears a cotton loincloth and clothes and has a meditation belt. His right hand is covering his knee and touching the earth, his left holding a kapāla full of nectar against his hip. He is sitting with his body erect and straight and his legs half-crossed. Shining in a hundred directions with the radiance of the gnosis of coemergent great bliss . . .
>
> Buddhagupta, to you respectfully we pay homage

and *śrī buddhaguptanātha hūṁ hūṁ*. {148}

Apart from these differences, the rest is as above.

As these examples show, the text says that one may adapt this ritual to any of the great siddhas in whom one especially has faith. It is sufficient to change the visualization, name, and name mantra in each case.

By this merit, may the blessings of the supreme siddhas
Permeate our streams of being.
May we attain realization and liberation at the same time
And find relief in the joyous city of the great celestial lands.

Although the author's colophon of this guru yoga is not clear, I am certain that it was written by the venerable omniscient Tāranātha. I, Lodrö Tayepai De, have arranged it as a liturgical text with the insertion here and there of some appropriate supplementary verses. I wrote it in the dharma college of Tashi Lhatse at Dzongsar.

May virtue and excellence increase.

# 5. A Precious Necklace

*Perfection Stage Teachings of the Eighty-Four Siddhas, the Root Text and a Commentary*[1]

THERE IS nothing like a good story to whet one's appetite for profound instructions. In this case, as related in Abhayadatta Shrī's commentary, a tale of jealousy and vengeance culminates in the principal character having molten copper poured over her. As a cure for her third-degree burns, she is prescribed a course of perfection stage (*rdzogs rim*) teachings, to be given by a number of mahāsiddhas who happen, conveniently, to be practicing in the charnel ground she inhabits. Despite her repeated complaints that she does not understand any of these teachings, the treatment slowly begins to work, and she finally attains realization and predicts Nāropa's meeting with his guru, Tilopa.

A literal translation of the commentary, which includes much repetition and explanation of ambiguities inherent in the language of the root text, would risk making for tedious if not incomprehensible reading. A certain amount of editing has proved necessary, but the essential meaning of this difficult text has, we hope, been retained.

{150}

**THE ROOT TEXT**

In Sanskrit: *Ratnamāla-nāma*
In Tibetan: *Rin chen phreng ba zhes bya ba*
[In English: *A Precious Necklace*]

Homage to the perfect, transcendent conqueror, the Lord of Speech!

Your reddish-brown hair streaming up,
Dark-blue eyes the color of utpalas,
Your terrifying roar—
Achala, to you I bow.

I have not set forth here
All that Dhamadhuma enjoyed
By seeing and hearing the eighty-four siddhas
Gathered in the realm of Manifest Joy.
Rather will I explain the precious necklace
Of the instructions to the yakṣhiṇī.

In the uninterrupted flow of insubstantiality
There is no periphery or center; it pervades everywhere.
That reality is extremely profound,
Like the fires of Mount Malaya.

Born from the ocean of substantiality,
You cling to the mire.
Without bees, flowers, and nectar,
What is there to taste?

Just as Brahmā knows the world and its inhabitants,
Certainty comes from definitive realization,
As with the season of warmth,
Yogurt culture, and oil in mustard seed.

It manifests as the very nature of space—
Inevident, invisible, and clear. {151}

The body that cannot be apprehended by anyone is utterly beautiful:
It is like a treasure vase, a wish-fulfilling tree, or a precious gem.

All cities are empty:
Ask yourself, What is it that created
The three worlds, the three existences, the body and speech?
The nature of the self is empty;
It does not dwell in any extremes whatsoever.

All cities are empty.
Where is there anything that exists substantially?

Because of dualistic grasping to the city
Of appearances, sounds, and thoughts, one is bound,
Like the unhappy silkworm trapped inside its own saliva.
Happiness comes when one lets go and does not grasp.

When you know how to not reject and not possess,
You will not enter the city.
As with Nanda and the jewel's light,
The city will become great bliss.

When people talk about phenomena,
Everything they say is a recollected thought.
And when they talk about nirvana,
Is that not too the faculty of thought?

All that appears—earth, water, fire, or wind—
Is simultaneous with emptiness.
The vivid appearances of gnosis {152}
Are identical with thought.

When you do not know how to unite the sun and moon,
All sorts of things manifest, like waves on water.
Because that very state is single,
Distinctions do not occur therein.

Here there is not even an atom of anything wrong.
This does not come about through effort.

Into the ocean of nonconceptuality
Sinks the mountain of conceptual thought.
The appearance of a subject is ultimate reality,
So where can there be the concept of an object?

In your vaselike body is the light of the elements,
And on top of it, the deity melts into nectar.

In a mass of light, ultimate reality,
The concepts related to the six consciousnesses are exhausted.

The various conceptual thoughts of the six classes of beings
Arise through the power of their full-grown obsession with evil.
Through the power of knowledge, which reverses it,
You awaken as buddha, so all your desires are fulfilled.

The appearances of the objects that cause them never cease;
They are like bubbles in water.
They are stopped by the subsequent antidote,
As if by a stick in the water.

It contains the seed of youth and beauty
That dwells in all beings, pervading them.
The highest faculty will apprehend its appearance;
It apprehends the appearance of gnosis alone.

It apprehends the sky and the forms of the clouds,
The mirror and the reflections that appear in it—
Thus it is when one examines it.
Darkness is of no use in illuminating that.
It is enjoyed by the power of secrets.

The seal that makes gnosis manifest
Is, for some, related to the vital point of the body.
By means of the magical machinery
The power of the faculties is developed.

As it is for the coconut tree,
What makes the fibrous husk,
The hard shell, and the white flesh grow
Is likewise the channels and winds.

In that which is without cause and without result
Everything is clearly revealed.
It is without analogy and cannot be designated.

What is the need for revealing something from which one is never separated?
Deviations and errors will not produce it. {153}
Free of wandering, it is the opposite of stagnation.

In the intermediate state between birth and death,
With regard to the concept of the body that is the ripening of karma,
Attachment is purified into luminosity.
Thus are the teacher's marvelous instructions.

Of the preparation and the main practice,
In the latter one must apprehend [one's dreams], refine them,
Bless them as illusions and get rid of fear,
And meditate without leaving thatness.

In the intermediate state of the transformation of consciousness,
One is driven by the body of habitual tendencies.
The connection, for the manifestation of dream,
In which bewilderment is transformed into luminosity,
Is made by one's strong aspiration.

When this body resulting from the ripening of karma perishes,
One has a mental body, with habitual tendencies.
Attachment manifests as luminosity.
Attachment to parents and so forth is abandoned.

The initial practice concerns the time,
Bodily control, and the object [of concentration].
The essential point of tummo is explained as four winds,
Which are held to be the four luminosities.

If death is unavoidable,
There are three kinds of transference:
The first is from the heart and from the navel.
Begin, in preparation, by closing the nine openings.

The double letter *kaṣa*,
Yellow and blazing with light—

The upright seed syllable
Keeps guard in the aperture of Brahmā.

The syllable of the bell is in the eye.
That which has the seed syllable of emptiness
Is placed on the tip of the ear.
The seed syllable of nectarous water
Is held on the tip of the tongue.

The stacked seed syllable of the lion
Guards the door of emanation and absorption.[2]
The stacked seed syllable of the tigress
Is to be placed on the breast.

The stacked seed syllable of the jackal
Is to be placed in the heart center.
In the navel, the vital center of burning, {154}
The seed syllable of power keeps guard.

Then, guard the lower opening as well
With the light-yellow seed syllable of water.
In the urethra and anus
Make the seed syllables blaze.

In the body, the seed syllable of the wind,
And in the mandala of mind and wind,
On the base of the final fading breath,
With a cry, the essence drop
Is to be guided by the mind.[3]

As a result of Dhamadhuma's virtuous deed
Of bringing to light all these [verses]
With the aim of helping the yakṣhiṇī,
May all beings attain the level of perfection.

This completes the short instruction text *A Precious Necklace.*

## The Commentary

Homage to the perfect, transcendent conqueror, the Lord of Speech!

For the benefit of beings,
With a devoted, single-pointed mind
I will compose a commentary on the *Precious Necklace*
Following my teacher's very words.

I will explain here *A Precious Necklace*, one of the five sections of the perfection stage teachings by the eighty-four siddhas summarized by the ḍākinīs Dharmavang and Kokala. For this I will give a brief exposition, commenting on it in three sections: (1) introduction; (2) main body of the text; and (3) conclusion. The first of these has three parts: (1) an explanation of the title; (2) homage; and (3) the promise to explain it.

### I. Introduction

### A. Explanation of the Title

In Sanskrit: *Ratnamāla-nāma*
In Tibetan: *Rin chen phreng ba zhes bya ba*
[In English: *A Precious Necklace*]

The title is indicated in Sanskrit by *Ratnamāla-nāma*, in Tibetan by *Rin chen phreng ba zhes bya ba*, [and in English by *A Precious Necklace*]. The titles in Sanskrit and Tibetan are equivalent.

What is the reason for mentioning it first? Because the translator Kawa Paltsek told the junior translators to do so. Moreover, the following specific explanation was given. {155}

It shows that the source is authentic and it inspires confidence, reminds one of the teacher,
Is auspicious, is not one's own invention,
Indicates the intention, is easy to understand, and indicates the subject that is taught—
By knowing the tradition of these eight branches of writing,
The wise should explain this shastra.

The phrase "In Tibetan" indicates that, in order to enable those who do not understand Sanskrit, the language of the gods, to understand the text, it was translated from Sanskrit into the language of our own country. So it is a grateful acknowledgment of the translator.

How was it translated? *Ratna* means "precious" and *māla* means "necklace." *Nāma* means "entitled."

Here the meaning of "precious" is shown by an analogy. A wish-fulfilling jewel is precious in that if one makes offerings to that jewel and venerates it on a grand scale, it brings numerous benefits. These can be summarized as of two kinds: it gets rid of all that is unwanted and unfavorable, and it brings about everything that one wants or needs.

"Necklace" is explained as follows. If there is a certain number of such jewels strung into a necklace, they will enable all beings to understand the meaning and to marvel. By analogy, this series of the precious instructions of the siddhas that get rid of unfavorable elements and have every kind of benefit are like a threaded necklace, and so they are given the title "Precious Necklace."

### B. Homage

Next, for the homage, there are two parts: (1) the homage by the paṇḍita who compiled this work and (2) the homage by the lotsawa who translated it.

#### 1. Compiler's Homage

> Homage to the perfect, transcendent conqueror, the Lord of Speech![4]

{156} A bhagavān—perfect, transcendent conqueror—is so called because he has conquered the four demons. These are the demon of defilements, the demon of the aggregates, the demon of death, and the demon "child of the gods." The first three interrupt one's span of life, while the demon child of the gods creates obstacles to the development of extraordinary qualities.[5] It is these demons that the bhagavān has conquered. This is summarized in an explanatory tantra:

> Power, a fine body,
> Glory, renown, gnosis,

And diligence—since he has these six
In abundance, he is "perfect."[6]

He is the Lord of Speech because he has mastery over, or enjoys, sameness, the pure gnosis devoid of stinginess and pride, or because he enjoys it, hence his being called "Lord." It is to that extraordinary object that homage is paid.

The individual who is paying homage is the compiler of these instructions, Suryarasmi. His purpose in doing so is so that no obstacles occur between the beginning and the end of this undertaking and to encourage others to pay homage as well.

### 2. Lotsawa's Homage

The homage by the lotsawa who translated it is made to the yidam deity:

Your reddish-brown hair streaming up,
Dark-blue eyes the color of utpalas,
Your terrifying roar—
Achala, to you I bow.

## C. Promise to Explain the Text

I have not set forth here
All that Dhamadhuma enjoyed
By seeing and hearing the eighty-four siddhas
Gathered in the realm of Manifest Joy.
Rather will I explain the precious necklace
Of the instructions to the yakṣhiṇī.

"Gathered in the realm of Manifest Joy" is explained as follows. "Manifest Joy" refers to the great charnel ground, the Sama Grove. It is called the "realm" of Manifest Joy because it is a realm in which the feast-offering mandala is performed, a place where the siddhas gather; {157} merely seeing or hearing of it makes fortunate beings joyful. "Gathered" means gathered in an assembly.

It was there that Dhamadhuma enjoyed the teachings that the eighty-four siddhas gave, enjoying them in the sense of seeing or listening to them, and so on. These teachings are not all recorded here. What then is presented in this text? The precious necklace of instructions to the yakṣhiṇī. The story of these instructions given to the yakṣhiṇī is as follows.

In that charnel ground there was a sort of hungry spirit, a carrion eater called Dukha. When she smelled flesh and blood, she would race unimpeded and arrive at the site in an instant, even from a distance of a hundred yojanas. At one time, in the northeast of that great charnel ground, there was a large tree, and since it was hollow, a female bear and her seven cubs made it their home. One day, a huge, fully grown rhinoceros fell asleep against the tree, which caused the tree to collapse, killing the bears living in it. The rhinoceros too had fallen over, and when the yakṣhiṇī found it, she immediately killed it. At this point, a rākṣhasa ogre called Koti from the south of the forest smelled the bears' flesh and blood and came looking everywhere for it. He begged the yakṣhiṇī for some meat but got none and consequently flew into a rage. On a large rock to the south, there were a number of copper smelters, so he stole some molten copper and poured it from the air above onto the yakṣhiṇī. {158} It burned the yakṣhiṇī's right hip down to the bone. Because of her karma from previous lives, it failed to kill her but it left her consumed by pain.

Just then, two ḍākinīs, Dharmadevī and Kokila, saw her. Taking pity on her, they chanted numerous mantras and healed the wounds in her flesh. The exposed bone, however, did not heal, and she continued to suffer. To put an end to the yakṣhiṇī's concepts, the two ḍākinīs made a request to the siddhas, who had gathered for a lengthy celebration of the feast offering, to teach her in accord with her particular predispositions. The masters granted this request, teaching her a series of topics strung together like a precious necklace, hence the title of these instructions, *A Precious Necklace*. It is these that the commentator is promising to explain to fortunate individuals of future generations, so that they may attain the peaceful, blissful state of nirvana.

## II. Main Body of the Text

First, Lūyipa gave an instruction on directly encountering appearances. When the yakṣhiṇī requested him to give an instruction that would help her, the master replied:

"The trouble is that you do not know your own nature. Once you know it, [you will know that] there are no appearances that exist, so how could physical appearances exist?"

"What is it to know one's own nature?" she asked.

"It is the gnosis of clear light, the exhaustion of the stream."

But she did not understand this, so he spoke the following verse: {159}

In the uninterrupted flow of insubstantiality
There is no periphery or center; it pervades everywhere.
That reality is extremely profound,
Like the fires of Mount Malaya.

"Insubstantiality" means there is nothing substantial whatsoever in anything: in the actual condition of things, there is nothing substantial. To make an analogy, although one can speak of a flower in the sky, it exists only in name: when one realizes that there is no such substantial thing, and that it cannot exist as something with shape and color, the concept of a flower in the sky ceases. In the same way, the actual condition of things is unborn; there is no substantial thing whatsoever that exists, and thus we speak of insubstantiality.

As soon as one realizes that there is nothing that exists, the stream of all the concepts of substantiality, appearances, emptiness, mind, mentation, and mental factors comes to an end. That is what we call the exhaustion of the stream, the gnosis of clear light.

In that case, when concepts come to an end, does gnosis also come to an end? If concepts have come to an end, how can there be a concept of a so-called gnosis? The nature of gnosis is clear light; it is uninterrupted.

With regard to that "uninterrupted flow," in what way is it uninterrupted? In its being clear light, in the same way that the radiance in a precious jewel never ceases.

What then are its characteristics? It is without periphery or center, and so it pervades everywhere. It is like [un]compounded space: without direction or bias, without boundary or center, and thus "pervasive," pervading everywhere from the peak of existence above to the terrifying hells below. {160}

That reality is extremely profound. "Reality" refers to the yakṣhiṇī's experiences[7] such as her physical ailments and her mental concepts and grasping at appearances. It is "profound" when one realizes that all those things are insubstantial, clear light.

"Like the fires of Malaya" is an analogy. Malaya is a huge mountain, and when it finds itself in the middle of fires blazing from the four directions, everything such as the roots, trees, branches, earth, rocks, and rivers—all the appearances that are encountered—serve to fuel the fire. Similarly, when one realizes everything as profound clear light, all appearances are destroyed as they are encountered and realized as clear light. Conceptual thoughts are killed[8] or destroyed in ultimate reality.

This teaching did not make any impression on the yakṣhiṇī, so she asked Lūyipa to clarify what he had taught. He replied with the following instruction:

> Born from the ocean of substantiality,
> You cling to the mire.
> Without bees, flowers, and nectar,
> What is there to taste?

You, Yakṣhiṇī, are attached to the ocean of substantiality, or the mire of existence. This is no good. In the first place, you have been born in the ocean of birth, aging, sickness, and death. Now too, on account of your body, ailments, and heat, you grasp at substantiality: because of your attachment to the mire of existence, you are not free from suffering.

When flowers, nectar, and bees come together, you get something that tastes sweet. But if you do not have these things {161} and they remain separate, you will never taste honey. In the same way, as long as you have not realized luminosity, as long as you consider your body as something special and are not free from the belief in substantiality, you will not experience the blissful flavor of the innate natural state. And until you experience that, how will you ever be free from suffering?

Next, Kokala gave an instruction on how to make use of this in one's mind stream.

> Just as Brahmā knows the world and its inhabitants,
> Certainty comes from definitive realization,
> As with the season of warmth,
> Yogurt culture, and oil in mustard seed.

While it is difficult for others to know the nature and the extent of this outer world and the existence of the sentient beings contained in it, the god Brahmā himself knows all these things without exception. Similarly, what you need to know by yourself is the nature of mind, whose essence is luminosity, which the teacher has shown you. Once you have recognized it, you need to make use of it in your mind stream. How you do this is indicated by "As with the season of warmth, yogurt culture, and oil in mustard seed."

You need to make use of it by not engaging with the outer apprehended object, as happens during the season of warmth. "The season of warmth" refers to the time almost three months after the New Year,[9] when the subtle wind withdraws and one remains without engaging with objects outside or pursuing concepts related to the six consciousnesses. Analogous to this, a person who makes use of the luminosity in their mind needs to turn away from the object, the conceptual thoughts related to the six consciousnesses, and {162} makes use in their mind stream of the object that is their own luminosity.

The analogy of the yogurt culture is as follows. When a yogurt culture is introduced into buffalo milk, the latter turns into yogurt. The milk itself has not been got rid of, but it has been transformed into yogurt and is no longer milk. Similarly, a person in whose mind stream luminosity has dawned has to make use of the transformation of the conceptual thoughts related to the six consciousnesses into gnosis without rejecting them.

How then does one know that the thoughts related to the six consciousnesses are gnosis? "Certainty comes from definitive realization, as with oil in mustard seed." Just as a mustard seed is pervaded by oil, the ground of all that characterizes sentient beings is pervaded by the natural state whose nature is luminosity. "Definitive realization" means that if you realize this without any doubts or uncertainties, you will not be mistaken.

What is the result of such realization? This question was answered by Chamaripa:

> It manifests as the very nature of space—
> Inevident, invisible, and clear.

"Inevident, invisible" refers to the fact that the body of truth is inevident and invisible, like space. It does not stand up to analysis in terms of anything: it is neither substantial nor insubstantial, nor mind, nor mentation, nor a mental factor, and therefore it is said to be "inevident, invisible."

In that case, if the body of truth is insubstantial, does the flow of compassion cease? Even though space has no identity, or shape or color, {163} or substantial attributes, the sun and moon, planets and stars, clouds, mist, rainbows, and so forth manifest clearly in it. Similarly, although the body of truth is invisible and uninterrupted, the flow of compassion never ceases:

it occurs automatically and uninterruptedly in the unceasing manifestation of the bodies of perfect enjoyment and manifestation, through the power of aspiration.

Saraha then said:

> The body that cannot be apprehended by anyone is utterly beautiful:
> It is like a treasure vase, a wish-fulfilling tree, or a precious gem.

The nature of mind, which is divested of the dualistic concepts of subject and object, is utterly beautiful. How can that be illustrated? It is as beautiful as a treasure vase, a wish-fulfilling tree, or a precious gem.

Next, the master Birvapa gave an instruction called "The Empty Cities."

> All cities are empty:
> Ask yourself, What is it that created
> The three worlds, the three existences, the body and speech?
> The nature of the self is empty;
> It does not dwell in any extremes whatsoever.

The "cities" of the three worlds or the three existences (on the outer level) or of the body, speech, and mind (on the inner level), or of the three times and so forth—these cities are empty. In what way are they empty? The outer universe is produced by four kinds of causal matter. It is produced from these four through interdependence and is therefore the resultant matter. "Body and speech" here include mind, and from the mind there arise the cities of conceptual thoughts related to the three times and so forth. All these cities are empty.

Why is that? Ask yourself, What is it that created these? {164} Were they created by the four kinds of causal matter or by the mentally produced self associated with the three times? If they were created by the four kinds of causal matter, those four kinds of matter must have an effect on one another, so they must be impermanent and empty. And since the cities of the three worlds are produced from the four kinds of matter, they too must be impermanent and therefore empty.

If they were created by the mentally produced self associated with the three times, were they made by a creator associated with the three times that exists substantially, or by an insubstantial entity? Supposing that they were made by something that exists substantially, since substantial entities are material things, and all material things are compounded, and all compounded entities are impermanent, the cities made by it must be empty. If they were made by an insubstantial entity, then that insubstantial entity would be making a substantial entity and it would follow that space could create flowers, so that cannot be the case either. The cities of all these, therefore, are empty.

Furthermore, when you ask yourself, Is it the self that created those cities, [the answer is that] there is no self; its nature is empty. You will never find an existent entity that constitutes a creator. It is empty. Is it all just a uniform emptiness? No. "It does not dwell in any extremes whatsoever." It is neither empty nor not empty, nor both empty and not empty, nor neither empty nor not empty. It does not dwell in any of these extremes.

The meaning of this was affirmed by Ḍombipa:

All cities are empty.
Where is there anything that exists substantially?

This point can be understood without being set out here.

Gorakṣha then gave the following teaching: {165}

Because of dualistic grasping to the city
Of appearances, sounds, and thoughts, one is bound,
Like the unhappy silkworm trapped inside its own saliva.
Happiness comes when one lets go and does not grasp.

"Appearances" refers to the world and its inhabitants and so on, which are physical phenomena, while "sounds" refers to conceptual, conventional labels. All these are nothing other than concepts, which is why Gorakṣha speaks of "the city of conceptual thoughts." Because of one's dualistic subject-object grasping at them as real, one binds oneself, like a silkworm that binds itself inside the cocoon secreted from its mouth.

"Happiness comes when one lets go and does not grasp." "Not grasping" is ceasing to believe in the true existence of the object outside. "Letting go" means giving up the belief in a substantially existing subject and resting in the natural state, ultimate reality. When one does so, one will be happy.

Tantipa spoke as follows:

When you know how to not reject and not possess,
You will not enter the city.
As with Nanda and the jewel's light,
The city will become great bliss.

"Not rejecting" refers to not rejecting all the outer and inner phenomena, the world and its inhabitants. In what way should one not reject them? One should not reject them because there is no existent creator of the world and its inhabitants, neither an atman nor anything to be rejected. You might argue that this is saying, "Do not reject delusion," and therefore that to say, "When you know that, you will not enter the city of delusion" is a non sequitur. That is true, but it is not that you enter the city of delusion as such: that delusion itself is by nature the ultimate nature and becomes the city of great bliss. "As with Nanda and the jewel's light, the city will become great bliss": {166} The analogy here is of Nanda, a nāga king, and a precious jewel. The nāga king can see the light of that jewel, but to others it is invisible. Similarly, when one knows the meaning of not rejecting it and simultaneously not possessing it, the city of conceptual thought will itself become great bliss.

Following this explanation of the master Birvapa's instruction on the city of bliss, the master Saraha gave the yakṣhiṇī the following instruction:

When people talk about phenomena,
Everything they say is a recollected thought.
And when they talk about nirvana,
Is that not too the faculty of thought?

This is the teaching by the great brahmin Saraha, an instruction on thought alone. "People" here means anyone who can talk.[10] "Phenomena" refers to all the phenomena mentioned in the scriptures. Whatever people say about these is only a recollected thought.[11] In what way? Whatever they speak about, whether samsara and nirvana, or sustained calm and profound insight, or meditation and postmeditation, or appearances and emptiness, all of these are recollected thoughts. Even when they say "nirvana," this is a word, and words are nothing but recollected thoughts. Everything one says is a recollected thought. Hence, "When they talk about nirvana, is that not too the faculty of thought?"

In what way?

All that appears—earth, water, fire, or wind—
Is simultaneous with emptiness.
The vivid appearances of gnosis
Are identical with thought.

{167} "All that appears—earth, water, fire, or wind" refers to everything that appears as external and internal products of those elements. These are all recollected thoughts. Yet at the very moment they appear, they are at the same time innately empty: they are "simultaneous with emptiness." At that moment of appearance, they are empty and yet simultaneously blissful. Thus those appearances are the appearances of the gnosis of emptiness; they are the vivid appearance of gnosis. Those appearances—recollected thoughts—are not independent[12] but are one with and indistinguishable from the appearances of gnosis, which are therefore "identical with thought."

Shavaripa then spoke:

When you do not know how to unite the sun and moon,
All sorts of things manifest, like waves on water.
Because that very state is single,
Distinctions do not occur therein.

The sun represents appearances, the moon emptiness. Alternatively, the sun represents skillful means and the moon wisdom. "Unite" refers to uniting appearances and emptiness or skillful means and wisdom. If one does not know how to do this, a multitude of things manifests, like the waves on water. Just as in the one ocean there are a multitude of waves, in the single ultimate nondual state there are many thoughts and recollections. But with regard to the union of sun and moon, "Because that very state is single, distinctions do not occur therein." "That very state" refers to the concepts of dualistic appearances explained above. "Single" means there are no independent thoughts in thatness, the natural state: the essential nature of thoughts is the same as the natural state. And therein, "distinctions do not occur." {168} What is meant by "therein"? In ultimate reality—the natural state, thatness—independent thoughts do not occur; thoughts are the same in the state of ultimate reality, the natural state.

Chauraṅgi added the following instruction:

> Here there is not even an atom of anything wrong.
> This does not come about through effort.

Here—that is, in ultimate reality, the natural state—there is not even an atom of anything wrong, meaning the independent thoughts mentioned above. This does not come about through effort. It is not something that comes about through the causal process of means leading to a result. It is simply the quality or appearance of the natural mode of being of the ultimate reality.

Vīnapa said:

> Into the ocean of nonconceptuality
> Sinks the mountain of conceptual thought.
> The appearance of a subject is ultimate reality,
> So where can there be the concept of an object?

Nonconceptuality is like an ocean, in which it is difficult to separate ultimate reality and mere thought. Into that ocean independent conceptual thoughts and recollections, which are like a mountain, sink, dissolving into ultimate reality. What is the reason for their dissolving? The moment one recognizes the appearance of an apprehending subject as ultimate reality, there is no concept of a substantially existing apprehended object, so where can there be the concept of an object?

After this teaching on Saraha's instruction on thought alone, the master Mīnapa gave an instruction on eating and clothing oneself with the elements.

> In your vaselike body is the light of the elements,
> And on top of it, the deity melts into nectar.
> In a mass of light, ultimate reality, {169}
> The concepts related to the six consciousnesses are exhausted.

The first line is an instruction from the point of view of the generation stage. First, one meditates that the palace of one's body becomes a single vaselike container. Inside it, one meditates on the light of the elements, as follows. From the syllable *yaṃ* comes the fire-wind, red in color like the sun's orb, one and a half earshots in diameter. Next, visualize that from the furious blowing of wind there appears a red syllable *raṃ*, emanating and reabsorbing light, from which appears red fire, equal in extent to the wind. From it there comes vapor and mist, from which one visualizes the red fire-water in the form of light. From the foam on it visualize a yellow syllable *su* emanating and reabsorbing light, from which there appears fire-earth, whose extent is the same as above.

On top of the palace of the light of the elements, there appears the radiance of the nature of mind, a white *hūṁ* having the nature of the deity. From the emanation and reabsorption of light, it melts into nectar and dissolves in stages into those elements. Those elements become one with the body-vase containing them. Then the nature of mind, the essence of the deity, which has the nature of fire, wind, and earth, becomes the nature of ultimate reality or manifests as a syllable *hūṁ* and melts into light. It is present inside the vase of light as ultimate reality in the form of a sphere, self-radiant like the heart of the sun. As a result of your concentrating on that, the conceptual thoughts related to the six consciousnesses are exhausted or cease, and as the six consciousnesses are turned inward, realization is born like a lamp inside a vase of radiant light. The sign of progress in that concentration is that the body becomes warm, clothed in the garments of the outer elements. Inwardly, the element of awareness is eaten as the food of concentration. {170}

The yakṣhiṇī, however, was unable to develop in her mind the concentration of clothing oneself in the elements and feeding on bodhichitta like this, so to help her practice and realize it, noble Nāgārjuna spoke to her as follows:

> The various conceptual thoughts of the six classes of beings
> Arise through the power of their full-grown obsession with evil.
> Through the power of knowledge, which reverses it,
> You awaken as buddha, so all your desires are fulfilled.

The six classes of beings, in other words, the sentient beings of the three worlds, take every possible kind of physical form and thus have a whole variety of possible thoughts and concepts. How do these arise? Through the power of their fully developed obsession with evil ways, that is, their attachment to wrong ways that are the opposite of the correct path. It is not that their conceptual thoughts each have individual causes. The thoughts associated with their obsession with evil are related to their respective habitual tendencies. Through the power of knowledge, the concepts of the six classes of beings that arise through their obsession with evil are reversed and they are turned toward the truth. And through the knowledge of the latter, there arise the qualities of great bliss. This is because one awakens as buddha—that is, one's mind awakens as buddha. As a result, all one's desires or wishes are fulfilled.

With this instruction, {171} Nāgārjuna told the yakṣhiṇī: "Because of your concepts related to the obsession with evil, you yourself continue to experience your body, its ailments, and so forth. If you were to develop the power of the nature of mind as a mass of light like the heart of the sun, there is no doubt that your suffering would arise as bliss."

Next, the master Shāntipa gave an instruction called "the six views, outer and inner, that reverse the consciousnesses of suddenly arisen appearances with subsequent understanding."

> The appearances of the objects that cause them never cease;
> They are like bubbles in water.
> They are stopped by the subsequent antidote,
> As if by a stick in the water.

The appearances of objects (which are the causal conditions for those appearances)—form (the object of the eye) and the other objects that act as the causes of perception by the ear, nose, body, mind, and so on—these appearances never cease. They arise suddenly in dependence on the objects. Like bubbles in water, whose sudden arising cannot be stopped, the appearances produced by sensory objects cannot be stopped. The consciousnesses of suddenly arising appearances cannot be stopped by a whole cavalry of lancers. This is the view of the six objects outside.

Is not this view of the six objects an erroneous view, since it concerns erroneous consciousnesses? No. They are termed six views in reference to reversing the grasping at the six objects as independently existing (which *is* an erroneous view) and using subsequent understanding[13] to recognize suddenly arisen appearances as ultimate reality.

What is it that recognizes this? The subsequent antidote, which reverses them like a stick in the water. What is the subsequent antidote? Although the consciousnesses of suddenly arising appearances cannot be turned back by a cavalry of lancers, {172} they are reversed by the understanding that cuts through perceptions, like a stick striking the water. At that moment, when the antidote transforms into gnosis, we speak of the six inner views. In the first place there is the suddenly arisen appearance, which is the defilement to be eliminated. The subsequent understanding is the antidote that eliminates it, like a sword striking the water. It is gnosis. The moment one realizes by this means that there are not two things—something to be eliminated and something that eliminates—there is only gnosis itself. This is what is referred to as the six inner views. "That," Shāntipa told the yakṣhiṇī, "is what you have to realize."

The two ḍākinīs now had the yakṣhiṇī practice five deity sādhanas, which they requested the siddhas to bestow on her. The master Khagarbha[14] gave her the instructions for the condensed sādhana of noble Achala, Kanaripa the sādhana of Prajñāpāramitā, Ḍombipa the quintessential sādhana of Chakrasaṃvara and Hevajra together, Chaloka that of Amitāyus, and Nāropa the confession ritual of the hundred-syllable mantra. After this, they put the yakṣhiṇī to practicing them. In her keenness to gain accomplishment quickly, the yakṣhiṇī practiced with the view that subject and object are independently existent and real. As a result, she did not get a single sign or mark of accomplishment, even as part of a dream. This led her to complain that there were no such things as so-called male and female deities, and not a single accomplishment to be had; meditating on nonexistent deities and counting mantras was making her extremely irritated.

To this the two ḍākinīs replied: "All the masters of the past attained accomplishment. {173} The fact that you have not is the fault of your not having purified your mind stream."

"I still don't understand what you mean by 'mind stream,'" she said. So to help her understand, they gave her the following explanation. Two topics are taught here: a teaching on the little nail of the pith instructions of the deity generation stage, and pith instructions of the method of symbols and meanings. First, the little nail of the deity generation stage.

> It contains the seed of youth and beauty
> That dwells in all beings, pervading them.
> The highest faculty will apprehend its appearance;
> It apprehends the appearance of gnosis alone.

"Youth and beauty" indicates what the deity in the generation stage is like: it has the fresh appearance of a beautiful youth—youthful because it does not have a body made up of the elements and is therefore free of the impurities of birth, aging, and youth; and beautiful because it is not flawed by conceptual imputations. The "seed" that gives rise to a likeness of the deity's youth and beauty refers to the essence of the sugatas[15] that is present in and pervades all beings. It is the seed present in all the beings of the six realms, pervading them all without exception, that enables them to generate the visualized deity regardless of their class {174} or status. Thus the apprehension of the deity is nothing other than the appearance of that seed, the nature of mind.

"The highest faculty will apprehend its appearance" refers to the faculty of the nature of the mind, which will apprehend the appearance of the deity, the best of habitual tendencies. Is this saying, then, that the best habitual tendency is the appearance of the deity or the highest faculty, and therefore that the highest faculty meditates on attributes? No. It is not that the manifold forms of the deity are independently existent and real, but rather that they are the manifestations of the nature of the mind or that they are recognized as an image. That is what we call "the highest faculty apprehending appearance." Why? Because it is the appearance of gnosis alone. There is no independent, truly existent deity. The deity that is pictured in the mind is, by nature, the body of perfect enjoyment. The uncontrived nature of the mind is the body of truth. Thatness, appearing in every way, does not exist, and yet it is not obstructed in any way. It pervades the two buddha bodies. Thus the text speaks of "the appearance of gnosis alone." When one understands this, one has mastered the pith instructions of the deity in the generation stage.

Next, the pith instruction of the method of symbols and meanings indicates with what symbols that is shown and what those symbols mean.

> It apprehends the sky and the forms of the clouds,
> The mirror and the reflections that appear in it—
> Thus it is when one examines it.
> Darkness is of no use in illuminating that.
> It is enjoyed by the power of secrets.

{175} The symbols here are first the sky and then the clouds, and similarly the mirror in which forms appear and then the reflections. The sky and mirror are analogies for the body of truth. The body of truth is the support of the second buddha body.[16] "Darkness" refers to bewilderment, and such bewilderment is of no use for seeing the two buddha bodies. When someone who is making an experience of that practices with the right commitment, that individual "enjoys it by the power of secrets." What are the secrets? There are ten secrets in all, which are enumerated in the *Tantra of the First Thought*:

> First, the teacher's conduct is secret,
> The yidam deity who bestows accomplishment is secret,
> The time when the blessings enter is secret,
> The secret name given by the teacher is secret,
> The innate view that liberates is secret,
> The signs of warmth that arise from experience are secret,
> The signs predicted by the ḍākinīs are secret,
> The spontaneous conduct free of concepts is secret,
> The samaya of the five nectars is secret,
> The accomplishment of the exhaustion of obscurations is secret.[17]

The meaning is that if one practices with the power of the ten secrets until one has attained the path of consummation, one will attain accomplishment.

This teaching on the little nail of the deity generation stage is now followed by the little nail of the instruction on the essential points of the channels and energies. {176} The two ḍākinīs explained many of the siddhas' instructions on the channels and winds to the yakṣhiṇī, and as soon as she applied these, her pain was relieved. But as she did not achieve bliss, she finally grew disenchanted. The teacher Tilopa therefore gave her this instruction:

> The seal that makes gnosis manifest
> Is, for some, related to the vital point of the body.
> By means of the magical machinery
> The power of the faculties is developed.

To make gnosis—the ultimate luminosity, the natural state—manifest, the tradition of the secret mantras includes the following ways. Practitioners on the path of transformation of the ground transform conceptual thoughts into the nature of the male and female deities and recognize them ultimately as the five kinds of gnosis. "For some" refers to another, different way. Those on the path of desire differ from them in that they make use of the essential point or seal of the body and determine gnosis by means of a clear understanding of the channels and winds. Those on the path of liberation determine gnosis simply as a magical display. Those on the great path of liberation determine that gnosis itself is nonexistent, and that neither is there any gnosis regarding that: defilements and concepts themselves do not exist and neither is there gnosis regarding that. It is like a flower in the sky.

Thus the seal that makes gnosis manifest is the determination of gnosis, for some, by making use of the vital point of the body. What is the vital point of the body? It is the essence drop, the chaṇḍalī. Through making use of that, the meaning of gnosis is made manifest. {177} An analogy for this is given in the last two lines. When a magician uses magical machinery to good effect, numerous manifestations appear. And although they are illusions, it is as though the magician has expanded one's eyesight. In the same way, when one makes use of the yogic exercises—the "magical machinery" of the essential point of the body—this makes gnosis manifest.[18]

To provide a symbolic analogy for this instruction on the essential point of the channels and winds, the master spoke as follows:

> As it is for the coconut tree,
> What makes the fibrous husk,
> The hard shell, and the white flesh grow
> Is likewise the channels and winds.

First, in what way is this symbolic? In what way are there factors that produce a coconut's husk outside, shell in the middle, and flesh inside?[19] Whether there are or not, this is simply an analogy. To explain this, the development of the fibrous husk is brought about by the spreading of the roots. The development of the hard shell is brought about by the trunk. And what makes the white flesh develop is the rising of the sap. Just as the coconut fruit develops in dependence on the roots and trunk, it is in dependence on the practice of the channels and winds that the result, the appearances of gnosis, arises as the three buddha bodies. {178}

The aim of all this is to enable one to attain ultimate reality, so after giving this instruction on the essential point of the channels and winds, the master taught the following pith instruction on the view and meditation:

> In that which is without cause and without result
> Everything is clearly revealed.
> It is without analogy and cannot be designated.

> What is the need for revealing something from which one is never separated?
> Deviations and errors will not produce it.
> Free of wandering, it is the opposite of stagnation.

Here he mentions what is the meaning of the view. The ultimate view is what is called the gnosis of luminosity. If one were to indicate it by an analogy, this is shown by "In that which is without cause and without result." "Without cause" refers to its being like space. What is [space] produced by? It is not produced by anything. Then is there a result or not? Since it has no cause, neither does it have a result. In that case, is it something that is nothing at all? No. In the body of truth there is no cause that produces something nor a result that is produced, yet it clearly displays a result, the two form bodies, unobstructedly. For example, in the great space, without there being any concept of a cause that produces and a result that is produced, "everything is clearly revealed." Although the essential nature of space itself is without activity, it provides a space for everything, and so "everything is clearly revealed." Similarly, the natural state, the nature of mind, luminosity, like the great space, is devoid, in its essential nature, {179} of activity, yet the two buddha bodies manifest clearly and unobstructedly.

The essential nature of the body of truth cannot be pointed out by anything. It is "without analogy and it cannot be designated." Can it be experienced then? It is something that one makes an experience of without being experienced, that one meditates on without anything to be meditated on, that one concentrates on unceasingly—a result without there being anything to attain. It is present from the very beginning, never separate from one, so there is no need to experience or reveal it. So, "What is the need for revealing something from which one is never separated?" In what way does it exist without ever separating? It never deviates anywhere, it never strays into error, it never gets lost in apathy, nor does it remain stagnant. It is the opposite of indifference.

When one says "deviate," where can it deviate? There are four kinds of deviations. The first is called "deviation with regard to emptiness-luminosity, the fundamental nature of phenomena." Some followers of the Great Vehicle of Characteristics, the Mādhyamikas and others, establish emptiness as neither one nor many and then meditate on emptiness as being like the heart of space, in other words, on a concept created by concepts. Followers of the

Mantra Vehicle dissolve the world and its inhabitants in stages or, with the *svabhāva* mantra, mentally make everything empty like perfectly pure space and then settle the mind on that. Both of these are mental creations and so constitute deviations.

Then there is the deviation into sealing luminosity-emptiness. This is to meditate by placing the seal of emptiness on the absence of concepts (in generosity, for example) of a recipient, a giver, and a gift. This too is a mental creation. {180}

The third deviation is the deviation into using luminosity-emptiness as an antidote to defilements. This is to settle the mind on whatever arises (attachment, aversion, and so forth) being empty—in that first it has not been born from anywhere, at present it does not exist as the essence of anything, and finally there is nothing to be stopped, or no cessation.

Finally there is the deviation with regard to the path of luminosity-emptiness. Practitioners with attachment consider that a good result exists elsewhere, and as their path or method, they train in making emptiness the object of the mind. By doing so, they are mentally creating the hope that they will attain the body of truth.

> At that time, emptiness is not means,
> Because if emptiness were means,
> Cause and result would conflict.
> Means is not emptiness.[20]

The actual condition of things, where these four deviations have been abandoned, is devoid of all conceptual thoughts and quite beyond the scope of the intellect.

The experiences of being pleased when bliss occurs and displeased when it does not are concepts. When they arise, one strays into the world of desire. When one apprehends [the experience of] absence of thought [in the same way], one strays into the formless world. If one is attached to or grasps at [these experiences] together, one strays into the state of the listeners and solitary realizers.

To remain stagnant is to rest in an unaltered state of consciousness in which those [errors] have been abandoned, and thus to stagnate in an unborn, thoughtless state.

To get lost in apathy is to remain indifferent when thoughts occur one after the other and to say to oneself: "There is no need to meditate; this is the body of truth." The opposite of that is to turn away from such indifference.

All this indicates the luminosity of the view. Next, Tilopa taught the meaning of meditation, which is not to separate from the view and to make them one. For this he taught the view of mind as luminosity and the body as the illusory body, their connection in dream and in the intermediate state, and the concentrations of transference and "entering a residence." {181} As the yakṣhiṇī still had not understood the teachings that the master Tilopa had given her, he gave her instructions to guide her on the path. The view of luminosity had already been taught above. How is it connected to the illusory body, and what is their connection in dream and the intermediate state? This he taught in three topics, each consisting of five points, making fifteen points in all: three intermediate states, three illusory bodies, three things that manifest, three mixings, and three connections. There now follows an explanation of the first of these topics with its five points.

> In the intermediate state between birth and death,
> With regard to the concept of the body that is the ripening of karma,
> Attachment is purified into luminosity.
> Thus are the teacher's marvelous instructions.

What we call the intermediate state between birth and death—that is, from when one is born until one dies—is a period when all kinds of conceptual thoughts manifest. Of the three kinds of body,[21] the body that is referred to is the body resulting from the ripening of karma, made from the elements, so we speak of "the concept of the body that is the ripening of karma." With regard to that concept, what is it that is manifesting? It is luminosity that manifests. What then is it mixed with? It is mixed with the defilement of attachment, hence, "attachment is purified into luminosity." How is it mixed with attachment? Practitioners on the path of transformation consider conceptual thoughts to be male and female deities; those on the path of desire [attain] bliss by making use of the channels, essence drops, and sound (*nada*), while those on the path of liberation achieve bliss by practicing the mystic heat (*tummo*). Those on the great path of liberation do not cling to these different kinds of bliss but realize them as luminosity, which is thus said to be mixed with attachment. {182}

What is it that makes the connection? "The teacher's marvelous instructions." It is the teacher's instructions that connect all the points explained above. In this case, they refer to the practice of what we call "incorporating dreams on the path," which is the practice on the path in this life.

> Of the preparation and the main practice,
> In the latter one must apprehend [one's dreams], refine them,
> Bless them as illusions and get rid of fear,
> And meditate without leaving thatness.

There are two stages: the preparation and the main practice. First the preparation is taught. If people who are beginning this [practice] do not have enduring good karma, have deteriorated their sacred commitments, have not accumulated merit, are lacking in respect for their teachers, and do not serve them properly, they cannot apprehend the dream state. They therefore have to confess their faults and recite the hundred syllables, develop intense devotion to the teacher and the Three Jewels, and be diligent in abandoning evil, purifying misdeeds, and accumulating merit. This is the preparation.

The main practice is divided into four parts: first, apprehending one's dreams; second, refining them; third, blessing them as illusions and getting rid of fear; and fourth, meditating on thatness.

First, apprehending one's dreams: How does one apprehend them? To begin with, you should have in mind a strong intention and clear interest in apprehending your dreams. During the day you should repeatedly bring to mind the thought "I must recognize my dreams as dreams." For this, think: "I will consider that whatever I think of, such as a tathāgata's buddha field, is a dream." Then, using a soft mat and thick pillow, lie down on the right side of your body, with your left arm stretched out on top of your thigh {183} and your right hand against your cheek. Consider that in your throat is a four-petaled red lotus, in the center of which is a white letter *A*, and lie there without falling into ordinary sleep. Then, as you fall asleep, retain mindfulness. As night falls, concentrate on a white sphere in between your eyebrows and, lying down, go to sleep. Then, at dawn, focus the mind on the letter *A* in your throat. If you have failed to apprehend your dreams when you are dreaming, you should feel a strong yearning, thinking, "I have woken up and failed to recognize any of my dreams." Once you are awake, understand that phenomenal existence is like a dream. Know that all phenomena are like a dream, like a magical illusion, like an optical illusion. By practicing in this manner day and night, you will manage to apprehend your dreams.

What are the signs of doing so? Whatever happens to you, such as floods, conflagrations, being chased, being murdered, and so on, you will sometimes think, "This is a dream." And when you are dreaming, you will think, "The teachings that all phenomena are like a dream are true" and feel intense faith and inspiration. This is apprehending your dreams.

Next, once you manage to apprehend your dreams, at dusk make a strong aspiration, thinking, "I must recognize the dream state *as* a dream." The teaching on apprehending your dreams is therefore followed by a teaching on refining the dream state (as indicated in the root verse by "refine"). How does one refine one's dreams? Make a strong aspiration, thinking, "Since it is a dream, I should train in it as just that." Then, during your dreams, do whatever there is in your mind—plunging into water, being burned in a fire, climbing a precipice, gazing at the Heaven of the Thirty-Three, looking at the twenty-four sacred places in India, trampling on the sun and moon, having a vision of the yidam deity and receiving teachings, {184} or seeing the buddha fields of the tathāgatas and hearing them teach. To train in getting used to this is to refine your dreams.

Understanding dreams to be illusions and getting rid of fear is indicated by "Bless them as illusions and get rid of fear." When you are training in the dream practice, if you still feel apprehensive or afraid when plunging into water and so on, meditate thinking, "This is a dream; dreams are not true, so how can I be afraid of it?" By doing so you get rid of fear.

Alternatively, meditate on thatness, as indicated by "meditate without leaving thatness." It is a dream, so what is there to refine? Recognize that it is your own mental delusion and meditate on thatness. The way to do that is to never separate from whichever of your teachers' instructions occur to you.

All the above concerns incorporating dreams on the path, which is a practice that one trains in in this life.

Next, the second intermediate state:

> In the intermediate state of the transformation of consciousness,
> One is driven by the body of habitual tendencies.
> The connection, for the manifestation of dream,
> In which bewilderment is transformed into luminosity,
> Is made by one's strong aspiration.

Here the intermediate state is held to be the intermediate state of dream; the body is the body of habitual tendencies; what manifests is dream, which is mixed with bewilderment; and the connection is made with mindfulness and aspiration.

To begin with, "In the intermediate state of the transformation of consciousness" refers to the intermediate state of dream. In what way is it the intermediate state of transformation of consciousness? In the dream state, the daytime consciousness is transformed, it follows habitual tendencies, and various delusions arise, {185} so it is called the intermediate state of the transformation of consciousness. The reason it follows habitual tendencies is that one is driven by the body of habitual tendencies. Now, the manifestation of those habitual tendencies as luminosity is brought about by the connection when dreams manifest. Mixing is with bewilderment, so that "bewilderment transforms into luminosity." And the connection is made by one's strong aspiration.

What is most important here is to enter luminosity when asleep. So when you go to sleep, meditate on a four-petaled lotus in the heart chakra which has in its center the syllable *hūṁ*, in front the letter *A*, on the right *nu*, behind *ta*, and on the left *ra*. When you are in your ordinary state, focus your mind on the *A*. Then, when the thoughts of the aggregates, elements, senses-and-fields, and so on dissolve,[22] as you fall completely asleep, concentrate on the letter *nu*. This mental appearance is known as "natural emptiness." Next, as subtle thoughts dissolve, concentrate on the *ta*. This mental appearance is called "great increase." Then, when the extremely subtle thoughts dissolve, at the moment of deep sleep, focus on the letter *ra*. This so-called mental appearance is the extremely empty state. After that, when you are completely asleep, gather your consciousness into the *hūṁ*. In that state, by sleeping [with your mind] one-pointedly on the nature of bliss-emptiness, you will experience sleep as bliss-emptiness and experience the bliss-emptiness of luminosity.

The third intermediate state is shown by:

> When this body resulting from the ripening of karma perishes,
> One has a mental body, with habitual tendencies.
> Attachment manifests as luminosity.
> Attachment to parents and so forth is abandoned. {186}

The intermediate state at this time is the intermediate state of becoming. The body is a mental body. What manifests is luminosity, which is mixed with aversion. And the connection is made by the father and mother, male and female deities.

"When this body resulting from the ripening of karma perishes" refers to the moment of the intermediate state of becoming. The body resulting from the ripening of karma is produced from the elements, from the father's semen and mother's ovum, from the wind of existence, and from the [karmic] accumulation in the ground-of-all. The intermediate state of becoming is said to be the period between such a body perishing and one's taking another body. During this time, "One has a mental body, with habitual tendencies." In that mental body, luminosity manifests and is mixed with attachment, so that "attachment manifests as luminosity."

What does all this mean? Were one to ask how the mind together with habitual tendencies is in that intermediate state, for someone with the best or middling faculties, after death, one remains unconscious for up to three, five, or seven days, without the arising of any thoughts whatsoever, as if one had fallen sleep. Then, when one regains consciousness, there is a movement of thoughts rather as in a dream, and one thinks, "My body has perished," or "I am dead," and all kinds of good thoughts, bad thoughts, and habitual concepts arise. At that time, those who have accumulated bad habitual tendencies in their previous lives proceed [to the next life] as one thought connects with the next. Those, on the other hand, who have accumulated good habitual tendencies recall their yidam deity and remember the view, and they will not see the three lower realms (the hells and so on) nor experience the sufferings there. {187} At that time, if one has not been carried away in an ordinary way by defilements in one's previous life, the deluded appearances of dream will not have arisen in an ordinary way, so that if one has not been carried away in one's dreams in an ordinary way, one's mind will not be carried away by thoughts in the intermediate state, and one will attain the state of luminosity, the body of truth.

As such, this is existence independent of taking birth. One has attained the perpetual body of truth and is thus connected to untainted habitual tendencies. One has realized luminosity in a session of sleep, and that is the very essence of the instruction.

"Attachment to parents and so forth is abandoned." In the body of the last intermediate state, it is aversion that has to be mixed. Attachment to beautiful women is not aroused but is taken as luminosity. Aversion to handsome men is not aroused but is taken as luminosity. This needs to be recognized in this life. Attachment to the mother is jealousy toward the father [and vice versa]. Considering the woman [or man] to be real is the link with delusion, but if one has no attachment to her [or him], nor aversion, it is that one has taken this on the path of luminosity. There is a separate instruction[23] on this above.

Therefore, the connection is that made by the father and mother, male and female deities.

In general, it is said that when the stages of the path in the three intermediate states are taught by means of the five topics, they are experienced gradually. Once one has experienced them all in this life, the second stage is to actually realize them.

After this teaching on dream, the intermediate state, illusory body, and luminosity, there now follows a teaching on concentration, and transference and entering a residence, for which there are two topics: mixing and transference. The first of these consists of meditating on the winds and luminosity.

> The initial practice concerns the time,
> Bodily control, and the object [of concentration].
> The essential point of tummo is explained as four winds, {188}
> Which are held to be the four luminosities.

"Time, bodily control, and the object [of concentration]" refers to the three essential points for training in the winds, for which there is, first, physical observance, and then meditation on the winds.

To begin with, "time" refers to the essential point of time. It is the time when the winds circulate in the avadhūtī. What one needs to know here is where the winds are moving from. Sometimes they move from the right; sometimes they move from the left. Meditating at the moment the winds move from both will invariably lead to the birth of gnosis. This covers the essential point of time.

Next, the essential point of controlling the body includes five points: crossed like interwoven netting, straight like an arrow, bent like a hook, tied like a knot, and tightened like *liri* grass [twisted into a rope],[24] making five in all.

"Crossed like interwoven netting" refers to the right leg being crossed over the left. One is held by a meditation belt or garment. The purpose of this is that the lower wind is naturally obstructed.

"Straight like an arrow" means that just as one cannot shoot a crooked arrow, so the purpose here is to naturally obstruct the upper wind.

"Bent like a hook" refers to the neck being slightly bent,[25] as a result of which the wind from both the right and left channels and the proliferation of thoughts is blocked. The purpose of this is to give rise to the absence of conceptual thought.

"Tied like a knot" refers to having the hands in the meditation gesture four finger widths below the navel. The purpose of this is to open the avadhūtī.

"Tightened like liri grass [twisted into a rope]" refers to holding the winds by concentrating mind and body. The purpose of this is to develop the heat.

As for the essential point of the object, in the middle of the chakras in the crown, throat, heart, and navel is the avadhūtī, [which starts] from the aperture of Brahmā at the top between the scalp and the skull. {189} The wind moves in the crane-like [side channels] between the bones down toward their lower ends [at the level] of the great wrinkle [of the belly], whence they bend up again to enter the avadhūtī. Now, does one concentrate on the four chakras? No, one does not. Where does one direct one's concentration? One concentrates on the point four finger breadths below the navel where the three channels join. There are three ways of concentrating on that. [Here] one concentrates on a sphere like the full moon, and nothing else.

The above is the teaching on the initial preparation, as shown by the words "The initial practice."

Now, "The essential point of tummo is explained as four winds." There are four essential points of the tummo practice. Tilopa's instructions say that the first two are merely to be understood: they are not put into practice. In particular, there is the instruction on the "short A" in the tummo practice. In the middle of two fingers below the navel and two fingers above it, make the gesture of meditation. As much as you can, squeeze the navel against the backbone. This opens the channel at the back that has been closed. In this way, the four inner winds are pushed down.[26] By your holding [the wind] at the navel and turning the wind to the right and left,[27] the fire is lit, appearing red inside as if blown on. Then, it is sent further and further,[28] reaching the heart or throat center, or simply a short way up—a finger span. Then expel the wind gradually and imperceptibly out through the nose. Consider that it goes out through the crown. Settle the residual wind for a short moment and train again and again. If one practices in this way for seven days, the first signs of heat will come. If one practices for two weeks, the heat will greatly develop and one will only need a single garment. If one practices for three weeks, {190} the [experience of] absence of thought will begin and it can be said that one is concentrating single-mindedly on the tummo fire. One will even be able to hold the mind on just a spark. When that happens in reality, one holds the mind on a flame as big as the biggest butter lamp.

All this is an accessory explanation to help one understand anything that has not been understood.

The one thing that one needs to know is that the essential point of time is when the five winds move into the avadhūtī. At that time, when the five essential points of controlling the body are applied, the mind concentrates on the essential point of the object, the tummo fire. This is what one trains in, and in general this will invariably give rise to gnosis.

By making an experience of this tummo practice and training in it, those with diligence attain enlightenment in this life. Even lazy practitioners will attain enlightenment in the intermediate state, so it is very important to mix ignorance and gnosis at the moment of death. Thus, in the intermediate state between birth and death, mixing as nonconceptual gnosis in the generation and perfection stages is taught, and then the four luminosities. These are mentioned in the last line of the verse and are associated with mixing dream and the illusory body in the intermediate state of dream. A person trains in the tummo during the day, and in the evening, when going to sleep, they first apprehend the luminosity of sleep and observe it.

There are four luminosities: the natural luminosity, the luminosity of meditation, the luminosity of sleep, and the luminosity of the moment of death.

The natural luminosity is the natural perfect purity of all the phenomena of samsara and nirvana. It is emptiness free of elaboration, present from the beginning as radiant light.

The luminosity of meditation: When a practitioner with much attachment takes the support of a consort to train in the tummo free of attachment, {191} the conceptual thoughts of the present are stopped. Until the subsequent understanding (the joy of absence of pleasure associated with the mind of discursive thought and subtle analysis) arises, the main practice is the luminosity of bliss-emptiness, the complete development of the experience of nondual bliss-emptiness.

The luminosity of sleep: As one sinks into deep sleep, gross thoughts of the present are stopped, and until one starts dreaming, there is the emptiness-luminosity of sleep, sleep free of elaborations.

The luminosity of the moment of death occurs after the gradual dissolution of the body's elements, during the first intermediate state, when thoughts of the present life stop. In this intermediate state, the wind has still not arisen, and at that time the luminosity of death occurs—emptiness free of elaborations, the body of truth as it is. This happens in the minds of all beings. Ordinary beings fail to recognize it because of their conceptual thoughts, and so they circle again and again in samsara.

Of these four kinds of luminosity, it is the luminosity of sleep that is apprehended or observed. For this, when the essential point of time occurs, lie down in the sleeping-lion posture[29] on a comfortable mat. First, you should be motivated by repeatedly thinking and yearning, "I must apprehend the luminosity of sleep, emptiness free of elaborations. And having apprehended it, I must also recognize it." Then, concentrate on the moment when you experience deep sleep and on the essential point of the object, the four letters *A, nu, ta,* and *ra*. Doing so will give rise to the complete experience of luminosity, the luminosity of sleep, inseparable from bliss and emptiness. From apprehending the luminosity of sleep in this way, if one trains in it diligently, one will attain enlightenment in this life. Lazy people will attain enlightenment in the intermediate state, {192} connecting the luminosity of awareness at the moment of death with sleep mixing. Mixing sleep and concentration is the perfection stage of luminosity.

Of the two instructions on mixing and transference, the above concerned mixing. Next, there is the teaching on transference.

> If death is unavoidable,
> There are three kinds of transference:
> The first is from the heart and from the navel.
> Begin, in preparation, by closing the nine openings.
> The double letter *kaṣa*,
> Yellow and blazing with light—
> The upright seed syllable
> Keeps guard in the aperture of Brahmā.
> The syllable of the bell is in the eye.
> That which has the seed syllable of emptiness
> Is placed on the tip of the ear.
> The seed syllable of nectarous water

Is held on the tip of the tongue.
The stacked seed syllable of the lion
Guards the door of emanation and absorption.
The stacked seed syllable of the tigress
Is to be placed on the breast.
The stacked seed syllable of the jackal
Is to be placed in the heart center.
In the navel, the vital center of burning,
The seed syllable of power keeps guard.
Then, guard the lower opening as well
With the light-yellow seed syllable of water.
In the urethra and anus
Make the seed syllables blaze.
In the body, the seed syllable of the wind . . .

This comprises the teaching for closing the openings, showing how the nine openings are closed in the case of superior and middling [transference].

Next, for the main practice, there is transference from the heart center and transference from the navel.

And in the mandala of mind and wind,
On the base of the final fading breath,
With a cry, the essence drop
Is to be guided by the mind.

This teaches the first kind of transference. After that there is transference lying down and forceful transference.

Entering a residence is divided into application, application to karma, and application to activities, referring to ejecting the consciousness and entering another [body], practicing clairvoyance in knowing that other one's mind, and subjugating kings and so forth. These are given as oral teachings.

The five instructions on the meaning of the view and four little nails of essential points make nine instructions, which, together with the seven on mixing and transference, make sixteen instructions that comprise the teachings in the source text.

There were also five [instructions] on the four armors and uprooting ignorance, which were transmitted orally.

The yakṣhiṇī realized the instructions on mixing and transference and, abandoning her evil body, transferred into the body of a yoginī called Sumati. Journeying to all the sacred places, {193} she venerated her teachers. At that time, to the west in Kashmir, she made the following prediction to Nāropa: "In a city to the east, called Telo, dwells the great Vajradhara, the buddha Telopa. For those who wish to bring an end to bewilderment and to realize the view, and those who wish to practice the path without a path, he enables them to realize the path and result. You should try to reach him."

Having also changed her name to the yoginī Sumati, the yakṣhiṇī went to a village called Sarrevartha to the west of the Sala charnel ground and described all her experiences, like jewels, to seven yogins and seven yoginīs. As a result, they were all liberated and brought to maturation. This teaching comprises sixteen small source texts.

## III. Conclusion

As a result of Dhamadhuma's virtuous deed
Of bringing to light all these [verses]
With the aim of helping the yakṣhiṇī,
May all beings attain the level of perfection.

The conclusion indicates the dedication of virtue not to some trifling goal but to the unsurpassed goal.

[This completes the short instruction text *A Precious Necklace*.]

This completes the commentary (*ṭīkā*) on *A Precious Necklace*. It was composed by Guru Abhayashrī and translated by Menyak Lotsawa.

## The Yakṣhiṇī's Realization: Oral Instructions on *A Precious Necklace*

Homage to the teachers.

Of the four topics on the dharma seal with which I have been blessed, the first is incorporating dreams on the path. For this there are two parts, preparation and main practice.

First, for the preparation, develop faith and respect for the teacher and the Three Jewels and confess breaches of samaya by reciting the hundred syllables, and so on.

For the main practice, there are four parts: apprehending dreams, refining them, training in them as illusory and getting rid of fear,[30] and meditating on thatness.

For this, when you are practicing apprehending dreams, as a preliminary, develop intense faith and yearning. {194} After that, pile your bed high with cushions. Lie down with your right side on the bed, stretching your left hand along the top of your thigh and placing your right hand against your cheek. In your throat center visualize a red four-petaled lotus. In its center visualize a white letter *A*. At dusk, directing your consciousness toward a white sphere between your eyebrows, go to sleep. Then, at dawn, concentrate on the *A*. If you have failed to apprehend your dreams while dreaming, you should feel a strong yearning, thinking, "I have woken up and failed to recognize any of my dreams." In the morning also, think, "I should understand that the whole of phenomenal existence is like a dream: there is no difference between it and last night's dream." During the daytime, repeatedly make the aspiration, "Tonight, I must recognize my dreams." By doing this day and night, you will apprehend your dreams. The sign of doing so is that various untoward things may happen to you in your dreams. You will have all kinds of dreams, of being in a great flood, being in an abyss from which you cannot escape, being chased by dogs, your body shining with light, and so on. Because of these, you will sometimes recognize them, thinking, "It is a dream." When this happens and during your dreams, you will feel strong faith and inspiration, thinking, "The teachings that all phenomena are like a dream are true." In the morning you should remember the previous night's dreams and feel strongly, "What is the difference between last night's dream and my present perceptions?" This is apprehending one's dreams.

After that, once you can apprehend your dreams, at dusk make a strong aspiration, thinking, "I must recognize my dreams *as* dreams." Then, to train in dream, {195} resolve, "Since it is a dream, no matter what I do, it will be all right." During the dream, do all the things that you think of—plunging into water, jumping into a fire, climbing a precipice, looking at the Heaven of the Thirty-Three, looking at all the sacred places in India, trampling on the sun and moon, having a vision of the yidam deity and receiving teachings, seeing the buddha fields of the tathāgatas and hearing them teach, and so forth. To train in habituating yourself in this way is to refine the dream state.

Next, for recognizing dreams as illusion and getting rid of fear, if you still feel apprehensive or afraid when jumping into water and so on during this training, meditate thinking, "It is a dream, it is an illusion, so what is there to be afraid of?" By doing so, you will free yourself of fear. This is recognizing dreams as illusion.

Then there is meditating on thatness. You should recognize that since it is a dream, what is there to refine? It is a delusion of your own mind. This is meditating on thatness. The way to meditate on that is to meditate on whatever you meditated on previously, and otherwise to focus on a sphere in the forehead center or in the secret center, whichever is suitable, and to aspire to bliss-emptiness. Merely doing this will give rise to extremely great bliss. This is the meditation on thatness in one's dreams. Incorporating dreams on the path is a practice that one trains in in this life.

## A Pith Instruction on Entering Luminosity in Deep Sleep

First of all, go to sleep. For this, begin by tiring out the body for three days. During that time, keep yourself from falling asleep in the evening by doing whatever virtuous activities you can. Massage your body {196} and build up your physical strength. Lie down on your right side.

The time is the period of sleep. The object is the heart center. In the heart chakra, visualize the four letters *A, nu, ta,* and *ra* on the four petals of a lotus, and the syllable *hūṁ* in the center. When you are in your ordinary state, focus your mind on the *A* in front. Then, when gross thoughts of the aggregates, elements, senses-and-fields, and so on have subsided, at the moment you start to fall asleep, concentrate on the letter *nu*. This is what is called mind appearing. After that, when subtle thoughts subside, concentrate on the *ta*. This is called the increase in mind appearing, the great emptiness. Then, when the extremely subtle thoughts subside, as your sleep becomes deeper, focus on the letter *ra*. This is called the attainment of appearances; it is extreme emptiness. Then, when you are completely asleep, gather your consciousness into the *hūṁ*, the nature of bliss-emptiness. As you maintain that, sleep is experienced as bliss-emptiness and you will experience the luminous bliss-emptiness. Preserving the dream state at that time is viewed as an adverse condition. Then, as you begin to rise out of a session of sleep, check whether you were in the sleep of ignorance or not, and then go to sleep as before. During the night, do four or five sessions, as suitable. Thus, in the last two or three sessions, meditate and sleep as before: the aggregates and so on dissolve into the subtle elements, the subtle elements dissolve in the mind, the mind again dissolves into the subtle mind, the subtle mind too dissolves into ignorance. In this way, as one falls asleep, ignorance will naturally cease and ordinary thoughts will vanish.

The result of this is that the nature of gnosis will dawn as luminosity. The sleep of ignorance {197} will be apprehended as if with a hook, and one's sleep in a state of bliss-emptiness will not be mixed with any consciousness. The sleep of luminosity will be experienced in reality.

Next, in the postmeditation period after waking from sleep, you should practice as follows. In front of you, put up a scroll painting of the yidam deity and look at it concentratedly. Visualize it clearly in your mind. When it is clear, meditate without concepts on that clarity as bliss-emptiness together. Again, make it clear by looking at the scroll painting. Then, visualize it clearly, exactly as in the scroll painting, and do the combined meditation on that as bliss-emptiness, meditating on the blissful taste arising vibrantly from emptiness. As you meditate in this way on the [visualization] as bliss-emptiness, the measure of your having trained is that you will remain in the unborn state of bliss-emptiness and arise in the experience of bliss. At that time, when you go to sleep in the evening and so on, do the meditation in your sleep.

From your meditating thus in the postmeditation, signs will occur, such as the body becoming light and comfortable. All appearances will arise vividly as bliss-emptiness. In this very life you will dwell in luminosity and attain the supreme accomplishment. Even if you do not achieve that in this life, in the intermediate state you will apprehend consciousness as luminosity. Then, in the intermediate state, you will attain enlightenment: for you, helplessly entering a womb will no longer be possible. If you have entered a womb, it is because when you take a body, you will have done so voluntarily in order to benefit others, and you will have entered the womb of your free accord. For someone who has meditated on the illusory body and someone who has trained in sleep as luminosity, their taking a body is not through becoming[31]—it is impossible for them to take a body in that way. {198} The master Lvavapa (Kambala) too declared that by doing sleep practice for twelve years one attains the supreme level. He practiced the two practices of illusory body and sleep luminosity together.

## [Intermediate States]

*namo guru*

There are three intermediate states, three illusory bodies, three things that manifest, three mixings, and three connections.

In the intermediate state between birth and death, the body is the body that results from the ripening of karma, what manifests is luminosity, and the mixing is mixing with attachment. Mixing with attachment means that practitioners on the path of liberation make use of the practice of tummo, and by doing so seal the body with bliss. Without grasping at that [bliss], they take luminosity as the path. The connection is made by the teacher's instructions.

In the intermediate state of dream, the body is the body of habitual tendencies, and what manifests is dream. The mixing is mixing with bewilderment. Mixing with bewilderment consists of refining dreams in deep sleep or in a balance[32] between deep sleep and light sleep, without one's getting lost in confusion. The connection is made through one's devotion and aspiration.

In the intermediate state of becoming, the body is a mental body, and what manifests is luminosity. The mixing is mixing with aversion. Mixing with aversion means that at the time of the last intermediate state, one takes luminosity as the path without developing aversion to the father or attachment to the mother [or vice versa]. [One recalls one's] teacher and yidam as in one's previous life. The connection is made with the father and mother, male and female deities.

## [Deviations and Errors]

*namo guru*

By avoiding the four deviations and four errors,[33] without remaining stagnant or getting lost in apathy, one arrives at a state of luminous space, an uncontrived consciousness that is the opposite of indifferent consciousness. Through one's meditating on this, it is said, the four kinds of yoga are developed. In this regard, first, here are the four deviations. {199}

Deviation into emptiness, the fundamental nature of phenomena: Those who follow the Vehicle of Characteristics establish emptiness as neither one nor many and then meditate on emptiness as being like the heart of space, in other words, on a concept created by concepts. Followers of the Mantra

Vehicle dissolve the outer world and inner beings in stages, or with the *svabhāva* mantra mentally make everything empty like perfectly pure space and then rest the mind on that. Both of these are mental creations and so constitute deviations.

Second, the deviation into sealing emptiness: This is to meditate by placing the seal of emptiness on the absence of concepts (in generosity, for example) of a recipient, a giver, and a gift. This too is a mental creation.

Third, the deviation into using emptiness as an antidote to defilements: This is to settle the mind on whatever arises (attachment, aversion, and so forth) being empty—in that first it has not been born from anywhere, at present it does not exist as the essence of anything, and finally there is nothing to be stopped, or no cessation.

Fourth, the deviation with regard to the path of emptiness: Practitioners on the path of desire consider that a good result exists elsewhere, and as their path or method, they train in making emptiness the object of the mind. By doing so, they are mentally creating the hope that they will attain the body of truth.

> If emptiness were the means,
> Then buddhahood would never occur,
> For cause and result would conflict.
> Means is not emptiness.

From believing that there is a result elsewhere—something good, a body of truth—even by mentally creating emptiness on that path and training in it, one will not attain that body of truth.

The actual condition of things, in which these four deviations have been abandoned, is free of all conceptualization and transcends the realm of the mind.

The four errors are as follows. As a result of being guided in meditation by a sublime teacher, the experience of bliss arises. When one asks the teacher whether this is the meditation or not, {200} one is told that it is and that one should preserve it. If, in doing so, one feels happy when the thrill of bliss happens and unhappy [when it does not], one's practice will lead to the error of one's straying into the world of desire. If one practices in the same way with regard to [the experience of] absence of thought, one will stray into the world of formlessness. Likewise, such a way of practicing when clarity arises will lead to one's straying into the world of form. If one is attached and grasps at these three together, one strays into the state of the listeners and solitary realizers, because these [states] are mind created.

If one settles in an uncontrived consciousness devoid of these [errors], one may become stagnant in a thoughtless inertia.

Getting lost in apathy is related to indifference, thinking to oneself, when thoughts occur one after the other, "There is no need to meditate; this is the body of truth."

The eighty-four siddhas taught *A Precious Necklace* to a yakṣhiṇī. Since she did not understand its meaning, the teacher Tilopa gave her instructions, of which this is the oral instruction from the yakṣhiṇī's realization.

## PART THREE

# Mitrayogin's Empowerments and Authorization Rituals for the Six Deities

The next eight texts all fall into the category of empowerments, although the only detailed empowerment (*dbang*) in this volume is that of Avalokiteshvara. It includes the preparatory sections concerning the teacher, the vases, and the disciples as well as detailed sections for the vase empowerment. It is followed by a supplement, apparently for use with that empowerment.* The remaining texts are authorization rituals (*rjes gnang*) for the other five of Mitrayogin's six deities and for Draklha Gönpo, the protector of these teachings. All these rituals were written by Öpak Dorje, with the exception of the Draklha authorization, which was written by Drakpa Rinchen.

An authorization ritual is a simple form of empowerment, in which the disciples receive the blessings of the teacher and yidam deity that authorize them to practice the related sādhana and recite the mantra. The detailed sections normally found in a full empowerment preparing them to enter the mandala are absent, and the process of conferring the four empowerments (vase, secret, wisdom, and word) is, in these texts, replaced by five stages in which the blessings of the deity's Body, Speech, Mind, Qualities, and Activities are conferred.

Mitrayogin was considered to be an emanation of Avalokiteshvara, the buddha of compassion, which perhaps accounts for the fact that both the empowerment and the instructions in the next section are more detailed

*Its listing in the Catalog (p. 108) as an authorization ritual is puzzling, as is the title, *The Glowing Jewel* (*Rin chen 'od 'phro*), apparently attributed to the empowerment ritual.

than those for the other deities whose teachings he received after he had practiced their sādhanas in the Sosaling charnel ground. Each of these deities is generally associated with a specific characteristic and, in this series of practices, with an aspect of enlightenment. Avalokiteshvara, the buddha of compassion, is associated with enlightened speech. Mañjushrī (or Mañjughoṣha) is the buddha of wisdom, associated with the enlightened body. Vajrapāṇi, "bearer of the vajra," is related to power and enlightened mind. Amitāyus, an aspect of Buddha Amitābha, is the buddha of long life and associated with enlightened qualities. And Green Tārā is the deity who grants protection from fear and danger and is associated with enlightened activities. Finally, there is an authorization ritual for Yellow Jambhala, a wealth deity whose practice bestows every kind of material and spiritual wealth. For Buddhist practitioners, the acquisition of riches by venerating Jambhala is not, of course, an end in itself but a means to ensure suitable conditions in which to further one's practice for enlightenment, to sponsor projects that accumulate merit and bring benefit to beings, and so forth.

This series of authorization rituals is supplemented by an authorization to practice the sādhana of Draklha Gönpo (Rock God Protector), the guardian of the teachings related to the aforementioned six deities. This authorization, as the colophon points out, was kept extremely secret until it was written down by Drakpa Rinchen.

These rituals are all quite similar in presentation. The ritual for Tārā is unusual in that the whole text, including the nonrecited sections in "small writing" (*yig chung*), has been composed in metered lines. For the sake of clarity, in this translation of what is essentially a series of instructions to a vajra master, no attempt has been made to reproduce the poetry of the original, attractive though it is in the Tibetan.

Teachers giving such empowerments have necessarily completed the relevant sādhana practices and moreover received specific training in conferring tantric initiations, many of which follow more or less standard ritual procedures. It is not surprising, therefore, that the instructions provided in empowerment texts assume that the reader, in this case the vajra master, already has the required knowledge to understand these instructions despite their often being presented in somewhat cryptic form. It should be borne in mind that certain passages may not make precise sense to most readers and indeed were never intended to do so. Some of the visualizations and prayers that the teacher or disciples need to recite are only indicated by their first lines, either because they are well known and common to such rituals or because the teacher is required to refer to the relevant sādhana texts or to adapt the visualizations provided in the instruction texts. The translations of these empowerment texts have kept as close to the meaning as possible without any attempt to decipher cryptic or ambiguous elements.

# 6. A River of Great Compassion

*The Empowerment for the Sādhana in the Stages of the Path of Noble Avalokiteshvara*[1]

{202}
Supreme lord, leader of the three worlds,
Without moving from the unborn expanse of reality
You guide all beings through numerous manifestations.
To you, Avalokiteshvara, I pay homage.

The way to bestow the empowerment of Avalokiteshvara
I shall now write down exactly as I heard it
In the words that blossomed lotus-like from my teacher's mouth,
Transmitted through the aural lineage in an uninterrupted series of
  empowerments.

Here is the ritual for bestowing the empowerment of the concentration of Avalokiteshvara. There are three main sections: (1) performing the sādhana of the deity and making offerings; (2) bestowing the empowerment; [and (3) the concluding stages].

## I. Performing the Sādhana of the Deity and Making Offerings

This is divided into making the preparations and practicing the sādhana.

### A. Making the Preparations

Draw a mandala, one cubit in size, consisting of a square measureless palace with four gates, arched pediments, and surrounding wall, and in the middle of it draw an eight-petaled lotus. Its center should be white, the four petals in the cardinal directions should be correspondingly colored, and the four petals in the intermediate directions beautifully painted. Distribute the colors with the east blue, the south yellow, the west red, the north green, and the center white. Lastly, around it arrange the outer offerings, the inner offerings, and the offering tormas. Set out the empowerment vase and the activity vase, with their ornamental stopper[2] and ribbon tied round the neck. Prepare a kapāla filled with nectar and a [mirror] covered with sindhūra powder, {203} on which are drawn, in the middle, the two letters *hrīḥ* and *baṃ*, and on the four petals, the letters *ha ri ni sa*. Prepare as well the vajra, bell, and other articles for the empowerment.

### B. Practicing the Sādhana

There are three parts: (1) self-visualization; (2) front visualization; and (3) vase visualization.

#### 1. Self-Visualization

This is divided into three: (1) purifying oneself with refuge and bodhichitta;[3] (2) gathering the accumulations with the seven branches; and (3) meditating on the generation stage and reciting the mantra.

##### a. Refuge

> I and all beings who have been my parents go for refuge in the teacher.
> We take refuge in the Buddha.
> We take refuge in the dharma.
> We take refuge in the sangha.
> We take refuge in the host of deities of noble Avalokiteshvara and their retinues.

Say this three times.

### b. The Seven Branches

Next, to arouse the mind set on supreme enlightenment, begin by gathering the accumulations with the seven branches:

> In an instant I become Avalokiteshvara. In my heart is the syllable *hrīḥ*, from which lights radiate, inviting Avalokiteshvara surrounded by buddhas and bodhisattvas. {204}

> *ārya avalokiteśvara vajra samaya ja jaḥ*
> *padma kamala ye stvaṃ svāhā*
> I pay homage to the Three Jewels.
> I venerate them with a multitude of offerings.
> I confess each and every one of my evil deeds.
> I rejoice in all virtue.
> I beseech you to turn the wheel of dharma.
> I pray to you to remain without passing into nirvana.
> By this merit, may we attain supreme enlightenment.

And:

> To the Three Jewels I go for refuge,
> All my evil actions I confess,
> And in the virtue of all beings I rejoice.
> The enlightenment of buddhahood I will hold in mind,
> And till enlightenment is reached
> I will take refuge in the Buddha, dharma, and supreme assembly.
> To achieve my own and others' aims,
> I'll arouse the mind intent on enlightenment.
> Having set my mind on supreme enlightenment,
> I invite all beings, each and every one, to be my guests
> And joyfully partake of the sublime ways of the bodhisattvas.
> To benefit all beings, may I achieve buddhahood!

and so on, as is found in the *Vajrapañjara Tantra*.[4] Repeat this three times. Then dissolve the field of accumulation.

### c. Meditating on the Generation Stage and Reciting the Mantra

Begin by meditating on the four boundless attitudes:

> May all beings come to possess happiness and the causes of happiness . . .[5]

and so on. Next, meditate on the generation stage with the five factors of awakening.

> *oṁ svabhāva śuddāḥ sarvadharmāḥ svabhāva śuddho 'haṃ*
> All phenomena are by nature empty and devoid of intrinsic existence.
>
> From the state of emptiness there arise the five elements, stacked in order, on top of which is the supreme mountain. On top of it is a multicolored lotus with a hundred thousand petals, and on it, a crossed vajra, from which light radiates, forming a vast protection circle. In the middle of it is the five-colored syllable *bhrūṃ*. It melts into light to become a measureless palace, which is square, with four doors and five-layered walls, four arched pediments, a top ornament, a vajra fence, and a mountain of flames—all the features of a measureless palace being complete. In the middle of it is the syllable *paṁ*, from which there appears a multicolored lotus with eight petals. From the letter *A* appears the mandala of a full moon, on which appear the white syllable *hrīḥ*, complete with visarga,[6] and the red syllable *baṁ*. From them infinite light rays emanate, benefiting immeasurable sentient beings and setting them on the level of Lord Avalokiteshvara. {205} The light rays are gathered back and transform into a white lotus plant, marked in its center with *hrīḥ* and *baṁ*, from which rays of light emanate, inviting all the buddhas and bodhisattvas in the form of Avalokiteshvara. They dissolve into the lotus, *hrīḥ*, and *baṁ*, which are transformed into oneself as noble Avalokiteshvara. His body is white in color, like a snow mountain with the sun shining on it. He has one face and four arms and is seated with his two legs crossed in the vajra posture. He is wearing upper and lower garments of multicolored celestial silks,

loosely tied with a jeweled sash. His first two hands are joined at the level of his heart, holding between them the wish-fulfilling jewel. Of his other two hands, the right one is holding a rosary of precious jewels and the left is holding an eight-petaled lotus by its stem, with the flower blooming at the level of his ear. His smiling face is adorned, between his almond eyes and long eyebrows, with a coil of white hair (*ūrṇā*). His hair is tied up to form a black crown, while locks of hair hang down to his waist, with a garland of flowers for a hair ribbon. He is adorned with two blue utpalas as ear ornaments. His left shoulder is draped with the skin of an antelope. He is adorned with the five-tipped crown, earrings, necklet, long necklace, bracelets, anklets, armlets, and girdle, all made of the five precious materials, and a garland of five kinds of pearls, together with a silken head ornament. He is seated in the middle of a dense mass of multicolored rays of light.

On his lap is his secret wisdom consort, who is red in color, like a ruby. {206} She has one face, two hands, and two legs, embracing the male deity around the waist. Her right hand is held up in the air, playing a golden dāmaru. Her left hand holds a kapāla filled with a stream of red nectar to the mouth of the male deity. Her mouth is smiling and peaceful, laughing slightly, while in her three eyes there is an angry smile. Her hair is tied in a topknot, with plaits hanging down to her waist. Her head is crowned with a tiara of five dry skulls crested with jewels. With her fully developed breasts and vulva, her peaceful smile, and her youth and charm, she has the marks of a sixteen-year-old. Adorned with the five bone ornaments, she emanates five-colored rays of light.

In their five centers, upon lotus and sun, are the syllables: *oṁ*, in the crown center, from which appears white Vairochana Avalokiteshvara with his consort; *hrīḥ*, in the throat center, from which appears red Padma Avalokiteshvara with his consort; *hūṁ*, in the heart center, from which appears blue Akṣhobhya Avalokiteshvara with his consort; *trāṃ*, in the navel center, from which appears yellow Ratnasambhava Avalokiteshvara with his consort; and *āḥ*, in the secret center, from which appears green Amoghasiddhi Avalokiteshvara with his consort. All of them have the same attributes as the principal deity.

To the east of him, arising from the letter *ha*, is the blue vajra ḍākinī; to the south, arising from *ri*, is the yellow ratna ḍākinī; to the west, arising from *ni*, is the red padma ḍākinī; and to the north, arising from *sa*, is the green karma ḍākinī. They all have one face, two hands, three eyes, and their four canine teeth slightly bared. In their right hands they each hold a curved knife; in their left, a skull cup full of blood. In the crook of their arms, they hold a khātvāṇga. With their two feet they dance, the left leg bent, the right one extended, dwelling in a mountainous expanse of flames and adorned with the five bone ornaments. All are surrounded by blazing wisdom fire. {207}

From the white *oṁ* in the crown center, the red *āḥ* in the throat center, and the blue *hūṁ* in the heart center, light rays emanate, inviting the wisdom deity similar to oneself from the natural expanse of reality.

*ārya avalokiteśvara vajra samaya ja jaḥ*
*jaḥ hūṁ baṃ hoḥ*—they become inseparable.

Again from *hūṁ* in the heart center, light radiates, inviting the buddhas of the five families and their retinues, with the prayer that the tathāgatas of the five families bestow empowerment, as a result of which one is empowered by the five families. The stream of nectar fills the inside of one's body, and from the excess nectar overflowing above, one's crown is ornamented by Amitāyus.

In one's heart center is a lotus and moon, on which is the thumb-sized wisdom deity (jñānasattva), similar to oneself. In his heart is the syllable *hrīḥ*, encircled by the mantra. Rays of light emanate from it, filling the whole of the body with the five families of Avalokiteshvara, as numerous as the atoms in the universe. They radiate outside, transforming the universe into a measureless palace and all the sentient beings inhabiting it into the form of Avalokiteshvara and his consort. All of them are reciting the secret mantra.

Visualizing this, recite the mantra with undistracted mind:

*oṁ maṇi padme hūṁ ḍākinī harinisa hūṁ*

At the end, pray:

> May the power of truth of Lord Avalokiteshvara enable me and all sentient beings to attain the supreme accomplishment, the Great Seal.

This recitation is to be performed either until three months have elapsed, or until thirty million recitations of the mantra have been counted, or until signs occur—in the best case, seeing Avalokiteshvara and consort in reality and receiving predictions from them; in the middling case, having experiences and visions; and in the worst case, dreaming of a white man or red woman bestowing accomplishment, of wrathful female deities gathering, and so on. {208}

### 2. Front Visualization

Cleanse the mandala of colored powder or of piles of grain with

> *oṁ amṛtakuṇḍali hana hana hūṁ phaṭ*

and purify it with

> *oṁ svabhāva śuddāḥ sarvadharmāḥ svabhāva śuddho 'haṃ*

Perform the meditation and recitation as for the self-visualization, from

> From the state of emptiness there arise the five elements, stacked in order, on top of which is the supreme mountain . . .

up to the recitation of the mantra.

### 3. Vase Visualization

Properly prepare the all-victorious vase and activity vase, containing the essential ingredients, with their ornamental stoppers and ribbons tied around the neck. Banish obstacle makers with

> *oṁ padmānta kṛta vajra krota hayagrīva hulu hulu hūṁ phaṭ*

[Then:]

> *oṁ svabhāva śuddāḥ sarvadharmāḥ svabhāva śuddho 'haṃ*
>
> All becomes emptiness.
>
> From the state of emptiness, there appears the syllable *bhrūṃ*, and from that a vase made of precious materials, with a round base, bulbous body, long neck, and spout. The neck is tied with a celestial silk ribbon, and the opening decorated with the wish-fulfilling tree. Inside is an ocean of milk, from the middle of which arises the syllable *paṃ*, and from it a lotus plant. From the letter *A* there appears the mandala of the moon, on top of which are the syllables *hrīḥ* and *baṃ*, from which rays of light emanate, benefiting immeasurable numbers of sentient beings and setting them on the level of Lord Avalokiteshvara. The light rays are gathered back and transform into a white lotus plant, marked in its center with *hrīḥ* and *bam* . . .

and so on, continuing the visualization as in the self-visualization, down to

> . . . are reciting the secret mantra

but replacing "In one's heart center . . ." with:

> In the heart center of the deity visualized in the vase . . .

and adapting the visualization accordingly. Consider that

> As all of them recite the secret mantra, a stream of nectar flows from their mouths, filling the vase.

And recite the mantra one hundred eight times:

> *oṁ maṇi padme hūṁ ḍākinī harinisa hūṁ*

Recite the following one a hundred times as well:

> *oṁ vajra uttaka svāhā*

At the end, pray:

May the power of truth of Lord Avalokiteshvara enable [me and all sentient beings to attain the supreme accomplishment, the Great Seal]. {209}

Then make the offerings, *arghaṃ* and so on. After that recite the praise:

Although you are inseparable from the body of truth, like space,
You manifest distinctly in the body of form, like a rainbow.
To you who have mastery of supreme means and wisdom—
To the sugatas of the five families I make homage and praise.

And:

Praised highly by all the buddhas,
You are a mine of all good qualities.
You who received the name All-Seeing,[7]
To you who are always full of love I make homage and praise.

Cleanse the activity vase with:

*oṁ padmānta kṛta vajra krota hayagrīva hulu hulu hūṁ phaṭ*

And purify it with:

*oṁ svabhāva śuddāḥ sarvadharmāḥ svabhāva śuddho 'haṃ*

From the state of emptiness there appears the syllable *paṃ*, and from it a lotus. From the syllable *raṃ* there appears the mandala of the sun, on top of which is the syllable *hrīḥ*, from which rays of light emanate and gather back, transforming into the wrathful Hayagrīva, who is red in color, with one face and two hands. The right hand holds a lotus stick; the left makes the threatening gesture. His right leg is bent, his left stretched out, and he is wearing a lower garment of tiger skin. His wrathful face has three eyes, and his four canine teeth are bared. His reddish-yellow hair streams upward. On the crown of his head is the green head of a horse, its neighs filling the ten directions and its red mane blazing like fire. He is adorned with snakes and precious ornaments and

> dwells amid a blazing mass of wisdom fire. From the white *oṁ* in his crown, red *āḥ* in the throat, and blue *hūṁ* in the heart center, light rays emanate, inviting the wisdom deity similar to himself.
>
> With *jaḥ hūṁ baṃ hoḥ*—they become inseparable.
>
> Again from *hūṁ* in the heart center, light radiates, inviting the buddhas of the five families and their retinues.
>
> The five families bestow empowerment, purifying stains, and from the excess nectar overflowing above, his crown is ornamented with Amitābha. {210}
>
> In his heart, upon a lotus and sun, is the syllable *hrīḥ*, encircled by the mantra, from which flows a stream of nectar, filling the vase.

With this in mind, recite the mantra one hundred eight times:

> *oṁ padmānta kṛta vajra krota hayagrīva hulu hulu hūṁ phaṭ svāhā*

At the end, make the offerings and recite the praise:

> Manifesting from the lotus family, free from attachment,
> In the guise of a nāga king, you tame all vicious beings.
> Great powerful one, blazing with majesty like the fire at the end of the kalpa,
> King of wrathful deities, Lord Hayagrīva, to you I make homage and praise.

Then pray for the fulfillment of all wishes.

### II. Bestowing the Empowerment

There are three parts: (1) the preparation, entering the mandala; (2) the main part, bestowing the four empowerments; and (3) the conclusion, giving authorization.

#### A. Preparation

The preparation, entering the mandala, is divided into thirteen parts: (1) praying; (2) taking the vows; (3) attaching the blindfolds; (4) giving the flowers; (5) protection; (6) arousing bodhichitta; (7) obeisance; (8) binding under oath; (9) the descent of gnosis and inquiry [as to what the disciple] sees; (10) throwing the flower; (11) opening the eyes; (12) revealing the deity; and (13) special utterances.

### 1. Praying

First, the disciples should perform ablutions, offer the mandala, and pray:

> Sole revealer of great joy,
> Who shows us the way of great enlightenment,
> To you, great protector, we pay homage.
> Bestow on us the sacred commitments,
> Bestow on us the bodhichitta,
> Bestow on us the triple refuge
> Of the Buddha, dharma, and sangha.
> Protector, please bring us
> Into the sublime city of great liberation! . . . and so on.

### 2. Taking Vows

First, the common vows are taken by reciting:

> In the Three Jewels we go for refuge . . . and so on.[8]

After that, the particular vows are taken by reciting three times:

> All you buddhas, bodhisattvas,
> And hosts of deities of Avalokiteshvara,
> Without exception, think of us. {211}
>
> Just as the buddhas, past, present, and to come,
> Resolved to attain enlightenment,
> We will arouse the sacred, unsurpassed
> Enlightened attitude of mind.
>
> For the yogic vows of the buddha [family],
> We will train in the discipline of restraint,
> Gather virtuous deeds,

And work for the benefit of beings,
Firmly keeping these three kinds of discipline.
And from this day onward we will firmly hold
The vows pertaining to the Buddha, dharma, and sangha—
The Three Jewels unsurpassed!
Never will we give them up.

For the supreme vajra family,
We will perfectly uphold
The seals of vajra and bell;
The masters too will we uphold.

For the delightful pledges
Of the great and supreme jewel family,
Every day on six occasions
We will constantly perform four kinds of generosity.

For the supreme lotus family,
We will uphold all the sacred teachings
Of the outer, inner, and secret vehicles,
Which have sprung from great enlightenment.

For the supreme action family,
All the vows that we have taken
We will perfectly observe
And make offerings as much as we are able.

Arousing the awakened mind,
Supreme and unsurpassed,
We will hold these vows without exception
For the benefit of every living being.
We will save all those as yet unsaved.
We will free all those as yet unfreed.
We will bring relief to those not yet relieved
And set all beings in the state beyond all pain.

### 3. Attaching the Blindfolds

*oṁ cakṣu bandha vara maṇaye svāhā*

### 4. Giving the Garlands of Flowers

*oṁ āḥ khaṃ vīra hūṁ svāhā* {212}

### 5. Protection

Cleanse with the mantra of Hayagrīva, then consider that:

Visualizing yourselves in an instant as Avalokiteshvara, in your crown center is the white syllable *oṁ*, in the throat center a red *āḥ*, and in the heart center a blue *hūṁ*.

And as you place a drop of scented water, say *oṁ āḥ hūṁ*.

### 6. Arousing Bodhichitta

Visualize upon a moon in the heart a white five-pronged vajra emanating rays of light.

And say:

*oṁ sarva tathāgata yoga citta upata yāmi*

Holding a vajra and flower at the heart center, recite:

*oṁ surate samaya stvaṃ hoḥ*
*siddha vajra ya vā su khaṃ*

### 7. Obeisance

Consider that you are led by the wrathful Hayagrīva, who leads you into the mandala. Consider that you pay homage to Ārya Avalokiteshvara.

Perform prostrations, saying:

*oṁ namo te hūṁ*
*oṁ namo me hūṁ*
*namo nama hūṁ*
*oṁ namo lokeśvarayā*

**8. Binding under Oath**

First, binding under oath with respect to the benefits:

> Today, you have entered the family of all the tathāgatas, but now I[9] must make the vajra gnosis develop in you. If, through gnosis, you will obtain the accomplishment of all the tathāgatas, what need is there to mention other accomplishments? Do not speak in front of those who have not seen this mandala, for you will deteriorate the sacred commitments.

Second, binding under oath with respect to both [the benefits and dangers]. Place the vajra at the heart center and say:

*oṁ* Today Avalokiteshvara himself
Has truly entered your heart.
If you speak of this to anyone,
Your head will be destroyed.

Third, binding under oath with respect to the dangers. Pouring the samaya water, say:

This is the water of your hell:
If you transgress the commitments, it will burn you up. {213}
If you keep the commitments, with this water of adamantine nectar
You will achieve accomplishment.
*oṁ amṛta udakaṭha*

Fourth, binding under oath with respect to the master. Proclaim the commitment as follows:

From now on, for you,
I am Avalokiteshvara.
Therefore, whatever I command,
You must carry it out.

### 9. The Descent of Gnosis and Inquiry

Bringing down the gnosis:

All you tathāgatas, bestow your blessings.
Pour down blessings on us, Avalokiteshvara.

After saying this, describe the following visualization:

From the state of emptiness, there appears the syllable *āḥ*, from which visualize yourselves as Amitābha, on whose feet, from *yaṃ*, appears the mandala of wind, a fluttering banner marked with *yaṃ*, raised by the two red syllables *jhaiḥ jhaiḥ*. At the junction [of the legs], from *raṃ* there appears the triangular mandala of fire, marked with a *raṃ* and blazing fire. In the heart center, from *laṃ* there appears the square mandala of earth, marked by a vajra in which is a sun marked by a blue *hūṁ*. In the throat center is the syllable *baṃ*, from which there appears the mandala of water, a vase with a moon marked with a red *āḥ*. In the head, from *yaṃ* there appears the blue mandala of wind, with a moon marked with a white *haṃ*. Rays of light from *jhaiḥ jhaiḥ* in the feet enter through the great veins of the legs. They mix with the fire at the junction of the legs and it burns brighter and brighter. It heats the mandala of earth in the heart center to a glowing red. The mandala of water in the throat center boils into a white misty vapor. From the *haṃ* in the crown center flows a stream of nectar. From *hūṁ* and *haṃ* rays of light emanate, radiating out through the tips of the hairs on the body and inviting the hosts of deities of Avalokiteshvara and the five classes of ḍākinīs. Like snow falling on a lake, they all dissolve into your body, speech, and mind.

Burn *gugul* and incense and bring about the descent of gnosis with:

*oṁ maṇi padme hūṁ ḍākinī harinisa hūṁ* {214}
*aveśaya stvambhaya ra ra ra calaya calaya hūṁ hāḥ aḥ jhaiḥ*

Then, inquire as to what color [the disciple sees in] the mandala and give predictions for the accomplishment of the four activities.

**10. Throwing the Flower**

Next,

> Consider that the garland of flowers, consecrated with *traṃ*, fresh, not wilted, and made radiant with *oṁ āḥ hūṁ*, is thrown over the head of Avalokiteshvara and his consort.

And

> These disciples whom I have introduced
> Into this mandala of the true secret—
> Deities, according to their merit,
> Place them in the appropriate family!
> Whatever the accomplishment they may gain,
> Whatever the family for which they are proper vessels,
> Whatever the power of their merit,
> May the mandala appear accordingly.
> *āḥ khaṃ vīra hūṁ pratīccha kusu māñca liṃ nātha hoḥ*

Saying this, throw the flower. Again, with

> *prati grihaṇa daṃ imaṃ svāhā mahābala*

tie the garland of flowers over the head.

**11. Opening the Eyes**

> *oṁ* Today Avalokiteshvara himself
> Has roused himself to open your eyes.
> The vajra eyes are unsurpassed;

They open the eyes to everything.
*oṁ jñāna cakṣu hūṁ āḥ svāhā*

### 12. Revealing the Face of the Deity

Say:

Oh, look at the vajra!

Then say:

Consider that it is showing the face of the deity, and thus you see it.
Now, by the force of faith,
Look at the very nature of this mandala.
You have been born in the family of the buddhas.
You have received the blessing of the mudrā and mantra.
You will attain all accomplishments
And have made the supreme commitment.
Using skillful means and wisdom,
Practice the secret mantras!

### 13. Special Utterances

*oṁ* I have entered into the great vajra mandala. {215}
I have seen the great yoga mandala.
I will bestow empowerment in the great secret mandala.

## B. The Main Part: Bestowing the Four Empowerments

This is divided into four: (1) the vase empowerment; (2) the secret empowerment; (3) the wisdom empowerment; and (4) the fourth empowerment or precious word empowerment.

### 1. Vase Empowerment

There are two parts: (1) the empowerment of the vajra disciples for their own fulfillment and (2) the empowerment of the vajra master for others' fulfillment.

### a. Empowerment of the Vajra Disciples for Their Own Fulfillment

This empowerment is divided into five: (1) the water empowerment of Akṣhobhya; (2) the crown empowerment of Ratnasambhava; (3) the vajra empowerment of Amitābha; (4) the bell empowerment of Amoghasiddhi; and (5) the name empowerment of Vairochana.

#### i. Water Empowerment of Akṣhobhya

This empowerment is divided into two parts: the request and the actual empowerment.

First, the request:

> Just as adamantine enlightenment
> Is the great offering bestowed upon the buddhas,
> In order to protect us, we pray,
> Bestow on us today the vajra space.[10]

Second, the actual empowerment. With the mantra of Hayagrīva and the water from the activity vase, cleanse the empowerment materials and the disciples:

> The master, disciples, and empowerment materials—

are purified with

> *oṁ svabhāva śuddāḥ sarvadharmāḥ svabhāva śuddho 'haṃ*
>
> From the state of emptiness there appears the syllable *hūṁ*, from which there arises Akṣhobhya Avalokiteshvara, blue in color, with one face, four arms, and Blue Gnosis (*ye shes sngon mo*), holding a vajra and vase. Both male and female deities are radiant with the major and minor marks and adorned with all the ornaments. In their crown, throat, and heart centers are the syllables *oṁ āḥ hūṁ,* radiating light, inviting the wisdom deities similar to themselves.
>
> *jaḥ hūṁ baṃ hoḥ*
>
> Consider that they become inseparable. Again, lights emanate, inviting the five families of empowering deities and their

retinues and invoking all the tathāgatas' intentions to bestow empowerment. A stream of nectar from the female buddhas enters through the crown, conferring the empowerment. {216} The vajra goddesses of charm sing. The bodhisattvas strew flowers and proclaim good auspices.

With this in mind, recite the auspicious prayer of the seven universal buddhas or the prayer of perfect auspiciousness. Next, bestow empowerment with the empowerment vase through the crown, as follows:

The great vajra empowerment,
Revered by the whole of the three worlds,
The vase empowerment of all the buddhas,
Is here and now conferred on you.
*oṁ sarva tathāgata udaka abhiṣiñca maṃ*

Again, from the heart of Avalokiteshvara and his consort there emanates a blue vajra ḍākinī holding a vase. Consider that with the water from the vase, she bestows empowerment.
*oṁ maṇi padme hūṁ vajra ḍākinī abhiṣiñca maṃ*—
With this, the flow of nectar confers empowerment.

May all the bodhisattvas' good auspices
Remain in the hearts of all sentient beings.
May I, the supreme lord of all families, revered by all, confer and give rise to great bliss in all sentient beings.
May everything be auspicious that here and now you receive the supreme empowerment.

In this way, say the prayer for auspiciousness.

The goddesses of charm sing vajra songs:
*oṁ sarva vajra su sang gra he*
*vajra manuttara ni*
*vajra dharmakāya ni*
*vajra karma karod bhave*

The wrathful deities banish obstacle makers:
*oṁ padmānta kṛta vajra krota hayagrīva hulu hulu hūṁ phaṭ*

With gugul incense and the like, a rain of flowers descends. The sound of the great drum and other musical instruments resounds. The inside of your body is filled with the flow of nectar and with forms of Avalokiteshvara as numerous as the atoms in the universe. The excess nectar overflows, adorning your crown as Akṣhobhya, and you become the nature of Akṣhobhya Avalokiteshvara, to whom the offering goddesses make offerings. {217}

With this in mind, make the five outer offerings and play music, offering them with:

*oṁ namaḥ sarva tathāgata vajra arghaṃ pratīccha ye svāhā*
*pādyaṃ . . .*
*vajra puṣpe pūja āḥ hūṁ*
*vajra dhūpe . . .*
*vajra āloke . . .*
*vajra gandhe . . .*
*vajra naivedye . . .*
*vajra śabda pūja āḥ hūṁ svāhā*

With this, consider that you have received the water empowerment of Akṣhobhya. The defilement of aversion is purified, the aggregate of consciousness is transformed, and you realize mirrorlike gnosis. You have the fortune to realize the level of the buddha Akṣhobhya Avalokiteshvara.

In this way, proclaim the realization that results from the empowerment.

### ii. Crown Empowerment of Ratnasambhava

This is divided into two parts: the request and the actual empowerment.

First, the request:

Just as the adamantine jewel
Is the great offering bestowed upon the buddhas,

In order to protect us, we pray,
Bestow on us today the vajra jewel.

Second, the actual empowerment:

From *oṁ āḥ hūṁ* in the three centers of the disciples and empowerment materials visualized as Ratnasambhava Avalokiteshvara with his consort, rays of light emanate, inviting the wisdom deities similar to themselves.

With *jaḥ hūṁ baṃ hoḥ* they become inseparable.

From their melting into light, consider that you are empowered with the precious crown.

The crown empowerment:

The great jewel empowerment,
Revered by the whole of the three worlds,
The crown empowerment of all the buddhas,
Is here and now conferred on you.

With:

*oṁ sarva tathāgata vajra mukuṭa abhiṣiñca hūṁ surati tvaṃ a haṃ*
*vajra tuṣya ho*
*oṁ hūṁ trāṃ hrīḥ āḥ*
*abhiṣiñca mi*

empowerment is bestowed.

Again, from the navel center of Avalokiteshvara and his consort visualized in front, there emanates a yellow ratna ḍākinī holding an empowerment vase. {218} Consider that with the water from the vase, she bestows empowerment.
*oṁ maṇi padme hūṁ ratna ḍākinī abhiṣiñca maṃ*—
With this, the flow of nectar confers empowerment.

As before:

> The bodhisattvas recite prayers for auspiciousness. The goddesses of charm sing vajra songs. The male and female wrathful deities banish obstacle makers. A rain of flowers descends. Music resounds. The inside of your body is filled with the empowerment water. The excess nectar overflows, adorning your crown as Ratnasambhava and [you become the nature of Ratnasambhava Avalokiteshvara] to whom the offering goddesses make offerings. With this, you have received the crown empowerment of Ratnasambhava. The defilement of stinginess is purified, the aggregate of feeling is transformed, and you realize the gnosis of equality. You gain the fortune to realize the level of Ratnasambhava Avalokiteshvara.

In this way, proclaim the realization that results from the empowerment.

**iii. Vajra Empowerment of Amitābha**

There are two parts. First, the request:

> Just as the padminī
> Is the great offering bestowed upon the buddhas,
> In order to protect us, we pray,
> Bestow on us today the vajra lotus.

Second, the actual empowerment. Consider that:

> The disciples and empowerment materials [dissolve into] the state of emptiness, from which visualize the syllable *jiṃ*, and arising from it a lotus marked with *jiṃ*. It emanates and gathers back rays of light, transforming into Amitābha Avalokiteshvara with his consort. The wisdom deities dissolve. From the [invitation of] buddhas of the five families, the empowerment materials [in the form of] Amitābha melt into light, and the empowerment of the vajra arising from that is bestowed.
>
> The great lotus empowerment,
> Revered by the whole of the three worlds,
> The vajra empowerment of all the buddhas,
> Is here and now conferred on you.

With *oṁ mahā vajra abhiṣiñca maṃ*
Empowerment is bestowed.

Again, from the throat center of [the deity] visualized in front there emanates a red padma ḍākinī holding an empowerment vase. Consider that with the water from the vase she bestows empowerment.

*oṁ maṇi padme hūṁ padma ḍākinī abhiṣiñca maṃ*—{219}

With this, the flow of nectar confers empowerment. The bodhisattvas recite prayers for auspiciousness. The [goddesses of charm] sing vajra songs. The wrathful deities banish obstacle makers. Offerings are made . . .

as above. Proclaim the realization [that results from the empowerment]:

With this, you have received the vajra empowerment of Amitābha. The defilement of attachment is purified, the aggregate of perception is transformed, and you realize the all-discerning gnosis. You gain the fortune to realize the level of Amitābha Avalokiteshvara.

In this way, proclaim the realization.

### iv. Bell Empowerment of Amoghasiddhi

There are two parts. First, the request:

Just as the supreme karma family
Is the great offering bestowed upon the buddhas,
In order to protect us, we pray,
Bestow on us today the vajra activity.

Second, the actual empowerment:

The disciples and empowerment materials [dissolve into] the state of emptiness, from which visualize the syllable *khaṃ*, and arising from it a sword marked with *khaṃ*. It emanates and gathers back rays of light, transforming into Amoghasiddhi Avalokiteshvara with his consort. The wisdom deities dissolve. Again, the buddhas of the five families and their retinues are invited. Consider that the empowerment is bestowed with the bell that arises from Amoghasiddhi melting into light.

The great empowerment of action,
Revered by the whole of the three worlds,
The bell empowerment of all the buddhas,
Is here and now conferred on you.
With *oṁ vajra adhipati staṃ abhiṣiñca maṃ tiṣṭha vajra samaya tvaṃ*
*oṁ vajra gandhe ā aḥ*
Empowerment is bestowed.

Again, from the heart center of Avalokiteshvara and his consort in the secret center of [the deity] visualized in front there emanates a green karma ḍākinī holding an empowerment vase. Consider that with the water from the vase she bestows empowerment.

With *oṁ maṇi padme hūṁ karma ḍākinī abhiṣiñca maṃ* empowerment is bestowed. {220}

The prayers for auspiciousness and so on are as before. Proclaim the realization that results from the empowerment:

With this, you have received the bell empowerment of Amoghasiddhi. The defilement of jealousy is purified, the aggregate of conditioning factors is transformed, and you realize the all-accomplishing gnosis. You [gain the fortune] to realize the level of Amoghasiddhi Avalokiteshvara.

In this way, proclaim the realization.

### v. Name Empowerment of Vairochana

There are two parts. [First, the request:]

Just as the adamantine enlightenment
Is the great offering bestowed upon the buddhas,
In order to protect us, we pray,
Bestow on us today the vajra enlightenment.

Second, the actual empowerment. Consider that:

> The disciples and empowerment materials

are purified with

> *oṁ svabhāva śuddāḥ sarvadharmāḥ svabhāva śuddho 'haṃ*
>
> From the state of emptiness visualize the syllable *bhrūṃ*, from which there arises a wheel marked with *bhrūṃ*. It emanates and gathers back rays of light, transforming into Vairochana Avalokiteshvara with his consort. The wisdom deities dissolve. The buddhas of the five families and their retinues bestow the name empowerment.
>
> The great buddha empowerment,
> Revered by the whole of the three worlds,
> The name empowerment of all the buddhas,
> Is here and now conferred on you.
> *oṁ vajra satva tvaṃ*
> *abhiṣiñca maṃ*
> *vajra nāma abhiṣekata*

So saying, [giving a name such as] Pema Dorje, at the end, also recite the mantra.

> Again, from the heart center of Vairochana Avalokiteshvara and his consort in the crown center of [the deity] visualized in front there emanates a white buddha ḍākinī holding an empowerment vase.
>
> Consider that with the water from the vase she bestows empowerment.
>
> With *oṁ maṇi padme hūṁ buddha ḍākinī abhiṣiñca maṃ* the flow of nectar confers empowerment.

The prayers for auspiciousness and so on are as before. Proclaim the realization that results from the empowerment:

> With this, you have received the name empowerment of Vairochana. The defilement of confusion is purified, {221} the aggregate of form is transformed, and you realize the gnosis of the expanse of reality. You [gain the fortune] to realize the level of Vairochana Avalokiteshvara.

In this way, proclaim the realization.

> With these, you have received the five empowerments of knowledge, which are the antidotes to ignorance.

### b. Empowerment of the Vajra Master for Others' Fulfillment

There are two parts. First, the request, as follows:

> Through your kindness
> We will be able to benefit ourselves and others.
> Treasure of compassion, please bestow on us
> The empowerment of the vajra master.

Second, the empowerment: Purify the disciples and empowerment materials with the *svabhāva* mantra.

> Consider that from the state of emptiness there appears the syllable *hūṁ*, and from it a vajra marked with a *hūṁ*. It emanates and gathers back rays of light, transforming into Vajrasattva Avalokiteshvara, who is white in color, with one face and four arms and his two legs crossed. He is in union with his consort Vajratopa, who is holding a vajra and bell. From the three syllables *oṁ āḥ hūṁ* in their three centers, lights radiate, touching the [deity] visualized in front. From the single body of the [deity] visualized in front infinite forms of the deity emanate, like a thousand lamps being lit from one, and dissolve into the bodies of the disciples.
> *oṁ maṇi padme hūṁ ḍākinī harinisa jaḥ hūṁ baṃ hoḥ*

Saying this, play music. Bestow empowerment on the crown with the body of Avalokiteshvara, saying:

The body empowerment of Avalokiteshvara
Is here and now bestowed on you.
In order to realize all the buddhas,
May you become Avalokiteshvara.

Again, from *hūṁ* in the heart center, rays of light emanate. Consider that the buddhas of the five families and their retinues bestow empowerment.

Give the vajra and bell in the two hands and say:

Take the great vajra and the great bell {222}
And receive the adamantine blessings.
Today you must become a vajra master
And gather disciples.

Next, bestowing empowerment with the water from the vase:

Empowerment is bestowed with the excellent purity
Of the pure water of the gods,
The stainless wisdom nectar
Arisen from the sacred commitment of the three
secrets.
*oṁ namaḥ sarva tathāgata abhiṣiñca maṃ*

Then, throwing flowers, say:

You are empowered as the dharma regent of the three worlds.

Second, the Speech authorization:

Consider that the mantra chain comes out of the mouth of the teacher, who is Avalokiteshvara. It enters the mouths of the disciples and dissolves into the *hrīḥ* in their heart centers.

Saying *oṁ maṇi padme hūṁ ḍākinī harinisa hūṁ* three times, place the crystal rosary on their heads and say:

> Bhagavān, bestow [the mantra] upon this person;
> Impregnate this person [with the mantra].

Third, the Mind authorization:

> The nature of the mind is radiant light, like a polished mirror, free of all conceptual thoughts. Rest in meditative equipoise in the state of clarity and emptiness that can only be known by itself.

Displaying the mirror, say:

> All phenomena are like a reflection,
> Pure and clear, free of impurity.
> Appearing infallibly in causes and deeds,
> They have no intrinsic essence; they dwell nowhere.
> Know phenomena to be thus
> And carry out the incomparable fulfillment of beings.

> Of the four mandalas [for conferring empowerment], it is the outer one, the mandala of colored powder [that has been used here].[11]
>
> Of the four teachers, it is the teacher in the body of manifestation [who has bestowed empowerment].
>
> Of the four empowerments, you have received the vase empowerment.
>
> Of the four kinds of obscurations, it is principally the obscurations of the body that have been purified.
>
> Of the four stages, it is the generation stage that you have been empowered to practice.
>
> Of the four joys, it is the gnosis related to joy that is born in your mind stream.
>
> Of the four results, {223} it is the adamantine level of the vajra body, the body of manifestation, that you have been given the fortune to realize.

With this, proclaim the realization that results from the empowerment.

## 2. Secret Empowerment

In order to receive the secret empowerment, a mandala should be offered. A young woman who has kept the sacred commitments is offered to the teacher, and the blindfolds are attached.

The request:

> Just as adamantine enlightenment
> Is the great offering bestowed upon the buddhas,
> In order to protect us, we pray,
> Bestow on us the secret empowerment.

> Visualize noble Avalokiteshvara with his consort in union. With the sound of great bliss of the teacher and his consort, *oṁ sarva tathāgata anu rāgana vajra svabhāva atma ko 'haṃ*, and the rays of light from his heart, the tathāgatas of the five families and their consorts descend onto the crown of the head. Consider that through the great passion of the male and female deities' union, they melt into light, becoming the nature of the white and red bodhichitta. They dissolve through the teacher's crown, stream down the central channel, and emerge from the vajra of skillful means. The bodhichitta that descends into the space of the consort is poured into the mouths of the disciples.

Give the disciples the nectar in the kapāla to drink, saying:

> Just as the buddhas of the past
> Empowered their bodhisattva heirs,
> With this excellent bodhichitta,
> Child, you are empowered.
> *oṁ maṇi padme hūṁ ḍākinī harinisa guhya abhiṣiñca āḥ*

So saying, give them the bodhichitta.

> The disciples, with the thought of gathering all the buddhas, say
> *a ho mahā sukha*

and drink it. Say:

Meditate that it passes through your speech [center], filling your whole being with great bliss.

Remove the blindfolds.

With this, in the mandala of relative bodhichitta:

Of the four teachers, it is the teacher in the body of perfect enjoyment [who has empowered you].

Of the four empowerments, {224} you have received the secret empowerment.

Of the four kinds of obscurations, it is the obscurations of the speech in this case that have been purified.

Of the four stages, it is the blessing of oneself that you have been empowered to practice.

Of the four joys, it is the gnosis related to supreme joy that is realized.

Of the four results, it is the level of the vajra speech, the body of perfect enjoyment, that you have been given the fortune to realize.

With this, proclaim the realization that results from the empowerment.

### 3. Wisdom Gnosis Empowerment

The mandala is offered. The blindfolds [are tied]. Considering that twenty-two wisdom consorts are offered to the teacher, [the disciples] make the following request:

Just as adamantine enlightenment
Is the great offering bestowed upon the buddhas,
In order to protect us, we pray,
Bestow on us the empowerment of wisdom gnosis.

Consider that the teacher has given you a wisdom consort with all the excellent marks and completely adorned with all the ornaments.

This beautiful consort
You should take as a support, so the buddhas have said.

By stages in the different chakras,
Through union, enjoy great bliss.

While that very goddess displays her sweet-smelling lotus,
Consider that she is saying:
"How wonderful! This is my lotus,
Possessed of every bliss.
If someone uses it according to the ritual,
I am present in front of them:
Whatever they do—the Buddha's teaching, and so on—
They do with the lotus.
King of great bliss,
I myself am always here.
*bha ja mokṣa hoḥ*

Then the disciples visualize themselves, from the syllable *hrīḥ*, as noble Avalokiteshvara, with one face and four arms. The first two hands are joined, embracing the consort. The lower two hold a garland of jewels and a white lotus. The two legs are crossed in vajra posture. He is fully adorned with all the silk garments and jewel ornaments. {225}

The wisdom consort is visualized from the syllable *baṃ* as the ḍākinī Guhyajñāna, who is coral red in color. She is smiling, and her whole being is filled with great bliss. In her right hand she is playing a golden ḍāmaru held up in the air. With her left hand she holds to the male deity's lips a skull cup full of red nectar. Her two legs are wrapped around the male deity's waist. She is adorned with the five bone ornaments.

In the crowns of both male and female deities are the syllables *oṁ*, in their throat centers *āḥ*, in their hearts *hūṁ*, in their navels *svā*, and in their secret centers *hā*. Meditate that from the male deity's secret center, beyond concepts, appears a *hūṁ*, from which arises the vajra jewel, whose opening is blocked by a yellow *phaṭ*. From the mudrā's secret center, beyond concepts, appears an *āḥ,* from which arises a red lotus, whose pistil cup is marked with a red *āḥ*. Through the union of the male and female deities, they utter the sounds of great bliss—
*oṁ śri śri śri ha ha ha svāhā oṁ sarva tathāgata anu rāgaṇa vajra svabhāva atma ko 'haṃ*—

invoking all the buddhas in the ten directions and their consorts, who arrive on the crown of one's head and perform union. Through their great passion, they melt into light and become inseparable from the bodhichitta of the syllable *haṃ* in the crown center. Meditate that it descends from the crown center to the throat, giving rise in your being to the gnosis of joy. From the throat center it descends to the heart, giving rise in your being to the gnosis of supreme joy. From the heart center it descends to the navel, giving rise in your being to the gnosis of special joy. And from the navel center it descends to the secret center, giving rise in your being to the gnosis of coemergent joy. Then, saying *hūṁ*, meditate that by your drawing the lower wind up, the four joys are experienced in ascending order, and rest in meditative equipoise in the state of the Great Seal, the coemergent bliss-emptiness. {226}

With this, of the four mandalas, it is in the mandala of letters, the bhaga, that of the four teachers, the truth-body teacher [has empowered you].

Of the four empowerments, you have received the wisdom gnosis empowerment.

Of the four kinds of obscurations, it is mainly the obscurations of the mind that have been purified.

Of the four stages of the path, it is the perfection stage of the ultimate luminosity that you have been empowered to practice.

Of the four joys, it is the gnosis related to special joy that has been born in your mind stream.

Of the four results, it is the level of the vajra mind, the body of truth, that you [have been given the fortune] to realize.

With this, proclaim the realization that results from the empowerment.

### 4. Precious Word Empowerment

The mandala is offered.

To request the empowerment, repeat after me:
Great being, through your kindness
We have received the three empowerments of the main deity.

> Today we pray, kindly protect us
> By bestowing the precious fourth empowerment.

Say this three times. Attach the blindfolds. Make the disciples sit with their bodies in the seven-point posture of Vairochana and read out the following:

> All phenomena are inconceivable by nature. Rest in meditative equipoise, in the nature of the great Vajradhara, the nature of the Great Seal that possesses the seven aspects.
>
> "This primordial wisdom is extremely subtle,
> Adamantine, like the midst of space,
> Free of defilement, ultimate, the state of peace;
> You yourself are the means for [realizing] it."[12]
> Thus has it been taught, and,
> "The fourth too is like that,"
>
> meaning that the third [empowerment] is an example, and the fourth reveals it in truth. The third indicates the cause; the fourth indicates the result. The third shows it to be like a shoot; the fourth shows it to be like the fruit. This is the meaning of the Great Seal possessing the seven aspects that has to be explained and introduced.

Then, remove the blindfolds.

> With this, of the four mandalas, it is in the ultimate mandala that, of the four teachers, {227} the teacher in the body of the essential nature [has empowered you].
>
> Of the four empowerments, you have received the precious word empowerment.
>
> Of the four kinds of obscurations, it is the obscuration of believing body, speech, and mind to be distinct that has been purified.
>
> Of the four stages of the path, it is the stage of the utterly non-dwelling union state that you have been empowered to practice.
>
> Of the four joys, it is the gnosis related to coemergent joy that has been realized.

> Of the four results, it is the level of the vajra gnosis, the body of the essential nature, that you [have been given the fortune] to realize.

With this, proclaim the realization that results from the empowerment. This is sufficient, as the most important thing is empowerment through concentration,[13] so the empowerment is now completed.

If you wish to do things in a detailed way, there is:

### C. Conclusion: Giving Authorization

There is nothing wrong in giving the practices to be observed, giving teachings to benefit others, reassuring [the disciples] with predictions, or giving praise to encourage them. The self-empowerment too should be taken with this same ritual procedure.

Next, the mandala should be offered and the following repeated three times:

> From now on, I offer myself
> To you as your servant.
> Accept me as your disciple,
> And use even the smallest part of me.

This completes the empowerment.

## III. Concluding Stages

Perform the offerings and praise. Enjoy the feast offering and send out the torma of the remainders. Pray for forgiveness and restore any deficiencies with the hundred syllables. Say the prayers of dedication and aspiration. Dissolve the wisdom deity into the supporting image. Dissolve the meditational deity into yourself. Apply the seal of nonconceptuality. Say prayers for auspiciousness. Throw the colored sand into a river, to the accompaniment of music. Leave no trace of the ritual. This completes the concluding stages.

From the reservoir of blessings of Lord Avalokiteshvara
May the river of the four empowerments of the unsurpassable tantra flow,

Purifying the four temporary stains of all beings
And swelling the ocean of the four joys and the four buddha bodies.

If, without first receiving instruction, one gives this empowerment to someone who has not kept the sacred commitments or indiscriminately, it will incur the punishment of the ḍākinīs, so do not do so.

Know that if one has received the empowerment and keeps the sacred commitments, one will obtain the supreme and common accomplishments. {228}

This visualization practice focusing upon the mandala of noble Avalokiteshvara, entitled *A River of Great Compassion*, was arranged in accordance with his glorious teacher's pith instructions and in compliance with the rituals of the tantras by the yogi Öpak Dorje on the Potala Mountain, blessed by noble Avalokiteshvara.

May it result in the teachings of the Vajrayāna enduring for great lengths of time.

May virtue and excellence increase.

# 7. An Offering Arrangement for the Empowerment Ritual of Noble Avalokiteshvara, "The Glowing Jewel," together with the Revelation of the Mandala[1]

{230}
After offering the torma, give praise:

Vairochana, sovereign of the gnosis of the expanse of reality,
Transformation of the form aggregate through the purification of confusion,
Sublime embodiment of the supreme unchanging nature—
To you, Vairochana Avalokiteshvara, homage and praise!

Vajrasattva, sovereign of mirrorlike gnosis,
Transformation of consciousness through the purification of aversion,
Sublime embodiment of the supreme unchanging nature—
To you, Akṣhobhya Avalokiteshvara, homage and praise!

Ratnakara, sovereign of the gnosis of equality,
Transformation of the feeling aggregate through the purification of pride,
Sublime embodiment of the supreme unchanging nature—
To you, Ratnakara Avalokiteshvara, homage and praise!

Amitābha, sovereign of all-discerning gnosis,
Transformation of perception through the purification of attachment,
Sublime embodiment of the supreme unchanging nature—
To you, Amitābha Avalokiteshvara, homage and praise!

Amoghasiddhi, sovereign of all-accomplishing gnosis,
Transformation of conditioning factors through the purification of jealousy, {231}
Sublime embodiment of the supreme unchanging nature—
To you, Amoghasiddhi Avalokiteshvara, homage and praise!

To you who perform the activity of pacification,
To the vajra ḍākinīs, homage and praise!

To you who perform the activity of increasing,
To the ratna ḍākinīs, homage and praise!

To you who perform the activity of bringing under control,
To the padma ḍākinīs, homage and praise!

To you who perform the activity of forcefully subduing,
To the karma ḍākinīs, homage and praise!

Pure nature of the water element,
Source of all the vajra goddesses—
To you, Māmakī, homage and praise!

Bliss and emptiness inseparable—
To you, secret ḍākinī, homage and praise!

Goddesses who pacify, increase, control, and subdue,
To you, ḍākinīs of the four families, homage and praise!

With this homage and praise we make to you,
Grant us the supreme and common accomplishments.
Help us to achieve the two fulfillments.

After that, for revealing the mandala, say:

> The palace of great liberation, whose nature is Vairochana, is made of different kinds of precious materials. It is square, with four doors, {232} arched pediments, terraces, vajra fence, and a mountain of fire. This is the mandala of your own mind. In it the different states of realization of the nature of the mind manifest as the thirty-seven elements that lead to enlightenment, symbolically indicated by the doors, ornaments, and so on, of the mandala. That is the ultimate mandala. The mind manifests as the aggregates, constituents, and senses-and-fields. Its nature is the exalted Lord Avalokiteshvara and his consort, arising as emptiness and compassion inseparable. Its unobstructed clarity-emptiness, earth and so on, manifest as the buddhas of the five families of Avalokiteshvara and their consorts, as the four ḍākinīs, and so on. Consider that you are truly seeing their faces in the mandala of noble Avalokiteshvara.

*namo guru*

The feast offering of the Great Compassionate One according to the aural lineage of Mitrayogin may be performed either during the approach and accomplishment, or during an empowerment or consecration ritual, or during the yogic practices of the activities, or on auspicious days such as the eighth day of the lunar calendar, the full moon, or the new moon. In an isolated locality, prepare a mandala as a support for accumulating merit as for the empowerment. If you do not have one, dispose piles of grain in numbers equal to the number of deities on a perfectly clean cotton or felt cloth. Set up an image of the Great Compassionate Teacher and his consort. Arrange the offerings and tormas in the same numbers as the deities, or no fewer than five or three. In front, place the ingredients for the feast offering and a kapāla full of liquor. Visualizing yourself as the deity, give the torma for the outer elemental spirits and banish obstacle makers. Set the boundaries and meditate on the protection circle. Then perform the seven branches and prayers. In the mandala in front, visualize the mandala [of deities], which is the support of accumulating merit. Bless all the outer and inner offerings like Avalokiteshvara. In particular, for the yogic practices of the activities consider that:

> From my two seed syllables appears the syllable *raṃ*, which burns up all faults and defects. From *yaṃ*, the wind scatters everything. And from *khaṃ*, the water rinses everything away. Then, from *trāṃ*, there appears a crossed vajra, and thence a vast and open container of precious materials, {233} with the essence it contains in the form of three *bhrūṃ* syllables.

Repeat *bhrūṃ* twenty-one times. Consider that:

> The *bhrūṃ* syllables melt to become wisdom nectar.

Then make the hand offering: With the ring finger of the left hand, stir the source of phenomena in the kapāla in front seven times, to bless it as wisdom nectar. Then with the ring finger of the right hand make five syllables in the palm of the left hand, visualizing the lord and his consort in the center and the four ḍākinīs in the four directions, and make the offering to all five. Offering the nectar with the ring finger of the right hand, make offering and praise many times with:

> *oṁ maṇi padme hūṁ ḍākinī harinisa hūṁ sura staṃ amṛta khāhi*

Consider that they melt into light. Place the hollowed hand over the nectar. Anoint your three centers with the same hand. Then, ringing the bell with the left hand, sprinkle the nectar with the vajra in the right hand over the deities of the mandala and consider that they are pleased.

> The feast torma is blessed as untainted nectar possessing the five qualities pleasurable to the senses.

Sprinkle yourself and consider that

> All my pores are pervaded by the lord and his consort.

Sprinkle the feast guests and consider that

> They are dākas and ḍākinīs.

At these times, recite the root mantra with the addition of the three syllables.

Next, the invitation. With the great incense and the great burnt offering, and to the sound of different musical instruments:

*hūṁ* From the measureless palace of the three bodies inseparable,
Very essence of the buddhas of the three times,
Compassionate ones who bring sentient beings to maturation,
Teachers of the instruction lineage, come, we pray.

From the measureless palace of the supreme natural state,
Deities of the three bodies surrounded by your retinues,
Embodiments of emptiness and compassion,[2]
Deities of the aural lineage, come, we pray.

From the palace of the Unexcelled, the expanse of reality,
All you hosts of deities of the mandala without exception,
Watching over beings with the eye of compassion,
Yidam deities, come, we pray.

From the measureless palace of the celestial land of Oḍḍiyanā,
You who bestow blessings and accomplishments,
Karma ḍākinīs, wisdom ḍākinīs, and other kinds,
Ḍākas and ḍākinīs, come, we pray.

From the measureless palace of the charnel ground, {234}
You who spread the Buddha's teachings
And dispel outer and inner obstacles,
Protectors and guardians of the dharma, come, we pray.

Requesting them to be seated:

*hūṁ* In this palace of manifold precious materials,
On thrones of multicolored lotuses,
Surrounded by beauty without measure,
Deities of secret accomplishment, pray be seated.

Next, paying homage:

*hūṁ* Though you never move from the state of sameness, the ultimate reality,
You appear like a rainbow in the body of perfect enjoyment
And manifest to guide all beings with compassion.
Avalokiteshvara, to you we pay homage.

After that, make the outer offerings:

*hūṁ* The water offerings, flowers, incense, and perfume,
Lamps, and every kind of food,
And offerings of sweet-sounding music—
Please accept these, Avalokiteshvara.

Beautiful forms, melodious sounds,
Sweet fragrances and delicious tastes,
Pleasurable sensations—the offerings to the senses—
Please accept these, Avalokiteshvara.

The five meats and five nectars;
The five aggregates, constituents, and senses-and-fields;
The five objects of the senses and the five elements—
Please accept these, Avalokiteshvara.

The four joys and eight kinds of bliss,
The four instants and five kinds of gnosis,
And the offering of the nondual joy and bliss—
Please accept these, Avalokiteshvara.

Bless the feast ingredients like the inner offering and say the condensed feast offering:

*namo* This vast feast offering of means and wisdom inseparable [we offer]
To the glorious teachers, roots of blessings—*kha raṃ kha hi*
To the hosts of yidam deities, root of accomplishments—*kha raṃ kha hi*
To the dharma protectors, roots of activities—*kha raṃ kha hi*

With this, serve the feast.

Next, to take the accomplishments, holding the ingredients related to skillful means and wisdom in the right and left hands:

> Look at these beautiful sacred substances, {235}
> It is wrong to have doubts concerning them.
> Consider that brahmins, dogs, and outcastes
> Are of the same nature, and enjoy!

With this vajra song, beginning with the master, it is offered to the brothers and sisters. The master makes the circular lotus gesture and accepts it, saying:

> To the sugatas in the body of truth,
> Free from the stains of desire-attachment,
> Completely rid of dualistic concepts,
> To the state of thatness I pay homage.
> *a la la ho*

The master receives a double [portion of the feast ingredients]. After that, the rest is to be enjoyed by the brothers and sisters. Then, after the remainders have been collected, the vajra master makes the gesture of the source of phenomena, sprinkles them and blesses them with *oṁ āḥ hūṁ*, sending them outside with *ucita balingta* . . . and so on.

For the concluding practices, offer whichever outer sense offerings there are, praise the host of deities, and go through the confession and vow to refrain. Make up excesses and omissions with the hundred syllables. Recite any suitable prayers for auspiciousness. Seal the practice with the final dedication and prayers of aspiration.

May this very clear arrangement of the sequence of offerings from the aural lineage of Avalokiteshvara benefit many sentient beings.

May virtue and excellence increase.

# 8. Authorization Ritual for Lord Mañjughoṣha[1]

{238}
To him whose wisdom is as vast as the sky
In which the sun of gnosis has fully risen,
Free of all obscuration and clouds of delusion—
To Mañjughoṣha, who clears away the darkness of ignorance, I bow.

In this text for giving the authorization ritual related to Lord Mañjughoṣha there are three main sections: (1) preliminaries; (2) main part; and (3) conclusion.

## I. Preliminaries

The preliminaries are divided into two: (1) material arrangements and (2) practicing the sādhana and taking the self-empowerment.

### A. Material Arrangements

Sprinkle a mandala plate with scented water, and on it paint an eight-petaled lotus, its center yellow, the eastern petal white, the southern yellow, the western red, the northern green, and the four intermediate petals beautifully painted. In the center, place a saffron-colored pile of grain to represent the deity. Around this place the offerings and tormas, and beside them set an activity vase. These constitute the material preparations.

### B. Practicing the Sādhana and Taking the Self-Empowerment

The self-empowerment is divided into four sections.

First, sit on a comfortable seat, go for refuge, arouse the mind set on supreme enlightenment, perform the seven branches, and meditate on the four boundless attitudes. This corresponds to the accumulation of merit.

Second, for the accumulation of wisdom, meditate on emptiness by saying *oṁ svabhāva śuddāḥ sarvadharmāḥ svabhāva śuddho 'haṃ.*

Third, for the visualization stage, visualize [the deity] as described in the instruction manual:

> With the five factors of awakening, [I visualize myself as]
> Mañjushrī, the color of saffron,
> With one face and two hands . . .

Dissolve the wisdom deity into this, receiving empowerment and applying the seal [of oneself as the deity]. Go through the mantra recitation. The front visualization is practiced in the same way. Do the visualization [for the activity vase] according to the source text:

> Inside the activity vase is Amṛitakuṇḍali . . .

Follow the source text for the empowerment and applying the seal. Recite the mantra, considering that:

> Then, in my heart center, the mantra garland turns and emanates rays of light.
> They enter the mouths of the deities visualized in front and in the vase.
> They encircle their heart centers, invoking their wisdom minds;
> As they pronounce the mantra, from all the parts of their bodies a stream of nectar flows down, filling the vase. {239}

Again, make the offerings and praises to them and offer the torma. Pray for the fulfillment of your wishes.

After that, at this point, following the order described below, take the self-empowerment by means of concentration.

## II. Main Part

The main part is divided into two: (1) the preliminaries for the authorization ritual and (2) the main authorization ritual.

### A. Preliminaries for the Authorization Ritual

Cleanse the disciples with the water from the activity vase and have them be seated. Offer the torma for obstacle makers and banish the obstacle makers. Meditate on the protection circle. Next, the disciples should request the teacher to give the authorization ritual by offering a mandala. The teacher then gives them the refuge vow, saying:

> Folding your hands together, repeat after me:
>
> > Master, think of us.
> > Until we reach the heart of enlightenment,
> > We go for refuge in the buddhas.
> > Likewise, we go for refuge in the dharma
> > And in the assembly of bodhisattvas.

Saying this three times, give them the vow. Then, give them the vow for arousing the bodhichitta.

> Just as the sugatas of the past
> Aroused the intent to attain enlightenment
> And practiced in stages
> The training of the bodhisattvas,
> Likewise, for the benefit of beings,
> We arouse the intent to attain enlightenment,
> And likewise will we also train in stages
> In that same training.
> We will take across those who have not crossed over;
> We will free those who have not been freed;
> We will bring relief to those who have not been relieved
> And set all beings in the state beyond suffering.

This should be said three times. Next, the disciples should accumulate merit with the seven branches:

To the essence of the Three Jewels,
The teacher Mañjughoṣha, we submit obeisance.
We offer outer, inner, and secret offerings.
Each and every one of our negative deeds we confess. {240}
We rejoice in beings' virtue.
Turn the wheel of dharma, we pray,
And stay without passing into nirvana.
We dedicate the merit to the great enlightenment.

This should be recited three times.

With this, the preliminaries have been completed.

**[B. Main Authorization Ritual]**

Next, for the second and main part, there are five sections: the authorizations for the Body, Speech, Mind, Qualities, and Activities.

First, to request the Body authorization, offer the teacher a mandala. Next, say this prayer:

O teacher, sovereign of compassion, Mañjughoṣha,
Fearful of samsara, we pray, hold us with compassion.
Frightened and threatened in the dark city of beings,
We pray to you.
As we touch the dust beneath your feet,
Grant us the authorization [to enter] the city of nirvana, great bliss.

This should be recited three times. After that, the master gives his assent:[2]

The sunlight of my compassion
Clears away the darkness of ignorance.
Your body, speech, and mind
Are blessed by the enlightened body, speech, and mind.

Next, cleanse the disciples with the *amṛta* mantra and purify them with the *svabhāva* mantra. Go through the visualization as in the sādhana:

In an instant [one arises] as Mañjughoṣha . . .

Then:

Consider that from the syllable *dhīḥ* in the heart of the master and the deity in the mandala, who are indistinguishable, lights radiate, touching all the buddhas and bodhisattvas in the ten directions. They all appear in the form of Mañjughoṣha, as countless tiny bodies, visualized clearly with their limbs and symbolic attributes, and dissolve into the bodies of the disciples. From the teacher's body too, countless bodies of Mañjughoṣha emanate {241} and dissolve into the disciples' bodies like snow falling on a lake.

Throw flowers or, alternatively, place an image of Mañjughoṣha on [the disciples'] heads, to the accompaniment of music and incense, as the master chants:

Noble Mañjughoṣha, bestow [your blessing] on this [person];
Impregnate this person [with your nature], I pray.
*ārya mañjuśrī jaḥ hūṁ baṃ hoḥ*

The benefits of receiving the Body authorization like this are both temporary and ultimate. On the temporary level, you will be at peace from all illnesses, negative forces, evil deeds, obscurations, and obstacles related to the body. On the ultimate level, you will acquire the enlightened body of Mañjughoṣha, adorned with the major and minor marks. That is its purpose.

Second, to request the Speech authorization, offer a mandala.

The request is as above.

Next, in the heart centers of both the master and disciples visualized as Mañjushrī are a lotus and moon, on which is a golden syllable *dhīḥ*, surrounded by the mantra garland
*oṁ a ra pa ca na dhīḥ namaḥ*.

It comes straight out of the mouth of the teacher Mañjughoṣha,

> enters the mouths of the disciples, and encircles the syllable *dhīḥ* in the heart. Concentrate on this.

Taking hold of the rosary, make [the disciples] repeat the mantra after you twenty-one times. At the end, touch the disciples at their throat centers with the rosary as you say:

> Noble Mañjughoṣha, bestow the knowledge mantra on this [person];
> Impregnate this person [with it], I pray.

Make the disciples too repeat these lines, adapting them accordingly.

> The benefits of this are both temporary and ultimate. On the temporary level, you will gain the great power of the mantra and proficiency in oral explanation, debate, and composition. {242} and on the ultimate level, you will accomplish words of truth and acquire the speech of the buddhas that possesses the sixty expressive qualities.
>
> Third, to request the Mind authorization, offer a mandala.

The request is as above. Instruct the disciples as follows:

> Next, the disciples should adopt the essential point of the body, the seven-point posture of Vairochana. Meditate on a syllable *dhīḥ* in the air in front, red in color like saffron, and shining with rays of light. Next, your body disappears into a rainbow body and dissolves into the syllable *dhīḥ* in the air in front. Direct your awareness on that. At the end, consider that the syllable *dhīḥ* disappears, like a rainbow vanishing in the sky. Remain in meditative equipoise, in the state free from all elaboration, the mind clear and empty, like the unblemished sky.
>
> The benefits of this are both temporary and ultimate. On the temporary level, you will develop extraordinary concentration in your mind stream, and on the ultimate level, you will realize ultimate reality as it is and know phenomena in all their multiplicity. That is its purpose.

Fourth, to request the Qualities authorization, offer a mandala.

The request is as above.

Next, the disciples should visualize themselves as Mañjughoṣha.

The master places a sword in the disciples' right hands and says:

This is the symbolic attribute of noble Mañjushrī, the sword of wisdom.
Use it to cut at the root the shoots of suffering of all sentient beings!

The benefits of this are both temporary and ultimate. On the temporary level, you will become learned in the five sciences. On the ultimate level, you will acquire the body, speech, mind, and qualities of the buddhas. {243}

Fifth, to request the Activities authorization, offer a mandala.

The request is as above. Instruct the disciples as follows:

Next, the disciples should visualize themselves as Mañjughoṣha.

The master places a volume of the scriptures in the disciples' left hands and says:

This is the tantra of noble Mañjushrī.
You should put it into practice yourselves and teach it to others on a vast scale.

The benefits of this are twofold. On the temporary level, you will accomplish the four activities and bring vast benefit to sentient beings. And on the ultimate level, you will accomplish the activities of the buddhas effortlessly and spontaneously.

After that, [the disciples] should make offerings of gratitude and perform the mandala offering to the teacher. Then they should say three times:

From now on, I offer myself
To you as your servant.
Accept me as your disciple,
And use even the smallest part of me.

Have them perform three prostrations and say, "Thank you!"

## III. Conclusion

Make the thanksgiving offerings and praise. Restore any excesses and omissions with the hundred-syllable mantra. Dedicate the merit to unsurpassable enlightenment. Say prayers for auspiciousness. If there is a support, request [the deity] to remain firmly in it. Otherwise,

With *vajra muḥ*, the wisdom deity departs;
The meditational deity dissolves into myself.

Leave no trace [of the ritual].[3]

This method is as taught by my teacher.
It is without errors or mistakes and unstained by anything I have made up.
I, Öpak Dorje, wrote it down exactly as it was taught.
By this merit may all beings attain the level of Mañjughoṣha.

There are a few oral clarifications, as follows.

Do the visualization according to the instruction manual. Dissolve the wisdom deity into it. Take empowerment and apply the seal. Recite the mantra. For the fourth part, again follow the procedure below. Take the feast offering and the self-empowerment at this point. {244}

Second, the main section is divided into five: (1) accepting the disciples; (2) an equivalent of the vase empowerment; (3) an equivalent of the secret empowerment; (4) an equivalent of the wisdom empowerment; and (5) an equivalent of the fourth empowerment.

First, accepting the disciples, for which there are four parts: (1) cleansing [the disciples]; (2) giving the torma for the obstacle makers; (3) banishing obstacle makers by peaceful and wrathful means; and (4) meditating on the protection circle. When you come to give the authorization ritual for the activities of Lord Mañjughoṣha, the mandala offering and request are as above. Then:

In the crown centers of both master and disciples visualizing themselves as Mañjughoṣha, visualize a white Mañjughoṣha, in the throat centers a red one, in the heart centers a blue one, in the navel centers a yellow one, and in the secret centers a green Mañjughoṣha.

Next, consider that the teacher and the deity in the mandala are indistinguishable, and that from the Mañjughoṣhas in their five centers, Mañjughoṣhas of the five families appear like lamps issuing forth from lamps. They dissolve into the disciples' five centers, as a result of which the five poisons are purified and transformed into the five kinds of gnosis. (NOTE: This is the equivalent of the second empowerment.)

Again, on the right shoulders of both master and disciples visualizing themselves as Mañjughoṣha, visualize a red Vajrabhairava, with one face and two arms. In his right hand he holds a curved knife with a lotus handle; his left holds a skull cup full of blood. His sharp blue horns gleam, and he is wrapped in bone ornaments. He is adorned with a long necklace of human heads, snake ornaments, and jeweled ornaments and is wearing an elephant skin.

On the left shoulders visualize a white Bhairava, holding a curved knife with a wheel handle and a skull cup.

On the right hips visualize a yellow Bhairava holding a curved knife with a jewel handle and a skull cup.

On the left hips {245} visualize a green Bhairava holding a curved knife with a crossed-vajra handle and a skull cup.

In the heart centers visualize a deep-blue Bhairava holding a curved knife with a vajra handle and a skull cup.

All these also have one face and two arms. Their faces are those of an enraged buffalo. Their sharp blue horns gleam, and they are wrapped in the six bone ornaments and adorned with a garland of human heads, and snake and bone ornaments.[4] They have an upper garment of elephant hide and are surrounded by blazing wisdom fire.

Next, consider that the teacher and deity in the mandala are indistinguishable, and from the five families of Bhairava in their bodies [five Bhairavas] appear, like lamps each emanating a second lamp. They dissolve into the five Bhairavas in the five places in the disciples' bodies, as a result of which bliss-emptiness, the vajra-like body, is realized. (NOTE: This is the equivalent of the third empowerment.)

After that, consider that the blue Bhairava in the heart center dissolves into the blue Mañjughoṣha in the heart center.

Likewise, consider that the red Bhairava on the right shoulder dissolves into the red Mañjughoṣha in the throat center, that the white Bhairava on the left shoulder dissolves into the white Mañjughoṣha in the crown center, that the yellow Bhairava on the right hip dissolves into the yellow Mañjughoṣha in the navel center, and that the green Bhairava on the left hip dissolves into the green Mañjughoṣha in the secret center.

Then the Mañjughoṣha in the secret center dissolves into the Mañjughoṣha in the navel. That in turn dissolves into the Mañjughoṣha in the heart center, which dissolves into the Mañjughoṣha in the throat center. {246} The latter dissolves into the white Mañjughoṣha in the crown center, which then melts into light. Visualize that it becomes a round essence drop—green, yellow, blue, red, and white—radiating five-colored rays of light.

Then one's own body melts into light and dissolves into the essence drop in one's crown center. Consider that the latter then disappears, like a rainbow vanishing in the sky. Settle in meditative equipoise, the mind clear and empty, in the state devoid of all elaboration, like pure space, without center or periphery. This is the ultimate authorization. (NOTE: This is the equivalent of the fourth empowerment.)

This is a point that has been clarified by the oral instructions.

Cleanse with the *amṛta* mantra and purify with the *svabhāva* mantra.

From the syllable *paṃ* appears a lotus, and from *A* a moon, on top of which is the syllable *bhrūṃ*, from which is visualized a precious vase.

On a lotus and moon is the syllable *hūṁ* and a crossed vajra, from which is visualized Amṛitakuṇḍali. He is blue-green and semiwrathful, holding a crossed vajra with the right hand at the heart center and a bell with a crossed-vajra handle in the left hand resting on the hip. He is seated cross-legged in the bodhisattva posture on the lotus and moon. In his crown center is the syllable *oṁ*, in the throat center the syllable *āḥ*, and in the heart center the syllable *hūṁ*. From *hūṁ* rays of light emanate, inviting the wisdom deity, like himself, who dissolves [into him] inseparably. Again, light rays emanate inviting the five families of empowering deities, who bestow empowerment. The excess nectar from the empowerment overflows and becomes Amoghasiddhi, ornamenting his crown.

Do the recitation with the visualization for the activity vase.

Great wrathful one, of awesome form, {247}
Having the nature of jealousy purified,
Tamer of all harmful beings without exception—
To Amṛitakuṇḍali, homage and praise!

With your right hand, you hold
A crossed vajra imposingly at your heart.
Your left rests on your hip, holding a bell.
To you who manifest thus I pay homage.

*sarva maṅgalaṃ*

# 9. A Mine of Blessings

*Authorization Ritual for Lord Vajrapāṇi*[1]

{250}
I pay homage to the ferocious wrathful one,
The vajra-bearing lord who dwells in the midst
Of a fiercely blazing fire of self-arisen gnosis,
Destroying all the defilements of the three worlds like firewood.

The order for his authorization ritual
I shall now write down, without mistake,
Exactly as I heard my teacher say.
For this, I ask for the blessings of the teacher and ḍākinīs.

This authorization ritual for the lord Vajra Ferocity has three main sections: (1) preliminaries; (2) main part; and (3) conclusion.

### I. Preliminaries

The preliminaries are divided into two: (1) material arrangements and (2) practicing the sādhana and taking the self-empowerment.

### A. Material Arrangements

Draw a blue mandala of a ten-petaled lotus, with multicolored petals, and in the middle of the lotus a blue wheel with ten spokes. On its hub and spokes draw ten blue *hūṁ* syllables. Around, arrange the offerings and tormas in a circle. Prepare the activity vase as well, with its ornamental stopper and ribbon tied around the neck.

## B. Practicing the Sādhana and Taking the Self-Empowerment

This second part is divided into seven sections. First, take refuge and arouse bodhichitta. Second, do the meditation and recitation of the hundred syllables. Third, accumulate merit by performing the seven branches. Fourth, meditate on the four boundless attitudes. These four sections follow the usual form.

Fifth, to meditate on the protection circle, dissolve everything into emptiness with the *svabhāva* mantra.

> From the state of emptiness there appears the syllable *hūṁ*, which transforms into a crossed vajra, its eastern section white, the southern yellow, the western red, and the northern green. The hub is blue, with a dark-blue *hūṁ* in its center, from which light radiates, [giving rise to] the ground of vajras underneath, the vajra fence and net in all the directions around, the vajra tent and canopy above, and, everywhere outside, the blazing wisdom fire.

Meditating on this constitutes the protection circle.

Sixth, the stages of the visualization are twofold: the self-visualization and the front visualization. For the first of these:

> From the state of emptiness there appears a syllable *paṃ*, which transforms into a multicolored lotus. From *raṃ* appears the mandala of the sun, on which are eleven blue *hūṁ* syllables, {251} emanating infinite rays of light, which subjugate all malicious spirits and obstacle makers and convert them to the doctrine. The light rays are gathered back and transform into myself as Vajra Ferocity. His body is blue in color, with a reddish hue. He has one face and two hands, and he is poised with his right leg bent and his left extended. He is wearing a skirt made of a fresh tiger skin. He has an enormous chest and belly and heavy limbs and appendages. His right hand holds a golden nine-spoked vajra up in the air, and from the tip of his threatening index finger issue forth garuḍa envoys. His left hand, in the threatening gesture, holds at the level of his heart a white silver bell, while from the tip of the index finger fire blazes forth. His mouth is open, baring his

> four white pointed canine teeth. His tongue is rolled against the palate. Grimacing wrathfully, he rolls his three red eyes, in which the fire of the end of the kalpa blazes. His orange hair streams upward, the rest hanging down. His head is adorned with the yellow [nāgas] Abundant Wealth and Guardian of the Conches. His earrings are the red [nāgas] Joyous and Friend. His bracelets and anklets are the white [nāgas] Lotus and Water God. And he is decorated with a belt and sash in the form of the black [nāgas] Eagle and Excellent. His upper garment is of blue silk, and he is adorned with the five kinds of jewels, radiating light. He has a silken crown and is present in the midst of the blazing fire of gnosis. The ten wrathful ones, with the same attributes as myself, are visualized with their faces looking in toward me.
>
> All these deities are marked with a white *oṁ* in the crown center, {252} a red *āḥ* in the throat center, and blue *hūṁ* in the heart center. From these, light radiates, inviting from the Willow Leaf buddha field the wisdom deities, in the same form as myself. With *jaḥ hūṁ baṃ hoḥ*, they dissolve into me inseparably. Once more, the buddhas of the five families are invited and bestow empowerment, purifying obscurations. As the nectar overflows, I consider that I am adorned on my crown with the buddhas of the five families, Akṣhobhya and the others.

This is the self-visualization.

Second, the front visualization. Just you did for the self-visualization, again visualize on the mandala in front Vajrapāṇi surrounded by the ten wrathful ones. Dissolve the wisdom deities into them and apply the seal of empowerment.

> Inside the activity vase is Amṛitakuṇḍali . . .

Go through this visualization as in the source text, and apply the seal of empowerment and so on in the general manner. Next:

> In my heart center, upon a lotus and sun,
> Is a blue vajra marked with a *hūṁ*,
> Surrounded by the mantra garland,
> *vajrapāṇi hūṁ*

or alternatively,

> *oṁ vajra caṇḍa mahā roṣaṇa hūṁ phaṭ*
> From it light radiates, touching the outer world and purifying it as the Willow Leaf buddha field. It touches the inhabitants and sets them on the level of Vajra Ferocity. The lights are gathered back, and I consider that all illnesses, negative forces, evil deeds, and obscurations are burned up. The mantra chain comes out of my mouth and enters the mouths of the deities visualized in front and visualized in the vase. As it circles their heart centers, their wisdom minds are invoked. And as the mantra resounds, from all the parts of their bodies a stream of nectar flows down, filling the vase.

Concentrating on this, recite the mantra. After that, make the offerings and praise to them, and offer the torma, praying for the fulfillment of your wishes.

Seventh, take the self-empowerment. In the order that occurs below, take the self-empowerment by means of concentration.

## II. Main Part

The main part is divided into two: (1) the preliminaries for the authorization ritual and (2) the main authorization ritual.

### A. Preliminaries for the Authorization Ritual {253}

Cleanse the disciples with the water from the activity vase and have them be seated. Give the torma for the obstacle makers, banish the obstacle makers, and meditate on the protection circle. Then, with

> In order to request the authorization from the teacher, offer a mandala,

have them offer the mandala. After that, the teacher gives the refuge vow:

> Teacher Vajrapāṇi, and buddhas and bodhisattvas, think of us.
> Until we reach the heart of enlightenment,

We go for refuge in the buddhas.
Likewise, we go for refuge in the dharma
And in the assembly of bodhisattvas.

By their saying this three times, the refuge vow is given. Next, taking the vow of bodhichitta:

Just as the sugatas of the past
Aroused the intent to attain enlightenment
And practiced in stages
The training of the bodhisattvas,
Likewise, for the benefit of beings,
We arouse the intent to attain enlightenment,
And likewise will we also train in stages
In that same training.
We will take across those who have not crossed over;
We will free those who have not been freed;
We will bring relief to those who have not been relieved
And set all beings in the state beyond suffering.

This should be said three times. Next, the disciples should accumulate merit with the seven branches:

To the essence of the Three Jewels,
The teacher Vajrapāṇi, we submit obeisance.
We offer outer, inner, and secret offerings.
Each and every one of our negative deeds we confess.
We rejoice in beings' virtue.
Turn the wheel of dharma, we pray,
And stay without passing into nirvana.
By the merit of this, may all beings attain buddhahood.

This should be recited three times.

With this, the preliminaries have been completed. {254}

### [B. Main Authorization Ritual]

> Next, for the second and main part, there are five sections: the authorizations for the Body, Speech, Mind, Qualities, and Activities. First, to request the Body authorization, offer the mandala with Mount Meru and the four continents.
>
> Next, say this prayer:
>
> O teacher, sovereign of compassion, Vajrapāṇi,
> Fearful of samsara, we pray, hold us with compassion.
> Frightened and threatened in the dark city of beings,
> We pray to you.
> As we touch the dust beneath your feet,
> Grant us the authorization [to enter] the city of nirvana,
> great bliss.

This should be recited three times. After that, the master gives his assent:

> The sunlight of my compassion
> Clears away the darkness of ignorance.
> Your body, speech, and mind
> Are blessed by the enlightened body, speech, and mind.

Next, cleanse the disciples with the *amṛta* mantra and purify them with the *svabhāva* mantra. Visualize Vajrapāṇi as in the sādhana.

> Consider that from the seed syllable in the heart of the master and the principal figure in the mandala, who are indistinguishable, lights radiate, touching all the buddhas and bodhisattvas in the ten directions. They all appear in the form of Vajrapāṇi, as countless tiny bodies, visualized clearly with their distinct features and symbolic attributes, vajras and bells. From the teacher's body too, countless bodies of Vajrapāṇi emanate. They [all] dissolve into the disciples' bodies like snow falling on a lake.

Burn incense and play music. The master places an image [of Vajrapāṇi] on the disciples' heads or, alternatively, throws flowers, chanting:

Lord Vajrapāṇi, bestow [your blessing] on this [person]; {255}
Impregnate this person [with your nature], I pray.[2]
*oṁ vajrapāṇi jaḥ hūṁ baṃ hoḥ*

Then say:

The benefits of receiving the Body authorization like this are both temporary and ultimate. On the temporary level, you will be at peace from all illnesses, negative forces, evil deeds, obscurations, and obstacles related to the body. On the ultimate level, you will acquire the powerful enlightened body of Vajrapāṇi.

Second, to request the Speech authorization, offer a mandala.

The request is as above.

Next, in the heart centers of both the master and disciples visualized as Vajrapāṇi are a lotus and sun, on which is a syllable *hūṁ*, surrounded by the mantra. The mantra chain, like a string of molten beryl, comes out of the [master's] mouth, enters the mouths of the disciples, and encircles [the syllable in] the heart. Concentrate on this.
*oṁ vajrapāṇi hūṁ phaṭ svāhā*
*oṁ vajra caṇḍa mahā roṣaṇa hūṁ phaṭ*

Taking hold of the rosary, make [the disciples] repeat the mantra after you twenty-one times. At the end, touch the disciples at the throat center with the rosary as you say:

Lord, bestow the knowledge mantra on this [person];
Impregnate this person [with it], I pray.

Make the disciples too repeat these lines, adapting them accordingly.

The benefits of this are both temporary and ultimate. On the temporary level, you will gain the great power of the mantra and proficiency in oral explanation, debate, and composition. And on the ultimate level, you will accomplish words of truth and acquire the speech of the buddhas that possesses the sixty expressive qualities.

Third, to request the Mind authorization, offer a mandala.

The request is as above.

Next, the disciples should adopt the essential point of the body, the seven-point posture of Vairochana. Concentrate on a blue syllable *hūṁ* in the air in front. {256} Next, your body disappears into a rainbow body and dissolves into the syllable *hūṁ* in the air in front. Direct your awareness toward that.

Consider that the *hūṁ* disappears, like a rainbow vanishing in the sky. Remain in meditative equipoise, in the state of mind free from concepts.

The benefits of this are both temporary and ultimate. On the temporary level, you will develop extraordinary concentration in your mind stream, and on the ultimate level, you will realize the actual condition of things—the body of truth, radiant light, the mind of the buddhas.

Fourth, to request the Qualities authorization, offer a mandala.

The request is as above.

Next, the disciples should visualize themselves as Vajrapāṇi.

The master places a vajra in the disciples' right hands and a bell in their left hands and says:

These are the symbolic attributes of Vajrapāṇi, the vajra and bell. If you always keep them with you, you will acquire all the qualities of the buddhas, who unite skillful means and wisdom. The benefits of this are both temporary and ultimate. On the temporary level, you will accomplish all the qualities of the path. On the ultimate level, you will achieve all the qualities of the buddhas.

Fifth, to request the Activities authorization, offer a mandala.

The request is as above.

Next, the disciples should visualize themselves as Vajrapāṇi and consider that their bodies are adorned with the eight great nāgas.

Give them the snake ornaments.

Consider that the upper part of the body is wrapped in the upper garment of blue silk and that the lower part of the body is wrapped in the skirt of tiger skin.

Wrap their upper bodies with the blue silk garment and their lower bodies with the tiger-skin skirt.

Next, {257} visualize in the five centers of both the master and disciples the five garuḍas of the five families.

Consider that from the garuḍas of the five families in the teacher's five centers, garuḍas of the five families emanate and dissolve into the five garuḍas in the disciples' five centers.

Place the five miniatures of the garuḍas in order at the disciples' five centers, as you say:

*oṁ buddha garuḍa cale cale hūṁ phaṭ*
*padma garuḍa cale cale hūṁ phaṭ*
*vajra garuḍa cale cale hūṁ phaṭ*
*ratna garuḍa cale cale hūṁ phaṭ*
*karma garuḍa cale cale hūṁ phaṭ*
*jaḥ hūṁ baṃ hoḥ*

The benefits of this are twofold. On the temporary level, you will accomplish the four activities and benefit sentient beings on a vast scale. And on the ultimate level, you will accomplish the activities of the buddhas effortlessly and spontaneously.

After that, [the disciples] should make offerings of gratitude and perform the mandala offering to the teacher. Then they should say:

> From now on, I offer myself . . .[3]

and so on.

## III. Conclusion

The concluding parts of the ritual, such as the thanksgiving offerings and praise through to the request to the deity to depart, are the same as in other [authorizations].

This completes the authorization ritual for Lord Vajrapāṇi entitled *A Mine of Blessings,* which the yogi Öpak Dorje wrote down in accordance with what his teacher had said.
*maṅgalaṃ*

# 10. Authorization Ritual for Lord Amitāyus[1]

{260}

I bow to the Buddha of Boundless Light,
Whose mountain-like body shines with infinite light,
Whose voice is as sweet as the divine sound of the celestial drum,
Whose mind has the power of knowing all there is to know.

These steps for his authorization ritual
Are the words of my sublime and glorious teacher,
Which I shall write down clearly, without mistake.
For this, I ask for the blessings of the teacher and ḍākinīs.

This authorization ritual for the lord and protector Amitāyus has three main sections: (1) preliminaries; (2) main part; and (3) conclusion.

## I. Preliminaries

The preliminaries are divided into three: (1) material arrangements; (2) practicing the sādhana; and (3) taking the self-empowerment.

### A. Material Arrangements

Prepare a mandala of an eight-petaled lotus, with a red center, the four directions in their respective colors, and the intermediate directions beautifully colored. In the middle, put the symbol of the deity or a pile of grain representing the deity. Around, arrange the offerings and tormas in a circle. On a tripod in the middle of the mandala, place the all-victorious vase [prepared] according to the source text. In addition, prepare the activity vase, with its ornamental stopper and ribbon tied around the neck. Besides these, collect and set out everything necessary [for the ritual].

**B. Practicing the Sādhana**

To practice the self-visualization and front visualization, in a secluded place, sit on a comfortable seat and begin by taking refuge, arousing bodhichitta, performing the seven branches, and meditating on the four boundless attitudes in the general manner.

For this particular practice, dissolve everything into emptiness with the *svabhāva* mantra.

> From the state of emptiness, the place in which I am appears as the completely pure Blissful buddha field, made of rubies, a beautiful and delightful [environment], in the middle of which is a throne made of different kinds of precious materials, supported by peacocks. On top of it, from the syllable *paṃ*, there appears a multicolored lotus, and from the letter *A*, the mandala of the full moon. In the middle of that, there is a red syllable *hrīḥ*, the nature of my own mind, from which light radiates, fulfilling the two goals. {261} [The light] is gathered back and [the syllable melts] into light, from which I visualize myself as the lord and protector Amitāyus. He is red in color, like a mountain of rubies, sitting with his two legs crossed in the vajra posture. His two hands are in the gesture of meditation, and on them he holds the vase of immortal life, filled with wisdom nectar. His smiling face is beautified by almond eyes, long eyebrows, a prominent nose, and his broad forehead with a coil of white hair between the brows. The hair on his head is dressed in a topknot, with locks hanging down. He is beautifully adorned with numerous precious ornaments—the crest ornament of five precious materials, earrings, necklet, long necklace, armlets, bracelets, belt, anklets, and so forth. The thirty-two major marks and eighty minor marks embellish and complete his beauty and perfection. He shines with rays of light, reaching to the ends of space.
>
> In his crown center is a white *oṁ*, in the throat center a red *āḥ*, and in the heart center a blue *hūṁ*. From them light radiates,

> inviting from the Blissful buddha field the lord, in the same form as myself, surrounded by the buddhas and bodhisattvas of the ten directions, who all dissolve inseparably into me. Once more, light radiates, inviting the buddhas of the five families and their retinues, who bestow empowerment, purifying obscurations. As the nectar overflows, I consider that I am adorned on my crown by the buddhas of the five families, Amitābha and the others.

After that,

> In my heart center, upon a lotus and moon, is a red syllable *hrīḥ*, the nature of my own mind, surrounded by the long mantra. From it lights radiate. As they touch the outer universe, it becomes the measureless palace; {262} as they touch the inhabitants, they become Amitābha. The rays of light are gathered back and dissolve into me. [The mantra] turns in my heart center.

Visualizing this, recite the mantra. Use this same method to practice both the front visualization and the vase visualization.

> Inside the activity vase, on a lotus and sun, is the syllable *hrīḥ*, from which I visualize Hayagrīva, who is red and poised with one leg extended, the other bent. His right hand holds a mace; his left gestures threateningly. His mouth is agape, baring his four white canine teeth. He rolls his three red eyes. His eyebrows and beard are orange. His yellow hair, tinged dark red, swirls over his head. Above his crown is the green head of a horse, neighing into space, its red mane blazing like the fire at the end of the kalpa. He is adorned with the snake and jewel ornaments and is wearing a tiger-skin skirt.
>
> The wisdom deity dissolves into him. The buddhas of the five families bestow empowerment, applying the seal of Amitābha.
>
> Then, from the syllable *hrīḥ* in my heart, surrounded by the mantra chain, rays of light emanate. They enter the mouths of the deities in the front visualization and the all-victorious vase, encircle their heart centers, and invoke their wisdom minds.
>
> As they pronounce the mantra, from all the parts of their bodies a stream of nectar flows down, filling the vase.

Concentrating on this, recite the mantra a hundred times or so.

> Again, from the *hrīḥ* in my heart center light radiates, invoking the wisdom mind of the deity in the activity vase . . .

and so on, as above. Visualize:

> From the *hrīḥ* in the heart center of Hayagrīva

surrounded by

> *oṁ padmānta kṛta vajra krodha hayagrīva hulu hulu hūṁ phaṭ*

After reciting [this mantra], make the offerings and praises to them, {263} offer the torma, and say prayers. Then, consider that:

> The deity in the activity vase melts into light and becomes the vase water.

### [C. Taking the Self-Empowerment]

Perform the cleansing with the vase water and, following the order described below, take the self-empowerment by means of concentration.

## II. Main Part

The main part is divided into two: (1) the preliminaries for the authorization ritual and (2) the main authorization ritual.

### A. Preliminaries for the Authorization Ritual

Cleanse the disciples with the water from the activity vase and have them be seated. Give the torma for the obstacle makers, banish the obstacle makers, and meditate on the protection circle. Next, [the disciples] should offer the teacher a mandala.

The teacher[2] then gives the refuge vow, saying:

> Fold your hands and repeat after me.

Master, think of us.
Until we reach the heart of enlightenment,
We go for refuge in the buddhas.
Likewise do we go for refuge in the dharma
And in the assembly of bodhisattvas.

By their saying this three times, the refuge vow is given. Next, the vow of bodhichitta:

Just as the sugatas of the past
Aroused the intent to attain enlightenment
And practiced in stages
The training of the bodhisattvas,
Likewise, for the benefit of beings,
We arouse the intent to attain enlightenment,
And likewise will we also train in stages
In that same training.
We will take across those who have not crossed over;
We will free those who have not been freed;
We will bring relief to those who have not been relieved
And set all beings in the state beyond suffering.

The vow is taken by the saying of this three times. Next, perform the seven branches:

To the essence of the Three Jewels,
The teacher Amitāyus, we submit obeisance.
We offer outer, inner, and secret offerings. {264}
Each and every one of our negative deeds we confess.
We rejoice in beings' virtue.
Turn the wheel of dharma, we pray,
And stay without passing into nirvana.
We dedicate the merit to the great enlightenment.

This should be recited three times.

With this, the preliminaries have been completed.

**[B. Main Authorization Ritual]**

> Next, for the second and main part, there are five sections: the authorizations for the Body, Speech, Mind, Qualities, and Activities. First, to request the Body authorization, offer the mandala with Mount Meru and the four continents.
>
> Now say this prayer:
>
> O teacher, sovereign of compassion, Amitāyus,
> Fearful of samsara, we pray, hold us with compassion.
> Frightened and threatened in the dark city of beings,
> We pray to you.
> As we touch the dust below your feet,
> Grant us the authorization [to enter] the city of nirvana,
> great bliss.

This should be recited three times. After that, the master gives his assent:

> The sunlight of my compassion
> Clears away the darkness of ignorance.
> Your body, speech, and mind
> Are blessed by the enlightened body, speech, and mind.

Next, cleanse the disciples with the *amṛta* mantra and purify them with the *svabhāva* mantra. Visualize Amitāyus as in the sādhana.

> Visualize in the hearts of the master and the [deity] in the mandala, who are indistinguishable, the syllable *hrīḥ*.
>
> From it, lights radiate, touching all the buddhas and bodhisattvas in the ten directions.
>
> They all appear in the form of Amitāyus, as countless tiny bodies, visualized clearly with their distinct features and symbolic attributes. {265}
>
> From the teacher's body too countless bodies of Amitāyus emanate.
>
> They [all] dissolve into the disciples' bodies like snow falling on a lake.

Throw flowers, or alternatively, place an image [of Amitāyus] on [the disciples'] heads, to the accompaniment of incense and music, as the master chants:

> Lord Amitāyus, bestow [your blessing] on this [person];
> Impregnate this person [with your nature], I pray.
> *oṁ hrīḥ amideva jaḥ hūṁ baṃ hoḥ*

> The benefits of receiving the Body authorization like this are both temporary and ultimate. On the temporary level, you will be at peace from all illnesses, negative forces, evil deeds, obscurations, and obstacles related to the body. On the ultimate level, you will acquire the enlightened body of Amitāyus, adorned with the major and minor marks. That is its purpose.

> Second, to request the Speech authorization, offer a mandala.

The request is as above.

> Next, consider that in the heart centers of the master and disciples visualized as Amitāyus are a red eight-petaled lotus and on it a moon disk. On top of that is a red syllable *hrīḥ*, complete with visarga, surrounded by the long mantra. Then the red mantra chain, like a string of red pearls, comes straight out of the teacher's mouth, enters the mouths of the disciples, and encircles the syllable *hrīḥ* in the heart. Concentrate on this.

Taking hold of the rosary, make [the disciples] repeat the long dhāraṇī after you twenty-one times. Then, touching the disciples at the throat center with the rosary, the master says:[3]

> Lord Amitāyus, bestow the knowledge mantra on this [person];
> Impregnate this person [with it], I pray.

Make the disciples too repeat these lines, adapting them accordingly. {266}

> The benefits of this are both temporary and ultimate. On the temporary level, you will gain the great power of the mantra and proficiency in oral explanation, debate, and composition. And

on the ultimate level, you will accomplish words of truth and acquire the speech of the buddhas that possesses the sixty expressive qualities.

Third, to request the Mind authorization, offer a mandala.

The request is as above.

Next, the disciples should adopt the essential point of the body, the seven-point posture of Vairochana. Concentrate on a red syllable *hrīḥ* in the air in front, glowing with light.

Next, your body disappears into a rainbow body and dissolves into the syllable *hrīḥ* in the air in front. Direct your awareness on that.

At the end, consider that that *hrīḥ* disappears, like a rainbow vanishing in the sky. Remain in meditative equipoise, without thinking of anything, in the state of mind beyond concepts, clear and empty, free of grasping.

This was the Mind authorization. The benefits of this are both temporary and ultimate. On the temporary level, you will develop extraordinary concentration in your mind stream, and on the ultimate level, you will realize the actual condition of things—the body of truth, radiant light, the mind of the buddhas.

Fourth, to request the Qualities authorization, offer a mandala.

The request is as above.

Next, the disciples should visualize themselves as Amitāyus.

The master places the all-victorious vase on the disciples' heads:

Consider that inside this vase is Amitāyus, and that from the vase in his hands a stream of nectar flows down. It enters the disciples' crowns, purifying all the negative deeds and obscurations in their bodies, {267} and the whole of the inside of their bodies is filled with wisdom nectar, suffused with red.

As you empower them with the vase, say:

> *oṁ hrīḥ amideva abhiṣiñca maṃ*

and give them the water from the vase to drink. Place the vase in the disciples' hands as they sit in meditation, and say:

> Meditate that I am giving you this vase full of nectar that Lord Amitāyus [holds] in his hands and that you thereby attain the accomplishment of immortal life and realize the level of Amitābha.

Give them the water from the vase to drink.

> This was the Qualities authorization. The benefits of this are both temporary and ultimate. On the temporary level, you will accomplish all the qualities of the path. On the ultimate level, you will achieve all the qualities of the body, speech, and mind of the buddhas.
>
> Fifth, to request the Activities authorization, offer a mandala.

The request is as above.

> Next, the disciples should visualize themselves as Amitābha, and as the master attaches the precious crown to the disciples' heads, consider that their bodies are adorned with the jewel ornaments, clothed in upper and lower garments of red silk, and adorned with the infinite qualities of the body of perfect enjoyment such as the major and minor marks of the buddhas.
>
> The benefits of this are twofold. On the temporary level, you will accomplish the four activities and bring vast benefit to sentient beings. And on the ultimate level, you will accomplish the activities of the buddhas effortlessly and spontaneously. {268} This is its purpose.

After that, [the disciples] should make the mandala offering in gratitude to the teacher. Then they should say three times:

From now on, I offer myself
To you as your servant.
Accept me as your disciple,
And use even the smallest part of me.

Prostrating to the teacher three times, they should say, "Thank you!"

### III. Conclusion

For the conclusion, make the thanksgiving offerings and praise. Restore any excesses and omissions with the hundred-syllable mantra. Dedicate the merit to unsurpassable enlightenment. Recite verses of auspiciousness. Request the wisdom deity to depart and dissolve the meditational deity into yourself.

Leave no trace [of the ritual].[4]

After that, the master and disciples should enjoy the feast.

This method is as taught by my teacher.
It is without errors or mistakes and conveys the complete sense.
I, the yogi Öpak Dorje, wrote it down with the intention of benefiting others.
By this merit may all beings attain the level of Amitābha.

May virtue and excellence increase.

# 11. Authorization Ritual for Tārā

*Who Protects Us from the Eight Fears and Frees Us from the Perilous Passage of Samsara*[1]

{270}
Lady, you who give us total freedom from the eight great fears,
Who have gained the state of fearlessness and vanquished Māra's
hordes,
A pilot saving us from the ocean of samsara,
Protect me and all beings, O venerable goddess.

This profound instruction for authorizing one to practice her,
Transmitted through the aural lineage, I shall now write down.

The authorization ritual has ten main sections: material preparations; visualization; taking the self-empowerment; admitting the disciples;[2] the authorization rituals for the body, speech, mind, qualities, and activities; and the concluding rituals.

First, the mandala is a circle with four segments. Its center is green, the east blue, the south yellow, the west red, and the north white. In the middle, place a [syllable] *taṃ* or else arrange a pile of grain to symbolize the deity. Around it, arrange the offerings, tormas, and activity vase.

Second, the refuge, bodhichitta, and seven branches and four boundless attitudes. Dissolve all into emptiness and then:

> From the state of emptiness appears a pure buddha field.
> In its center meditate on the protection circle and visualize the
> sublime measureless palace,

With porch and pinnacle, and in its center, a blue lake and grassy isle,
And in the middle, upon an utpala and full moon, is Tārā.
She is the color of an emerald, with one face and two hands,
The right [foot] stretched out, the left folded in; she wears a silken skirt.
Her right hand is in the gesture of supreme gift and holds a fully bloomed utpala;
Her left hand holds the stem of an utpala at heart level,
With its fully bloomed petals at the level of her ear.
Her smiling face is beautified by almond eyes and long eyebrows.
The locks of her hair are embellished by a jeweled crown,
And she is beautifully adorned with earrings, a necklet, bracelets, anklets,
And a headdress of multicolored silk.
With her fully developed breasts, she has the appearance of a sixteen-year-old maiden.
Though she appears, she has no intrinsic existence, like the image in a mirror.
Visualize her clearly
and then dissolve the wisdom deity.

Empowerment is taken, sealed with gnosis. Such is the self-visualization.

In the heart center is a lotus, moon, and *taṃ*, {271}
Surrounded by the mantra garland, from which lights purify the world and its inhabitants.

In this manner, do the front visualization and perform the offerings and praise.

Third, to the deities of the mandala in front, offer the mandala, pray, and take empowerment by means of concentration.[3]

Fourth, give the vows of refuge and bodhichitta and the commitments of the seven branches:

Master, think of us.
Until we reach the heart of enlightenment,
We go for refuge in the buddhas.

Likewise, we go for refuge in the dharma
And in the assembly of bodhisattvas.

By their saying this three times, the refuge vow is given. Next, the vow of bodhichitta:

Just as the sugatas of the past
Aroused the intent to attain enlightenment
And practiced in stages
The training of the bodhisattvas,
Likewise, for the benefit of beings,
We arouse the intent to attain enlightenment,
And likewise will we also train in stages
In that same training.
We will take across those who have not crossed over;
We will free those who have not been freed;
We will bring relief to those who have not been relieved
And set all beings in the state beyond suffering.

The bodhichitta is aroused by their saying this three times. Next, perform the seven branches:

To the essence of the Three Jewels,
The teacher Tārā, we submit obeisance.
We offer outer, inner, and secret offerings.
Each and every one of our negative deeds we confess.
We rejoice in beings' virtue.
Turn the wheel of dharma, we pray,
And stay without passing into nirvana.
We dedicate the merit to the great enlightenment.

This should be recited three times.

Fifth, to the deity in the mandala and the teacher, who are inseparable, offer the mandala, make the request, and [go through] the stages of the authorization:[4]

From the body of the teacher, Tārā, light radiates, {272}
And countless [deities' bodies] dissolve into the disciples' bodies.

Consider that blessings for obtaining the body of Tārā enter you.[5]
*oṁ tāre tuttāro jaḥ hūṁ baṃ hoḥ*
This was the authorization for Tārā's body.
The benefits of this are both temporary and ultimate.
Temporarily you will purify all physical misdeeds and
obscurations,
And ultimately you will acquire the body of Tārā,
Endowed with the major and minor marks—that is its purpose.

Sixth, the Speech authorization, for which a mandala is offered and the request made:

O teacher, sovereign of compassion, Mother Tārā . . .

and so on.[6]

Or alternatively:

Just as the revered noble Tārā
Gave authorization to Mitra himself,
Likewise, Teacher, grant us, please,
The authorization of the Body.[7]

In similar manner, adapt this verse to the context, to read "[authorization of the] Speech," "Mind," "Qualities," or "Activities."

As for what to concentrate on:

Consider that in the heart center of the teacher Tārā, upon a lotus
and moon,
Is the syllable *taṃ* surrounded by the mantra garland, which issues
forth
From the teacher's mouth and enters the disciples' mouths,
Dissolving into the *taṃ* in their hearts.

Holding the *mālā*, recite the mantra twenty-one times.

This was the authorization for Tārā's speech.
The benefits of this are both temporary and ultimate.
Temporarily, you will gain the great power of the mantra

And proficiency in oral explanation, debate, and composition.
And ultimately, you will accomplish words of truth
And acquire the speech of the buddhas
Endowed with the sixty expressive qualities.

This is the proclamation of the [resultant] realization.

Seventh, the Mind authorization, for which a mandala is offered and the request made:

In the sky in front is the green syllable *taṃ*:
Your mind and body dissolve into light.
Rest in meditative equipoise, the unborn state, clear and empty. {273}
This was the authorization for Tārā's mind.
The benefits of this are both temporary and ultimate.
Temporarily, extraordinary concentration will develop in your mind stream,
And ultimately, you will know the ultimate reality as it is
And all phenomena as many as there are—that is its purpose.

Eighth, the Qualities authorization:

Consider that the utpala in the teacher Tārā's hand
Is entrusted to you and becomes your symbolic attribute
And that you acquire all Tārā's qualities.
This was the authorization for Tārā's qualities.
The benefits of this are both temporary and ultimate.
Temporarily, you will achieve all the qualities of the path.
Ultimately, you will gain all the qualities
Of Tārā's body, speech, and mind—that is its purpose.

Ninth, the Activities authorization:

Visualize yourself as Tārā, and in your five centers
Clearly visualize the five families of Tārā.
After that, the green Tārā in the secret center
Dissolves into the yellow Tārā in the navel. The yellow one in turn
Dissolves into the blue Tārā in the heart center. The blue one in turn

Dissolves into the red Tārā in the throat center. The red one in turn
Dissolves into the white Tārā in the crown center. Everything
[Dissolves] as if the sky were filled with rainbow light.
Rest in meditative equipoise without fabrication, in the state of clarity-emptiness.
This was the authorization for Tārā's activities.
The benefits of this are both temporary and ultimate.
Temporarily, you will accomplish the four activities
And bring vast benefit to sentient beings, and ultimately
The activities of the buddhas will occur, effortlessly and spontaneously—
That is its purpose.

This is the proclamation of realization.

Tenth, make offerings and praise, say prayers, make the request to depart, and pray, dedicate, and say prayers for auspiciousness.

These are the steps for giving the authorization for Tārā. {274}

This method is an essential pith instruction
Taught by my teacher, which I have set down in writing.
By this merit may all beings attain
The sublime level of the Lady Tārā.

May virtue and excellence increase.

# 12. Authorization Ritual for Noble Jambhala[1]

{276}
In the unborn space of the body of truth
The great clouds of the body of enjoyment gather
And the supreme body of manifestation rains down accomplishments.
To the spontaneous presence of the three buddha bodies,[2] the deity
Jambhala, I bow.

This authorization ritual for the venerable Jambhala has three main sections: (1) preliminaries; (2) main part; and (3) conclusion.

### I. Preliminaries

The preliminaries are divided into two: (1) material arrangements and (2) practicing the sādhana and taking the self-empowerment.

### A. Material Arrangements

Draw a mandala of an eight-petaled lotus, with a yellow center, the four directions in their respective colors, and the intermediate directions beautifully colored. On each of the eight petals draw a jewel. Around it, arrange the offerings and tormas in a circle. In addition, prepare the activity vase, with its ornamental stopper and ribbon tied around the neck. Besides these, collect and set out everything necessary for the authorization ritual.

## B. Practicing the Generation Stage

In a secluded place, sit on a comfortable seat, facing east, and begin by taking refuge, arousing bodhichitta, performing the seven branches, and meditating on the four boundless attitudes in the general manner.

In particular, dissolve everything into emptiness with the *svabhāva* mantra.

> From the state of emptiness appears a throne made out of many precious materials, decorated with intertwined vases. On top of it, from the syllable *paṃ* appears a multicolored lotus, and, from *A*, a full-moon disk, on which is a bījapūra fruit marked with the syllable *jaṃ*. From it rays of light emanate, making offerings to the hosts of noble beings and benefiting sentient beings. They are gathered back and transform into oneself as Jambhala, whose body glows like the purest gold. He is sitting with his two legs in the posture of royal ease. He wears an upper garment of multicolored silks, tied with a golden belt marked in the middle with a jewel. He has a large belly and well-developed limbs and joints. His right hand is resting on his knee in the gesture of supreme gift, holding a pañcapuraka fruit,[3] its center marked with a wish-fulfilling jewel. {277} In his left hand he holds a pouch in the form of a mongoose regurgitating different kinds of jewels. His face is slightly wrathful, slightly smiling, expansive like the mandala of the sun. His hair is tied up in a topknot, with the rest hanging down, and it is adorned with flower garland hair ribbons and a crown of five wish-fulfilling jewels glowing with light. He is adorned with many precious ornaments—earrings, necklet, armlets, bracelets, girdle, anklets, and a long necklace and tassels of precious gems and blue utpalas. He is beautified by a garland of five kinds of pearls and a silken headdress. He is seated in the middle of wreaths of five-colored light rays encircling him.
>
> In his crown center is a white *oṁ*, in the throat center a red *āḥ*, and in the heart center a blue *hūṁ*. From the *hūṁ* light radiates, inviting from the Willow Leaf buddha field the wisdom deity, who is like oneself. It dissolves inseparably.

Again, light radiates, inviting the buddhas of the five families, who bestow empowerment, purifying obscurations.

Consider that:

The excess nectar overflows and one's crown is ornamented by the buddhas of the five families, Ratnasambhava and the others.

In one's heart center is a lotus and moon, upon which is a jewel shining with light, its center marked with the syllable *jaṃ*, surrounded by the mantra. From it light radiates, touching the outer world, which transforms into the measureless palace, and touching its inhabitants, which become Jambhala. Gathered back, [the light] dissolves into oneself. Consider that it encircles the heart. Jambhalas present on the tips of the light rays cause a rain of five kinds of jewels to fall.

Concentrating on this, recite the mantra.

Next, the front visualization. On the mandala in front, visualize Jambhala just as you did for the self-visualization. Dissolve the wisdom deity. Receive empowerment and apply the seal.

Inside the activity vase is Amṛitakuṇḍali . . . {278}

Go through this visualization as in the source text, and apply the seal of empowerment and so on in the general manner. Then:

From one's heart center surrounded by the mantra chain, light radiates. It enters the mouths of the [deities] visualized in front and visualized in the vase, encircles their heart centers, and invokes their wisdom minds. As they pronounce the mantra, from all the parts of their bodies a stream of nectar flows down, filling the vase.

Concentrating on this, recite the mantra a hundred times or so. After that, make the offerings and praise to the deities, offer the torma, and say prayers for the fulfillment of wishes. Then, at this point, following the order described below, take the self-empowerment by means of concentration.

## II. Main Part

The main part is divided into two: (1) the preliminaries for the authorization ritual and (2) the main authorization ritual.

### A. Preliminaries for the Authorization Ritual

Cleanse the disciples with the water from the activity vase and have them be seated. Banish the obstacle makers and meditate on the protection circle. The mandala is offered. Then, to give the refuge vow, say:

> Fold your hands and repeat after me.
>
> > Master, think of us.
> > Until we reach the heart of enlightenment,
> > We go for refuge in the buddhas.
> > Likewise, we go for refuge in the dharma
> > And in the assembly of bodhisattvas.

By their saying this three times, the refuge vow is given. Next, give the vow of bodhichitta:

> Just as the sugatas of the past
> Aroused the intent to attain enlightenment
> And practiced in stages
> The training of the bodhisattvas,
> Likewise, for the benefit of beings,
> We arouse the intent to attain enlightenment,
> And likewise will we also train in stages
> In that same training.
> We will take across those who have not crossed over;
> We will free those who have not been freed;
> We will bring relief to those who have not been relieved
> And set all beings in the state beyond suffering.

The vow is taken by the saying of this three times. Next, perform the seven branches: {279}

> To the essence of the Three Jewels,
> The teacher Jambhala, we submit obeisance.

We offer outer, inner, and secret offerings.
Each and every one of our negative deeds we confess.
We rejoice in beings' virtue.
Turn the wheel of dharma, we pray,
And stay without passing into nirvana.
We dedicate the merit to the great enlightenment.

This should be recited three times.

With this, the preliminaries have been completed.

## [B. Main Authorization Ritual]

Next, for the second and main part, there are five sections: the authorizations for the Body, Speech, Mind, Qualities, and Activities. First, to request the Body authorization, offer the mandala. Next, say this prayer:

O teacher, sovereign of compassion, Jambhala,
Fearful of samsara, we pray, hold us with compassion.
Frightened and threatened in the dark city of beings,
We pray to you.
As we touch the dust below your feet,
Grant us the authorization [to enter] the city of nirvana,
great bliss.

Say this prayer three times. After that, the master gives his assent:

The sunlight of my compassion
Clears away the darkness of ignorance.
Your body, speech, and mind
Are blessed by the enlightened body, speech, and mind.

Next, cleanse the disciples with the *amṛta* mantra and purify them with the *svabhāva* mantra. Visualizing Jambhala as in the sādhana,

From the seed syllable in the hearts of the master and the [deity] in the mandala, who are indistinguishable, light radiates, touching all the buddhas and bodhisattvas in the ten directions. They all appear in the form of Jambhala, as countless tiny bodies,

> visualized clearly with their distinct features and symbolic attributes. From the teacher's body too, countless bodies of Jambhala emanate. {280} These flowers, inseparable from them, dissolve into the disciples' bodies like snow falling on a lake.

With this visualization, throw flowers, burn incense, and play music. Placing an image [of Jambhala] on the disciples' heads, the master chants:

> Lord, bestow [your blessing] on this [person];
> Impregnate this person [with your nature], I pray.
> *oṁ jambhala jalendraye jaḥ hūṁ baṃ hoḥ*

> The benefits of receiving the Body authorization like this are both temporary and ultimate. On the temporary level, you will be at peace from all illnesses, negative forces, evil deeds, obscurations, and obstacles related to the body. On the ultimate level, you will acquire the enlightened body of Jambhala, adorned with the major and minor marks. That is its purpose.

> Second, to request the Speech authorization, offer a mandala.

Make the request as above.

> Next, consider that in the heart centers of the master and disciples visualized as Jambhala is a moon disk, and on top of it a yellow syllable *jaṃ* surrounded by the mantra. Then the mantra chain, like a string of molten gold, comes straight out of the teacher's mouth, enters the mouths of the disciples, and encircles the syllable *jaṃ* in their hearts. Concentrate on this.

Taking hold of the rosary, make [the disciples] repeat the mantra after you twenty-one times.

> *oṁ jambhala jalendraye svāhā*

Then, touching the disciples at the throat center with the rosary, the master says:

Lord, bestow the knowledge mantra on this [person];
Impregnate this person [with it], I pray.

The benefits of this are both temporary and ultimate. On the temporary level, you will gain the great power of the mantra and proficiency in oral explanation, debate, and composition. And on the ultimate level, you will accomplish words of truth and gain the speech of the buddhas that possesses the sixty expressive qualities.

Third, to request the Mind authorization, offer a mandala. {281}

The request is as above.

Next, the disciples should adopt the essential point of the body, the seven-point posture of Vairochana. Concentrate on a yellow syllable *jaṃ*, the color of gold, in the air in front.

Next, your body disappears into a rainbow body and dissolves into the syllable *jaṃ* in the air in front. Direct your awareness on that.

Consider that the syllable *jaṃ* disappears, like a rainbow vanishing in the sky. Remain in meditative equipoise, in the state of mind free of all elaboration, clear and empty, like the perfectly pure sky.

This was the Mind authorization.

The benefits of this are both temporary and ultimate. On the temporary level, you will develop extraordinary concentration in your mind stream, and on the ultimate level, you will know the nature and multiplicity of ultimate reality. That is its purpose.

Fourth, to request the Qualities authorization, offer a mandala.

The request is as above.

Next, the disciples should visualize themselves as Jambhala.

The master places a jewel in the disciples' right hands, while saying:

This is the wish-fulfilling jewel, the symbolic attribute of noble Jambhala;
It will grant all wishes that are made in accord with the dharma.

Placing a mongoose in the disciples' left hands, he says:

This is the mongoose, noble Jambhala's symbolic attribute. Simply holding it will bring a rain of everything you could want or need. The benefits of this are both temporary and ultimate. On the temporary level, you will accomplish all the qualities of the path. On the ultimate level, you will achieve all the qualities of the body, speech, and mind of the buddhas.

Fifth, to request the Activities authorization, offer a mandala. {282}

The request is as above. Next,

The disciples should visualize themselves as Jambhala,
With jewels on their five limbs and on the five limbs of the deity in the mandala and the teacher, who are indistinguishable.
On the crown of the head is a white wish-fulfilling jewel,
On the right shoulder a red jewel,
On the left shoulder a blue jewel,
On the right hip a yellow jewel,
And on the left hip a green jewel, all glowing with light.
From these five, lights emanate and gather back in the form of jewels;
The wealth of buddhas and bodhisattvas in the ten directions;
Of Brahmā, Indra, and other gods,
Of the universal monarch, ruler of the billionfold universe;
And of the eight great nāgas, Jeweled Crest and the others,
And all the resources of the world and its inhabitants.
They dissolve into the jewels in the five locations of the deity in the mandala and the teacher, who are indistinguishable.
From those jewels, visualize numerous jewels of the five kinds emanating and dissolving into the jewels on the disciples, pouring down wealth like rain.

Touch [the disciples'] five places with the jewels, saying:

> With these five jewels, all the activities of pacification, increase, bringing under power, and forceful subjugation will be spontaneously accomplished, and everything you could want or need will be showered down on you.
>
> The benefits of these are both temporary and ultimate. On the temporary level, you will accomplish the four activities and bring vast benefit to sentient beings. And on the ultimate level, you will accomplish the activities of the buddhas effortlessly and spontaneously. That is its purpose.

After this, [the disciples] should make the mandala offering in gratitude to the teacher and then say three times:

> From now on, I offer myself . . . {283}

and so on.[4]

## III. Conclusion

Make the thanksgiving offerings and praise. Restore any excesses and omissions with the hundred-syllable mantra. Dedicate the merit to unsurpassable enlightenment. After that, say prayers for auspiciousness. Request the wisdom deity to depart and dissolve the meditational deity into yourself.

Leave no trace [of the ritual].[5]

This order of the authorization ritual for Lord Jambhala
Was arranged by Öpak Dorje without error or mistake,
Exactly as his teacher taught it.
By this merit may all beings swiftly attain enlightenment.

*sarva dāka lyāṇa bhavatu*

# 13. Routing the Hordes of Obstacle Makers

*An Authorization Ritual for the Protector of the Teachings, Draklha Gönpo*[1]

{286}
To the supreme refuge, peerless guide, protector of beings,
Who leads beings on the path to freedom in great bliss,
Who emanates light rays of great wisdom—
To Avalokiteshvara, possessor of enlightened mind, I bow.

From the complete teachings of the ocean of pith instructions
Of the graded path to enlightenment that came from him,
The instructions on those who were renowned as six deities
Were arranged without mistake by the supreme teacher,
Girti Ratna, in whose presence Buddhashrī
Prayed devotedly and wrote them down as six instructions.

This authorization ritual for the guardian of those teachings
Has been requested by the learned spiritual friend Sangye Özer.
Therefore, in order to benefit a few, I will arrange it here.

The powerful great deity, Glorious Protector,
Is dark red, with one face, two arms, and three eyes,
His four canines bared, his mouth agape, tongue rolled up.
His hair streams up, crowned with five dry skulls.
His right hand holds a club, his left a small vessel,
And he is adorned with a garland of fifty fresh skulls and a tiger-skin skirt.

He has two legs, one stretched out, the other folded in, and wears a
cloak of black silk.
Extremely awesome, his laugh resounds like thunder.
To you who pulverizes those who harm the teachings,
To glorious Drakgön I make homage and praise.

Here is a method for giving the authorization for the guardian of Avalokiteshvara's teachings on the graded path to enlightenment, the dharma protector Draklha Gönpo. It is divided into four main sections: (1) material preparations; (2) preliminaries; (3) the main part; and (4) the conclusion.

## I. Material Preparations

The first of these is divided into two: material preparations and preliminaries.

### A. Material Preparations

Set up a table an arrow's length square, and sprinkle it with the blood of a human, a horse, and a dog. On top of it draw a dark-blue triangle, with vajra [fence] and mountain of fire. In the middle of that set up an image of the protector or, alternatively, in the center, a dark-red *hūṁ*. Over it[2] place a tripod on which is displayed a triangular torma of the protector, beautifully ornamented with meat and blood. Plant an arrow with dark-red silk streamers. Arrange the offerings and tormas around in a circle. Prepare an activity vase containing the five medicinal substances, five fragrant ingredients, and so on. Recite the *amṛta* mantra and the mantra of Amṛitakuṇḍali and leave it [ready for use]. Prepare the torma for the local deities and the torma for the obstacle makers. The vajra master should then sit on a comfortable seat. {287}

### B. Preliminaries

The preliminaries are divided into two sections.

For the first, purify the offerings and tormas with the *yakṣa* mantra. Go through the refuge and bodhichitta and the generation stage, with stable visualization of the yidam deity. Give the torma for the local deities and command them.

For the torma for the obstacle makers, to summon them and make them enter, say the "power of truth," and dedicate [the torma] with the *ākāro* mantra. Banish them with the *sumbhani* mantra. Then, with the stable visualization of [oneself as] the yidam deity, create the protection circle.

## II. Preliminaries

For the preliminaries, there are four subsections. First, for the self-visualization, do the visualization[3] according to the sādhana. Second, for the front visualization, making the torma and mandala inseparable, follow the same order as the self-visualization. Third, for the vase visualization, visualize in the activity vase the deity that destroys the obstacle makers, invoke the wisdom deity, visualize the empowerment, and apply the seal.

> Then, from the heart center of myself visualized as the yidam deity, the mantra chain winds along the mantra thread, goes out, and touches the mouth of the wrathful deity,[4] so that through the resounding of the mantra and light rays from the mantra a stream of nectar flows down, filling the vase.

Concentrating on this, recite the mantra:

> *oṁ āḥ vighnān takrit ta hūṁ phaṭ*

At this point, make the offerings and praise in the general manner.

Fourth, take the self-empowerment. Take the self-empowerment in the same way as empowerment is bestowed on the disciples, described below.

## III. Main Part[5]

There are two parts: the preliminaries and the main authorization ritual.

### A. Preliminaries

The preliminaries to the main authorization ritual consist of seven sections: cleansing [the disciples], [giving] the torma for the obstacle makers, [offering] the mandala, giving refuge, bodhichitta, the seven branches, and requesting [the authorization].

First, lead the disciples outside the temple and, reciting whichever mantra is suitable, wash them with scented water, saying:

> With the most exquisite scents . . .[6]

or

> As from the moment of your birth . . .[7]

Then, have them take their seats inside.

Second, the torma for the obstacle makers. Dedicate it as above.

Third, the mandala offering. {288} Someone suitable should stand up and offer the mandala. It is good to offer it in the manner of this tradition.

Fourth, refuge. Telling the disciples to say their respective names, have them repeat three times:

> I, who am called . . . (*name*),
> Take refuge in the buddhas, supreme beings among humankind.
> I take refuge in the sacred dharma, supreme among all that is peaceful and free of attachment.
> I take refuge in the noble sangha of nonreturners, supreme among assemblies.

Fifth, arousing the bodhichitta.

> I will take across beings who have not crossed over;
> I will free those who have not been freed;
> I will bring relief to those who have not been relieved
> And set all beings in the state beyond suffering.

Sixth, the seven branches:

> To the Three Jewels I go for refuge . . . *down to*
> . . . To benefit beings all, may I achieve buddhahood.[8]

Seventh, the request, which is as below.

### [B. Main Authorization Ritual]

Second, the main part, for which there are six sections, related to body, speech, mind, qualities, activities, and entrustment.

For each of these, begin with the offering of the mandala and the prayer to request the authorization and proceed with the visualization, bestowal, and mantra recitation; throw flowers; and play music.

First, to request the Body authorization, offer a mandala. Now say the following prayer:

Just as the great wisdom protector
Gave authorization to Mitra himself,
Likewise, teacher, please bestow on us
The authorization for his body.

This prayer should be said three times. For the visualization, place the torma on the disciples' heads and transmit to them the detailed visualization of the glorious protector, saying,

Meditate that [the deity] is inseparable from this torma,

have them meditate with a clear visualization [of the deity]. {289}

Next, from the protector's body, or from his forehead, countless white protectors issue forth and dissolve into the disciples' bodies, so that illnesses, negative forces, evil deeds, and [untoward] circumstances and obstacles are removed.

Concentrating on that, recite the root mantra, with at the end *aveśaya a aḥ*, and play music and throw flowers.

Second, to request the Speech authorization, offer a mandala.

Just as the great wisdom protector
Gave authorization to Mitra himself,
Likewise, teacher, please bestow on us
The authorization for his speech.

After this request, for the visualization:

> Consider that in the protector's throat center is a red syllable *āḥ,* from which countless dark-red forms of the protector issue forth, dissolving into the disciples' speech. All [their] verbal misdeeds and faults are purified.

Placing the torma at the [disciples'] throat centers, say the root mantra, play music, and throw flowers, as before.

Third, to request the Mind authorization, offer a mandala.

The request should be made as above. For the visualization:

> Consider that in the protector's heart center is a syllable *hūṁ*, from which countless dark-blue forms of the protector issue forth, dissolving into the disciples' heart centers. All [their] mental misdeeds and faults are purified.

Placing the torma on the [disciples'] heart centers, say the root mantra, play music, and throw flowers, as before.

Fourth, to request the Qualities authorization, offer a mandala.

The request should be made as above. For the visualization:

> Consider that in the protector's navel center is a yellow syllable *ho,* from which countless dark-yellow forms of the protector issue forth, dissolving into the disciples' navel centers.

Placing the torma on the [disciples'] navel centers, play music, as before.

Fifth, to request the Activities authorization, offer a mandala.

The request should be made as above.

> Consider that in the protector's secret center is a green syllable

> *kṣa*, {290} from which countless green forms of the protector issue forth, dissolving into the disciples' secret centers.

Holding the torma on the [disciples'] secret centers, say the root mantra, play music, and throw flowers, as before. Then, have the disciples say:

> Wisdom Protector, bestow [your blessing] on me;
> Impregnate me [with your nature], I pray.

The teacher too should say:

> Lord, bestow [your blessing] on this [person];
> Impregnate this person [with your nature], I pray.

Sixth, entrustment. Placing the torma in the disciples' hands, say:

> Wisdom Protector,
> Until this disciple, whose name is . . . , attains buddhahood,
> Remove adverse conditions for practicing the path,
> Bring about favorable conditions [for doing so],
> Extend their dharma lineage and family line,
> And accomplish all their commands and activities.
>
> The protector gives his assent. Then the protector melts into light and transforms into nectar, inseparable from the torma. Consider that as a result of its being given to you, you will attain the two kinds of accomplishment.

[The disciples] should eat the torma. Do not give it to animals.

### IV. Conclusion

The disciples should offer the mandala in gratitude and say three times:

> Whatever the Lord commands,
> I will do.
> From now on, I offer myself

To you as your servant.
Accept me as your disciple,
And use even the smallest part of me.

As they say this three times, they should acknowledge [the teacher's] kindness.

After that, enjoy the feast offering. Go through the sections of requesting to depart, dissolving, dedicating, and saying prayers of aspiration and auspiciousness. Restore any excesses and omissions with the hundred-syllable mantra. Keep the sacred commitments properly, and do not give the colored powder of the mandala or the torma to those who are not included in the mandala.

This most profound authorization, the nectar from the mouth of
The supreme guardian of the teachings, who compassionately guides beings, {291}
Is an oral instruction transmitted just as Mitra and Shrīputra taught it.
It came down through the aural lineage of peerless Girti Ratna.[9]
To that incomparable being the master Sangye Özer
Respectfully made repeated requests and prayed.
This beautiful string of pearls, the nectar of his speech,
He arranged in writing without mistake, in the same perfect words.
By this merit, may we swiftly accomplish the level of the Great Compassionate One.

This authorization ritual for the great protector of the teachings Draklha Gönpo, entitled *Routing the Hordes of Obstacle Makers*, is even more profound than extremely profound teachings. It was requested by the learned great master Sangye Özer, who repeatedly beseeched the peerless Girti Ratna. In response to his request, Drakpa Rinchen, a practitioner of the supreme protector, composed this in the monastery of Dochen Pal. The scribe was Buddha Vajra. It should not be propagated to anyone except disciples who are suitable vessels, as there is a strict seal of secrecy not to do so.

Virtue!

PART FOUR

# Mitrayogin's Instructions on the Practices of the Six Deities

For each of the empowerments in the previous section there is a corresponding set of instructions, again all written by Öpak Dorje, with the exception of the Draklha sādhana, which was written by Drakpa Rinchen. And as with the empowerments, it is the instructions related to Avalokiteshvara that are the most detailed. They begin with a poem, *Vajra Verses on the Graded Path of Avalokiteshvara*, a highly condensed presentation of the entire path to enlightenment, from the preliminary practices, through the visualizations and mantra recitation of the generation stage, to the different practices of the perfection stage, culminating in the teachings on the intermediate state, or bardo. The *Vajra Verses* form the basis for the three texts that follow it: a complete sādhana, including an offering to the dharma protector and the feast offering; detailed instructions on the preliminary practices and generation and perfection stages—effectively a commentary on the *Vajra Verses*; and a supplement in the form of pith instructions.

The instructions for the other deities—Mañjushrī, Vajrapāṇi, Amitāyus, Green Tārā, and Yellow Jambhala—cover more or less the same ground but are less detailed. Sādhana texts for these deities are absent from *The Treasury of Precious Instructions*, which makes one suspect that they either have been lost or were never written down.

The section concludes with a prayer to the lineage teachers of the Avalokiteshvara sādhana (which can presumably serve equally for the practices of the other deities) and the sādhana of the protector of these teachings, Draklha Gönpo. Added on at the end of the lineage prayer is a sort of super-mantra combining the mantras of all the deities in this tradition.

# 14. Vajra Verses on the Graded Path of Avalokiteshvara[1]

Whether Mitrayogin received this poem from Avalokiteshvara and used it as the basis for the sādhana, pith instructions, and guide that he subsequently transmitted to his disciple Shrīputra or whether he himself composed it as a concise presentation of the teachings he received from Avalokiteshvara is not clear from the colophon. In any case, these few pages essentialize the instructions contained in the three texts that follow. Their condensed form is impossible to understand fully without the relevant commentary provided in those texts. The subject of the poem covers the entire path, from reflecting on the precious human life, through the preliminary practices, to the visualizations and mantra recitation of the generation stage and the different practices of the perfection stage, culminating in the teachings on the intermediate state, or bardo.

{294}
In Sanskrit: *Āryāvalokiteśvara bodhi māra gobha vakrama nāma*
In Tibetan: *'Phags pa spyan ras gzigs dbang phyug gi byang chub lam bsgom pa'i rim pa zhes bya ba*
In English: *Stages to Be Practiced on the Path to Enlightenment of Noble Avalokiteshvara*
I pay homage to noble Avalokiteshvara.

Those who have obtained the supreme empowerment
Should [go to] a blessed place possessing auspicious signs,

An isolated place where all the conditions are favorable.
In such a place the wise should practice.

Meditate on the difficulty of finding the freedoms and advantages,
This precious human life,
In terms of cause and effect, its nature, and analogies and their meanings;
Developing ever greater diligence, practice!

Meditate on the impermanence of the world and its inhabitants:
Death is certain; one will definitely die,
And the time of death is unpredictable.
At death, the things of this life will not help one, so renounce them.

The result of nonvirtue is suffering;
With virtuous deeds happiness is gained;
Mixed deeds give rise to a mixture of pain and joy,
So, beginning with the smallest things, take up virtue and give up evil.

In samsara, everywhere and all the time,
One is never exempt from the three kinds of suffering.
Those who wish for certain deliverance from that
Must meditate properly on this truth.

Those who fear[2] the sufferings of samsara
Go for refuge in the Three Jewels.
They guard the precepts of the refuge,
Valuing them as much as their own bodies.

For the sake of all beings, who pervade the whole of space,
Arouse the mind intent on supreme enlightenment.
The children of the conquerors train constantly
In the precepts of the six transcendent perfections.

Those who skillfully combine means and wisdom in confessing,
On relative and absolute levels,
Their accumulated evil deeds, both natural and in violation of vows,
Train in the instruction on the syllable *hrīḥ* and the four applications.

Offer the outer, inner, and secret mandalas,
Together with the seven branches.
Knowing that all phenomena are like magical illusions, {295}
Train as well in the accumulation of wisdom.

In the body of the teacher Amitāyus,
Watch the nature of all that is supreme.
Through prayer and the four empowerments, you will be matured.

Through purity[3] and the five [factors of] awakening,
Visualize Avalokiteshvara and his consort
Like a reflection, like a rainbow,
And, meditating on the subtle yoga,
Train constantly in conduct and the practice.
Through the application of the seed syllable in the heart center,
Meditate on the [four] boundless attitudes, equalizing and exchanging.

The result of meditation on causes and categories
Is that body and body-and-mind are perfectly still.
Through habituation to sustained calm,
One will obtain a trained body and mind.

Relying on all the causes of profound insight
And meditating on the categories,
Make skillful use of the way of the result
And meditate on the conceptless, self-arisen gnosis.

With all-discerning wisdom
Look for a mind that ignorantly believes in a self;
Then you will know that it is neither one nor many.
It is like a magical illusion or a dream.

Accumulating merit with the offering of the illusory body,
View all phenomena as like those in a magical illusion.
Mingle wind and mind, and meditate on the deity's form,
A magical illusion that is your own self-experience.

Purifying yourself as the five elements,
Apprehend dreams, transform, and multiply.
Ascertain, subjugate obstacle makers, and train in pure realms,
And train in dream as the body of perfect enjoyment.
Adopt the essential point of the body and gaze
And concentrate on a *hrīḥ* in the heart:
Like the sun, like the moon in water, and like the sky,
Meditate on the mind, with the ten signs of luminosity complete.

Those who have trained and are skilled in the points of transference
[Know] the signs of death, and appearance, increase, and full
attainment,
And tread the path of coemergent luminosity;
They transfer by means of the deity's body, speech, and mind.

To attain the state of Avalokiteshvara in the bardo,
Meditate on the pith instructions for mixing
The illusory body and the body of perfect enjoyment,
And birth and taking a supreme manifestation body. {296}

It is not from reading these points
But by meditating on them that in this very life
One will definitely, it is taught,
Accomplish the supreme level of Avalokiteshvara.

Those who practice his generation and perfection stages
Were predicted as supreme beings
Who for up to seven generations
Are blessed by Avalokiteshvara.

This completes the *Stages to Be Practiced on the Path to Enlightenment of Noble Avalokiteshvara* that the lord of yogis Shrī Jagatamitrānanda bestowed on the great paṇḍita Shrīputra. The latter had a literal translation made and taught it to Jetsun Drakpa Rinchen, who in turn transmitted it to Öpak Dorje, and he to Buddhashrī, who bestowed it on me.

Virtue!

# 15. A Stream of Nectar

*The Approach and Accomplishment of Noble Avalokiteshvara*[1]

Of the six deities from whom Mitrayogin received the instructions included in this volume, Avalokiteshvara appears to be only deity for which a sādhana text is provided. The structure of the sādhana is slightly unusual in that the offering and praise sections come after the recitation of the mantra instead of before it.

{298}
*namo lokeśvara*
Sublime sovereign of those who guide the three worlds,
To Avalokiteshvara I pay homage.
I will write the stages for approaching and accomplishing him,
Along with a feast offering for auspicious occasions.

This [sādhana] is divided into three parts: (1) preliminaries; (2) main practice; and (3) conclusion.

## I. Preliminaries

The preliminaries are treated under seven headings: (1) time; (2) place; (3) material preparations; (4) preliminary torma; (5) blessing the offerings; (6) refuge and bodhichitta; and (7) the field of accumulation.

### A. Time

The times [for doing this sādhana] are periods of approach and accomplishment, occasions [such as] empowerments and consecrations, activity practices, or auspicious days such as the full moon, new moon, and eighth of the month.

### B. Place

The place is as described in the instruction texts.

### C. Material Preparations

Set up a mandala, the support for accumulating merit, as for the empowerment. If you do not have one, on a perfectly clean cloth arrange piles of grain in the same number as the number of deities. Set out images of the teacher and the Great Compassionate One and his consort. Arrange the offerings and tormas in numbers equal to the number of deities, or five, or three, but no fewer. In front arrange the ingredients for the feast offering, of good quality and in great quantity, {299} and a kapāla full of nectar. Having made sure you have a vajra, bell, and hand drum, and all the other necessary articles, sit on a comfortable seat.

### D. Preliminary Torma

In an instant I [appear as] the wrathful king, the heruka
Hayagrīva, red in color, with one face,
Two hands, three eyes, and his four canine teeth bared.
His hair and whiskers blaze like fire.
On his crown is a green horse's head, neighing.
His right hand brandishes a stick in the air;
His left, level with his heart center, is making the threatening gesture.
One leg is stretched out, the other is bent, and he is adorned with snakes[2] and precious ornaments.
He [wears] a tiger-skin skirt
And is present amid a blazing [mass] of wisdom fire, inseparable from the wisdom deity.

In his heart center is the syllable *hrīḥ* surrounded by the mantra.
*oṁ hrīḥ padmāntakṛta vajra krota hayagrīva hulu hulu hūṁ phaṭ*

Saying this, cleanse the torma with Hayagrīva's activity mantra and {300} purify it with *oṁ svabhāva śuddāḥ sarvadharmāḥ svabhāva śuddho 'haṃ.*

It is transformed into emptiness.
From the state of emptiness appears the syllable *bhrūṃ*, which melts to produce a vast, open, precious vessel.
Inside it, the syllables *oṁ āḥ hūṁ* melt to become a torma endowed with pleasurable qualities.

Visualizing this, with the *hūṁdzad* mudra, summon with:

*namo* Through the power and blessings of the truth of the sublime and glorious teacher and those of the exalted root and lineage masters,
The truth of the hosts of deities of the yidam mandala,
And the truth of the Three Jewels, rare and supreme,
All you hosts of obstacle makers and elemental spirits and all who dwell in this place, come here for the offering of the torma!
*ṭākki rāca hūṁ jaḥ*

Opening the vajra hand-clasp [mudra], offer the torma:

*namaḥ sarva tathāgatebhyo viśhvamukhebhyaḥ sarvathā khaṁ udgate spharaṇa imaṃ gagana khaṁ ghrīḥaṇa dam baliṅgtaye svāhā*

Say this three times.

You spirits who delight in the activities of accomplishing the mandala,
Enjoy and be satisfied with this torma, and carry out the activities in accord with the dharma.
All you different obstacle makers who should not hear or see the ritual, take satisfaction from this torma and depart to your own abodes.

Saying this, take the torma outside. Banish the obstacle makers with

*oṁ hrīḥ padmāntakṛta vajra krota hayagrīva hulu hulu hūṁ phaṭ*
*oṁ sumbhāni . . .*

Burn gugul incense and play loud music. Brandish the vajra and meditate on the protection circle.

*hūṁ* Everywhere, above and below and in the cardinal and
intermediate directions,
Is a fence of ḍākinīs, a tent of vajras,
And a swirling, turbulent mass of kalpa-ending fire.
All you obstacle makers, products of conceptual thought,
I forbid you to ever trespass
Inside the limits that I have set.
*oṁ vajra rakśa rakśa hūṁ*

### E. Blessing the Offerings

Cleanse the offerings with the mantra *oṁ hrīḥ padmāntakṛta vajra krota hayagrīva hulu hulu hūṁ phaṭ* and purify them with *oṁ svabhāva śuddāḥ sarvadharmāḥ svabhāva śuddho 'haṃ.*

They are transformed into emptiness. {301}

From the state of emptiness appears the letter *A*, and from that a vast, open skull cup. Inside it, the syllables *oṁ āḥ hūṁ* melt to become drinking water, water for washing the feet, flowers, incense, lamps, scented water, food, and musical instruments—inconceivable clouds of limitless offerings, both real and imagined, as occur in the life story of noble Samantabhadra.

Saying:

*oṁ vajra arghaṃ āḥ hūṁ*
*oṁ vajra pādyaṃ āḥ hūṁ*
*oṁ vajra puṣpe āḥ hūṁ*
*oṁ vajra dhūpe āḥ hūṁ*
*oṁ vajra āloke āḥ hūṁ*

*oṁ vajra gandhe āḥ hūṁ*
*oṁ vajra naivedye āḥ hūṁ*
*oṁ vajra śabda āḥ hūṁ*

bring down the blessings, to the accompaniment of music.

### F. Going for Refuge and Arousing Bodhichitta

I and all sentient beings, my old mothers, go for refuge in the teacher and the host of deities of Lord Avalokiteshvara.
We go for refuge in the buddhas, virtuous and transcendent conquerors.
We go for refuge in the sacred dharma.
We go for refuge in the sangha of noble beings.
We go for refuge in the ḍākas, ḍākinīs, and dharma protectors and guardians.

Say this three or more times. Then arouse bodhichitta, saying three times:

To the Buddha, the dharma, and the supreme assembly
I go for refuge until enlightenment is reached.
By the merit of my practicing the approach and accomplishment,
May I attain enlightenment for the benefit of beings.

There also exists a tradition of meditating on Vajrasattva at this point.

### G. Field of Accumulation

In an instant I become Avalokiteshvara, in whose heart center is a syllable *hrīḥ*, from which light radiates,
Inviting from the Potala into the sky in front noble Avalokiteshvara, crowned by the teacher Amitābha and surrounded by buddhas and bodhisattvas.

With the vajra gathering gesture, [say]:

*ārya avalokiteśvara sapārivāra vajra samajaḥ*
*padma kamalāya stvaṃ svāhā*

Gather the accumulations by offering the seven branches to those present in the sky in front:

To the Three Jewels I submit obeisance.
I venerate them with masses of offerings. {302}
I confess each and every one of my negative deeds.
I rejoice in all virtuous deeds.
I exhort the turning of the wheel of dharma.
I pray that [the teachers] may stay without passing into nirvana.
Through this virtue, may enlightenment be swiftly attained.

Taking the vow:

To the Three Jewels I go for refuge,
All my evil actions I confess,
And in the virtue of all beings I rejoice.
The enlightenment of buddhahood I will hold in mind,
And till enlightenment is reached
I will take refuge in the Buddha, dharma, and supreme assembly.
To achieve my own and others' aims,
I'll arouse the mind intent on enlightenment.
Having set my mind on supreme enlightenment,
I invite all beings, each and every one, to be my guests
And joyfully partake of the sublime ways of the bodhisattvas.
To benefit all beings, may I achieve buddhahood!

Say this three times. Then take the vows of the five families, from "Buddhas, bodhisattvas . . ." to ". . . and set all beings in the state beyond pain."[3]

A prayer to the teachers of the lineage:

To the body of truth, Amitābha, I pray.
To the body of enjoyment, the Great Compassionate One, I pray.
To the body of manifestation, Mitrayogin, I pray.
To the great paṇḍita Shrīputra I pray.
To the realized yogi Girti Ratna I pray.
To Jetsun Buddhashrī I pray.
To my immensely kind root teacher I pray.

To the yidam deities, ḍākinīs, and dharma protectors I pray.
Bestow on me the four empowerments and bless me.

The different beings in the mandala of the teacher and yidam deity dissolve into me.

With *oṁ āḥ hūṁ*, they dissolve.

## II. Main Practice

The main practice is divided into the self-visualization, the front visualization, and the related offerings and praises.

### A. Self-Visualization

The self-visualization consists of training in the generation stage by means of the five factors of awakening. First of all,[4] meditate on the four boundless attitudes:

May all sentient beings be happy and possess the causes of happiness.
May they be rid of suffering and the causes of suffering. {303}
May they never be parted from happiness, free of suffering.
May they dwell in equanimity, free of attachment to those close to them and aversion to those who are not.

Meditate on this three times.

*oṁ svabhāva śuddāḥ sarvadharmāḥ svabhāva śuddho 'haṃ*
All phenomena are devoid of intrinsic nature and are without self.
From the state of emptiness there appear the five elements, one above the other, and on top of them the supreme mountain.
On top of that is a thousand-petaled, multicolored lotus, and in its center the syllable *hūṁ*, which transforms into a vajra marked with a *hūṁ*.
From it light radiates to form a vast protection circle.
In its center is a five-colored syllable *bhrūṁ*.

It melts into light, from which appears the measureless palace of great liberation—square, with four gates, walls of five layers,
Four arched pediments, and top ornaments.
It is encircled outside by the vajra fence and mountain of fire.
In the center of the measureless palace, whose attributes are all present and complete, appears the syllable *paṁ*, and from it an eight-petaled multicolored lotus.
In its center, from the letter *A*, appears a full-moon disk,
And on top of that a white syllable *hrīḥ* with its visarga
And a red syllable *baṁ*, from which infinite rays of light emanate,
Benefiting countless sentient beings
And setting them all on the level of Lord Avalokiteshvara.
The light rays are gathered back and transform into a lotus,
Marked in its center with *hrīḥ* and *baṃ*, from which light radiates,
Inviting all the buddhas and bodhisattvas in the form of Avalokiteshvara.
They dissolve into the lotus, *hrīḥ*, and *baṃ*.
Through their transformation, I take the form of noble Avalokiteshvara,
White in color, like a snow-capped mountain lit by the sun.
He has one face and four arms
And is seated with his two legs crossed in the vajra posture.
He is wearing upper and lower garments of celestial multicolored silk,
Loosely tied with a jeweled belt. {304}
Between his first two hands, palms joined at the level of his heart, he holds the wish-fulfilling gem, king of all jewels.
The second right hand holds a rosary of a hundred white precious jewels.
The second left hand holds the stem of an eight-petaled lotus in full bloom,
Its blossom opening level with his ear.
His smiling face is beautified by almond eyes,
Long eyebrows, and a coil of white hair.[5]
His hair is tied up to form a black crown,
With locks of hair falling down to his waist,
A garland of flowers for a hair ribbon,

And two blue utpalas adorning the tops of his ears.
The skin of an antelope covers his left breast,
And he is adorned with a tiara of five jewels,
Earrings, short necklace,
Long necklace, bracelets, anklets,
Armbands, girdle, a garland of five kinds of pearls,
And a silken head ornament.
He is seated in the midst of dense rays of five-colored light.
On his lap is his secret consort, a wisdom ḍākinī, ruby red in color,
With one face, two arms, and two legs clasping the male deity's waist.
Her right hand is playing a golden ḍāmaru in the air.
With her left she is holding to the male deity's lips a skull cup filled with a stream of red nectar.
Her face is wrathful with a slight smile.
She has three eyes.
Her hair forms a topknot, with [loose] locks covering her waist.
She is crowned with a tiara of five dry skulls crested with jewels.
Her breasts and vulva are fully developed.
Her smile is peaceful; she is youthful and graceful,
Aged sixteen years, adorned with the five bone ornaments, and emanating rays of five-colored light.
In each of the male deity's five centers is a lotus and moon seat.
In the crown center, from the syllable *oṁ* there appears upon it white Vairochana Avalokiteshvara and his consort;
In the throat center, from *hrīḥ*, red Amitābha Avalokiteshvara and his consort; {305}
In the heart center, from *hūṁ*, blue Akṣhobhya Avalokiteshvara and his consort;
In the navel center, from *trāṃ*, yellow Ratnasambhava Avalokiteshvara and his consort;
And in the secret center, from *āḥ*, green Amoghasiddhi Avalokiteshvara and his consort.
All of them are seated with the same attire as the main deity and his consort.
To the east of them, from the syllable *ha*, there appears a blue vajra ḍākinī,

To the south, from *ri*, a yellow ratna ḍākinī,
To the west, from *ni*, a red padma ḍākinī,
To the north, from *sa*, a green karma ḍākinī.
All of them have one face, two arms, three eyes, and four slightly bared canine teeth;
Their right hands hold a curved knife, their left hands a skull cup full of blood.
In the crook of their arm, they hold a khātvāṇga.
They are adorned with the five bone ornaments
And are standing with their two feet in dancing posture, the right one bent, the left extended,
In the midst of a blazing wisdom fire.

From the white syllable *oṁ* in all these deities' crown centers, red *āḥ* in their throat centers, and blue *hūṁ* in their heart centers rays of light emanate, inviting from the natural expanse of reality the wisdom deities who are their corresponding likenesses.
*ārya avalokiteśvara saparivāra vajra samaya ja jaḥ*
*jaḥ hūṁ baṃ hoḥ*

They become inseparable from the meditation deities.
Again, from the *hūṁ* in the heart center, light rays emanate,
Inviting the five families of tathāgatas and their retinues.
*vajra samaya jaḥ*

Tathāgatas, please bestow empowerment!

In response to this prayer,
The deities of the five families and their consorts bestow empowerment with a stream of nectar from their vases, filling the inside of one's body.
The excess [empowerment] water overflows and one is crowned with Amitābha.

Next, perform the recitation:

> In my heart center is a lotus and moon, on top of which is the wisdom deity, who is like myself, {306} the size of a thumb. In his heart center is a lotus and moon, and on top of them rests the syllable *hrīḥ*, encircled by the mantra. From it, rays of light emanate, filling the entire inside of the body with the [deities of the] five families of Avalokiteshvara, as numerous as the atoms in the universe.
>
> The light radiates out, touching the containing world, which becomes the measureless palace, and the sentient beings inhabiting it, who all take the form of Avalokiteshvara and his consort, from whose mouths the mantra resounds.

Visualizing this, recite the mantra with an undistracted mind as much as possible.

> *oṁ maṇi padme hūṁ ḍākinī harinisa hūṁ*

At the end of the session, pray:

> By the truth of Lord Avalokiteshvara, I pray, help me and all sentient beings to attain the supreme accomplishment, the Great Seal.

Make a condensed offering and praise. It is good to do the hand offering at this point; see below. The duration of this recitation should be, in terms of time, three months; in terms of numbers, thirty million recitations of the mantra; or when the following signs occur: in the best case, one sees the deity and his consort in reality and receives predictions; in the middling case, one has experiences and visions; and in the worst case, one dreams of white men and red women bestowing accomplishments, of large gatherings of people, and so on.

### B. Front Visualization

Cleanse the mandala in front with the activity mantra.

> *oṁ svabhāva śuddhaḥ sarvadharmāḥ svabhāva śuddho 'haṃ*

All becomes emptiness.
From the state of emptiness appear the five elements, one above the other, and on top of them . . .

and so on, as above, down to

. . . from which infinite rays of light emanate,
Making offerings to the noble beings
And benefiting sentient beings. The lights are gathered back and transform into
Noble Avalokiteshvara, who is white in color . . .

and so on, as above, down to

. . . and blue *hūṁ* in their heart centers.

There is also a tradition, when one is doing the front visualization, in which the Avalokiteshvaras with their consorts in the throat, heart, navel, and secret centers mentioned above are seated clockwise around, starting in front. The four ḍākinīs are disposed in the four intermediate directions. {307}

From *hūṁ* in the heart centers of the self-visualized deity and the deity visualized in front rays of light emanate,
Inviting from the natural expanse of reality into the sky in front the teachers of the instruction lineage,[6]
The hosts of yidam deities, ḍākas and ḍākinīs, and dharma protectors and guardians.
*vajra samaya jaḥ*

Holding incense and musical instruments:

*hrīḥ* From the measureless palace of the three bodies inseparable,
Very essence of the buddhas of the three times,
Compassionate ones who bring sentient beings to maturation,
Teachers of the instruction lineage, come, I pray.

From the measureless palace of the supreme natural state,
Hosts of deities of the three bodies surrounded by your retinues,
Embodiments of emptiness and compassion,
Deities of the aural lineage, come, I pray.

From the palace of the Unexcelled, the expanse of reality,
All you hosts of deities of the mandala without exception,
Watching over beings with the eye of compassion,
Hosts of yidam deities, come, I pray.

From the measureless palace of the celestial land of Oḍḍiyāna,
You who bestow blessings and accomplishments,
Karma ḍākinīs, wisdom ḍākinīs, and other kinds,
Ḍākas and ḍākinīs, come, I pray.

From the measureless palace of the charnel ground,
You who spread the Buddha's teachings
And dispel outer and inner obstacles,
Protectors and guardians of the dharma, come, I pray.

The request to be seated:

*hrīḥ* In this palace made of all kinds of precious materials,
Upon seats of multicolored lotuses and moons,
In the immeasurably beautiful delightful palace,
Deities of the aural lineage, please be seated.
*jaḥ hūṁ baṃ hoḥ*
They become inseparable from the meditation deities . . .

and so on, as above, down to

. . . is crowned with Amitābha.

At this point, if you wish to recite the mantra, do so as above.

## [C. Offerings and Praises]

Next, paying homage:

> *hūṁ* Though you never move from the expanse of reality, the state of sameness,
> You manifest in the body of perfect enjoyment, like a rainbow,
> And compassionately guide all beings without exception. {308}
> To the deities of Avalokiteshvara, I pay homage.

After that, make the outer offerings:

> *hrīḥ* Water, flowers, incense,
> Lamps, scented water, food,
> Musical instruments and cymbals—all these offerings,
> Deities of the mandala, please accept.

Offering the inner offerings:

> Beautiful forms, pleasing sounds,
> Fragrant smells and sweet tastes,
> And pleasurable sensations—all these offerings,
> Deities of the mandala, please accept.

Also make the "inner offering" of amṛita. Offer the secret offering:

> The five fleshes and five nectars;
> The five aggregates, constituents, and senses-and-fields;
> The five objects of the senses and the five elements—
> Deities of the mandala, please accept.
>
> The four joys, eight kinds of bliss,
> Four instants and five kinds of gnosis,
> And the nondual joy and bliss—
> These offerings, deities of the mandala, please accept.

The offering of thatness:

The knowledge that offerer, offering, and object of offering
Are like magical illusions and dreams
Is the ultimate offering, free of elaboration.
This offering, deities of the mandala, please accept.

Next, the praise. Repeat these four lines:

Through your kindness
[Great bliss arises in an instant:
To the teacher whose body is like a precious jewel,
At the lotus feet of the vajra being I bow down.]

And this four-line homage:

You are pure white, unsullied by defects.
[Your crown is adorned with the perfect buddha.
You watch over beings with eyes of compassion.
To you, Avalokiteshvara, I pay homage.]

And make the following praise and prayer:

*hrīḥ* You who personify Vairochana, bewilderment purified,
The aggregate of form transformed into the gnosis of the expanse of reality,
Master of the supreme immutable nature—
To you, Vairochana Avalokiteshvara, homage and praise!

You who personify Vajrasattva, aversion purified,
The aggregate of consciousness transformed into mirrorlike gnosis,
Master of the supreme immutable nature—
To you, Akṣhobhya Avalokiteshvara, homage and praise!

You who personify Ratnasambhava, pride purified,
The aggregate of feeling transformed into the gnosis of equality,
Master of the supreme immutable nature—
To you, Ratnasambhava Avalokiteshvara, homage and praise!

You who personify Amitābha, attachment purified, {309}
The aggregate of perception transformed into all-discerning gnosis,
Master of the supreme immutable nature—
To you, Amitābha Avalokiteshvara, homage and praise!

You who personify Amoghasiddhi, jealousy purified,
The aggregate of conditioning factors transformed into all-accomplishing gnosis,
Master of the supreme immutable nature—
To you, Amoghasiddhi Avalokiteshvara, homage and praise!

Bliss and emptiness inseparable,
To Secret Wisdom, homage and praise!

Ground from which the deities of the expanse of reality arise,
Space completely purified—
To Dhātishvarī, homage and praise!

Ground from which the deities of the vajra family arise,
The water element completely purified—
To Māmakī, homage and praise!

Ground from which the deities of the ratna family arise,
The earth element completely purified—
To Buddhalochanā, homage and praise!

Ground from which the deities of the padma family arise,
The fire element completely purified—
To Pāṇḍaravāsinī, homage and praise!

Ground from which the deities of the karma family arise,
The wind element completely purified—
To Samayatārā, homage and praise!

To you who carry out the activities of pacifying,
Vajra ḍākinīs, homage and praise!

To you who carry out the activities of increasing,
Ratna ḍākinīs, homage and praise!

To you who carry out the activities of magnetizing,
Padma ḍākinīs, homage and praise!

To you who carry out the activities of forcefully subjugating,
Karma ḍākinīs, homage and praise!

As a result of my homage and praise to you,
Grant the supreme and common accomplishments
And help me to achieve the twofold goal.

Bless the hand offering of nectar as follows. Cleanse it with the activity mantra and purify it with the *svabhāva* mantra.

From the state of emptiness appears the syllable *yaṁ*, and from it the wind. {310}
From *raṁ* fire appears, and from three *kaṃ* syllables appear three hearthstones in the form of skulls. Upon them, from the letter *A* appears a kapāla, white on the outside and red on the inside, vast and open.
Inside it, on a moon seat,
From *go, ku*, *da*, *ha*, and *na*, the five fleshes marked with those same syllables,
And on top of them, from *vi*, *mu*, *ma*, *ra*, and *shu*, the five nectars marked with those same syllables.
On top of that, from *hūṁ*, *bhrūṁ*, *aṃ*, *jriṃ*, and *khaṃ*, the five gnoses,
Topped by the syllables *oṁ*, *āḥ*, and *hūṁ*.
From *hūṁ* in one's heart center rays of light emanate, as a result of which
The wind blows, fanning the fire;
It heats up the skull cup, in which the ingredients boil.
The steam touches the syllables *oṁ*, *āḥ*, and *hūṁ*,
And from them a stream of nectar flows down.
With the *oṁ*, *āḥ*, and *hūṁ*, it descends into the skull cup and becomes a great ocean of untainted nectar.

Bless it by saying three times

*oṁ āḥ hūṁ ha ho hrīḥ*

With each line, sprinkle the nectar with the left ring finger as you say:

To the gracious root teacher [I offer], *oṁ āḥ hūṁ.*
To Lord Amitābha [I offer], *oṁ āḥ hūṁ.*
To noble Avalokiteshvara [I offer], *oṁ āḥ hūṁ.*
To the accomplished practitioner Mitrayogin [I offer], *oṁ āḥ hūṁ.*
To the great paṇḍita Shrīputra [I offer], *oṁ āḥ hūṁ,*
To the realized yogi Girti Ratna [I offer], *oṁ āḥ hūṁ.*
To peerless Öpak Dorje [I offer], *oṁ āḥ hūṁ.*
To my gracious root teacher [I offer], *oṁ āḥ hūṁ.*
As well as them, to the holy teachers who bestow empowerment and teach the tantras and pith instructions [I offer], *oṁ āḥ hūṁ.*
To the hosts of deities of the Great Compassionate One, Lord of the World [I offer], *oṁ āḥ hūṁ.*
To the five classes of ḍākinīs and other ḍākinīs of the three sacred places [I offer], *oṁ āḥ hūṁ.*
To Draklha Gönpo and the other protectors and guardians of the teachings [I offer], *oṁ āḥ hūṁ.*
To Brahmā and the guardians of the ten directions, and the other worldly protectors [I offer], *oṁ āḥ hūṁ.*
To the twelve tenmas who protect Tibet and Kham and the other indigenous local deities [I offer], *oṁ āḥ hūṁ.*
May all the beings of the six realms, included in the six classes of beings, the five paths of being, {311} and the four modes of birth, be satiated by [this] nectar and swiftly attain the precious level of buddhahood.

## III. Conclusion

Third, the conclusion. There are two parts: the feast offering and the thanksgiving offering.

### A. Feast Offering

First, bless the feast ingredients as for the inner offering. Then:

> *namo* This copious feast offering in which skillful means and wisdom are inseparable, whose nature is perfectly pure, marked with the perfectly pure vowels and consonants whose essence is unborn, and sealed with the perfectly pure five fleshes and five nectars—all this
>
> [I offer] to the teachers of the instruction lineage, the root of blessings, *oṁ āḥ hūṁ*;
>
> [I offer] to the host of yidam deities, the root of accomplishments, *oṁ āḥ hūṁ*;
>
> [I offer] to the dharma protectors and guardians, the root of activities, *oṁ āḥ hūṁ*.
>
> *pañca amṛta la khā hi*
> *gaṇacakra la khā hi*

This is a condensed version. To make the offering more elaborately, recite the following invitation:

> *hrīḥ* Teacher and teachers of the lineage,
> All you yidam deities without exception,
> Ḍākinīs and dharma protectors, with your retinues,
> I invite you to a feast of food, please come!

Then, offer up the feast:

> Above the crown of my head, upon seats of lotus and moon,
> Are the assembled deities of the bodies of truth, enjoyment, and manifestation
> And the teachers of the instruction lineage and their retinues—
> To you I offer the feast of food.
> May it delight you with great bliss.
> A la la, enjoy!
>
> In the wheel of great bliss in my crown
> Are Vairochana and his consort

And the assembled deities of the buddha family.
To you I offer the feast of food.
May it delight you with great bliss.
A la la, enjoy!

In the wheel of enjoyment in my throat
Are Amitāyus and his consort
And the assembled deities of the lotus family.
To you I offer the feast of food.
May it delight you with great bliss.
A la la, enjoy!

In the wheel of ultimate reality in my heart center {312}
Are Vajra Akṣhobhya and his consort
And the assembled deities of the vajra family.
To you I offer the feast of food.
May it delight you with great bliss.
A la la, enjoy!

In the wheel of manifestation in my navel
Are Ratnasambhava and his consort
And the assembled deities of the qualities family.
To you I offer the feast of food.
May it delight you with great bliss.
A la la, enjoy!

In the bliss-preserving wheel in my secret center
Are Amoghasiddhi and his consort
And the assembled deities of the action family.
To you I offer the feast of food.
May it delight you with great bliss.
A la la, enjoy!

To the male and female bodhisattvas,
Who are the pure aspects of the senses-and-fields of the eye and so forth,
To you I offer the feast of food.

May it delight you with great bliss.
A la la, enjoy!

To the ten male and female wrathful deities,
Who are the pure aspects of the head and other parts of the body,
To you I offer the feast of food.
May it delight you with great bliss.
A la la, enjoy!

To all the assembled ḍāka deities without exception,
Who are the pure aspects of the subtle channels,
To you I offer the feast of food.
May it delight you with great bliss.
A la la, enjoy!

To all the wisdom ḍākinīs without exception,
Who are the pure aspects of the subtle winds,
To you I offer the feast of food.
May it delight you with great bliss.
A la la, enjoy!

To all the assembled deities of the secret mantras
Who are the pure aspects of the essence drops,
To you I offer the feast of food.
May it delight you with great bliss.
A la la, enjoy!

To the buddhas and bodhisattvas
Who are the pure aspects of the atoms of the body, {313}
To you I offer the feast of food.
May it delight you with great bliss.
A la la, enjoy!

To the assembled deities of the vajra body
Who are the pure aspects of my own body,[7]
To you I offer the feast of food.

May it delight you with great bliss.
A la la, enjoy!

To the assembled deities of the vajra speech
Who are the pure aspects of my own speech,
To you I offer the feast of food.
May it delight you with great bliss.
A la la, enjoy!

To the assembled deities of the vajra mind
Who are the pure aspects of my own mind,
To you I offer the feast of food.
May it delight you with great bliss.
A la la, enjoy!

From the eight sites of the great cemeteries,
Worldly ḍākinīs with miraculous powers,
Come here, accept this offering of the feast
And accomplish the four activities, I pray.

From the eight great samaya sites,
Ocean-like loyal protectors, please come.
Come here, accept this offering of the feast.
Carry out your deeds as messengers and servants.
*pañca amṛta la khā hi*
*gaṇacakra la khā hi*

Offer the feast liquor in the same way as the hand offering, sprinkling it in the air. Separate the first part of the feast and offer it to the mandala and to the torma. Cleanse the torma with the above activity mantra and purify it with the *svabhāva* mantra. Bless it as with the hand offering above. Invite the torma guests and offer it to them:

All you teachers and hosts of yidam deities, come before me in the sky—
*vajra samaya ja jaḥ*
*pheṃ pheṃ*

> They penetrate the torma with their tubular vajra tongues and consume it.
> *namo guru ratna idam baliṅgta kha kha khā hi khā hi*

Say this three times for [the offering to] the teacher. And make the offering three times with:

> *oṁ āḥ hūṁ hrīḥ oṁ maṇi padme hūṁ ḍākinī harinisa hūṁ idam baliṅgta kha kha khā hi khā hi*

On other occasions too, insert the [offering to the] yidam deity after this. {314} Make the offerings with *arghaṃ* and so on, and pray as follows:

> Teachers and hosts of deities of the mandalas of Avalokiteshvara and the others, may this delight your body, speech, and mind: Grant me and all sentient beings, I pray, all the supreme and common accomplishments without exception.

The torma for the dharma protectors. Cleanse and purify the torma as above, blessing it as the flesh and blood of the enemies and obstacle makers. The following is a condensed visualization ritual.

> *oṁ svabhāva* . . . and so on.
> All becomes emptiness.
> From the state of emptiness, in the sky before me appears a tent of rows of spears and swords.
> In the middle of mobbing mamos and swirling dust devils
> Is a blazing dark-blue triangular mandala.
> On top of male and female obstructor-enemies, face down and face up,
> In the middle of a thousand-spoked wheel of meteoric iron,
> On a seat of lotus and sun appears a syllable *hūṁ* and thence a curved knife, from which arises the glorious wisdom protector Draklha, dark red in color, with one face, two arms, and three eyes looking with angry glares in the ten directions,
> His mouth fearfully agape and four canine teeth bared,
> Tongue darting like lightning, orange hair streaming upward.

In his right hand he holds a four-faceted club, marked on its tip with a jewel and emitting sparks.
His left hand holds a small vessel with the heart of an enemy inside it.
He is adorned with a crown of five dry skulls,
A long necklace of fifty fresh heads,
And a shoulder belt and hand and foot ornaments of vicious black snakes.
On his lower body he is wearing a skirt of a fresh tiger skin.
His right leg is bent, his left leg extended.
He wears a gown of black silk.
His body emits fiery sparks,
Burning up all evil beings.
In front of him is his henchman, Black Mönpa, who is dark blue in color and has one face, two arms, and three eyes, wide open.
His yellowish-red hair streams upward.
His right hand brandishes a curved knife in the air.
With his left hand he offers his master a skull cup containing an enemy's heart. {315}
Besides him, the protector is surrounded by wisdom protectors massed like clouds,
Activity protectors and worldly protectors swirling around like the wind,
And countless hosts, as well, of mamos and lords of death.
On the protector's forehead is the syllable *oṁ*, on his throat the syllable *āḥ*, and on his heart center the syllable *hūṁ*.
From these light radiates, inviting the wisdom deities from the Shītavana Cool Grove.

If you wish to make a detailed invitation, recite the following:

*hūṁ* As, with faith and [pure] commitments . . .

and so on.[8]

With *jaḥ hūṁ baṃ hoḥ* they become inseparable.
The tathāgatas bestow empowerment, the [empowerment] water overflows, and the excess becomes Akṣhobhya, adorning his crown.

His tubular vajra tongue penetrates the torma.
*oṁ mahākāla dhurusva hūṁ hūṁ phaṭ phaṭ idam baliṅgta kha kha khā hi khā hi*

Say this three times and with the *śāsana* mantra, make the offering to the general protectors. Visualize Palden Lhamo as you usually do, and use her own mantra, or alternatively:

*trag rakṣa mahā rakṣiṇ nagmo dunting bhyo idam baliṅgta khā hi*

Glorious wisdom protectors with your consorts and retinue of sons, accept this vast torma, offered and given;
Protect me and the Buddha's teachings,
Bring about favorable conditions,
Repel adverse conditions,
And destroy enemies and obstacle makers, I pray.

For the general torma to the ḍākinīs, invite them and offer it with their respective mantras, or alternatively:

All you manifestation bodies who dwell in the retinues of the five ḍākinīs,
Who dwell in the thirty-two sacred lands,
The twenty-four sacred places,
And the eight great charnel grounds,
Dwelling there for the benefit of sentient beings,
To you [I offer this torma]—*khā hi*.
May it delight your body, speech, and mind:
Grant the supreme and common accomplishments.

The torma for the local protectors. Bless the white torma, then:

To the twelve tenmas, who protect Tibet, the local protectors of each region, {316}
And the loyal protectors of mountain solitudes, along with your retinues, to you I also make this offering.
Pleased and satisfied by this, be my friends, helping me to practice the dharma.
And may all beings included in the six realms, the five paths of

being, and the four modes of birth be satiated by this torma
and swiftly attain the precious state of buddhahood.

Make offerings with *argham̩* and so on, and also offer the inner offering. Then do the praise:

Merely thinking of you destroys
All the faults of samsara
And brings one to unsurpassed enlightenment—
To all you teachers I make homage and praise.

*hrīḥ* You who personify Vairochana, bewilderment purified, . . .

and so on, down to

. . . And help me to achieve the twofold goal.

Mighty Black One arisen from *hūṁ*,
Loyal guardian of Lord Avalokiteshvara's words,
Draklha Gönpo, lord of the hundred thousand protectors,
Great protector of the Buddha's doctrine, to you I give praise.

*bhyo* By the force of your body, speech, and mind,
You overpower the whole world of desire.
Mistress of the world of desire,
Queen of the world of desire, to you I bow.

Eight classes of mahādevas and your retinues,
Eight classes of nāgas and your retinues,
Eight guardians of the world and your retinues,
All you hosts of yakṣhas,
All you hosts of preta spirits,
All you hosts of flesh-eating demons,
All you hosts of demons that produce insanity,
All you hosts of demons that produce oblivion,
All you hosts of mamos,
All you hosts of ḍākinīs,
And all you hosts of other spirits, without exception,

Come to this place and think of me. {317}
Accept this torma, offered and given,
And for us practitioners and our followers
Bring about freedom from disease, longevity, power,
Glory, renown, good luck,
And wealth, all on a vast scale.
Grant us the accomplishment of the activities
Of pacifying, increasing, and the rest.
Keep your promise to protect us,
And help us attain all the accomplishments.
Keep us from untimely death, and rid us
Of sicknesses, negative forces, and obstacles.
Put an end to nightmares, bad omens,
And evil activities.
Increase happiness in the world,
Good harvests, and supplies of grain;
Spread the dharma and bring about perfect happiness
And the accomplishment of all we desire.

After that, enjoy the feast. The master of ceremonies takes the ingredients of skillful means and wisdom, crossing his hands one above the other and saying:

O vajra master, listen to me.
Look at these beautiful sacred substances;
You should have no doubts about them.
Consider that brahmins, dogs, and outcastes
Are of the same nature, and enjoy!
*a ho mahā sukha hoḥ*

He takes it to the master. Making the circular lotus gesture, the master says:

*hūṁ* To the sugatas' body of truth,
Free of attachment and other stains,
Free of subject-object duality.
To the ultimate nature, respectfully I pay homage.
*a la la ho*

In this way, take it also to the brothers and sisters. They all enjoy the feast while [preserving] the state of their bodies being deities, their speech being mantra, and their minds being ultimate reality. After that, collect the left-overs in a single container. The vajra master makes the blazing mudra and sprinkles them with saliva. Saying,

*oṁ vajra ārali ho pheṃ pheṃ*

with the blazing mudra, he makes a circular movement from left to right between his eyebrows.

*yaṃ raṃ khaṃ oṁ āḥ hūṁ*
The torma of the first-portion leftovers becomes an excellent, vast [offering],[9]
Inexhaustible and possessed of the five pleasurable qualities. {318}
*oṁ āḥ hūṁ oṁ ucchiṣṭa baliṅgta bhakśa bhakśayi svāhā*
May it satisfy all the beings who have a right to the leftovers.

Offering the leftovers:

*hūṁ* All you karma ḍākinīs too,
You who have the skill and power of speed,
Worldly ḍākinīs with magical powers,
You who display terrifying wrath,
Flesh-eating ḍākinīs with magical powers,
You who have control over the billion worlds,
And all you messengers swift in your activities—
By virtue of your commitments, come!
Accept the torma of the first-portion leftovers and rinsing water.
Guard the teachings of the Three Jewels.
Subdue the enemies and obstacle makers—wrong views.
Carry out the activities that the practitioners entrust you with.

Scatter it in an open place. Offering the rinsing water:

All you tenmas, guardians of Tibet,
Who protect the world in the ten directions,

Come here and accept this torma of rinsing water.
Carry out the activities the practitioners have assigned.

Scatter it in the air. Next, turning the torma container upside down, perform the torma dance.

*hūṁ* In the infinite mandala of the expanse of reality,
Deities who have control over phenomenal existence,
Ḍākinīs who have dominion over all—
With your terrifying laughter, resounding *hūṁ*,
A billowing ocean of ḍākinīs,
Dancing gracefully, in continuous movement,
Come to this place, and reduce to dust
Those who are hostile to the teachings.
*oṁ maṇi padme hūṁ ḍākinī harinisa hūṁ phaṭ svāhā all harmdoers staṃ bhaya nan nan*

With this, consider that all the enemies and obstacle makers are crushed underneath Mount Meru.

### B. Concluding Ritual[10]

If you wish to do this elaborately, bless the offerings and make the detailed offerings with, for example, the *tsang jar ma* [torma offering].[11]

For a condensed version, make the offerings as above with:

*oṁ sarva tathāgata lokeśvara saparivāra vajra arghaṃ . . .*

and so on. Offer the inner offering of nectar as well. Then do the praise: {319}

Praised by numerous buddhas,
You are a treasure of sublime qualities.
To you, Avalokiteshvara and all your retinue,
Constant in your compassion, I give homage and praise.

After that, request forgiveness, reciting the hundred-syllable mantra three times and praying:

Whatever faults I have made in this virtuous practice
On account of ignorance,
And whatever additions or omissions I have made in the ritual,
I beg the deities of the mandala to forgive.

Next, say the dedication:

All you teachers, yidam deities, buddhas, and bodhisattvas
dwelling in the ten directions, think of me.
As a result of this virtuous practice,
May I swiftly accomplish the teacher-yidam
And, not leaving out a single being,
May I set them all on his level.

Prayer for auspiciousness:

True manifestations of all the buddhas, precious teachers,
Whose perfect and abundant qualities are as great as the expanse
of reality,
You who guide all us beings,
Teachers of the instruction lineage, may all be auspicious!

Deities on whom my flower fell,
Avalokiteshvara and the rest,
You to whom I am linked by karma and fortune,
Yidam deities, may all be auspicious!

You whose bodies of air are unobstructed wherever you go,
Great illusionists, with bodies you can change at will,
Who accompany me in the guise of loving mothers and
sisters,
Outer and inner ḍākinīs, may all be auspicious!

You who in Lord Buddha's presence
Promised to protect, as you would your children,
Those who are striving for accomplishment,
Dharma protectors and guardians, may all be auspicious!

> Mighty Black One arisen from *hūṁ*,
> Loyal guardian of Lord Avalokiteshvara's words,
> Draklha Gönpo, lord of the hundred thousand protectors,
> Great guardian of the Buddha's doctrine, may all be auspicious!

After saying this prayer for auspiciousness, request [the deities] to remain firmly [in the images].

> Lord and all you who possess great compassion, {320} as long as they are not damaged by the elements earth, water, fire, and wind, please remain firmly in these images and act as the supreme refuge and protector for me and all sentient beings.
> *oṁ supra tiṣṭha vajra ye svāhā*

If there are no images, request [the deities] to depart:

> *oṁ* You who do everything for beings' welfare,
> Grant accomplishment accordingly.
> Return to the land of the buddhas,
> And in order to benefit sentient beings,
> Come again, I pray.

With *vajra muḥ*, let them depart.

> The meditational deities dissolve into myself.

With *oṁ āḥ hūṁ*, they dissolve. Snapping your fingers, say *sarva bhūta gaccha* and:

> Worldly deities, please return to your own abodes.

After that, settle in meditative equipoise for a long while in the state[12] of ultimate emptiness, transcending everything that acts as a support—a container and contents—from the measureless palace to the seed nāda. Again, arise in the union body and properly practice the instructions on generation and perfection as above. For details of the practice of daily activities and the perfection stage, refer to the great sādhana.

The sādhana of Avalokiteshvara (NOTE: in Mitra's tradition)[13]
I (NOTE: Öpak Dorje) arranged in response to someone else's (NOTE: Chatang Chöje's) request,
According to the transmission and the teacher's pith instructions
In a form suitable (NOTE: for those of modest intellect), for the sake of ease and clarity.
I beg the ḍākinīs to pardon any errors,
And I dedicate the merit for the benefit of sentient beings.
Through this, may they come to hold the sacred teachings of the conquerors.

May virtue and excellence increase.

# 16. A Banquet of Nectar

*A Complete Instruction on Noble Avalokiteshvara's Graded Path to Enlightenment*[1]

{322}
Born from the great treasure of the ocean of virtue and excellence,
Precious jewel spontaneously accomplishing the two goals,
Completely fulfilling all the wants and needs of beings—
Lineage teachers, at your feet I bow.

He who, countless cosmic eons before,
With Avalokiteshvara gave rise to supreme bodhichitta
And carried out on a vast scale the activities of the lord—
Unexcelled siddha Mitrayogin, at your feet I bow.

Guided by Avalokiteshvara,
You in turn guided Shrīputra,
And he in turn guided my sublime teacher.
These instructions are his pith instructions,
Perfectly transmitted down the lineage and uncorrupted by intellectual inventions.
May the teachers and ḍākinīs bless my being
That I may write down the stages [of the path] just as they were taught,
Without forgetting anything, in order to benefit beings.

Here I will reveal the instructions on Avalokiteshvara's graded path.[2] For this there are four main topics: {323} (1) historical background[3] of the instructions; (2) pith instructions on the preliminary practices; (3) instructions on the generation stage and the related [practices] of love, compassion, and bodhichitta; and (4) instructions on the perfection stage.[4]

## I. Historical Background of the Instructions

Ninety-one kalpas ago the mahāsiddha Mitrayogin took birth as the monk Emanated Light and was the teacher who taught the dharma to the prince Lokeshvara. In Tibet, he took birth as Tönmi Sambhota, traveled to India, became a translator, and propagated the teachings of Shākyamuni in Tibet. Later, knowing that the time had come to train disciples in India, he took birth and, having acted out the sādhana of Avalokiteshvara, attained the immortal vajra body. For the benefit of sentient beings, he displayed numerous paradoxical paired miracles,[5] taught, practiced, bestowed maturing empowerments, and trained beings according to their needs. In such ways he effortlessly and spontaneously worked for the welfare of sentient beings. {324} Moreover, that great siddha journeyed to the Sosaling charnel ground. There he practiced the five yidam deities and accomplished them. They appeared to him in reality, each teaching him the graded instructions on their respective generation and perfection stages. In that way, Mañjughoṣha gave him the Body instruction, *The Wheel of Ornaments of Gnosis That Makes Wisdom Grow*. Avalokiteshvara taught him the Speech instruction, *A Banquet of Nectar*, a complete instruction on the whole graded path to enlightenment. Vajrapāṇi taught him the Mind instruction, *The Spreading Rays of Light That Vanquish the Hordes of Demons*. Amitāyus gave him the Qualities instruction, the method for *Accomplishing the Immortal Vajra Body*. Tārā taught him the instruction that protects one from the eight fears, called *Spontaneous Activities That Free One from the Perilous Path of Samsara*. And Yellow Jambhala gave him the instruction called *A Shower of Accomplishments*. These six instructions are the respective graded instructions that each of the deities taught him.

These deities told him to put these instructions into practice and to reveal them to one other lineage holder, saying that their blessings would carry for up to seven generations of lineage holders. In particular, they predicted that for seven generations the individuals who practiced these instructions would be exclusively ones blessed by Avalokiteshvara.

The great siddha Mitrayogin's disciple was the paṇḍita Shrīputra. The latter's disciple was the realized being Girti Ratna. As far as him, there has been only a single lineage holder [at a time], [holding] the pith instructions transmitted through an aural lineage. To prevent my forgetting them, I have put them down in writing. This, then, is the transmission lineage of these instructions.

## II. Pith Instructions on the Preliminary Practices

The preliminary practices are divided into sections: (1) the common and (2) the specific preliminaries. {325}

### A. Common Preliminaries

The common preliminaries are divided into four: meditation on the difficulty of finding the freedoms and advantages; meditation on death and impermanence; meditation on action, cause and effect; and meditation on the defects of cyclic existence. The procedures for these are the same as in other instruction manuals.

### B. Specific Preliminaries

The specific preliminaries are divided into four: (1) instructions on going for refuge and arousing bodhichitta, which make everything one does become the path to liberation; (2) a pith instruction on the four applications of the syllable *hrīḥ*, which enable one to swiftly purify all one's negative deeds and obscurations; (3) instructions on the mandala practice, which enables one to complete the two accumulations; and (4) instructions on the guru yoga, which enables one to quickly receive blessings.

#### 1. Instructions on Going for Refuge and Arousing Bodhichitta

In the sky before one, raised by herculean men and lions, is a vast, spacious throne with a multicolored lotus of a hundred thousand petals. On top of it is a full-moon disk, in the middle of which is one's own root teacher [in the form of] Amitābha, wearing the attributes of the body of perfect enjoyment. He is surrounded by the teachers of the instruction lineage. In front of him is the yidam deity, the Great Compassionate One, surrounded by an ocean of yidam deities. On his right is Buddha Shākyamuni surrounded by an ocean of buddhas, such as the thousand buddhas of the good kalpa. Behind is the Great Mother[6] surrounded by an ocean of the sacred dharma in the form of books and volumes of the scriptures. On the left are the eight close bodhisattva sons and the eight sublime listeners, surrounded by an ocean of the sanghas of the Great and Lesser Vehicles. All the directions and intermediate directions are filled with ḍākas and ḍākinīs. He is surrounded below by an ocean of protectors who guard the teachings—the six-armed Mahākāla, Draklha Gönpo, and others, {326} who are present as a defense.

Considering that you and all the infinite beings are under their protection, repeat the following aloud, many times, as you develop devotion and respect:

> All sentient beings, my mothers, as numerous as space is vast, take refuge in the glorious holy teachers in the ten directions.
> We take refuge in the infinite yidam deities in the ten directions.
> We take refuge in the infinite buddhas in the ten directions.
> We take refuge in the infinite sacred dharma teachings in the ten directions.
> We take refuge in the infinite sanghas in the ten directions.
> We take refuge in the infinite ḍākinīs in the ten directions.
> We take refuge in the infinite dharma protectors in the ten directions.
> Keep us perfectly under your protection, we pray.

Meditate on the four boundless attitudes. After that, the sources of refuge melt into light and dissolve into you, so that they are inseparable from your own body, speech, and mind, like water poured into water. To settle in that state without contrivance is the ultimate [practice of] taking refuge.

### 2. A Pith Instruction on the Four Applications of the Syllable *hrīḥ*

a. While remaining in your ordinary form, visualize on the crown of your head a white syllable *hrīḥ*, complete with visarga, radiating light. Nectar flows down from it like milk, washing away all the negative deeds and obscurations inside your body. Consider that from the pores of your body, from the anus and urethra, and from your legs and feet, including your toenails, they emerge as black matter oozing out in the form of smoke and liquid charcoal. Imagine that the whole of the inside of your body is completely filled with the white nectar of primordial wisdom. This is the application that purifies one's negative deeds.

b. The application that purifies illness and negative forces consists of five parts. {327}

   i. The application for purifying fevers involves considering that from the syllable *hrīḥ* a stream of nectar flows down as a cooling stream of water, like meltwater or camphor, so that one's body becomes cool.[7]

   ii. To purify cold diseases, one considers that the stream of nectar flowing down is hot, like boiling molten metal, so that waves of heat like a blazing fire flow into one's body.

   iii. To purify illnesses due to multiple imbalances, one considers that five-colored nectar flows down, blissful in nature, so that one's body becomes vibrant with bliss-emptiness. [These three] comprise the application that purifies illness.

   iv. The application that purifies negative forces consists of the following visualization. From the syllable *hrīḥ* infinite small wrathful emanations in the form of Vajrapāṇi and Hayagrīva appear, with the details of their tiny bodies—their limbs, expressions, and everything—all very clear, laughing terrifyingly, holding all sorts of weapons in their hands, and surrounded by blazing wisdom fire. Their mouths roar *hūṁ hūṁ* and *ha ha phaṭ phaṭ*. As a result, all the negative forces inside your body are expelled through the hairs of your body. This is the application that purifies negative forces.

   v. The application of emanating and gathering back rays of light that cleanses away all negative deeds and obscurations. From the syllable *hrīḥ* five-colored rays of light emanate, like the light of a thousand suns, purifying all the negative deeds and obscurations within your body and cleansing them away like the rising sun dispelling darkness. The inside of your body is filled with rays of light. After that, visualize five-colored rays shining outward, purifying the illnesses, negative forces, negative deeds, and obscurations of all sentient beings. This is the application that cleanses all obscurations. {328}

In all these cases you should also recite the syllable *hrīḥ*. At the end, your body melts into light and dissolves into the *hrīḥ*. The [different elements] of the syllable *hrīḥ* dissolve in stages—[first] into the *rata*,[8] then the *rata* into the body of the syllable, the body into the *gigu*,[9] which itself dissolves like a rainbow vanishing in the sky. Settle in the nonconceptual state. This is the great purificator.

All this was the instruction on the four applications of the syllable *hrīḥ*.

### 3. Instructions on the Mandala Practice

The instructions on the mandala practice are divided into three: (1) the outer mandala, the universe presented as a mandala; (2) the inner mandala, the body presented as a mandala; and (3) the secret mandala, the channels presented as a mandala.

#### a. Outer Mandala

This has two aspects: (1) the accomplishment mandala and (2) the offering mandala.

i. The accomplishment mandala should be one made of the five kinds of precious materials, or, if you do not have one, an earthen base, sprinkled with scented water. On it should be disposed the piles, composed of various precious materials, [representing] the four continents and Mount Meru, on top of which is the measureless palace, made of different precious materials, with its four sides, four gates, ornaments, arched pediments, terraces, and top ornament. In its center is a throne of precious materials, on which is a lotus and moon disk, and on top of that, in the middle, one's own root teacher appearing as Buddha Amitābha, surrounded by the lineage teachers. In front are the yidam deities; to the right, the buddhas; behind, the sacred dharma; to the left, the sangha; and below, the ḍākinīs and dharma protectors. Visualizing all these, set out the piles and say:

*guru buddha dharma saṅgha maṇḍal la vajra samaya jaḥ jaḥ hūṁ baṁ hoḥ padma kamalā ya stvaṃ*

ii. Next, prepare the offering mandala. This should be a mandala of precious material such as gold or silver, on which the piles should be spaced correctly. {329} If you do not have two mandalas, visualize the deities of the accomplishment mandala up in the air in front of you and use the same accomplishment mandala on which to set out the piles, as follows.

*oṁ vajra bhumi āḥ hūṁ*—corresponding to the mighty golden ground.

*oṁ vajra rekhe āḥ hūṁ*—corresponding to the outer ring of iron mountains, in the middle of which is Mount Meru, made of the five kinds of precious materials.

In the east is Pūrvavideha, which is semicircular and made of crystal, embellished with uncultivated crops of grain. In the south is Jambudvīpa, which is trapezoidal and made of precious beryl, embellished with jewels. In the west is Godānīya, which is round and made of ruby, embellished with bountiful cows. In the north is Uttarakuru, which is square and made of precious gold, embellished with wish-fulfilling trees. They are flanked by the eight subcontinents. In the sky to the southeast is the sun, made of fire crystal. In the sky to the northwest is the moon, made of water crystal. In the sky to the northeast is the yellow Ketū, and in the sky to the southwest is the black Rāhu.[10] In the space in between are the seven attributes of royalty, namely the precious wheel, the precious jewel, the precious queen, the precious elephant, the precious minister, the marvelous and precious horse, and the precious general; and the eight auspicious symbols, namely the precious parasol, the banner of universal victory, the golden fish, the utterly beautiful lotus, the conch that resounds to the melodious sound of the dharma, the vase of great treasure, the eternal knot that fulfills all needs and desires, and the wheel that turns the wheel of dharma. Besides these, {330} there are the four outer offering maidens—the lady of flowers, the lady of incense, the lady of lamps, and the lady of perfume—and the four inner offering maidens: the lady of song, the lady of dance, the lady of garlands, and the lady of charm.

In short, [everything] is completely filled with the many riches of gods and humans, with nothing missing, and these, along with your own body and possessions, are offered to the teacher and the Three Jewels and infinite objects worthy of veneration. Saying "Accept these with compassion for the sake of beings, and grant your blessings, I pray," make this offering twenty-one, fourteen, or seven times.

### b. Presentation of One's Body as the Inner Mandala

*oṁ vajra bhumi āḥ hūṁ*—one's skin corresponds to the mighty golden ground.

*oṁ vajra rekhe āḥ hūṁ*—one's innards correspond to the outer ring of iron mountains. In the middle of them is the backbone, the central Mount Meru.

The head corresponds to the Mansion of Complete Victory, the right arm to the eastern continent of Pūrvavideha, the right leg to the southern continent of Jambudvīpa, the left leg to the western continent of Godānīya, and the left arm to the northern continent of Uttarakuru.

The two eyes correspond to the sun and moon, the two ears to Rāhu and Ketū, the nose to the vase of great treasure, the tongue to the bountiful cow, the ten toes to the ten outer goddesses, the fingers to the ten inner goddesses, the eight main articulations to the eight auspicious symbols, the seven internal organs to the seven attributes of royalty. The hair on the head and body hairs correspond to the bountiful riches of gods and humans, with nothing missing. All these are "offered to the holy root and lineage teachers, to the Three Jewels, and to the hosts of yidam deities, ḍākinīs, and dharma protectors until samsara has been emptied. Accept them with compassion for the sake of beings." {331}

### c. Presentation of One's Channels as the Secret Mandala

The supreme channel in the secret center corresponds to the mighty golden ground. The channels in the limbs correspond to the outer ring of iron mountains.

In the middle is the avadhūtī, corresponding to Mount Meru, the king of mountains. The heart center corresponds to Pūrvavideha in the east, the navel center to Jambudvīpa in the south, the throat center to Godānīya in the west, and the crown center to Uttarakuru in the north. The rasanā channel is the sun, the lalanā the moon, the lower end of the avadhūtī is Rāhu, and the upper end is Ketū.

The five chakras—the wheel of dharma in the heart, the wheel of manifestation in the navel, the wheel of enjoyment in the throat, the wheel of great bliss in the crown, [and the bliss-preserving chakra in the secret center]—correspond to the five goddesses of the sense pleasures. The radial channels are the eight auspicious symbols, the seven attributes of royalty, and the riches of gods and humans, with nothing missing.

All these "are offered to the root and lineage teachers and the yidam deities. Accept them with compassion for the sake of beings."

> The virtue gathered by myself and others, with our body, speech,
> and mind, in the past, present, and future,
> Together with all the offerings of precious mandalas and offerings
> made in the manner of Samantabhadra,
> I take mentally and offer to the teachers and yidam deities.
> Accept them with compassion for the sake of beings,
> And accepting them, grant your blessings, I pray.
> *guru maṇḍala pūja megha samudra spharaṇa samaye hūṁ*

Make this offering one hundred eight or twenty-one times. After that, the hosts of deities that constitute the object of offering dissolve into you. Settle your body, speech, and mind in meditative equipoise in the uncontrived state. This corresponds to the accumulation of wisdom.

This is the instruction on the mandala, which enables one to complete the two accumulations. {332}

## 4. Instructions on the Guru Yoga

The guru yoga, which enables one to quickly receive blessings, is treated under four headings.

### a. Visualizing the Teacher

Above the crown of your head visualize a vast, spacious throne made of many precious materials, and on it a multicolored lotus with a hundred thousand petals and a full-moon disk. On that is your root teacher, and above his head, the great paṇḍita Shrīputra. Above the latter's head is the siddha Mitrayogin, who is white in color, playing a gold ḍāmaru in his right hand, and ringing a sweetly sounding silver bell in his left. Wearing a skirt of white cotton and the six bone ornaments, he is gazing into space. Above his head is Avalokiteshvara, who has one face and four arms and is seated in the vajra posture on a lotus and moon. He is adorned in silks and jewels. Above his head, visualize Amitābha as the lord of the family.

All these teachers are surrounded by rainbows, their bodies resplendent, their voices as melodious as Brahmā's, their minds full of blessings. Their crown centers are marked with a white *oṁ*, their throat centers with a red *āḥ*, their heart centers with a blue *hūṁ*, and their navel centers with a yellow *hoḥ*. From these emanate white, red, blue, and yellow rays of light, gathering with the light rays all the root and lineage teachers in the ten directions, the yidam deities, Three Jewels, ḍākinīs, and dharma protectors. They dissolve into the teachers' four centers. Consider that they thus become the great beings embodying all the teachers, yidams, and buddhas, the dharma, the sangha, the ḍākas and ḍākinīs, and the dharma protectors.

### b. Making Offerings {333}

First submit obeisance. Mentally make prostration with such prayers as

> Through his kindness
> [Great bliss arises in an instant:
> To the teacher whose body is like a precious jewel,
> To the lotus feet of the vajra being, I bow down.]

Make outer, inner, and secret offerings and complete these with the seven branches.

### c. Praying

> To the conqueror Amitābha I pray.
> To Lord Avalokiteshvara I pray.
> To the great siddha Mitrayogin I pray.
> To the great paṇḍita Shrīputra I pray.
> To the realized yogi Girti Ratna I pray.

To my precious teacher, embodiment of all teachers, I pray.
To my precious teacher, embodiment of all yidam deities, I pray.
To my precious teacher, embodiment of all buddhas, I pray.
To my precious teacher, embodiment of all the sacred teachings, I pray.
To my precious teacher, embodiment of all the sanghas, I pray.
To my precious teacher, embodiment of all the ḍākinīs and dharma protectors, I pray.

Then, pray for the fulfillment of your wishes:

Bestow the four empowerments on my stream of being, I pray.
Help me to develop the gnosis of the four joys, I pray.
Help me to train in pure perception and devotion, I pray.
Help me to acquire stability in the generation stage, I pray.
Help me to train in love and compassion, I pray.
Help me to unite sustained calm and profound insight, I pray.
Help me to merge the mother and child luminosities, I pray.
Help me to train in the illusory body and dream practices, I pray.
Help me to transfer to the body of truth at the moment of death, I pray.
Help me to attain the body of enjoyment in the intermediate state, I pray.
Bless me to achieve buddhahood in a single lifetime. {334}

### d. Receiving Empowerment

Empowerment is divided into four sections.

#### i. Purification with the Empowerment of Rays of Light

On a wheel in the crown center of each of the teachers is a white syllable *oṁ*, on a lotus in their throat centers a red syllable *āḥ*, on a vajra in their heart centers a blue syllable *hūṁ*, and on a kalpa's-end fire in their navel centers a yellow syllable *hoḥ*. From these, white, red, blue, and yellow light rays emanate, touching your own four centers—crown, throat, heart, and navel. Consider that the four obscurations—those of the body, speech, and mind and habitual tendencies—are purified; the four joys of the path are born in your mind stream; and you realize the result, primordial wisdom.

### ii. Purification by Means of the Four Waters of the Empowerment of the Stream of Water

From the four syllables in the four centers there spring streams of liquid, respectively like milk, like rubies, like molten beryl, and like refined gold. They dissolve into your own four centers. Consider that the four obscurations are purified, the four joys are developed, and the four buddha bodies are realized.

### iii. The Confirming Empowerment of Seed Syllables

The seats[11] and seed syllables in the teachers' four centers suddenly shoot out and dissolve into your own four centers. Consider that the four obscurations are purified, the four joys are developed, and the four buddha bodies are realized.

### iv. Empowerment of Completion

The teachers one by one melt into light and dissolve into your root teacher. Consider that your own body, speech, and mind become indivisible with the glorious teacher's body, speech, and mind, and, adopting the seven-point posture of Vairochana, settle your body, speech, and mind in the uncontrived state. {335} This is guru yoga—uniting with the teacher's true nature. It is by this means that you will swiftly receive blessings.

This completes the instruction on the guru yoga, and with it, the instructions on the preliminary practices.

We come now to the main practice,[12] which is divided into the generation stage and perfection stage.

## III. Instructions on the Generation Stage

The instructions on the generation stage are divided into three.

## A. The Body Instruction on Training in the Generation Stage with the Five Factors of Awakening

Concentrating on the four pure states,[13] with *oṁ svabhāva śuddāḥ sarvadharmāḥ svabhāva śuddho 'haṃ*, settle in meditative equipoise in the state free of all elaboration, in which all phenomena are empty and devoid of self, like the pure expanse of the sky at midday. This is the awakening related to the ground, the state of emptiness.

From that state of emptiness there appears a syllable *paṃ*, from which there appears a multicolored lotus with a hundred thousand petals. On top of it, from the letter *A*, appears the mandala of the full moon. To hold the mind on this is the awakening related to the throne, lotus, and moon.

On top of that there appears a white syllable *hrīḥ*, complete with visarga, emanating rays of light, which make offerings to the noble beings and benefit sentient beings. This is the awakening related to speech, the seed syllable.

From that there appears a white lotus in full bloom, its center marked by the syllable *hrīḥ*. To concentrate on this is the awakening related to the mind, the attribute. The *hrīḥ* melts into light, and one arises as noble Avalokiteshvara. He is white in color, like a snow-capped mountain, and has one face and four arms. He is sitting with his two legs crossed in the vajra posture. He has a skirt of celestial silk and a jeweled sash hanging down. Between his first two hands, palms joined at the level of his heart, he holds the wish-fulfilling gem, king of all jewels. The lower right hand fingers a rosary of one hundred eight white crystals. {336} The lower left hand holds the stem of a white lotus in full bloom, its blossom opening level with his ear. He has a smiling face, with almond eyes and long eyebrows. His broad forehead is adorned with a coil of white hair. Half his hair is tied up; the remaining half is loose, the locks and tresses reaching over his shoulders and down to his waist. In the midst of his hair is Amitābha, in the attire of the body of manifestation. On his head is a crown of the five precious materials, and he is adorned with earrings, a short necklace, long necklace, armbands, bracelets, anklets, a garland of five kinds of pearls, and multicolored silks. Visualize him clearly, like an image reflected in a mirror—appearing yet devoid of intrinsic existence.

In the three centers are arranged the three syllables. From the *hūṁ* rays of light emanate, inviting the wisdom deity, who dissolves [into one] inseparably.

If you can do the bestowal of empowerment and applying the seal, do so. If not, it has been taught that it is acceptable to not do it.

This is the awakening related to the body, complete and perfect.

### B. The Speech Instruction on the Recitation of the Mantra

The recitation of the mantra is divided into four sections.

#### 1. The Outer Way of Reciting according to the Sutra Vehicle

The appropriate times for this are at dawn and late in the evening. Concentrating on the *hrīḥ* in the heart center and on the body, do the recitation aloud and distinctly.

#### 2. The Inner Way of Reciting according to the Mantra Vehicle

In your heart center is a red eight-petaled lotus, in whose center is a moon disk, and on top of it a white syllable *hrīḥ*, complete with visarga, around which the six syllables circle clockwise. From them, five-colored rays of light emanate, filling the inside of your body. Again, the light radiates outward, touching the containing world {337} and turning it into the Blissful buddha field. It touches the beings who inhabit it, transforming them into Avalokiteshvara. Consider that they are all chanting the mantra. Recite only [as loudly] as can be heard inside the room. This is to be done in the morning and afternoon.

#### 3. The Secret Way of Reciting, Silently

The appropriate times for this are at noon and at midnight. Recite the mantra on the tip of the tongue, with clear concentration.

#### 4. The Ultimate Way of Reciting

Clearly visualize yourself as Avalokiteshvara, and in your heart center the syllable *hrīḥ*, from which rays of light shine forth, filling the inside of your body, and all the pores, with the forms of the Great Compassionate One. As the light rays touch the outer containing world, [it is transformed] into the Blissful buddha field; and as they touch the sentient beings inhabiting it, they all become Avalokiteshvara. In short, everything that appears as form becomes the body of Avalokiteshvara; everything that resounds as sound reminds one of the six syllables. In this way, recite [the mantra] mentally. This is done in the cool of the morning and in the late afternoon.

This completes the speech instruction on reciting the mantra.

### C. The Mind Instruction, Using the Emanation and Reabsorption of Light Rays as a Support for Training in Love, Compassion, and Bodhichitta

Meditating on the thought that all the sentient beings in the three worlds have been your parents, visualize yourself as the Great Compassionate One. In his heart center, upon a lotus and sun, is the white syllable *hrīḥ*, complete with visarga, emanating rays of light, filling your body. The light rays emanate outward, touching all sentient beings. Consider that all those sentient beings' negative deeds and obscurations are purified. Expel the stale air completely three times. {338} Again, visualize from the *hrīḥ* in the heart center white rays of light like lassos and hooks emanating in the ten directions. All the parent beings in the ten directions are drawn by their hearts joyfully in front of you. Consider that all the illnesses, negative forces, negative deeds, obscurations, and sufferings afflicting those sentient beings are collected by the rays of light and dissolve into the *hrīḥ* in your own center, so that, like a fire to which fuel has been added, the *hrīḥ* glows ever brighter and becomes more resplendent, your own mind feels joyful, and the whole of your body feels comfortable. Draw the lower wind up and press the upper wind back, and hold the vase breath as much as you can. When you expel the wind, consider that all your happiness and virtue dissolves into all sentient beings, so that, on the temporary level, their whole bodies and minds are filled with bliss, and on the ultimate level, they complete the two accumulations and all become the Great Compassionate One in reality. Train in sending and taking until you are able to actually do it.

At the end, the outer world dissolves into the Great Compassionate Ones, the inner Great Compassionate Ones dissolve into you, you dissolve into the syllable *hrīḥ* in your heart center, and the *hrīḥ* [dissolves] like a rainbow vanishing in the sky. Rest in the state free of concepts. This is the ultimate generation stage.

The practice for enhancing compassion is known from an oral instruction. It completes the relative generation stage, which is now followed by the ultimate perfection stage.

## IV. Instructions on the Perfection Stage[14]

The perfection stage is divided into seven sections: (1) sustained calm; (2) profound insight; (3) the illusory body; (4) dream; (5) luminosity; (6) transference; and (7) the intermediate state.

### A. Sustained Calm

Sustained calm is treated under three headings: (1) sustained calm making use of conceptual attributes; (2) sustained calm focusing on conceptual thoughts; {339} and (3) sustained calm settling in a state without conceptual thoughts.

#### 1. Sustained Calm Making Use of Conceptual Attributes

There are two parts: (1) holding the mind on an object outside and (2) holding the mind on an object inside.

##### a. Holding the Mind on an Object Outside

This is divided into two aspects: (1) impure and (2) pure.

###### i. Holding the Mind on an Impure Object

With your body held in the seven-point posture of Vairochana, and with the proper gaze, hold the mind undistractedly on a suitable object in front of you, such as a pillar, vase, stick, or pebble, all the while respecting the essential point of the body and the correct gaze. For this, do not get involved in distraction or entertain conceptual thoughts. Relax as you settle the mind directly on it. Should wildness or dullness occur, you should know how to focus the mind up or down or right or left.

### ii. Holding the Mind on a Pure Object

This consists of holding the mind on a buddha image. Place in front of you an image of Lord Amitābha. Alternatively, if you do not have one, visualize it. Do not get scattered in thoughts or get involved in distraction. Just rest the mind on the image, relaxed and undistracted. This is holding the mind on a pure object, an image of a buddha.

### b. Holding the Mind on an Object Inside

Holding the mind on an object inside also has two aspects: (1) impure and (2) pure.

### i. Holding the Mind on an Impure Object

This consists of holding the mind on a sphere. Concentrate on a pea-sized white sphere emanating rays of light on a lotus and moon in your heart center. While doing so, do not get scattered in thoughts or involved in distraction. This is a pith instruction for incorporating thoughts on the path without rejecting them.

There now follows a pith instruction for incorporating thoughts on the path of sustained calm by directing the mind at that very thought and holding the mind on it.

### ii. Holding the Mind on a Pure Object

This involves concentrating on the form of a buddha. {340} Hold the mind on a thumb-sized form of Avalokiteshvara on a lotus and moon in your heart center, radiating light. For this, do not entertain conceptual thoughts or get involved in distraction. If wildness or dullness occurs, for both pure and impure objects, visualize the object in the forehead or navel center and hold the mind there.

All this is sustained calm making use of conceptual attributes.

### 2. Sustained Calm Focusing on Conceptual Thoughts

Especially when thoughts proliferate, look directly, without any concepts, at the nature of any thoughts that arise, whether virtuous or unvirtuous—

thoughts related to samsara (the five poisons or three poisons, defilements, dualistic concepts of subject and object) or thoughts related to the ten virtuous deeds, or to the six or ten transcendent perfections, and so on. In this way, they will be destroyed, without being grasped at, and awareness, clear and empty, will arise vividly yet intangibly. Preserve that state of pure awareness, self-recognizing and self-liberating. Again, whatever thoughts arise, focus the mind on them and recognize them as your own nature without rejecting them or accepting them. In this way, put into practice the pith instruction of taking thoughts on the path.

### 3. The Ultimate, Resultant Sustained Calm, Settling in a State without Conceptual Thoughts

In an isolated, dark room, on a soft cushion, adopt the seven-point posture of Vairochana and direct your eyes blankly into the empty surrounding space. Cut off all thoughts related to the three times that pass through your mind—thoughts of the past, present, and future and virtuous, unvirtuous, and indeterminate thoughts. Do not think of anything. Settle the mind in clarity and emptiness beyond grasping, like the unblemished sky—still, vivid, and awake. By this means, the sustained calm of bliss, clarity, and absence of thought occurs. {341} In that very state, check whether you are involved in attachment, aversion, clinging, grasping, or wildness or dullness, and, distinguishing the faults and virtues in these, identify them.

## B. Profound Insight

Profound insight is treated under three headings.

### 1. [The Causal Profound Insight: Examining the Mind]

For the causal profound insight, one trains by investigating the mind, as follows. Examine and analyze the essential nature of the mind's arising, ceasing, and staying, asking yourself, From where has this mind of mine arisen? Where does it stay? Where will it cease?

Examine and check, asking yourself, Has it arisen from the five elements or from my own body? Does it dwell there? Will it die there?

Check further: Does the mind have a color—white, red, yellow, green, or multicolored? Or is it colorless? Moreover, was this mind of mine produced with a shape—the form of earth, water, fire, wind, or space, or round, square, semicircular, oblong, or oval, and so on? Or is it shapeless? Are thoughts something other than the mind, or are thoughts the mind? Again, check: Does the mind arise from appearances outside, or do appearances outside arise from the mind?

Now, mentally examine and look at the examining mind. Does that mind exist or not? Check: Is it clear or unclear? Happy or unhappy? Is it a self or not? {342} Is it permanent or impermanent? Is it calm or restless? Is it visible or invisible?

Moreover, what is the mind that rests in meditative equipoise like? What is the mind that is not meditating like? In this way, use your own mind to thoroughly investigate itself. And you should also thoroughly investigate the nature of awareness of the meditator. Investigate whether those minds are one and the same or distinct and different.

When you do this, you might conclude that the essential nature of the mind is devoid of any arising, staying, and ceasing. Its essential nature is intrinsically empty. It is like the expanse of space. It is naturally radiant. It is the unobstructed display of awareness, arising in every kind of way, and all these appearances are of the same taste in being unborn, nondwelling, and unceasing. Its nature is emptiness, its character is luminous clarity, its manifestation is unobstructed: awareness arising in many ways—appearance and emptiness inseparable. It is inconceivable like space, clear, aware, and empty, with neither periphery nor center.

Recognize that this is thatness, the nature of your own mind, in which all good qualities [are present]—the triad of ground, path, and result; the quartet of view, meditation, conduct, and result; the four truths; four joys; four boundless qualities; six transcendent perfections; ten levels; five paths; the duo of skillful means and wisdom; the two truths; refuge; confession; the observance of vows; bodhichitta; the two accumulations; compassion; the generation stage; the perfection stage; sustained calm and profound insight; the Three Jewels; three buddha bodies; the five kinds of gnosis; and so on. {343} On that basis, you should become proficient in recognizing it.

## 2. [The Essential Profound Insight, Putting Recognition into Practice]

Next, having been introduced to the fresh, "ordinary" mind,[15] you should simultaneously experience it, as follows.

The nature of mind is devoid of the limits of birth, cessation, and destruction.[16] It is free from the dualistic apprehension of subject and object that grasps at "I" and "mine." Its nature is emptiness, its character luminous clarity. Its manifestation is unobstructed: awareness, without object, yet appearing clearly in a multitude of ways. It transcends any field of apprehension—something to be seen and someone seeing. It is free of any field of reference, something to be meditated on and someone meditating. It neither thinks of something nor does it not think. It is not something that is contrived, so it is a state of relaxation. It is devoid of all activity, so there is nothing to be done. There is no identifying whatever arises, so it is free of grasping. The mind of meditative equipoise is unadulterated by contrivance, so it is free of thoughts. Free of grasping at attributes, it is utterly empty. Naturally radiant, it is vividly clear. Uncontaminated by dualistic thoughts, it is fresh and naked. Recognizing its own nature, it is fully awake. Since apprehension of object and subject have been destroyed, appearance and mind are inseparable, all-penetrating, and even. Since it rests naturally in uncontrived awareness, it is the ordinary mind. And since it does entertain chains of thoughts, it is what is known as "fresh awareness." This is the main practice, the essence of making an experience of profound insight.

Furthermore, the nature of mind is also Avalokiteshvara—the All-Seeing One. It is the All-Seeing One because the eyes of great compassion[17] gaze on the totality of beings impartially. It is the All-Seeing One because the eye of omniscience that transcends the ordinary intellect, being devoid of conceptual limits, sees all phenomena distinctly and self-cognizingly, like reflections. {344} It is the All-Seeing One because the eye of self-cognizing wisdom sees the meaning of unborn ultimate reality. It is the All-Seeing One because the eye in which dualistic apprehension has been purified in the ultimate expanse sees the nature of mind, which is luminosity free of elaboration. This is how the nature of mind is introduced.

### 3. The Ultimate Practice of the Union of Sustained Calm and Profound Insight

To settle in the state of emptiness and clarity inseparable, like space (for the mind is devoid of birth, cessation, and dwelling), is sustained calm. To see and recognize the nature of that is profound insight. The nature of mind is the union of sustained calm and profound insight, which is the actual way things are, free of the two extremes. Since the nature of mind is unborn, it is free of the extreme of eternalism. And since it has no cessation, it is free of the extreme of nihilism.

Its nature is to dwell as emptiness, so it is free of the extreme of eternalism. Yet it is aware and manifests clearly in multifarious ways, so it is free of the extreme of nihilism. The nature of the mind has no existence as color or shape, so it is free of the extreme of eternalism. But its character is luminous clarity, so it is free of the extreme of nihilism. Since the three buddha bodies are spontaneously present in it, it is free from the extreme of nihilism.[18] The nature of the mind is empty and without self, beyond the ordinary mind, so it is free from the extreme of eternalism. Its manifesting power appears in all sorts of ways, so it is free from the extreme of appearance.[19] Thus, transcending the conceptual extremes of eternalism and nihilism, it is the inseparable union of clarity, awareness, and emptiness. The manner in which this union is put into practice is as follows.

The settling of the mind on the illusion-like skillful means, the accumulation of merit, is sustained calm; knowing and seeing that these are devoid of intrinsic nature and therefore empty {345} is profound insight. Settling the mind on devotion in the practice of guru yoga is sustained calm, while seeing that the essential nature of that mental state is emptiness, transcending the intellect, is profound insight. Settling the mind on the visualization in the generation stage, which is like the reflection of the moon in water, is sustained calm, while seeing that its nature is emptiness is profound insight. Settling the mind on all appearances being the self-experience of the mind, like the reflection of the moon in water, is sustained calm; seeing that appearances are interdependent and unborn—appearance and emptiness inseparable—is profound insight. Settling the mind on the great bliss, the culmination of the path, is sustained calm; seeing that very state as emptiness, without clinging, is profound insight. Settling the mind on the natural luminosity of the mind is sustained calm, while seeing its essential nature as emptiness, free of elaboration, is profound insight. Settling the mind on the fresh state of awareness uncontaminated by contrivance is sustained calm; seeing it as no-self, awareness and emptiness inseparable, is profound insight.

In short, there is no emptiness that is other than appearances, which are like the reflection of the moon in water, a reflection in a mirror, or an echo. And there are no appearances that are other than emptiness. To realize the inseparability of appearances and emptiness, like a rainbow appearing in the sky, and to settle in the essential nature of that is what we call the union of sustained calm and profound insight.

This completes the perfection stage instruction on the union of sustained calm and profound insight.

### C. Illusory Body

Meditation on the illusory body involves training during the day. It is divided into four parts.

#### 1. The Preliminary Practice for the Illusory Body, the Kusulu's Gathering of the Accumulations

Visualize in the air above the crown of your head a white wisdom ḍākinī, holding a curved knife in her right hand and a skull cup full of blood in the left. She is in the dancing posture {346} and adorned with jewel and bone ornaments. Visualize your own consciousness as a white letter *A*, resting in your secret center, and meditate that it is ejected like a shooting star through the aperture of Brahmā in your crown and dissolves into the heart center of the goddess. After that, you yourself become the wisdom ḍākinī. In front of you is a manifested hearth of three skulls, on top of which is a kapāla, white outside and red inside, sliced from your own head at the level of the brow. Visualize it as the size of the billionfold universe, and inside it the flesh and blood of your own body, chopped into pieces and poured into it. Underneath it, the fire ignites. As you say *oṁ āḥ hūṁ*, the fire melts all the flesh and blood into white nectar. Then, as you again say *oṁ āḥ hūṁ*, it is blessed as wisdom nectar.

Visualize in your heart center the syllable *hrīḥ*. From it, boundless rays of light like lassos and hooks emanate, touching the root and lineage teachers in the ten directions; the hosts of deities of the four classes of tantra; the Buddha, dharma, and sangha; all the ḍākinīs and dharma protectors and guardians; and all the beings in the six realms. All of them become the Great Compassionate One and are drawn by their hearts, summoned by the light rays and taking their places in front of you. Consider that they sip up the white nectar and that their whole bodies are thus filled with untainted bliss, as you say:

To the lips of the root and lineage teachers [I offer], *oṁ āḥ hūṁ.*
To the lips of the hosts of yidam deities [I offer], *oṁ āḥ hūṁ.*
To the lips of the precious buddhas [I offer], *oṁ āḥ hūṁ.*
To the precious teachings [I offer], *oṁ āḥ hūṁ.*
To the lips of the precious sanghas [I offer], *oṁ āḥ hūṁ.* {347}
To the lips of the buddhas and bodhisattvas [I offer], *oṁ āḥ hūṁ.*
To the lips of the ḍākas and ḍākinīs [I offer], *oṁ āḥ hūṁ.*
To the lips of the dharma protectors and guardians [I offer], *oṁ āḥ hūṁ.*
To the lips of the local deities [I offer], *oṁ āḥ hūṁ.*
To the lips of the six classes of beings [I offer], *oṁ āḥ hūṁ.*

Consider that they are all satisfied. Visualize that they all become Avalokiteshvara and Tārā, murmuring the six-syllable mantra. Meditate thinking: "All this is a magical illusion; it is a dream." Indeed, apart from its being created by your own mind, it has no separate existence; it is a fiction. You should make an experience of this yourself.

### 2. General Training in the Illusory Body

All the phenomena included in the relative realm of appearance and existence, samsara and nirvana, are impermanent and unstable, like magical illusions or dreams. How to meditate on the meaning of this is as follows.

If we investigate these phenomena of samsara and nirvana, asking ourselves where they come from—whether from above or below, or from the cardinal and intermediate directions—and where they go, we should understand that they come from nowhere, they go nowhere, and they do not stay anywhere. They are no more than the pure and impure perceptions of the mind, which, apart from merely appearing, have no intrinsic existence, like the apparitions in a magical illusion, a dream, or a city of gandharvas.

From where, then, does this so-called samsara arise? It arises through our sense of self and sense of possession.[20] We therefore need to investigate where this self comes from—whether our sense of self and possession come from the five elements or from some part of the body. After that, once we have seen that samsara originates in our grasping at an "I" and "mine," {348} we should investigate whether that grasping at "I" and "mine" is something that has already passed, something that will come in the future, or something that is arising right now. If it is related to the past, it has already passed, so such a self cannot exist. If it is related to the future, it has not yet come into being, so it cannot be taken as an observable object. And if it is related to the present, it cannot exist even for a moment as the nature of an instant of awareness. It is emptiness. Thus, we should understand that the sense of self and possession, which is the root of samsara, has no intrinsic existence.

Now, while they may not exist, phenomena appear in many forms, like the apparitions in a magical illusion or a dream. They come into being through conditions, like an echo, the reflection of the moon in water, or an image in a mirror. They are impermanent and fleeting, like lightning in the sky, dewdrops, bubbles, clouds, and mist. They appear, yet they have no real existence, like a mirage, an optical illusion, a rainbow, or a city of gandharvas. Thus all these external appearances, while not existing, are nothing but the deluded appearances of the mind. We should realize that all phenomena are like the many different dreams that someone might have while asleep but which have no intrinsic reality or existence. We have to understand that that is how all phenomena are, and thence make an effort to even out the eight ordinary preoccupations.[21]

### 3. Specific Training in the Illusory Body

Once we have thus trained generally in illusion, we should proceed to the specific training, for which there are three parts.

### a. Training in the Body Being Apparent yet Empty

Place a mirror in front of you. As your reflection appears in it, praise and criticize it. Look at whether you are pleased or displeased. If you are displeased, train in being so as an illusory body. {349} As well as that, imagine that on your right is the hideous-looking Lord of Death chopping you up with a fiery ax, while on your left is a beautiful goddess rubbing you with sandalwood ointment. Watch the state of your mind to see whether it is pleased or displeased, and recognize that both the Lord of Death and the goddess are simply your own perceptions. The mind has no intrinsic reality; its appearances are like magical illusions and dreams. Train in the illusory body realizing that all mental states related to attachment and aversion are devoid of intrinsic existence and are therefore essentially the same.

### b. Training in Speech Being Like an Echo

Go to a place where there is an echo and shout [to create] an echo. You will be answered with the words you shouted. Those words you shouted do not exist beyond merely being external perceptions. Thus train in all sounds being of the same taste, like echoes.

### c. Training in the Mind Being Like a Dream, a Magical Illusion, or a Mirage

The mind is like a dream, a magical illusion, a mirage. Nothing in it exists, and although, when we are deluded, things seems to be there, in truth they have no intrinsic existence. If we look at their essential nature, they are like space. So train in whatever conceptual thoughts arise as being devoid of self, without grasping, in the state of clarity-emptiness that transcends intellect.

### 4. Training in the Pure Illusory Body

Meditate that all appearances are the Great Compassionate One. Meditate that all sounds are the murmuring sound of the six syllables. Meditate thinking that these deities do not arise from anywhere; they do not go anywhere; they are simply the appearances of your own mind, like dreams and magical illusions. And rest in the state free of elaboration. This is how to train in the pure illusory body.

### D. Dream

The dream practice involves training at night. It is divided into four parts.[22] {350}

### 1. Preliminary Practice

The preliminary for the dream practice is the kusulu's gathering of the accumulations, as above.

## 2. Training in Dream

The dream practice itself is divided into (1) general training and (2) specific training.

### a. General Training

Meditate on manifestations and transformations, reflecting, "These appearances outside are dream appearances; this body too is a dream body. The objects in a dream and the body have no true existence. However they manifest or transform, they are all the same."

### b. Specific Training

Imagine in front of you a great pit in the ground, or a high mountain, or an enormous cliff, and that you are falling from it. At that moment, mingle your mind with the earth, thinking: "This is a dream, an illusion. The objects in a dream are fictional. The dream and my mind have no intrinsic existence. This cliff is a dream cliff. The earth is by nature Ratnasambhava. Who would be afraid of him?" And meditate that the whole earth[23] is Ratnasambhava. Venerate him with clouds of offerings and meditate that everything emits the sound of the teachings.

Again, imagine that you are falling into a large lake or a great river in front of you, and mingle your mind with the water, thinking: "I am sleeping. This is a dream body and dream water. They do not exist truly. The nature of water is Akṣhobhya. Who would be afraid of him?" And meditate that all the water is Akṣhobhya.

Again, imagine that you are falling into a firepit or a huge, blazing furnace in front of you, and mingle your mind with the fire, thinking: "I am sleeping. This is a dream body and dream fire. {351} They do not exist truly. The nature of fire is Amitābha. Who would be afraid of him?" And meditate that all the fire is Amitābha.

Again, imagine in front of you a deep black whirlwind, which sucks you up and whirls you around. Mingle your mind with the wind, thinking: "I am sleeping. This is a dream body and dream wind. They do not exist truly. The nature of wind is Amoghasiddhi. Who would be afraid of him?" And meditate that all the wind is Amoghasiddhi.

Finally, imagine that you are falling into a void expanse in front of you.

Mingle your mind with space, thinking: "I am sleeping. This is a dream body and dream space. They do not exist truly. The nature of space is Vairochana. Who would be afraid of him?" And meditate that the whole of space is filled by Vairochana.

This is the specific training.

### 3. Apprehending Dreams

Apprehending one's dreams is treated under three headings.

#### a. For Those with the Best Faculties, Apprehending Dreams in the State Free of Concepts

Visualize above the crown of your head the Great Compassionate One, the size of a thumb. Visualize in your secret center a red secret wisdom ḍākinī, the size of a thumb. Then, from the Great Compassionate One on your crown there emanates a white essence drop, which comes into your heart center, purifying ignorance. From the secret wisdom [ḍākinī] in your secret center there emanates a red essence drop, which reaches your heart center and purifies attachment. The two drops come closer together, purifying aversion. Next, the drops go around in a circle, as if chasing each other: this corresponds to the vase empowerment. {352} They touch, corresponding to the secret empowerment. The arising of bliss from their contact corresponds to the wisdom empowerment. They dissolve into each other and melt into light, corresponding to the fourth empowerment. After that, being quite certain in your mind that all phenomena are magical illusions and dreams, and that the nature of illusions and dreams is beyond concepts, go to sleep with your mind undistracted in the state of clarity and emptiness. This is apprehending dreams by relying on nonconceptuality.

#### b. For Those with Middling Faculties, Apprehending Dreams through Aspiration

Apprehend dreams by concentrating on the ten points of the method of training described above. In particular, make a strong aspiration: "These appearances outside are dream appearances. This body of mine too is a dream body. The objects and body in a dream have no true existence. How can I transform them?"

First, fix your awareness on a sphere in the heart center. Then, in that hazy moment when you are going to sleep in the evening, practice the dream yoga without straying from your aspiration, relaxing your body and maintaining undistracted mindfulness. Simply by doing this, you will apprehend your dreams.

### c. For the Least Capable Individuals, Apprehending Dreams through Concentration

This practice is divided into three sections.

i. Visualizing your teacher above the crown of your head, take the empowerments with concentration. Pray to recognize your dreams. Then, concentrating on an eight-petaled red lotus in your throat center, in the center of which is a red sphere radiating light, go to sleep[24] and thus recognize your dreams.

ii. Apprehending dreams by taking the support of a seed syllable of buddha speech. If you direct your concentration on a brightly shining red syllable *hrīḥ* in the center of an eight-petaled[25] red lotus in your throat center, you will recognize your dreams.

iii. Apprehending dreams by taking the support of the buddha body. {353} This involves concentrating on the Great Compassionate One, the size of a thumb, radiating light, on the center of an eight-petaled red lotus in your throat center and then recognizing your dreams.

All these are the stages of apprehending dream. In this regard, it has been taught that one should know that one needs to have [the means] for removing obstacles and eliminating excessive mental states.[26]

### 4. Manifesting and Transforming and Multiplying

Once you can apprehend your dreams, you should manifest as the five elements—earth, water, fire, wind, space, and so on—and manifest as Indra and the universal monarch, all-knowing horses, elephants, garuḍas, and many kinds of sentient beings. Next, for transformation, you should transform earth into water, water into fire, fire into wind, wind into space, space into the beings of the six realms, and the beings of the six realms into the deities of Kriyā, Upa, Yoga, and Anuttara. At times make yourself visible; at other times make yourself invisible. Similarly, you should learn how to manifest and transform the gross into the subtle, the subtle into the gross, the many into a single, the single into many, and so on. This completes manifestation and transformation.

Next, multiplying. After manifesting and transforming as many beings, multiply them from one to ten, from ten to a hundred, from a hundred to a thousand, from a thousand to ten thousand, a hundred thousand, a million, ten million, a hundred million, and so on. Similarly, manifest and transform as numerous deities of Kriyā, Upa, Yoga, and Anuttara, and in particular just Avalokiteshvara and the deities of Anuttara, and so forth. {354} And multiply them from one to a hundred million, reciting the *maṇi* and other mantras.

### 5. [Further Instructions on Dream Practice]

These are taught under three headings: (1) ascertaining object appearances; (2) training in pure realms; and (3) subduing obstacle makers.

#### a. Ascertaining Object Appearances

Those with the best faculties will ascertain object appearances from the state of luminosity free from conceptual thoughts.

Those with middling faculties will ascertain object appearances by means of some mental activity.

Those with the most modest faculties will ascertain object appearances by manifesting as vultures and so on and traveling. For this, it is said that one begins by clearly ascertaining the objects in one's own house and bedroom, and then ascertains other objects outside.

#### b. Training in Pure Realms

Having manifested as a garuḍa, for example, one should travel to the Blissful land, the land of Manifest Joy, the land of Beryl Light, the Joyful Heaven, and other pure lands. There, one should manifest many offerings to the buddhas dwelling in those buddha fields, venerate them, and request teachings. Likewise, one should manifest multiple buddha fields oneself, make infinite manifested offerings, and receive teachings. This is how to train in pure realms.

### c. Subjugating Obstacle Makers

Manifesting as Hayagrīva, for example, one subjugates the likes of the king of evil spirits. One manifests as a garuḍa to subjugate the nāgas; as Vajrapāṇi to subjugate the mamos; as Vajrabhairava to subjugate the gods and demons in general. If an evil spirit manifests as water, one manifests oneself as a thousand suns and dries it up. To an evil spirit manifesting as fire, one appears as water to extinguish it. {355} To evil spirits manifesting as vultures and so forth, one appears as a garuḍa and subdues them. To evil spirits manifesting as hawks, one appears as an eagle and subdues them. Likewise, to dogs one manifests as a tiger, to little birds as a hawk, to deer and antelope as a beast of prey, to [lesser] beasts of prey as a lion, to lions as a mass of fire, and so on, manifesting as whatever is inimical to them to subdue them and induce them to offer one their vital mantras.

At the end, meditate on love, compassion, and bodhichitta, and settle in the state of emptiness. This is how to tame evil spirits.

## E. Luminosity[27]

Luminosity is taught under three headings.

### 1. Identifying the Ground Luminosity, the Ultimate Reality, the Actual Way Things Are

The nature of the mind is luminosity; it is devoid of birth, remaining, and destruction; it is thatness, free of elaboration, free from extremes. Whether or not sentient beings have realized it, it is present as their essential nature, pervading all beings since time without beginning. Because they have not realized the meaning of thatness, and they grasp at a self where there is no self, the luminous nature of mind is obscured by the stains of the delusion of an apprehending subject and an apprehended object, and thus beings wander in samsara. Nevertheless, what we call the ground luminosity is present as one's own naturally luminous mind, whether or not it is freed of obscurations, which are like the clouds in the sky, mist in the air, or mud in water. It is like a lamp in a pot or a priceless treasure in a pauper's house.

### 2. Developing Proficiency in the Path Luminosity

Developing proficiency is divided into two parts.

#### a. Luminosity Practice during the Day

This is the practice of applying the crucial points of the channels, winds, and essence drops, {356} through which one actualizes luminosity. For this there are three sections.

i. In a completely sealed dark room, on a soft seat with a raised meditation cushion, [adopt] the essential points for the body: legs crossed in the vajra posture; hands as vajra fists placed on the thighs; shoulders well apart like a vulture's wings; spine as straight as an arrow; throat drawn in like a hook; eyes gazing motionless—up toward the crown of the head if one is drowsy, past the tip of the nose if one is restless,[28] and into space level with the eyebrows if the meditation is balanced.

ii. The [essential point of the] speech involves binding the winds. This refers to holding the winds with the vase exercise.

iii. By means of the above, the essence drops are bound by themselves and there will arise the universally supreme concentrations of bliss, clarity, and no-thought, [with] the ten signs of luminosity and many indefinite signs. One is introduced to the luminosity that is the mind's own natural radiance, the body of truth, the inseparability of the ultimate expanse and awareness.

#### b. Luminosity Practice at Night

The best practitioners go to sleep in the state of luminosity, the nature of the mind, and thereby apprehend luminosity. If one cannot apprehend it by this means, one should do so by relying on concentration: Visualize yourself as the Great Compassionate One, clear and radiant outside and inside, and in your heart center, upon a moon disk, the white syllable *hrīḥ*, with the visarga, emanating rays of light brighter than a hundred thousand suns. The outside and inside of your body and the whole of the billionfold universe, with its four continents, become clear and radiant outside and inside. By concentrating on this as you go to sleep, you will apprehend luminosity.

### 3. Realizing the Resultant Luminosity

The resultant luminosity is introduced as follows. The nature of the mind is free of subject-object duality. {357} It is self-cognizant and naturally luminous. It is the inseparability of the object that is known—ultimate reality supreme in all aspects—and the self-cognizant gnosis whose essence is knowing. It is devoid of birth, cessation, and dwelling. It is the body of truth free from the extremes of existence and nonexistence, truth and falsity, eternalism and nihilism.

## F. Transference

Transference comprises two parts.[29]

### 1. Training

Visualize your own body as Avalokiteshvara, as in the sādhana. In the middle of this body, visualized as clear and empty, is the central channel, white on the outside, red on the inside. Consider that the opening at its lower end, pointing toward the secret center, is blocked by the syllable *phaṭ*, and that the upper end pierces your crown, clear and empty like an open skylight. Visualize each of the nine orifices blocked by a red syllable *hrīḥ*.

After that, for the destination of transference, visualize in the sky, an arm span above the crown of your head, a precious throne, with a lotus and moon seat piled above it. Upon that visualize the Great Compassionate One, his body adorned with the major and minor marks, in the attire of the body of perfect enjoyment.

Next, for training in the transference, there are three points.

#### a. Transference by Means of the Deity's Mind

In your heart center visualize a lotus and moon, upon which is the essence of your consciousness, a brilliant white sphere, round and glossy, and emanating rays of five-colored light. Then, the Great Compassionate One above your head, reciting the six-syllable mantra, says: "Fortunate child, transfer into my mind." The moment he says this, visualize that from that sphere, a white sphere shoots up, passes up the central channel, touches the heart of the Great Compassionate One for a moment, {358} and then comes down again, dissolving into the original sphere in your heart. Train in this way one hundred or twenty times, and so on, until the signs occur.

### b. Transference by Means of the Deity's Speech—the Seed Syllable

The stages of visualizing yourself as the Great Compassionate One, visualizing the channel in the center of your body, and concentrating on the teacher above the crown of your head are the same as above. In this case, visualize in your heart center, upon a lotus and moon, a red syllable *hrīḥ*, shining with light. Consider that from the *hrīḥ* another *hrīḥ* shoots up and remains for a short while in the teacher's heart center. It then dissolves back into the original *hrīḥ*. Train in this as above.

### c. Transference by Means of the Deity's Body

Visualize the deity, central channel, and teacher in the same way as before. For the specific visualization, visualize on a moon in your heart center the Great Compassionate One, crystal clear, shining with light, the size of a thumb. From him, another shoots up and touches the teacher's heart center, remaining there for a moment. Then it dissolves back into the original deity. Train in this manner.

### 2. Putting Transference into Practice

Once the signs of death are all present, completely cut the ties of clinging and attachment and, maintaining love, compassion, and devotion, visualize your body as the deity, meditate on the central channel in the middle, and visualize your teacher above the crown of your head. On a lotus and moon in your heart center, visualize successively the sphere, the syllable *hrīḥ*, and the form of the deity. Then, consider that they, together with their seats, shoot out and, propelled like shooting stars, dissolve into the teacher's heart center. Meditate on this until you are able to transfer. At the end, consider that the teacher too dissolves into the heart center of Amitābha in the Blissful buddha field, Sukhāvatī. {359} This is how one puts transference into practice.

### G. The Intermediate State

The intermediate state (*bardo*)[30] is considered under four headings.

#### 1. Training in the Intermediate State

Pray to your teacher to train in the intermediate state. Then meditate thinking: "All these appearances outside are bardo appearances. This body of mine is a bardo body. All forms are bardo forms. All sounds are bardo sounds. Smells, tastes, and physical sensations are all bardo [experiences]. All happiness and suffering are bardo appearances. They are illusions, dreams. The bardo body has no intrinsic existence." Leave the self-illuminating mind in equipoise, free of elaboration, in the sky-like state, the sameness of all phenomena, where there is nothing to adopt or reject. To do so is to train in the bardo as the body of truth.

Meditate that all the forms that you perceive are the body of Avalokiteshvara, all sounds are the speech of Avalokiteshvara, and all thoughts are the generation stage of Avalokiteshvara. To make an experience of these is to train in the bardo of the body of perfect enjoyment.

Meditate that all objects of perception outside are the Blissful buddha field, all sentient beings are manifestation-body buddhas, all sounds are the sounds of the sacred dharma, and all thoughts are the display of gnosis. This is the training in [purifying phenomena as a] manifestation-body buddha field.

#### 2. Checking the Signs of Dissolution

The outer signs of the earth element dissolving into the water element are that the body loses its radiance, one cannot smell things, and one's perceptions seem to become dark and heavy. The inner signs are the experience like vapor or steamy breath.

The signs of the water element dissolving into the fire element are {360} that the mouth and nose become dry and the lips pucker. The inner signs are experiences like dust and mirages.

The signs of the fire element dissolving into the wind element are that the warmth of the body withdraws from the extremities and one has difficulty breathing in. The inner signs are experiences like a lamp being raised up or like fireflies.

The signs of the wind dissolving into the consciousness are a dark spot on the tongue and one gapes. The inner signs are experiences like clear sky or snow falling.

The signs of the consciousness dissolving into luminosity are, outwardly, experiences like a cloudless sky and, inwardly, experiences like the sun rising at daybreak.

This is what one checks for as the signs of dissolution.

### 3. How to Put the Bardo of the Three Buddha Bodies into Practice

a. The instructions on attaining buddhahood as the body of truth in the bardo of ultimate reality are as follows. After the dissolution of the five elements, the subtle wind dissolves into the central channel. When this stage has been completed, the blood constituent obtained from one's mother is gathered upward, and there is an experience of redness. The seminal constituent obtained from one's father falls downward and whiteness is experienced. Then the white and red constituents and the dhanaṃjaya wind, together with the consciousness, are gathered into the vasanta channel in the heart center, and the universally supreme luminosity will manifest,[31] the sky-like state of bliss, clarity, and no-thought without center or periphery. At that time, everything that appears as form is the natural form of the body of truth, luminosity, the nature of mind. All sounds are the natural sound of the body of truth, the nature of mind. All smells, tastes, physical sensations, and consciousness are the display of ultimate reality, luminosity, the nature of the mind. {361} By thus recognizing one's own nature and remaining in meditation in that state, one will attain buddhahood in the bardo of luminosity, the expanse of the body of truth.

b. For those who have proceeded into the bardo of becoming, the practice for the body of perfect enjoyment is as follows. Someone who possesses the pith instructions on all the signs of the bardo should remain undistracted from considering all appearances as the Blissful buddha field, Sukhāvatī (visualizing themself and all beings as Avalokiteshvara in union with his consort), all sounds as the six-syllable mantra, and all thoughts as the generation phase. In this way, they will be liberated in the body of perfect enjoyment.

c. The practice for the body of manifestation in the last bardo is as follows. Having transformed all objects perceived outside as the Blissful buddha field and oneself and all sentient beings as manifestation-body buddhas, and transformed all sounds as the sound of the teachings, and transformed all thoughts as the play of gnosis, one should perform such deeds as teaching sentient beings the dharma. Furthermore, taking support of transformations, one should travel by miraculous power to buddha fields such the Blissful, Joyful, and Manifest Joy, listen to the teachings, manifest multiple offerings and venerate the buddhas there, and so on. By this means, one will attain buddhahood in the last bardo in a manifestation-body buddha field.

These were the instructions on the bardo.

### 4. Blocking the Entrance to the Womb

If you are unable to attain liberation in the three bardos, you should at least block the entrance to the womb. When you perceive a male and female having sex and a place such as a house, visualize all males as Avalokiteshvara and all females as Vajravarāhī, {362} and meditate on all sounds as the six syllables and all thoughts as the generation and perfection stages from the state devoid of attachment and grasping. If you do so, the entrance to the womb will be closed and you will be reborn in a pure buddha field.

## V. Concluding Edicts

Mitra sealed these instructions with four commands:

1. Teach this instruction to a single lineage holder.
2. Offer the feast and flowers of gold.[32]
3. Do not give the instruction [simply] by reading transmission.
4. Having received it, practice it.

This method for attaining enlightenment in one lifetime
The great siddha Mitra received from Avalokiteshvara
And passed on to the great Indian paṇḍita Shrīputra.
From him, through the aural lineage of pith instructions, they came to Girti Ratna,
Who granted me the brimming vase
Of these essential instructions, poured without mistake.

These I have written down, with no errors in word or meaning.
By this merit, may I attain the level of Lord Avalokiteshvara
And thus become a guide for all beings.

These condensed instructions on the stages of the path of noble Avalokiteshvara, entitled *A Banquet of Nectar*, were written down by the yogi Öpak Dorje. By the mass of merit from this, may all sentient beings swiftly be set in the heart of enlightenment.

This prayer of dedication completes the instructions. By this merit may all beings attain buddhahood.

Virtue!

# 17. The Luminous Golden Wand of Pith Instructions

*An Appendix to the Instructions on Noble Avalokiteshvara's Graded Path to Enlightenment*[1]

In the Vajrayāna, it is the "pith instructions" an authentic vajra master gives their disciple, often in response to a particular question or to address a particular difficulty, that transform the formal instructions into a living practice. Many of them are never written down and, as is pointed out below, do not appear in any texts. It is usually to save such vital pieces of advice from being lost that they are eventually recorded in texts such as this one.

The pith instructions in this text need to be read in conjunction with the relevant sections in the two preceding texts. Some of them provide considerable extra detail to the instructions in those texts, others discuss points that are barely touched upon, and yet others condense the practice into the essential points that might otherwise be forgotten when one is concentrating on the details.

{364}
I bow at the feet of the teachers, supreme guides,
Whose sublime bodies are buddhas lighting up the world,
Whose voices clarify all there is to know, banishing the darkness of
 ignorance,
Whose minds are omniscient and see the true mode of being of all
 phenomena.

In order to clear away the fog of unknowing,
The dualistic delusion of all beings,
I will record in note form this precious golden wand,
The pith instructions spoken by my teacher.

To begin with, here are the pith instructions on taking refuge. At daybreak, and at other times, visualize yourself in an instant as Avalokiteshvara, resting upon a lotus and moon. He has one face and four arms and is sitting with his legs crossed in the vajra posture. His first two hands are held, palms joined, at the level of his heart, the right hand holding a crystal rosary, the left a white lotus. His mouth is smiling, and he has long ears and nose and almond eyes. His hair is tied up with a crown, and above his head is Amitābha. His secret wisdom consort is red, with the appearance of a sixteen-year-old maiden. Half her hair is tied up, the other half left loose. Her right hand is playing a ḍāmaru; her left holds a skull cup filled with nectar. Her two legs are wrapped round the male deity's waist.

All this is visualized in an instant, appearing yet devoid of intrinsic nature, like the reflection of the moon in water. Above the crown of the head is Mitrayogin, white in color, tinged with red, with a ḍāmaru in his right hand and a silver bell in his left. He is wearing the six bone ornaments.

From the heart center of Avalokiteshvara clearly visualized in this manner, rays of light issue forth, inviting into the sky in front Avalokiteshvara and consort, surrounded by the buddhas and bodhisattvas. {365} [Recite:]

> Through his kindness
> Great bliss [arises in an instant:
> Teacher, whose body is like a precious jewel,]
> To Avalokiteshvara we bow respectfully.
>
> To the very essence of the Three Jewels,
> The teacher Avalokiteshvara, I submit obeisance.
> I offer outer, inner, and secret offerings.
> Each and every one of my evil deeds I confess.
> I rejoice in the virtue of beings.
> I urge you to turn the wheel of dharma
> And pray that you remain without passing into nirvana.
> I will attain, for the benefit of beings,

The supreme level of Avalokiteshvara,
And in order that all beings may attain buddhahood,
I arouse the mind intent on supreme enlightenment.

May sentient beings be happy.
May they be free from suffering.
Rejoicing at their everlasting happiness,
I remain impartial in the state of sameness.

Consider that all the objects of refuge melt into a ball of light and dissolve into you. This is the pith instruction on taking refuge and arousing bodhichitta.

When you are making the mandala offering, for the ultimate mandala offering, the mighty golden ground represents the perfectly pure ultimate reality, the ring of iron mountains represents the multifarious appearances, Mount Meru represents bewilderment purified, Pūrvavideha in the east is aversion purified, Jambudvīpa in the south is pride purified, Godānīya in the west is attachment purified, and Uttarakuru in the north is jealousy purified. The eight subcontinents are the eight consciousnesses purified, the sun and moon are skillful means and wisdom, and Rāhu and Ketū represent the apprehended object and apprehending subject purified. The eight auspicious symbols represent freedom from the eight extremes, the seven attributes of royalty the seven collections, {366} the four outer offering goddesses the four boundless attitudes, and the four inner offering goddesses the four joys. The inconceivable clouds of offerings represent all the phenomena included in appearance and existence, samsara and nirvana. All these are offered to the teacher, precious buddha, who is the embodiment of the three buddha bodies. Saying, "Please accept these in the inseparable state of sameness," make the offering of the ultimate mandala.

For the instruction on the guru yoga, visualize the hosts of teachers and ḍākinīs all gathered together, one above the other, in the air above the crown of your head. Underneath them, imagine yourself and all sentient beings murmuring the prayer together, with such devotion that in the best case tears well up in your eyes, in the middling case you feel a powerful yearning, and at the very least your hairs stand on end. At the end the teacher melts into light and dissolves into you.

As for the activities related to this, if you wish for the supreme accomplishment, concentrate on Vajradhara. If you wish for wisdom, concentrate on the teacher in the form of Mañjushrī. For love and compassion, concentrate on the teacher in the form of Avalokiteshvara. For miraculous powers, concentrate on Vajrapāṇi; for protection from danger, on Tārā; for a long life, on Amitāyus; for relief from illness, on the Medicine Buddha; for great wealth, on Vaishravaṇa or Ratnasambhava. If you wish to pacify, visualize Vajrasattva; for increasing, visualize Ratnasambhava; for bringing under power, visualize Amitābha and Kurukulle; and for forcefully subjugating, visualize Vajrabhairava and the dharma protectors. It has been taught that by doing so and praying for the fulfillment of your wishes, you will accomplish the particular activity in each case.

All this comes from the paṇḍita's teachings. He said they do not occur in any texts.

In the context of the generation stage, [first] there is blessing oneself. {367} In an instant, you visualize yourself as the Great Compassionate One with his consort, seated or, when you are moving around, standing. In his heart center is a moon, and on top of that, a white syllable *hrīḥ*. In the consort's heart center is a lotus and moon, and on top of that, a red syllable *baṃ*. From these emanate white and red rays of light. The white light touches all the male sentient beings, and they are blessed as Avalokiteshvara. The red light touches all the female sentient beings, who are blessed as Secret Wisdom (Guhyajñāna). All the sentient beings become the Great Compassionate One and his consort. Considering that they are murmuring the *maṇi*, recite the mantra.

Second, blessing the place. In your heart center is the wisdom deity together with the syllable *hrīḥ*. From it light radiates, touching your dwelling place. Consider that it is transformed into the measureless palace, made of many precious materials. It is transparent, square, with four gates, ornaments, pediments, balustrades, and a central upper story, together with the top ornament. Rays of light emanate outward, touching in stages the region, the four continents, and the billionfold universe, and filling everything to the very limits of space. Consider that all the impure elements are purified and that everything becomes the pure buddha field, the Blissful, made of many precious materials. This is how the place is blessed.

Third, blessing your clothes. Consider that you, the Great Compassionate One with consort, are wearing the multicolored garments of the gods—

upper and lower garments that are translucent, light, soft, and warm. Bless them with *oṁ āḥ hūṁ* and offer them. In this way, by considering that your clothes are offered to all the deities in your body and in the outer world, {368} and by wearing those clothes, you will complete the [two] accumulations.

Fourth, blessing your food. From the state of emptiness there appears the syllable *yaṃ*, and from it the wind; the syllable *raṃ*, and from it fire; and the syllable *kaṃ*, and from it three skull hearthstones. On top of them, from the letter *A* there appears an authentic, one-piece kapāla.[2] Inside it is a moon disk, on top of which are the vowels and consonants (*ālikāli*). From *go ku da ha na* there appear the five fleshes, from *bi ra shu ma ha* the five nectars. *oṁ hūṁ trāṃ hrīḥ mu* manifest as the five wisdoms. On top of those are a half moon and half vajra. From *oṁ āḥ hūṁ* light radiates, igniting the fire. The skull cup heats up and the ingredients boil. The steam touches the half moon and vajra, which melt into nectar. From *oṁ* in the foam light radiates, gathering back wisdom nectar, and [they become] inseparable. Say *oṁ āḥ hūṁ oṁ maṇi padme hūṁ ḍākinī harinisa hūṁ* three times.

[To eat the food,] visualize yourself as Avalokiteshvara with one face and four arms. In the crown center is Vairochana Avalokiteshvara surrounded by Mitrayogin and the other teachers of the lineage. In the throat center is the lotus family Avalokiteshvara; in front of him, the yidam deities; to the right, Shākyamuni; behind, the dharma in the form of the Great Mother, Prajñāpāramitā; and to the left, the lords of the three families[3] surrounded by an immeasurable sangha. In the heart center is Avalokiteshvara of the Akṣhobhya family, surrounded by the yidam deities, the buddhas of the four classes of tantra. In the navel center is Avalokiteshvara of the Ratnasambhava family, surrounded by an ocean-like host of dharma protectors such as the six-armed Mahākāla and Lord Draklha. In the secret center is Avalokiteshvara of the Amoghasiddhi family, surrounded by all the sentient beings of the six realms. {369}

In the consort's crown center is the buddha ḍākinī surrounded by the ḍākas and ḍākinīs of the buddha family. In her throat center is the padma ḍākinī surrounded by the ḍākas and ḍākinīs of the lotus family. In her heart center is the vajra ḍākinī surrounded by the ḍākas and ḍākinīs of the vajra family. In her navel center is the ratna ḍākinī surrounded by the ḍākas and ḍākinīs of the jewel family. In her secret center is the karma ḍākinī surrounded by the ḍākas and ḍākinīs of the action family.

The male deity's senses-and-fields (those of the eyes, and so on) are the six bodhisattvas. The consort's six senses-and-fields are their six vajra consorts.

His four arms are the four doorkeepers. Her four arms are the four mothers. The hairs on the heads and bodies of the male and female deities are buddhas and bodhisattvas. Visualizing all this and your ten fingers as the ten outer and inner goddesses, consider that the deities are making offerings to the deities, and enjoy the food considering it as a feast offering of nectar. This is a pith instruction on the yoga of eating food.

As well as this, all your everyday activities [should be adapted as follows]: When you are walking, consider that you are going to meet Avalokiteshvara and that you are circumambulating him. When you are sitting, train in the generation stage. When you rise, consider that you are rising for Avalokiteshvara and prostrating to him. When you lie down, go to sleep concentrating on Avalokiteshvara and his retinue. In short, it has been taught that in everything you do—walking, moving around, lying down, or sitting still—take the display of Avalokiteshvara as the path. All this is a pith instruction for the generation stage related to the enlightened body, with the five factors of awakening.

For the recitation, do the visualizations according to the instructions on the generation stage. As for the perfection stage, {370} it has been taught that one should train in the state without concepts, like an echo in empty space.

Next is a pith instruction for meditating on love, compassion, and bodhichitta, based on the emanation and reabsorption of the rays of light from the heart. If one has not trained in compassion, here is a method for doing so, in five steps. Begin by meditating on your own parents. When you were in the belly of those mothers, they experienced a lot of difficulties. As soon as you were born, they dressed you in soft clothes. They gave you all the delicious food you needed. When you were freezing cold, they warmed you up. They breast-fed you and even used their mouths to wipe away your dribble and snot. As you were growing up, they gave you their own food rather than eat it themselves; they gave you their own drink rather than drink it themselves; they dressed you in their own clothes rather than wear them themselves. They could not bring themselves to enjoy any of their own belongings but unstintingly handed them over to you. They taught you the proper way to do things, including how to walk, how to sit, and how to talk. When something unpleasant happened to you, they looked unbearably affected. When you were ill, they gave you medicine. Fearing that you were dying, they had rituals performed for you. So, with tears of anguish welling up in your eyes at the thought of how sad it is that these old mothers underwent so much suffering because of you, train until you can truly let go of your body and possessions and feel the same compassion and affection for them. After that, meditate on compassion for your fathers and relatives: these are easy subjects for developing compassion.

Second, meditate on beings who suffer greatly. For this, reflect on the sufferings of the hell beings, hungry spirits, and animals. Since time without beginning, they have, on countless occasions, been like the mother you have had in this life. Think how pitiful they are and, emanating rays of light from the syllable *hrīḥ* [in your heart], summon them in front of you and train in sending and taking (*tonglen*). {371}

Third, meditate on beings with very bad karma—loud-mouthed individuals who, although they are wealthy and powerful, do a lot to hurt people. They have no compassion and create an enormous amount of negative karma, engaging in actions that destroy both themselves and others. Thinking how pitiful they are, meditate on compassion for them, and try to help them, either directly or in your thoughts. For this, earnestly practice sending and taking, using the training method with the *hrīḥ*.

Fourth, meditate on those for whom it is difficult to arouse compassion. This refers to beings who are hostile toward you and harm you greatly in return for your having helped them: negative forces that are attracted by past karma, and likewise anyone who harms you and for whom it is difficult to feel compassion on account of past karma. Think of them as follows: "These harmful beings have been my kind parents since time without beginning, but I harmed them in the past, so they are now paying me back. When they were my parents, they were never anything but kind to me, so I should repay the harm they are doing me now by helping them." In this way, meditate intensely on compassion for those who have not recognized this and are now harming you. [At the same time] train in rejoicing at the harm they are doing you, thinking how enormously kind beings who wrong you are, as they are assisting you on the path to enlightenment and helping you to train in patience. And do whatever you can to help them.

Fifth, [meditate] on the beings of the six realms filling the whole of space. Summon them in front of you with the practice of the syllable *hrīḥ* and train in sending and taking. For this, make use of the light rays from the syllable *hrīḥ* to summon all the beings in the different directions—east, south, west, north, the four intermediate directions, and the zenith and nadir—and practice sending and taking.

The above comprises a pith instruction on training in bodhichitta. It was taught that this gives rise to immense merit.

Even if you have given rise to compassion, {372} if you are unable to practice sending and taking, come close to someone who is sick or suffering in some way and, touching the sick person's right nostril with your left nostril, meditate that the other person's suffering happens to you. Breathe in and hold the vase breath: consider that the suffering dissolves into the *hrīḥ*. Meditate that your own virtue goes out through your left nostril and into the other person's right nostril, giving rise in their mind stream to the extraordinary concentration of bliss-emptiness, and they feel comfortable. By this means, you will be able to send and take.

If you get a headache[4] or other problem from holding the vase breath, focus your consciousness on a golden crossed vajra below the navel, draw in your toes, raise the lower door, and from time to time perform a *bep*.[5] Again, if you feel depressed or uneasy, consider that on top of an eight-petaled lotus in your heart center there is your root teacher in the form of Avalokiteshvara, resplendent and yellow in color, and perform a *bep*. As you do so, consider that you dissolve, with your heart, into the mighty golden ground, and bring the consciousness down. This will get rid of [your mood].

Again if the lower doors are obstructed, with retention of urine and feces, meditate that between the two passages a wind goddess opens the passages, and forcefully open and close the lower door. This will help. If it does not, for a woman, apply stick therapy between the passages. For a man, tap below the navel with a stick. This will clear the blockage. It removes obstacles to the vase exercise.

Here is a pith instruction on mixing with all kinds of objects, as in an illusion or dream, which enhances the meditation of the Great Seal, the union of sustained calm and profound insight. {373} Whatever forms you see—white, red, blue, yellow, or green in color; round, square, semicircular, or triangular in shape; whether good, bad, or neutral—you should recognize that they are all by nature the deluded appearances of the mind, and settle in equipoise on that, in a state beyond intellect, without mental activity. Whatever sounds you hear—whether pleasant, unpleasant, or neutral; gentle words or harsh—recognize them as the Great Seal, resounding yet empty, like an echo, and settle in equipoise in the state free of thoughts. Similarly, for sweet fragrances, delicious tastes, things that are soft or rough to the touch, and good or bad thoughts, whatever arises, recognize them as thatness and rest in equipoise in the state free of thoughts. Moreover, all the time, during the four modes of everyday conduct—walking, moving around, lying, and sitting—rest in equipoise, in the vivid, relaxed, unconstrained state, without fabrication and free of attachment to concepts of adopting and avoiding, blocking and encouraging.

To mix the visualization with the pure ground and the Great Seal with dharma activities, practice as follows. Having clearly visualized the form of the deity like a rainbow, [recognize it] as clarity-emptiness, like a reflection in a mirror or the reflection of the moon in water, and settle in meditative equipoise on that without grasping. Besides this, mix what appear to be idle chatter, running and jumping, thoughts related to the five poisons, and indulgence in the eight ordinary preoccupations[6] with the meditation on the Great Seal. If they do not mix, train in this again.[7]

Whether you are using your speech to recite a short or long mantra or to chant a sutra, recite in the nonconceptual state of recognizing it as sound-emptiness. Similarly, whatever you are doing, such as performing the seven branches, {374} doing circumambulations, offering tormas, making *tsatsa*s, or performing daily rituals, carry out all dharma activities in the state of clarity-emptiness beyond intellect, without grasping. In that way, those activities will gather the two accumulations together. If you see that you are not progressing, stay in solitude and persist in the practice of meditative equipoise. Check repeatedly whether you are able to mix. If you can mix, you will be practicing the two accumulations together and will spontaneously accomplish the two goals.

In brief, whatever form of dharma activity you undertake, if you recognize its very nature and it arises vividly as clarity-emptiness, freely as appearance-emptiness, clearly as absence of thoughts, then, it was said, you are progressing. All this is how to progress in sustained calm and profound insight.

Next is a pith instruction on the illusory body. When you go somewhere inhabited and it happens that you hit someone, for example, and they hit you back, watch whether you feel attachment or aversion to that person and grasping at self. If you do, then you still need to train in the illusory body. Similarly, when people engage in pleasant or unpleasant talk, train in it as being like an echo. Likewise, watch whether you feel attached or averse to things that smell nice or disgusting and to things that taste sweet or foul. If you do, then you need to train in the illusory body. Watch whether you feel a difference between wearing cotton and silk. Look whether you feel any difference between someone on your right trying to set you on fire and another person on your left anointing you with perfume. Look whether your thoughts arise as dharma and whether you recognize negative thoughts. Experiencing all these as devoid of self, like the eight examples of illusion—magical illusion, dream, echo, and so on {375}—preserve that experience of a single flavor, free of all attachment. If you are making no progress with this, again train in solitude. In those situations too, experience all singing, dancing, music, and dharma activities as illusion and dream. By doing so, you will make progress.

Here is a pith instruction for eliminating four excessive mental states during the dream practice.

Being too awake refers to waking up just at the moment you apprehend your dream. To avoid this, focus your consciousness on a black sphere in your feet or in the secret center, and relax and go to sleep. This will solve the problem.

Too much delusion occurs when you are slightly able to apprehend your dreams but you immediately fall into delusion—in other words, there occurs a solid belief in their reality. You should therefore emphasize the training in illusion and dream. In particular, it is important not to lose mindfulness when apprehending dreams.

From being too forgetful, you may be able to apprehend your dreams a little, but once you wake up you forget them. To remedy this, stabilize your mindfulness of illusion, and focus your mindfulness on a white sphere between your eyebrows.

Being too impervious is the result of neglecting the practice and becoming an impervious practitioner. For this, it is important to meditate on impermanence in particular, to determinedly cut worldly ties, and to persevere in the practice.

A pith instruction on luminosity: Four essential points were taught for the arising of luminosity: keeping the body straight, which is the essential point regarding the channels; holding the winds; stability of the subtle elements; and keeping one's mind free of the obscuring veils of dualistic subject-object concepts.

Two essential points were taught concerning transference: not to be attached to anything and to be undistracted in focusing the awareness above the crown of the head. {376}

Three essential points were taught concerning the intermediate state: stability in the generation stage, directing one's aspirations toward a pure buddha field, and recognizing everything as one's own nature.

Some essential points to be observed regarding the whole practice were taught as follows: the command that it is wrong to give [only] the reading transmission of the book;[8] the command not to give it to one who does not offer a feast and a mandala of gold; the command to make the promise to practice this teaching once one has received it; and the command not to give these instructions to unsuitable vessels.

The oral instructions of Mitrayogin were bestowed upon the great paṇḍita Shrīputra, who gave them to Girti Ratna. The latter gave me the pith instructions without any omissions or additions.

With the sole intention of benefiting others,
I put the golden wand of the pith instructions into writing.
By the merit of my doing so, may I and all sentient beings
Attain the supreme level of Avalokiteshvara.

This completes *The Luminous Golden Wand of Pith Instructions*.
*śubhaṃ*

# 18. The Wheel of Ornaments of Gnosis That Makes Wisdom Grow

*The Instructions of Mañjushrī, the Deity Related to the Enlightened Body*[1]

{378}

With respect, I pay homage to the teacher and Lord Mañjushrī.

These graded instructions of the Lord Mañjushrī consist of three topics: (1) preliminaries; (2) main practice; and (3) conclusion.

## I. Preliminaries

The preliminaries are divided into three parts: (1) the history of the lineage of teachers; (2) the common preliminaries; and (3) the specific preliminaries.

### A. History of the Lineage of Teachers

Here is how the instructions of noble Mañjushrī originated. When the glorious great siddha Mitrayogin practiced the five yidam deities in the charnel ground of Sosaling, the deities each revealed themselves to him and gave him their respective graded instructions: *The Wheel of Ornaments of Gnosis That Makes Wisdom Grow*, instructions on Mañjushrī, the deity related to the enlightened body; *A Banquet of Nectar*, complete instructions of Avalokiteshvara, the deity related to enlightened speech, which include all the stages of the path to enlightenment; *The Spreading Rays of Light That Vanquish the Hordes of Demons*, instructions of Vajrapāṇi, the deity related to enlightened mind; {379} *Accomplishing the Immortal Vajra Body*, instructions of Amitāyus, the deity related to enlightened qualities; *Spontaneous Activities That Liberate from the Perilous Path of Samsara*, instructions of

Tārā, the deity related to [enlightened activities] who protects from the eight fears; and *A Shower of Accomplishments*, instructions of the Yellow Jambhala. These six sets of instructions are the six instructions that each of the deities gave him individually. They told him to practice these instructions and to reveal them to one other lineage holder, saying that their blessings would carry for up to seven generations and predicting that the yogis who practiced these instructions would all be individuals whom they had blessed. The great siddha [Mitrayogin] then bestowed these instructions on paṇḍita Shrīputra, who gave them to Jetsun Girti Ratna, who in turn gave them to me.

### B. Common Preliminaries

The instructions on the common preliminaries—namely, meditation on the difficulty of finding the freedoms and advantages; on death and impermanence; on action, cause and effect; and on the defects of cyclic existence—are the same as are generally taught. {380}

### C. Specific Preliminaries

These are divided into four: (1) instructions on going for refuge and arousing bodhichitta, which is what makes everything one does become the path of enlightenment; (2) instructions on the meditation and recitation of Vajrasattva, which enables one to purify one's negative deeds and obscurations; (3) instructions on the mandala practice, which enables one to complete the two accumulations; and (4) instructions on the guru yoga, which enables one to receive blessings—this consists of meditating on the teacher, whose nature is Mañjushrī, and praying.

## II. Main Practice

The main practice consists of (1) instructions on the generation stage and (2) instructions on the perfection stage.

### A. Instructions on the Generation Stage

The instructions on the generation stage are divided into four: (1) instructions on the visualization; (2) instructions on appearances as the deity's body, which introduce the manifestation body by means of the emanation and reabsorption of light rays from the five families of Mañjushrī; (3) instructions on sounds as the deity's speech, which introduce the body of perfect enjoyment by means of meditation on the Noble Lord of Speech and the emanation and reabsorption from attributes and syllables; and (4) instructions on thoughts as the deity's mind, which introduce the body of truth by visualizing oneself as Bhairava, establishing Bhairavas in the five centers, purifying the five poisons into their natural state, and making the five wisdoms grow.

### 1. Visualization

In an isolated place, begin with the four pure states.[2] Then, with *oṁ svabhāva śuddāḥ sarvadharmāḥ svabhāva śuddho 'haṃ*, meditate on emptiness. From the state of emptiness, the whole outer world is laid out as the buddha field of Mañjushrī. The ground is made of the five kinds of precious materials; it gives when one steps on it and springs back when one lifts one's foot. There are magical trees made of many precious substances and strung with bells and tinklers, and different kinds of birds, from all of which resounds the sound of the sacred dharma. [Rivers of] nectar and scented water, {381} endowed with the eight qualities of pure water,[3] murmur the words of the Perfection of Wisdom. In short, [everything] is a perfectly pure buddha field, with these and other qualities.

In its center, on a throne made of many precious materials, is a thousand-petaled multicolored lotus. In its center, from the letter *A*, there appears a moon disk, and on top of it the syllable *dhīḥ*, the color of molten gold. From it five-colored rays of light emanate in the ten directions, making offerings to the noble beings and purifying the obscurations of sentient beings. They gather back and dissolve into the *dhīḥ*, which is completely transformed into yourself as noble Mañjushrī, who is golden red, the color of fresh saffron. He has one face and two arms and is seated with his legs in the vajra posture. He is wearing a lower garment of five-colored silk. His right hand is adorned with the sword of wisdom which he is turning above him; it blazes with wisdom fire and emits sparks. Between the thumb and ring finger of his left hand he is holding at his heart center the stem of an utpala, which is blossoming at the level of his ear and is adorned with a volume of the Perfection of Wisdom. He has a smiling face, with long eyebrows, almond eyes, and a long nose, and his broad forehead is adorned with a coil of white hair.

His hair is tied up in a crown on top of his head, and the remaining locks reach down to his waist. He has the beauty of youth and is adorned with all the thirty-two major marks and eighty minor marks of a buddha. He is seated amid a dense mass of five-colored rays of light. In his crown center is a white syllable *oṁ*, in his throat center a red *āḥ*, and in his heart center a blue *hūṁ*. From these, rays of light emanate, inviting the wisdom deity, who is identical to himself. The wisdom deity dissolves inseparably into you. {382} Again, rays of light emanate, inviting the buddhas of the five families, with their consorts and retinues. They bestow empowerment, purifying your obscurations. The nectar [of the empowerment] overflows, and your head is crowned by Vairochana and the other buddhas of the five families.

In your heart center, on a red lotus and moon disk, is the syllable *dhīḥ*, encircled by [the mantra] *oṁ a ra pa ca na dhīḥ namaḥ*. From all these syllables, rays of light emanate. They touch the outer world, purifying it as a buddha field, and touch the sentient beings inhabiting it, so that they all become Mañjushrī. Considering that they are all reciting the mantra, perform the practice of approach. At the end, consider that they all melt into light and dissolve into you. You dissolve into the *dhīḥ* in your heart center. The *dhīḥ* disappears like a rainbow into space. Then rest in the state of nonconceptuality.

**2. Instructions on the Deity's Body**

With the five factors of awakening, visualize yourself as Mañjushrī as before. In each of your five centers—crown, throat, heart, navel, and secret center—is a lotus and moon disk, on which is the syllable *dhīḥ*: white, red, blue, yellow, and green respectively. From each of these appears a Mañjushrī—respectively white, red, blue, yellow, and green—with one face and two hands, and two legs crossed in the vajra posture. In their right hands they are turning a sword above their head. In their left hands they hold the stem of an utpala at their heart centers. They have smiling faces, with long eyebrows, almond eyes, and long noses, and their broad foreheads are adorned with a coil of white hair. Their locks are tied up in a crown, decorated with a hundred thousand precious substances. Visualize them all as having the nature of clear light, appearing clearly yet empty, like a reflection in a mirror. {383}

In their crown, throat, and heart centers are arranged the three syllables, from which lights radiate. The wisdom deities identical to them enter, and empowerment is bestowed, as before. In each of their heart centers there is again a lotus and moon, and upon these is the syllable *dhīḥ*—white, red, blue, yellow, and green respectively. From them, rays of light emanate in the ten directions, enhancing the power of the body, speech, mind, qualities, and activities of the buddhas and bodhisattvas in the ten directions, venerating them with clouds of offerings, and inviting (in the form of white, red, blue, yellow, and green light rays) the blessings of the body, speech, mind, qualities, and activities of the buddhas and bodhisattvas in the ten directions, and all the power of their wisdom and knowledge. These dissolve into the Mañjushrīs of the five families in one's own crown center, throat, heart, navel, and secret center. Consider that you thus realize the enlightened body, speech, mind, qualities, and activities and the qualities of the gnosis of the expanse of reality, all-discerning gnosis, mirrorlike gnosis, gnosis of equality, and all-accomplishing gnosis.

Again, from the five Mañjushrīs in the five centers, rays of light emanate as before. They touch the bodies, voices, and minds of all the sentient beings of the six realms in the ten directions and purify their five poisons—bewilderment, attachment, aversion, pride, and jealousy. They are brought to the level of Vairochana Mañjushrī, Amitābha Mañjushrī, Akṣhobhya Mañjushrī, Ratnasambhava Mañjushrī, and Amoghasiddhi Mañjushrī, and they realize the five kinds of gnosis—the gnosis of the expanse of reality, all-discerning gnosis, mirrorlike gnosis, gnosis of equality, and all-accomplishing gnosis. {384} After that, all the power of their body, speech, mind, qualities, and activities, whose essence is gnosis and wisdom, is gathered back in the form of white, red, blue, yellow, and green rays of light. Consider that they dissolve into your five centers. During these stages, when you send the light rays out, you should also breathe out. When you gather in the qualities, you should breathe in and hold the breath in the vase for a while, pressing down. This is a pith instruction.

### 3. Instructions on the Deity's Speech

From the state of emptiness there appears a fully bloomed lotus and moon disk. On it is the syllable *sa*, from which appears a blue lion, looking downward. On top of that is a moon disk, and in its center a yellowish-red syllable *dhīḥ*. It emanates rays of light, making offerings to the noble ones and benefiting sentient beings. They are gathered back, and it transforms into oneself as the noble Lord of Speech,[4] who is a radiant ruby red and is seated with his two legs in the posture of royal ease. He is wearing a skirt of five-colored silk. He holds his two hands in the teaching gesture. With the thumb and finger of his right hand, he holds the stem of a lotus, marked with a sword; with the thumb and finger of his left hand he holds an utpala, on top of which is a precious volume of the scriptures. He has a smiling face, with long eyebrows and almond eyes, and his [forehead] is adorned with a coil of white hair. Half of his hair is tied up in a topknot; the other half is loose, hanging down and curling up at the waist. His hair is bound with a garland of flowers and decorated with a multitude of jewels and five-colored pearls, and he is beautifully adorned with a silken crown. {385} Visualize him clearly in this manner.

In his crown, throat, and heart centers are the syllables *oṁ*, *āḥ*, and *hūṁ*, from which light radiates, inviting the wisdom deity, identical to himself, who dissolves into you. Again, consider that the buddhas of the five families are invited and bestow empowerment, and that you are crowned by Vairochana. In each of the lord's five centers—crown, throat, heart, navel, and secret center—in the midst of spheres of rainbow-colored light, upon a lotus and moon, is a precious volume of the scriptures, marked with a sword of wisdom blazing with fire, the handle [marked with] the syllable *dhīḥ*. The sword is standing on top of the volume, pointing upward. In the crown center, the sword of wisdom is white, and similarly red in the throat center, blue in the heart center, yellow in the navel center, and green in the secret center; and each is marked with a white, red, blue, yellow, or green syllable *dhīḥ*. From them, light radiates, venerating all the buddhas of the ten directions with clouds of offerings and making the wisdom of their body, speech, mind, qualities, and activities shine ever brighter. It touches all sentient beings, dispelling all the darkness of their ignorance and purifying the five poisons; they are brought to the level of the five families of Mañjushrī. Consider that the light of the five gnoses grows. Keep this in mind as you breathe out. As you breathe in, consider that the blessings of the body, speech, mind, qualities, and activities of all the buddhas and bodhisattvas present as the five families of Mañjushrī, along with their gnosis and qualities; their knowledge, love, and power; and all the wisdom and power of their teaching, debating, and composing, together with their unforgetting powers of retention—all these are gathered in the form of white, red, blue, yellow, and green rays of light {386} and dissolve into the attributes in your own five centers, which are Mañjushrī by nature. Hold the breath, considering that they have the nature of the five gnoses and that the power of the wisdom of teaching, debating, and composing, along with unforgetting memory, dissolves, as you [continue to] hold the breath. Consider that, as a result, you yourself have the five forms of gnosis, and the light of the wisdom of teaching, debating, and composing, along with unforgetting memory, increases, and you realize the level of Mañjushrī.

At the end, consider that the world and its inhabitants dissolve into you. The spheres and attributes dissolve in turn from the bottom into the crown center. Your own body too dissolves into the attributes in the crown, which vanish into rainbow light, filling space. Rest in the state of nonconceptuality. This is the instruction on realizing speech as the body of perfect enjoyment.

### 4. Instructions on the Deity's Mind

With the five factors of awakening, visualize yourself clearly as Mañjushrī. Through his being transformed, visualize yourself on a lotus, sun, and corpse as Vajrabhairava, with dark-blue body and one face and two arms. His right leg is stretched out, his left leg bent. He is adorned with human heads and bones. His phallus is erect, his belly distended. He has his two hands crossed at the level of his heart, holding a curved knife and skull cup full of blood. His head is the extremely wrathful head of a buffalo. He is rolling his tongue and baring his canine teeth. His three red eyes flash. His sharp horns are of blue copper, rattling with the six bone ornaments. In the middle of his upward-swirling, yellowish-red hair is the golden-faced Mañjushrī, {387} in peaceful form. On the upper part of his body he is wearing an elephant skin, and he is adorned with a vicious black serpent as a shoulder belt. He wears a long necklace of fifty human heads and has a crown of jewels and five skulls. As well as these, he is adorned with the six jewel and bone ornaments. His roars of laughter—*ha ha* and *hūṁ hūṁ*—resound like thunder. Visualize him as the great being who, in a single instant, terrifies the three worlds.

In his five centers—crown, throat, heart, navel, and secret center—upon lotus and sun, are respectively the five syllables *oṁ*, *āḥ*, *hūṁ*, *trāṃ*, and *hrīḥ*. These melt and appear as the lord White Yamāntaka, slayer of bewilderment, in the crown; Red Yamāntaka, slayer of attachment, in the throat; Black Yamāntaka, slayer of aversion, in the heart; Yellow Yamāntaka, slayer of miserliness, in the navel; and Green Yamāntaka, slayer of jealousy, in the secret center. Their appearance and attributes are similar to those of the main deity. Visualize each of them holding in their right hand a curved knife marked respectively with a wheel, lotus, vajra, jewel, and crossed vajra.

In each of their heart centers are a lotus and sun, on which are the five attributes—respectively wheel, lotus, vajra, jewel, and sword—marked with the five syllables *oṁ*, *āḥ*, *hūṁ*, *trāṃ*, and *hrīḥ*. From these, rays of white, red, blue, yellow, and green light emanate, making offerings to the buddhas and bodhisattvas in the ten directions and enhancing the power of their bodies, voices, minds, qualities, and activities. After that, the rays touch the six classes of beings in the ten directions, purifying the bewilderment, attachment, aversion, pride, and jealousy of the six realms and {388} bringing them to the level of Yamāntaka the slayer of bewilderment, Yamāntaka the slayer of attachment, Yamāntaka the slayer of aversion, Yamāntaka the slayer of pride, and Yamāntaka the slayer of jealousy. Consider that they realize the gnosis of the expanse of reality, all-discerning gnosis, mirrorlike gnosis, the gnosis of equality, and all-accomplishing gnosis. As you do so, breathe out. When you breathe in, consider that all the blessings of their body, speech, mind, qualities, and activities, and the five buddha bodies, gnoses, knowledge, love, and power are all gathered in the form of white, red, blue, yellow, and green rays of light, which then dissolve into your crown, throat, heart, navel, and secret center. All the blessings of body, speech, mind, qualities, and activities, and of the five buddha bodies, gnoses, knowledge, love, and power, enter you. Consider that you realize the level of the five families of Yamāntaka and hold the vase breath. From time to time, it has been taught, you should recite the name mantra or the essence mantra (*oṁ yama rāja hūṁ phaṭ oṁ hrīḥ ṣṭiḥ vi kṛtā na na hūṁ phaṭ*) or the long mantra.

At the end, the action Yamāntaka in the secret center dissolves into the one in the navel center. It in turn dissolves into that in the heart center, which dissolves into the throat center, which dissolves into the crown center. That one vanishes like a rainbow in space. Settle in meditative equipoise with the mind free of contrivance, in the state of clarity-emptiness, without center or circumference, free of arising, ceasing, and staying, as pure as the sky at noon, clarity-emptiness devoid of all elaborations. This is the graded instruction on the mind, meditating on the five families of Bhairava.

### B. Instructions on the Perfection Stage

The ultimate perfection stage {389} is divided into four parts: (1) sustained calm; (2) profound insight and their union; (3) transference; and (4) the intermediate state.

### 1. Sustained Calm

Sustained calm is treated under three sections: (1) sustained calm making use of conceptual attributes; (2) sustained calm focusing on conceptual thoughts; and (3) sustained calm settling in [a state] without conceptual thoughts.

#### a. Sustained Calm Making Use of Conceptual Attributes

Sustained calm making use of conceptual attributes is divided into two parts: (1) holding the mind on an object outside and (2) holding the mind on an object inside.

##### i. Holding the Mind on an Object Outside

This is divided into two aspects: (1) impure and (2) pure.

###### A) Holding the Mind on an Impure Object

Adopt the seven-point posture of Vairochana and hold the mind on anything with attributes that you can see—a pillar, vase, lamp, stick, pebble, or whatever—all the while maintaining the right physical posture and gaze. Without getting distracted or getting involved in thoughts, settle the mind on it without conceptual thoughts, in an uncontrived, relaxed state. Should wildness or dullness occur, you should know how to focus the mind up or down or right or left.

###### B) Holding the Mind on a Pure Object

For this one holds the mind on a buddha image. In front of you place an image of Mañjushrī or, if you do not have one, visualize him. Do not get scattered in thoughts or involved in distraction. To settle the mind on it in a relaxed way, without any distraction, hold the mind on a pure object, an image of a buddha.

#### ii. Holding the Mind on an Object Inside

Holding the mind on an object inside has two aspects: (1) impure and (2) pure.

#### A) Holding the Mind on an Impure Object

This consists of holding the mind on a sphere. Visualize in your heart center a pea-sized, smoke-colored sphere, emanating rays of light. Hold the mind on it without getting distracted or involved in thoughts.

#### B) Holding the Mind on a Pure Object

This {390} consists of concentrating on the form of a buddha. Hold the mind on a thumb-sized form of Mañjushrī on top of a lotus and sun disk in your heart center. Without wandering or getting involved in thoughts, concentrate on it without any distraction.

#### b. Sustained Calm Focusing on Conceptual Thoughts

When a thought suddenly arises, recognize it and look at it clearly with the eye devoid of concepts. By this means, you will destroy it without grasping, and natural awareness, clear and empty, devoid of object, will vividly arise. Focusing on the nature of any thought that arises, recognize your own nature and preserve that state. This is concentrating on conceptual thoughts.

#### c. Sustained Calm Settling in [a State] without Conceptual Thoughts

Adopt the seven-point posture of Vairochana and gaze into space. Cutting off all thought movements related to the past, present, and future, without thinking of anything, rest in meditative equipoise in the state of clarity-emptiness, without extremes or middle, the uncontrived nature of the mind free of concepts, vivid and awake. This will give rise to the concentration of the sustained calm of bliss, clarity, and absence of thought.

### 2. Profound Insight

Profound insight is treated under three headings:

### a. Causal Profound Insight: Examining the Mind

Examine the essential nature of the mind's arising, ceasing, and staying, asking yourself, From where has this mind of mine arisen? Where does it stay? Where will it cease?

Examine and check, asking yourself, Has it arisen from the five elements or from my own body? Does it dwell there? Will it die there?

Check further: Does the mind have a color—white, red, blue, yellow, or green? Or is it colorless? {391} Was this mind of mine produced with a shape—the form of earth, water, fire, wind, or space, or round, square, semicircular, triangular, oblong, or oval, and so on? Check whether it is single or multiple. Are thoughts something other than the mind, or are thoughts the mind? Again, does the mind arise from appearances outside, or do appearances outside arise from the mind?

Now, use the mind to examine and analyze the mind that is analyzing. Does that mind exist or not? Check: Is it clear or unclear? Happy or unhappy? Is it permanent or impermanent? Is it visible or invisible? Is it aware or unaware? Is there a self or no self?

When you check like this, you will see that the essential nature of the mind is devoid of arising, staying, and ceasing. Its essence is emptiness, like space. It is naturally radiant. It is unobstructed awareness, arising in every kind of way, and all these appearances are of the same taste in being unborn; they are of the same taste in not dwelling and not ceasing. By examining and analyzing, you will see its ultimate nature, which is clarity and awareness, appearance and emptiness inseparable, inconceivable like space. In that way, as you realize the nature of mind, you will be introduced to thatness, in which all the qualities of the ground, path, and result are complete.

### b. Path Profound Insight {392}

The fresh, "ordinary" mind[5] is introduced and simultaneously experienced as follows.

The nature of mind is devoid of the conceptual extremes of existence and nonexistence, of birth, cessation, and dwelling. It is free of the dualistic concepts of subject and object that grasp at "I" and "mine." It is beyond something to be seen and something that sees. Its nature is emptiness; its character is luminous clarity. Its manifestation is unobstructed awareness, appearing clearly in a multitude of ways. Unspoiled by fabrication, it is uncontrived. Naturally radiant, it is vividly clear. Recognizing its own nature, it is fully awake. Uncontaminated by dualistic concepts, it is fresh and naked. There being nothing to meditate on, it is free of mental activity. Since there is no modifying or fabricating the nature of the mind, it is a state of relaxation. There is no identifying whatever arises, so it is free of grasping. Since it rests naturally as it is, without grasping or contrivance, it is the ordinary mind. And since it does not continuously indulge in chains of thoughts, it is known as the "fresh" state. This is an introduction to experiencing the main practice of profound insight.

### c. Ultimate Profound Insight: Practicing Sustained Calm and Profound Insight Together

To settle in the uncontrived state of clarity, awareness, and emptiness inseparable, the mind being devoid of birth, cessation, and dwelling, is sustained calm. To see and recognize the nature of that is profound insight. The nature of mind, free of the two extremes, is the union of sustained calm and profound insight, which is the actual way things are. Since the nature of mind is unborn, it is free of the extreme of eternalism. And since it has no cessation, it is free of the extreme of nihilism. It has no existence as color or shape, so it is free of the extreme of eternalism. Its manifesting power appears in all sorts of ways, so it is free from the extreme of nihilism. {393} Its nature is to dwell as emptiness, so it is free of the extreme of eternalism. Yet it is aware and manifests in multifarious ways, so it is free of the extreme of nihilism. Thus, since it transcends the conceptual extremes of eternalism and nihilism, it is the inseparable union of clarity, awareness, and emptiness. The manner in which this union is experienced is as follows.

When one looks directly at the nature of one's mind, to rest in a state of bliss, clarity, or absence of thought, devoid of the extremes of an apprehended object and apprehending subject, is sustained calm, while to see that its nature is naturally pure is profound insight. To settle the mind on devotion to the teacher is sustained calm, while to see that the essence of [that state of mind] is emptiness, transcending the intellect, is profound insight. Settling the mind on the visualization in the generation stage, which is like the reflection of the moon in water, is sustained calm, while seeing that its nature is emptiness, beyond birth, cessation, and dwelling, is profound insight. Settling the mind on love and compassion embracing all sentient beings is sustained calm, while seeing that their nature is emptiness is profound insight. Settling the mind on the illusion-like skillful means, the accumulation of merit, [is sustained calm,] while seeing that these are devoid of intrinsic nature and empty is profound insight. Settling the mind on the great bliss is sustained calm; seeing that very state as emptiness, without clinging, is profound insight. Settling the mind on all appearances being the appearances of the mind, on appearance and emptiness inseparable like the reflection of the moon in water [is sustained calm]; seeing that those appearances are interdependent and unborn, like the reflection of the moon in water, is profound insight. Settling the mind on the fresh state of awareness uncontaminated by contrivance [is sustained calm]; seeing that there is no-self, awareness and emptiness, without there being an object,[6] is profound insight. {394}

In short, there is no emptiness that is other than appearances, which are like the reflection of the moon in water, a reflection in a mirror, or an echo. And there are no appearances that are other than emptiness. To realize the unborn nature[7] of appearances and emptiness, like a rainbow appearing in the sky, and to settle in that state [is sustained calm], while seeing one's own nature, the nature of the mind, is profound insight. This is the union of sustained calm and profound insight.

This is the meaning of the nature of the mind being present since the beginning as the nature of the three buddha bodies inseparable. By purifying all dualistic concepts and developing the gnosis of pure awareness, one becomes what is called a buddha, and that state is also Mañjughoṣha—the youthful Mañjushrī. Because he has purified the five poisons, he is called Gentle and Glorious.[8] Because he possesses the glory of the two accumulations of the union of sustained calm and profound insight, he is called Glorious. And he is called Youthful in that his form body is adorned with the major and minor marks, and that the truth body is beyond birth or death. That is the meaning of the nature of mind being present since the beginning as the nature of the three buddha bodies. This is an introduction to the fact that all the qualities included in the path and result, such as those of the three bodies and five gnoses, are complete in the mind.

### 3. Instructions on Transference at the Moment of Death

This has two parts: (1) training and (2) putting transference into practice.

### a. Training

Visualize yourself as Mañjushrī. In the five centers, visualize the Mañjushrīs of the five families, emanating and reabsorbing rays of light. After that, the Mañjushrī in the secret center melts into a green sphere, which then dissolves into the Mañjushrī in the navel center. That becomes a yellow sphere and dissolves into the Mañjushrī in the heart center. That one becomes a blue sphere and dissolves into the Mañjushrī in the throat center, who in turn becomes a red sphere and dissolves into the Mañjushrī in the crown center. {395} He becomes a white sphere, which is expelled through the aperture of Brahmā as if through an open skylight. There, in the sky above, on top of a precious throne, lotus, and moon disk, one above the other, is Mañjushrī, around whose heart center the white sphere turns. After that, it comes back down through your crown center and, one by one, becomes the five Mañjushrīs in the respective centers. Train in this visualization, holding the breath.

### b. Putting Transference into Practice

When the signs of approaching death are all present, abandon all mundane clinging and attachment. Then visualize the five Mañjushrīs of the buddha families transforming in turn into a green, yellow, blue, red, and white sphere, from the secret center up, and dissolving into spheres in the navel, heart, throat, and crown centers. Expel this last sphere through the aperture of Brahmā and consider that it dissolves into space: the whole of space is filled with dense rainbow-colored light. Settle there in the nonconceptual state. This is what is known as the rainbow transference.

## 4. Instructions on the Intermediate State

The instructions on the intermediate state (bardo) comprise three parts.

### a. Training

Train by means of the generation stage and perfection stage. For this, you should imagine with conviction: "I am dead. This is the bardo. The bardo body has no true existence." And meditate that the whole world around you is set out as the buddha field of Mañjushrī, and that you yourself and all sentient beings are Mañjushrī. Visualize the five Mañjushrīs in the five centers and practice the instructions on the emanation and reabsorption of light rays. At the end, train in the perfection stage, settling in the state without mental activity, where all is like a magical illusion, a dream, or the reflection of the moon in water—inconceivable, unborn clarity-emptiness. {396}

### b. The Moment of Death

During the dying process, the sign that the earth element is dissolving into the water element is that the body feels heavy. The sign that water is dissolving into fire is that one's mouth and nose dry up. The sign that fire is dissolving into wind is that one's bodily heat draws in from the extremities. The sign that wind is dissolving into space is that the outer breath ceases. The sign that space is dissolving into consciousness is that one loses consciousness for a while. The inner signs that occur during these stages are respectively the appearance of smoke, a mirage, fireflies, a lamp, and a cloudless sky. After that, the seminal essence obtained from one's father descends and the white experience occurs. The red essence obtained from the mother is gathered upward and the red experience occurs. The white and red essences together with the dhanaṃjaya wind [are gathered] at the level of the heart within the central channel, and one will remain in a state of bliss, clarity, and no-thought for a day. If one recognizes this as one's own nature, one will in a single instant attain perfect buddhahood.

### c. The Bardo of Becoming

When you transmigrate into the bardo of becoming, you should meditate that everything you perceive is the display of the buddha field of Mañjushrī. Meditate that you yourself and all sentient beings are Mañjushrī. Emanate and gather back rays of light from the buddhas of the five families in your five centers. Consider that all sounds are the sound of mantra. Recognize all thoughts as the unborn body of truth. Make the repeated aspiration[9] to travel miraculously to the Unexcelled realm, Akaniṣhṭha, or to the Blissful realm, Sukhāvatī. There, in the bardo, you will accomplish Mañjushrī in the body of perfect enjoyment and seize the buddha field of the body of perfect enjoyment. {397}

## [III. Conclusion][10]

By the power of increasing in virtue, as if extending the earth,
May I complete the tenth level—[rare as the] manifestation of the
utpala—
And, like the peerless lord Mañjushrī,
May I too become a protector of beings.

This completes the graded instructions of Mañjushrī, the deity related to the enlightened body aspect, entitled *The Wheel of Ornaments of the Light of Gnosis That Makes Wisdom Grow*.[11] They were maintained in the aural lineage, but the yogi Öpak Dorje wrote them down so that they are not completely forgotten and lost.

Virtue!

# 19. The Spreading Rays of Light That Vanquish the Hordes of Demons

*The Instructions of Lord Vajrapāṇi, the Deity Related to Enlightened Mind*[1]

{400}
Immutable, beyond the realm of others' imagination,
Embodiment of the power of past, present, and future conquerors,
Vajra holder who destroys all of beings' confusion—
To the teacher together with the Holder of Secrets I bow.

The graded instructions on his generation and perfection stages—
The words of the Buddha and the teachers' pith instructions—
I will set down in writing, for fear of forgetting them.
For this, Vajra Ferocity, please bless my stream of being.

Here are the *Spreading Rays of Light That Vanquish the Hordes of Demons*, the instructions of Vajrapāṇi, the deity related to enlightened mind, who embodies the essence of the secrets of all the buddhas of the three times and who is the transcendent perfection of their power. These instructions comprise three topics: (1) preliminaries; (2) main practice; and (3) conclusion.

## I. Preliminaries

The preliminaries are divided into three parts: (1) the history of the lineage of teachers; (2) the common preliminaries; and (3) the specific preliminaries.

## A. History of the Lineage of Teachers

The lord of yogis Mitrayogin practiced five yidam deities {401} in the great charnel ground of Sosaling: Amitābha, Mañjushrī, the Great Compassionate One, Vajrapāṇi, and Tārā. As result of his accomplishing them, these deities each revealed themselves to him and, through concentration, bestowed empowerment. They taught him the instructions of the generation and perfection stages and authorized him to teach them to a single lineage holder, saying that for seven generations they would all be individuals whom they had blessed. They also said that Jambhala and the protector Draklha would bring about favorable conditions and protect the teachings.

The lord of yogis heard these instructions from Vajrapāṇi in person and then bestowed them on paṇḍita Shrīputra. He in turn gave them to Tokden Girti Ratna, who gave them to me. This is how these instructions came down through the lineage.

## B. Common Preliminaries

The common preliminaries consist of four parts: namely, {402} meditation on the difficulty of finding the freedoms and advantages; on death and impermanence; on action, cause and effect; and on the defects of cyclic existence. These are the same as found in other teachings.

## C. Specific Preliminaries

These specific preliminaries are divided into four.

### 1. Instructions on Going for Refuge and Arousing Bodhichitta, Which Is What Makes Everything One Does Become the Path of Enlightenment

In the space in front of you visualize a supremely vast and spacious throne made of many precious materials and rendered pure by multicolored divine silks. On top of it, in the center of a lotus with a hundred thousand petals, is a full moon, and on this throne is seated your root teacher, having the appearance of Vajradhara, surrounded by the ocean-like buddhas of the ten directions. In front of him is the yidam deity Vajrapāṇi, surrounded by the hosts of yidam deities of the four tantras. On his right is Buddha

Shākyamuni, surrounded by infinite buddhas such as the one thousand two buddhas.[2] To the rear is the Great Mother,[3] surrounded by volumes of the scriptures. To the left is Lord Maitreya, surrounded by the ocean-like sanghas of the Supreme and Lesser Vehicles. In all the intermediate directions are gathering clouds of ḍākas and ḍākinīs. Below is an ocean-like assembly of dharma protectors.

Considering that you and the whole infinity of sentient beings are under their protection, and arousing the intention, "For the benefit of all sentient beings who are as numerous as the sky is vast, I will attain the level of Vajrapāṇi," take refuge and arouse the bodhichitta, reciting the same prayer as in the instructions on Avalokiteshvara: "All sentient beings, my mothers, as numerous as space is vast, take refuge in the teacher, precious Buddha," and so on. {403}

At the end, the objects of refuge melt into light and dissolve into you. Their enlightened body, speech, and mind become inseparable from your body, speech, and mind, like water poured into water. Rest in meditative equipoise in that uncontrived state.

## 2. Instructions on the Meditation and Recitation of Vajrasattva, Which Enables One to Swiftly Purify One's Negative Deeds and Obscurations

On the crown of your head visualize a letter *paṃ*, from which there appears a multicolored lotus, and a letter *A*, from which a full-moon disk appears. On top of it is the syllable *hūṁ*, from which appears a white five-pronged vajra marked with the syllable *hūṁ*. It emanates rays of light, making offerings to the noble ones and benefiting sentient beings. The lights are gathered back, and it transforms into Lord Vajrasattva. He is white, with one face and two arms, and seated with his two legs crossed in the vajra posture. In his right hand he holds a golden five-pronged vajra, pointing toward his heart center. His left hand is resting on his hip, holding a vajra-handled bell. He has a smiling face, with almond eyes. Half of his hair is tied up in five hair knots, and the remaining locks reach down to his waist. He is adorned with a jeweled head ornament, earrings, short necklace, long necklace, armlets, bracelets, belt, and so on, and a silken crown. In his crown center is a white *oṁ*, in his throat center a red *āḥ*, and in his heart center a blue *hūṁ*. From these, rays of light emanate inviting the wisdom deity, who is identical to himself. As you say *jaḥ hūṁ baṃ hoḥ*, consider that the wisdom deity dissolves inseparably into the meditational deity.

Then pray: "Lord, bless me and the whole infinity of sentient beings and purify all our negative deeds and obscurations." {404} As a result of this prayer, a stream of nectar descends from his big toe, gushing out as if unplugged. It enters you through the aperture of Brahmā on the crown of your head. All illnesses, negative forces, negative deeds, and obscurations are forthwith expelled through the soles of your feet and through your anus and urethra, in the form of liquid smoke and liquid charcoal. They dissolve nine levels below the surface of the earth. The whole of your body is completely filled with white wisdom nectar. As you concentrate on this, recite the hundred-syllable mantra. At the end, Vajrasattva melts into light and dissolves into you. With Vajrasattva's enlightened body, speech, and mind [mingled] with your body, speech, and mind like water poured into water, rest with no contrivance regarding your body, speech, and mind. Train in this way until signs occur that you have purified your illnesses, negative forces, negative deeds, and obscurations.

### 3. Instructions on the Mandala Practice

These concern (1) the accomplishment mandala and (2) the offering mandala.

#### a. The Accomplishment Mandala

On a mandala made of the five precious materials, set out five piles of flowers. Then visualize the outer ring of iron mountains, and in its center the four continents and Mount Meru, made of the five precious materials, and on top of that the measureless palace, made of the five precious materials. It is square, with four gates, pediments, and terraces, and decorated with a top ornament. In its center is a lotus and moon disk, on which is seated one's teacher. In front is the yidam deity; to the right, the Buddha; at the rear, the sacred dharma; and to the left, the sangha, with, in the cardinal and intermediate directions, hosts of ḍākas, ḍākinīs, and dharma protectors. In each one's crown center is a white syllable *oṁ*, in the throat center a red *āḥ*, and in the heart center a blue *hūṁ*. From these, rays of light emanate inviting the wisdom deities, {405} who dissolve inseparably into them. This constitutes the accomplishment mandala.

### b. The Offering Mandala

If you have two mandala plates, arrange them separately. If not, [visualize the deities] up in the air in front of you. Then, for the offering mandala:

*oṁ vajra bhumi āḥ hūṁ*—corresponding to the mighty golden ground.

*oṁ vajra rekhe āḥ hūṁ*—corresponding to the outer ring of iron mountains, in the middle of which is Mount Meru, made of the five kinds of precious materials.

In the east is Pūrvavideha, which is semicircular and made of crystal, embellished with uncultivated crops of grain. In the south is Jambudvīpa, which is trapezoidal and made of beryl, embellished with jewels. In the west is Godānīya, which is circular and made of ruby, embellished with bountiful cows. In the north is Uttarakuru, which is square and made of precious gold, embellished with wish-fulfilling trees. They are flanked by the eight subcontinents.

In the sky to the southeast is the sun, made of fire crystal. To the northwest is the moon, made of water crystal. To the northeast is Ketū, and to the southwest is Rāhu. Above Mount Meru are the seven attributes of royalty, namely the precious wheel, the precious jewel, the precious minister, the precious queen, the precious elephant, the marvelous and precious horse, and the precious general; the eight auspicious symbols, namely the precious parasol, the banner of universal victory, the fish made of gold, the utterly beautiful lotus, the conch that proclaims the melodious sound of the dharma, the vase of great treasure, the eternal knot that fulfills all needs and desires, and the wheel that turns the wheel of the teachings; {406} the four outer offering maidens (the lady of flowers, the lady of incense, the lady of lamps, and the lady of perfume); and the four inner offering maidens—the lady of charm, the lady of garlands, the lady of song, and the lady of dance.

In short, everything is completely filled with the many riches of gods and humans, with nothing missing, and these, along with [one's own] body and possessions, one offers to the teacher and the Three Jewels, along with infinite objects worthy of veneration. Saying, "Accept this with compassion for the sake of beings, and, accepting it, grant your blessings, I pray," make this offering twenty-one, seven, or ten times. In this way, gather the accumulation of merit.

This completes the instruction on the mandala, which enables one to complete the two accumulations.

### 4. Instructions on the Guru Yoga, Which Enables One to Swiftly Receive Blessings

The guru yoga is divided into four parts.

#### a. Visualizing the Teacher above the Crown of One's Head

Above the crown of your head visualize a vast, spacious throne made entirely of many precious materials, and on it a multicolored lotus with a hundred thousand petals and a full-moon disk. On that is one's root teacher appearing as Vajradhara. Above his head is Tokden Girti Ratna, above his head Shrīputra, and above his head the siddha Mitrayogin, who is white in color, playing a gold ḍāmaru in his right hand, and ringing a sweetly sounding silver bell in his left. He has a lower garment of white cotton and is wearing the six bone ornaments. His eyes are gazing into space. Above his head is Vajrapāṇi, who has one face and two arms and is seated cross-legged on a lotus and moon. {407} In his right hand he holds a vajra, in his left a bell. He is adorned with silks and jewel ornaments. In [each one's] crown center is a white *oṁ*, in the throat center a red *āḥ*, and in the heart center a blue *hūṁ*. From these, white, red, and blue rays of light emanate. The light rays gather back the teachers and yidam deities of the ten directions; the Buddha, dharma, and sangha; and the ḍākinīs and protectors. They dissolve into the upper and lower bodies of the teachers, who become the embodiments of all teachers.

#### b. Making the Offerings of Praise, the Seven Branches, and the Mandala

#### c. Praying

Recite the prayer, "All beings, as numerous as the sky is vast, pray to the Teacher, precious Buddha," and so on. At the end, pray for the fulfillment of wishes.

#### d. [Receiving Empowerment]

From the white *oṁ*, red *āḥ*, and blue *hūṁ* in the teacher's crown, throat, and heart centers, rays of light issue forth and touch your own body, speech, and mind. Consider that your obscurations are purified and that you receive the empowerments of the enlightened body, speech, and mind. Again, from the three syllables *oṁ*, *āḥ*, and *hūṁ* streams of white, red, and blue nectar issue forth, filling your body, so that you receive the empowerments of the enlightened body, speech, and mind. At the end, the three syllables and their associated attributes[4] shoot out and dissolve into your three centers. Consider that in this way the three empowerments are sealed. After that, the lineage teachers, one by one, melt into light and dissolve into each other, all dissolving into your root teacher. The latter melts into light and dissolves into you. Your body, speech, and mind mingle inseparably with the teacher's enlightened body, speech, and mind, {408} like water poured into water. Rest in meditative equipoise, naturally relaxed with your body, speech, and mind in a state free of contrivance. To do so is the ultimate guru yoga.

Having gone through the specific preliminaries with these [we come now to the main practice].

## II. Main Practice[5]

### A. Instructions on the Generation Stage

The generation stage comprises three sections.

#### 1. Actual Generation Stage

Keeping the four boundless attitudes in mind, banish the obstacle makers with the *amṛta* mantra. Purify everything with the *svabhāva* mantra. From the state of emptiness the earth becomes the Willow Leaf buddha field. In its center, upon a lotus and sun, is the syllable *hūṁ*, radiating light. This gives rise to the ground of vajras below—hard, firm, and immutable; all around is the vajra fence and lattice; above is the vajra tent and canopy. This is surrounded by a thousand-spoked wheel made of meteoric iron. Outside that is a forest of sharp weapons and a blazing mountain of fire. This is the visualization of the protection circle.

In the center, visualize the syllable *bhrūṃ*, from which there appears the measureless palace, with its four sides, four doors, ornaments, and pediments. In the middle of that is the letter *paṃ*, from which appears a ten-petaled multicolored lotus, and in its center the letter *raṃ*, and from it eleven sun disks, on top of which, from the *hūṁ* syllables, appear blue vajras marked with a *hūṁ*. From them light radiates, making offerings to the hosts of noble ones, subjugating all harmful beings, and converting them to the Buddha's doctrine. The lights are gathered back and transform into oneself as Vajrapāṇi, who is sky-blue in color, with one face, two arms, and two legs in the striding posture of a warrior. He is wearing a skirt of a freshly flayed tiger skin. He has an enormous belly and fully developed torso. With his right hand he brandishes in the air a golden nine-pronged vajra. {409} His left hand is making the threatening gesture and holding a bell at the level of his heart. His mouth is wide open, his four canine teeth bared, and his tongue curled back. His face is wrinkled in anger, and his three eyes blaze with light, like the fire at the end of the kalpa. His beard, mustache, and eyebrows flash, and his light-yellow hair swirls upward. He has a huge body and massive limbs and appendages. He is adorned with the variegated white head ornament of the warrior caste, the variegated yellow earrings of the merchant caste, the variegated red necklet of the brahmin caste, the variegated green bracelets and anklets of the servant caste, and the variegated black sash and shoulder belt of the lowest castes. He is adorned with the five jewel ornaments, shining with light, and beautified with the silken crown. He is standing amid a blazing mass of wisdom fire.

The ten *hūṁ* syllables on the petals of the lotus [transform into] the ten wrathful ones, who have the same attributes as oneself and are standing with their faces looking in toward the center. In the crown center of each of these deities is a white *oṁ*, in their throat center a red *āḥ*, and in their heart center a blue *hūṁ*. From these, light radiates, inviting from the Willow Leaf buddha field wisdom deities identical to themselves. With *jaḥ hūṁ baṃ hoḥ*, they dissolve inseparably into you. Again, with the emanation of light, the tathāgatas of the five families are invited, the request for empowerment is made, and you are empowered by the buddhas of the five families. Consider that the inside of your body is filled with wisdom nectar, which overflows, so that you are adorned on your crown by Akṣhobhya.

In your heart center visualize a lotus and sun disk, upon which there is a blue vajra, and in its hub the syllable *hūṁ* is surrounded by [the mantra] *oṁ vajrapāṇi hūṁ*, like a string of beryls. {410} To concentrate on this is the peaceful approach.

For the wrathful approach, concentrate on the syllables *oṁ vajra caṇḍamahāroṣaṇa hūṁ phaṭ* in a circle in the form of hot, burning red light. This is the wrathful approach.

Again, from the *hūṁ* in your heart center, rays of light emanate. Consider that they touch the world outside so that it becomes the Willow Leaf buddha field. They touch the beings inhabiting it, so that they become Vajrapāṇi, all intoning the sound of the mantra.

This is the instruction on the approach, which should be practiced until the signs [of accomplishment] are complete.

At the end, the outer world dissolves into its inhabitants. The inhabitants dissolve into you, and you dissolve into the *hūṁ* in your heart center. The *hūṁ* vanishes like a rainbow dissolving in the sky. Rest in the state without concepts.

All this is the instruction on the generation stage.

## 2. Instructions on the Emanation and Reabsorption of Light Rays, Related to the Five Families

These instructions comprise two parts.

### a. The Emanation and Reabsorption of Light Rays of the Five Families of Vajrapāṇi

Visualize yourself clearly as Vajrapāṇi, as before, and in the five centers (crown, throat, heart, navel, and secret center) upon a lotus and sun, five *hūṁ* syllables (white, red, blue, yellow, and green) from which there appear [the five] bhagavāns: in the crown, white Vairochana Vajrapāṇi, in the throat, red Padma Vajrapāṇi, in the heart, blue Vajra Vajrapāṇi, in the navel, yellow Ratnasambhava Vajrapāṇi, and in the secret center, green Karma Vajrapāṇi. They are attired like Vairochana and present in the middle of a mass of fire. As you visualize them emanating white, red, blue, yellow, and green rays of light, making inconceivable clouds of offerings to the buddhas and bodhisattvas of the ten directions, {411} concentrate on breathing out. As you breathe in, consider that the body, speech, mind, qualities, and activities of the buddhas and bodhisattvas in the ten directions, and their power, ability, wisdom, deeds, blessings, and splendor are all gathered in the form of the five Vajrapāṇis and dissolve into your crown, throat, heart, navel, and secret centers, and hold the breath for a short while. Again, as you breathe out, emanate five-colored rays of light. Consider that they touch the beings of the six realms—gods, demigods, humans, animals, hungry spirits, and hell beings—purifying their obscurations and five poisons and bringing them to the level of the five Vajrapāṇis. When you breathe in, consider that all the power, wisdom, qualities, deeds, activities, splendor, and blessings of their body, speech, mind, qualities, and activities are gathered in the form of the five Vajrapāṇis as white, red, blue, yellow, and green rays of light, which dissolve into the five Vajrapāṇis in your crown, throat, heart, navel, and secret centers, so that you yourself acquire the infinite power, wisdom, deeds, splendor, and blessings of their enlightened body, speech, mind, qualities, and activities. With this visualization, hold the vase breath in the five centers.

At the end, the world melts into light and dissolves into the sentient beings. All the sentient beings dissolve into the buddhas, the buddhas and bodhisattvas dissolve into you, and you dissolve into the *hūṁ* in your heart center. The *hūṁ* vanishes like a rainbow in the sky. Rest in meditative equipoise in the nonconceptual state. {412} This is the perfection stage.

### b. The Emanation and Reabsorption of Light Rays of the Five Families of Garuḍas

This is section is divided into three.

#### i. Visualizing the Garuḍas Crowning One's Head

On the crown of your head is the white garuḍa of the buddha family. On the forehead is the blue vajra garuḍa. Behind the right ear is the yellow ratna garuḍa. On the back of the head is the red padma garuḍa. And behind the left ear is the green karma garuḍa. They all have beaks made of meteoric iron, outstretched vajra wings, and two sharp horns, between which they are adorned with a jewel. In their two hands they hold a venomous snake, which they are devouring. They are present in the midst of a blazing mass of fire. From these garuḍas, five-colored rays of light emanate, making offerings to the buddhas and bodhisattvas and touching the beings of the six realms, purifying their five poisons and bringing them to the level of the five families of garuḍas. After that, all the power, ability, wisdom, splendor, and blessings of their enlightened body, speech, mind, qualities, and activities are gathered back in the form of white, red, blue, yellow, and green rays of light, or in the form of the five garuḍas, and dissolve into the five garuḍas crowning your head. Consider that you obtain all the power, ability, wisdom, splendor, and blessings of their enlightened body, speech, mind, qualities, and activities, and hold the vase breath.

### ii. Manifesting the Garuḍas in the Five Centers

Visualize yourself as Vajra Ferocity with, in the crown center, a white buddha garuḍa, in the throat center a red padma garuḍa, in the heart center a blue vajra garuḍa, in the navel center a yellow ratna garuḍa, and in the secret center {413} a green karma garuḍa. They all have beaks made of meteoric iron, outstretched vajra wings, and two sharp horns, between which they are adorned with a jewel. Their two hands hold a venomous snake, which they are devouring. They are present amid a blazing mass of fire. From these garuḍas of the five families, rays of light—white, red, blue, yellow, and green—emanate one after the other,[6] making offerings to the buddhas and bodhisattvas and purifying sentient beings of their five poisons and setting them on the level of the five families. After that, all the power, ability, wisdom, deeds, splendor, and blessings of their enlightened body, speech, mind, qualities, and activities are gathered back as five-colored rays of light in the form of the garuḍas of the five families and dissolve into the garuḍas in your five centers. Considering that you possess all the boundless power, ability, wisdom, deeds, splendor, and blessings of their enlightened body, speech, mind, qualities, and activities, hold the vase breath.

### iii. Manifesting the Garuḍas on the Five Limbs and Subjugating the Nāgas

On your head is a white buddha garuḍa, on your right arm a blue vajra garuḍa, on your left arm a yellow ratna garuḍa, on your right thigh a red padma garuḍa, and on your left thigh a green karma garuḍa. They all have three eyes, beaks made of meteoric iron, outstretched vajra wings, and two sharp horns, between which they are adorned with a blazing precious jewel. Their two hands are holding a venomous snake, which they are devouring. They are present amid a fiercely blazing mass of fire. From these garuḍas of the five families, rays of white, {414} red, blue, yellow, and green light emanate, making outer, inner, and secret offerings, and touching the six classes of beings and bringing them to the level of the five families of garuḍas. In particular they touch the nāgas related to the five castes—the warrior caste, merchant caste, servant caste, brahmin caste, and lowest castes—purifying their five poisons and setting them on the level of the five garuḍa families. All the power, ability, wisdom, and deeds of their enlightened body, speech, mind, qualities, and activities in the form of white, red, blue, yellow, and green rays of light are gathered and dissolve into the garuḍas of the five families. Consider that power, ability, wisdom, deeds, splendor, and blessings of their enlightened body, speech, mind, qualities, and activities become more powerful in you, and hold the vase breath. In this way, for each of the five families of Vajrapāṇi and the five families of garuḍas, hold the vase breath.

At the end, all appearances dissolve into the sentient beings. They dissolve into the buddhas, and they in turn dissolve into you. You dissolve into the *hūṁ* in your heart center, which vanishes like a rainbow. Rest in meditative equipoise in the state beyond intellect, devoid of mental activity.

### 3. Instructions on the Recitation, Enlightened Speech

These instructions are divided into two: (1) the recitation of Vajrapāṇi and (2) the garuḍa recitation.

#### a. Recitation of Vajrapāṇi

This recitation has three parts.

##### i. Outer Recitation

Visualize yourself as Vajrapāṇi with the five families of Vajrapāṇi. In your heart center is a lotus and sun, on top of which is the syllable *hūṁ* surrounded by the mantra *oṁ vajrapāṇi hūṁ*, like a string of blue beryls. Concentrating on this, recite *oṁ vajrapāṇi hūṁ*.

##### ii. Inner Recitation

Visualize yourself as Vajrapāṇi. In your heart center is a lotus and sun, on top of which is a blue vajra blazing with fire. {415} In its hub is the syllable *hūṁ* surrounded by the ten-syllable mantra, whose nature is that of hot, burning red light. As it turns, it fills the inside of your body with the blazing fire of wisdom. Considering that all your sicknesses, negative deeds, and obscurations are being burned up like feathers in a fire, recite *oṁ vajra caṇḍa mahāroṣaṇa hūṁ phaṭ*.

### iii. Secret Mental Recitation

Visualize yourself very clearly as Vajrapāṇi. In your heart center is a lotus and sun, on top of which is the syllable *hūṁ* surrounded by the peaceful and wrathful mantras, from which five-colored rays of light emanate. They fill the inside of your body and issue forth from the tips of the hairs on your body, touching the outer world and turning it into the Willow Leaf buddha field. They touch the sentient beings, which are transformed into the five families of Vajrapāṇi. Consider that they are murmuring the sound of the mantra. The light rays are gathered back and dissolve into your body. Your whole body and all the hairs on it become the bodies of the five families of Vajrapāṇi. Visualize them all looking outward, amid a mass of fire, intoning the sound of the mantra. After that, the light rays enter your body, and the whole of the inside of your body is filled to bursting with the bodies of the five families of Vajrapāṇi. Visualize them all looking inward, intoning the mantra, and do the recitation.

## b. Instructions for the Garuḍa Recitation

These instructions are divided into three sections.

### i. Outer Recitation

In the heart center of each of the five garuḍas, visualize a lotus and sun, on top of which is a syllable *khroṁ*, respectively white, red, blue, yellow, and green, surrounded by the mantra *oṁ garuḍa cale cale hūṁ*. This is the instruction on performing the approach, the outer recitation.

### ii. Inner Recitation {416}

In the heart center of each of the five garuḍas, visualize a lotus and sun, on top of which is a syllable *khroṁ*, respectively white, red, blue, yellow, and green, surrounded by the mantra *oṁ hūṁ trāṃ hrīḥ āḥ garuḍa cale cale hūṁ phaṭ,* which is hot and blazing with fire. Recite the mantra, considering that the illnesses, negative forces, negative deeds, and obscurations inside your body are burned up like feathers burned in a fire and that the inside of your body is filled with the fire of wisdom.

### iii. Secret Mental Recitation

On a lotus and sun in the heart center of each of the five garuḍas, visualize a syllable *khroṁ*, respectively white, red, blue, yellow, and green, surrounded [by the mantra], from which rays of light in the five colors emanate. They fill the inside of the body, and from the roots of the hairs of your body they radiate outward, transforming the world into the Willow Leaf buddha field. They touch the buddhas and bodhisattvas, who all transform into garuḍas of the five families. Touching the beings of the six realms, they transform them all into garuḍas of the five families. Consider that they are loudly intoning the sound of the mantra. The rays of light are reabsorbed, and the hairs on your head and body all become infinite tiny garuḍas of the five families with their limbs projecting out and completely covering your body. Visualize them facing outward, reciting the mantra. After that, the light rays are gathered back inside your body, and the whole of the body is filled to bursting with the five wisdom garuḍas, looking inward, in the midst of masses of fire, and intoning the sound of the mantra. In this way, recite the mantra mentally, without getting distracted.

At the end, the world and its inhabitants dissolve into you, and you dissolve into the seed syllable in your heart center. The syllable [dissolves]: rest in equipoise in the nonconceptual state.

All these are the instructions on enlightened speech, the recitation. {417}

## B. Instructions on the Perfection Stage[7]

The perfection stage comprises the enlightened-mind instructions on the nature of mind. There are four topics.

### 1. Sustained Calm

The development of sustained calm is divided into three sections.

#### a. Holding the Mind on Conceptual Attributes

Begin by holding the mind on [an object with] conceptual attributes. For this, there are four kinds of objects.

### i. Holding the Mind on an Impure Object Such As a Pillar or Vase

Hold the mind on a pillar, vase, stick, pebble, or other suitable object, all the while maintaining the right physical posture and gaze. Without getting distracted or getting involved in thoughts, settle the mind on it without conceptual thoughts, in an uncontrived, relaxed state. Should wildness or dullness occur, you should know how to focus the mind up or down or right or left.

### ii. Holding the Mind on a Pure Object Such As an Image of a Buddha

In front of you place an image of Vajrapāṇi or, if you do not have one, visualize him. Do not get involved in thoughts or get carried away by distraction. To settle the mind on it in a relaxed way, without any distraction, is concentration on a pure object, the form of a buddha.

### iii. Holding the Mind on an Impure Object, a Sphere, Inside

Visualize in your heart center a brilliant blue sphere the size of a pea. Hold the mind on it without letting your attention wander or getting involved in thoughts.

### iv. Holding the Mind on a Pure Object, the Form of a Buddha, Inside

Hold the mind on a lotus and sun disk in your heart center, and on them a thumb-sized form of Vajrapāṇi, surrounded by fire. Without wandering or getting involved in thoughts, concentrate on it without any distraction.

In both pure and impure forms of concentration, if dullness occurs, concentrate on [the image in] the forehead.

### b. Concentrating on Conceptual Thoughts

When a thought suddenly arises, recognize it {418} and look at it directly with the eye devoid of concepts. By this means, you will destroy it without grasping, and natural awareness, clear and empty, devoid of object, will vividly arise. Focusing on the nature of any thought that arises, preserve the recognition of your own nature, awareness. This is concentrating on thoughts.

### c. Holding the Mind on [a State of] Absence of Thoughts

Adopt the seven-point posture of Vairochana and gaze into space. Cutting off all thought movements related to the three times—past, present, and future—without thinking of anything, settle in meditative equipoise in the state of clarity-emptiness, without extremes or middle, the thought-free uncontrived nature of the mind, vivid and awake. If a thought arises out of that, cut off its sudden arising. Then again settle in equipoise in the state free of conceptual thoughts and devoid of all mental activity. In this way, the experiences of bliss, clarity, and no-thought will occur.

All this concerned [the practice of] sustained calm.

## 2. Profound Insight

Profound insight is treated under three headings.

### a. Causal Profound Insight: Examining the Mind

Examine the nature of the mind's arising, ceasing, and dwelling, asking yourself, From where has this mind of mine arisen? Where does it stay? Where will it cease?

Examine and check, asking yourself, Does it arise, stay, and disappear in the five elements or in my own body? Check further: Does the mind have a color—white, red, blue, yellow, or green? Or is it colorless? Check whether this mind of yours was produced with a shape—the form of earth, water, fire, wind, or space, {419} or round, square, semicircular, triangular, oblong, or oval, and so on. Are thoughts something other than the mind, or are thoughts the mind? Moreover, does the mind arise from appearances outside, or do appearances outside arise from the mind?

Now use the mind to examine and analyze the mind that is analyzing. Does that mind exist or not? Check: Is it clear or unclear? Happy or unhappy? Is it permanent or impermanent? Is it visible or invisible? Is it aware or unaware? Is there a self or no self?

When you examine in this way, you will see that the essential nature of the mind is devoid of arising, dwelling, and ceasing. Its essence is by nature emptiness, like space. It is naturally radiant. It is unobstructed awareness, arising in every kind of way, and all these appearances are of the same taste in being unborn; they are of the same taste in not dwelling and not ceasing. By examining and analyzing, you will see its ultimate nature, which is clarity, awareness, appearance, and emptiness inseparable, inconceivable like space. In that way, as you realize the nature of mind, you will be introduced to thatness, in which all the qualities of the ground, path, and result are complete.

### b. Essential Profound Insight: Simultaneously Experiencing the Fresh "Ordinary" Mind {420}

The nature of mind is devoid of the extremes of birth, cessation, and dwelling. It is bliss, clarity, and absence of thought, like space. It is free of the dualistic apprehension of subject and object that grasps at "I" and "mine." Its nature is emptiness, its character luminous clarity. Its manifestation is unobstructed awareness, without object, yet appearing in a multitude of ways. It transcends any field of apprehension, something to be seen and someone seeing. All concepts of something to be meditated on or someone meditating have been destroyed. There is nothing to think about, so it is devoid of mental activity. Being uncontrived, it is a state of relaxation. As it is devoid of all effortful activity, there is nothing to be done. There is no identifying whatever arises, so it is free of grasping. Since the mind of meditative equipoise is unadulterated by contrivance, it is free of thoughts. Free of attributes, it is utterly empty. Naturally radiant, it is vividly clear. Uncontaminated by dualistic thoughts, it is fresh and naked. Recognizing its own nature, it is fully awake. Since it rests naturally in uncontrived awareness, it is the ordinary mind. And since it does not continuously indulge in chains of thoughts, it is known as fresh awareness. It is free of the concepts of subject and object. Appearances and mind being inseparable, it is unobstructed. Being devoid of grasping, it is uniform. This is how the main practice of profound insight, experiencing the state of awareness that recognizes and sees its own nature, is introduced.

### c. Ultimate Profound Insight: Practicing Sustained Calm and Profound Insight Together

To settle in the space-like state of bliss, clarity, and absence of thought, the mind being devoid of birth, cessation, and dwelling, is sustained calm. To see and recognize the nature of that {421} is profound insight. The nature of mind, free of the two extremes, is the union of sustained calm and profound insight, which is the actual way things are. Since the nature of mind is unborn, it is free of the extreme of eternalism. And since it has no cessation, it is free of the extreme of nihilism. Its nature is to dwell as emptiness, so it is free of the extreme of eternalism. Yet there is awareness and clarity, manifesting in multifarious ways, so it is free of the extreme of nihilism. The nature of the mind has no existence as color or shape, so it is free of the extreme of eternalism. Yet its manifesting power arises in all sorts of ways, so it is free from the extreme of nihilism. Thus, it transcends the concepts of eternalism and nihilism. It is the union of clarity, awareness, and emptiness inseparable. The manner in which this union is experienced is as follows.

Settling the mind on the illusion-like skillful means, the accumulation of merit, is sustained calm. Seeing that all that is emptiness, devoid of intrinsic nature, is profound insight. Settling the mind on devotion in the practice of guru yoga is sustained calm, while seeing that its essence is emptiness, devoid of birth, cessation, and dwelling, is profound insight. Settling the mind on love and compassion embracing all sentient beings is sustained calm, while seeing that their nature is emptiness is profound insight. Settling the mind on the great bliss, the culmination of the path, is sustained calm; seeing that very state as emptiness, without clinging, is profound insight. Settling the mind on all appearances being the deluded appearances of the mind, like a city in a dream, [is sustained calm]; seeing that those appearances are interdependent and unborn is profound insight. Settling the mind on the state of luminosity, the nature of the mind, {422} [is sustained calm]; seeing that its nature, free of elaboration, is unborn clarity-emptiness is profound insight. Settling the mind on the fresh state of awareness uncontaminated by contrivance [is sustained calm]; seeing that there is no-self, awareness and emptiness, without there being an object,[8] is profound insight.

In short, there is no emptiness that is other than appearances, which are like the reflection of the moon in water, a reflection in a mirror, or an echo. And there are no appearances that are other than emptiness. Realizing the inseparability of appearances and emptiness, like a rainbow appearing in the sky, and settling in that state, one purifies all dualistic clinging and develops the gnosis of awareness, and this is what has been taught as "buddha."[9] It is also called Vajrapāṇi, "Vajra in the Hand." *Pāṇi* ("in the hand") signifies the union of great compassion (related to skillful means and relative truth) and the form body. *Vajra* signifies the essential nature (emptiness and transcendent wisdom) and the body of truth. This is an introduction to the fact that all the qualities included in the path and result, such as the three buddha bodies and the five kinds of gnosis, are complete in the mind.

### 3. An Instruction on Transference at the Moment of Death

There are two sections: (1) training in transference and (2) putting it into practice.

#### a. Training in Transference

Visualize your body as a hollow frame.[10] In the middle of the body is the central channel, which is white on the outside and red inside, empty, vividly clear, and as thin as a reed. Its lower end, reaching down to the secret center, is blocked by the syllable *phaṭ*; its upper end, penetrating the crown of the head, opens straight out, like an open skylight. In the air directly above your head, six feet above, clearly visualize the palace of the pure Willow Leaf buddha field. In its center, on a throne of lotus and sun piled one on top of the other, {423} is Lord Vajrapāṇi, indistinguishable from your teacher, surrounded by the ten wrathful deities and the buddhas and bodhisattvas.

Next, visualize two spheres located in the secret center, blue and red, the nature of your mind, one on top of the other. Like one lamp shooting out of another, the blue one sets off from inside the central channel in the manner of a guide. It circles the syllable *hūṁ* visualized in your heart center and bursts straight out through the aperture of Brahmā, touching the heart center of Vajrapāṇi. Again, it circles the *hūṁ* visualized in your heart center, and circles the red sphere, the base. At that time, when you project it up, shout *hik!* When it descends again,[11] say *ka* and visualize it dissolving into the base sphere. Train in this way twenty-one times. At the end, consider that the teacher dissolves into you, and that your aperture of Brahmā is blocked by a crossed vajra. This is the training.

#### b. Putting Transference into Practice

When all the signs of approaching death are present, abandon all mundane clinging and attachment. Visualize the central channel as before and visualize the syllable *hūṁ* in your heart center and the blue and red spheres in your secret center. Begin with the blue sphere, which shoots up and dissolves in the syllable *hūṁ*, as a result of which the syllable *hūṁ*, like a shooting star, dissolves into Vajrapāṇi's heart center. Concentrate firmly on the visualization and wind and mind. At that time, do this repeatedly until transference occurs. At the end, having miraculously arrived in the Willow Leaf buddha field, where Vajrapāṇi and your own mind are inseparable, you will definitely transfer to the Willow Leaf buddha field. {424}

### 4. Instructions on the Intermediate State

The instructions on the intermediate state (bardo) comprise three parts.

#### a. Training

Train by means of the generation stage and perfection stage. First, you should imagine with conviction: "I am dead. This is the bardo. These are the perceptions of the bardo. My body has no true existence." And meditate that all appearances are the palace of the Willow Leaf buddha field. With the firm pride that you are Vajrapāṇi, meditate that all sentient beings are the nature of Vajrapāṇi. Practice the emanation and reabsorption of light rays based on the five families as described above in the instructions on the generation stage. At the end, train in the perfection stage, settling in the state without mental activity, where all is like a magical illusion, a dream, or the reflection of the moon in water, the inconceivable, unborn clarity-emptiness.

#### b. The Moment of Death

During the dying process, the sign that the earth element is dissolving into the water element is that the body feels heavy. The sign that water is dissolving into fire is that one's mouth and nose dry up. The sign that fire is dissolving into wind is that one's bodily heat draws in from the extremities. The sign that wind is dissolving into space is that the outer breath ceases. The sign that space is dissolving into consciousness is that one loses consciousness for a while. The inner signs that occur at these times are respectively the appearance of smoke, fireflies, a lamp, a cloudless sky, and so on.[12]

After that, the seminal essence drop obtained from one's father descends, and the white experience occurs. The red blood essence obtained from the mother is gathered upward, and the red experience occurs. Mind and wind and the white and red essences rest together within the vasanta channel at the level of the heart, and at first the experience of utter blackness occurs, after which the vajra-like concentration of bliss, clarity, and no-thought arises. If one remains in that state, one will attain buddhahood in the first bardo, in the truth-body buddha field. {425}

### c. The Bardo of Becoming

When you transmigrate into the bardo of becoming you should meditate that everything you perceive is the Willow Leaf buddha field. Meditate that you and all sentient beings are Vajrapāṇi. Perform the emanation and reabsorption of rays of light from the five families located in the five centers. Meditate that all sounds are the sound of mantra. Recognize all thoughts as being your own nature, the unborn body of truth. Direct your aspirations again and again to Vajrapāṇi's Willow Leaf buddha field. By doing so, you will accomplish Vajrapāṇi as the body of perfect enjoyment and be reborn in Vajrapāṇi's Willow Leaf buddha field.

This completes the graded instructions on the generation and perfection stages of Lord Vajra Ferocity.

## [III. Conclusion]

May these instructions spread like the fire at the end of time
And burn up all the obscurations of beings in the three worlds.
May those beings attain the level of the vajra holders of the three bodies
And attain the supreme level of Vajrapāṇi.

These graded instructions from the lineage of the great siddha Mitrayogin, the instructions of Vajrapāṇi, the deity related to enlightened mind, entitled *The Spreading Rays of Light That Vanquish the Hordes of Demons*, came down through the oral lineage. In order that they should not be forgotten, the yogi Öpak Dorje wrote them down. By the mass of merit of doing so, may all beings accomplish the supreme level of Lord Vajrapāṇi, the Vajra Holder. Through this also, may everything be virtuous and auspicious for the Buddha's teachings in all circumstances, everywhere and forever.
*sarvadā śubhaṃ*

# 20. Accomplishing the Immortal Vajra Body

*The Instructions of the Lord Protector Amitāyus, the Deity Related to Enlightened Qualities*[1]

AMITĀYUS (*Tshe dpag med*), the buddha of infinite life, is an aspect of Buddha Amitābha (*'Od dpag med*), the buddha of infinite light, and as his name suggests, he is associated with practices that promote longevity. In these instructions, both names are used to refer to the same deity.

{428}
Your body is adorned with ten million jewels.
You are resplendent as a mountain of rubies,
Shining like a hundred thousand suns at daybreak—
To you, our guide Amitābha, I pay homage.

Seated cross-legged on a lotus and moon, you hold a treasure;
In your hands placed in meditation is the excellent vase filled with nectar;
Smiling peacefully, you are adorned with the major and minor marks—
Lord Amitābha, take care of me!

In the light of the lord's wisdom
Glorious Mitrayogin blossomed, lotus-like,
Bestowing a honeyed feast of pith instructions
On a single lineage holder, the scholar Shrīputra.

From that excellent vase, the sublime ambrosia was poured
Into him who bears the name of Drakpa.
This stream of honeyed nectar, perfectly handed down,
I drank and thus was filled with the nectar of tantra.

Here are the instructions of the lord protector Amitāyus, the deity related to enlightened qualities, {429} which enable one to accomplish the immortal vajra body. There are four parts.

### I. History of the Lineage of These Instructions

When the lord of yogis Mitrayogin practiced five yidam deities in the great charnel ground of Sosaling, he had a direct vision of them, and they each taught him the graded instructions, telling him that for up to seven generations all [those who practiced them] would be fortunate individuals blessed by themselves. Subsequently, the instructions were passed from one lineage holder to the next: the lord protector Amitāyus gave these instructions to Mitrayogin; the latter taught them to paṇḍita Shrīputra, who gave them to Drakpa Rinchen, who in turn bestowed them on Buddhashrī. This is how these instructions came down through the lineage.

### II. Preliminary Practices

The preliminary practices are divided into two: (1) common preliminaries and (2) specific preliminaries.

### A. Common Preliminaries

The common preliminaries consist of the four practices of reflecting on the difficulty of finding the freedoms and advantages; reflecting on death and impermanence; {430} reflecting on action, cause and effect; and reflecting on the defects of cyclic existence.

### B. Specific Preliminaries

The specific preliminaries are divided into four.

### 1. Instructions on Going for Refuge and Arousing Bodhichitta, Which Is What Makes Everything One Does Become the Path of Enlightenment

In the sky above your head is a vast and spacious throne made of many precious materials, supported by peacocks. On it is a lotus with a hundred thousand petals in full bloom, and a moon disk, on top of which is your root teacher in the form of Amitābha. He is in the attire of the body of perfect enjoyment and is surrounded by the teachers of the instruction lineage. In front of him is an ocean-like gathering of the yidam deities, to his right are the infinite buddhas, behind are the infinite scriptures, and to his left are the infinite sanghas. The space below is filled with oceans of ḍākinīs and dharma protectors, and in all the directions and intermediate directions are all the buddhas and bodhisattvas massed like billowing clouds. Consider that you and the whole infinity of sentient beings are under their protection and imagine all of you faithfully intoning the refuge prayer. As you do so, go for refuge and arouse the mind set on supreme enlightenment.

At the end, the objects of refuge melt into light and dissolve into you. Leave your body, speech, and mind without contrivance in the state of the Great Seal—completely even in the absence of conceptual thoughts, totally free in the absence of grasping, vivid and lucid as clarity-emptiness. This is the ultimate going for refuge.

### 2. Instructions on the Four Applications of the Syllable *hrīḥ* That Purify One's Negative Deeds and Obscurations

#### a. The Application That Purifies Negative Deeds

On the crown of your head visualize a red syllable *hrīḥ*, with the visarga. From it a continuous stream of nectar, white as flowing milk, descends, {431} driving out all the illnesses, negative forces, negative deeds, and obscurations inside your body in the form of liquid smoke and charcoal, which are expelled through your anus, urethra, and even your fingernails. They dissolve into the depths of the earth nine levels below. The whole of your body is completely filled with white wisdom nectar. This practice is the application that purifies negative deeds.

### b. The Application That Purifies Illnesses

For fevers, meditate on cooling nectar, like a glacial stream or liquid camphor. For chills, meditate on warming nectar, like boiling molten metal. For illnesses due to multiple imbalances, meditate on the nectar spreading,[2] like melted butter. Visualize these different nectars descending and curing every kind of sickness.

### c. The Application That Purifies Negative Forces

From the syllable *hrīḥ* many tiny forms of Hayagrīva appear, with the details of their limbs and attributes all very clear, in the midst of blazing wisdom fire. They fill the inside of your body and burn up and destroy all negative forces. Consider that they are expelled through your anus, urethra, and pores in the form of spiders and scorpions.

### d. The Application of Light Rays

From the syllable *hrīḥ* visualize five-colored rays of light emanating, like the light of a thousand suns. They fill the inside of your body, purifying all your illnesses, negative forces, negative deeds, and obscurations. They issue out and purify the illnesses, negative forces, negative deeds, and obscurations of all sentient beings.

In all these cases, you should verbally recite the syllable *hrīḥ*. At the end, your body melts into light and dissolves into the *hrīḥ*. The syllable *hrīḥ* vanishes like a rainbow in the sky. Settle in the nonconceptual state, maintaining the correct bodily posture and gaze. Doing this is the ultimate confession.

## 3. Instructions on the Mandala Practice, Which Enables One to Complete the Two Accumulations {432}

The instructions on the mandala are divided into two.

### a. The Accomplishment Mandala

Visualize Mount Meru surrounded by the four continents and the eight subcontinents, on top of it the measureless palace made of different precious materials, and inside it the objects of refuge as visualized [earlier]. As you do so, set out piles of flowers.

### [b. The Offering Mandala]

After that, if you have two mandala plates, leave that one as it is and offer the offering mandala in front of it. Otherwise, [visualize] the deities up in the air and use the same mandala plate as for the accomplishment mandala. Mentally manifest Mount Meru and the four continents, the seven attributes of royalty, the eight auspicious symbols, and multitudes of offering goddesses making the outer and inner offerings, and offer the mandala in the general fashion twenty-one times. This will complete the accumulation of merit.

At the end, the deities that comprise the object of veneration melt into light and dissolve into you. Leave your body, speech, and mind in the uncontrived state, inseparable from them. This corresponds to the accumulation of wisdom.

### 4. Instructions on the Guru Yoga, Which Enables One to Receive Blessings Swiftly

Above the crown of your head visualize a vast, spacious throne made of many precious materials, and on it a multicolored lotus with a hundred thousand petals and a moon disk. On top of that is your root teacher in the form of Amitābha, in the attire of the body of perfect enjoyment. Above his head is the great paṇḍita Shrīputra, and above his head is the siddha Mitrayogin. He holds a ḍāmaru in his right hand and a bell in his left. His eyes gaze into space. On his body he has a lower garment consisting of white cotton shorts, and he is wearing the six bone ornaments. Above his head is Avalokiteshvara, who has one face and four arms and is adorned with jewel ornaments. {433} All these teachers are present in the midst of rainbows, their bodies resplendent, their voices divinely melodious, their minds full of blessings. Their crown centers are marked with a white *oṁ*, their throat centers with a red *āḥ*, their heart centers with a blue *hūṁ*, and their navel centers with a yellow *ho*. From these emanate rays of light, inviting with the light rays all the root and lineage teachers in the ten directions, the yidam deities, the Three Jewels, ḍākinīs, and dharma protectors. They dissolve into the teachers' crown, throat, heart, navel, and secret centers, as enlightened body, speech, and mind. Thinking of your teacher as the essence embodying all teachers, make the mandala offering. Pray and request empowerment. The latter is divided into four stages, as follows.

### a. Purification by Rays of Light

From the syllables in the teachers' centers—white *oṁ* in their crown centers, red *āḥ* in their throat centers, blue *hūṁ* in their heart centers, and yellow *ho* in their navel centers—visualize rays of white, red, blue, and yellow light respectively issuing forth. They touch your four centers, purifying the obscurations related to the four occasions,[3] and you receive the four empowerments.

### [b. Empowerment by Nectar]

From the four syllables in the teachers' four centers visualize nectar streaming forth like a stream of milk, of liquified rubies, of liquified sapphires, and of molten gold, respectively. They enter you in turn through the aperture of Brahmā, filling your body and purifying the four obscurations. The gnosis of the four joys is born in you; you receive the four empowerments and realize the four buddha bodies.

### c. Confirmation by Syllables

The four syllables, {434} together with their associated attributes,[4] suddenly shoot out and dissolve into your four centers. Consider that as a result, again the four obscurations are purified, the four joys are developed, the four empowerments are sealed, and the four buddha bodies are realized.

### d. Complete Empowerment

The lineage teachers melt into light, one after another, and dissolve into the root teacher. The root teacher melts into light and dissolves into you, so that the teacher's enlightened body, speech, and mind, and your body, speech, and mind become inseparable. Settle in the uncontrived state of the nature of mind, relaxed, aware, without concepts, without grasping, free. This is the unsurpassable, ultimate yoga.

## III. Instructions on the Generation Stage

The generation stage is treated in four sections.

### A. Meditating on the Protection Circle

From the state of emptiness appears a syllable *hūṁ*, and from that a multicolored crossed vajra, its hub marked with the syllable *hrīḥ*. From it light radiates, transforming into the ground of vajras below, the vajra fence and lattice all around, and the vajra tent and canopy above. The outside is filled with all kinds of weapons and a blazing mass of wisdom fire. In the middle of this, from the syllable *hrīḥ*, you appear as Hayagrīva, who is red, with one face and two arms. He is standing with his two legs on a lotus and sun seat, one leg stretched out, the other bent in. His right hand is brandishing a club in the air, his left hand held at the level of his heart in the threatening gesture. His mouth is agape, with his tongue curled back, and he is baring his four sharp white canine teeth. He is rolling his three eyes. His eyebrows and hair are ablaze, and on the crown of his head is a green horse's head with a red muzzle and mane, blazing like fire. He is wearing a tiger-skin skirt and adorned with manifold serpents and jewels. {435} Visualize him present amid the blazing great fire at the end of the kalpa. From his body infinite tiny wrathful ones like him emanate, destroying and burning up all negative forces and obstacle makers. On the outside of the protection circle, they block the smallest opening, looking outward to guard against obstacles. Others are looking inward, blocking the smallest openings and standing guard. This visualization constitutes the instruction on the protection circle.

### B. Instruction on Accomplishing Immortal Vajra Life through the Main Practice

Begin with the four boundless attitudes, then visualize the inside of the body that you inhabit ordinarily as a light red hollow framework.[5] Above the crown of your head is a vast and spacious throne made of many precious materials, and on it is a lotus with a hundred thousand petals and moon disk. On top of that is the syllable *hrīḥ*, which radiates lights fulfilling the two goals. As they are reabsorbed, it transforms into the lord protector Amitāyus. His body is ruby red, and he is sitting with his legs crossed in the vajra posture. In his two hands, held in the gesture of meditation, is the vase of immortal vajra life filled with wisdom nectar. He has almond eyes and long eyebrows, adorned with a coil of white hair. His hair is tied up in a topknot, with a silken crown, and he is adorned with a head ornament, earrings, necklet, long necklace, armlets and bracelets, belt, and anklets made of the five precious materials, and with a silken crown and the five kinds of pearls. He is embellished with the thirty-two major marks and eighty minor marks. Visualize him as the sovereign whose rays of light illumine all the realms in the universe. {436}

In his crown center is the white syllable *oṁ*, in his throat center the red syllable *āḥ*, and in his heart center the blue syllable *hūṁ*. From these, light radiates, inviting Amitāyus surrounded by the buddhas and bodhisattvas of the ten directions, who dissolve inseparably into that Amitāyus.

In the middle of the vase in the lord's hands visualize a red syllable *hrīḥ*, complete with visarga, from which rays of light emanate in the ten directions, venerating the buddhas and bodhisattvas of the ten directions with manifold clouds of offerings and gathering back with the light rays all their immutable longevity, merit, glory, resplendence, and enlightened body, speech, mind, qualities, activities, and gnosis, which dissolve into the *hrīḥ* inside the vase. Again, rays of five-colored light like hooks and lassos emanate in the ten directions. They touch all sentient beings in the ten directions, in particular the gods, nāgas, yakṣhas, gandharvas, demigods, garuḍas, kinnaras, and mahoragas, so that they are all brought to the level of Amitābha. All their qualities—their longevity, merit, glory, wealth, renown, and gnosis—are gathered back by the light rays and dissolve into the *hrīḥ* inside the vase. Again, visualize rays of light emanating, and all the vital essence of the earth, water, fire, wind, and space in the ten directions, of the sun and moon, the wish-fulfilling tree, the five precious jewels, and so on, and their power, luster, radiance, light, and qualities all dissolving into the *hrīḥ*.

Next, venerating the lord with manifested offerings, {437} pray: "Lord Amitābha, empower me and all sentient beings with your body, speech, mind, qualities, activities, longevity, and gnosis and grant us accomplishment." As a result of this prayer, from the inside of the vase, a stream of nectar like milk flows down through your aperture of Brahmā and confers empowerment. Then, expel the stale winds three times, and as you breathe in, swallow your saliva; press the wind down at the navel and draw up the lower wind, and hold the vase breath. As you do so, consider that the stream of nectar completely fills the secret center with whiteness and concentrate on this. Likewise, imagine it completely filling the navel, heart, throat, and crown centers in turn with whiteness and concentrate on these in turn. This is what has been taught.

In this way, practice developing the visualization. If you are adept at this, combine each wind exercise with the filling of a chakra, training repeatedly in filling the five chakras one after another in this first visualization stage.

Again, for the four remaining visualization stages, the visualization of Amitābha and emanation and reabsorption of light rays is the same as above. Streams of nectar, respectively red like molten rubies, blue like molten beryl, yellow like molten gold, and green like [molten] emeralds, flow down through the aperture of Brahmā. As you concentrate on these, expel the stale winds three times, swallow your saliva, turn it below the navel center, and forcibly press the upper wind down; draw up the lower wind and hold the vase breath. {438} Visualize the secret center and the navel, heart, throat, and crown centers filling with the five nectars. If you are doing the detailed practice, go through each visualization in turn.

If you are not adept at this, for each visualization stage, do everything together with each color nectar. In that way, visualize the stream of red nectar descending and completely filling the whole body with red. Similarly, visualize a stream of blue, yellow, or green nectar descending. At that time, visualize your body as well in the form of one of the five families of Amitābha, depending on the particular color, and think that you have attained immortal vajra life.

When you have completed these, Amitābha melts into light and dissolves into you. Your whole body is filled to bursting with Amitābhas the size of mustard seeds, and all the roots of your body hairs too are filled with forms [of Amitābha]. Rest with your body, speech, and mind in the uncontrived state.

### C. Instructions Related to Speech: Accomplishing Immortal Speech

Visualize on the crown of your head a glass with a stem, its base acting as a stopper and its mouth facing upward. In the middle of it is a white syllable *āḥ*, emanating rays of light like hooks and lassos in the ten directions. They make offerings to the buddhas and bodhisattvas and gather back their longevity and merit. They touch the beings of the six realms, set them on the level of Amitābha, and gather back their longevity and merit and the quintessence of the elements. The visualization for this is the same as above. Similarly, say the prayer as above, as a result of which a stream of white nectar, as if overflowing, descends and fills your secret center. In the same way, visualize it filling the {439} navel, heart, throat, and crown centers. Press the gentle breath, together with the saliva, below the navel and, drawing up the lower wind, hold the vase breath.

For the second visualization, visualize from the syllable *āḥ* a stream of red nectar descending, and do the vase exercise as before, meditating on the filling of the five chakras one after another, and combining the holding of the breath and the visualization.

When it is time to conclude, from the white *āḥ* other white *āḥ* syllables issue forth like a shower of rain. Consider that the whole of the inside of your body is completely filled with *āḥ*s, and all the roots of your body hairs too are filled with *āḥ*s. For this, it has been taught that you may also repeat *āḥ*.

At the end rest in meditative equipoise with your body, speech, and mind in the uncontrived state.

### D. Instructions Related to Mind: Accomplishing Immortal Vajra Life

Visualize your body in its ordinary form as a light-red hollow framework. Above your head is a red eight-petaled lotus, and on its pistil cup is a brilliant red essence drop, round and glossy. From it rays of light like hooks and lassos emanate in the ten directions, making offerings to the buddhas and bodhisattvas in the ten directions and gathering back their longevity and merit and the quintessence of the elements. These visualizations are the same as in the instructions for the body. Again, pray as described above. Then, expel the stale winds three times. After that, practice as follows. From the essence drop a continuous[6] stream of red nectar issues forth, descending as far as the secret center and filling it. Meditate that, in the same way, the navel, heart, throat, and crown centers are filled one after another. {440} Press down the gentle breath, together with the saliva, below the navel and, drawing up the lower wind, hold the vase breath.

At the end, from the essence drop infinite essence drops issue forth and, like rain falling, fill the whole of the inside of your body. Consider that it is filled to bursting with red essence drops. Imagine that all the roots of your body hairs are also completely filled with red essence drops. Then settle with your body, speech, and mind in the uncontrived state.

## IV. Instructions on the Perfection Stage

The perfection stage is divided into three parts: (1) sustained calm; (2) profound insight; and (3) transference.

### A. Sustained Calm

Sustained calm is treated under four headings.

#### 1. Holding the Mind on an Object Outside

Holding the mind on an object outside has two aspects.

##### a. Holding the Mind on an Impure Object Such As a Pillar or Vase

Without getting distracted, hold the mind on a pillar, vase, stick, pebble, or other suitable object in front of you, while maintaining the correct physical posture and gaze. Do not engage in distraction or entertain conceptual thoughts. Likewise, should wildness or dullness occur, you should know how to focus the mind up or down or right or left.

##### b. Holding the Mind on a Pure Object, a Buddha Image

Place in front of you an image of Amitābha. Alternatively, if you do not have one, visualize it. Do not indulge in thoughts or get involved in distraction. Just rest the mind on the image, relaxed and undistracted. This is holding the mind on a pure object, an image of a buddha.

#### 2. Holding the Mind on an Object Inside

This section also has two parts.

##### a. Holding the Mind on an Impure Object, a Sphere

Concentrate on a pea-sized shining white sphere in your heart center. {441}

### b. Holding the Mind on a Pure Object, the Form of a Buddha

Concentrate on a thumb-sized Amitābha seated on a lotus and moon in your heart center, emanating rays of light. If wildness or dullness occurs, deal with it as above.

### 3. Holding the Mind on Conceptual Thoughts

When you recognize the sudden arising of a thought and look directly at that thought, it will be destroyed without being grasped at, and awareness, clear and empty, will arise vividly. Whatever thoughts arise, meditate directly on them. In that way, without rejecting thoughts, you incorporate them into the path. This is a pith instruction.

### 4. The Ultimate, Resultant Sustained Calm: Holding the Mind on [a State of] Absence of Thoughts

In an isolated, dark room, on a soft cushion, adopt the seven-point posture of Vairochana and direct your eyes blankly into space. Without thinking of anything at all, settle in meditative equipoise in the state of empty space, uncontrived, without thoughts, clear and awake. This is concentrating on absence of thoughts.

These comprise the practice of sustained calm.

## B. Profound Insight

Profound insight is treated under three headings.

### 1. Causal Profound Insight: Examining the Mind

Examine and analyze the essential nature of the mind's arising, ceasing, and staying, asking yourself, From where has this mind of mine arisen? Where does it stay? Where will it go? Check whether it arises from the five elements or from your own body. Examine further: Does the mind have a color—white, red, blue, yellow, or green? Or is it colorless? Check whether this mind of yours has a shape—the form of earth, water, fire, wind, or space, {442} or round, square, semicircular, triangular, oblong, or oval, and so on. Or is it shapeless? Are thoughts something other than the mind, or are thoughts the mind? Check: Does the mind arise from appearances outside, or do appearances outside arise from the mind?

Now examine and analyze the mind that is analyzing. Does that mind exist or not? Check: Is it clear or unclear? Happy or unhappy? Is it permanent or impermanent? Is it visible or invisible? Is it aware or unaware? Is there a self or no self?

When you check like this, you will see that the essence of the mind is empty, like space. It is naturally radiant. It is unobstructed awareness, arising in every kind of way, and all these appearances are of the same taste in being unborn; they are of the same taste in not dwelling; they are of the same taste in not ceasing. You will see its ultimate nature, which is clarity, awareness, and emptiness; appearance and emptiness inseparable, beyond the intellect, like space. In that way, you will be introduced to thatness, in which all the qualities of the ground, path, and result are complete.

### 2. Path Profound Insight That Is Experienced Simultaneously

The nature of mind is devoid of the extremes of birth, cessation, and dwelling. {443} It is devoid of the dualistic attributes of subject and object, the grasping at "I" and "mine." There is nothing to see and nothing that sees. Its nature is emptiness, its character luminous clarity. It is unobstructed awareness, without object, yet appearing clearly in a multitude of ways. Unadulterated by contrivance or alteration, it is vividly clear. Recognizing its own nature, it is fully awake. Uncontaminated by dualistic thoughts, it is fresh and naked. Since in awareness there is no contrivance or artifice, it is the "ordinary" mind. Since it does not continuously indulge in chains of thoughts, it is said to be fresh. This is how the main practice of experiencing the essence of profound insight is introduced.

### 3. Ultimate, Resultant [Profound Insight]: The Practice of Sustained Calm and Profound Insight Together

Settling the mind on devotion in the practice of guru yoga is sustained calm, while seeing that its essence is emptiness, devoid of existence, is profound insight. Settling the mind on the visualization in the generation stage, like the moon reflected on water, is sustained calm, while [understanding that] its nature is empty, devoid of birth, cessation, and dwelling, is profound insight. Settling the mind on love and compassion embracing all sentient beings is sustained calm, while settling the mind on their nature being emptiness is profound insight. Settling the mind on the illusion-like skillful means, the accumulation of merit, is sustained calm. Seeing that all that is emptiness, devoid of intrinsic nature, is profound insight. Settling the mind on all appearances, which are the mind's own forms, like moons reflected on water, is sustained calm, while seeing them nakedly as being unborn, like moons reflected on water, is profound insight. Settling the mind on the mind's natural luminosity is sustained calm; seeing that its nature free of elaboration {444} is unborn clarity-emptiness is profound insight. Settling the mind on the fresh state of awareness uncontaminated by contrivance is sustained calm; seeing that there is no-self, that awareness and emptiness are inseparable, is profound insight.

In short, there is no emptiness that is other than appearances, which are like the reflection of the moon in water, a reflection in a mirror, or an echo. And there are no appearances that are other than emptiness. Realizing the inseparability of appearances and emptiness, like a rainbow appearing in the sky, and settling in that state, one purifies all dualistic clinging and develops the gnosis of awareness, and this is what is called buddha.[7] It is also what we call union. It is the ultimate point.

All this was profound insight.

### C. Instructions on Transference at the Moment of Death

These instructions are divided into two parts: (1) training and (2) putting transference into practice.

#### 1. Training

Visualize your body as a hollow frame.[8] In the middle of the body is the central channel, which is white on the outside and red inside and hollow, the size of a bamboo. Its lower end is blocked by the syllable *phaṭ*; its upper end opens straight out at the aperture of Brahmā, like an open skylight. In the air directly above your head, six feet up, visualize the pure buddha field, the Blissful, perfect in its layout. At its center is a precious throne supported by a lotus, and seated upon it is your root teacher, Amitābha, in the attire of the body of perfect enjoyment, surrounded by a retinue of the buddhas and bodhisattvas of the ten directions. Visualize this clearly, like the moon's reflection in a clear lake.

Next concentrate on two spheres (the nature of your mind), white and red, below your navel. The white sphere circles the red one three times and then, as white as a shooting star, {445} shoots up through the crown and touches Amitābha's heart center. At that moment, you should say *hik*. And then, as you say *ka*, it comes down again and circles the red sphere three times. Again, say *hik*, and it shoots up as before and comes down again. In this way, counting a cycle of shooting up and coming down again as one, train in this one hundred eight times in each session, until, after a thousand or so times, you have gained proficiency.

### 2. Putting Transference into Practice

When all the signs of approaching death are present, give up all mundane clinging and attachment. Without letting the mind get distracted, begin by practicing love and compassion, and then visualize your teacher above your head. In the middle of your body, visualize the channels and visualize the two spheres becoming one. With *hik*, join the wind and mind firmly together at your crown, ejecting your awareness like a shooting star and transferring it into Amitābha's heart center. Concentrate on this repeatedly, with one-pointed awareness, until you are able to transfer. Then consider that you have arrived in the Blissful Land of your teacher, Amitābha. By doing so, you will definitely transfer to the Blissful buddha field.

These excellent explanations are a ship laden with jewels,
A fount providing every need, fulfilling every wish.
I have written down the essence of these pith instructions as my teacher
taught them.
By the merit of my doing so, may all beings attain buddhahood.

The instructions of Amitāyus, the deity related to enlightened qualities, entitled *Accomplishing the Immortal Vajra Body* were set down in writing by the yogi Öpak Dorje as his teacher had spoken them.
*śubhaṃ*

# 21. Liberation from the Perilous Path of Samsara

*The Instructions of Tārā, the Deity Related to Enlightened Activities Who Protects from the Eight Fears*[1]

{448}
Blooming in the lake of the two accumulations,
The utpala flower of self-arisen gnosis manifests miraculously,
Giving off the fragrance of nonconceptual compassion.
Lady Tārā, I pray, protect all beings.

Brahmā, powerful gods, the four guardians of the world,
And the world's haughty spirits respectfully
Take your two feet as a lotus crown on their heads.
At the feet of noble Tārā I bow my head.

The graded pith instructions on the practice
That Lady Tārā gave to Mitrayogin,
This great treasure of nectar transmitted through the aural lineage,
I will now set down in writing in order to rid beings of their torments.

Here I will reveal the instructions of Lady Tārā, the deity related to enlightened activities who protects from the eight fears, entitled *Liberation from the Perilous Path of Samsara*. There are three sections: (1) preliminaries; (2) main practice; and (3) conclusion.

### I. Preliminaries

The preliminaries are divided into two: (1) common preliminaries and (2) specific preliminaries.

#### A. Common Preliminaries

There are four common preliminaries, consisting of meditation on the difficulty of finding the freedoms and advantages; {449} on death and impermanence; on action, cause and effect; and on the defects of cyclic existence. These are as generally taught.

#### B. Specific Preliminaries

There are four specific preliminaries: instructions on going for refuge and arousing bodhichitta, which is what makes everything one does become the path of enlightenment; instructions on the meditation and recitation of Vajrasattva, which enables one to purify one's negative deeds and obscurations; instructions on the mandala practice, which enables one to complete the two accumulations; and instructions on the guru yoga, which enables one to receive blessings swiftly. These four are as generally taught.

These comprise the preliminary stages.

### II. Main Practice

The main practice is divided into (1) the generation stage and (2) the perfection stage.

#### A. Generation Stage

The generation stage has three parts.

##### 1. Instructions on the Visualization of the Body

Begin with the four boundless attitudes. Then, with *oṁ svabhāva śuddāḥ sarvadharmāḥ svabhāva śuddho 'haṃ*, everything is purified as emptiness. From the state of emptiness, the whole earth appears as the Potala Mountain or as the buddha field Turquoise Leaf Array. In its center is a clear blue lake, in the middle of which is a grassy meadow full of beautiful flowers. {450} In its center there appears a syllable *paṃ*, from which appears a blossoming utpala, its stem made of gold, its stamens, leaves, and petals stirred by the wind, giving rise to the sound of the sacred dharma. In the heart of the flower is the letter *A*, from which a moon disk appears. On top of that appears the syllable *tāṃ*, and from it, a green utpala marked with a *tāṃ*. It emanates rays of light in the ten directions, making offerings to all the buddhas and bodhisattvas and purifying the obscurations of all beings, bringing them to the level of Tārā. They are gathered back and transform into oneself as noble Tārā. She is blue green in color, with one face and two arms. Her right foot is stretched out, the left bent in. She is wearing a silk skirt. With her right hand in the gesture of supreme gift, she holds an utpala flower. In her left hand, held at the level of her heart, between the thumb and ring finger she grasps the stem of an utpala, whose blossom is level with her ear. She has fully developed breasts, almond eyes, and long eyebrows. The locks of her hair are tied up on top of her head, with tassels falling down to her waist. She is dignified, peaceful, and attractive and has reached young adulthood—a maiden of sixteen years. She is adorned with a head ornament, earrings, necklet, armlets, bracelets, anklets, belt, and long necklace made of the five precious materials, and with a silken crown and clusters of pearls. Behind her is a moon. Visualize all this as appearing yet without intrinsic existence, like a reflection in a mirror.

In Tārā's crown center is a white syllable *oṁ*, in her throat center a red *āḥ*, and in her heart center a blue *hūṁ*. From the *hūṁ* rays of light like hooks emanate, inviting from the Potala or Turquoise Leaf Array the wisdom deity, who is identical with her and becomes inseparable from you. Again, rays of light emanate, {451} inviting the buddhas of the five families. They bestow empowerment, purifying stains. The empowerment nectar overflows, and one is crowned with Amoghasiddhi.

In the heart center, on top of an utpala, is a moon disk, in the middle of which is a green syllable *tāṃ*. From it appears the mantra garland, which is the color of emerald. From this, light radiates, filling the inside of your body and purifying it of the five poisons. It radiates outward, turning the world into a measureless palace of light and touching sentient beings, setting them on the level of Tārā. The light rays are gathered back, and as you concentrate on the mantra turning clockwise, consider that the sound of the mantra resounds from the mouths of all, and recite the mantra *oṁ tāre tuttāre ture svāhā*.

At the end, all appearances melt into light and dissolve into the buddha field's inhabitants. The latter melt into light and dissolve into you. Your body melts into light and dissolves into the syllable *tāṃ* in the heart center. The syllable *tāṃ* dissolves into the nāda, which in turn vanishes like a rainbow in the sky. Settle in the uncontrived state, free of concepts.

This is the visualization stage.

## 2. Instructions on Visualizing the Above and Emanating and Reabsorbing Rays of Light

Visualizing yourself as Tārā as before, in your crown center, on a lotus and moon, is the enlightened body aspect, Vairochana Tārā, as white as the moon, with one face and two arms, seated with her right leg stretched out and her left leg bent. Her right hand, in the gesture of supreme gift, holds an utpala. The thumb and ring finger of her left are grasping, at the level of her heart, the stem of an utpala, which is flowering next to her ear. She has a smiling face, with almond eyes and long eyebrows, and so on—the rest of the visualization is as before. In her heart center, upon a lotus and moon, is a white syllable *tāṃ*, from which appears the white mantra garland turning like a string of pearls. From it infinite rays of white light emanate. {452} They fill your cranial cavity, purify the obscurations of your body, and cleanse you of bewilderment. The light radiates outward to the ten directions. It touches the bodies of the buddhas and bodhisattvas in the ten directions, making their bodies shine with splendor. All the blessings of their bodies are gathered back in the form of white rays of light and dissolve into the Tārā[2] in your crown center. You receive the blessings of enlightened body and realize the gnosis of the expanse of reality. As you meditate on this, recite the mantra.

In your throat center, on a lotus and moon, is the enlightened speech aspect, Amitābha Tārā. She is red, and in her heart center, upon a lotus and moon, is a red syllable *tāṃ*, with the mantra garland, the color of rubies. From it rays of red light emanate. They fill the inside of your throat center, purify the obscurations of your speech, and cleanse you of attachment. The light radiates outward to the ten directions. It touches the voices of the buddhas and bodhisattvas in the ten directions, making them manifest the sixty expressive qualities of buddha speech. All the blessings of their voices are gathered back in the form of red rays of light and dissolve into your throat center. You receive the blessings of the sixty expressive qualities of buddha speech and realize the all-discerning gnosis. As you meditate on this, recite the mantra.

In your heart center, on a lotus and moon, is the enlightened mind aspect, Akṣhobhya Tārā. She is blue, and in her heart center, upon a lotus and moon, is a blue syllable *tāṃ*, with the mantra garland, the color of beryl. From it rays of light emanate. They fill the inside of your body, purify the obscurations of your mind, and cleanse you of aversion. The light radiates outward to the ten directions. It invokes the minds of the buddhas and bodhisattvas in the ten directions. All the wisdom of their minds, whose nature is luminosity and which have realized the nature of ultimate reality and know the whole multitude of phenomena, {453} is gathered back in the form of blue rays of light and dissolve into the Tārā in your heart center. You receive all the blessings of enlightened mind and realize mirrorlike gnosis. As you meditate on this, recite the mantra.

In your navel center, on a lotus and moon, visualize the enlightened qualities aspect, Ratnasambhava Tārā. She is the [yellow] color of monastic robes, and in her heart center, upon a lotus and moon, is a yellow syllable *tāṃ*, from which the golden-colored mantra garland appears and turns. From it rays of light emanate. They fill the inside of your body and purify the obscurations that come from desire and pride. The light radiates outward to the ten directions. It touches all the buddhas and bodhisattvas in the ten directions, enhancing extraordinary qualities. All their qualities are gathered back in the form of yellow rays of light and dissolve into the Tārā in your navel center. You receive all the blessings of the enlightened qualities and realize equalizing gnosis. As you meditate on this, recite the mantra.

In your secret center, on a lotus and moon, is the enlightened activities aspect, Amoghasiddhi Tārā. She is green, like oneself, and in her heart center, upon a lotus and moon, is a green syllable *tāṃ*, from which the mantra garland appears and turns like a string of emeralds. From it green rays of light emanate. They fill the whole of your secret center and purify attachment and jealousy. The light radiates outward to the ten directions. It touches all the buddhas and bodhisattvas in the ten directions, enabling the spontaneous accomplishment of their activities. All the blessings of their activities are gathered back in the form of green rays of light and dissolve into your secret center. You attain the accomplishment of enlightened activity and realize all-accomplishing gnosis. As you meditate on this, recite the mantra.

Again, {454} from the five Tārās (white, red, blue, yellow, and green) in your five centers (crown, throat, heart, navel, and secret center) respectively, rays of white, red, blue, yellow, and green light fill the five centers of your body, cleansing you of bewilderment, attachment, aversion, pride, and jealousy. The light radiates to the ten directions and touches the six classes of beings in the ten directions, purifying their bewilderment, attachment, aversion, pride, and jealousy and causing them to realize the gnosis of the expanse of reality, all-discerning gnosis, mirrorlike gnosis, equalizing gnosis, and all-accomplishing gnosis. They are brought to the level of the enlightened body, speech, mind, qualities, and activities, or of Vairochana, Amitābha, Akṣhobhya, Ratnasambhava, and Amoghasiddhi. The lights are gathered back and dissolve into each center. You receive the blessings of enlightened body, speech, mind, qualities, and activities, purify the five poisons, realize the five kinds of gnosis, and attain the five buddha bodies. As you concentrate on this, recite the mantra.

All these are the visualizations for the instructions on emanating and reabsorbing rays of light. These instructions on the generation stage are the object of the vase empowerment and enable one to realize the body of manifestation.

### 3. Instructions on the Recitation with the Emanation and Reabsorption of Mantras

Visualize yourself as Tārā as before. In your five centers visualize the five Tārās of the different buddha families—white in the crown center, red in the throat center, blue in the heart center, yellow in the navel center, and green in the secret center. In each of their heart centers, upon a lotus and moon, visualize the syllable *tāṃ*—white, red, blue, yellow, and green—surrounded by the mantra garland: white like a string of pearls, red like a necklace of rubies, blue like a string of sapphires or beryls, yellow like a gold necklace, {455} and green like an emerald necklace. From them rays of light emanate in the form of the mantra garlands or of the vowels and consonants, respectively white, red, blue, yellow, and green. The lights radiate in turn to the ten directions, touching all the buddhas and bodhisattvas in the ten directions; enhancing all the displays of their enlightened body, speech, mind, qualities, and activities; and venerating them with outer, inner, and secret offerings. As you visualize this, expel the stale winds three times. Then breathe in and hold the vase breath. All the essence of the enlightened body, speech, mind, qualities, and activities of all the buddhas and bodhisattvas in the ten directions is gathered in the form of white, red, blue, yellow, and green mantra chains and dissolves into the mantra circles in the hearts of the white, red, blue, yellow, and green Tārās in your crown, throat, heart, navel, and secret centers. The obscurations related to bewilderment, attachment, aversion, pride, and jealousy are purified. You realize the five kinds of gnosis (the gnosis of the expanse of reality and the all-discerning, mirror-like, equalizing, and all-accomplishing gnosis), attain the five buddha bodies, and receive the blessings of enlightened body, speech, mind, qualities, and activities. Concentrating on this, hold the vase breath for as long as you can.

In the same manner, from the heart center of each of the five Tārās, white, red, blue, yellow, and green mantra chains emanate, filling the five centers of your body and purifying the five poisons. After that, light rays emanate in the ten directions. They touch the sentient beings in the six realms in the ten directions, purifying them of their bewilderment, attachment, aversion, pride, and jealousy. The beings realize the five kinds of gnosis {456} and are brought to the level of the five Tārās of the body, speech, mind, qualities, and activities families. As you concentrate on this, breathe out. Then consider that you receive all the power of their enlightened body, speech, mind, qualities, and activities and, in particular, give rise to boundless compassion for all sentient beings. Gather back the light rays in the form of mantra chains and hold the vase breath for as long as you can.

This is the practice of the mantra chains using the support of the vase breath.

After that the world and its inhabitants dissolve into you. The Tārā in your crown center dissolves into the Tārā in your throat center. The Tārā in your throat center dissolves into the Tārā in your heart center. The Tārā in your secret center dissolves into the Tārā in your navel center. The Tārā in your navel center dissolves into the Tārā in your heart center. Your body dissolves into the Tārā in your heart center. The Tārā in the heart center dissolves into the syllable *tāṃ*. The *tāṃ* dissolves like a rainbow vanishing in the sky. Settle in meditative equipoise in the nonconceptual state beyond intellect.

These are the instructions on the mantra chains using the vase breath as a support to purify one's speech and winds. They are the object of the secret empowerment and enable one to realize the body of perfect enjoyment.

### B. Perfection Stage

The perfection stage is divided into four parts: (1) sustained calm; (2) profound insight; (3) luminosity; and (4) transference.

#### 1. Sustained Calm

Sustained calm is treated under three headings: (1) sustained calm making use of conceptual attributes; (2) sustained calm focusing on conceptual thoughts; and (3) sustained calm settling in [a state] without conceptual thoughts.

##### a. Sustained Calm Making Use of Conceptual Attributes

There are two kinds: (1) holding the mind on an object outside and (2) holding the mind on an object inside.

##### i. Holding the Mind on an Object Outside

There are two kinds of object: (1) impure and (2) pure.

##### A) Holding the Mind on an Impure Object Outside

Adopting the correct bodily posture and gaze, hold the mind without distraction on a suitable object in front of you, such as a pillar, vase, stick, or pebble. {457} Do not get distracted or get involved in thoughts. Moreover, if dullness or wildness occurs, you should know how to focus the mind up or down or right or left.

##### B) Holding the Mind on a Pure Object Outside

Hold the mind in a relaxed way, without any distraction, on an image of Tārā in front of you or, if you do not have one, visualize her. Do not let thoughts proliferate or get involved in distractions. This is holding the mind on a pure object, an image of a buddha.

### ii. Holding the Mind on an Object Inside

There are two kinds of object: (1) impure and (2) pure.

### A) Holding the Mind on an Impure Object, a Sphere

Hold the mind on a pea-sized reddish-yellow sphere in your heart center, radiating light. Do not let thoughts proliferate or get involved in distractions.

### B) Concentrating on a Pure Object, the Form of a Buddha

Hold the mind on a thumb-sized, radiant form of Tārā on a lotus and moon in your heart center. Do not let thoughts proliferate or get involved in distractions. Should dullness or wildness occur, deal with them as mentioned above.

All this is sustained calm making use of conceptual attributes.

### b. Sustained Calm Focusing on Conceptual Thoughts

When there is an excessive proliferation of thoughts, whatever positive or negative thoughts arise, whether thoughts related to samsara—the three poisons, five poisons, defilements, and dualistic concepts of subject and object—or thoughts related to the ten virtuous actions and the ten transcendent perfections, look directly, without concepts, at their essential nature. When you do this, they will be destroyed, without grasping, and natural awareness, clear and empty, devoid of object, will vividly arise. Preserve that undistractedly in the state of pure awareness, self-recognizing and self-liberating. Again, whatever thoughts arise, look directly at their nature and {458} recognize them as your own nature, without rejecting them or accepting them. Thus, put into practice the pith instructions on taking thoughts as the path.

### c. Ultimate Sustained Calm: Settling in a State Free of Thoughts

In an isolated, dark room, on a soft cushion, adopt the seven-point posture of Vairochana and direct your eyes blankly into the empty surrounding space. Cut off all thoughts related to the three times that pass through your mind—thoughts related to the past, present, and future and virtuous, unvirtuous, and indeterminate thoughts. Do not think of anything. Settle the mind in clarity and emptiness beyond grasping, like the unblemished sky—pervasive, vivid, and awake. By this means, the sustained calm of bliss, clarity, and absence of thought will arise.

## 2. Profound Insight

Profound insight is treated under three headings.

### a. Causal Profound Insight

The causal profound insight involves examining the mind and training as follows. Examine and analyze the essential nature of the mind's arising, ceasing, and staying, asking yourself, From where has this mind of mine arisen? Where does it stay? Where will it cease? Check whether it arose from the five elements or from your own body. Does it dwell there? Will it die there? Check further: Does the mind have a color—white, red, blue, yellow, or green? Or is it colorless? Moreover, is the mind produced with a shape—the form of earth, water, fire, wind, or space, or round, square, semicircular, oblong, or oval, and so on? Or is it shapeless? Check and analyze: Are thoughts something other than the mind, or are thoughts the mind? {459} Investigate further: Do appearances outside arise from the mind, or does the mind arise from appearances? Mentally look at the mind that is investigating. Does that mind exist, or does it not exist? Is it clear, or is it unclear? Is it happy, or is it unhappy? Is there a self or not? Is it permanent or impermanent? Is it calm or restless? Check whether it is visible or invisible. Moreover, what is the mind that settles in meditative equipoise like? What is the mind that is not meditating like? In this way, use your own mind to thoroughly investigate itself. And thoroughly investigate as well the nature of the mind that settles in meditative equipoise.

When you check like this, you might conclude that the essential nature of the mind is devoid of arising, staying, and ceasing. Its nature is intrinsically empty. It is like the expanse of space. It is naturally radiant. It is the unobstructed display of awareness, arising in every kind of way, and all these appearances are of the same taste in being unborn, nondwelling, and unceasing. Its nature is emptiness, its character luminous clarity. Unobstructed awareness arises and appears in many ways; it is inseparable, inconceivable like space, clear, aware, and empty, with neither periphery nor center.

Recognize that this is thatness, the nature of your own mind, in which all good qualities [are present]—such as the triad of ground, path, and result; the quartet of view, meditation, conduct, and result; the four truths; four joys; four boundless attitudes; six transcendent perfections; ten levels; five paths; the duo of skillful means and wisdom; {460} the two truths; refuge; confession; the observance of vows; bodhichitta; the two accumulations; compassion; the generation stage; sustained calm and profound insight; the Three Jewels; the three buddha bodies; and the five kinds of gnosis. In that way you should become proficient in discovering it.

### b. Essential Profound Insight

This involves being introduced to the fresh, ordinary mind and simultaneously experiencing it.

The nature of mind is devoid of the extremes of birth, cessation, and dwelling. It is freed of the dualistic apprehension of subject and object that grasps at "I" and "mine." Its nature is emptiness, its character luminous clarity. It is unobstructed awareness, without object, yet appearing clearly in a multitude of ways. It transcends any object of apprehension—something to be seen and someone seeing. It is free of any reference—something to be meditated on and someone meditating. There is nothing to think about, so it is devoid of mental activity. Being uncontrived, it is a state of relaxation. As it is devoid of all activity, there is nothing to be done. There is no identifying whatever arises, so it is free of grasping. Since the mind of meditative equipoise is unadulterated by contrivance, it is free of thoughts. Free of conceptual attributes, it is utterly empty. Naturally radiant, it is vividly clear. Uncontaminated by dualistic thoughts, it is fresh and naked. Recognizing its own nature, it is fully awake. Since apprehension of object and subject have been destroyed, appearance and mind are inseparable, all-penetrating, and uniform. Since it rests naturally in uncontrived awareness, it is the ordinary mind. And as the mind does not continuously indulge in chains of thoughts, it is what is known as fresh. This is the main practice, that of experiencing the essence of profound insight.

This itself is the nature of the noble Lady Tārā. "Noble" signifies that she is above samsaric ignorance and dualistic grasping. {461} "Lady" signifies that she recognizes her own nature by means of the spontaneous manifestation of wisdom. "Savior-" (Tārā) means that her unobstructed display of great compassion works effortlessly for the benefit of sentient beings. And "-ess"[3] means that because she is endowed with the essence of emptiness and compassion, she spontaneously fulfills the two goals. Thus, it is the nature of the mind, noble Tārā, that we have to realize and that is introduced here.

### c. The Ultimate Practice of the Union of Sustained Calm and Profound Insight

The nature of mind is free of birth, dwelling, and destruction. Since it has no cessation, it is free of the extreme of nihilism. Since it dwells naturally as emptiness, it is free of the extreme of eternalism. Since it is multifariously aware, it is free of the extreme of nihilism. Since the mind in essence has no color or shape, it is free of the extreme of eternalism. Since the essential nature of the mind is emptiness, no-self, beyond the intellect, it is free of the extreme of eternalism. Its expressive power manifests in all kinds of ways, so it is free of the extreme of nihilism. Thus, since it is beyond the conceptual extremes of nihilism and eternalism, it is clarity, awareness, and emptiness inseparable.

The way to practice this union is as follows. Settling the mind on the illusion-like means, the accumulation of merit, [is sustained calm,] and knowing and seeing that they are emptiness, devoid of intrinsic nature, is profound insight. Settling the mind on devotion in the practice of guru yoga is sustained calm, while to see that the nature of that mental state is emptiness, transcending the intellect, is profound insight. Settling the mind on the visualization in the generation stage, which is like the reflection of the moon in water, is sustained calm, while seeing that its nature is emptiness is profound insight. Settling the mind on appearances, which are the self-experience of the mind, like reflections of the moon in water, [is sustained calm,] and {462} seeing that they are interdependent and unborn, appearance and emptiness inseparable, is profound insight. Settling the mind on the great bliss, the culmination of the path, is sustained calm. Seeing that very state as emptiness, without clinging, is profound insight. Settling the mind on the natural radiance of the mind is sustained calm. Seeing its essential nature as emptiness, free of elaboration, is profound insight. Settling the mind on the fresh state of awareness uncontaminated by contrivance is sustained calm. Seeing it as unborn, devoid of self, is profound insight.

In short, there is no emptiness that is other than appearances, which are like the reflection of the moon in water, a reflection in a mirror, or an echo. And there are no appearances that are other than emptiness. To realize the unborn [nature of] appearances and emptiness, like a rainbow appearing in the sky, and settle in the essential nature of that is what we call the union of sustained calm and profound insight.

This completes the perfection stage instruction on the union of sustained calm and profound insight.

### 3. Luminosity

The practice for apprehending luminosity is as follows. Visualize yourself as Tārā. In your heart center is a wheel, green or white, the color of mercury. From it, rays of light emanate, filling the inside of your body. They radiate outward, so that the whole outside of your body is lit with light greater than that of a thousand suns. Then everything up to a league away is filled with light. Then the whole of Jambudvīpa, then the four continents, and then the whole of the great universe of a billion worlds is filled with light. It touches all sentient beings, and they become light. Visualize everything, subject and objects alike, being filled with light, shining even more than the light of a hundred thousand suns. Then, from the nonconceptual state of the mind's natural luminosity, {463} rest in meditative equipoise in the thoughtless state devoid of all elaborations and meditate on luminosity.

At night too, if you rest in meditative equipoise in this manner, your sleep will arise as luminosity. These are the stages of meditation on luminosity.

### 4. Transference

Transference is divided into two parts: (1) training and (2) putting transference into practice.

#### a. Training

Consider that your body is a hollow frame.[4] In the heart center is an utpala in full bloom, on top of which is a moon disk. On that, visualize a green syllable *tāṃ*. Visualize a hole in the aperture of Brahmā on the crown of your head. In the air fifteen inches above that, clearly visualize a precious throne, and on it an utpala blossom, on which is seated noble Tārā. As she utters the mantra *oṁ tāre tāṃ svāhā*, a green sphere shoots up from the syllable *tāṃ* in your heart center, passes through the aperture of Brahmā on your crown, and touches the heart center of the Tārā above your head. Then it returns down and dissolves into the *tāṃ* in your heart center. Again, the green sphere shoots up from the *tāṃ* and, shining with light, dissolves into the heart center of the Noble Lady. Perform this visualization twenty-one or a hundred times or so. At the conclusion of the session, consider that the Tārā above your head closes your aperture of Brahmā with a moon disk in her right hand. This is a countermeasure. This is how to train.

### b. Putting Transference into Practice

When all the signs that you are dying are present, {464} free yourself of all clinging and attachment. Then, in the heart center of your body, which is transparent and empty, on a moon disk, visualize the green syllable *tāṃ*, emanating five-colored rays of light. The crown of your head is like an open skylight, and in the air about six feet above it, visualize Tārā, summoning you with the sound of the mantra she is saying: *oṁ tāre tāṃ svāhā*. Like a shooting star in the sky, the syllable *tāṃ*, together with its seat, shoots up and dissolves into Tārā's heart. As you concentrate on this, energetically direct your wind and mind above your head, while uttering *hik*. By doing so, you will accomplish transference. This is the transference to the body of manifestation.

Transference to the body of perfect enjoyment is as follows. Consider that Tārā appears in the sky and that she then dissolves into the heart of Vairochana in Akanishṭha, or into the heart of Amitābha in the Blissful buddha field, becoming inseparable from those buddhas. In this way you will transfer to the body of perfect enjoyment.

For transference to the body of truth, meditate that those form bodies vanish into nonconceptuality and direct your awareness into the space above, free of grasping, clarity-emptiness. This is [how to accomplish] transference to the body of truth.

All this was the main practice.

## III. Conclusion

By this vast merit
May I attain the supreme level of Tārā for the benefit of beings

And bring the hosts of beings who have not been freed by previous buddhas
To the level of buddhahood.

With these words, make the prayer of dedication and aspiration. This is the conclusion.

These graded instructions of noble Tārā,
In which the preparation, main practice, and conclusion are complete, {465}
Tārā bestowed on Mitrayogin,
Who took Shrīputra as his disciple.
The latter took as his disciple Mikyö Dorje,
Who, through the aural lineage of these instructions,
As if pouring nectar into a vase,
Taught them to me, Öpak Dorje.
For fear of them being forgotten, I wrote them down.
By the merit of my doing so, may all beings without exception
Attain the sublime level of Lady Tārā.

May virtue and excellence increase.

# 22. A Shower of Accomplishments

*Instructions of the Yellow Jambhala*[1]

{468}

You who have completed the ocean-like two accumulations
And constantly thereby rain down on beings all that they desire or need,
You were empowered by water[2] to ripen their crop of merit—
Lord Protector, to you I pay homage.

The instant people pray to you,
You grant, spontaneously and effortlessly,
A wealth of everything that's fortunate and good.
Lord Jambhala, please care for me!

The graded practice of your pith instructions,
The sublime teachings transmitted aurally that fulfill all desires and needs,
I will now write down for the benefit of beings.
Teachers, ḍākinīs, Jambhala, grant your blessings!

Here are the instructions of noble Jambhala, entitled *A Shower of Accomplishments*. They comprise three sections: (1) preliminaries; (2) main practice; and (3) conclusion.

## I. Preliminaries

The preliminaries are divided into three: (1) the history of the lineage of teachers; (2) the common preliminaries; and (3) the specific preliminaries.

### A. History of the Lineage of Teachers {469}

When the lord of yogis Mitrayogin performed the practices of five yidam deities in the great charnel ground of Sosaling, he accomplished those deities, and each of them appeared to him and bestowed on him the graded instructions, predicting that their blessings would be [transmitted] for seven generations. At that time, the lord, noble Jambhala, told him: "For yogis who practice these instructions, I will shower down a rain of all they could need and wish for, and in the future, until the end of time, I will accomplish all their needs and desires. They will be protected and be happy and well." Saying this, he taught the graded instructions on the generation and perfection stages.

The lord of yogis Mitrayogin took as his disciple the great paṇḍita Shrīputra, who in turn took as his disciple the peerless Girti Ratna.

### B. Common Preliminaries

There are four common preliminaries, consisting of meditation on the difficulty of finding the freedoms and advantages; meditation on death and impermanence; meditation on action, cause and effect; {470} and meditation on the defects of cyclic existence. These are the same as are generally taught.

### C. Specific Preliminaries

There are four specific preliminary practices.

#### 1. Instructions on Going for Refuge and Arousing Bodhichitta, Which Is What Makes Everything One Does Become the Path of Enlightenment

In the air in front of you, on a vast and spacious throne made entirely of many kinds of precious materials, visualize your precious root teacher surrounded by an ocean of teachers. They are surrounded by the infinite yidam deities in front, the infinite buddhas to the right, the infinite dharma scriptures behind, and the infinite sanghas to the left. Go to them for refuge. At the end, the sources of refuge dissolve into you. Rest in nonconceptuality.

### 2. The Meditation and Recitation of Vajrasattva, Which Enables One to Purify One's Negative Deeds and Obscurations

This is as generally taught.

### [3. Instructions on the Mandala Practice][3]

### 4. Instructions on the Guru Yoga, Which Enables One to Swiftly Receive Blessings

Above your head, visualize a precious throne and a lotus and moon, upon which is your root teacher, who embodies all the teachers of the lineage, the yidam deities, the buddhas, dharma, and sangha, ḍākinīs, and dharma protectors.

Offer the mandala and pray that all your needs and wishes may be showered down on you like rain. Receive the three empowerments. At the end, the teacher dissolves into you. Rest in meditative equipoise in the uncontrived state.

These preliminaries are similar to those in Mitrayogin's five sets of detailed instructions.

## II. Main Practice

The main practice is divided into two: (1) the generation stage and (2) the perfection stage.

### A. Generation Stage

There are two parts: (1) the generation stage and (2) the recitation.

### 1. Generation Stage

The generation stage is divided into three.

#### a. Instructions on the Approach

In a pleasant, isolated location, concentrate on the four pure states, and then meditate that all phenomena are emptiness. From the state of emptiness there appears the ground, a measureless palace made of the five precious materials. It is square, with four gates, ornaments, pediments, and four terraces, {471} topped with dharma wheels and parasols. The central tier is adorned with a jewel as a top ornament. It is surrounded by a wall and turrets. The whole is encircled by a vajra fence and pleasure gardens with the eight auspicious symbols and the seven attributes of royalty.

In the center of the measureless palace is a vast and spacious throne made of many precious materials and embellished with intertwined vases filled with the five kinds of precious materials. On top of it is a multicolored lotus with a hundred thousand petals, and on it, appearing from the letter *A*, a full-moon disk. On top of that is a yellow yakṣha[4] fallen on his back, and on top of it the syllable *jaṃ*, the color of gold. From it boundless rays of five-colored light emanate in the ten directions. They venerate the buddhas and bodhisattvas of the ten directions with clouds of offerings. They touch all sentient beings, purifying all their negative deeds and obscurations, in particular miserliness, and setting them on the level of Ratnasambhava. The lights are gathered back, transforming the *jaṃ* into a bījapūra fruit,[5] marked with a *jaṃ*. This transforms into oneself as Jambhala. He is the color of refined gold, blazing with light. He is seated with his two legs in the posture of royal ease and is wearing a multicolored silken lower garment, tied with a golden belt marked in the middle with a jewel. He has a large belly and well-developed limbs and joints. His right hand rests on his knee in the gesture of supreme gift, holding a pañcapuraka fruit,[6] its middle marked with a wish-fulfilling jewel blazing with light. With his left hand he is holding a mongoose regurgitating various precious substances. Jambhala's face is a little wrathful, with a slight smile, as splendidly radiant as the orb of the sun. {472} His hair is tied up in a topknot, the rest hanging loose, and adorned with flower-garland hair ribbons and a crown ornament of five wish-fulfilling jewels blazing with light. He is beautified with earrings, a necklace, armlets, bracelets, leg bands, and anklets of many precious materials and with beautiful hanging garlands of five-colored utpala flowers, strings of five kinds of pearls, and a silken crown. He is seated in the midst of five-colored rays of light encircling him.

On eight lotus petals are present eight wealth deities, whose attributes are similar to one's own. Visualize this great being surrounded as well by a retinue of many hosts of gods, nāgas, yakṣhas, gandharvas, the sun god, the moon god, rākṣhasas, wealth deities, and the like. In the crown center of each of them is a white syllable *oṁ*, in the throat center a red *āḥ*, and in the heart center a blue *hūṁ*. From these, light radiates, inviting the wisdom deity like oneself from the Willow Leaf buddha field; they dissolve inseparably into oneself. Again light radiates, inviting the buddhas of the five families, who bestow empowerment, purifying one's negative deeds and obscurations. The excess nectar overflows, and you are crowned with Ratnasambhava and the other buddhas of the five families.

In Jambhala's heart center, upon a lotus and moon, is a jewel marked with a yellow *jaṃ*. As well as this are the letters of the mantra, each on a lotus and moon—in the crown center is the syllable *oṁ*, on the forehead *jaṃ*, on the tongue *bha*, at the throat *la*, at the heart *ja*, at the navel *len*, on the right thigh *dra*, on the left thigh *ye*, on the right foot *svā*, and on the left foot *hā*. All these letters shine with reddish-yellow light. From them rays of light emanate, with the form of the noble being on the tip of each ray, {473} all holding in their hands a jewel and a mongoose, from which a rain of the five kinds of precious materials falls. Concentrating on this, perform the approach, reciting the mantra *oṁ jaṃbhala jalendraye svāhā*. During the approach, light radiates from the mantra letters, touching the world outside and transforming it into the measureless palace. It touches its inhabitants, turning them into Jambhala. From the mouths of all of them the sound of the mantra resounds, and a great rain of the five kinds of precious materials falls. Concentrating on this, recite the mantra.

At the end, the world and its inhabitants dissolve into you; you dissolve into the seed syllable. Leave that in the nonconceptual state.

### b. Instructions on Enhancing the Power of Merit and Gnosis Relying on the Buddhas of the Five Families

Visualize yourself as Jambhala as you did for the approach. In your crown center, upon a lotus and moon, is Vairochana, whose color is white. His right hand at his heart center holds a wheel; his left, resting on his hip, holds a bell with a wheel handle. In his heart center, on a lotus and moon, is a white jewel marked with a white syllable *oṁ*.

In your throat center, upon a lotus and moon, is Amitābha, who is red, holding in his right hand at his heart center a lotus, and in his left, resting on his hip, a lotus-handled bell. In his heart center, on a lotus and moon, is a red jewel marked with a *hrīḥ*.

In your heart center, upon a lotus and moon, is Akṣhobhya, who is blue, holding in his right hand at his heart center a vajra, and in his left, resting on his hip, a vajra-handled bell. In his heart center, on a lotus and moon, is a blue jewel marked with a *hūṁ*.

In your navel center, upon a lotus and moon, is Ratnasambhava, who is yellow, holding in his right hand at his heart center a jewel, and in his left, resting on his hip, a jewel-handled bell. {474} In his heart center, on a lotus and moon, is a yellow jewel marked with a *trāṃ*.

In your secret center, upon a lotus and moon, is Amoghasiddhi, whose body is green. He is holding in his right hand a crossed vajra turned toward his heart center, and in his left, resting on his hip, a bell with a crossed-vajra handle. In his heart center, on a lotus and moon, is a green jewel marked with an *āḥ*.

Visualize all of them with one face and two arms, with their legs crossed in the vajra posture. They are adorned with multiple silks and precious ornaments and bear the attributes of the body of perfect enjoyment.

From the five wish-fulfilling jewels, together with their seed syllables, rays of white, red, blue, yellow, and green light emanate, venerating all the buddhas and bodhisattvas in the directions with inconceivable clouds of offerings. The buddhas and bodhisattvas are delighted with the offerings, and all the power of their enlightened bodies, speech, minds, qualities, and activities and of their five kinds of gnosis and their merit is gathered back in the form of white, red, blue, yellow, and green rays of light, which dissolve into the jewels and seed syllables in the heart centers of the [five buddhas] in your five centers. Consider that the power of your merit and gnosis increases, and hold the vase breath.

Again rays of white, red, blue, yellow, and green light emanate. They touch the sentient beings in the six realms, purifying their attachment, aversion, bewilderment, pride, and jealousy and bringing them to the level of the five families of buddhas. Their longevity, merit, glory, renown, power, and splendor are gathered back in the form of white, red, blue, yellow, and green rays of light and dissolve into your five centers. Consider that all your longevity, merit, glory, renown, power, and splendor grow, and hold the vase breath. {475}

Again from the jewels and seed syllables in your five centers, rays of light of the five colors emanate and gather back, as five-colored light rays, the wealth of the gods of the world of form and the riches of the gods of the world of desire, and of its demigods, nāgas, yakṣhas, gandharvas, kinnaras, and humans—in short, the light of the sun and moon, the vital essence of the five elements, and all the brilliance, radiance, and good qualities there are. Consider that on your dwelling and the whole country too a great rain of wealth and precious things pours down, and hold the vase breath.

Each of these three specific visualizations should include all five chakras. If you are doing the practice in a detailed way, do the specific visualization for each chakra, making five visualization stages. By means of this practice, the power of your merit will increase and a great rain of riches will pour down. There is an oral instruction concerning visualizing the deities on the tips of the rays of light.

### c. The Activity of Bringing Particular Objects under Control by Means of Pacifying, Increasing, Magnetizing, and Wrathful Subjugation

Visualize yourself as Jambhala as you did before during the approach. In your five centers are the Jambhalas of the five families, similar to yourself: in your crown center, white Vairochana Jambhala; in your throat center, red Padma Jambhala; in your heart center, blue Vajra Jambhala; in your navel center, yellow Ratnasambhava Jambhala; and in your secret center, green Amoghasiddhi Jambhala. All of them are seated on a precious throne and lotus and moon, with the same attributes as yourself. In each of their heart centers, upon a lotus and moon, visualize a jewel—white, red, blue, yellow, or green.

#### i. Bringing under Control by Pacifying

In your crown center is Vairochana Jambhala, and in his heart center, on a lotus and moon, is a white wish-fulfilling jewel, blazing with light. {476} From it, infinite lasso- and hook-shaped rays of white light emanate. They touch the siddhas, khecharas,[7] vidyādharas, and scholars learned in the five sciences—in short, all the teachers—between the eyes, delighting their hearts and filling them with bliss. Consider that they cannot help being drawn into your crown, and the teachers are brought under your control. They are greatly pleased, and your mind stream is blessed by their enlightened body, speech, and mind. This is gathering the teachers under control.

Second, bringing the yidam deities under control. The rays of white light like lassos and hooks touch the heart centers of the yidam deities, filling their minds with bliss-clarity. Because they have great compassion, they are powerless not to come and dissolve into the jewel in your crown center.

Consider that you receive the supreme and common accomplishments. This is bringing the yidam deities under control.

Third, bringing revered beings such as spiritual friends under control. The rays of white light like lassos and hooks touch the crowns of the spiritual friends. Consider that they cannot resist being drawn to you and dissolve into the jewel in your crown center. In this way you will bring revered beings under control.

Fourth, bringing kings under control. The rays of white light like lassos and hooks touch the heads of the kings on their various headdresses, turning them into Jambhala. Consider that they are powerless to resist being pleased with you, and they gather in front of you and dissolve into the jewel in your crown center.

Fifth, bringing ministers and other laymen under control. {477} The rays of white light like lassos and hooks take hold of the ministers or others by the heart. They are attracted to you, gain faith, are happy, and cannot resist being gathered under your power. Consider that they dissolve into the jewel [in your crown center].

Sixth, bringing women such as queens under control. The rays of white light like lassos and hooks take hold of the queens or other women by the navel and the anthers of the lotus. Consider that they cannot resist delighting in you and being gathered under your control and that they dissolve into the jewel in your crown center.

Seventh, bringing wealth under control. From the jewel in your crown center and the seed syllable, rays of white light like lassos and hooks emanate. Consider that all the riches in the world, the five kinds of precious materials, all kinds of grain, all forms of clothing, all kinds of food, and all fields, grazed or cultivated, are gathered by the light rays and dissolve into the jewel [in your crown center].

Eighth, bringing everything under control. From the jewel in the heart center of Jambhala in your crown center, rays of white light like lassos and hooks emanate, touching all the teachers, buddhas, and bodhisattvas and pleasing them with offerings. They touch all sentient beings and turn them into Jambhala. They touch the world outside, purifying it as a buddha field made of the five kinds of precious materials. Then all these are gathered up by the light rays and dissolve into the jewel in your crown center. By concentrating on this you will bring everything under control.

Before beginning all these eight activities, expel the stale winds {478} three times and consider that the five obscurations such as miserliness are purified. As you breathe in, the rays of white light like hooks and lassos touch the objects of the practice in their respective centers. At that moment, consider that they fill their whole bodies and minds with joy and great bliss and that they feel faith, devotion, and deep affection for you; they are helplessly gathered in front of you, transform into Vairochana Jambhala, and sit down in front of you. After that, simply from being touched by the rays of light, they all melt into white light and dissolve into the jewel in the heart center of Jambhala in your crown center. At that time, consider that from the jewel and symbolic attributes of Jambhala in your crown center there falls a torrential rain of all the riches one could need or desire, filling the whole of the inside of your body and your dwelling, and hold your breath.

This is bringing under control by pacifying.

### ii. Bringing under Control by Magnetizing

Visualize yourself as Jambhala and in your throat center a precious throne, with a lotus and moon. On it is a red Jambhala, similar to yourself, his heart center marked with a red jewel. It emanates rays of red light like lassos and hooks, touching and bringing under control first the teachers, second the yidam deities, third the spiritual friends, fourth the kings, fifth the ministers and other laymen, sixth the queens and other women, seventh riches and other wealth, and eighth everything together. As a result of the lights' touching their respective centers, as described above, all their bodies and minds are filled with joy and great bliss, {479} and they feel faith, devotion, and deep affection for you; they are helplessly brought under control, becoming Padma Jambhala, seated in front of you. Again the rays of light touch them, as a result of which they develop joy and great bliss and gradually melt into a mass of red light and dissolve into the jewel in the heart of Padma Jambhala in your throat center. You receive both the supreme and common accomplishments, and a torrential rain of all kinds of riches falls, [filling] the inside of your body and the whole place. Concentrating on this, hold your breath. This is bringing under control by magnetizing.

### iii. Bringing under Control by Increasing

Visualize yourself as Jambhala and in your navel center a precious throne, with a lotus and moon. On it is [yellow] Ratnasambhava Jambhala, similar to yourself, and in his heart center, upon a lotus and moon, a yellow jewel marked with a yellow *jaṃ*. From it rays of yellow light like lassos and hooks emanate in the ten directions, touching all the teachers and so forth in the ten directions. As before, they are helplessly attracted, transform into Ratnasambhava Jambhala, and sit in front of you. Again the rays of light touch them, and they develop joy and great bliss; they all melt together into a mass of light and dissolve into the jewel in the heart center[8] of Ratnasambhava Jambhala in your navel center. As a result, you receive both supreme and common accomplishments, and a torrential rain of riches falls, filling the inside of your body and the whole of your dwelling. Concentrating on this, hold the vase breath. This is bringing under control by increasing.

### iv. Bringing under Control by Wrathful Subjugation

Visualize yourself as Jambhala and in your secret center {480} a precious throne, with a lotus and moon. On it is a dark-green or black Karma Jambhala, and in his heart center, upon a lotus and moon, a green jewel marked with a black *jaṃ*. From it rays of dark-green light like lassos and hooks emanate in the ten directions, touching all the teachers and so forth in the ten directions, bringing them and the other objects under control in the eight ways. As before, the light touches their respective centers, filling their whole bodies and minds with joy and great bliss. In particular, it makes all the objects of the practice tremble with fear. Frightened and confused, they are powerless to resist being brought under control. They turn into Karma Jambhala and sit in front of you. Again the rays of light touch them, and they develop joy and great bliss; they all melt together into a mass of green light and dissolve into the jewel in the heart center of Jambhala in your secret center. As a result, you receive the supreme and common accomplishments, and a torrential rain of the five kinds of enjoyment falls, filling the inside of your body and the whole of your dwelling. Concentrating on this, hold the vase breath. This is bringing under control by means of wrathful subjugation.

### v. Bringing under Control by Means of Multifarious Activities

Visualize yourself as Jambhala and in your heart center a precious throne, with a lotus and moon. On it is a blue Akṣhobhya Jambhala, similar to yourself. Alternatively, it has been taught that you may visualize a black, wrathful Jambhala. Whichever the case, in his heart center, upon a lotus and moon, is a blue jewel marked with a blue *jaṃ*. From it infinite rays of white, red, blue, yellow, green, and five-colored light shaped like lassos and hooks emanate in the ten directions, touching all eight objects of the practice, all the teachers, {481} yidams [and so forth] in the ten directions, bringing them under control in the eight ways. As before, the light touches their respective centers, filling their whole bodies and minds with joy and bliss, and they are blessed and feel faith, devotion, and deep affection for you; they are helplessly brought under control. They turn into Akṣhobhya Jambhala and sit in front of you. Again, the five-colored rays of light touch them, and they develop joy and great bliss. Consider that they all transform into a mass of blue light. That in turn melts into five-colored rays of light, which dissolve into the jewel in the heart center of Jambhala in your heart center. As a result, you receive both the supreme and common accomplishments, and a torrential rain of the five kinds of precious materials and all kinds of riches falls, filling the inside of your body and the whole of your dwelling. Concentrating on this, hold the vase breath. This is bringing under control by means of multifarious activities.

In the context of the above practices, you should know that there is an oral instruction for visualizing the deities on the tips of the rays of light and also for the arrangement of the eight wealth deities in the body.

### 2. Instructions on Speech, the Recitation

These instructions are divided into outer, inner, and secret.

#### a. Outer Recitation

Visualize yourself as Jambhala. In your crown center is the syllable *oṁ*, on the forehead *jaṃ*, on the right shoulder *bha*, on the left shoulder *la*, at the heart *ja*, at the navel *len*, on the right thigh *dra*, on the left thigh *ye*, on the top of the right foot *svā*, and on the top of the left foot *hā*. On the tips of the rays of light emanating from them are the ten syllables, from which a rain of the five kinds of precious materials descends. Concentrating on this, recite the mantra.

#### b. Inner Recitation

Visualize yourself as Jambhala as before, {482} and in your five centers the Jambhalas of the five families. In their hearts are five jewels marked with the syllable *jaṃ*. From these appear the mantra, in five corresponding colors, encircling them. Concentrating on this, recite the mantra.

#### c. Secret Recitation

Visualize yourself as Jambhala, and in your five centers the five Jambhalas. In their heart centers, upon a lotus and moon, are five jewels marked with five *jaṃ* syllables corresponding to the five families. From these appear the mantra garlands in the five colors, encircling them. They emanate rays of light, the tips of which emanate the Jambhalas of the five families. The whole of the inside of your body is filled to bursting with Jambhalas of the five families. They issue forth outside, filling all your pores with Jambhalas. They touch the world outside, transforming it into a buddha field. And they touch all the sentient beings inhabiting it, who all become Jambhala. The whole of the intervening space is filled, and on the tips of all those rays of light dwell the five Jambhalas. From the mouths of all of them the melodious murmuring sound of the mantra resounds. Consider that a torrential rain of the five precious materials and all kinds of riches pours down, and recite the mantra mentally. This is the secret recitation, which completes the instructions on recitation, related to enlightened speech.

## B. Perfection Stage

The instructions on the perfection stage are divided into three: (1) sustained calm; (2) profound insight; and (3) transference.

The first two are the same as for the graded path of Avalokiteshvara, so they have not been written down here.

### 3. Transference

Visualize yourself as Jambhala, and in your five centers—crown, throat, heart, navel, and secret center—visualize the Jambhalas of the five families. The Jambhala in your secret center transforms into a green essence drop, which dissolves into the Jambhala in your navel center. That Jambhala transforms into a yellow essence drop, {483} which dissolves into the Akṣhobhya in your heart center. Akṣhobhya transforms into a blue essence drop and dissolves into Amitābha in your throat center. Amitābha transforms into a red essence drop and dissolves into Vairochana in your crown center. Vairochana transforms into a radiant white essence drop and shoots up out of your crown and dissolves into the heart center of your teacher [inseparable from] Ratnasambhava, visualized above your head. The teacher transforms into a five-colored rainbow in the sky, and the whole of space is filled with lights and rainbows. Concentrating on this, settle in meditative equipoise in the nonconceptual state of the Great Seal. This is known as the rainbow transference, after the manner of both the training and its actual application.

This completes the instructions on the main practice.

### III. Conclusion

Seal the practice with prayers of dedication and aspiration, and do this practice regularly. As a result, the common and supreme accomplishments will occur spontaneously.

These instructions bear the seal of secrecy: they should be given only to lineage holders and people who one is certain are suitable vessels; they should not be given to unsuitable vessels.

Now that through my teacher's kindness
I have truly seen that wishing gem, the source of all one needs or wants,
Whose instructions lead to the two accomplishments,
I have written them down to benefit all beings.

By the merit of my doing so, may all beings traverse the ocean of samsara
And discover the wish-fulfilling jewel of the nature of the mind.
Freeing themselves and others from the sufferings of samsara,
May they achieve the level of supreme great bliss.

This completes, for the time being, the instructions of the noble lord Jambhala entitled *A Shower of Accomplishments*, which the yogi Öpak Dorje wrote down in accordance with what his teacher had taught.

Virtue! Virtue! Virtue!

# 23. Ocean of Blessings

*A Prayer to the Lineage of the Teachers of the Graded Path of Avalokiteshvara*[1]

THIS PRAYER to the lineage masters of the Avalokiteshvara sādhana employs a typical structure, beginning with the truth-body teacher (in this case, Amitābha) and the enjoyment-body teacher (Avalokiteshvara), and then listing each of the manifestation-body teachers from Mitrayogin down in chronological order. Each master is described in four lines, followed by an aspirational refrain.

{486}
*oṁ svasti*
Vast space of the body of truth, with its strengths and other qualities,
Complete embodiment of the thousand lights of the major and minor
  marks,
Sublime buddha possessed of the light of the five kinds of gnosis—
To the guide Amitābha we pray:
Bless us that we may train in generation and perfection, in love and
  compassion,
And gain mastery of sustained calm, profound insight, the illusory
  body, dream,
Luminosity, transference, and the intermediate state,
To accomplish buddhahood in a single life.

Master of the tenth level, embodiment of all the buddhas' speech,
Manifesting bodies pervading the entire expanse of space,

Leading all beings on the path to enlightenment—
To Lord Avalokiteshvara we pray:
Bless us that we may train in generation and perfection, in love and compassion,
And gain mastery of sustained calm, profound insight, the illusory body, dream,
Luminosity, transference, and the intermediate state,
To accomplish buddhahood in a single life.

Sublime bodhisattva, manifestation of Avalokiteshvara,
Guiding all beings by means of your infinite miraculous powers,
You attained the vajra body beyond birth and death—
To Mitrayogin we pray:
Bless us that we may train in generation and perfection, in love and compassion,
And gain mastery of sustained calm, profound insight, the illusory body, dream,
Luminosity, transference, and the intermediate state,
To accomplish buddhahood in a single life.

Regent of the buddhas, sublime sovereign of the doctrine,
Your lifestyle emulated the vast activities of the bodhisattvas,
Setting the inhabitants of Jambudvīpa on the path of benefit and happiness—
To Shrīputra we pray:
Bless us that we may train in generation and perfection, in love and compassion,
And gain mastery of sustained calm, profound insight, the illusory body, dream,
Luminosity, transference, and the intermediate state,
To accomplish buddhahood in a single life.

Accepted as a disciple by Shrīputra, who saw in you a suitable vessel for the instructions,
You possessed the eye of preternatural knowledge and realized the way things truly are;
Sublime teacher, vast mine of pith instructions—
To the noble Drakpa Rinchen we pray:

Bless us that we may train in generation and perfection, in love and compassion, {487}
And gain mastery of sustained calm, profound insight, the illusory body, dream,
Luminosity, transference, and the intermediate state,
To accomplish buddhahood in a single life.

As a result of previous training, you realized the meaning of the two truths;
Because of your aspirations, you spontaneously accomplished the two goals
And propagated the activities of Avalokiteshvara—
To the realized yogi Buddhashrī we pray:
Bless us that we may train in generation and perfection, in love and compassion,
And gain mastery of sustained calm, profound insight, the illusory body, dream,
Luminosity, transference, and the intermediate state,
To accomplish buddhahood in a single life.

This prayer to the lineage of the teachers of the graded path of Avalokiteshvara, entitled *Ocean of Blessings*, was composed by the yogi Öpak Dorje.

A unified compilation of the mantras of the deities in the six instructions of Mitrayogin.

*oṁ amitābhāva hūṁ*
*oṁ hrīḥ padmānta kṛta vajra krodha hayagrīva hulu hulu hūṁ phaṭ*
*oṁ āḥ hūṁ hrīḥ*
*oṁ maṇi padme hūṁ baṃ ḍākinī harinisa hūṁ*
*oṁ hūṁ hriṁ hriṁ āḥ*
*oṁ guru āyuḥ jñāna siddhi hūṁ hrīḥ*
*oṁ amāraṇi jīvāntiye svāhā*
*oṁ a ra pa ca na dhīḥ namaḥ*
*oṁ vāgrīśvari muṃ*
*oṁ yama rāja hūṁ phaṭ*
*oṁ hrīḥ ṣṭrīvi kṛtānana hūṁ phaṭ*

*oṁ vajrapāṇi hūṁ*
*oṁ vajra caṇḍa mahāroṣaṇa hūṁ phaṭ*
*oṁ bhiruṭa cale cale hūṁ phaṭ*
*oṁ tāre tuttāre ture svāhā*
*oṁ tāre tāṃ svāhā*
*oṁ jaṃbhala jalendraye svāhā*
*oṁ vajra mahākāla durusvi hūṁ phaṭ*
*trak rakmo baliṅgta mahā rakṣa ṇa nagmo dun ting bhyo*
*oṁ śrī mahākāla ya śāsana upa hariṇa eṣvā paści makalo a yaṃ idam ratnā traya apakariṇa ati pratijña smara satidā idam duṣṭaṃ kha kha khā hi khā hi māra māra ghrīḥaṇa ghrīḥaṇa bandha bandha* {488} *hana hana daha daha paca paca dina mekena māraya hūṁ hūṁ phaṭ phaṭ svāhā*
*oṁ vajra satva hūṁ*
*oṁ padma satva samaya manu pāla ya padma satva tvenopa tiṣṭha ḍri ḍho mebhava suto ṣyo mebhava supo ṣyo mebhava anurakto mebhava sarva siddhi meprayaccha sarva karma sucame cittaṃ śreyaḥ kuru hūṁ ha ha ha ha ho bhagavān sarva tathāgata padma māme muñca padma bhava mahā samaya satva āḥ hūṁ phaṭ*
*a ā i ī u ū ri rī li lī e ai o au aṃ aḥ ka kha ga gha nga ca cha ja jha ña ṭa ṭha ḍa ḍha ṇa ta tha da dha na pa pha ba bha ma ya ra la va śa ṣa sa ha kṣa*
*oṁ yedharmā hetu prabhavā hetunteṣān tathāgato hy avadat teṣāñ ca yo nirodha evaṃ vādī mahāśrāmaṇaḥ ye svahā*

May virtue and excellence increase.

# 24. Sādhana of the Dharma Protector Draklha Gönpo[1]

Draklha, an aspect of the dharma protector Mahākāla, is the protector associated with all the teachings transmitted by Mitrayogin. He has already featured in the Avalokiteshvara sādhana in chapter 15. The present text is a sādhana dedicated entirely to him, but it would normally be practiced within a yidam deity sādhana, perhaps along with other prayers and offerings to the dharma protectors. In any case, it is necessary to visualize oneself as one's yidam deity before visualizing the protector in front of oneself, making offerings, and entrusting him with the activities of guarding the teachings and protecting those who practice them.

{490}
Homage to Avalokiteshvara.

Sublime lord, protector of the teachings in the realm where they are
  taught,
You constantly stand guard over the Buddha's doctrine:
Chief of the Nāthas, Great Mahākāla,
Praise to lord Draklha Gönpo, black protector of the teachings.

For others' benefit, I will here set down
The sādhana of his manifestation
Exactly as my teacher taught it,
Without error or mistake, as lovely as a necklace of pearls.

You who wish to accomplish the Great Black One (Mahākāla) should begin by taking refuge and arousing bodhichitta. Then, purify everything as emptiness with the *svabhāva* mantra.

> From the state of emptiness, I visualize myself as the yidam deity.
> In front of me, amid an array of spears and swords,
> A mobbing multitude of mamos,
> And a swirling expanse of multiple dust devils,[2]
> Is a blazing, dark-blue, triangular measureless palace.
> In its center, on top of male and female hostile obstacle makers, face down and face up,
> Is a thousand-spoked wheel of meteoric iron,
> In the center of which is a lotus and sun throne, and on it the syllable *hūṁ*.
> From it there appears a dark-red curved knife, its center marked with a *hūṁ*,
> From which rays of light emanate, making offerings to the noble ones,
> Fulfilling the hopes of sentient beings, and subjugating all harmful forces.
> The rays of light are gathered back and dissolve into the curved knife and the syllable *hūṁ*,
> Which is thereby transformed into the wisdom protector.
> He is dark red in color, with one face, scowling wrathfully.
> His three eyes cast angry glances in the ten directions.
> His four canine teeth are completely bared,
> His terrifying mouth agape, tongue darting like lightning,
> And orange hair streaming upward.
> In his right hand he holds a four-faceted club for slaughtering hostile forces and obstacle makers, emitting sparks and with its tip marked with a jewel. {491}
> His left hand holds a small vessel, inside which is an enemy's heart.
> He is crowned with five skulls
> And adorned with a long necklace of fifty-one freshly severed heads
> And a shoulder belt and hand and foot ornaments of vicious black snakes.
> On his lower body he wears a skirt of a freshly flayed tiger skin.

His right leg is drawn in,
His left stretched out,
And he is wearing a cloak of black silk.
Emitting sparks of fire,
He burns up all evil forces.
In front of him is his henchman, Black Mönpa,
Dark blue in color, with one face and two arms,
Three eyes wide open,
Dark reddish-yellow hair streaming upward.
His right hand brandishes a curved knife in the air;
His left holds a skull cup containing an enemy's heart,
Which he is holding to the lips of the main deity.
Besides him, the protector is surrounded by massed clouds of wisdom protectors,
A whirlwind of activity protectors and worldly protectors,
And infinite hosts, as well, of mamos and lords of death,
Hungry for flesh, thirsting for blood, pitiless,
In infinite terrifying forms and hideous colors.
In the protector's forehead is the syllable *oṁ*,
In his throat center the syllable *āḥ*,
And in his heart center the syllable *hūṁ*.
These emanate rays of light,
Inviting the wisdom protectors and their retinues from the Cool Grove (Shītavana).

Visualizing this, and making the vajra gathering gesture:

*hūṁ* As, with faith and [pure] commitments,
I invite the glorious wisdom protector,
Because of your promise and compassion, {492}
Please come to this place in order to protect the teachings.

Make the offerings with *arghaṃ* and so on.

With *jaḥ hūṁ baṃ hoḥ*, [the wisdom deity] dissolves inseparably.
The tathāgatas bestow empowerment,
The [empowerment] water overflows, and the excess becomes Akṣhobhya, adorning his crown.

On a seat of lotus and sun in the protector's heart center
I visualize a dark-red *hūṁ*,
Surrounded clockwise by the mantra:
*oṁ mahākāla durusva hūṁ hūṁ phaṭ phaṭ*

Recite this as the principal recitation, and the long *śā sa ṇa* mantra, as generally taught, until signs of accomplishment occur. As the sacred commitment, do not throw stones at black dogs or birds.

## Offering the Torma to the Protector

Set up the torma in front of you in a skull cup or precious container. Cleanse it with the *amṛta* mantra and purify it with the *svabhāva* mantra.

From the state of emptiness, there appears the syllable *yaṃ*, and from it, the wind.
From *raṃ* appears fire;
From *kaṃ*, three human heads as hearthstones;
And from the letter *A*, a vast and spacious kapāla container.
Inside it, from *go ku da ha na* appear the five fleshes;
From *vi mu ma ra śu*, the five nectars;
From *hūṁ bhrūṃ aṃ jiṃ khaṃ*, the five wisdoms.
On top of them is a moon mandala in the form of a lid for the skull cup.
In its center is a half vajra standing upright, marked inside with *oṁ āḥ hūṁ*.
From my heart center rays of light emanate,
Touching the torma.
The wind blows and the fire flares up,
Warming the skull cup.
Impurities are boiled out like froth,
And the steam issues upward in the form of light rays,
Reminding all the buddhas and bodhisattvas of their pledges.
Wisdom nectar is drawn down from their heart centers
And mixes with the meditational nectar.
After that, the vajra marked with *oṁ āḥ hūṁ* and the moon cover fall into the skull cup, {493}

And everything becomes inseparable, a great ocean of nectar.
The protector and his retinue dip their vajra-pipe tongues into the torma and partake of it.

Visualizing this, offer [the torma] three or seven times, as appropriate, with the root mantra and the *śā sa ṇa* mantra to which is added *idaṃ baliṅgta kha kha khā hi khā hi*. At the end, make the offerings with *arghaṃ* and so on, and the praise, as follows:

*hūṁ* From the measureless palace of a terrifying skeleton-filled charnel ground,
Within a tent-like array of spears and swords,
And in the center of a whirlwind of mamos and ḍākinīs,
Is a blazing dark-red triangular measureless palace.
In it, on top of enemy obstacle makers, face up and face down, and a wheel of meteoric iron,
On a throne of lotus, sun, and moon, one on top of the other,
Is the syllable *hūṁ*, from which arises the Black Powerful One.
You who keep the commitment to guard the teachings of Lord Avalokiteshvara,
Draklha Gönpo, lord of the hundred thousand gönpos,
Protector of the Buddha's doctrine, Black One, to you I bow!

*hūṁ* Dark red in color, with one face and two arms,
Unchanging ultimate reality, possessed of skillful means and wisdom,
Mouth agape, fangs bared, three angry, restless eyes
Scrutinizing[3] birth and death, clearly seeing past, present, and future—
Black Lekden, to you homage and praise!

Your hair streams upward; you are adorned with five skulls
Marked with the five gnoses that put to flight the demigods.
Grimacing and snorting,
You keep your promise to subdue evil spirits.
Protector of the teachings, Black One, to you homage and praise!

Your tongue is curled back, proclaiming the sound of the secret teachings.
You liberate those who do harm and protect those who keep the sacred commitments. {494}
Wearing a necklace of fresh skulls and adorned with vicious snakes,
You are clothed in cemetery attire and subdue the four classes of nāgas.
You who war with the enemies of the practice, Black One, to you I give praise!

In your right hand is a jeweled club, in your left a fresh skull.
You subdue negative forces and fulfill beings' hopes.
Wearing a tiger-skin skirt and a cloak of black silk,
You attract the mamos and gather the loyal protectors under your power.
Black protector of the Buddha's teachings, to you I give praise!

Your two legs in the striding posture, your body poised majestically,
You liberate the enemies and obstacle makers and subdue all the armies of demons without exception.
Supreme deity, Black One, to you I give praise!

Great Black One, you perfectly fulfill the hopes
Of practitioners who keep the sacred commitments.
This pure torma, the first portion of the feast, ornamented with red meat and blood,
Beautifully decorated with dark-red ribbons and a silk canopy
(NOTE: Also refers to a burning pennant planted in the torma.)
And sprinkled with strong drink, the sublime, nectarous liquor,
I offer to the glorious Draklha Gönpo and your retinue.
Please accept it in order to guard the teachings of the Buddha.
Please accept it that we practitioners may accomplish the activities.
Remember the promise and commitment you made in former times

In the presence of Lord Avalokiteshvara
And carry out the activities that we practitioners entrust you with.

After this offering and praise, make the feast offerings and so forth on a grand scale. At the end, be diligent in going through the concluding sections: the request to depart, dissolution, dedication, aspiration prayers, prayers for auspiciousness, and so forth.

This sādhana of glorious Draklha Gönpo, along with the torma dedication, offerings, and praise, is a pith instruction of Jetsun Mitra, transmitted through the aural lineage to a single disciple at a time. {495} It is as precious as refined molten gold and had never been written down. But in response to the learned master Sangye Özer's repeated prayers requesting Jetsun Drakpa Rinchen [to write it down] so that a few others could benefit from it, the sublime lord, the yogi Girti Ratna, compiled it in a hermitage at Dochen Monastery.

The copyist was Buddha Vajra.
May all beings be guided by virtue.
Keep this utterly pure composition secret and do not show it to anyone.
*maṅgalaṃ*

PART FIVE

# Mitrayogin's Mahāmudrā Instructions

The final section of this volume contains a number of profound pith instructions introducing the disciple to the nature of the mind. The most important of these is the teaching Avalokiteshvara gave Mitrayogin in a vision, entitled *Resting in the Nature of One's Own Mind* or simply *Resting in the Nature of Mind* (*sems nyid ngal gso*). This poem of twenty-five verses is the source text for six other texts in this volume and the inspiration for *Thirty Verses Expressing Realization*, the song Mitrayogin sang on hearing Avalokiteshvara's words. Both these works are included in the Derge Tengyur. Unlike Gyalwa Longchenpa's famous text of the same name, in which the author presents the whole path of the Great Perfection, beginning with a chapter on the precious human life, Mitrayogin's *Resting in the Nature of Mind* concentrates from the beginning on the view of the Great Seal, Mahāmudrā, with a series of introductions aimed, according to Jamyang Khyentse Wangpo's commentary, at practitioners with different levels of understanding.

The source text of *Resting in the Nature of Mind* is complemented by a detailed commentary by Khyentse Wangpo, a work by the omniscient Butön correlating the verses with sources from the sutras and tantras, Jamyang Khyentse Wangchuk's *Notes* on how to put Mitrayogin's verses into practice, a song of experience inspired by these instructions, a guide on how to teach the text, and a lineage prayer, along with a supplement updating the visualization for the guru yoga practice in the *Notes*.

Included with the source text in the same set of pages in the Tibetan are *Thirty Verses Expressing Realization*, along with an explanation by Tropu Lotsawa Jampa Pal, and two short pith instruction texts, *Three Essential Introductions* and *Cherished Essence*. The author of these is not mentioned, but their inclusion here would lead one to assume that Mitrayogin himself gave them to Tropu Lotsawa. In order to keep *Resting in the Nature of Mind* and its related texts together in this translated volume, these additional pith instructions have been moved to the end of the *Resting* collection.

The volume concludes with yet another pith instruction by Mitrayogin, *Three Quintessential Points*, which is followed by a lineage prayer and Jamyang Khyentse Wangpo's guide on how to put these three points into practice, along with the relevant liturgies.

# 25. Resting in the Nature of One's Own Mind

*A Pith Instruction Given to the Mahāsiddha Mitrayogin by Noble Avalokiteshvara*[1]

{498}

*oṁ svasti*

These twenty-five verses on resting in the nature of one's own mind comprise three sections: (1) introduction; (2) main body of the text; and (3) conclusion.

## I. Introduction

The introduction is divided into (1) an exposition of the title and (2) the translator's homage.

### A. Title

In Sanskrit: *Svacittaviśrāmopadeśapañcaviṃśatikāgāthā*
In Tibetan: *Rang gi sems ngal gso ba'i man ngag tshigs su bcad pa nyi shu rtsa lnga pa*
[In English: *A Pith Instruction in Twenty-Five Verses on* Resting in the Nature of One's Own Mind]

### B. Translator's Homage

Homage to Glorious Vajrasattva

## II. Main Body of the Text

The main body of the text has several parts.[2]

### A. Introduction of the Three Ways of Resting Naturally

Wonder! One's own mind is, from the beginning, unborn.
Nowhere else is there the cause for creating samsara and nirvana.
Present in the center of one's own heart,
It will be known through the teacher's instructions.

Whatever is born is the natural state,
So if one remembers this, mindful of whatever arises,
It arises as emptiness.
This, there is no doubt, is the king of yogas.

All that arises is thatness,
And that does not arise as anything.
So, whatever is born is itself unborn;
While unborn, it appears to be born.

### B. Three Verses of Introduction by Means of Analogies of the Three Worlds

Right leg stretched out, left leg bent, he makes the threatening gesture, {499}
And looking with the vajra view,
He keeps the supreme horse gently coming and going,
Experiencing the many as one.

The feet rest in the great ocean.
The hands wander all over the earth.
The two eyes gaze into space.
The mind does not move anywhere.

Like a beautiful woman's mirror, a powerful athlete,
A prisoner, a queen,
A sweeper, or a courtesan,
Keep the company of a single companion.

### C. Introduction by Means of Outer, Inner, and In-Between Analogies

Like a tiger, lion, or elephant,
A camel, deer, or monkey,
Sandalwood, a tree, or human corpse—
Adept, do the practice of emptiness.

Like a mountain torrent or a great lake,
The mother of an only child, an elephant keeper,
A snow mountain, or a pure crystal—
If you are free of reference, the foundation has been laid.

In the beginning, middle, and end, respectively,
Phenomena have no root, essential nature, or function,
Like a lamp in a dream.
Through training in compassion, without moving, all is accomplished.

### D. Introduction by Means of Three Direct Approaches

The three aspects of purity and emptiness
Regarding arising, remaining, and ceasing in going, coming, and staying
Are great bliss, luminosity, and absence of thought. {500}
Thus do the wise settle in equipoise.

By settling, first, with great compassion,
Looking continuously at that state without distraction,
And meditating on the deity and the teacher,
Practitioners will find rest.

Listen, child: whatever thoughts you have,
Because they neither bind nor free you here,
Do not be distracted, do not fabricate, leave things as they are—
Behold, find rest from weariness!

### E. Introduction by Means of Three Trainings

Reflections and forms, echoes and sounds,
Real events and dreams—for the mind that thinks of these,

Combine concentration and the meditation
Of connection and exhaustion.

Discernment, absence of basis,
And constant, unbroken meditation
Are like gold, like fire, like space,
Understanding, dissolving, and purifying.

Nonappearance, appearance, and circumstantial appearance
Are like space, a mirror, and a pure crystal.
This is realized by means of concentration,
Gnosis, and the power of memory.

### F. Introduction Related to the Three Doors

Perception, in equipoise, is luminosity,
At which time perception has not arisen.
Remaining one-pointed, utterly free of concepts,
One is freed of the dust of distraction.

Wherever the wind goes, the mind goes too.
But if you hold it prisoner inside the body's house,
You'll put to death the ordinary mind;
Without a mount, where can the mind go?

The nature of all is uncontrived:
All thoughts depend on conditions.
If one knows the three natures,
Thoughts make thoughts themselves disappear.

### G. Introduction by Means of Three Affirmations and Negations

Existence when we perceive
And nonexistence when we scrutinize are just concepts.
Nothing whatsoever here exists.
O child, meditate on space!

Camphor and its smell are interrelated:
One cannot have one without the other.
Likewise, conditions and absence of conditions
Are not separate, so meditate leaving things as they are.

The mind of sameness brings movement to an end;
Mindfulness binds unsameness.
At that time resting in equipoise free from those
Puts to death conceptual thoughts.

### H. Introduction Related to the Four Empowerments {501}

Wash, and wear the clothes of space;
Perform the fire offering of conceptual thoughts;
And on the bank, purify the ashes of thoughts
With water and wind together.

Container and contents, winds and mind stream, the fixed and the
motile;
Sky, sun, moon, and Rāhu;
Firefly, rain, and bee—with these analogies
One masters the samaya mudrā.

In the multicolored flower of the mind
One takes the essence of the four joys:
When one experiences the innate,
The mind, like a person, is satiated.

Bind the body, speech, and mind
With the mudrās of body, wind, and the great channel.
There will be no impediment to attaining warmth.
Do not be fixed in conduct.

## III. Conclusion

The conclusion is divided into (1) a statement marking the completion of the text and (2) the translator's colophon.

### A. Statement Marking the Completion of the Text

This completes the song of realization pointing out the authentic state of thatness, called *A Pith Instruction in Twenty-Five Verses That Enables Practitioners to Find Rest in Their Own Minds.*

### B. Translator's Colophon

These verses that Lord Avalokiteshvara gave in person to the great master of yogis who had attained accomplishment, Shrī Jagatamitrānanda, were translated by him and the translator Jampa Pal in a summerhouse in the Ambara[3] forest at the golden pagoda of Shrī Pashupati.

# 26. The Quintessence

*A Commentary on the Root Text of the Great Seal* Resting in the Nature of Mind *That Noble Avalokiteshvara Taught the Mahāsiddha Mitrayogin*[1]

{526}

*oṁ svasti siddhaṃ*

Bowing down respectfully to the sublime teacher,
Lord of the World, Treasure of Compassion,
I shall compile a slightly essentialized commentary
On *Resting in the Nature of One's Own Mind.*

This commentary is divided into two sections: (1) the historical background and (2) the actual instructions.

## I. Historical Background

The great siddha universally known as Mitrayogin, who was a manifestation of noble Avalokiteshvara, was born into the kṣhatriya caste in a large city in the province of Raḍā, in the east of the noble land of India. From an early age, he awakened to the family of sublime beings and, abandoning the kingdom like spit in the dust, he set out to seek the dharma. The tales of his attainments at that time, known as "the twenty wondrous deeds," are music to the ears of [all] noble and learned beings. Here are these stories.[2]

First, he was guided by Lālitavajra, who was a direct disciple of Tillipa. As a result of his meditating on Khasarpāṇi for twelve years, noble Avalokiteshvara and his retinue appeared to him in person on top of a wooden mandala[3] as smooth as a mirror and taught him the dharma. {527} By this means, he gained accomplishment. This was the first [wondrous deed], when he was named Ajitamitragupta, or [in Tibetan] Mipham Bepai Shenyen—Invincible Secret Friend.

When Ekajaṭī taught him the path of skillful means, he prepared a wooden mandala in front of her and prayed. All his wishes were fulfilled. This was the second wondrous deed.

At Otantapūri, a dispute arose among the twelve thousand monks living there, with one side supported by the Burshing king, who led his troops against the monastery. Mitrayogin hurled a wheel, causing the whole army to take fright and flee, leaving the sangha and monastery unharmed. This was the third wondrous deed.

During the reign of King Sultān Khan, troops from Vārāṇasī, raising so much dust that it darkened the sky, began suppressing the Buddha's doctrine in Magadha. Mitrayogin stripped naked and let out a great roar of laughter. The earth shook, petrifying all the people and livestock. The king begged for forgiveness, and Mitrayogin restored the petrified beings to their former state. This was the fourth wondrous deed.

King Yashas, taking the monks of the four schools of Buddhism as witnesses, ruled that if [the tīrthikas] could move his wooden throne, he would give them a thousand gold coins, and the Buddhists would have to convert to the tīrthikas' religion. {528} If they failed to move it, the tīrthikas would have to convert to Buddhism. He set the wooden throne in a wide field. [Because of Mitrayogin's powers] no one could move it even slightly. Thus the tīrthikas were converted to Buddhism. This was the fifth wondrous deed.

King Upatra covered a cesspit with a cloth and invited the master to sit there, as a result of which he fell into the pit. The king then closed the opening with a lot of wood and stones. However, the master managed to get to the marketplace and said, "Take me to the king's palace!" The king repented and took the master's feet on his head. This was the sixth wondrous deed.

Again, the king ordered wood to be collected and had the master sit on top of it. For three days he set fire to the [pyre], but the master was not burned. This was the seventh wondrous deed.

When he related five verses of profound [teachings] to the king of Vārāṇasī, a rain of flowers fell from the sky and he showed him a vision of a god offering a vase of nectar. This was the eighth wondrous deed.

When the king requested empowerment, Mitrayogin said that all the colored dust [of the mandala] would need to be made of precious materials. Fearing that Mitrayogin was trying to dupe him, the king began to regret [having made the request], whereupon Mitrayogin rose into the air and displayed himself sitting in the midst of the clouds. This was the ninth wondrous deed.

Then, filled with intense remorse, the king spent a week praying to him, as a result of which Mitrayogin [descended] onto a pool and sat there on top of it. This was the tenth wondrous deed.

After that, the king offered a town of sixteen hundred thousand households for the master's use, and the master, having built an almshouse, practiced charity there for three years. At the end of the three years he departed to an unknown destination. This was the eleventh wondrous deed.

To the south, in the region around Kuru Vihāra, he subjugated two yakṣhas who were devouring an old person and a young person from the town every day. He also built a temple [there]. This was the twelfth wondrous deed.

In order to inspire greater faith among the monastics, he adopted a yogic gaze and ordered all the birds in the sky to settle on his hands, {529} and they obeyed. This was the thirteenth wondrous deed.

Without even speaking to the eighty-four lords of Vārāṇasī, he simply directed his mind at them, as a result of which they gave rise to the perception of [everything being] skeletons, and so on, and they departed to forest hermitages, their minds freed of mundane concerns. This was the fourteenth wondrous deed.

Next, he induced King Jayasena and Paṇḍita Ānanda, who lacked faith and were a danger to his life, to adopt the meditation gesture, and he concentrated on the meaning of a single verse. As a result, without rising from that very seat, they were liberated. This was the fifteenth wondrous deed.

To the king of Vārāṇasī he gave the following prediction: "Since you have doubts regarding me, you will not attain accomplishment in this life, but you will attain it in the intermediate state." This was the sixteenth wondrous deed.

The king of Vārāṇasī thought, "I will not let this master go anywhere else," and he forced him to stay in the temple, locking the door. Despite this, Mitrayogin was seen playing on top of a boulder outside and [simultaneously] sitting inside the temple. This was the seventeenth wondrous deed.

On another occasion, when he was residing in a house in the city of Tapasi, two monks saw people going in and out of the house and, looking through a hole, they saw Mitrayogin teaching the dharma to the eight classes of spirits. This was the eighteenth wondrous deed.

At the Bamboo Temple he was cared for by Devadāki and met Avalokiteshvara, who authorized him: "Fortunate child, for the benefit of sentient beings of the future, bestow the empowerments of the four classes of tantra together." Accordingly, he performed these practices, and as a result, up to the present time the river of empowerments of the one hundred eight major tantras has not dried up. This was the nineteenth wondrous deed.

The king of Vārāṇasī prayed to him for seven days, and so he displayed the miraculous power of universal vajra speech in simultaneously bestowing the empowerments of all the classes of tantra in a single mandala. This was the twentieth wondrous deed.

When Tropu Lotsawa Jampa Pal {530} was receiving teachings from the paṇḍita Buddhashrī, he heard that this great siddha, who possessed such wondrous abilities, had arrived at Swayaṃbhūnath, whereupon he brought some betel, offered it to him, and inquired after his health. Mitrayogin did not answer but sat with his face turned toward Tibet. Thinking that this meant he might accept an invitation to come to Tibet, the lotsawa requested Mitrayogin to do so, but the latter did not make any promises. After he had received a short teaching on arousing bodhichitta, the lotsawa was stricken with fever and came close to death. The great siddha slowly began the journey [back] to India. As soon as the lotsawa had recovered from his illness, though still not having fully regained his health, he set out to catch up with him. [He found] Mitrayogin staying in a border fort, surrounded by an escort of fearsome Tirahuti soldiers. An āchārya with whom he was acquainted led him inside, and the lotsawa met up with Mitrayogin on the roof of the fort. He again entreated Mitrayogin to come to Tibet, but the latter did not agree. Thinking, "Now that I have met such a great siddha, I would rather die than return to Tibet without him," he uttered numerous prayers that he might be the master's disciple in his next life and, without hesitation, leaped from the top of the fort. The great siddha caught him with his hand and, laughing, "Don't do that!" he held him close. "For me to go to Tibet," he explained, "you had to purify your obscurations. The fever purified many of your obscurations. Now, by giving your life for me, you have purified all your obscurations without exception. So now I will go to Tibet." They then proceeded to Tibet, and Mitrayogin stayed in Upper Tsang for eighteen months, teaching the dharma to numerous scholars and monks. He also blessed the land for building Tropu Monastery and erecting a giant buddha image.[4]

In particular, the lord himself received directly from noble Avalokiteshvara the twenty-five verses of pith instruction *Resting in the Nature of One's Own Mind,* {531} on the basis of which, over a long period, he explained the experiential instructions to the lotsawa, and in a summerhouse in the Ambara forest at the golden pagoda of Shrī Pashupati, they translated it. The great lotsawa in turn conferred it on his own heart son, Tropu Sempa Chenpo, and others. After that, the supreme scholar of Tropu, Tsemai Kyebu Sönam Gön, transmitted it to the teacher Yang Tsewa Rinchen Senge, from whom Omniscient Butön Rinchen Drup, [appearing in this] Age of Strife, received it and practiced it. It is a most extraordinary instruction, which the most accomplished disciples have assiduously upheld in the form of heart advice, and the lineage of experiential instructions has continued unbroken to the present day.

The great siddha himself subsequently returned to India and displayed all kinds of illusion-like manifestations, benefiting countless beings. He attained the immortal wisdom body and continues to be present.

In short, [Mitrayogin] was an Indian siddha who came to Tibet and displayed the true signs of accomplishment, appearing as the great master Padmasambhava during the earlier period when the Buddhist teachings were introduced and as this great siddha during the later period of their propagation. Truly, no one can match him, as the great scholars have stated.

## II. Explanation of the Main Body of the Text

The main explanation has three parts: (1) introduction; (2) main body of the text; and (3) conclusion. The introduction comprises (1) the title and (2) the translator's homage.

### A. Introduction

#### 1. Title

The Sanskrit title is *Svacittaviśrāmopadeśapañcaviṃśatikāgāthā.*

When translated into Tibetan, it is *Rang gi sems ngal gso ba'i man ngag tshigs su bcad pa nyi shu rtsa lnga pa,* [which in English means] *A Pith Instruction in Twenty-Five Verses on* Resting in the Nature of One's Own Mind.

The import of this is as follows. The nature of one's mind is innate gnosis, naturally pure from the very beginning. However, we have not realized that, {532} and as a result, we have long been exhausting ourselves in the ocean of samsara because of the dependent nature—the duality of an apprehending subject and apprehended object. This is a text that enables us to find rest on the precious island of the natural state, the Great Seal. It is a pith instruction that, in a few verses, reveals an almost unfathomable great meaning in a way that is easy to understand. As for the size of the text, it consists of twenty-five verses. That is why it bears this title.

#### 2. Translator's Homage

Homage to Glorious Vajrasattva.

This is easy to understand.

### B. Main Body of the Text

The main body of the text consists of (1) the ground, an introduction to the natural state, and (2) the path, incorporating conceptual thoughts on the path.

The first of these comprises (1) general points and (2) subsidiary points.

#### 1. The Ground, an Introduction to the Natural State

##### a. General Points

The Great Lotsawa[5] said that in general the condensed essence of how to practice and introduce the profound instructions can be introduced with three topics: (1) preliminaries; (2) main practice; and (3) conclusion.

###### i. Preliminaries

There are three preliminaries. The common preliminaries consist of purifying one's mind stream through such practices as the seven branches. The uncommon preliminaries for blessing one's being consist of such practices as meditating on Vajrasattva and reciting the hundred-syllable mantra. The extraordinary preliminaries consist of mastering one's mind stream by praying with the fifty syllables.

### ii. Main Practice

The seal of the body consists of sitting on a comfortable seat in an isolated location and adopting the prerequisites for concentration. The seal of speech consists of letting one's breath flow naturally. The seal of the mind is at first to relax, then to settle, vividly awake, and finally to let go completely.

For the first of these, relaxing, there are three points: (1) the advantages of relaxing; (2) the disadvantages of not relaxing; and (3) how to relax.

### A) Advantages of Relaxing

The mode of being of the mind's natural state is something unfabricated, so if one's mind is relaxed, one will necessarily approach that mode of being and thus realize how the natural state is. {533}

### B) Disadvantages of Not Relaxing

These are the opposite of that. If one applies oneself forcefully and fails to relax, one's perception of how things are will become distorted, and one cannot but experience confusion and delusion.

### C) How to Relax

This has two aspects: (1) the method for relaxing and settling and, connected to that, (2) how to dispel obstacles.

### 1) Method for Relaxing and Settling

Abandon all worldly pursuits. Never have any expectations concerning the development of concentration or misgivings about its not developing. Do not have any intellectual concepts or analytical thoughts. Do not grasp at characteristics—likes and dislikes. The very thought "I must not conceptualize or analyze" compounds delusion, so let the mind relax in its own state. When one leaves that relaxation in its own state, there is a particular way in which it manifests. What is that way of manifesting? It is a state where there is no correcting and nothing to be done.[6] Relaxing without contriving the thought of not contriving is the very principle of the profound method.

Do not think, "What is the use of relaxing in a state without contrivance?" Just as one refers to someone who hits the target as a marksman, relaxing into that uncontrived state is called the "flow." Indeed, not contriving is the basis of all the teachings. If you wish to realize that state, sameness, you should rest quietly in loose relaxation without any mental involvement with an object. This is how it has been taught.

## 2) Dispelling Obstacles

Having settled in a relaxed state, when the movement and proliferation of thoughts ceases, one arrives at a complete absence of thoughts. If one tries to stop both, this is dumb meditation. Therefore, rather than settling in that, remedy it by arousing wakeful awareness and settling in a lofty state—aware, pure, limpid.

At that time, the manifestations of awareness arise, and one is unable to part with the clarity aspect that has arisen. This is the dualistic phenomenon of grasping at the characteristic of clarity. {534} So rather than resting in that state, remedy it by settling without even a hair's breadth of mixing with the lowly consciousness [that distinguishes this and that].

Then again, in the state of balanced awareness with no thoughts whatsoever, there arises a state of limpid bliss. This is called a spontaneous experience of bliss created by the mind. In that case, you should not rest in that either, but instead let the mind relax freely.

Even if you think you are not clinging to the experience of bliss that has occurred, it can act as a cause for being caught by the clinging of being unable to part with the bliss aspect. And when there is clinging, from subtle inner clinging and desire, the defilements of existence will grow. For it is said that by clinging to bliss, one will fall into the world of desire.

Even if you think you are not clinging to the experience of clarity that has occurred, it can act as a cause for being caught by the clinging of being unable to part with the clarity aspect. And when there is clinging, subtle inner clinging leads to karmic deeds with clinging, which produce existence in the world of form. For it is said that by clinging to clarity, one will err in the worlds of form.

Even if you think you are not clinging to the experience of no-thought that has occurred, it can act as a cause for being caught by the clinging of being unable to part with the no-thought aspect. And it is impossible for it not to become subtle inner clinging, as a result of which there are subtle karmic deeds with clinging, which again produce existence in the formless world. For it is said that by clinging to meditation on no-thought, one will migrate to the formless world.

Thus, if one has clinging to bliss, clarity, or no-thought, one will never attain liberation from the three worlds of existence. So it is very important, whatever manifests when you settle, not to cling to that manifestation, and to rest loosely in uncontrived awareness. Settling without anything to settle on is the great dwelling without settling. Dwelling without anywhere to dwell is the sublime meditation of not dwelling. Meditating without anyone meditating is the unsurpassable concentration of meditation. {535}

After that, in the middle resting vividly aware and at the end letting go completely are to be known from the procedure described above.

For beginners to meditate like this, as a result of following a great being, they will gradually equalize the highs and lows in a contrived way, and when they are on the verge of achieving evenness, like a balance that is properly calibrated for weighing gold, they will recognize the uncontrived innate state that is the nature of their own mind. It has been taught that this is introduced through one's being cared for with the blessings of a holy teacher, along with the nectar of their teachings, and through one's having accumulated merit by practicing properly over a long period.

### iii. Conclusion

The three things to be done in conclusion are (1) after being introduced, not separating from that for a long time; (2) incorporating appearances into the path; and (3) making everything one does beneficial for others. All three are necessary.

A) Recognizing the experience you have been introduced to in the main practice, you should practice applying it to whatever various appearances arise as soon as they arise.
B) In the state of recognition of your own nature as a result of being introduced to it, train in whatever arises—happiness or suffering—as being the display of thatness, without blocking it.
C) Dedicate the spontaneous freedom that results from recognizing your own nature, thinking, "May all sentient beings, numerous as the sky is vast, also be spontaneously free." And apply everything you do physically, verbally, and mentally to the welfare of others,

with compassion inseparable from the state free of clinging. So it has been taught. Greater detail on all this can be found in the practice manual.[7]

### b. Subsidiary Points

As a general rule, the introductions for the different kinds of beings—those with the highest, middling, or least faculties—were taught separately. Of these, for those with the highest faculties, there is the introduction to the three ways of resting naturally, the first of which is given in one verse:

> Wonder! One's own mind is, from the beginning, unborn.
> Nowhere else is there the cause for creating samsara and nirvana.
> Present in the center of one's own heart,
> It will be known through the teacher's instructions.

The meaning of this verse as follows. It is because one fails to realize the mind's true mode of being that one is bound in samsara. Realizing it makes one free. This is something to be marveled at, which is why {536} the text begins by saying "Wonder!"

What is it that is so marvelous? The mode of being of one's mind. From the very beginning, it is unborn; it does not exist as the essence of anything at all. It remains like that whether or not the buddhas of the three times have come, whether or not the teachers have introduced it, and whether or not people have realized it. If one does not realize it, one possesses the cause or seed that creates samsara. If one does realize it, one has the cause or seed that leads to nirvana. Its essence is not to be sought anywhere else than oneself. Its location is in the middle of one's own heart. There, whenever awareness arises, it can be known through the skillful means, the practice based on a holy teacher's instructions.

### 2. Incorporating Conceptual Thoughts on the Path

This is divided into two parts: (1) pith instructions for practitioners who progress gradually on the path, who are freed by means of symbols, and (2) pith instructions for those who gain accomplishment at a single stroke, who are freed by the power of blessings.

### a. Pith Instructions for Practitioners Who Progress Gradually on the Path

These comprise (1) those of the highest faculties, for whom thought movements cause them to awaken to their own state, and (2) those of middling and basic faculties, for whom thoughts are liberated by other means.

#### i. Those of the Highest Faculties

For beings of the highest faculties, there are two of the introductions to the three ways of resting naturally.

##### A) First, an Introduction to Being Mindful of Whatever Is Born and Whatever Arises

> Whatever is born is the natural state,
> So if one remembers this, mindful of whatever arises,
> It arises as emptiness.
> This, there is no doubt, is the king of yogas.

Just as the waves are not anything other than the ocean, whatever thoughts arise, they are not anything other than the natural state, the state that is free from coming and going. Therefore, if one remains mindful in recognizing everything that arises as one's own nature and does not forget this, even though those things appear in their different forms, they will appear as the essential essence, emptiness. There is no doubt that this is the king of yogas.

As for how one remains unforgettingly mindful, there are three aspects: first, to not forget the perceiver; in the middle, to not forget the apprehender; and finally, to not forget the agent who is attached. {537}

##### B) The Second Introduction

> All that arises is thatness,
> And that does not arise as anything.
> So, whatever is born is itself unborn;
> While unborn, it appears to be born.

All the thoughts that arise never move from thatness, the true natural state. That natural state, one's own mind, while not arising as anything that exists intrinsically, appears in every kind of way, like the reflection of the moon in water.

So, from the point of view of delusion, whatever is born appears clearly as if it were born. From the point of view of awareness, it is unborn. But the fact of its being unborn does not contradict its apparently being born, just as, while it is true that in a dream no child is born, this does not contradict the fact that from the point of view of the distortion that sleep brings, it may seem as if a child has been born.

It has also been taught that the above three verses correspond to the introduction to the unborn natural state in stages, the introduction to perfect purity instantaneously, and the introduction to their inseparable union.

#### ii. Those of Middling and Basic Faculties

This is divided into two: (1) introduction for beings with middling faculties and (2) introduction for beings with the most basic faculties.

#### A) Beings with Middling Faculties

The introduction for beings with middling faculties is divided into three: (1) introduction for the best beings with middling faculties by means of analogies of the three worlds; (2) introduction for the middling beings with middling faculties by means of outer, inner, and in-between analogies; and (3) introduction for the lowliest beings with middling faculties by means of the three direct approaches.

#### 1) The Best Beings with Middling Faculties

There are three analogies.

#### a) Analogy of a Wrathful Deity's Demeanor above the Earth

> Right leg stretched out, left leg bent, he makes the threatening
> gesture,
> And looking with the vajra view,

He keeps the supreme horse gently coming and going,
Experiencing the many as one.

His right leg stretched out signifies his skillful means, arousing the vast attitude of great compassion. His left leg drawn in signifies that his mind is turned inward by wisdom—emptiness. Holding his hand in the threatening gesture signifies recognizing the meditator, meditating on both emptiness and compassion. The vajra view is that of looking nonconceptually at the absence of duality—of something to be looked at and someone looking. Looking in that way, he trains in the gentle coming and going, in and out, of the supreme horse of the breath, on which thoughts are mounted, and dwells in the profound vajra recitation. By this means, the many suddenly arising thoughts are to be experienced as one taste in the natural state of the mind. {538}

### b) Analogy of the Nāga Kings Playing under the Earth

The feet rest in the great ocean.
The hands wander all over the earth.
The two eyes gaze into space.
The mind does not move anywhere.

When the nāga kings are playing on festive occasions, although their lower bodies are stretched out in the ocean, their upper bodies roam all over the earth.[8] Their eyes gaze at the sky, yet their minds do not move from their own abode. By analogy, their lower bodies placed in the great ocean signifies meditating on sustained calm with the mind remaining one-pointed in the uncontrived state. Their upper bodies roaming all over the earth signifies meditating on profound insight, enjoying the unobstructed display of manifestations appearing in multifarious ways while realizing them as the inseparability of appearance and emptiness. Their eyes gazing into space signifies looking undistractedly from the state of sustained calm and profound insight combined, enjoying everything while having no concepts whatsoever of doer or deed. Practicing in this way, at all times and in all situations, the mind should never move from its natural repose, free from activity, beyond concepts.

### c) Analogy of the King's Courtiers on the Earth

Like a beautiful woman's mirror, a powerful athlete,
A prisoner, a queen,
A sweeper, or a courtesan—
Keep the company of a single companion.

Here the analogy is divided into six: two analogies indicating the preparation, two indicating the main practice, and two indicating the conclusion.

Like a beautiful woman looking in a mirror, look again and again in the spotless mirror of awareness. Like a powerful athlete, destroy, through their self-liberation, all conceptual thoughts that apprehend attributes.

Like a convicted prisoner, never part, day or night, from the wish to be free from all the bonds of thoughts related to defilements. Like a king's queen, make all your physical, verbal, and mental activities a means by which your practice delights the king of gnosis, the nature of mind, {539} but without the slightest pretense in listening, explaining, and so on, like a common subject doing ordinary activities.

Like a sweeper, be diligent in clearing away, through their self-liberation, all thoughts related to virtue and nonvirtue, without any distinction between good and bad. Like a courtesan, develop the power of realization with regard to whatever arises, whatever appearances are encountered, but without being more interested in the great or the good.

This makes six analogies in all. "Keeping the company of a single companion" is an instruction to keep the company of the whole variety of appearances within a single mindfulness and develop the power of concentration.

### 2) Middling Beings with Middling Faculties

Middling beings with middling faculties are introduced by means of outer, inner, and in-between analogies, comprising three sections.

### a) Nine Outer Analogies

Like a tiger, lion, or elephant,
A camel, deer, or monkey,
Sandalwood, a tree, or human corpse—
Adept, do the practice of emptiness.

These nine analogies indicate three ways to give rise to concentration where it has not yet been developed; three branches that transform the development of concentration into the path; and three crucial points that enable one to travel the path to its end.

(1) In the beginning, by being courageous and not losing heart in overcoming all one's thoughts and defilements, one is like a tiger. (2) Later, one has no dread or fear whatever happens, regardless of outer and inner obstacles or imminent death, so one is like a lion. (3) In the end, in spite of all sorts of adverse circumstances such as sinking or wildness, one never turns back from the path, and one is like an elephant plunging into a river. These three analogies refer to the three methods that enable one to develop concentration.

(4) For the development [of concentration] to become the path of the Great Vehicle, one has to be particularly skilled in the methods for benefiting others, and the ability to benefit others depends on the deity and teacher, so in the intense longing of one's devotion, one is like a camel. (5) Because of one's wish to help others, compassion comes naturally, {540} and one is like a gentle deer. (6) By means of the methods for benefiting others, training whoever needs training, the various conceptual elaborations are carried on the path, and one is like a monkey.

The three crucial points that enable one to travel the path to its end are as follows: (7) Because [one's practice] possesses the three qualities of cooling the scorching fires of desire, dissipating the fever of the defilements, and being the best of all great teachings, it is like sandalwood. (8) Because the root is never shaken by adverse circumstances, the top does not bend with favorable circumstances, and it rises higher than all the majority of mind streams—with these three qualities, one's [mind] is like the trunk of a tree. (9) Because the faculty of grasping at attributes is blocked, attachment is dead, and one is not colored by acceptance and rejection—with these three qualities, one is like a human corpse.

Those who are adept at practicing the profound meaning, as indicated by these nine analogies, should do the practice of emptiness.

### b) Six In-Between Analogies

> Like a mountain torrent or a great lake,
> The mother of an only child, an elephant keeper,
> A snow mountain, or a pure crystal—
> If you are free of reference, the foundation has been laid.

(1) Three characteristics make one's [mind] like a rushing mountain torrent: the forceful production of many different thoughts, the lack of interruption of thoughts by no-thought or equanimity, and the mind's moving as fast as lightning. (2) Three qualities make one's mind like a great lake: all thought movements are of even taste in ultimate reality; one rests motionless in the state free of conceptual thoughts; and whatever thoughts concerning things outside may occur, they are pacified in the uncontrived state. These two analogies refer to the method that enables the mind to stay still.

(3) Three qualities make one like a mother with an only child: one cherishes genuine realization more than one's own heart; one can never bear to part from such realization; and {541} whatever arises through the manifesting power of realization, one does not regard it as a fault. (4) Three qualities make one like an elephant keeper: skill in reining in, relaxing, and alternating. These two analogies refer to branches that enable one to bring stability in meditation.

(5) On account of three qualities one is like a snow mountain: height, for one is not attached to lower views; coolness, as one is free from the scorching torments of dualistic apprehension; and immutability in the face of whatever misfortunes occur. (6) On account of three qualities one is like a pure crystal: purity, for one is free of the impurities of gross clinging; clarity, since one is not obscured by any outer objects or inner cognitive phenomena; and adaptability in being ready for transformation by such conditions as faith, compassion, and the path of skillful means. These two analogies are crucial points that enable one to perfect stability.

Through training in this way, one's mind will naturally become still without deliberately focusing on an object, and it is said that when this happens, the foundation of concentration has been laid.

### c) One Inner Analogy

> In the beginning, middle, and end, respectively,
> Phenomena have no root, essential nature, or function,
> Like a lamp in a dream.
> Through training in compassion, without moving, all is
>   accomplished.

Every one of the thoughts that arise is, to begin with, devoid of the root of the four conditions—namely, the objective, dominant, causal, and immediately preceding conditions—and it is therefore like a horse or elephant in a magical illusion. Then, its essential nature is similarly nonexistent, and apart from merely being labeled with a name, it is ultimately empty, like the child of a barren woman. Finally, it is devoid of function, like an ax in one's dream that is used to fell a tree in the dream. In short, all the phenomena that appear or are thought are similar to the appearances in a dream.

In what way are they similar? Although a lamp in a dream {542} appears to shine, the four causal factors or roots of the lamp (namely, the oil reservoir, wick, oil, and flame) are all devoid of intrinsic existence. The same is true of its essential nature (the shining red light) and its function (the dispersing of light), and the darkness that is dispelled. Likewise, all phenomena that appear or are thought like this are devoid of intrinsic existence: they are empty. If one trains in great compassion without moving from the knowledge of that, all concepts will be naturally undone and the pure activities will be spontaneously accomplished.

### 3) The Lowliest Beings with Middling Faculties

For the lowliest beings with middling faculties, who are introduced by means of three direct approaches, there are three introductions.

#### a) Introduction to Awakening the Uncontaminated Mind That Is to Be Accomplished by Means of Three Ways of Dealing Directly with Experiences

> The three aspects of purity and emptiness
> Regarding arising, remaining, and ceasing in going, coming, and staying
> Are great bliss, luminosity, and absence of thought.
> Thus do the wise settle in equipoise.

The aspects that have to be accomplished are bliss, clarity, and no-thought; the three freedoms from going, coming, and staying, which are the nature of the three aspects; and their mode of being, the three doors of perfect liberation—emptiness, absence of attributes, and absence of expectancy.

In that regard they are devoid of thoughts that go, come, and stay—they are emptiness, devoid of any thoughts for which there is, in the first place, a cause for their arising; in the middle, an essence that stays; and in the end, a result that ceases. They are pure as the three doors of perfect liberation. These correspond to untainted great bliss, intrinsic luminosity, and total absence of thought. Good practitioners with the pure eye of intelligence regarding the profound meaning should always settle in meditative equipoise in the state of realization of this resultant bliss, clarity, and absence of thought.

### b) Introduction to the Perfect Meditation That Enables One to Attain Accomplishment by Means of Three Direct Applications

By settling, first, with great compassion,
Looking continuously at that state without distraction,
And meditating on the deity and the teacher,
Practitioners will find rest.

First, the application of skillful means. Beginning with the thought, as boundless as the ocean, {543} of great compassion for beings as numerous as space is vast, one should promise to accomplish the limitless activities of the bodhisattvas' practice, which is as immense as Mount Meru.

Second, the application of wisdom. Recognizing, by observation and analysis with discerning wisdom, the nature of that same attitude and practice, watch constantly without distraction.

Third, the application of blessings. Meditate on the yidam deity and pray with the guru yoga. By means of these applications, practitioners will tire of their mental elaborations and find rest in the state of great bliss.

### c) Incorporating Conditions That Hinder Accomplishment into the Path by Means of Three Ways of Dealing Directly with Thoughts

Listen, child: whatever thoughts you have,
Because they neither bind nor free you here,
Do not be distracted, do not fabricate, leave things as they are—
Behold, find rest from weariness!

"Child" refers to [the author's] own spiritual heir, whom he is addressing familiarly, instructing them to listen without getting distracted. What they should listen to is as follows. First, what has to be incorporated into the path is all the various thoughts that arise in your mind stream. Second, the reason that it is possible to incorporate them into the path is that in the beginning those thoughts have not bound one here in the ocean of samsara, and in the end they do not free one. To make an analogy, when the reflection of the moon appears in a bowl of water, there is no binding of the reflection in the water bowl. And when the bowl is broken and the water flows away, there is no releasing of the moon's reflection. The moon in the sky has not changed in nature. Similarly, thoughts merely appear and there is no moving from their original state, ultimate reality. Third [is] how to practice taking thoughts as the path. First, settle without distraction, like a swordsman entering the fray. In the middle, be skilled in simply watching,[9] like an elephant keeper looking after an elephant. {544} In the end, be skilled in leaving things as they are, like a bird flying from the top of a ship.[10] These are as they appear in detail in the instruction manual.[11] This instruction is the very essence of this source text. It is an extraordinary means for making thoughts the path. This is why [the last line] begins with "Behold," an expression implying a sense of wonder, and instructs sentient beings, who from the very beginning have worn out their minds in the ocean of suffering that is samsara, to rely on this method for resting in the natural state, the intrinsically radiant expanse of reality.

### B) Beings with the Most Basic Faculties

For beings with the most basic faculties, there are three introductions. For the best of those with the most basic faculties, there is the introduction to three trainings that show that one's own awareness is free of contaminants. For middling beings with the most basic faculties, there is the introduction to cutting the root of dualistic grasping in relation to the three doors. For the lowliest of beings with the most basic faculties, there is the introduction to three affirmations and negations that dissolve concepts into the expanse of reality.

#### 1) The Best Beings with the Most Basic Faculties

The introduction for the best of those with the most basic faculties is given in three verses.

### a) Three Analogies That Show Same Taste in the Union of Sustained Calm and Profound Insight

Reflections and forms, echoes and sounds,
Real events and dreams—for the mind that thinks of these
Combine concentration and the meditation
Of connection and exhaustion.

If one carefully examines the mind that thinks of reflections and actual forms, echoes and actual sounds, direct perceptions with the sense organs and experiences in a dream, one will understand that while the appearance aspects such as reflections appear, the entities such as actual forms do not exist intrinsically: all phenomena, apart from merely appearing, have no true existence. Since all the objects that give rise to attachment and aversion do not exist intrinsically, the subjective consciousness does not have any true existence,[12] and if one recognizes this, all dualistic subject-object apprehension will naturally dissolve. On this basis one should practice the combined meditation of sustained calm, remaining one-pointed in concentration, {545} and of profound insight, by which causal relationships are established and the methods for eliminating conceptual attributes are exhausted. First, one begins with one-pointed concentration on the object of meditation. Then, by recognizing that one-pointedness as one's own nature, one leaves it as it is. Finally, by not conceptualizing even that, one should put an end to the mind's fine distinctions.

### b) Dispelling the Darkness of Obscurations by Lighting the Lamp of the Three Kinds of Superior Understanding

Discernment, absence of basis,
And constant, unbroken meditation
Are like gold, like fire, like space,
Understanding, dissolving, and purifying.

By using discerning wisdom to examine all the thought movements that one recognizes, one comes to understand that they are devoid of intrinsic existence. In the end, one understands that that discerning wisdom too is without any basis. And there is the superior understanding that comes from constant, unbroken meditation on the state in which the mental apprehension of a knower and something to be known is stilled. These three kinds of superior understanding that one should develop in one's mind stream are respectively like gold that has been flamed, cut, and polished; like fire that burns up fuel; and like the sky, which is unaltered by clouds, mist, and so forth. They enable one respectively to understand the exact mode of being of an apprehended object or something to be eliminated, to naturally dissolve the concepts of an apprehending subject or a remedy, and to purify the two adventitious obscurations along with habitual tendencies.

### c) Opening the Door of Precious Qualities by Awakening the Gnosis of the Three Aspects of Appearance

> Nonappearance, appearance, and circumstantial appearance
> Are like space, a mirror, and a pure crystal.
> This is realized by means of concentration,
> Gnosis, and the power of memory.

The ground is naturally devoid of appearance;[13] yet, because of the path, there is appearance; and the result, brought about through transformation by conditions, is appearance in all kinds of different ways. These three aspects of appearance are illustrated by the following analogies, respectively: the sky, which is devoid of intrinsic nature; a mirror, in which reflections appear, and a pure crystal, in which, because of conditions, all sorts of colors appear. {546}

Through one's making an experience of this and meditating on it, a treasury of precious qualities is opened. As a result of one's being awakened into the uncontrived state of nonappearance, one dwells one-pointedly in that state and the door of concentration is opened. From one's being awakened to appearances being one's own self-experience, self-experience dissolves into itself and the door of gnosis is opened. And from one's being awakened to circumstantial appearances—the appearances of dependent origination—interdependent connections are purified and the door of the power of memory is opened. Thus, from the ground of concentration, the essence of gnosis is accomplished. And through the power of memory, one holds these inseparably. Because of that, ultimately there arises in one's mind stream the realization, respectively, of the body of truth, the body of perfect enjoyment, and the body of manifestation.

### 2) Middling Beings with the Most Basic Faculties

The introduction for middling beings with the most basic faculties is given in three verses.

#### a) Getting Rid of the Grasped Object and the Dust of Distraction in Relation to the Door of the Body's Five Senses

> Perception, in equipoise, is luminosity,
> At which time perception has not arisen.
> Remaining one-pointed, utterly free of concepts,
> One is freed of the dust of distraction.

When one perceives the five sense objects through the door of the five sense organs, if one settles in a loosely relaxed and blank equipoise, in the natural state of the perceiver, the appearing object is not blocked and there arises a luminosity in which there is no grasping at the object. At that time, whatever one perceives is, in truth, not perceived, and the reason is that dualistic clinging to it has not arisen. By resting one-pointedly in that utterly nonconceptual luminosity, one is freed of the dust of distraction by conceptual attributes.

#### b) Killing the Grasping Mind in Relation to the Door of Speech, the Subtle Winds

> Wherever the wind goes, the mind goes too.
> But if you hold it prisoner inside the body's house,
> You'll put to death the ordinary mind;
> Without a mount, where can the mind go?

The mind[14] is the rider of the subtle wind, so wherever the subtle wind goes, the mind goes and stays. By applying the vase exercise in the central channel of the dwelling place that is one's body, one holds the subtle wind prisoner, {547} and one [can] stab the ordinary mind[15] with the weapon of recognition of one's own nature, putting it to death in the expanse free of deliberate activity. Thus, without the subtle wind to ride on, where can the mind go? It will be like a cripple and remain where it is.

### c) Destroying the Habitual Tendencies of Both an Apprehending Subject and Apprehended Object by Realizing the Nature of Conceptual Thought in Relation to the Door of the Mind

> The nature of all is uncontrived:
> All thoughts depend on conditions.
> If one knows the three natures,
> Thoughts make thoughts themselves disappear.

The nature of all conceptual thoughts is nothing other than the essence that is the uncontrived natural state. All conceptual thoughts arise in dependence on conditions. If one properly understands the true state of the three natures, as soon as thoughts arise, they make the thoughts themselves intrinsically nonexistent. What are the three natures? The uncontrived state, the nature of the essence; appearance in multiple forms, the nature of conditions; and the single taste, the nature of nonduality.

## 3) The Lowliest of Beings with the Most Basic Faculties

The introduction for the lowliest of beings with the most basic faculties is made in three ways.

### a) Dissolving the Concepts of Establishment and Refutation into the Expanse of Reality through the Practice of Meditation on Space

> Existence when we perceive
> And nonexistence when we scrutinize are just concepts.
> Nothing whatsoever here exists.
> O child, meditate on space!

When one perceives knowable objects, one postulates that they exist. And when one scrutinizes them with wisdom, one establishes their nonexistence. These are nothing other than conceptual imputations. But here in the fundamental nature of the mind itself, from the beginning, there is nothing whatsoever that exists. Therefore, O child, instructs the author, addressing us familiarly, meditate on space. There are three ways to meditate on space. The outer way is to stare at the sky, unobscured by anything. The inner way is to settle the rational mind on the uncontrived, spacelike state of mind. And the secret way is to meditate on space without any outer or inner references, as it is. {548}

### b) Dissolving the Concepts of Absence of Conditions into the Expanse of Reality through the Practice of Leaving-As-It-Is

> Camphor and its smell are interrelated:
> One cannot have one without the other.
> Likewise, conditions and absence of conditions
> Are not separate, so meditate leaving things as they are.

Camphor and its smell both depend on each other: they can be separated as aspects, but their nature is inseparable. Without camphor, there cannot be the smell of camphor. And if the smell of camphor is absent, camphor too must be absent, nor would one ever think that it is present. In the same way, with regard to the nature of the mind, there are two aspects: delusion, with its adventitious conditioned perceptions, and gnosis, which is unconditioned, spontaneous, fresh. But these two aspects are not distinct and separate; they are indistinguishable. So, instructs the author, meditate leaving things just as they are.

There are three ways in which one meditates leaving things as they are. Settle in the fundamental, uncontrived, fresh state, as it is. Whatever thoughts arise as its display, leave them as they are; let them go as they arise. And when they have just arisen, as they are, the unborn nature, experience it as the same taste in being unborn, without having any concept of there being anything to arise.

### c) Dissolving Concepts of Sameness and Not Sameness in the Expanse [of Reality] through the Practice of Killing Conceptual Thoughts

> The mind of sameness brings movement to an end;
> Mindfulness binds unsameness.
> At that time resting in equipoise, free from those,
> Puts to death conceptual thoughts.

Inwardly, the mind of the great all-encompassing sameness brings to cessation momentary mental movements. Externally, the rope of mindfulness of the instructions on the great sameness also enable one to bind the many different[16] phenomena and varied perceptual experiences such as mirages. By one's experiencing things in this way, there comes a time when there is no grasping at either sameness or unsameness. This is the great equipoise, which enables one to kill all conceptual thoughts. There are three methods for killing conceptual thoughts: killing them by being mindful of ordinary thoughts; killing them by recognizing the thought of mindfulness as one's own nature; and killing them with the sameness of the thought of recognition. {549}

### b. Pith Instructions for Those Who Gain Accomplishment at a Single Stroke, Who Are Freed by the Power of Blessings

These pith instructions are given in four verses.

#### i. Training in Bringing Thoughts to an End by Means of the Purifying Vase Empowerment

> Wash, and wear the clothes of space;
> Perform the fire offering of conceptual thoughts;
> And on the bank, purify the ashes of thoughts
> With water and wind together.

Outwardly, wash with the water from the vase. Inwardly, purify yourself with mantras such as the *svabhāva* mantra. Secretly, cleanse yourself with the knowledge that in the ultimate nature of all phenomena there is not as much as a sesame seed's worth of impurity. Then, training in the state of naked awareness, dress in the clothes of space, free of even the odor of concepts of purity. Meditating that conceptual thoughts are devoid of any basis, make the fire offering in which they are burned up in spontaneous liberation. And on the banks of bliss, clarity, and no-thought (experience, gnosis, and concentration, respectively), simultaneously clean away even the ashes of subtle thoughts and tendencies with the water of concentration and the wind of gnosis. Thus does the author instruct us.

### ii. Mastering the Samaya Mudrā by Means of the Secret Consort Empowerment

Container and contents, winds and mind stream, the fixed and the motile;
Sky, sun, moon, and Rāhu;
Firefly, rain, and bee—with these analogies
One masters the samaya mudrā.

The body and subtle winds are like a container and its contents, for the winds depend on the body and dwell in it. What accompanies the wind is the mind stream. Thus the body (mentioned first in the root verse) is fixed, while the wind and mind (mentioned second) are motile. The sky is the naturally luminous expanse. The sun is the fire of tummo, the moon is kuṇḍa,[17] and Rāhu is the union of wind and mind. The experience of luminosity that is produced from that is [like] a firefly. These and others are the signs that appear. Rain refers to no-thought: like heavy rain falling uninterruptedly from the clouds, no thought arises through the manifesting power of bliss and luminosity combined. Bliss is a bee: like a bee extracting the essence of honey, bliss arises from experiencing the union of luminosity and no-thought. {550} Through the gnosis of the secret empowerment, exemplified by these, one will master the channels, winds, and essences—the samaya mudrā.

### iii. Tasting the Flavor of Coemergent [Wisdom] by Means of the Empowerment of Wisdom and Gnosis

In the multicolored flower of the mind
One takes the essence of the four joys:
When one experiences the innate,
The mind, like a person, is satiated.

The multicolored flower of the mind refers to the outer, inner, secret, and thatness mudrās. By making use of these correctly, one takes the essence of the four joys—joy, supreme joy, extraordinary joy, and innate joy. Based on the experience of the coemergent melting bliss, the practitioner's mind, illustrated here by analogy with a person, is satiated with gnosis.

### iv. Observing the Spontaneous Conduct of a Wanderer by Means of the Empowerment of the Manifestation of Mudrā

Bind the body, speech, and mind
With the mudrās of body, wind, and the great channel.
There will be no impediment to attaining warmth.
Do not be fixed in conduct.

"Body" refers to the pure body, the visualization of the deity's body; the sublime body considered as an illusion; and the perfect body purified as clear light.

"Wind" [is of three kinds]: Through the ability to apply the activities to the moving wind, one accomplishes the outer and inner summoning and drawing, and so on. Through the ability to hold the stable wind like a vajra, one is immune to harm from spirits. And when one holds the indestructible wind, one is able to develop the gnosis of the union of bliss and emptiness.

"Channel" [is again of three kinds]: The great illusory channel is the trained central channel. The great space channel refers to meditation on the ultimate state of all phenomena. And the great inconceivable channel is the realization of the expanse of reality.

If one seals and binds one's body, speech, and mind with these mudrās, there will be no impediment to one's attaining "warmth," the signs of progress. There are four such signs: bliss, clarity, no-thought, and equal taste. Having attained these, one should not be one-sided and fixed in one's conduct, meaning that {551} one should maintain the limitless and impartial activities pervading all space by conducting oneself without concepts.

## C. Conclusion

The conclusion is divided into two: (1) a statement marking the completion of the text and (2) the translator's colophon.

### 1. Statement Marking the Completion of the Text

This completes the song of realization pointing out the authentic state of thatness, called *A Pith Instruction in Twenty-Five Verses That Enables Practitioners to Find Rest in Their Own Minds.*

This text is called "a pith instruction in twenty-five verses that enables practitioners" who apply their minds to the profound meaning of the union of skillful means and wisdom "to find rest in own their minds," wearied by the multifarious elaborations of dualistic apprehension. Its subject is the method for pointing out the authentic state of thatness, the actual condition of all phenomena. And what conveys this is a dohā—a song of realization—for it does so in an uncontrived or effortless manner. This source text of vajra verses has been taught in full, with no omissions, so it is now completed.

## 2. Translator's Colophon

> These verses that Lord Avalokiteshvara gave in person to the great master of yogis who had attained accomplishment, Shrī Jagatamitrānanda, were translated by him and the translator Jampa Pal in a summerhouse in the Ambara forest at the golden pagoda of Shrī Pashupati.

"Lord" signifies the Sanskrit word *ārya*, meaning "noble and exalted," a term applied to one's yidam deity. Who is this referring to? To him who is universally known as Avalokiteshvara, so called because he is foremost among the bodhisattvas, the buddhas' heirs, constantly watching over all beings with the eye of great compassion.[18] This dohā in twenty-five vajra verses is consistent with the summary of the whole content of the *Perfection of Wisdom* into twenty-five doors of concentration in the Dharmodgata chapter.[19] Avalokiteshvara gave it in person to someone who had attained the supreme accomplishment, the Great Seal, namely the great master of yogis Shrī Jagatamitrānanda (Glorious Joyful Teacher of Beings), [who is described] as a "yogi" because he applied his mind to the meaning of union, as a "master" because he was the chief of such yogis, and as "great" because he attained the noble levels. {552} Mitrayogin was given the name Glorious Joyful Teacher of Beings because during his birth as a prince, when father and son met in the midst of a great crowd, he delighted all beings, divine and human. The translator, [who came from] the aristocratic lineage of Nup Namkhai Nyingpo, was commonly known as Jampa Pal. He and Mitrayogin translated the original Sanskrit text into Tibetan in the summerhouse of Parpati in the sacred focal point known as the forest of Ambara at the golden pagoda of Shrī Pashupati in Nepal.

For this source text there have appeared the detailed and concise commentaries by the great Tropu Lotsawa, a text by the omniscient Butön Rinpoche correlating it with the sutras and tantras, and a few incidental explanations. Of these, I have summarized the essential meaning of Tropu Lotsawa's writings, mainly drawing on the word-by-word commentary. These extraordinary instructions have come through the oral tradition of the incomparable leader of accomplished beings. You should understand that to ascertain their meaning by hearing them and reflecting on them and to put them into practice by meditating on them is the very best way to make full use of one's precious human body with its unique freedoms and advantages.

Through the virtuous deed of having condensed
The commentary on *Resting in the Nature of Mind*,
Sublime among all the instructions on the Great Seal,
May all beings attain the supreme union state.

The renunciate who has given up busying himself with extensive learning, Khyentse Wangpo, the joyful servant of the teacher Mañjughoṣha, summarized the thinking of the ancient commentary without sullying it with confusing elements of his own invention, writing it in the form of notes. May it serve to increase virtue and excellence.

# 27. Correlations between the Root Verses of the Great Seal Text *Resting in the Nature of Mind* and the Scriptural Sources in the Sutras and Tantras[1]

Buddhist writers have always laid great emphasis on scriptural authority by quoting extensively from the sutras and tantras. In this way they can authenticate their work and demonstrate that their explanations have not simply been made up but are based on original sources. In this text, the omniscient Butön correlates the different verses of *Resting in the Nature of Mind* with passages from *The Perfection of Wisdom in Eight Thousand Lines* on the one hand and a selection of tantras on the other.

{554}
The introductions in *Resting in the Nature of Mind* were taught in the Dharmodgata chapter in *The Perfection of Wisdom in Eight Thousand Lines*.[2]

> **Wonder! One's own mind is, from the beginning, unborn.**
> **Nowhere else is there the cause for creating samsara and nirvana.**
> **Present in the center of one's own heart,**
> **It will be known through the teacher's instructions.**

The point [expressed here is to be found in the following line from the Dharmodgata chapter]:

It is thus: the perfection of wisdom is the same inasmuch as all things are the same.

Likewise,

**Whatever is born is the natural state,**
**So if one remembers this, mindful of whatever arises,**
**It arises as emptiness.**
**This, there is no doubt, is the king of yogas.**

[equates with:]

The perfection of wisdom is void inasmuch as all things are void.

**All that arises is thatness,**
**And that does not arise as anything.**
**So, whatever is born is itself unborn;**
**While unborn, it appears to be born.**

The perfection of wisdom is unmoving inasmuch as all things are unmoving.

**Right leg stretched out, left leg bent, he makes the threatening gesture,**
**And looking with the vajra view, {555}**
**He keeps the supreme horse gently coming and going,**
**Experiencing the many as one.**

The perfection of wisdom does not create conceit inasmuch as all things do not create conceit.

**The feet rest in the great ocean.**
**The hands wander all over the earth.**
**The two eyes gaze into space.**
**The mind does not move anywhere.**

The perfection of wisdom is devoid of arrogance inasmuch as all things are devoid of arrogance.

**Like a beautiful woman's mirror, a powerful athlete,**
**A prisoner, a queen,**
**A sweeper, or a courtesan,**
**Keep the company of a single companion.**

The perfection of wisdom is of a single flavor inasmuch as all things are of a single flavor.

**Like a tiger, lion, or elephant,**
**A camel, deer, or monkey,**
**Sandalwood, a tree, or human corpse—**
**Adept, do the practice of emptiness.**

The perfection of wisdom is limitless inasmuch as all things are limitless. {556}

**Like a mountain torrent or a great lake,**
**The mother of an only child, an elephant keeper,**
**A snow mountain, or a pure crystal—**
**If you are free of reference, the foundation has been laid.**

The perfection of wisdom is unborn inasmuch as all things are unborn.

**In the beginning, middle, and end, respectively,**
**Phenomena have no root, essential nature, or function,**
**Like a lamp in a dream.**
**Through training in compassion, without moving, all is accomplished.**

The perfection of wisdom is unimpeded inasmuch as all things are unimpeded.

**The three aspects of purity and emptiness**
**Regarding arising, remaining, and ceasing in going, coming, and staying**
**Are great bliss, luminosity, and absence of thought.**
**Thus do the wise settle in equipoise.**

The perfection of wisdom is limitless inasmuch as the sky is limitless.

**By settling, first, with great compassion,**
**Looking continuously at that state without distraction,**
**And meditating on the deity and the teacher,**
**Practitioners will find rest.**

The perfection of wisdom is limitless inasmuch as the ocean is limitless.

**Listen, child: whatever thoughts you have,**
**Because they neither bind nor free you here,**
**Do not be distracted, do not fabricate, leave things as they are—**
**Behold, find rest from weariness!**

The perfection of wisdom is multifaceted inasmuch as Mount Meru is multifaceted.

**Reflections and forms, echoes and sounds,**
**Real events and dreams—for the mind that thinks of these,**
**Combine concentration and the meditation**
**Of connection and exhaustion.**

The perfection of wisdom is devoid of conceptual thought inasmuch as the sky is devoid of conceptual thought.

**Discernment, absence of basis,**
**And constant, unbroken meditation**
**Are like gold, like fire, like space,**
**Understanding, dissolving, and purifying.**

The perfection of wisdom is limitless inasmuch as form is limitless. {557}

**Nonappearance, appearance, and circumstantial appearance**
**Are like space, a mirror, and a pure crystal.**

**This is realized by means of concentration,**
**Gnosis, and the power of memory.**

Similarly, the perfection of wisdom is limitless inasmuch as feeling, perception, conditioning factors, and consciousness are limitless.

**Perception, in equipoise, is luminosity,**
**At which time perception has not arisen.**
**Remaining one-pointed, utterly free of concepts,**
**One is freed of the dust of distraction.**

The perfection of wisdom is limitless inasmuch as the earth element is limitless.

**Wherever the wind goes, the mind goes too.**
**But if you hold it prisoner inside the body's house,**
**You'll put to death the ordinary mind;**
**Without a mount, where can the mind go?**

Similarly, the perfection of wisdom is limitless inasmuch as the water element, fire element, and wind element [are limitless].

**The nature of all is uncontrived:**
**All thoughts depend on conditions.**
**If one knows the three natures,**
**Thoughts make thoughts themselves disappear.**

The perfection of wisdom is limitless inasmuch as the space element [is limitless].

**Existence when we perceive**
**And nonexistence when we scrutinize are just concepts.**
**Nothing whatsoever here exists.**
**O child, meditate on space!**

The perfection of wisdom is limitless inasmuch as the consciousness element is limitless.

**Camphor and its smell are interrelated:**
**One cannot have one without the other.**
**Likewise, conditions and absence of conditions**
**Are not separate, so meditate leaving things as they are.**

The perfection of wisdom is sameness inasmuch as the vajra-like dharma is sameness.[3]

**The mind of sameness brings movement to an end;**
**Mindfulness binds unsameness.**
**At that time resting in equipoise free from those**
**Puts to death conceptual thoughts. {558}**

The perfection of wisdom lacks differentiation inasmuch as all things lack differentiation.

**Wash, and wear the clothes of space;**
**Perform the fire offering of conceptual thoughts;**
**And on the bank, purify the ashes of thoughts**
**With water and wind together.**

The perfection of wisdom is devoid of reference inasmuch as all things are devoid of reference.

**Container and contents, winds and mind stream, the fixed and the motile;**
**Sky, sun, moon, and Rāhu;**
**Firefly, rain, and bee—with these analogies**
**One masters the samaya mudrā.**

The perfection of wisdom is indestructible inasmuch as all things are indestructible.

**In the multicolored flower of the mind**
**One takes the essence of the four joys:**

**When one experiences the innate,**
**The mind, like a person, is satiated.**

The perfection of wisdom is without activity inasmuch as all things are without activity.

**Bind the body, speech, and mind**
**With the mudrās of body, wind, and the great channel.**
**There will be no impediment to attaining warmth.**
**Do not be fixed in conduct.**

The perfection of wisdom is inconceivable inasmuch as all things are inconceivable—thus should it be known.

Thus is it stated in the sutra.

## Correlations between the Root Verses of the Great Seal Text *Resting in the Nature of Mind* and Scriptural Sources in the Tantras

"Wonder" [finds its source in] the *Later Guhyasamāja Tantra* [in which it is said]:

Wonder, this exceedingly great marvel;
Wonder, peace beyond the senses;
Wonder, the stream of samsara purified;
Wonder, sublimely beyond sorrow.[4]

**From the beginning, unborn.**

In the *Guhyasamāja* we read:

Free of all substantiality,
The aggregates, constituents, senses-and-fields, {559}
Form, and apprehender all eliminated,
Phenomena, devoid of self, are sameness,
So one's own mind, unborn from the very beginning,
Is the nature of emptiness.[5]

**The cause for creating samsara and nirvana.**

In the *Saṃpuṭa Tantra* it is said:

> Overcome by the darkness of the many thoughts filling it,
> Crazed and darting like lightning,
> Tainted by the stubborn stains of attachment and the rest—
> That mind, the Vajra Holder said, is samsara.
> Luminous by nature, free from conceptual thoughts,
> Unstained by attachment and the like,
> Devoid of dualistic apprehension—that mind, supremely brave,
> He spoke of as being sublime nirvana.[6]

**Nowhere else is there . . .**

The *Saṃpuṭa Tantra* says:

> That which is the cause of the manifold aggregate of suffering
> Is not the slightest bit different from this.
> That which is the source of infinite happiness
> Does not go somewhere other than that.
> Those who wish to bring to an end all suffering without exception,
> Who wish to attain the supreme bliss of perfect buddhahood,
> Should make the mind stable and examine it assiduously
> And put an end to its substantial nature.
> As long as people's minds are obscured by the thick veil of the darkness of conceptualization,
> There is no end to suffering.
> Once they are divested of it,
> There is no difference from vast happiness.
> Sameness, the ultimate point of all that delights the noble ones,
> Ends all that. Therefore, increase your own efforts
> And watch them become accessories to it.[7]

**Present in the center of one's own heart.**

The *Saṃpuṭa Tantra* says:

Thatness is transcendent wisdom, {560}
Taking form in relative aspects.
Thatness transcends place;
It is present in all beings' hearts.[8]

**It will be known through the teacher's instructions.**

[The same tantra states:]

**Since it dwells within,**
**It will be found through the teacher's instructions.**[9]

And in the *Tantra of the Ornament of the Vajra Essence* we read:

Just as, with a lamp inside a pot,
The light is not visible outside,
But when the vase is broken,
After that the lamp will shine,
So too when the vase of one's body
Is shattered by the teacher's words,
They connect us to lamp-like thatness
And reveal the ultimate.[10]

**Whatever is born is the natural state.**

The *Guhyasamāja* states:

Since these things are unborn,
There are no phenomena and no nature of phenomena.
Like space, there is no self.
This is how enlightenment is shown.[11]

**All that arises is thatness.**

The *Guhyasamāja* states:

The nature of phenomena is clear light,
Pure from the beginning, like the sky.

There is no enlightenment, no realization.
This is how enlightenment is shown.[12]

**Right leg stretched out, left leg bent, he makes the threatening gesture.**

The *Saṃpuṭa Tantra* states:

Those with compassion
Should never turn their backs on sentient beings.
"Beings exist, they don't exist"—
Never should they reason like this.
The nature of freedom from elaboration
Is widely known as wisdom.
Compassion is a wish-fulfilling gem,
Benefiting all without exception.
Wisdom dwelling in nonconceptuality
And the great nonconceptual compassion
Are innate to the mind,
Like space in space.[13]

**The feet rest in the great ocean.** {561}

The *Prophecy of the Intent* states:

Sustained calm is called the father.
Profound insight is explained as being the mother.
From them, knowledge of suchness is born.
Peace is the yogi's nourishment.[14]

**Keep the company of a single companion.**

The *Saṃpuṭa Tantra* states:

All the forms one sees,
The sounds one hears,
The words and jokes one tells,
The tasty things one eats,

And all the acts one perpetrates
Will constantly arise as the practice
Of a yogi who recognizes thatness
Without letting the mind proceed elsewhere.[15]

**Adept, do the practice of emptiness.**

The *Saṃpuṭa Tantra* states:

There are no aspects, no doubts,
No desire, and no evil.
Free from concepts of beginning and end,
The meditation of the wise is like space.[16]

**If you are free of reference, the foundation has been laid.**

The *Guhyasamāja* states:

There is no thing, no meditation;
It is not meditation on something to be meditated.
Thus, since it is substantial and insubstantial,
The meditation is devoid of reference.[17]

**Like a lamp in a dream.**

The *Guhyasamāja* states:

All phenomena are like a dream.
In essence, they are unborn.
By nature they are pure.
Regarding that,
The illusory vajra was taught.[18]

**Regarding arising, remaining, and ceasing in going, coming, and staying [. . . ]**

[*The Prophecy of the Intent* states:]

Thus, going, coming, and staying
Do not exist in the slightest.
With the practice of staying without a place,
Staying is the nature of the sky.[19]

**Looking continuously at that state without distraction.**

The *Tantra of the Ornament of the Vajra Essence* states:

Scrutinize the most profound state
In going, sitting, and resting.
For those who know the path of the gnosis of luminosity,
With this application of concentration
By a yogi who has understood reality, {562}
The jewel of the mind will become stable.[20]

**Do not be distracted, do not fabricate, leave things as they are.**

The *Tantra of the Ornament of the Vajra Essence* declares:

After engaging in that way,
As long as the mind does not weary
It is good to keep the mind in equipoise,
And one should train assiduously in that.
After that, if one combines it
With whatever conduct one pleases,
Characterized by the slight opening of the eyes,
One will attain vast enlightenment.
Until that happens,
Whether one is laughing, speaking, attracting,
Or sometimes dancing,
Hold on to the mind of meditation.
A mantrika who keeps that sacred commitment
And has no concepts
Will abandon fixed schedules
And attain unsurpassable enlightenment.[21]

**Reflections and forms, echoes and sounds [. . .]**

The *Prophecy of the Intent* states:

> Echoes, reflections,
> Magical illusions, mirages,
> And likewise, the moon in water and dreams—
> All phenomena are like them.[22]

**Discernment, absence of basis** [. . .]

The *Prophecy of the Intent* states:

> Take an example, fortunate child:
> A hand drill and hearth board
> And the movement of a person's hands—
> From these conditions smoke will rise,
> And thence will fire appear as well.23
> But in the hand drill and the rest,
> Examined individually,
> There is no fire present anywhere.[24]

**Nonappearance, appearance, and circumstantial appearance.**

The *Awakening of Vārāhī* states:

> Resting in the state of absence of appearance,
> Truly rely on nonappearance.
> In phenomena that are not examined
> There are no phenomena and no nature of
> phenomena.
> Interdependent phenomena are like space, {563}
> Without substance and without attributes.[25]

**Perception, in equipoise, is luminosity** [. . .]

The *Saṃpuṭa Tantra* declares:

> With the yoga of not meditating
> On the nature of the sense organ

And its sphere,
One always achieves perfect meditation.[26]

**Wherever the wind goes, the mind goes too.**

The *Prophecy of the Intent* states:

The winds in subtle form
Mix fully with the consciousnesses
And emerge through the gates of the senses
To then engage with their objects.[27]

**The nature of all is uncontrived.**

The *Tantra of the Ornament of the Vajra Essence* declares:

Phenomena are by nature radiant light,
Pure and unclouded from the very first.
There are no beings, no life,
No buddhahood, no enlightenment.
The mind of enlightenment,
Appearing like a dream or illusion, is constant.[28]

**O child, meditate on space!**

*The Supreme* states:

Everything has the characteristics of space,
And space has no characteristics.
Through union with space,
All is perceived as supreme sameness.[29]

[...] **Are not separate, so meditate leaving things as they are.**

The *Saṃvarodaya Tantra* states:

Likewise, that mind is devoid of mind.
To those who have realized the one and the multitudinous

And abandoned distinctions of substantial and insubstantial
The nature of innate joy is clear.[30]

**Puts to death conceptual thoughts.**

The *Saṃpuṭa Tantra* declares:

The great ignorance of conceptual thoughts
Is what makes one fall into the ocean of samsara.
If one abides in the concentration of no-thought,
One will become free of impurities, like the sky.[31]

**Perform the fire offering of conceptual thoughts.**

The *Vajraḍāka* states:

Consider that with the wind of activity
The wisdom fire sets ablaze the twigs of the aggregates and so forth
In this mandala of the navel. {564}
The fire of Brahmā dwells at the junction.
The filling ladle is said to be the lalanā channel.
The mouth of the pouring ladle is the rasanā channel.
At the end of the jeweled vajra handle,
As far as one's own vajra,
The skull is the container for the fire offerings.
The offerings to be burned are the whole of [phenomena].
Expressed successively in this way,
The unsurpassable fire offering
Is explained to you, goddess.[32]

**One takes the essence of the four joys.**

The *Saṃpuṭa Tantra* states:

The first joy is the ḍāka.
Supreme joy is the yoginī.33
The joy of extreme bliss is certainty of everything.
From the means to that bliss comes knowledge of everything.[34]

**One masters the samaya mudrā.**

The *Saṃpuṭa Tantra* states:

> Having found a mudrā, lovely-eyed,
> In the first bloom of youth,
> Take her as a wisdom consort,
> And after training in the stages of refuge,
> Proclaim all the stages
> Of the secret, mantra, and tantra.
> Through sound or tongue upon the lower path,
> Thus penetrate the true nature on top.
> Knowing the aspects of all, practice this in various ways.
> With the two stages, [she who] possesses
> Earrings, a girdle, necklace,
> Anklets, and bracelets
> Will thus bestow sublime accomplishment.[35]

**Do not be fixed in conduct.**

The *Saṃpuṭa Tantra* states:

> There is no eating anything here,
> Nor is there anything to eat
> Or anyone eating—all is free.
> In this meditation on the ultimate,
> It is said there is no accomplisher,
> No praising anything,
> Not the slightest rejection.
> There is not even a teacher in the mind.
> View everything as like a gandharvas' city,
> Like a magical illusion or mirage,
> Like the moon's stolen reflection in water,
> Or like playing in a dream.[36]

For each of the root verses of *Resting in the Nature of Mind*, the monk Rinchen Drup has shown the corresponding scriptural source in the tantras. {565}

*sarvadvā maṅgalaṃ*

# 28. Notes on *Resting in the Nature of Mind*[1]

Jamyang Khyentse Wangchuk (1524–1568) was a disciple of Tsarchen Losal Gyatso (1502–1566), whose oral teachings on Mitrayogin's source text he recorded in these *Notes*. Rather than simply commenting on the meaning of the twenty-five verses, these teachings provide a guide for actually putting their essential message into practice.

I pay homage and take refuge for all time in the presence of the venerable vajra holder Losal Gyatso Drakpa Gyaltsen Palzangpo, essence of all the buddhas of the three times. I pray to him to care for me with his great love.

The mahāsiddha called Mitrayogin, who was a manifestation of noble Avalokiteshvara, practiced for twelve years, at the end of which the noble Great Compassionate One Khasarpāṇi, on a wooden mandala as smooth as a mirror, revealed himself in person. Gathering the entire contents of the *Perfection of Wisdom* into twenty-five points of access comprising methods by which the minds of all sentient beings, worn out by suffering since time without beginning, would find rest, he recited a song of realization of twenty-five vajra verses. On hearing it, Mitrayogin attained the supreme accomplishment. From this lord of yogis, the great Tropu Lotsawa received these pith instructions in full and put them into practice. The way to practice these instructions, known as *Resting in the Nature of Mind*, consists of three sections: (1) preliminaries; (2) main practice; and (3) conclusion. The first of these is again divided into three: (1) common; (2) uncommon; and (3) specific preliminaries.

## I. Preliminaries

### A. Common Preliminaries

Sit on a comfortable seat in the meditation posture and discontinue [the activities of] your body, speech, and mind and relax, leaving these in their natural state. Then, consider that the place where you are is a vast pure realm, produced through the spontaneous manifestation of gnosis. In its center {566} is a lofty, broad precious throne supported by lions. On it is a gleaming multicolored lotus, and in its center a full-moon disk. It is encircled by countless other jeweled thrones, together with their lotuses and moons, which are at a slightly lower level.

On the central throne is your root teacher, appearing as he or she is, youthful, sitting cross-legged in the bodhisattva posture, with a leg slightly stretched out in the posture of royal ease or youthful play. On the row of thrones outside are seated the teachers of the *Resting* lineage, appearing as they are, from Lord Khasarpāṇi to the great Jetsun Doringpa,[2] encircling the root teacher clockwise, like a string of pearls. On the successive rows of thrones outside them are the root and lineage teachers of the three times with whom you have a connection; the assemblies of yidam mandala deities; the buddhas of the body of perfect enjoyment; the sacred dharma in the form of volumes piled up like a mountain and displayed inside their silk wrappings; the sangha of those who have adopted the ways of the bodhisattvas, solitary realizers, and listeners; and the ḍākas and ḍākinīs and dharma protectors, all disposed in a circle clockwise.

With you, in the center of the ground directly in front of them, are your father on your right and your mother on your left. In front of you are demons and enemies headed by the wicked Māra, and all around, all the sentient beings of the six realms along with the beings who are in the intermediate state. Thinking that all of you are using your body, speech, and mind to take refuge together, recite aloud the six-line refuge prayer as occurs in our particular lineage:

> I and all sentient beings who have been my old mothers,
> numerous as the sky is vast, from now on and until we attain the heart of enlightenment, take refuge in the glorious holy teachers, my root teacher and the teachers of the lineage. {567}
> We take refuge in the Buddha.

We take refuge in the dharma.
We take refuge in the sangha.
We take refuge in the hosts of deities of the yidam mandalas.
We take refuge in the ḍākas and ḍākinīs and dharma guardians
and protectors who possess the eye of gnosis.

Alternatively, it is also acceptable to use the condensed, four-line prayer. Take refuge in this way a hundred times or more until a change occurs in your body and mind. At the end, join your vajra hands at your heart and recite the verse for requesting refuge.[3]

For arousing bodhichitta, thinking of all sentient beings, recite three times:

With the wish to liberate beings . . .[4]

Next recite the seven-branch prayer from the *Prayer of Good Conduct* three times (or, if you do not know it, say three times the four-line prayer beginning "What little merit . . . ")[5] while reflecting on its meaning, as follows:

- the obeisance, in which you and all other beings emanate bodies equal in number to the atoms [in the universe] and pay homage (this is the branch that makes encounters meaningful);
- making offerings (this is the branch that gives meaning to one's possessions);
- confessing negative actions by employing the four strengths (regretting your past negative deeds as if you had swallowed poison, resolving not to commit them henceforth even if your life is at stake, and so on);
- rejoicing in order to vastly increase the mass of merit;
- exhorting [the teachers] to turn the wheel of dharma in order that the doctrine may endure for a long time;
- praying that [the teachers] do not pass into nirvana; and
- dedicating all sources of good related to the three times, beginning with and represented by the above branches.

Offer the seven-element mandala as many times as you can, either physically or mentally, reciting the prayer "The ground is purified with scented water . . . *niryātayāmi*."[6]

Then pray from the depth of your heart, many times:

I pray to the teacher and the Three Jewels. {568}
Please help me to recognize the meaning of the fundamental
natural state.

Consider that they clearly give their assent, saying, "Fortunate child, all your negative deeds are purified."

When you want to conclude the session, consider that the hearts of the objects of refuge emanate rays of light, touching all sentient beings. As a result they are all transformed into a single body of untainted light. The objects of refuge too melt into light, one by one from the outside, and dissolve into the root teacher. The root teacher gradually melts into light, starting from the big toe of the right foot and dissolving into the crown of the head, which evaporates like a rainbow vanishing in the sky. Rest for a while in the inexpressible state of awareness. Conclude in the proper manner by dedicating the merit and so on. Practice assiduously like this in four or so sessions. This is how it has been taught.

### B. Uncommon Preliminaries

The uncommon preliminaries consist of blessing one's stream of being by doing the meditation and recitation of the hundred syllables.

Go through the refuge, bodhichitta, and seven branches as above. At the end, [visualize] on the crown of your head a syllable *paṃ*, from which there appears a white lotus; a white letter *A*, from which there appears a moon disk; and on top of that, a white *hūṁ*. The latter transforms into glorious Vajrasattva, whose body is as white as the moon in autumn. In his right hand, at his heart, he holds a five-pronged gold vajra; in his left, resting on his hip, a silver bell with a gold half vajra for a handle. He is adorned with silks and jewels and embellished with the major and minor marks. He is sitting with his legs in the posture of youthful play, his big toe touching your aperture of Brahmā.

In his heart center visualize a moon disk and on it a white syllable *hūṁ* encircled by the white garland of the hundred-syllable mantra, upright and turning clockwise. {569} Light radiates from the mantra garland and touches the *hūṁ*, which in turn radiates light, [invoking] all the blessings of the body, speech, and mind of all the tathāgatas in the ten directions, who appear in the form of white light, densely filling the whole of space. They enter through the crown of Vajrasattva's head and dissolve into the *hūṁ* in his heart. The *hūṁ* grows bigger and becomes thumb-sized,[7] ambrosial in nature, the nectar overflowing through the *zhapkyu*,[8] from which it descends in a pure white stream, completely filling the whole of Vajrasattva's body. It gushes out from the tip of the big toe on his right foot as if a cork has been removed and flows into you through the aperture of Brahmā, filling the whole of your body and completely purifying all your negative deeds, obscurations, downfalls, and breaches of the sacred commitments, like the rising sun dispelling darkness. As you visualize this, recite the hundred syllables. Every forty-nine recitations, repeat the emanation and reabsorption of light rays as above. When you have finished reciting as much as you can—one hundred, one thousand, or so—it is good to say the confession and vow using the usual formula ("I, through ignorance . . ." and so on). However, it is not stipulated here, so it is also acceptable to not do so. Consider that Vajrasattva is pleased at your having purified your negative deeds and obscurations and, as if congratulating you, he intones clearly, "Fortunate child, all your negative deeds and obscurations are purified. All your deteriorations and breaches are restored." Then he melts into light and dissolves into you. Your body becomes like a polished crystal, your speech gains in power, and your mind is freed in the nondual state of bliss-emptiness. Thinking that you have achieved your own and others' fulfillment, rest as long as you can without focusing your mind on anything.

## C. Specific Preliminaries

The specific preliminaries consist of mastering one's mind stream by [reciting] the fifty syllables.

Above your head visualize a seat consisting of a jeweled throne borne by lions, {570} a multicolored lotus, and a moon disk, and on top of this our root teacher, Vajradhara Tsarchen.[9] He is dark red in color, smiling wrathfully, utterly resplendent, and dressed in a roughly sewn blanket. His hands are in the meditation posture, placed over his knees. His huge form just fits on his throne.

Above his head is Jetsun Doringpa, whose body is red with a maroon tinge. He has an attractive, wrathfully smiling face, and his eyes are staring into space. His head is bald, and he is wearing a fur cloak.

Above his head is the gracious Khyenrap Chöje. His body is white, tinged with red, and he has thick hair.

Above him is Trulzhik Tsultrim Gyaltsen, who has an attractive appearance and gleaming triangular eyes.[10]

Above his head is Khechok Tsandra Shri, who is tall and slim and has a slightly long neck and thick white hair on his head.

Above him is Chögyal Namkhai Tsenchen. He is very large.

Above his head is Tukse Sempa Chenpo, who is impressive and well built, with a wide parting on his head.

Above him is the Omniscient Dharma Lord,[11] who has a reddish body. His right hand is in the teaching gesture, his left in the gesture of meditation.

Above his crown is Lama Yangtsewa Rinchen Senge, bright yellow and very thin.

Above his head is Tsemai Kyebu.

Above his head is Tropu Sempa Chenpo, whose body is white tinged with red. He is corpulent, with a caring face.

Above him is Lachen Sönam Wangchuk. He is dark red in color and wearing a felt cloak.

Above his head is Tropu Lotsawa. He is white tinged with red and slightly short but attractive.

All these lineage teachers are monks and, unless otherwise specified, have their hands in the gesture of meditation.

Above Tropu Lotsawa's head is the great siddha Mitrayogin, aged sixteen years, his body white tinged with red, {571} dressed in yogi's attire. (NOTE: An old text mentions that he is wearing a lower garment of yellow cotton and is adorned with a garland of flowers.) His right hand is in the teaching gesture, his left in the gesture of meditation, holding a skull cup filled with nectar. In the crook of his arm he holds a wooden mandala.

Above his head is the mahāsiddha Lālitavajra, attired as a paṇḍita. His right hand displays the teaching gesture; his left holds a volume of the scriptures.

Above him is Tilo Sherap Zangpo, who is smoke-colored, with his hair tied in a topknot and wearing bone ornaments. He holds his right hand in the teaching gesture and his left in the gesture of meditation.

Above his head is the bodhisattva Matiratna (Lodrö Rinchen), with a complexion like pure gold. He is wearing celestial dress. His right hand is in the teaching gesture and his left holds a bright stalk of wheat at his heart, with the brilliantly shining ear of grain level with his ear.

Above his head is noble Khasarpāṇi, who is white in color. His right hand displays the gesture of supreme gift, and in his left hand he holds a lotus at his heart. He is seated in the posture of youthful play.

In each of their heart centers visualize a full-moon disk, in the center of which is a white syllable *hūṁ*, each *hūṁ* encircled by the fifty syllables turning clockwise. Each of these syllables is upright, with the foot of the syllable touching but not sticking to the top of the moon disk, for they are, by nature, light.

Next, from the *hūṁ* in Avalokiteshvara's heart center light radiates, invoking all the blessings, ability, and power of the body, speech, and mind of all the root and lineage teachers, yidam deities, buddhas, and bodhisattvas in the ten directions. These enter him through his crown and dissolve into the *hūṁ* in his heart. {572} As you visualize this, recite seven or twenty-one times:

> *oṁ āḥ vajrasattva*[12] (NOTE: Vajrasattva)
> *guru śrī* (NOTE: Glorious Teacher)
> *khasarpāṇi* (NOTE: Khasarpāṇi)
> *lokanātha* (NOTE: Lord of the World)
> *sarva buddha* (NOTE: all the buddhas and)
> *bodhisattva* (NOTE: bodhisattvas)
> *svabhāva* (NOTE: naturally)
> *adhiṣṭanaṃ* (NOTE: through the blessings)
> *ma ma cittam* (NOTE: in my heart)
> *vajra traṭ* (NOTE: the vajra descent)
> *jñāna jvala jvala* (NOTE: let wisdom blaze and blaze)
> *spharaṇa spharaṇa* (NOTE: spread and spread)
> *hūṁ hūṁ phaṭ svāhā* (NOTE: the mantra ending to make it stable)

Then say the following prayer with intense devotion three times:

> Sublime noble Great Compassionate One, I pray to you.
> Please bless my mind stream.

Consider that as a result of your prayer, the moon disk, *hūṁ* syllable, and mantra garland in Avalokiteshvara's heart all melt into light, overflowing and completely filling every part of his body. Like rain falling from a cloud or a glacial torrent from a snow mountain, from every part of his body a rain of nectar sprinkles down. It enters the bodhisattva Matiratna through his crown and dissolves into the *hūṁ* and mantra garland in his heart, gathering [into it] all the blessings of the Great Compassionate One. Again, rays of light emanate from the *hūṁ*, bringing all sentient beings to maturation and liberation. The light rays invoke all the blessings of the body, speech, and mind of all the buddhas and bodhisattvas in the ten directions, which dissolve into the *hūṁ*. Concentrating on that, recite the fifty syllables and pray three times: "Bodhisattva Matiratna, I pray to you . . ." and so on. The moon disk, *hūṁ* syllable, and mantra garland in his heart all melt into light {573} and fill his whole body with nectar. From every part of his body a stream of nectar flows down. It enters Tilo Sherap Zangpo through his crown and dissolves into the *hūṁ* in his heart.

Repeat this, going through the emanation and reabsorption of light rays and so on as above, all the way down to our sublime root teacher, not simply mouthing the prayer but involving your whole body, speech, and mind together.

At the end, the moon disk, *hūṁ* syllable, and mantra garland in the root teacher's heart all melt into light, filling the whole of his body. Like water falling from a cloud or a stream from a snow mountain, it flows down from all the parts of his body as a shimmering white stream of wisdom nectar inseparable from his enlightened mind, whose nature is great bliss. It enters you through the crown of your head and fills your whole body, completely purifying all your negative deeds and obscurations like the rising sun dispelling the darkness. Think that all blessings of the body, speech, and mind of your teacher and lineage teachers enter you. Rest in that state without grasping. Finally, the teacher and lineage teachers intone clearly: "Fortunate child, you now possess all the perfect qualities." As a result, your whole being experiences an extraordinary happiness and you rest in that state of joy. Then the teacher and lineage teachers dissolve like a rainbow vanishing in the sky. Remain as long as you can in the thought that your own mind has merged inseparably with emptiness. Conclude properly by dedicating the merit and so on.

If you do not know the fifty-syllable mantra, it is acceptable, according to what the lineage teachers have said, to visualize the *hūṁ* in the heart center encircled by *oṁ āḥ hrīḥ hūṁ* and to recite that. {574}

Unless you practice all these preliminaries very assiduously, and in particular the guru yoga, you will never benefit from the main practice, and even if, after a long time, you receive some partial benefit, it will never be stable. In short, nothing will happen as it should. This is why it is said to be so important to put intense effort into practicing the preliminaries.

Oh, for a time when I can abandon
The swirl of pointless distractions in this life
And, in lonely valleys where no one lives, practice earnestly
These words of my revered teacher, free of delusion.

## II. Main Practice

The main practice consists of putting into practice the meaning of five of the twenty-five vajra verses, those that comprise the method for introducing the natural state. (NOTE: In the source text, these are the verses from "Listen, child: whatever thoughts you have . . ." to ". . . One is freed of the dust of distraction.")[13]

What does one mean by "the natural state of the mind"? In the same way that we speak of an assembly of monks or nuns who are permanently resident in a monastery as being a "naturally established sangha,"[14] because the mind, from the very beginning, remains uncontrived and naturally pure, it is referred to as the natural state—the uncontrived state, the fresh state, or ordinary mind.[15] From the point of view of its essential nature, it is unchanging, but from the point of view of its aspects, it does change. Take three examples of a single substance such as brass: a dog's bowl, an ornament, and a buddha statue. There is not a hair's worth of difference in the quality of the brass in them, yet from the point of view of their different uses [they are utterly different]: one is repulsive, another can be used as an adornment, and the third is an object that everyone venerates. Similarly, from the Hell of Torment Unsurpassed up to buddhahood, the essential nature of mind itself is no better or worse. Yet when one fails to recognize one's own nature, we speak of samsara; when the holy teacher's pith instructions make one's impurities somewhat fainter, we speak of traveling the spiritual path; and when all one's impurities have been eliminated, we speak of buddhahood. That is the only difference. {575} In this regard, it is said:

> Sentient beings are buddhas,
> Yet they are obscured by adventitious stains.[16]

The nature of the mind, which is clear light, is buddha at the time of the ground, but because we do not recognize that this is so, it arises as multifarious appearances. And because we engage in attachment to true existence in what arises, we experience the deluded perceptions of samsara, nonexistent though they are. We are buddhas, but we are unable to perform the activities of the buddhas. This is what is called the causal continuum. The cause is a continuum in both samsara and nirvana: it is present without interruption from the sentient being state right up to buddhahood, so we speak of a continuum. "Rid of those stains"[17] refers to the means continuum, where using the holy teacher's pith instructions to practice the means for purifying the adventitious stains attenuates our deluded appearances. "They are truly buddhas" refers to what is called the result continuum,[18] where as a result of that path, all the [obscurations] that have to be eliminated are eliminated and all the [qualities] that have to be obtained are obtained, and we realize buddhahood endowed with the two purities.[19]

Practicing the means for realizing that consists of (1) decisively establishing the view with wisdom and (2) practicing meditation with skillful means.

### A. Decisively Establishing the View with Wisdom

For establishing the view with wisdom, there appear to be two aspects: leaving the nature of the object as it is and leaving the subject in the view of nondual gnosis. It is the second of these that is dealt with here, and this concerns the means for realizing thatness, the natural luminosity of one's own mind, as was indicated above. This has two aspects: training in relaxation and getting rid of hindrances.[20]

Training in relaxation involves what are commonly designated the three isolations, or the three immovabilities or, in this case, the three seals. The seal of the body is to properly adopt the seven-point posture of Vairochana, with the hands in the gesture of meditation and the thumbs joined. The seal of speech {576} is to let the breath come and go naturally. The seal of the mind is to abandon all the thoughts relating to the three times and to focus the eyes at a level about seven hand spans in front of the point between the eyebrows. In settling [in this way], the most important thing is to settle with the mind relaxed deep within.

The problem with not relaxing is that one's mind runs here and there looking for the meditation and that becomes a distraction. On the other hand, the advantage of relaxing is that when one lets go and relaxes, the mind will recognize its own nature, nakedly and clearly. An analogy for this is that the more one tries to make muddy water clear, the cloudier it will become, whereas if one leaves it to settle by itself, it will quickly become clear. So, with the three seals, leave the mind clear and limpid: without entertaining any hopes and doubts, wondering whether you are actually meditating or not, settle in a clear, relaxed state, leaving the mind as it is.

When one rests like that, it does not last long. It is in the nature of things that thoughts suddenly pop up from time to time. Whatever thoughts occur, cut them off without following them. The previous thought is past; the next thought has not arisen. And there, in between them, there nakedly arises ordinary mind. Rest in that very state. When one practices like that without being distracted for an instant, there comes a time when the belief that external appearances truly exist disintegrates and there dawns the realization that all these appearances are one's own mind. Thus is born in one's mind stream the Chittamātra view of Mind Only. This is how the first stage of finding rest for the weary mind is introduced.

When one looks further at the nature of this recognition that appearances and the mind are inseparable, in the first place, one does not perceive any arising—from such and such a place, with such and such a shape, for such and such a length of time. Then, {577} one cannot find a so-called place, from the top of one's head to the tips of one's toes, like a universe and beings or samsara and nirvana, that is characterized as outside or inside the body, or anything that one can say has a shape, color, or attributes. So, in the middle, there is no staying that exists. Since there is no arising and no staying, neither is there any corresponding ceasing: one cannot find anything that at a precise moment ceases in a particular way or has come to an end. In short, one will come to realize that it is devoid of arising, staying, and ceasing and, by extension, it is free from the four or eight extremes, such as existence and nonexistence, eternalism and nihilism. This how the Madhyamaka view of the Middle Way takes birth in one's mind stream, or how the second stage of finding rest for the weary mind is introduced.

When you are meditating like that, if the mind cannot stay still as it is and you have many scattered and agitated thoughts, and so on, you should again practice the guru yoga as explained above. Pray [to the teacher] until your body and mind are worn out. Then dissolve the teacher and your mind inseparably into space and rest in a relaxed, uncontrived manner in that state. In short, if you pray to the teacher with intense devotion, not just once but from the depth of your heart, their blessings will enter you and unadorned realization of the actual condition, the original state, of your mind will arise spontaneously from within. Unless you have absorbed the teacher's blessings, however much you meditate, you will only get a vague, general, theoretical idea, and genuine realization will not occur. This is why it is so important to unremittingly concentrate on devotion to the teacher.

Oh, for a time when, wholly and sincerely practicing
The consummate path of devotion to the teacher,
I may behold the sublime vision of my own mind,
The uncontrived natural state, spontaneously and directly.

### B. Practicing Meditation with Skillful Means

Even if you glimpse the essential nature of the mind in this way, {578} unless you preserve the continuity of that, your recognition of the natural state will be obscured by the habitual tendencies to which you have been accustomed in samsara since time without beginning, like the sun coming in and out of the clouds. So in order for this not to happen, you need to preserve that state at all times and in all situations without distraction. How to do this is described in three phases.

#### 1. The Means for Stilling Unsettled States

The initial phase involves being proficient in training undistractedly, "like skilled swordsmen going into battle." In India, when battles were fought, whether they were grasping their swords or wielding slings, the swordsmen were never put off by indecision and wielded their weapons undistractedly. As a result, no one could harm them, and they would defeat all their opponents and were certain to be victorious in battle. But if their minds were distracted or they hesitated, their opponents would stab them, and not only would they die but their country would be defeated. In the same way, if yogis who have seen the nature of the mind put that insight into practice without a moment's distraction, not only are they not be affected by their thoughts but they can overcome all of them. On the other hand, if, on account of doubts and distractions, they are unable to settle in that state, they will be overpowered by distraction, delusion, and dissipation. They will fall into this ocean of samsara and there will never come a time when they will be freed. So it is very important to be mindful and undistracted, all the time and in all situations. This is how it has been taught.

Starting from when you take refuge and until you can rest in the natural state of mind free of elaboration, as above, settle in that very state without ever being distracted. Whatever thoughts occur, cut them off and again settle without grasping. When you get used to this again and again, the mind will remain clear and free of elaborations. This is how the third stage of finding rest for the weary mind is introduced. {579}

## 2. The Means for Making the Settled State Stable

The intermediate phase involves being proficient in watching without contrivance, "like a skilled elephant keeper looking after an elephant." An elephant is one of the strongest and wildest of creatures, so to keep it requires someone who knows when to proceed and when to hold back. If one tries to hurry things up with much use of the whip, hook, and so on, the elephant will become furious and carry one off where it wants. If one does not control it, it will not take the right road. Therefore, when it goes the right way by itself, leave it alone. When it starts to take the wrong way, if you discipline it with a whip or hook and so on, it will go where you want.

It is the same with this mind. If you leave it to its own devices, it will drift off into delusion. If you are too busy applying lots of antidotes, again that will just add to the confusion. So while outwardly relaxed yet inwardly alert, without being too forceful, post an undistracted lookout. Then, if the mind stays as it is, leave it quiet in that state. If it moves, use mindfulness to hold it tight. Whatever thoughts arise, leave them completely [alone] without grasping at them. When you rest like that, a thought will arise. By looking at its nature you will see the one face of the mind, the natural state, vividly, without grasping. Yet, as the illustration shows, you cannot stop the movements of thoughts, so whatever arises, do not get involved with grasping at it but let it go its own way. As you get used to this, any thoughts that arise you will recognize nakedly as your own nature. This is referred to as "thoughts being dissolving in their own state." This is how the fourth stage of finding rest for the weary mind is introduced.

## 3. Once Stability Is Achieved, Making Progress

The final phase involves being proficient in leaving as it is, "like a bird flying from the top of a ship." In ancient India, merchants going to sea [in search of jewels] would use pigeons, crows, and other birds to look out for reefs and large marine predators. {580} As long as they were still close to the land, the birdkeepers would be careful to keep the birds caged so that they would not escape, otherwise they would fly back to land, thus defeating the purpose of taking them. Hence the need to prevent them from flying. However, once the merchants were well out to sea and over the horizon, it was not necessary to cage them, and they could be let free and allowed to fly wherever they wanted. Since they would then be unable to fly anywhere else and could not alight on the water, they would return to the boat.

Similarly, for the mind, until thoughts dissolve by themselves, one has to discipline the mind in not being distracted. Whatever thoughts arise, if one fails to maintain the state of nongrasping, the mind will get distracted toward the object. Apart from achieving some intellectual understanding of virtuous practice, one will be unable to accomplish the path to liberation and omniscience, and so one's practice will be useless. Once one can recognize thought movements as self-liberating, one needs to check whether this recognition is stable or not, and for this, one should deliberately think of an object that gives rise to a defilement such as attachment or aversion, completely letting go and exercising the ability to liberate that thought. When one does so, even if that particular defilement is vividly present as a mental image, its nature will be experienced nakedly as nondual gnosis. Without resting on that object, the mind itself should remain relaxed in the inexpressible state. When one gets used to this, one can go to haunted places and mix [one's experience] with the apparitions of obstacle makers and mix with fire, water, weapons, and so on in turn. As a result, these things will be incapable of harming one, and on top of that one's experiences and realization will progress more and more. This is how the fifth stage of finding rest for the weary mind is introduced. {581}

Oh, for a time when, long cared for by the nurse of undistracted
  mindfulness,
With all phenomena freed in the expanse of the uncontrived natural
  state,
Unbound, I may let things be, recognizing their nature,
And realize the actual condition of things without mistake.

### C. Getting Rid of Hindrances[21]

It is with these three phases of skillful means that one meditates on the view that one has established with wisdom. When one practices these without being distracted for an instant, at some stage the experiences of bliss, clarity, and no-thought will occur. If one is attached to these, they will act as causes for rebirth in the three worlds of samsara, and one will not proceed on the path to omniscience. For this reason, it is necessary to dispel such hindrances. On the one hand, without these experiences, one cannot continue on the path, so first one must persevere until they do occur. On the other hand, if one clings to these experiences, the path will be interrupted, so one needs to nurture them as the path. An analogy can be made with traveling to Bodhgaya in India. On the way to Bodhgaya there are pleasant, attractive plains like Palmo Paltang, and there are dangerous passages through narrow paths, gorges, and so on. Without traveling through them, one will be unable to reach Bodhgaya. On the other hand, if one becomes attached to those places and stops there, or becomes frightened and turns back without being able to continue, those places will prevent one from ever getting to Bodhgaya. It is the same with meditation. When one is meditating like that, all thought movements may cease, but if one fails to recognize this nakedly as the mind's natural state, [one will find oneself in] a dull state called "stagnant sustained calm" or "the experience of no-thought." If one clings to this, not only will one be reborn as a god in the formless world, but one's practice will not serve as the path to omniscience. To dispel this hindrance, therefore, keep the body straight, lift[22] your gaze, sharpen your awareness, and rouse your consciousness. When you rest in the uncontrived state of mind, vivid, clear, open, and awake, you will achieve the union of clarity and emptiness.

When you train in that again and again, {582} an experience of clarity will occur, lucid and awake, and with it, the belief that the clarity aspect is truly existent, as if the mind cannot bear to part from that clarity. If you are attached to this, you will be reborn as a god in the world of form. Therefore, to dispel that hindrance, you should relax deeply physically, lower your gaze, relax your consciousness within, and leave it quietly as it is. In this way, you will achieve the union of no-thought and clarity.

When clarity and emptiness are united like that, through the interdependence of skillful means and wisdom, an inexpressible bliss occurs very vividly. Do not cling to any experience of bliss, for attachment to it will result in your being reborn in one of the realms of the world of desire, and you will not achieve the path to omniscience. Therefore, without clinging to the nature of the bliss, the mind should let go completely, expanding the consciousness to the limits of space. By resting without grasping, one will achieve the union of bliss and emptiness. In short, as with spinning wool, keep [meditating naturally, while shifting the focus]: when clarity is predominant, focus on no-thought; when no-thought is predominant, focus on the skillful means of bliss;[23] when bliss is predominant, focus on emptiness. By this means, all clinging and grasping is purified and one will rest in the state of the natural state of mind.

Thus, the body of truth at the time of the ground is the mind itself, resting in its uncontrived original state. The body of truth at the time of the path is the mind practicing the means for settling in the uncontrived state. And the body of truth at the time of the result is the resulting naked recognition by the mind itself of its uncontrived, natural state. This is what we call "buddha." If there were a body of truth somewhere other than the mind, we would not be able to seize it, and even if we could, it would be difficult to integrate with.

In short, when all the adventitious stains that prevent one from recognizing the nature of one's own mind dissolve into the expanse of reality, one realizes the nature of the mind, endowed with the two purities, and this is what is given the name "buddha." This is how it was taught.

All the above {583} comprises [my] notes on what has to be meditated on as the stage of the main practice.

Oh, for a time when the experiences of clarity, emptiness, and bliss may arise in me,
When I may practice them in union, without clinging to them separately,
And realize the Great Seal endowed with the two purities,
My own mind, the inconceivable natural state!

## III. Conclusion

The means for preserving [the nature of the mind] in the long term is to remain mindful of the meaning of freedom from elaboration, without distraction, as explained above, so that one makes an experience of it without being distracted for a single second. As a result, even one's dreams at night will be infused with virtue. In short, one should practice constantly, day and night, with intense diligence.

The means for incorporating appearances on the path is to direct the mind more and more onto whatever arises—sickness, negative forces, defilements, and the like. As one perfects one's skill in this, one will rest serenely in uncontrived awareness, and so on. To summarize, whatever appearances arise, without evaluating those appearances, one should relax and settle on their nature.

The means for making everything one does beneficial for beings is as follows. Although the natural state of the mind, free of all elaboration, is inherently present in all sentient beings, because of adventitious impurities they do not recognize that it is there, even though it is. As a result, they experience nothing but deluded perceptions. Thinking, "How sad that is. What can I do to help them?" be diligent in any ways for making whatever you do beneficial for sentient beings. This is what was taught.[24]

Oh, for a time when, with my constant virtuous practice beyond
meditation and postmeditation,
Appearance and existence may arise as the body of truth, great bliss,
And in that state may I, directly and indirectly,
Bestow on those who have been my kind mothers infinite benefit and
happiness.

These words were written down by one named Khyentse,
Who gained mastery of the realm of dharma
Through the inseparable connection he made, bowing his diademed
head
At the feet of the Lord of Tsarpa, embodiment of all the buddhas. {584}

By the merit of this, may those who have been my mothers,
Wearied by their extensive wanderings through the realms of existence,
Find rest on the couch of the natural state and attain untainted bliss,
The union state exceeding space, the level of the Lord of the World.

*sarvadā maṅgalaṃ*

## 29. Nectarous Moonbeams

*A Song of Experience of the Great Seal Instructions* Resting in the Nature of Mind, *the Thought of Which Dispels the Anguish of the Heart*[1]

---

This song of experience was composed by Jamyang Khyentse Wangpo's teacher in the lineage of *Resting in the Nature of Mind*, Rinchen Losal Tenkyong (b. 1804). It testifies to the fact that some eight hundred years after Mitrayogin gave this teaching to Tropu Lotsawa, the lineage was still very much alive and the teachings were still being practiced. Rich in metaphor, with an unusual twelve-syllable meter and other poetic devices, it sadly loses much of its impact in English translation.

---

Ah! Embodiment of compassion, you who hold a lotus in your hand,
Dharma lord, omniscient Butön, lord of the cool land of Tibet,
Gracious root teacher dwelling above my crown—as I, a humble monk,
Make this heartfelt prayer, protect me with compassion; may we never be apart.

The essence of the siddha Mitrayogin's enlightened mind, quintessence of the vast and profound teachings,
These nectarous moonbeams, mind instructions the thought of which is soothing to the heart,
Passed down through the aural lineage by omniscient Butön to liberate on hearing and give rest for the mind,
A yoga that I have had the fortune to inherit—sweet balm upon my ear.

In the fertile field of faith, tilled by the common path,
I planted the seed of practice—refuge, bodhichitta, and the hundred syllables—
And gathered the perfect and abundant shoots of a pure mind,
Truly practicing diligence with the three doors.

In the buddha field of the root and lineage teachers, where the light of blessings radiates,
My heart so fortunate bloomed with a thousand petals of devotion, and in its center
My prayers, the melodious recitation of the fifty syllables, buzzed like bees,
Regurgitating the honey of experience and realization. Revered teacher, you know all things!

With the support of the three seals, I straightened the crucial points of channels, winds, and mind;
I saw all the phenomena of appearance and existence, samsara and nirvana, as the play of my mind;
And, deciding on the nature of the mind, free of the four extremes, bliss-emptiness like space,
I reached the state of freedom of the Middle Way, the king of views. {585}

I perfected the three skills in sustained calm, by means of the crucial points concerning tightening and relaxing,
As illustrated by the analogies of a swordsman, an elephant keeper, and a crow flying from a ship.
I clearly saw transparent emptiness, divested of all mind-made elaborations,
And trained in the unsurpassed yoga of space, of dwelling and nondwelling.

Never separating from the experience of ineffable great bliss, holding it with mindfulness,
I took as the path whatever arose as being ultimate reality, without rejection or adoption,

And with nonconceptual compassion, transforming everything I did
into altruistic good,
My conduct was spontaneous, unobstructed, so that buddhahood burst
forth in my mind.

Since the paṇḍitas and siddhas of India have divulged their secret
teachings,
There are many ways of giving the profound instructions, scattered like
the planets and stars reflected in a lake,
But the most heartfelt advice the teacher can give his children, holders
of the threefold confidence,
Is this profound introduction to resting in the nature of the mind.

These days, only the dregs of the teachings are left, and brass sells better
than gold.
I think how times have changed and my heart heaves with sadness.
Whatever activities I consider, they are not even a little worthwhile.
I will give myself to what is essential—practicing in a mountain
hermitage.

This song of experience of *Resting in the Nature of Mind* was composed by the monk Losal Tenkyong.

*sarvadā kalyāṇaṃ bhavatu*

# 30. The Nectarous Light of the Words of the Teacher

## *A Guide for Teaching the Great Seal Text* Resting in the Nature of Mind[1]

The existence of this text is a reminder that even if texts like the root verses and *Notes on Resting in the Nature of Mind* were available in Tibet in book form, no practitioner would study them on their own without having them explained by a teacher, who would at the same time give the reading transmission (*lung*). In this text Jamyang Khyentse Wangpo provides advice on how to use Khyentse Wangchuk's *Notes*—which he refers to as a guide or instruction manual (*khrid yig*)—to teach disciples and guide them on a daily basis as they try to put Mitrayogin's pith instructions into practice. He describes how to teach the text over a period of three days, with instructions on what the disciples should do between each day of teaching. The additional information included here complements that in the *Notes*, making this text as useful a reference for students who have received the transmission as it is for the teacher.

Bowing down respectfully to the teacher, Padmapāṇi,
Wisdom body of all the buddhas and their heirs,
I shall shed a little nectarous light on how to explain
His instructions, *Resting in the Nature of Mind*.

Here is a way to guide fortunate disciples to the level of buddhahood by means of the graded path related to *Resting in the Nature of Mind*, a teaching of the Great Seal, which is the essence of the great siddha Mitrayogin's enlightened mind.

## [Day 1]

First of all, {586} the master themself should sit on a comfortable seat, adopting the meditation posture, and consider what are the most appropriate subjects to give the disciples who are present that day. After that the disciples—who should have trained their minds by means of the common path, received in full the four empowerments in any suitable mandala of the Unexcelled Yoga, and have kept their sacred commitments and vows—should cleanse themselves, perform prostrations and make offerings, and then sit in their respective rows. At the master's prompting, they should recite the lineage prayer and, led by the shrine master, make the offering of the thirty-seven-heap mandala. Then the master should softly recite three times the mantra for subjugating negative forces. After that, with unconditional love and great compassion (the wish to free beings from samsara), the master should remind the disciples of the correct motivation by giving the following instruction.

Think: "Oh, for the sake of all sentient beings, our mothers, who are as numerous as the sky is vast, I must do whatever I can to attain—swiftly, in this very life—the level of the great union Vajradhara, the state of perfect buddhahood. To that end, I will listen to the profound graded instructions on the most profound of teachings and practice them properly." With this thought, arouse the mind intent on supreme enlightenment. Furthermore, you should adopt the correct conduct for listening to the teachings, as is mentioned in the *Series of Lives*:

> Sit on a very low seat,
> Cultivate the virtue of self-control,
> Look with joyful eyes,
> And drink the words like nectar;
> With a pure and unstained mind,
> Listen like a patient to the doctor:
> Make offerings and listen to the dharma.[2]

Accordingly, you should avoid the three defects of the pot—namely, the defect of being like an upside-down pot, whereby you fail to pay attention to the words of the teaching and their meaning; the defect of being like a leaky pot, whereby even if you pay attention, you do not retain the teaching with mindfulness and vigilance; {587} and the defect of being like a contaminated pot, whereby even if you do retain the teaching with mindfulness and vigilance, you are contaminated by any of the six stains, as listed in the *Well-Explained Reasoning*:

> It is a stain to listen with pride,
> With lack of faith, or without interest,
> While distracted outwardly,
> Introverted, or discouraged.[3]

As the antidote to these [faults] you should listen while keeping in mind four notions: think of yourself as someone who is sick, think of the teacher as a doctor, think of the teaching as medicine, and think of your assiduous practice as the treatment for your sickness.

In particular, here in the context of the unexcelled Vajrayāna, if one clings to ordinary appearances, one is not a suitable vessel for receiving the teachings. Therefore, with regard to your physical posture, you should sit up straight. And with regard to your mental attitude, you should avoid perceiving your surroundings as an ordinary location, but see it with pure perception as the measureless palace of great liberation, produced through the spontaneous manifestation of nondual gnosis, with all its proportions and attributes complete. In its center is your present vajra master teaching the dharma. Think that they too are not in their ordinary form but are the sublime Padmapāṇi[4] in person, the single embodiment of the gnosis of the great compassion of the buddhas and bodhisattvas of the three times.

You too should have the pride of being your postmeditational yidam deity, whichever it may be, and in that way consider that the melodious sound of the teachings resounds as unborn sound-emptiness, its clear sounds clearing away all the troubles of existence and peace.

With this in mind, I request you to listen undistractedly in the state of clarity and emptiness, without grasping.

The teaching that you are going to receive is the profound graded path of *Resting in the Nature of Mind*, a teaching of the Great Seal, which [has come down to us] through the lineage from the great siddha Mitrayogin.

As for the way to explain it, {588} there are two parts: (1) the history of the teaching, which inspires confidence and confirms its authenticity, and (2) the actual instructions whose history has been related.

## I. History of the Teaching

The history of the teaching is divided into (1) the historical background of the teaching that is being explained and (2) the history of the teaching lineage.

### A. Historical Background of the Teaching

Our Teacher,[5] who was skilled in means and had boundless compassion, gave an inconceivable number of ambrosial teachings in accord with the respective characters, faculties, attitudes, and predispositions of the sentient beings he was benefiting. In terms of their subject matter, all these teachings can be condensed into the three trainings,[6] and in terms of the texts that present them, into the three scriptural collections.[7] These again are included in the two vehicles—the Basic Vehicle and the Great Vehicle, of which the Great Vehicle is superior in having seven distinguishing features.[8] And the Great Vehicle again has two aspects: the causal vehicle of the transcendent perfections and the resultant vehicle of the mantras. The latter comprises the four great tantra systems, and the highest of all these is the cycle of the *Tantra of Ekajaṭa*,[9] the king of the Unexcelled Mahāyoga tantras, which has two aspects: the maturing empowerment and the liberating instructions on the paths of the generation and perfection stages. The present teaching concerns the extremely profound perfection stage, the Great Seal cycle called *Resting in the Nature of Mind*.

### B. History of the Teaching Lineage

Regarding the extraordinary tradition of this teaching, the general [lineage begins with] Lord Avalokiteshvara, who transmitted it to his direct disciple, a bodhisattva in the celestial realms called Matiratna.[10] He transmitted it to the great siddha Tilopa, whose disciple was the great siddha Lālitavajra. The latter's disciple was Lord Mitrayogin. {589} Widely known as Mahāsiddha Mitrayogin, he was an emanation of noble Avalokiteshvara who manifested taking birth as a prince in the east of India. From the moment he was born, he developed faith, renunciation, and great compassion. Abandoning the kingdom like spit [in the dust], he [traveled to] the city of Bhagabhiṭara, where he received three extraordinary instructions from the great siddha Lālitavajra. He subsequently dedicated himself one-pointedly to the essential practice on Khasarpāṇi's mountain. After twelve years, the Great Compassionate One, noble Khasarpāṇi, appeared in person in front of him, on top of a wooden mandala as smooth as a mirror, and said "Son,[11] what do you want?"

"Since the very beginning, my mind has been worn out in the ocean of suffering that is samsara. Will you please show me a way to enable it to find rest?" he asked. Khasarpāṇi responded to this request by uttering a dohā of twenty-five vajra verses, beginning, "Wonder! One's own mind is, from the beginning, unborn." They summarize the content of the *Perfection of Wisdom* in twenty-five points, providing a way for the minds of all sentient beings, worn out from the beginning by the sufferings of samsara, to find rest. On hearing these verses, Mitrayogin attained the supreme accomplishment. This was the first of the twenty deeds in his wondrous life story.

The Lord of Yogis transmitted this teaching in full to the great Tropu Lotsawa, Nup Jampa Pal, who practiced it and transmitted it in turn. In due course, it came down to Butön Rinchen Drup, the "Omniscient One in the Time of Strife," and he gave it to his closest disciples in the form of heartfelt advice. From them, it has come through an uninterrupted lineage as far as our glorious holy teacher.[12] {590}

### II. The Actual Instructions Whose History Has Been Related

How to guide the disciples with these instructions comprises three sections: (1) preliminaries; (2) main practice; and (3) conclusion.

### A. Preliminaries

How to explain and put into practice the preliminary practices is divided into (1) a brief introduction in the form of an outline and (2) a detailed explanation of how to practice.

### 1. Brief Introduction in the Form of an Outline

As a brief introduction, the practice can be condensed into three essential points:

- the common preliminaries, comprising the practices of refuge, bodhichitta, and accumulating merit;
- the uncommon preliminary practice, consisting of the meditation and recitation of the hundred syllables, which enables the blessings to descend into one's mind stream; and
- the specific preliminary practice, the guru yoga, in which one's mind stream is empowered with the fifty syllables.

## 2. Detailed Explanation of How to Practice

First, for the common preliminaries, begin with taking refuge. Go through the instruction manual[13] starting from "Sit on a comfortable seat in the meditation posture . . ." and so on up to and including the six-line refuge prayer.* For a condensed version, it is also acceptable to use the four-line prayer, because the yidam deities are included in the Jewel of the Buddha, and the ḍākas and ḍākinīs, dharma guardians and protectors, and wealth deities are included in the Jewel of the sangha. Whichever the case, take refuge in this way a hundred times or more until a change occurs in your body and mind. At the end, join your vajra hands at your heart and recite the following words requesting refuge three times:

> In the Buddha, the dharma, and the supreme assembly
> We take refuge until we attain enlightenment.
> By the merit of practicing generosity and the like,
> May we attain buddhahood for the benefit of beings.

Next, arouse the mind intent on enlightenment. Visualizing all around you the totality of sentient beings, think: "All these beings {591} have been my mother and father, who have shown me nothing but kindness. And they have not been my parents just once: there is no counting how many times they have been so. Each time they were my parents, they helped me immeasurably in just the same way as my present parents. They protected me from being harmed in countless ways. These beings full of kindness are wandering[14] endlessly in samsara. How pitiful! How sad!"

Thinking this and leaving it at that will not help them, so you should arouse the bodhichitta in aspiration by thinking, "I must quickly set them

*See ch. 28, pp. 552–53.

on the level of buddhahood!" And you should arouse the bodhichitta in action by thinking, "In order to do that, I will put into practice the profound path of the Great Seal, the profound yoga of resting in the nature of mind, and attain the level of the great union Vajradhara, not sometime in the distant future but very soon!" In this way, train earnestly in bodhichitta in aspiration and in action. Taking the objects of refuge as your witness,[15] go for refuge in them as the support for your arousing bodhichitta by saying three times:

> With the wish to liberate beings,
> Until I reach the heart of enlightenment,
> I will constantly take refuge
> In the Buddha, the dharma, and the sangha.

Then arouse the mind set on enlightenment as many times as you can with the following prayer:

> With wisdom, compassion, and diligence,
> For the sake of sentient beings,
> In the presence of the buddhas
> I arouse the mind set on perfect enlightenment.

After that, for the main practice of gathering the accumulations, in the presence of the objects of refuge that you visualized previously, go through the instructions on practicing the seven branches from the *Prayer of Good Conduct*, which should be performed three times.* If you do not know that prayer, recite three times any other suitable condensed version of the seven branches.

Considering that you are offering your body, possessions, and ocean-like accumulation of merit, from which there appear {592} the four continents, Mount Meru, the ring of iron mountains, and all the sense offerings of the celestial and human worlds, all piled up with nothing lacking, offer the seven-element mandala as many times as you can, either physically or mentally, reciting the prayer "The ground is purified with scented water and strewn with flowers . . . *idam guru ratna maṇḍala kaṃ niryātayāmi*."[16] Then pray from the depth of your heart:

*See ch. 28, p. 553.

I pray to the teacher and the Three Jewels . . .

and so on.*

Continue [the instructions] until "This is why it is said to be so important to put intense effort into practicing the preliminaries."† And when you are going through the guru yoga, add as an addendum the "Supplement for the [visualization of the] Lineage Teachers in the Guru Yoga."‡

Having explained in detail how to practice the above, go through the essential points of the different parts of the practice again, as follows:

Starting from this evening, sit on a comfortable seat in your respective rooms, adopting the meditation posture. Rest for a little while until your breathing naturally becomes peaceful. If a thought suddenly arises, instead of falling under its power, begin the practice, starting with the prayer to the lineage and continuing from there. First, for the common preliminaries, go through the instructions on taking refuge, from ". . . consider that the place where you are is a vast pure realm . . ." as far as "Thinking that all of you are using your body, speech, and mind to take refuge together . . . ."§ Say the six-line prayer or the four-line prayer a hundred times or more until a change occurs in your body and mind. At the end, join your vajra hands at your heart and recite the words for requesting refuge.

For arousing the mind intent on enlightenment, visualizing all around you the totality of sentient beings and thinking, "In order to bring them all to perfect buddhahood, I must properly practice the excellent path," {593} recite three times the prayer, "With the wish to liberate beings . . . ."¶ Then, in the presence of the objects of refuge, perform the seven branches three times, starting with obeisance. Alternatively, if you do not know [the *Prayer of Good Conduct*], any other condensed version is acceptable. Continue from "Offer the seven-element mandala as many times as you can, either physically or mentally . . ." through to "Rest for a while in the inexpressible state of awareness."**

Then continue from "The uncommon preliminaries consist of blessing one's stream of being by doing the meditation and recitation of the hundred

*See ch. 28, p. 554.
†See ch. 28, p. 559.
‡See ch. 32.
§See ch. 28, p. 552.
¶See p. 579.
**See ch. 28, pp. 553–54.

syllables. Visualize on the crown of your head a syllable *paṃ*, from which appears a white lotus . . ." as far as "it is acceptable, according to what the lineage teachers have said, to visualize the *hūṁ* in the heart center encircled by *oṁ āḥ hrīḥ hūṁ* and to recite that."*

In addition, give the following instruction. If you cannot achieve a clear visualization of the lineage teachers, or if you adopt a less detailed visualization, you can practice as follows. Above your head visualize a seat consisting of a precious throne supported by lions, a multicolored lotus, and a moon disk, and on top of this your gracious root teacher, appearing as they are, youthful, their right hand in the teaching gesture, the left in the gesture of meditation. They are sitting cross-legged in the bodhisattva posture, with the right leg stretched out in the posture of royal ease or youthful play. In their heart center, in the middle of a full-moon disk, is the white syllable *hūṁ* encircled by *oṁ āḥ hrīḥ hūṁ*. From it rays of light emanate, inviting the teachers of the lineage, who dissolve into the root teacher. Consider that the root teacher is the embodiment of all the lineage teachers. Instead of the fifty-six-syllable mantra, recite *oṁ āḥ hrīḥ hūṁ*. Apart from this, the other details of the gathering and dissolving of the wisdom nectar, the stream of nectar flowing down, the purification, and so forth should be practiced as in the detailed explanation. Either way of doing this has been taught as being acceptable.

After practicing the detailed or condensed guru yoga like this, {594} at the end, when you wish to conclude the session, seal the practice by dedicating the merit to buddhahood and making pure aspirations with such prayers as:

> By the merit of this
> May I swiftly accomplish the glorious teacher
> [And, not leaving out a single being,
> May I establish them all in his level].

And

> In all my lives, may I never separate from an authentic teacher,
> [May I enjoy the glory of the dharma,
> And, completing the qualities of the levels and paths,

*See ch. 28, pp. 554–58.

May I swiftly attain the level of Vajradhara].

All the time between sessions, employing mindfulness and vigilance, spend your time in virtuous conduct, beginning with training in never neglecting to maintain devotion to the teacher and the Three Jewels as the path. Go through these stages of the practice in one session this evening and one session tomorrow. If you do not practice the two sessions, you will not be able to receive the experiential instructions, so you should definitely be diligent in practicing these. Please do just these practices as your practice commitment for tonight and tomorrow morning.

Say [the dedication prayer], "By this merit . . . " and so on, and conclude.

## Day 2

On the second day, the master should do the practice and then gather the disciples and do the lineage prayer, mandala offering, and so on, as before. After that, the master should go through [the instructions] from "Think: 'Oh, for the sake of all sentient beings, our mothers, who are as numerous as the sky is vast . . ." and so on, through to "How to guide the disciples with these instructions comprises three sections: (1) preliminaries; (2) main practice; and (3) conclusion," as on the first day.*

Then go through the detailed explanation again, as on the first day, from "The first of these is again divided into three: common, uncommon, and specific preliminaries. First, the common preliminaries . . ." through to "This is why it is said to be so important to put intense effort into practicing the preliminaries."†

All this has been given as a repetition of yesterday's instructions. Today I will give you some new instructions:

### B. Main Practice

The main practice should be presented under three headings: (1) a brief introduction; (2) a detailed explanation of how to practice by using listening and reflection to remove doubts and come to a clear understanding and by meditating; {595} and (3) a summary essentializing the practice.[17]

*See pp. 574–77.

†See ch. 28, pp. 552–59.

As a brief introduction, the main practice comprises (1) removing doubts and coming to a clear understanding by hearing and reflecting on what one is going to meditate on and (2) combining the points that have been investigated into a meditation and then practicing it. The latter consists of establishing the view with wisdom, practicing meditation with skillful means, and getting rid of hindrances.[18]

Now, for the detailed explanation of how to practice these, we begin by removing doubts and coming to a clear understanding by hearing and reflecting.

Go through the instructions from "The main practice consists of putting into practice the meaning of five of the twenty-five vajra verses in the root text of *Resting in the Nature of Mind* that comprise the method for introducing the natural state."* Read out these verses:

> Listen, child: whatever thoughts you have,
> Because they neither bind nor free you here,
> Do not be distracted, do not fabricate, leave things as they are—
> Behold, find rest from weariness!
>
> Reflections and forms, echoes and sounds,
> Real events and dreams—for the mind that thinks of these
> Combine concentration and the meditation
> Of connection and exhaustion.
>
> Discernment, absence of basis,
> And constant, unbroken meditation
> Are like gold, like fire, like space,
> Understanding, dissolving, and purifying.
>
> Nonappearance, appearance, and circumstantial appearance
> Are like space, a mirror, and a pure crystal.
> This is realized by means of concentration,
> Gnosis, and the power of memory.
>
> Perception, in equipoise, is luminosity,
> At which time perception has not arisen.

*See ch. 28, p. 559.

Remaining one-pointed, utterly free of concepts,
One is freed of the dust of distraction.

Then continue [going through the instructions] until "refers to what is called the result continuum, where as a result of that path, all the [obscurations] that have to be eliminated are eliminated and all the [qualities] that have to be obtained are obtained, and we realize buddhahood endowed with the two purities."*

Then, having cleared away doubts regarding the meaning of these by listening and reflecting, making use of scriptural authority, logic, and pith instructions, go through from "Practicing the means for realizing that . . ." {596} to "This is why it is so important to unremittingly concentrate on devotion to the teacher."† Then, from "B. Practicing Meditation with Skillful Means" to "This is how the fifth stage of finding rest for the weary mind is introduced."‡ And from "C. Getting Rid of Hindrances" to "This is what is given the name 'buddha.'"§

Having, with these sections, explained in detail the way to remove doubts and come to a clear understanding concerning the meaning of the main practice by listening and reflecting and the stages for practicing the points that have been investigated, go through the essential points of the practice again, beginning with, "Starting from this evening . . ." and continuing, "begin the practice, starting with the prayer to the lineage and continuing from there" through refuge to the guru yoga, as before.¶

After that, remove doubts by listening and reflecting on the presentation of the ground, path, and result. Then, for putting into practice the method for realizing that, which has the two parts—establishing the view with wisdom and practicing meditation with skillful means—go through the first part, "Training in relaxation," and continue through to "This is why it is so important to unremittingly concentrate on devotion to the teacher."**

Then go through the *Notes* from "B. Practicing Meditation with Skillful

*See ch. 28, p. 560.
†See ch. 28, pp. 560–62.
‡See ch. 28, pp. 562–64.
§See ch. 28, pp. 564–66
¶See pp. 580–82.
**See ch. 28, pp. 560–62.

Means" to "This is how the third stage of finding rest for the weary mind is introduced."* [Then say to the disciples:]

When you get used in this way to the method for settling the mind, gradually practice the methods for making the settled state stable, enhancing stability, and dispelling hindrances to these, as explained before. When you are preparing to conclude the session of the main practice of meditation, first arouse great nonconceptual compassion for sentient beings who have not realized this natural state and then conclude the session and continue into the postmeditation by dedicating the merit to the essence of enlightenment, saying such prayers as:

> By the merit of this, may all beings
> Complete the accumulation of merit and wisdom
> And attain the two supreme bodies,
> Which arise from merit and wisdom.

Seal the practice with prayers of pure aspiration. {597} All the time between sessions, employing mindfulness and vigilance, spend your time in virtuous activities, in particular training in conserving the flavor of whatever you experienced in the main practice, without pursuing any perceptions of the six senses that may arise.

Explain the procedure for going through these stages of the practice as on the first day† and conclude.

## Day 3

On the third day, the master should prepare as before, and then go through the instructions from "Think: 'Oh, for the sake of all sentient beings . . ." through to ". . . there are two parts: (1) the history of the teaching, which inspires confidence and confirms its authenticity, and (2) the actual instructions whose history has been related."‡ Now say:

The latter comprises three sections: (1) preliminaries; (2) main practice; and (3) conclusion. Of these I have already given you a full explanation of the stages of the preliminaries. Now, for the second, the main practice, there

*See ch. 28, pp. 562–63.
†See p. 582 ("Go through these stages of the practice . . .").
‡See pp. 574–75.

are two parts: (1) removing doubts by hearing and reflecting on what one is going to meditate on and (2) how to combine the points that have been investigated into a meditation and then practice it.

For the first of these—removing doubts and coming to a clear understanding by hearing and reflecting—go through the detailed explanation, as on the second day, by going through the instructions from "The main practice consists of putting into practice the meaning of five of the twenty-five vajra verses in the root text of *Resting in the Nature of Mind* . . ." to "This is what is given the name 'buddha.'"*

Continue through the *Notes* from "III. Conclusion: The means for preserving [the nature of the mind] in the long term . . ." through to ". . . be diligent in any ways for making whatever you do beneficial for sentient beings. This is what was taught."†

## [C. Conclusion]

After successfully completing the main part of the instructions, conclude by saying, "I will now offer you the supporting reading transmissions," and give the transmissions by reading through the vajra verses of the root text, the correlations with the source scriptures, the lineage prayer composed by Khyenrap Chöje, the *Notes* by Jamyang Khyentse Wangchuk, the *Song of Experience of Resting in the Nature of Mind* by the lord teacher (Rinchen Losal Tenkyong), and so on. After that, say: "With these, you have properly received the experiential instructions and the reading transmissions, so to repay the teacher's kindness, I request you to make the offering of the mandala."

In response to this request, the disciples, led by the shrine master, should offer the mandala.

"I have now {598} finished making you a perfect offering, without any additions or omissions, as I received them directly from our glorious sublime teacher, ______ Rinpoche, of the complete instructions and reading transmission of the Great Seal teaching *Resting in the Nature of Mind*, which has come down to us through an uninterrupted lineage from Mitrayogin—the great lord of siddhas who was a manifestation of the most noble Padmapāṇi, the single embodiment of the gnosis of the great compassion of

*See ch. 28, pp. 559–66.

†See ch. 28, pp. 566–67.

the buddhas and bodhisattvas of the three times. So now I request you to conclude by nonconceptually dedicating all the sources of good gathered in the three times, symbolized by the merit that has been produced by listening to the teaching and explaining it, for the benefit of yourselves and all other sentient beings filling space. Please practice this profound path yourselves and explain and propagate it to others, and by so doing act on a vast scale for the benefit of yourselves and others."

Say dedication prayers, long or short, as appropriate, and prayers of aspiration for the spread of the teachings, and other prayers, and conclude.

By the nectarous light of *Resting in the Nature of Mind*,
The heart essence of ten million siddha lords,
May the spring-blossoming lotus of the four bodies of liberation
Forever grace the three worlds.

On the basis of my own wish to write a guide for teaching Jamyang Khyentse Wangchuk's instruction manual for the Great Seal teaching *Resting in the Nature of Mind*, and being further encouraged to do so by the peerless sovereign of all the buddha families and mandalas, Tenpai Nyima Jamyang Namkha Gyaltsen Pal Zangpo, I was inspired by the eloquent instructions of my lord Zhalu Losal Tenkyong, the thought of whom dispels the anguish of my heart, to write this work. I, the worthless, do-nothing mani mumbler {599} Jamyang Khyentse Wangpo, completed it at Tartse, the lama's residence of Glorious Ewaṃ Chöden, the source of many precious qualities, on the first day of the second month of the year of the female earth bird also called "Peace" (1849). May the merit of doing so lead to this profound path being nurtured and proclaimed for infinite kalpas.
*sarvadā maṅgalaṃ*

# 31. A Prayer to the Lineage Teachers of *Resting in the Nature of Mind* in the Places Associated with Them[1]

This prayer to each of the lineage holders of this teaching demonstrates Tibetan Buddhists' veneration not only of the teachers but also of the places in which they lived or stayed. Most of the places mentioned here are situated in the regions around Tropu and Zhalu monasteries. Although Tibetan place names often have particular meanings—for example, Ripuk (*ri phug*), meaning mountain cave or hermitage—it has seemed more logical to retain the Tibetan names in most cases. Marginal notes in the Tibetan text appear to explain the locations of some of these sites.

{601}
*namo guru*
I pray to the buddha, great Vajradhara,
Who dwells in the Unexcelled, the palace of the expanse of reality.
Precious teacher, as I pray to you,
Grant your blessing, kind dharma lord.

I pray to noble Lokeshvara,
Who dwells in the Potala Mountain.
Precious teacher, as I pray to you,
Grant your blessing, kind dharma lord.

I pray to the bodhisattva Matiratna,
Who dwells in a manifested celestial palace.

Precious teacher, as I pray to you,
Grant your blessing, kind dharma lord.

I pray to Tilo Sherap Zangpo,
Who dwells in the eastern manifested city of Maya.
Precious teacher, as I pray to you,
Grant your blessing, kind dharma lord.

I pray to Lord Lālitavajra,
Who dwells in the monastic seat of Vajrāsana.
Precious teacher, as I pray to you,
Grant your blessing, kind dharma lord.

I pray to Lord Mitrayogin,
Who dwells in Khasarpāṇi's abode.
Precious teacher, as I pray to you,
Grant your blessing, kind dharma lord.

I pray to Lord Jampa Lotsawa,
Who dwells in Tropu Gaden.
Precious teacher, as I pray to you,
Grant your blessing, kind dharma lord.

I pray to Lachen Sönam Wangchuk,
Who dwells in the glorious monastery of Jangpu.[2]
Precious teacher, as I pray to you,
Grant your blessing, kind dharma lord.

I pray to Khenchen Sönam Senge,
Who dwells in the middle monastic seat.
Precious teacher, as I pray to you,
Grant your blessing, kind dharma lord.

I pray to Khechok Tseme Kyebu,
Who dwells in the monastic seat of Tropu.
Precious teacher, as I pray to you,
Bless me, kind lord of dharma.

I pray to Omniscient Dharma Lord,
Who dwells in the dharma palace of Gaden.
Precious teacher, as I pray to you,
Grant your blessing, kind dharma lord.

I pray to Tukse Sempa Chenpo,
Who dwells in the dharma palace of Ripuk.
Precious teacher, as I pray to you,
Grant your blessing, kind dharma lord.

I pray to Chögyal Namkhai Tsenchen,
Who dwells in Gepel Chözong (NOTE: near Zhalu Pu Nesar).
Precious teacher, as I pray to you,
Grant your blessing, kind dharma lord.

I pray to Khedrup Dawa Palrin,
Who dwells in Sangye Ling (NOTE: to the west of Zhalu).
Precious teacher, as I pray to you,
Grant your blessing, kind dharma lord.

I pray to Trulzhik Tsultrim Gyaltsen,
Who dwells in Samding Yang Gön (NOTE: Denam).
Precious teacher, as I pray to you,
Grant your blessing, kind dharma lord.

I pray to Kuzhang Khyenrap Chöje,
Who dwells in the hermitage of Sharchen (NOTE: Ripuk).
Precious teacher, as I pray to you,
Grant your blessing, kind dharma lord.

I pray to Jetsun Kunpang Chenpo,
Who dwells in Kha'u Kyelhe (NOTE: Sakyapu).
Precious teacher, as I pray to you,
Grant your blessing, kind dharma lord.

I pray to the powerful vajradhara of Tsarchen,
Who dwells in Ripuk Ladrang.

Precious teacher, as I pray to you,
Grant your blessing, kind dharma lord.

I pray to Jamyang Khyentse Wangchuk,
Who dwells in the teaching hall of Zhalu's golden pagoda. {602}
Precious teacher, as I pray to you,
Grant your blessing, kind dharma lord.

I pray to Pakchok Jampa Kalzang,
Who dwells in a pure buddha field.
Precious teacher, as I pray to you,
Grant your blessing, kind dharma lord.

I pray to the sublime guide Wangchuk Rapten,
Who dwells in Dechen Podrang.
Precious teacher, as I pray to you,
Grant your blessing, kind dharma lord.

I pray to the kind Sönam Chokdrup,
Who dwells in Chökhor Sharchen.
Precious teacher, as I pray to you,
Grant your blessing, kind dharma lord.

I pray to the embodiment of all, Rinchen Jampal,
Who dwells in Chökhor Yangtse.
Precious teacher, as I pray to you,
Grant your blessing, kind dharma lord.

I pray to the sublime guide Lozang Khetsun,
Who dwells in Dechen Pal.
Precious teacher, as I pray to you,
Grant your blessing, kind dharma lord.

I pray to the peerless Jampal Tsultrim,
Who dwells in Jangling Chökyi Podrang.
Precious teacher, as I pray to you,
Grant your blessing, kind dharma lord.

I pray to Chetsun Tenzin Trinle,
Who dwells in countries far and wide.
Precious teacher, as I pray to you,
Grant your blessing, kind dharma lord.

I pray to the sovereign Yeshe Paljor,
Who dwells in Samten Khangpu.
Precious teacher, as I pray to you,
Grant your blessing, kind dharma lord.

I pray to Rinchen Losal Tenkyong,
Who dwells in Drupkhang Namröl Yangtse.
Precious teacher, as I pray to you,
Grant your blessing, kind dharma lord.

I pray to my gracious root teacher,
Who dwells on a sun and moon throne above my head.
Precious teacher, as I pray to you,
Grant your blessing, kind dharma lord.

I pray to the yidam deity, the Great Compassionate One,
Who dwells in the mandala of buddhas in my own body.
Precious teacher, as I pray to you,
Grant your blessing, kind dharma lord.

I pray to the sublime teaching, *Resting in the Nature of Mind*,
Who dwells inseparably in the middle of my heart.
Precious teacher, as I pray to you,
Grant your blessing, kind dharma lord.

Bless me that I may master the yoga of the preliminaries,
Accumulating merit, purifying obscurations, and reciting the fifty syllables.
Bless me that I may realize the union view
Of the body of truth, the unborn, luminosity free of elaboration.
Bless me that I may give up grasping and, by means of the teacher's instructions,
Attain the result that comes through meditation.

This prayer to the lineage teachers of *Resting in the Nature of Mind* mentioning the places associated with them was written by Vajradhara Khyenrap Chöje, with additional verses added progressively by his successors in the lineage; the verses from Tsarchen down were added by Janglingpa Sönam Chokdrup, and the subsequent verses by Vajradhara Losal.
*sarvadā mangalambhavatu*

# 32. A Supplement for the [Visualization of the] Lineage Teachers in the Guru Yoga[1]

THE VISUALIZATION of the lineage teachers described by Jamyang Khyentse Wangchuk in the guru yoga section of his *Notes* does not, for obvious reasons, include any of the teachers who succeeded him. This text, therefore, contains the visualization details of the teachers in the lineage between Jamyang Khyentse Wangchuk and Jamyang Khyentse Wangpo, which are to be inserted into the description in the *Notes*.* It appears to have been compiled incrementally by the some of the teachers described here. There is no colophon, but the fact that Jamyang Khyentse Wangpo refers to this supplement in his teaching guide† would suggest that he or perhaps Jamgön Kongtrul added the visualizations of the two most recent lineage holders.

{603}

Above your head visualize a seat consisting of a jeweled throne borne by lions, a multicolored lotus, and a moon disk, and on top of this our gracious root teacher, Vajradhara Jamyang Khyentse Wangpo. He is well built, tall, and dignified, with a wrathful smile and a calm look. He is wearing the three dharma robes and holds his right hand in the teaching gesture and his left in the gesture of meditation. His voice clearly intones the words of the

*See ch. 28, p. 555.

†See ch. 30, p. 580.

teachings, and his mind is in meditative equipoise, in numerous doors of concentration. He looks pleased with you.

Above his head is Zhalu Choktrul Rinpoche, Losal Tenkyong, who body is thin and emaciated. He is looking straight ahead.

Above him is Janglingpa Drupwang Yeshe Paljor, who is tall and lean. He has thick white hair and looks resplendent, with a slightly emaciated face.

Above his head is Jetsun Tenzin Trinle, whose body is dark red and slightly bent forward.

Above him is Jangling Jampal Tsultrim, whose hair is as white as a conch, and his eyebrows are white. His body is light blue and lustrous.

Above his head is Chetsun Lozang Khetsun, who is imposing in appearance and well built. His eyes are staring into space.

Above his head is Khenchen Rinchen Jampal, who is large and corpulent, with round eyes.

All of them are wearing the three dharma robes and holding their right hands in the teaching gesture and the left in the gesture of meditation. They are seated with their legs crossed in the bodhisattva posture.

From Yeshe Paljor to this point was written by Vajra[dhara] Losal Tenkyong.

Above Khenchen Rinchen Jampal's head is Khenchen Sönam Chokdrup, who is tall and white in color, tinged with red. {604} He has a beautiful, smiling face and is dressed in the style of a listener arhat. His hair is almost completely white. His hands are in the meditation position, and his gaze is fixed, looking straight ahead. He is sitting with his legs crossed in the vajra posture.

This [visualization] was added by Rinchen Jampal. Those from the next teacher as far as Khyentse [Wangchuk] were written by Khenchen [Sönam Chokdrup].

Above Sönam Chokdrup's head is Vajradhara Wangchuk Rapten, who is white tinged with red and dressed as a monk. He has thick white hair. He is sitting with his legs crossed in the vajra posture and his hands in the gesture of meditation. He is looking fixedly into space.

Above his head is Pakchok Jampa Kalzang. He is white tinged with red, has thick gray hair, and is beautifully dressed.

Above his head is Jamyang Khyentse Wangchuk, who is white tinged with red. In his right hand at the level of his heart center he holds a five-spoked gold vajra. In his left hand, held in the gesture of meditation, is a kapāla full of nectar.

From here, continue through the text with "Above his head is Vajradhara Tsarchen . . ." and so on.[2]

# 33. Thirty Verses Expressing Realization[1]

{509}

In Sanskrit: *Triṃśatiavabodha*
In Tibetan: *rTogs*[2] *pa brjod pa sum cu pa*
In English: *Thirty Verses Expressing Realization*

Homage to Lord Avalokiteshvara

Vajra Holder, crowning Brahmā and Indra,
Lord of the World in the center of a great lotus,
By bestowing empowerment with a stream of light rays
You purify the three stains—how marvelous. (1)

With the body as stable as a mountain,
The mind free of elaboration is like space.
Continuously binding the wind, the moving mind—
By this means is the yogi fully freed. (2)

The mind is all-pervading, like space:
The body, whose nature is the five chakras,
The life and fierce winds, and the sun and moon
Are bound by the noose of adamantine great bliss. (3)

The five impurities are purified by the five,
Body, speech, and mind are Body, Speech, and Mind.
These are uncontrived, unborn.
Wonder! What is there to meditate on here? (4)

As the fire blazes from the essence of the ocean,
A chariot passing up the life tree of the supreme mountain,
The rain falls down[3] from Brahmā's peak.
Look how means brings absence of means! (5)

Ignorance is emptiness.
Entanglement is a grove of bliss.
Aversion shines brightly as luminosity.
What negativity can fetter the supreme deity? (6)

In the navel, the lamp dispels the darkness.
In the heart center, the lotus of wisdom blooms.
In the crown, the gnosis of great bliss drips.
Now[4] one's own body attains accomplishment. (7)

In the center, where the three channels are gathered as the chakras,
The essential drops of great bliss reside, {510}
And in their midst, absence of concepts,
The immaculate eye of gnosis. (8)

Like the sun rising in the sky,
The light[5] of realization [shining] on the darkness of duality
[Reveals] that duality does not dwell there nor anywhere else.
Goodness! How extremely profound that state is. (9)

The whole world is bound by the sky,
Obscured by the clouds in that sky.
When the clouds of conceptual thought clear,
What is there that appears here? (10)

An illusory city is conquered[6] by an illusion;
The mind is deceived by the mind:
On this point, someone like myself should not be fooled.
How wonderful, how amazing is the teacher's kindness! (11)

Below, one is bound by the wheel of karma.
In between, one is bound by the vajra knot.

Above, the letter is turned upward.
This method one discovers within oneself. (12)

The body held like a mountain,
The speech restrained as if damming the flow of air,
The mind like the very nature of space—
Inseparable in the true nature, the reality of everything. (13)

With the inanimate, the body used as a chariot,
And the animate brought into the path of the life tree,
The concentration of binding in this way
Brings attainment of the sky-like accomplishment of deathlessness. (14)

The sky-like yoga, no-thought;
The true deity, great bliss;
Their union, clear light—
The wise find rest in these states. (15)

Holding the vajra is Vajradhara.
The vajra king is vajra bliss.
Vajrasattva is the hero, emptiness.
How wondrous is the vajra, omniscience! (16)

You might see the flower but not the honey.
You might see ice but not the water.
So behold the body and take the bliss;
See the mind, though there is nothing to see. (17)

Someone's reflection in water is whose child?
A city in a dream has no owner.
A reflection in a mirror comes from where?
All these beings are just like that. (18)

No place to stay, no cause for their arising,
No time when they cease—
Regarding these phenomena, whose nature is space, {511}
Well, what is there to fear? (19)

These things that appear are just images.
That awareness is devoid of awareness.
Everything is an aware thought, a conscious thought:
And even those thoughts are without thought. (20)

These all-accomplishing beings
View anger as sun-like luminosity;
They practice attachment as moonlike bliss,
And they overcome confusion with the eclipse of no-thought. (21)

Like clouds in the sky, waves on the ocean,
The nectar in flowers, camphor and its smell,
Reflections in a mirror, and a white crystal,
Conceptual thought and absence of thought are actually inseparable. (22)

These beings are born from karmic deeds,
And deeds from defilements,
Whose cause is assigning conceptual attributes.
When they know that, beings have no concepts and are free. (23)

The elephant of conceptual thought is coerced with a hook,
The bee of the mind is attracted by nectar,
The swan of concentration sports in a lake,
And the lotus of wisdom blossoms in the sunlight. (24)

The lamp of the mind dispels the darkness.
The bees drink from the flower of bliss.
The waves of grasping subside into the ocean.
The clouds of happiness and suffering vanish in the sky. (25)

When the three letters are used for the symbolic pointing-out,
One realizes that there are no letters.
The king of practices is the supreme letter,
Which does not exist as other than the mind. (26)

Without going anywhere, where can this goer
Be said to stay?

What does not stay is the expanse of reality:
How do you think it will ever cease? (27)

Forever free of any agent, there is no bewilderment;
Anger and attachment are forever destroyed.
This is sublime peace, beyond all suffering.
Know that this great treasure is present within you. (28)

The world is produced from illusory karma,
And that illusion by the illusory mind.
When one recognizes that all that is an illusion,
One is free, as in an illusion. (29)

By realizing all as illusion, one destroys the concept of true existence,
But it does not remain a conceptless illusion.
Without remaining, through diligence in benefiting beings,
Wonder!—One finds a precious jewel. (30)

{512}

This completes *Thirty Verses Expressing Realization*.

It was translated by Nup Lotsawa Jampa Pal in the presence of the lord of yogis, the great siddha Mitrayogin.

# 34. An Explanation of the Words of the Vajra Song *Thirty Verses Expressing Realization*[1]

{512}
To the gracious, most venerable lords I pay homage.

With great respect I bow my head to the dust on the lotus feet
Of the king of great siddhas, Mitrashrī, who was blessed
By the lord of compassion, glorious Avalokiteshvara,
And the ultimate single taste of wisdom, Ekajaṭī.

Here I shall tell of the realization of that eighty-fifth lord of yogis. First of all, for twelve years he practiced the sādhana of Avalokiteshvara in the great temple of Shrī Khasarpāṇi, at the end of which he beheld in reality the adamantine form of the Lord of the World, on a wooden mandala together with an ablutions mirror, inconceivably resplendent, the size of two cubits and a finger. Avalokiteshvara uttered the twenty-five-verse dohā that gives rest to the mind. When Mitrayogin heard it, there immediately arose in him the highest realization of the union of emptiness and compassion. When Avalokiteshvara's physical form disappeared, he was tormented with grief, but then he saw that he was internally the deity and he settled in meditative equanimity. As a result, he gained a clear understanding of the experience that had been kindled in him by the vajra song, or dohā, the melodious teaching he had received earlier. Clear, unobstructed realization dawned in him, like the reflection of the moon in a clear lake or the imprint left by a seal, and his mind was filled with untainted joy and bliss. Like mushrooms suddenly sprouting in a meadow, these thirty verses expressing his realization arose in his mind and poured from his mouth.

They should be understood under three headings: in the beginning, an expression of realization in terms of gratitude; {513} in the middle, an expression of realization in terms of introduction; and in the end, an expression of realization in terms of accomplishing the great goal by seeing the practice through to its culmination.

## I. An Expression of Realization in Terms of Gratitude

Vajra Holder, crowning Brahmā and Indra,
Lord of the World in the center of a great lotus,
By bestowing empowerment with a stream of light rays
You purify the three stains—how marvelous! (1)

When someone who possesses the three supreme methods unceasingly practices the guru yoga and prays with the teacher [visualized] above their head, they will be permeated by the teacher's blessings. And, by never separating from the practice of the yidam deity [visualized] in their heart center (referred to in the root verse by "lotus"), and uninterruptedly doing the recitation and meditation of the generation and perfection stages together, they will attain the accomplishment of the Great Compassionate One. "With a stream of light rays"—from both the teacher and yidam deity rays of bright light stream forth and "bestow" on that person the "empowerments" of their enlightened body, speech, and mind, purifying the three impurities associated with conceptual attributes and perceptions. And the verse concludes, "How marvelous!" indicating how they have cared for that person.

## II. An Expression of Realization in Terms of Introduction

The expression of realization in terms of introduction consists of (1) expressing realization in terms of the main introduction and (2) expressing realization in terms of supplementary introductions.

### A. Expressing Realization in Terms of the Main Introduction

With the body as stable as a mountain,
The mind free of elaboration is like space.

Continuously binding the wind, the moving mind—
By this means is the yogi fully freed. (2)

Someone who has the seven seals of concentration makes their body as stable as a mountain and settles with undistracted mind in meditative equipoise in the uncontrived [state] free of elaboration, like space. And by means of the four applications—inhaling the moving [wind], filling, pushing, and expelling it up like an arrow, they bind [the wind] at the level of the navel. By training continuously in this way, they are introduced to how one's own mind is—the uncontrived nature of the mind.

### B. Expressing Realization in Terms of Supplementary Introductions

There are two parts: (1) expressing realization in terms of the instantaneous path and (2) expressing realization in terms of the graded path.

#### 1. Expressing Realization in Terms of the Instantaneous Path

The mind is all-pervading, like space:
The body, whose nature is the five chakras,
The life and fierce winds, and the sun and moon
Are bound by the noose of adamantine great bliss. (3)

When an instantaneous practitioner practices the yogic exercises, {514} at that time their vast mental yogic practice pervades everything like Vishnu[2] and they meditate on the profound nature, the sky-like emptiness. The physical yogic exercise concerns the five chakras: the chakra of great bliss in the crown center, the chakra of enjoyment in the throat, the chakra of dharma in the heart center, the chakra of manifestation in the navel, and the chakra of activity in the secret center. Through the binding of the five sense organs, the supports of the five sense consciousnesses, inside, the five consciousnesses are automatically brought under control. This is the skillful means for doing so.

The yogic exercise of speech comprises expertise in mastering mind (life) and wind (energy) and expertise in mastering the white and red bodhichitta essences, the sun and moon.

By mastering these three yogic exercises, one experiences bliss and emptiness inseparable, giving rise to realization of the path instantaneously. This is referred to as "adamantine great bliss."

## 2. Expressing Realization in Terms of the Graded Path

The expression of realization in terms of the graded path is divided into three: (1) expressing ordinary realization related to those with the most basic faculties; (2) expressing uncommon realization related to those of middling faculties; and (3) expressing extraordinary realization related to those with the highest faculties.

### a. Expressing the Ordinary Realization of Those with the Most Basic Faculties

Ordinary realization is divided into nine sections: expressing the realization of (1) the self-liberation of appearances; (2) the skillful means of blazing and dripping; (3) uprooting the three poisons; (4) the gnosis of the tummo practice; (5) gathering the three chakras; (6) leaving duality as it is; (7) equalizing one's mind and space; (8) recognizing deception; and (9) making great bliss the path.

#### i. Expressing the Realization of the Self-Liberation of Appearances

> The five impurities are purified by the five,
> Body, speech, and mind are Body, Speech, and Mind.
> These are uncontrived, unborn.
> Wonder! What is there to meditate here? (4)

On the outer level, the defects in the five aggregates are purified by the buddhas of the five families. On the inner level, the consciousnesses of the five senses are purified by the recognition of their own nature. And on the secret level, the five poisons or defilements are purified by one's knowing them to be perfectly pure as gnosis. The perceptions of their being impure dissolve spontaneously. The body is liberated as the deity's body, speech is liberated as mantra, and the mind is liberated as enlightened mind: {515} this is the self-liberation of the three doors.

Their mode of liberation is indicated by "These are uncontrived," meaning that since they are pure as the innate gnosis that is self-arisen from the very beginning, they are already devoid, already divested, of something to be meditated on and a meditator.

### ii. Expressing the Realization of the Skillful Means of Blazing and Dripping

As the fire blazes from the essence of the ocean,
A chariot passing up the life tree of the supreme mountain,
The rain falls down from Brahmā's peak.
Look how means brings absence of means! (5)

As a skillful means for realizing self-liberation, one meditates on the blazing and dripping from the innate two syllables in the self-arisen body. As one holds the wind in the navel center, from the syllable *baṃ* (the "essence of the ocean") below it the wisdom fire of the tummo blazes and, [rising] through the hollow interior of the avadhūtī (the "life tree of the supreme mountain") it melts the *haṃ* in the crown, "Brahmā," and fills and spreads through all the insides of the channels of the five chakras, as a result of which the experiences of bliss, clarity, and emptiness naturally occur. From this, the realization free of means that occurs through skillful means occurs. What an amazing thing that is to see!

### iii. Expressing the Realization of Uprooting the Three Poisons

Ignorance is emptiness.
Entanglement is a grove of bliss.
Aversion shines brightly as luminosity.
What negativity can fetter the supreme deity? (6)

The causal factors that fetter all sentient beings are the three defilements or poisons. Through the recognition of the very nature of ignorance, the realization that it is emptiness, devoid of essence, dawns. Through the recognition of the very nature of attachment, entanglement is naturally purified and blazes as great bliss. And through the recognition of the very nature of aversion, conflict is naturally purified and is transformed into luminosity. In this way, all fetters are realized as self-liberating.

### iv. Expressing the Realization of the Gnosis of the Tummo Practice

In the navel, the lamp dispels the darkness.
In the heart center, the lotus of wisdom blooms.

In the crown, the gnosis of great bliss drips.
Now one's own body attains accomplishment. (7)

Physically adopting the "stove-fuel" posture,[3] one holds the wind with the vase exercise and keeps the mind on the three vajra syllables. As a result, the fire of the tummo blazes from the letter *A* in the navel center, filling the lower part of the body, so that the sun of clear light rises. From the *haṃ* in the crown a stream of nectar flows down, so that great bliss descends. As one concentrates one-pointedly on the *hrīḥ* or *hūṁ* in the heart center, the lotus flower of wisdom free of conceptual thoughts opens. Thus, {516} through one's own body one attains one's own accomplishment.

### v. Expressing the Realization of Gathering the Three Chakras

In the center, where the three channels are gathered as the chakras,
The essential drops of great bliss reside,
And in their midst, absence of concepts,
The immaculate eye of gnosis. (8)

At the head of the central channel in the body, the *roma* and *kyangma* unite in the crown [to form] the chakra of great bliss. They unite in the heart center to form the chakra of dharma. And they unite in the navel center to form the chakra of manifestation. When these three chakras are brought under one's control, the essential drops, source of bodhichitta, are gathered like butter from churning cream, and the self-arisen nonconceptual gnosis arises in the dhūtī like a reflection appearing in a clear mirror, appearing as the immaculate eye of gnosis.

### vi. Expressing the Realization of Leaving Duality as It Is

Like the sun rising in the sky,
The light of realization [shining] on the darkness of duality
[Reveals] that duality does not dwell there nor anywhere else.
Goodness! How extremely profound that state is. (9)

Both the apprehended object toward which the mind moves and the apprehending mind that clings to [the object as having] attributes are one's own nature. Recognizing this is like realizing, when one wakes up, that neither one's dream nor the objects in the dream exist. As a result of that recognition, both subject and object dissolve by themselves, without there being any need to eliminate them. As when the sun rises in a cloudless sky, under the light of realization, [one sees that] ignorance and gnosis do not dwell in those states, nor have they gone anywhere else. This is an extremely profound [point].

### vii. Expressing the Realization of Equalizing One's Mind and Space

> The whole world is bound by the sky,
> Obscured by the clouds in that sky.
> When the clouds of conceptual thought clear,
> What is there that appears here? (10)

All sentient beings who perceive like this are bound by their own sky-like minds, and that sky is clouded over by delusion. But when the obscuring clouds of conceptual thought clear by themselves, in the uncontrived sky-like state there occur no good or bad perceptions whatsoever.

### viii. Expressing the Realization of Recognizing Deception

> An illusory city is conquered by an illusion;
> The mind is deceived by the mind:
> On this point, someone like myself should not be fooled.
> How wonderful, how amazing is the teacher's kindness! (11)

An antidote that destroys an obscuration that has to be eliminated is like an army in a magical illusion conquering an illusory city. The mind emptied of defilements fools the defiled mind. When, thanks to the teacher's kindness, this deception takes place, one realizes that there is no being fooled on this point and one has recognized deception as gnosis. {517}

### ix. Expressing the Realization of Making Great Bliss the Path

> Below, one is bound by the wheel of karma.
> In between, one is bound by the vajra knot.
> Above, the letter is turned upward.
> This method one discovers within oneself. (12)

Below, the secret gate is bound by the wheel of karma. In the middle, the vajra knot is tied at the level of the navel. Above, the letter of Brahmā is turned upward. By this means, one achieves bliss and emptiness inseparable without depending on another's body.

This series of nine verses should be understood as describing in three sets of three verses each the realization of the most basic of basic practitioners, of middling basic practitioners, and of the best of basic practitioners, respectively.

### b. Expressing the Uncommon Realization of Those with Middling Faculties

The uncommon realization of those with middling faculties also has nine parts, expressing the realization of (1) the application of activities of the three doors; (2) gathering the inanimate and animate world under one's power; (3) finding rest in space; (4) knowing all, the vajra of one's own mind; (5) taking the essence; (6) whatever arises being a deceptive appearance; (7) unfavorable conditions being groundless; (8) pride being purified in its own place; and (9) transforming the three poisons.

#### i. Expressing the Realization of the Application of Activities of the Three Doors

> The body held like a mountain,
> The speech restrained as if damming the flow of air,
> The mind like the very nature of space—
> Inseparable in the true nature, the reality of everything. (13)

With the body in the vajra posture, as immovable as a mountain; the speech and flow of the breath held tight within, as if tied up in a bag; and the mind completely free of grasping, like the center of space, one settles in meditative equipoise in the ultimate reality of all phenomena.

#### ii. Expressing the Realization of Gathering the Inanimate and Animate World under One's Power

> With the inanimate, the body used as a chariot,
> And the animate brought into the path of the life tree,

The concentration of binding in this way
Brings attainment of the sky-like accomplishment of deathlessness. (14)

With the stove-fuel posture, one takes the inanimate body as if using a chariot. By one's introducing the animate breath alone into the life tree that is the central channel, the concentration of inseparable luminosity is spontaneously achieved, and in this manner one attains the sky-like accomplishment of immortality.

### iii. Expressing the Realization of Finding Rest in Space

The sky-like yoga, no-thought;
The true deity, great bliss;
Their union, clear light—
The wise find rest in these states. (15)

On the inner level, one finds rest in the sky-like state of absence of thought. On the outer level, one finds rest in the state of great bliss, the yoga of the true deity. And one finds rest in the clear radiance of the innate union of bliss and emptiness, {518} the state of luminosity. As a result of one's finding rest in these three ways, the beginningless weariness of samsara dissolves by itself.

### iv. Expressing the Realization of Knowing All, the Vajra of One's Own Mind

Holding the vajra is Vajradhara.
The vajra king is vajra bliss.
Vajrasattva is the hero, emptiness.
How wondrous is the vajra, omniscience! (16)

First by relaxing in the uncontrived state, one takes birth as the self-born Vajradhara. From that state, there appears in multifarious ways the vajra king, ultimate reality, pervading its whole realm. As everything that arises dissolves by itself, there is Vajrasattva, the hero of emptiness. That is buddhahood, awakening to omniscience.

### v. Expressing the Realization of Taking the Essence

You might see the flower but not the honey.
You might see ice but not the water.
So behold the body and take the bliss;
See the mind, though there is nothing to see. (17)

Take the honey of bliss-emptiness from another's body, as if from a flower. Train in melting the ice of your own mind into the water of emptiness. By using the body to practice the incorporeal union of the bliss and clarity, as if taking essential medicine, one will see one's own mind in the manner of the mind not seeing itself, and thus behold ultimate reality and attain the ultimate state.

### vi. Expressing the Realization That All That Arises Is a Deceptive Appearance

Someone's reflection in water is whose child?
A city in a dream has no owner.
A reflection in a mirror comes from where?
All these beings are just like that. (18)

Whatever arises, nobody has created any arising entity: it is like a person's reflection in water. There is no existent entity in the sense organ that is the support of that [arising]: it is like a city in a dream. There is no support for the arising to stay: it is like a reflection in a mirror. When one understands this, one concludes that all living beings are deceptive appearances.

### vii. Expressing the Realization that Unfavorable Conditions Are Groundless

No place to stay, no cause for their arising,
No time when they cease—
Regarding these phenomena, whose nature is space,
Well, what is there to fear? (19)

For all phenomena, there is no place to stay,[4] as it is for people in a dream. There is no cause for their arising, as it is for the mistaken impressions in a magical illusion. There is no time when they cease, as it is for a lamp in a dream. When one realizes that the whole of space is empty by nature, one is no longer afraid of unfavorable circumstances and obstacles.

### viii. Expressing the Realization of Pride Being Purified in Its Own Place

> These things that appear are just images.
> That awareness is devoid of awareness.
> Everything is an aware thought, a conscious thought:
> And even those thoughts are without thought. (20)

Objects, whether true or false, are appearance-emptiness. Whatever happiness or suffering one knows of is awareness-emptiness. {519} When one concludes, therefore, that apparent objects are consciousness and that whatever the mind knows is awareness, those conclusions themselves are empty of thought, so they dissolve by themselves.

### ix. Expressing the Realization of Transforming the Three Poisons

> These all-accomplishing beings
> View anger as sun-like luminosity;
> They practice attachment as moonlike bliss,
> And they overcome confusion with the eclipse of no-thought. (21)

The defilement of aversion is transformed by the sunlight of luminosity into the vajra luminosity. Attachment is transformed by the moonlight of the experience of bliss into the vajra great bliss. Confusion is destroyed by the eclipse[5] of no-thought and thus transformed into Vajradhara, the absence of conceptual thought.

This series of nine verses should be taken as three sets of three verses each, concerning practitioners of middling faculties—respectively, the most basic middling practitioners, middling middling practitioners, and the best middling practitioners.

## c. Expressing the Extraordinary Realization of Those with the Highest Faculties

The extraordinary realization of those with the highest faculties is described in nine verses expressing the realization of (1) those who possess skillful means (with six analogies); (2) the self-liberation of attributes; (3) having the method of skillful means; (4) naturally dissolving grasping; (5) letters and absence of letters; (6) absence of going, staying, and ceasing; (7) discovering treasure in one's own mind; (8) everything being an illusion, with no true existence; and (9) illusion being free of illusion.

### i. Six Analogies Expressing the Realization of Those Who Possess Skillful Means

Like clouds in the sky, waves on the ocean,
The nectar in flowers, camphor and its smell,
Reflections in a mirror, and a white crystal,
Conceptual thought and absence of thought are actually inseparable. (22)

Of the six analogies, here is the first. Like clouds suddenly appearing in the empty sky, conceptual thoughts suddenly occur in empty ultimate reality.

Second, like waves that rise up from the ocean and again dissolve back into it, everything one perceives, the experiences that arise in the unborn state, again dissolve back into it.

Third, just as there is nectar to be taken from flowers, there is bliss-emptiness to be taken in the body.

Fourth, just as camphor is inseparable from its smell, appearance and emptiness are inseparable.

Fifth, just as a reflection appears in a clear mirror, uncontaminated awareness appears as all sorts of knowable phenomena. {520}

Sixth, like a white crystal, which is not changed by the colors of other things, the uncontrived state is not changed into something else by the power of conditions.

Those who have the skillful means of knowing these six analogies realize that conceptual thoughts and absence of conceptual thought are inseparable.

### ii. Expressing the Realization of the Self-Liberation of Attributes

These beings are born from karmic deeds,
And deeds from defilements,

Whose cause is assigning conceptual attributes.
When they know that, beings have no concepts and are free. (23)

All the happiness and suffering of living beings in the higher realms and lower realms are produced by their karmic deeds, and good and bad deeds spring from defilements. The causal factor for these is improper use of the mind and other concepts that assign attributes. When one recognizes those very attributes as one's own nature, it is that there are no attributes, and thus one realizes the self-liberation of attributes.

### iii. Expressing the Realization of Skillful Methods by the Wise

The elephant of conceptual thought is coerced with a hook,
The bee of the mind is attracted by nectar,
The swan of concentration sports in a lake,
And the lotus of wisdom blossoms in the sunlight. (24)

There are four special skillful methods that easily give rise to the experience of the wise:[6] (1) reining in by recognizing that the thoughts that go out toward the various kinds of objects and the thinker are one's own nature, like coercing an elephant with a hook; (2) taking support of the experience of bliss with one's own body and another's body, like bees drawn by the nectar in a flower; (3) playing in the concentration of luminosity, the state of great bliss, like a swan sporting on a clear lake; and (4) dispelling obstacles by means of prayer and opening the lotus of realization, like the sun's rays making the "mud-born" lotus blossom. By means of these skillful methods, one realizes the pith instructions by which the wise integrate the path.

### iv. Expressing the Realization of Naturally Dissolving Grasping

The lamp of the mind dispels the darkness.
The bees drink from the flower of bliss.
The waves of grasping subside into the ocean.
The clouds of happiness and suffering vanish in the sky. (25)

The above four special means give rise in the wise to the following direct experiences, which constitute the benefits of training in them. By means of the skillful method that is like coercing an elephant with a hook, the lamp of naturally radiant awareness dispels the darkness of the [ordinary] mind. By means of the skillful method that is like attracting bees to nectar, the bees of conceptual thought drink up the nectar of bliss. By means of the skillful method that is like a swan playing in a lake, the waves of grasping dissolve into the ocean. {521} And by means of the skillful method that is like the sun's rays making the lotus blossom, the clouds of happiness and suffering disperse and vanish in the sky of freedom from elaboration.

### v. Expressing the Realization of Letters and Absence of Letters

When the three letters are used for the symbolic pointing-out,
One realizes that there are no letters.
The king of practices is the supreme letter,
Which does not exist as other than the mind. (26)

The three letters are *A*, *sa*, and *ka*. *A a ma ni* indicates that the mind that realizes is devoid of mental engagement. *Sa pa ra mārtha*[7] indicates that what is to be realized does not truly exist; it is the ultimate, emptiness. *Ka ka ja* means that the result of the practice, the mind realizing the point that is to be realized, is the self-liberation of conceptual attributes. In this way, the three letters show that there are no letters, so one realizes the king of letters as absence of letters.

### vi. Expressing the Realization of Absence of Going, Staying, and Ceasing

Without going anywhere, where can this goer
Be said to stay?
What does not stay is the expanse of reality:
How do you think it will ever cease? (27)

Just as it is impossible for a mother who dies in a dream to go anywhere, it is impossible for any thought to go from a particular place and time to another place and time. And just as a father appearing in a dream has no place to stay, thoughts too have no location, outer, inner, or in between. Everything that does not stay is the expanse of reality, and just as the sky has no cessation, thoughts have no cessation. In this way, one realizes the meaning of going, staying, and ceasing.

### vii. Expressing the Realization of Discovering Treasure in One's Own Mind

Forever free of any agent, there is no bewilderment;
Anger and attachment are forever destroyed.
This is sublime peace, beyond all suffering.
Know that this great treasure is present within you. (28)

Purifying bewilderment with bewilderment is the great treasure of the absence of obscuration, because what creates bewilderment is being obscured by ignorance, but like darkness in a dream, at the time one is obscured there is no obscuring agent. Purifying anger with anger is the great treasure of absence of conflict. What creates anger is the mind being in complete turmoil but, like the tumultuous flames in a magical illusion, at the time one is in conflict, there is no disturbing agent. Purifying habitual tendencies or attachment with [attachment] is the great treasure of absence of clinging and entanglement, {522} because what creates attachment is clinging and entanglement, and like a snake freeing its coils by itself, at the time one is entangled there is no entangling agent. This purification of the three poisons is the treasure of peace transcending suffering. You should understand that it does not exist elsewhere but is present in yourself.

### viii. Expressing the Realization of Everything Being an Illusion, with No True Existence

The world is produced from illusory karma,
And that illusion by the illusory mind.
When one recognizes that all that is an illusion,
One is free, as in an illusion. (29)

The world that appears like this is produced from illusion-like deeds, and those illusion-like deeds are produced from the illusory mind. In the same way that robbers, once they have been identified, can no longer steal, when one recognizes things to be illusory, clinging to true existence is reversed and suffering is automatically stopped.

### ix. Expressing the Realization of the Illusion Being Free of Illusion

This is described in two lines:

> By realizing all as illusion, one destroys the concept of true existence,
> But it does not remain a conceptless illusion. (30ab)

When, with profound wisdom, one realizes everything to be illusion, one no longer has the concept of true existence. But because of one's great compassion, one does not leave it as mere illusion but acts on a vast scale for the welfare of sentient beings, thus mastering the accomplishment of wisdom and compassion united.

It should be understood that this series of nine verses is to be taken as three sets of three verses each, concerning the practitioners with superior faculties—respectively, the most basic superior practitioners, middling superior practitioners, and the best superior practitioners.

## III. An Expression of Realization in Terms of Accomplishing the Great Goal by Seeing the Practice Through to Its Culmination

This is described in two lines:

> Without remaining, through diligence in benefiting beings,
> Wonder!—One finds a precious jewel. (30cd)

When the realization of the union of wisdom and compassion occurs, as has just been mentioned, one finally reaches the culmination and result of practice over a long period. On account of one's skillful means and wisdom, instead of remaining in either samsara or nirvana, one perfectly fulfills one's own and others' goals. This is like finding the precious sovereign of all gems.

As soon as the Lord of the World pronounced the vajra song,
The king of guides {523} experienced realization, imprinted on his heart
as by a seal.
This he expressed in thirty verses,
Of which I have here given a brief explanation.

By this merit, may the dark gloom of inborn ignorance
In the hearts of my followers be cleared away,
And may the awareness of all mother beings filling space who follow
them
Blaze with uncontaminated spontaneous realization.

The explanation of the words of the vajra song *Thirty Verses Expressing Realization* was written by the monk who bears the name Glory.[8]

# 35. Three Essential Introductions: A Pith Instruction That Is Like Distilled Ambrosia[1]

{501}

To my gracious, most venerable lords I pay homage.

This introduction to the essential point, one's own mind, has three topics: (1) receiving blessings through prayer; (2) essential pith instructions introducing one to one's own nature; and (3) incorporating appearances on the path by sealing and dedication.

## I. Receiving Blessings through Prayer

Install yourself in a solitary place and prepare the appropriate sacred substances. Then take refuge and arouse the bodhichitta. Adopt the posture of concentration, with your body sitting cross-legged in the meditation position and so on.

On the crown of your head, visualize a lion throne, lotus, and moon seat, on which is seated your root teacher with the gesture of supreme concentration, in the process of blessing you. In your heart visualize a red four-petaled lotus, half open, half closed. {502} Inside it, clearly visualize your root yidam deity, whichever it may be. Next, lead all the sentient beings in the three worlds in making the common, uncommon, and extraordinary offerings. Of these, the first consists of offering flowers, incense, lamps, scented water, food, music, and praises on an infinite scale. Offer a mandala of the universe and its inhabitants, filled with all kinds of precious things, and in particular the wish-fulfilling gem, the wish-fulfilling tree, the bountiful cow, the treasure vase, bathing pools, and so on, as much as you can imagine.

The uncommon offering consists of wholeheartedly and sincerely offering yourself—every bit of you, from the crown of your head to the soles of your feet—as an attendant and servant. The extraordinary offering consists of offering all the virtuous actions that you and all sentient beings have performed, so that [the teacher's] wishes may be fulfilled.

Next, join your hands and, with the three supreme methods [in mind], recite the following prayer again and again:

> For the sake of my mother beings who are as numerous as the sky is vast,
> Teacher, Great Compassionate One, I pray,
> Help me to develop the highest realization.
> Look on me with your wisdom, hold me with your compassion.

Consider that as a result of your fervent prayer, boundless rays of light emanate from both the teacher and the deity, purifying all your faults and obscurations without any trace of them left. At the same time, recite *oṁ āḥ hrīḥ hūṁ* or the hundred-syllable mantra as much as you can.

This completes the preliminaries.

## II. Essential Pith Instructions Introducing One to One's Own Nature

The pith instruction for the main practice consists of three essential introductions to one's own nature: (1) in the beginning, settling without distraction, like a skilled swordsman going into battle; (2) in the middle, watching without contrivance, like a skilled elephant keeper looking after an elephant; and (3) in the end, leaving things as they are, like a bird flying from the top of a ship.[2]

First, abandoning all physical and mental activities, {503} settle in a relaxed state—vividly clear, direct, unadulterated, naked, even. Whatever thoughts arise, do not see them as anything wrong. Do not follow them. Prolonging the natural state without losing the previous uncontrived state of relaxation, rest in that.

Second, from that state, whatever outer and inner appearances arise, however elevated or base, never try to stop the phenomena that have arisen, but relax and let them arise. When they arise, the agent that is arising should recognize its own nature. The best practitioners leave [whatever arises] as it is. Middling practitioners recognize it. The practitioners of least ability trace the movements of thoughts. Having done so and not found anything, in that state, devoid of all effort, practice the yoga of the flow of a river.

Third, without there being [separate] stages of meditation and post-meditation, hold your attention without separating from your previous experience. Let the consciousness move freely toward the various objects. Everything that arises, whether attachment or aversion, pleasure or pain, is its own uncontrived display, so all you have to do is recognize it as your own nature. Compassion for sentient beings who have not realized that will come naturally, and with that motivation, you will practice on a vast scale the good of others as the unobstructed display of awareness-luminosity. As we find in the *Dohā of Lālitavajra*:

> The poison of appearances is driven into emptiness.[3]
> The creative power of emptiness is trained by appearances.
> Progress in both is made by both.
> Through meditation without duality, dualistic beliefs are brought to an end.

### III. Incorporating Appearances on the Path by Sealing and Dedication

The concluding activities consist of sealing and dedication. Do not rest in the practice of emptiness alone, but integrate it with the skillful means of the deity yoga, so that the outer world is sealed as the measureless palace, its inhabitants as male and female deities, your body as the form of the deity, your speech as mantra, your mind as concentration, beings as your retinue, their conversation as mantra recitation, food as {504} the feast offering, what you wear as dharma robes, and all your activities as the practice of dharma. In this way, uniting the ground appearance and emptiness and practicing the path with skillful means and wisdom, you will gather the two accumulations of merit and wisdom simultaneously and thus complete the result, the union of the body of truth and the form body. It is therefore very important to dedicate whatever you have accomplished, by making the dedication prayer:

> Through this vast and unadulterated virtue,
> May all beings clear away the two obscurations forever,
> And by joining the nectarous streams of the two accumulations,
> May they swiftly attain the result of the two buddha bodies.

This completes *Three Essential Introductions: A Pith Instruction That Is Like Distilled Ambrosia.*

# 36. Cherished Essence

*The Most Precious Pith Instruction, Also Called*
The Three-by-Three Pith Instruction[1]

---

The alternative title of this profound collection of pith instructions refers to its division into three sections, each of which is further divided and subdivided into sets of three.

---

{504}
To my gracious, most venerable lords I pay homage.

I bow to the Glorious One who guides the totality of beings
By blessing them with the three supreme methods,
Thence introducing one's own mind as the three buddha bodies
And maintaining the great means of the three mindfulnesses.

This pith instruction comprises three points: (1) the preliminary, praying with the three supreme methods; (2) the main practice, the essential introduction to the three buddha bodies; and (3) the conclusion, skillful means related to three aspects of mindfulness.

## I. Preliminary: Praying with the Three Supreme Methods

> For the sake of my mother beings who are as numerous as the sky is vast,
> Teacher, Great Compassionate One, I pray,

Help me to develop the highest realization.
Look on me with your wisdom; hold me with your compassion.

The meaning of this is as follows.

Visualize above your head your root teacher, and in your heart center Lord Avalokiteshvara. Venerate them with vast and profound offerings, take refuge, confess your negative deeds, rejoice, arouse the mind set on supreme enlightenment, and fervently pray: "For the benefit of all sentient beings as numerous as the sky is vast, teacher and Great Compassionate One, help me to develop extraordinary realization within my mind stream!"

In all this, it is very important to consider that you are making a commitment, {505} to have an intense yearning in your mind stream, and to have a powerful aspiration for realization.[2]

After that, as the teacher dissolves into you, consider that the teacher's realization spreads into you. As Lord Avalokiteshvara dissolves into you, meditate on his body, speech, and mind.

To acquaint ourselves with praying like this in greater detail, there are three topics: (1) the reasons for praying; (2) essential points in praying; and (3) how to pray.

### A. Reasons for Praying

The reasons for praying have three aspects: (1) three benefits of praying; (2) three disadvantages of not praying; and (3) three examples of how prayers bear fruit.

#### 1. Three Benefits of Praying

One swiftly achieves one's goals, like a merchant finding goods on their travels.
One will have few difficulties,[3] as when clay is pressed into a mold.
One achieves perfection, like a lotus growing out of the mud.

#### 2. Three Disadvantages of Not Praying

One will never find what one wants, like a poor person looking for money.
One will have a lot of difficulties, like someone trying to take water with their cupped hands.

One will never achieve perfection, like an inadequate, clumsy person.

### 3. Three Examples of How Prayers Bear Fruit

In terms of the support,[4] it fulfills all one's needs and desires without thinking about it, like the wish-fulfilling jewel.
In terms of oneself, the power of the prayer induces one's aspiration, as when yearning causes tears to well up.
There is a profound connection between the two, as when tinder catches fire.

## B. Essential Points in Praying

There are three essential points when one prays:

Being well set[5] in one's body as a support.
Using one's voice to recite the ritual.
Giving rise to yearning in one's mind.

## C. How to Pray

There are three ways to pray:

With the urgency of a mother who has not seen her child for a long time.
With the anguish of a camel that has lost its calf.[6]
With the hope of someone in a dangerous place[7] looking for an escort.

## II. Main Practice: The Essential Introduction to the Three Buddha Bodies

Establish the perceiver as your own nature.
Transform absence of appearances into great compassion.
Transform all you encounter into the path of nonduality.
Without distraction, without contrivance, leave things free.[8] {506}

The meaning of this is as follows.

After having prayed, however awareness manifests as appearances, you yourself, the perceiver, are empty, devoid of any reality. Recognize this as your own nature and keep your mind on that. This is an instruction that the perceiver is liberated in its own state and the uncontaminated body of truth is thus realized.

[Realizing] absence of appearances on its own will not benefit beings, so one must train in bodhichitta, transforming the absence of appearances into great compassion for beings who have not realized uncontaminated wisdom. This is the essential point of completely pure great compassion arising as the body of the perfect enjoyment of the dharma by oneself and others.

From that state, whatever good or bad mental states arise, if you recognize them as your own nature, they will dissolve by themselves. This is a complete, infallible, easy, and swift causal factor that leads to one's own perfect fulfillment. Dedicating it to the welfare of others, saying, "May all sentient beings too be liberated just like that!" is a complete, infallible, easy, and swift causal factor that leads to others' perfect fulfillment. This incorporation into the path of whatever suddenly arises, whatever you encounter, is the essential point for arising as the unimpeded body of manifestation that acts to benefit and tame beings of all kinds and in all kinds of ways.

In all this, it is important in the beginning to settle without getting distracted, in the middle to watch without contrivance, and in the end to preserve that free state.

To acquaint oneself with this introduction in greater detail, there are three points: (1) the reasons for such an introduction; (2) essential points that are introduced; and (3) ways of introduction.

### A. Reasons for Such an Introduction

There are three reasons: (1) the benefits of introduction; (2) the disadvantages of no introduction; and (3) examples of success in introduction.

#### 1. Benefits of Introduction

There are three benefits:

> One discovers the buddha in oneself, like a poor person finding a treasure in their home.
> Suffering is transformed into happiness, like iron being transformed alchemically into gold.

Defilements arise as friends, like poison over which mantras have been chanted.[9] {507}

### 2. Disadvantages of No Introduction

There are three disadvantages of not being introduced:

One will not recognize one's own nature, and one will be like a madman possessed by an evil spirit.
Whatever one does will lead to suffering, as when one eats poisoned food.
Rejecting defilements will not eliminate them, as when a fire spreads through a forest.[10]

### 3. Examples of Success in Introduction

There are three examples of successful introduction:

In terms of appearances, self-appearances[11] dissolve into emptiness, as when one recognizes that ice is water.
In terms of emptiness, emptiness arises as appearances, like the moon's reflection in water.
And in terms of both, one realizes that appearances and emptiness are inseparable, like a rainbow in the sky.

## B. Essential Points That Are Introduced

There are three essential points:

One is introduced to leaving as-it-is, the natural state.
One is introduced to the self-liberation of thought movements.
Everything one encounters serves as a continuous introduction.

## C. Ways of Introduction

There are three ways by which introduction is made:

In the beginning, one should rest without getting distracted, like a skilled swordsman going into battle.

In the middle, one should watch without contrivance, like a skilled elephant keeper looking after their elephant.
In the end, one should leave things as they are, like a bird flying from the top of a ship.[12]

## III. Conclusion: Skillful Means Related to Three Aspects of Mindfulness

Meditation and postmeditation are linked by mindfulness from one moment to the next;
Mindfulness is sealed by applying the seal of continuity;
The innermost essence is maintained by mindfulness of others' welfare.
In all [these], clear awareness without attachment is most important.

The meaning of this is as follows.

When one arises from concentration, one might then get distracted by this or that thought as one tries, with the attitude that everything is like an illusion, to benefit all beings. But by being mindful of the connection between meditation and postmeditation, one will join meditative and nonmeditative states, realizing that they are by nature the same.

The unbroken link of mindfulness seals [one's practice] uninterruptedly until one attains buddhahood.

By being mindful of benefiting others, one genuinely gives away the whole of one's sources of good to all the beings in the three worlds without any concern for oneself.

In all these, {508} it is very important to remind oneself from time to time of keeping the connection constant and regular,[13] and applying the seal, and ultimately engaging wholeheartedly in benefiting others.

If we were to categorize these skillful means related to three kinds of mindfulness in greater detail, there are three points: (1) the reasons for putting them into practice; (2) essential points in putting them into practice; and (3) how to put them into practice.

### A. Reasons for Putting Them into Practice

There are three reasons: (1) the benefits of putting them into practice; (2) the disadvantages in not doing so; and (3) examples of successful practice.

### 1. Three Benefits [of Putting Them into Practice]

Even without meditating, they fulfill the function of meditating, like a wheel that never separates from its linchpin.
One is uninterruptedly connected with merit, like a glacial stream and the ocean.
Whatever one does, one hits the essential point, like a skilled archer's arrow.

### 2. Three Disadvantages of Not Putting Them into Practice

The connection between meditation and postmeditation is broken, as with a chariot that has a broken linchpin.
One's efforts, results, and accomplishment decline, like a red-hot iron fading when the fire goes out.
One's spiritual austerities are hollow and worthless, like a grown plantain tree.

### 3. Three Examples of Successful Practice

By being constant and regular, one simultaneously achieves ability and power together, like yogurt being used to seed another batch of yogurt.
By maintaining continuity, one's practice is saved from interruption by ordinary states, as if by a yogi's protection circle.
By accomplishing others' welfare by means of both, one will be like the trunk of a medicinal tree growing from the seed.

## B. Essential Points in Putting Them into Practice

There are three essential points:

Remember without forgetting.
Fix the linchpin of refreshing the memory.
Cut desire and attachment from within.

## C. Ways to Put Them into Practice

There are three ways:

Know how to be constant and regular, like someone who is proficient at spinning.
Refresh [your experience] a bit at a time, like adding wood to a fire.
Look trustingly to others, like a mother to her only child.

These are the three [pith instructions]: preliminaries, main practice, and concluding {509} means.

I received these pith instructions, which are like a stream of nectar,
From my teacher, who is like a wish-fulfilling jewel.
May the fruit, which is like that of the wish-fulfilling tree, ripen,
And may we complete the accumulations without concepts, like the sky.

This completes the most precious[14] pith instruction entitled *Cherished Essence* and also *The Three-by-Three Pith Instruction*.

# 37. The Root Vajra Verses of the Pith Instruction on the *Three Quintessential Points* Composed by the Great Siddha Mitrayogin[1]

{606}

*namo guruve*

To explain this instruction, there are three points.

## I. Brief Introduction

In this life, meditate on the yidam deity continuously.
At the moment of death, practice the instructions on transference.
In the intermediate state, meditate on mixing.
To meditate continuously is the essence of all.

## II. Detailed Exposition

This has three sections: (1) the essence of practice in this life, meditating continuously on the yidam deity; (2) the essence of practice at the moment of death, practicing transference; and (3) the essence of practice for the intermediate state, training in mixing.

### A. The Essence of Practice in This Life: Meditating Continuously on the Yidam Deity

This has four parts.

#### 1. A Pith Instruction on the Condition, Inciting [One to Practice]

> Keep in mind impermanence and suffering,

#### 2. The Cause: Arousing the Mind Set on Supreme Enlightenment

> And give rise thoroughly to great compassion.

#### 3. A Pith Instruction on Praying to the Teacher and Yidam Deity

> On the crown of your head, the teacher; in your heart, the deity.

#### 4. A Pith Instruction on Meditating on the Unborn Nature, One's Mind

> Meditate that your mind is unborn.

### B. The Essence of Practice at the Moment of Death, Practicing Transference

This also has four parts.

#### 1. Offering the Illusory Body to Accumulate Merit

> Offer and give your own body,

#### 2. Cutting Mental Ties

> And completely abandon[2] all your ties.

### 3. Opening the Great Path to Liberation

By meditating on a tube of light, {607}

### 4. Transferring the Consciousness Higher

Direct your mind into the Tuṣhita heaven.

## C. The Essence of Practice for the Intermediate State: Training in Mixing

This too has four parts.

### 1. Keeping in Mind the Antidote to Not Recognizing the Intermediate State

Knowing that this is the intermediate state,

### 2. Keeping in Mind the Antidote to Clinging to the Intermediate State as Ordinary

Transform outer, inner, and secret.

### 3. Keeping in Mind the Antidote to Taking Rebirth through Attachment or Aversion

By means of the yoga of emptiness and compassion,

### 4. Keeping in Mind the Antidote to an Unpredictable Rebirth

Skillfully make the connection with a new rebirth.

## III. Concluding Summary with a Pith Instruction on the View, Meditation, and Conduct

> To recognize whatever arises is the crucial point of the view.
> To not be distracted in that is the crucial point of the meditation.
> Mindfulness and even taste comprise the crucial point of conduct.
> These are the instructions of the great siddha.

These [last] words indicate the source of these instructions. The first quatrain comprises the actual words of the Great Compassionate One. The other verses were composed by Tropu Lotsawa, Nub Jampa Pal, as a commentary on their meaning.

# 38. Bestowal of the Supreme Blessings

*A Prayer to the Lineage Teachers of the* Three Quintessential Points[1]

While the tantric teachings tended, in the earlier years, to be transmitted to a single lineage holder at a time, over the centuries it became less unusual for a master to have several lineage successors, resulting in numerous branch lineages. According to this prayer, the teaching was transmitted down the lineage as far as the omniscient Butön, who then passed it on to Jangchup Tsemo on the one hand and Zhönu Sönam Jamgön on the other. Some three centuries later, the master Jamyang Drakpa received the transmission from their successors in both these lineage streams, which thus came together again, like a river split by an island. Jamyang Drakpa's successors then passed the transmission down the lineage to Jamyang Khyentse Wangpo. This lineage prayer appears, therefore, to give us an *à la carte* choice as to which lineage masters we can pray to.

To the Great Compassionate One, Matiratna, {608}
The mahāsiddhas Tilopa and Lalīta,
Mitrayogin, and Tropu Lotsawa I pray,
Bestow on me the two accomplishments.

To Sönam Wangchuk, Sönam Senge,
Rinchen Senge, the omniscient Rinchen Drup,
Jangchup Tsemo, and Drakpa Gyaltsen I pray,
Bestow on me the two accomplishments.

To Chokle Namgyal, Jamyang Drakpa,
Dawa Gyaltsen, Khyenrap Chöje,
Kunpang Chenpo, and Losal Gyatso I pray,
Bestow on me the two accomplishments.

To Khyentse Wangchuk, Jampa Kalzang,
Wangchuk Rapten, Lord Shalupa,[2]
Jamyang Drakpa, and Gelek Gyatso I pray,
Bestow on me the two accomplishments.

To the Jamgön Lama, the omniscient Jikme Wangpo,
Könchok Gyaltsen, Tenpa Rapgye,
And my peerless, gracious root teacher I pray,
Bestow on me the two accomplishments.

Alternatively, after Rinchen Drup, say:

Zhönu Sönam Jamgön, and his son I pray,
Bestow on me the two accomplishments.

To Chökyi Gyaltsen, Lekpa Chöjor,
Gendun Gyatso, Sönam Trapai De,
Sönam Gyatso, and Sönam Palzang I pray,
Bestow on me the two accomplishments.

To Chöpal Zangpo, Paljor Lhundrup,
Trinle Rapgye, Lozang Gyatso,
Jamyang Drakpa, [and Gelek Gyatso I pray,
Bestow on me the two accomplishments.]

From here on is the same as above. At the end, pray as follows:

May I be ever mindful of impermanence and suffering, and with determination to be free
May I go for refuge, arouse the mind intent on enlightenment,
And realize the profound and luminous yoga of teacher and deity
And the unborn true condition of the mind.

May I make an offering and gift[3] of my tainted aggregates
And give up attachment to my family and friends, possessions, and body.
With the hook of light rays, may my mind {609}
Be transferred into the heart of the invincible protector, Avalokiteshvara.

May I think of him in my waking life, in dreams, and in the intermediate state,
And may the world and its inhabitants appear completely pure, as the great appearance-emptiness.
Through emptiness and compassion, may attachment and aversion dissolve by themselves,
And may I swiftly attain the level of union.

This prayer was written by a young monk of the Shākya lineage who bears the name Khyentse, in whose mind deep faith in the teachings of the non-sectarians blossomed like an utpala.
*siddhirastu*

# 39. The Chariot of Supreme Accomplishment

*A Concise Practice on the* Three Quintessential Points, *the Direct Instructions of the Highest of Noble Beings, the Great Compassionate One*[1]

*namo guru lokeśvaraya*
Embodiment of all the buddhas' compassion, holder of a white lotus,
Manifesting as a saffron-robed monk—lord of dharma,
Glorious teacher, to you I bow respectfully
As I disclose a little of the practice of his quintessential instructions.

Here is a summary of the profound instruction *Three Quintessential Points*, noble Avalokiteshvara's direct instructions that have come down through the lineage from the lord of siddhas Mitrayogin, showing how to put them into practice. The root text begins:

> In this life, meditate on the yidam deity continuously.
> At the moment of death, practice the instructions on transference.
> In the intermediate state, meditate on mixing.
> To meditate continuously is the essence of all.

The essence of the practice in this life is the daily practice of the yidam deity. The essence of the practice at the moment of death is the practice of transference. The essence of the practice in the intermediate state is meditation on mixing.

Regarding the first of these points:

Keep in mind impermanence and suffering,
And give rise thoroughly to great compassion.
On the crown of your head, the teacher; in your heart, the deity.
Meditate that your mind is unborn.

To practice this point, sit on a comfortable seat {610} in an attitude of meditation. Even if you have obtained an extraordinary support like this [human body endowed with] the freedoms and advantages that are so difficult to find, you cannot be confident that you will not die this very night. And after you die, only your positive and negative deeds will follow you, and wherever you are reborn in the three worlds, you will have nothing but suffering. So, thinking, "I must do whatever I can to set out on the path to liberation right now," give rise to intense renunciation. In that state, visualize in the sky in front of you a four-petaled white lotus rising out of a wish-fulfilling tree. In its center is your teacher, around whom are disposed the Buddha in front, the dharma on the right, the sangha on the left, and an assembly of ḍākas, ḍākinīs, and dharma protectors and guardians behind. Visualize them as if they are actually present, and with one-pointed yearning say three times:

With the wish to liberate beings,
Until I reach the heart of enlightenment,
I will constantly take refuge
In the Buddha, the dharma, and the sangha.

or

Until I and all beings reach the heart of enlightenment,
I take refuge in the Three Jewels.
With the wish to attain buddhahood for the benefit of others,
I will perform the practice of noble Avalokiteshvara.

Then:

Above the crown of my head is the Stupa of Enlightenment,
Made out of white crystal and with all the attributes complete,
Having four terraces and a thousand gates. In its center,
On a lotus and moon, is noble Avalokiteshvara,

Surrounded by the ocean-like assemblies of the Three Jewels, our refuge.
The thousand buddhas of the Good Kalpa occupy the thousand gates,
Taking the form of the tathāgatas of the four families.
In my heart center, in the middle of a thousand-petaled lotus,
Is my own mind [in the form of] Khasarpāṇi, the highest of noble beings,
And on the thousand petals one thousand white *A* letters,
Shining like strings of pearls.
The three centers of the deities are marked with the three syllables. {611}
Lights radiate,[2] inviting the wisdom deities, who dissolve inseparably.

Say the detailed lineage prayer[3] or this condensed prayer:

Actual embodiment of the knowledge, love, and power
Of all the buddhas and bodhisattvas of the three times,
Teacher Avalokiteshvara, to you I pray.
Please bestow on me empowerment and blessings.

Say this as many times as you can. At the end:

With this prayer, from the teacher's body above my head
A stream of white ambrosia flows down.
It fills the inside of my body, purifying sickness, negative forces, and obscurations.
I receive all the blessings and accomplishments.

From that state, complete in an instant's recollection,
I appear on a white lotus and moon as Avalokiteshvara,
Brilliant white in color, with one face and four arms.
The first two hands are joined at the level of the heart;
The lower right and left hands hold a crystal rosary and white lotus.
He is adorned with breathtakingly beautiful silks and jewel ornaments

And seated with his two legs crossed in the vajra posture.
He is visualized as the great union of appearance and emptiness.
In his heart center is the wisdom deity, in the middle of whose heart,
Upon a moon disk, is the syllable *hrīḥ*, encircled by the mantra garland turning clockwise.
From it light radiates, filling the whole of the six realms
And completely cleansing away each one's suffering along with its cause.
The outer world becomes the pure Potala buddha field;
All the beings inhabiting it take the form of the Great Compassionate One,
Their voices proclaiming the sound of the six-syllable mantra;
All thoughts are a single taste, the radiant body of truth.

Say this and then, with this visualization in mind, recite as many times as possible:

*oṁ maṇi padme hūṁ*
The teacher above my head, the yidam deity in my heart,
And the perfect buddhas dissolve into the thousand *A* letters.
The stupa fades away like a rainbow in the sky. {612}
The world and its inhabitants melt into light and dissolve into me:
I too gradually dissolve into light and become emptiness.

After this, without being interrupted by other thoughts, rest in meditative equipoise for as long as you can, in the state of emptiness free of elaboration, the union of sustained calm and profound insight.

As you prepare to conclude the session, again visualize yourself in an instant as the Great Compassionate One and recognize all phenomenal existence, the world and its inhabitants, as being like a magical illusion. Thinking with great compassion of all the beings who have not realized that, say the prayer of dedication and aspiration:

As a result of this source of good, may I swiftly
Attain the level of the Great Compassionate One
And, not leaving out a single one of all the beings filling space,
May I establish them all on that level.

All the time between sessions, train in never separating from the view that appearances, sounds, and perceptions are the display of the Noble One's three secrets.

The second point:

> Offer and give your own body
> And completely abandon all your ties.
> By meditating on a tube of light,
> Direct your mind into the Tuṣhita heaven.

To practice this point, visualize the field of accumulation in the sky in front, as for the guru yoga. Shoot your mind far away in the form of the Great Compassionate One. Set it in front of the teacher, the Great Compassionate One, above your head, and pray, "Please make my accumulation [of merit], using these aggregates of mine, vast and complete."

From the teacher's heart center rays of light emanate, striking your old aggregates, which become fat, large, and oily. They cut off and restore your head three times, to make a fireplace of three skulls as hearthstones. From the teacher's heart center four offering goddesses wielding curved knives emanate. They cut off the [top of the] skull of your aggregates at the level of the eyebrows and place the skull cup on the hearth. Inside it, [they put] your body, cut up into pieces. The teacher utters *oṁ āḥ hūṁ* three times, purifying all the impure contents into pure wisdom nectar, and multiplying them so they become as vast as space.

Again, infinite offering goddesses emanate, carrying skull cups in their right hands. They scoop up the stream of nectar and offer it to all the root and lineage teachers, the yidam deities, buddhas and bodhisattvas, ḍākas, ḍākinīs, and {613} dharma protectors and guardians. The two accumulations are completed and the two obscurations purified. The remainder of the nectar is given to the guests of the six realms, transformed into whatever they desire. As they enjoy it, their bodies and minds are satiated with untainted bliss. With this in mind, recite *oṁ āḥ hūṁ* as many times as possible and concentrate assiduously on the visualization. At the end, rest in the nonconceptual state. Then, recognizing that one can never be sure who is an enemy and who is a friend, and that one's possessions and body are essentially worthless, completely sever all ties with them.

In the middle of the perfectly arrayed Tuṣhita heaven in the sky above the

Heaven of the Thirty-Three on top of Mount Meru, visualize the buddha Lord Maitreya, his face turned toward us in Jambudvīpa. Visualize your own body as completely empty, with the central channel in the middle, its lower end closed about four finger widths below the navel, and the upper end opening out in the aperture of Brahmā. At the level of your heart visualize the yidam deity Avalokiteshvara, the essence of wind and mind inseparable, and pray:

> Embodiment of all sources of refuge,
> Teacher, Lord Maitreya, to you I pray.
> Grant the blessing that the ties of my belief in a self be severed
> And my consciousness transferred to the Joyous realm.

As a result of your praying like this, a yellow tube of light emerges from the heart center of Buddha Maitreya and penetrates your crown. At the same time, from within it a hook of light stretches down through the central channel and catches the hair of the Great Compassionate One—your own mind—in your heart center. As you pray fervently with the three notions in mind—the notion of that light as the path, the notion of yourself taking that path, and the notion of transferring into the heart of the lord—imagine that {614} your mind is drawn up completely and that the moment it touches Maitreya's heart center, the Buddha's mind and your own mind mingle inseparably. Then, consider that it returns to its own place. Train in this way again and again. At the close of the session, consider that the tube of light is cut off and that your aperture of Brahmā is blocked by a yellow plug.

When the time comes to enact the transference, instead of visualizing it coming down, mingle your own mind and Buddha Maitreya's mind inseparably and settle in meditative equipoise in that very state.

The third point:

> Knowing that this is the intermediate state,
> Transform outer, inner, and secret.
> By means of the yoga of emptiness and compassion,
> Skillfully make the connection with a new rebirth.

To practice this point, begin by considering that all your perceptions during the day are a dream. Having trained in that, you should make a fervent aspiration to recognize your dreams as dreams and to remember that all your daytime perceptions are the intermediate state. When you get used to that, the whole of the world outside is transformed into a pure buddha field, all its inhabitants are transformed into the form of the Great Compassionate One, and all these are transformed as being like the reflection of the moon in water or like a rainbow—appearing yet having no intrinsic existence. You will abruptly abandon clinging to ordinary appearances. In particular, since in the intermediate state thoughts of attachment and aversion to parents will prevent you from taking a good rebirth, you should make the determined wish, "As the antidote to attachment, I must thoroughly analyze birth, cessation, and staying and apply the seal of bliss-emptiness. As the antidote to aversion, I should voluntarily take birth as I wish, out of great compassion, remembering that all beings have been my parents. {615} I must do whatever I can so that in all my lives, I acquire the extraordinary support [of a human body] with all the freedoms and advantages, I am accepted as a disciple by an authentic spiritual teacher who teaches this path, and I practice it properly, so that I can attain the union level in one lifetime." Make the aspiration, "May I be able to do that!" And pray, "Teacher, Three Jewels, that I may be able to do that, I put my trust in you!" Be diligent in integrating these three together.[4]

In summary:

> To recognize whatever arises is the crucial point of the view.
> To not be distracted in that is the crucial point of the meditation.
> Mindfulness and even taste comprise the crucial point of conduct.
> These are the instructions of the great siddha.

At all times and on all occasions, recognize whatever thoughts arise, knowing that they lack true existence, like space. This is the crucial point of the view.

In that state, avoid faults such as dullness and agitation and settle one-pointedly in meditative equipoise. This is the crucial point of the meditation.

And in the postmeditation period, be mindful that all appearances are like dreams and like magical illusions and thus equalize happiness and suffering. This is the crucial point of the conduct.

To make practicing in this way the most essential thing is the complete, unmistaken path for accomplishing buddhahood, the profound instruction of the great siddha Mitrayogin, who was noble Avalokiteshvara appearing in human form and was graced by twenty wondrous deeds. You should therefore make as much use of it as you can while you have a human body with the freedom to do so.

In this chariot that travels the unique excellent path
Of the supreme siddhas of India and Tibet,
May boundless beings sport delightedly {616}
And reach forthwith the city of the quintessence—enlightenment!

On the occasion of my giving guidance on this path to some serious practitioners, including my own disciple, the monk Jampal Tenzin, who devotes himself one-pointedly to renunciation and meditation, I, the fortunate one named Khyentse, composed[5] this text at Tarpa Tse, the lama's residence at Ewaṃ Chöden. May the merit of doing so lead to all beings swiftly reaching the level of the highest of noble beings Padmapāṇi.

*sarva maṅgalaṃ*

# 40. An Essential Recitation Text for the Daily Practice of Mitrayogin's Tradition of the Great Compassionate One's Direct Instructions[1]

This appears to be an appendix to the preceding text, supplying the elements that need to be recited when one is putting the teaching on the *Three Quintessential Points* into practice.

*oṁ svasti siddhi*

The heart essence of the lord of yogis, the great siddha Mitrayogin, who was noble Avalokiteshvara in person, is the direct instruction of the Great Compassionate One, which has come down to us through an uninterrupted [lineage] of learned and accomplished holy beings and is known as the *Three Quintessential Points.*

[Of these three points,] the essence of the practice in this life is the daily practice of the yidam deity. Here is a brief summary of the way to do this. Visualizing the object of refuge, take refuge by saying:

> With the wish to liberate beings,
> Until I reach the heart of enlightenment,
> I will constantly take refuge
> In the Buddha, the dharma, and the sangha.

Recite this as many times as you can. Then arouse the bodhichitta three times:

> With wisdom, compassion, and diligence,
> For the sake of sentient beings,
> In the presence of the buddhas
> I arouse the mind set on perfect enlightenment.

After these preliminaries, begin the practice of the teacher and deity:

> Above the crown of my head is the Stupa of Enlightenment,
> Made out of white crystal and with all the attributes complete,
> Having four terraces and a thousand gates. In its center,
> On a lotus and moon, is the teacher Avalokiteshvara,
> Surrounded by the ocean-like assemblies of the Three Jewels, our refuge.
> The thousand buddhas of the Good Kalpa occupy the thousand gates, {617}
> Taking the form of the tathāgatas of the four families.
> In my heart center, in the middle of a thousand-petaled lotus,
> Is my own mind [in the form of] Khasarpāṇi, the highest of noble beings,
> And on the thousand petals one thousand white *A* letters,
> Shining like strings of pearls.
> The three centers of the deities are marked with the three syllables.
> Lights radiate, inviting the wisdom deities, who dissolve inseparably.

Say the detailed lineage prayer[2] or this condensed prayer:

> Actual embodiment of the knowledge, love, and power
> Of all the buddhas and bodhisattvas of the three times,
> Teacher Avalokiteshvara, to you I pray.
> Please bestow on me empowerment and blessings.

Say this as many times as you can. At the end:

> With this prayer, from the teacher's body above my head
> A stream of white ambrosia flows down.

It fills the inside of my body, purifying sickness, negative forces,
and obscurations.
I receive all the blessings and accomplishments.

From that state, complete in an instant's recollection,
I appear on a white lotus and moon as Avalokiteshvara,
Brilliant white in color, with one face and four arms.
The first two hands are joined at the level of the heart;
The lower right and left hands hold a crystal rosary and white lotus.
He is adorned with breathtakingly beautiful silks and jewel
ornaments
And seated with his two legs crossed in the vajra posture.
He is visualized as the great union of appearance and emptiness.
In his heart center is the wisdom deity, in the middle of whose
heart,
Upon a moon disk, is the syllable *hrīḥ*, encircled by the mantra
garland turning clockwise.
From it light radiates, filling the whole of the six realms
And completely cleansing away each one's suffering along with its
cause.
The outer world becomes the pure Potala buddha field;
All the beings inhabiting it take the form of the Great
Compassionate One, {618}
Their voices proclaiming the sound of the six-syllable mantra;
All thoughts are a single taste, the radiant body of truth.

Say this and, with this visualization in mind, recite as many times as possible:

*oṁ maṇi padme hūṁ*
The teacher above my head, the yidam deity in my heart,
And the perfect buddhas dissolve into the thousand *A* letters.
The stupa fades away like a rainbow in the sky.
The world and its inhabitants melt into light and dissolve into me:
I too gradually dissolve into light and become emptiness.

After this, without being interrupted by other thoughts, rest in meditative equipoise for as long as you can, in the state of emptiness free of elaboration, the union of sustained calm and profound insight.

As you prepare to conclude the session:

> Again I visualize myself in an instant as the Great Compassionate One.

Recognize all phenomenal existence, the world and its inhabitants, as being like a magical illusion. Thinking with great compassion of all the beings who have not realized that, conclude with prayers of dedication and aspiration such as:

> By the merit of this, may I swiftly
> Accomplish the Great Compassionate One
> And, not leaving out a single being,
> May I establish them all on his level.

Then engage in daily activities, and in all situations, train in never separating from the practice of integrating appearance, sounds, and thoughts with the path, seeing them as the Noble One's three secrets.

If you wish to train in the yogas of transference and mixing, you should refer to the practice instruction manual.[3]

I, the do-nothing maṇi mumbler Jamyang Khyentse Wangpo, compiled this essential recitation text with the wish to help those of very limited intellect. May the merit of doing so lead to all beings swiftly reaching the level of the Great Compassionate One.
*sarva maṅgalaṃ*

# Appendix

THE FOLLOWING is a selection of prayers that are referred to in the texts in this volume only by their first lines.

## Bathing Offering (*ji ltar bltams pa . . .*)

As from the moment of your birth
You were bathed by all the celestial beings,
Likewise, with pure celestial waters,
We make the offering of bathing you.

This glorious and sublime ablution
Is the unsurpassable water of compassion:
Through the blessing with wisdom water
May you grant accomplishment in accordance with our wishes.
*oṁ sarva tathāgata abhiṣékata samaya śrī ye hūṁ*

## Mandala Offering (*sa gzhi spos kyis . . .*)

The ground is purified with scented water and strewn with flowers;
It is adorned with Sumeru, the four continents, and the sun and moon;
Thinking of it as a blessed buddha field, I offer it:
May all beings enjoy the happiness of the perfectly pure buddha fields.
*idam ratna maṇḍala kaṃ niryātayāmi*

### Refuge and Bodhichitta (*sangs rgyas chos dang tshogs kyi mchog rnams la . . .*)

In the Buddha, the dharma, and the supreme assembly
I take refuge until I reach enlightenment.
By the merit of practicing generosity and the rest,
May I attain buddhahood for the benefit of beings.

### Four Boundless Attitudes (*sems can thams cad bde ba dang . . .*)

May all beings come to possess happiness and the causes of happiness.
May they come to be free from suffering and the causes of suffering.
May they never separate from the happiness that is without suffering.
May they come to rest in the boundless equanimity which is free
from both attachment to loved ones and hatred for others.

### Common Vows (*dkon mchog sum la bdag skyabs mchi . . .*)

To the Three Jewels I go for refuge,
All my evil actions I confess,
And in the virtue of all beings I rejoice.
The enlightenment of buddhahood I will hold in mind,
And till enlightenment is reached
I will take refuge in the Buddha, dharma, and supreme assembly.
To achieve my own and others' aims,
I'll arouse the mind intent on enlightenment.
Having set my mind on supreme enlightenment,
I invite all beings, each and every one, to be my guests
And joyfully partake of the sublime ways of the bodhisattvas.
To benefit all beings, may I achieve buddhahood!

### Vows of the Five Families (*sras bcas sangs rgyas . . .*)

Buddhas, bodhisattvas,
Dākas and yoginīs,
I pray you all to think of me!
I who am named . . .

From this day forward
And until enlightenment is gained,
Just like all the buddhas, past, present, and to come, (*ji ltar dus gsum . . .*)
Generate the sacred, unsurpassed
Enlightened attitude of mind,
I will generate it, too.
Training to control myself,
Accumulating virtuous action,
And acting for the sake of beings—
These three kinds of discipline I will firmly keep.
Buddha, dharma, sangha,
Three Jewels unsurpassed!
From this day forward I will firmly keep the vows
Arising from the Buddha yoga tathāgata family.
For the supreme vajra family,
I will perfectly uphold
The vajra, bell, and mudrā of the deity.
And I will perfectly uphold the masters.
For the delightful pledges
Of the great and supreme jewel family,
Every day on six occasions
I will constantly perform four kinds of generosity.
For the supreme lotus family,
I will uphold all sacred teachings
Of the outer, inner, and secret vehicles,
Which have sprung from great enlightenment.
For the supreme action family,
All the vows that I have taken
I will perfectly observe
And make offerings as much as I am able.
Bringing forth the ultimate awakened mind,
Supreme and unsurpassed,
I will hold these vows without exception
For the benefit of every living being.
I will save all those as yet unsaved.
I will free all those as yet unfreed.
I will bring relief to those not yet relieved
And establish beings in the state beyond all pain.

## Taking the Vow (*gtso bos ji ltar . . .*)

Whatever the lord commands,
I will do.

## Offering Oneself (*deng nas brtsam te . . .*)

From now on, I offer myself
To you as your servant.
Accept me as your disciple
And use even the smallest part of me.

## Dedication (*bsod nams 'di yis thams cad . . .*)

By this merit may we attain omniscience
And overcome our enemies, evil deeds.
May beings, buffeted by the waves of birth, old age, sickness, and death,
Be freed from the ocean of existence.

## Prayers for Auspiciousness

Possessed of all perfection, like a mountain of gold, (*phun sum tshogs pa mnga' ba . . .*)
Protector of the three worlds, free of the three stains,
Buddha whose eyes are like fully bloomed lotuses—
Today may you grant us peace and auspiciousness.

Your sublime teachings are undeceiving,
Renowned in the three worlds and venerated by gods and humans:
Sacred dharma that brings peace to living beings—
Today may you grant us peace and auspiciousness.

Possessed of the sacred dharma, enriched with the fortune of hearing,
You, the sangha, are venerated by devas, humans, and asuras:

Supreme assembly, ground of excellence and a sense of
propriety—
Today may you grant us peace and auspiciousness.

May the morning be blessed (*nyin mo bde legs . . .*),
May the noon as well be blessed,
May the day and night, all the time, be blessed.
Three Jewels, grant this today!

# Abbreviations

| | |
|---|---|
| Catalog | Jamgön Kongtrul Lodrö Taye, *The Catalog of The Treasury of Precious Instructions*, translated by Richard Barron (Chökyi Nyima) (New York: Tsadra Foundation, 2013). |
| Dg.K. | Derge Kangyur (sDe dge bka' 'gyur): Derge edition of the Tibetan canonical collection of sutras and tantras. |
| Dg.T. | Derge Tengyur (sDe dge bstan 'gyur): Derge edition of the Tibetan canonical collection of commentarial treatises. |
| DNZ | Jamgön Kongtrul Lodrö Taye, *The Treasury of Precious Instructions. gDams ngag rin po che'i mdzod.* 18 vols. (Shechen printing) (Delhi: Shechen Publications, 1999). |
| DNZ-K | Jamgön Kongtrul Lodrö Taye, *The Treasury of Precious Instructions. gDams ngag rin po che'i mdzod.* 12 vols. (Kundeling printing) (Delhi: N. Lungtok and N. Gyaltsan, 1971–1972). |
| DzLL | *Collection of Texts from Dzongsar Lama Lhakhang in Derge. Khams sde dge rdzong sar bla ma lha khang du bzhugs pa'i dpe rnying*, vol. 209. (BDRC: W3PD988). |
| GKZ | Jamgön Kongtrul Lodrö Taye, *The Treasury of Extensive Teachings. rGya chen bka' mdzod.* 13 vols. (Shechen printing) (Delhi: Shechen Publications, 2002). |
| Toh. | *A Complete Catalogue of the Tibetan Buddhist Canons*, edited by Hakuju Ui et al. (Sendai, Japan: Tohoku University, 1934). |
| ch. | chapter |
| f., ff. | folio, folios |
| p., pp. | page, pages |
| vol., vols. | volume, volumes |

# Notes

## Series Introduction

1. 'Jam dbyangs mkhyen brtse dbang po (1820–1892), mChog 'gyur bDe chen gling pa (1829–1870), Mi pham rgya mtsho (1846–1912), and many more masters were involved in this movement, including Kongtrul's guru Si tu Pad ma nyin byed (1774–1853). See E. Gene Smith, "'Jam mgon Kong sprul and His Friends," in *Among Tibetan Texts*, pp. 247–50; Jamgön Kongtrul, *Treasury of Knowledge: Esoteric Instructions*, pp. 25–48; Ringu Tulku, *The Ri-me Philosophy of Jamgön Kongtrul the Great*, etc.
2. The specific text by Shes rab 'od zer that expounds the eight chariots is *Meditation's Ambrosia of Immortality* (*sGom pa 'chi med kyi bdud rtsi*). A study of this has been done by Marc-Henri Deroche: "'Phreng po gter ston Shes rab 'od zer (1518–1584) on the Eight Lineages of Attainment." According to Deroche, "This text may be considered as an (if not the) original source of the '*ris med* paradigm' of the eight lineages of attainment" (p. 17). It is interesting to note that the eight lineages are arranged in a different sequence in that text—Nyingma, Kadampa, Shangpa Kagyu, Lamdre, Marpa Kagyu, Zhije, Jordruk, Dorje Sumgyi Nyendrup—which may have been more chronological than Kongtrul's preferred order.
3. One finds this idea developed in the volume on esoteric instructions in *The Treasury of Knowledge*, where Kongtrul describes in incredibly condensed detail the basic principles and sources of these eight lineages. It is expounded in the catalog of *The Treasury of Precious Instructions* (DNZ, vol. 18), published in English as *The Catalog of The Treasury of Precious Instructions*, trans. Richard Barron (Chökyi Nyima). Also see Stearns, *Luminous Lives*, pp. 3–8.
4. Jamgön Kongtrul Lodrö Taye, Catalog, p. 21.
5. *The Treasury of Precious Instructions. gDams ngag rin po che'i mdzod* (DNZ), 12 vols. (Delhi: N. Lungtok and N. Gyaltsan, 1971–1972). Known as the Kundeling printing.
6. *The Treasury of Precious Instructions. gDams ngag rin po che'i mdzod* (DNZ), 18 vols. (Delhi: Shechen Publications, 1998). Known as the Shechen printing.

## Translator's Introduction

1. See George N. Roerich, trans. *The Blue Annals*, 1949, 2nd ed. (Delhi: Motilal Banarsidass, 1976).
2. The Indian name Kīrtiratna translated into Tibetan would be *grags pa rin chen* (Drakpa Rinchen). Throughout this volume, his Indian name is rendered variously as Girti Ratna, Gīrti Ratna, and Ghirti Ratna. For the sake of consistency we have used the first of these spellings throughout.
3. Further details of Mitrayogin's and Tropu Lotsawa's extraordinary lives can be found on the Treasury of Lives website (treasuryoflives.org).

## 1. The Source of All Blessings, Accomplishments, and Qualities

1. *sGrub brgyud shing rta chen po brgyad kun 'dus kyi bla ma mchod pa'i chog byin rlabs dngos grub yon tan kun gyi 'byung gnas*, in DNZ, vol. 16 (*ma*), pp. 1–55.
2. *phyi nang ram par bskor bsham bya*. This assumes the setting up of a central altar with the offerings arranged on all sides of it.
3. DNZ here reads *lus srul* ("rotten bodies"), but it seems preferable to follow Jonang Lotsawa's *Veneration of the Teacher* (*bla ma mchod pa*), on which the present text is based, which has *lus gsum*, the three bodies. These refer to a body produced by the ripening of karma, a body produced by habitual patterns, and a mental body.
4. *oṁ sumbhani sumbhani hūṁ ghṛhaṇa ghṛhaṇa hūṁ ghṛhaṇa pāya ghṛhaṇa pāya hūṁ ānaya hoḥ bhagavān vidyārājaya krodha hūṁ phaṭ*
5. See *Treasury of Knowledge, Book 8, Part 3: The Elements of Tantric Practice*, p. 90.
6. For the three brothers and other lineage masters of the Eight Chariots mentioned in the lines that follow, see *Treasury of Knowledge, Book 4: Buddhism's Journey to Tibet*, pp. 333–73.
7. *lus gnad byed* (corrected from *phyed*) *bcing*, the posture of a yogi doing the practice of channels and winds.
8. *g.ya' med mtsho smad*. We have chosen to follow the Jonang bla mchod's *g.yeng med 'tsho sla*.
9. A medicine made from solidified animal bile.
10. The two stages of liberation (*thar pa'i rim gnyis*) refers either to liberation from the lower realms and liberation from samsara, or to liberation from samsara and the great liberation of buddhahood.
11. *oṁ rnal 'byor dbang po sogs*. Probably the prayer beginning *oṁ rnal 'byor dbang po ye shes mthar phyin pa*.
12. *ji ltar dus gsum mgon po rnams sogs*. See Appendix, vows of the five families.
13. *sgrol ba'i mgon po*, more commonly known as Tāranātha.
14. *bZang po spyod pa'i smon lam*, the famous prayer at the end of the *Gaṇḍavyūha Sūtra*.

15. *bLa ma lnga bcu pa'i don bsdus*. This may refer to Jamgön Kongtrul's own prayer in the *rGya chen bka' mdzod*, vol. 9, (*ta*) (GKZ) that summarizes the *Gurupañcāśikā* by the tenth-century author Ashvaghoṣha: *dPal ldan bla ma dam par mnyes pa tshul bzhin 'grub pa'i smon lam bla ma lnga bcu pa'i bsdus don dang 'brel ba mdo sngags kun gyi yang snying*.
16. Jonang Lotsawa Lodrö Pelzang, 1299–1353/1354.
17. The two Jamgön lamas are Jamyang Khyentse Wangpo and Jamgön Kongtrul Lodrö Taye.
18. Khenchen Tashi Özer (1836–1910), a disciple of Jamyang Khyentse Wangpo and Jamgön Kongtrul Lodrö Taye.
19. Karma Tashi Chöpel was a disciple of Jamgön Kongtrul.

## 2. The Stream of Accomplishment

1. *bLa ma rdo rje 'chang grub thob brgyad cu rtsa bzhi'i byin rlabs lhan cig tu bya ba'i tshul dngos grub chu rgyun*, in DNZ, vol. 16 (*ma*), pp. 57–100; DNZ-K, vol. 11 (*ta*), pp. 1–44.
2. Jamyang Khyentse Wangpo. See *Catalog*, p. 108.
3. *rnam rgyal bum pa* ("all-victorious vase").
4. *dpal gtor* ("glorious torma").
5. *nang mchod*, a small kapāla containing nectar.
6. *sgrub mchod*.
7. As described in the *Mahāyānasūtrālaṃkara*, ch. 20, v. 59–60, the Great Vehicle is superior to lesser vehicles on account of its great reference, great accomplishment, great gnosis, great application of diligence, great skill in means, great consummation, and great activities. See Maitreya/Mipham, *A Feast of the Nectar of the Supreme Vehicle*, trans. Padmakara Translation Group (Boulder: Shambhala Publications, 2018).
8. *Prajñāpāramitāsaṃcayagāthā*, *Shes rab kyi pha rol tu phyin pa sdud pa tshigs su bcad pa* (Toh. 13), Dg.K., sher phyin, *ka*, f. 9a6.
9. *Hevajratantra*, *Kye'i rdo rje'i rgyud* (Toh. 417), Dg.K., rgyud, *nga*, f. 10a2–3.
10. We have been unable to trace the source of this quotation.
11. *bdag cag gi ston pa*, "our Teacher," refers to the buddha of our time, Buddha Shākyamuni.
12. *A Precious Necklace* (*Rin chen phreng ba*) appears in ch. 5 of this volume.
13. See Abhayadatta, *Buddha's Lions: The Lives of the Eighty-Four Siddhas*, trans. James B. Robinson (Berkeley, CA: Dharma Publishing, 1979); and Keith Dowman, *Masters of Mahāmudrā: Songs and Histories of the Eighty-Four Buddhist Siddhas* (Albany: State University of New York Press, 1985).
14. See Appendix, mandala offering.
15. *ji ltar bltams pa sogs*. See Appendix, bathing offering.
16. The three perceptions (*'du shes gsum*) are blessing the secret space, blessing the vajra, and blessing oneself and the consort as deities.

17. *bral 'bras*, divestment of the stains that obscure one's own nature.
18. In other words, this state is beyond cause and effect.
19. Kṛiṣhṇasāra, the Indian blackbuck.
20. Gorakṣha is also known as Gorakṣhanātha.
21. *mudra nag po*. Whether "black" refers to the color of the earrings or has some other significance is not certain.
22. *gcen bu* in DNZ should read *bcer bu* as in DNZ-K.
23. Vīnapa's instrument is qualified in the Tibetan by an Indic term (possibly a corrupt form), *jantara*. We have not been able to identify this precisely.
24. Tilopa is presented here using his alternative name, Tillipa.
25. The name given here is Dhupiraja, which would appear to be another name for Dhombipa or Dhobīpa, the washerman.
26. *ku ji pa* in DNZ-K is more correct than *ku ri pa* in DNZ. This siddha is more commonly known as Kuchipa.
27. *'chis pa* in DNZ should read *'chos pa,* as appears clearly in DzLL and rather faintly in DNZ-K.
28. *kunda byang sems dkar po*.
29. *rakta byang sems dmar po*.
30. The three corresponding paths are the path of the generation stage; the path of skillful means, relying on your own body; and the path of the wisdom messenger, relying on another's body.
31. Rapten is the name of an elephant in the gods' realm which the gods make drunk before sending it into battle against the demigods with a sword tied to its trunk.
32. In inserting the name of the siddha to which each verse is attributed, we have relied on the attributions in Vīraprabhāsvara, *Essence of the Eighty-Four Siddhas' Realization*, Dg.T., rgyud 'grel, *zhi* (Toh. 2292). Some of these names have been modified for the sake of consistency.
33. The translation follows Vīraprabhāsvara, *Essence of the Eighty-Four Siddhas' Realization*, f. 153b4, which reads *skyes pa de* rather than *skyes pa deng* in DNZ.
34. The original version of this verse in the Tengyur (Dg.T., rgyud 'grel, *zhi*, f. 154b1–2) appears to lay greater emphasis on the difference between worldly and spiritual weapons: "A worldly warrior brandishing his weapons / May constantly do battle with his enemies / But will be overpowered by suffering."
35. This quatrain does not appear in Vīraprabhāsvara, *Essence of the Eighty-Four Siddhas' Realization*, but is to be found in Abhayadatta's account of the life of Babhahi.
36. In Vīraprabhāsvara, *Essence of the Eighty-Four Siddhas' Realization*, f. 155b7, this verse reads: "In the petaled lotus in the crown, / The motile seed leads to joy, / The essence is drawn (*snying po 'byin pa*), and supreme joy, / Innate joy, and unsurpassed joy of absence are obtained."
37. For *so mal* in DNZ and DNZ-K, *sol mal* (in Dg.T., rgyud 'grel, *zhi*, f. 156a5) is probably more correct.

38. Rāhu, according to Indian astromythology, is a spirit responsible for eclipses when its decapitated head devours the sun or moon, which disappear as they are swallowed and then reappear from Rāhu's neck. The "lunar circle" refers to a white circle or drop in the crown chakra into which Rāhula's teacher instructed him to absorb relative concepts, and which is then to be "eclipsed" by nondual space and awareness.
39. Although DNZ reads *thad ka ma de gnyug mar gnas*, we have followed *thog ma med de* in the Tengyur (Dg.T., rgyud 'grel, *zhi*, f. 156b7).
40. DNZ and DNZ-K have *rje bo 'dzin*, but all other versions have *rdo rje 'dzin* (Dg.T., rgyud 'grel, *zhi*, f. 157a4).
41. *mi ro'i khog par nges par zhugs*. According to Khenchen Pema Sherab, this may be a reference to the transference practice of "entering a residence" (*'pho ba grong 'jug*), transferring one's consciousness into a corpse and then using that reanimated body to undertake the work of benefiting beings. Note that the Tengyur version reads *ri mo'i khang par nges par zhugs* ("One is certain to enter a painted house"). Dg.T., rgyud 'grel, *zhi*, f. 157a7.
42. The first two lines refer to an event in Sakara's life story, when he stopped a famine by coercing the nāga kings to bring rain and food to the suffering people. In the last four lines, this is taken as a metaphor for spiritual realization.
43. The translation follows Dg.T., rgyud 'grel, *zhi*, f. 158a3: *'khor ba snying po med pa yin* in place of DNZ: *'khor ba snying po med pa yi*.
44. The identity of Dorje Denpa (*rdo rje gdan pa*) here is not clear. It could refer to the mahāsiddha Āchārya Lālitavajra.
45. Repeat the section on p. 78, adapting the words accordingly.
46. *gtso bos ji ltar sogs*. See Appendix, taking the vow.
47. *deng nas brtsam te sogs*. See Appendix, offering oneself.
48. *bsod nams 'di yis thams cad sogs*. See Appendix, dedication.
49. We have followed DNZ-K *renṭha*. DNZ reads *reṭṭha*. DzLL is not very clear but looks more like *renṭha*.

### 3. The Source of Accomplishments

1. *'Phags yul gyi grub chen brgyad cu rtsa bzhi la mchod cing gsol ba gdabs pa'i cho ga dngos grub kun 'byung*, in DNZ, vol. 16 (*ma*), pp. 101–31; DNZ-K, vol. 11 (*ta*), pp. 45–75.
2. *ba byung*. According to Kriyātantra, five ingredients collected under specific circumstances are especially pure: they are the milk, butter, curds, urine, and dung of a red cow, born at an auspicious moment, and which has just calved for the first time. These have to be obtained during a lunar eclipse by a monk who has held full ordination for fifteen years without breaking his vows and who now renews his vows before milking the cow.
3. For *byin dpa'* in DNZ read *byin dbab* (DNZ-K and DzLL).
4. See Appendix, refuge and bodhichitta.

5. See Appendix, four boundless attitudes.
6. See Appendix, bathing offering.
7. Ratnakarashānti is also known as Shāntipa.
8. Here Tantipa's name appears as Chantipa.
9. Kṛiṣhṇāchāri is also known as Kāṇḥapa.
10. Shyalipa is also known as Shalipa.
11. The name used here is Dhuti, another name for Dhombipa.
12. Ḍiṅgipa is known elsewhere as Ṭeṅgipa.
13. Kujipa is also known as Kuchipa.
14. One of Mahila's alternate names, Mahipa, is used here.
15. Shāntideva is also referred to by the name Bhusuku.
16. Togchepa is also known as Koṭali.
17. Jālandhara is referred to here as Jālandhari.
18. Saṅkaja is also known as Paṅkaja.
19. Chaliki is also known as Chaluki.
20. Naguṇa is also known as Niguṇa.
21. Dhilepa is also known as Telopa.
22. Charpaṭipa is also known as Chaparipa.
23. Udhilipa is also known as Udhili and Udheli.
24. Kiravalapa, also known as Kirava or Kilapa, is referred to here as Karavalajar.
25. Putalipa is referred to here as Sutali.
26. Pahanapa is also known as Panaha.
27. Kokilapa is also known as Kokali.
28. Anonga is also known as Anaṅga.
29. *The Play in Full* lists eight great forms of merit, the first of which results in rebirth as a universal monarch, and the others as various celestial beings or gods from a supreme ruler in the Heaven of the Four Great Kings through to Brahmā.
30. The translation follows DNZ-K *grol ba* instead of DNZ *phrog pa*.
31. Kāṇḥapa is another name of Kṛiṣhṇāchāri.
32. Dhombipa is called Dhutipa here.
33. The Tibetan here uses the same verb for both lines: *zad pa* (pf. of *'dzad pa*), meaning "spent, consumed, exhausted, lost."
34. Bhusuku, another name by which Shāntideva is known, refers to someone who does nothing but eat, sleep, and wander about.
35. The text reads "Kotali," one of Togchepa's alternate names.
36. Rāhu is the planetary spirit in Indian mythology that swallows the moon or sun, thus causing an eclipse. A more literal rendering of these two lines might read: "The Rāhu of realization of nonduality ate (or swallowed) the moon of dualistic grasping into the expanse of reality."
37. *'jig rten chos brgyad*. The normal preoccupations of unrealized people without a clear spiritual perspective: gain and loss, pleasure and pain, praise and criticism, and a good or bad reputation.
38. The translation follows DNZ-K *gsol ba gdab pa* instead of DNZ *gsol ba gnas pa*.

39. See pp. 107–108.
40. *khu khrag 'dres pa'i byang sems* ("the bodhichitta that is a mixture of semen and blood").
41. *zhing dang nye ba'i zhing sogs bcu gnyis*. See *Treasury of Knowledge, Books 9 & 10: Journey and Goal*, pp. 155–58, for an explanation of how the levels in the Vajrayāna are named. The two mentioned here are the third and fourth levels.
42. See p. 45.
43. For these last two prayers, see Appendix, prayers for auspiciousness.

## 4. Collecting the Essence Drops of Accomplishment

1. *Grub mchog spyi la brten pa'i bla ma'i rnal 'byor rgya gar lugs dngos grub thig le 'khyil ba*, in DNZ, vol. 16 (*ma*), pp. 133–48; DNZ-K, vol. 11 (*ta*), pp. 76–91.
2. See note 2 in ch. 3.
3. *gsungs pa* ("it is said" or "he said"), presumably referring to Tāranātha, whose text Jamgön Kongtrul used as the basis for this one.
4. *puṣpe sogs sbyar*. At the end of each of the following quatrains, the Sanskrit offering formula should be used incorporating the appropriate offering material: respectively, *puṣpe* for flowers, *dhūpe* for incense, *āloke* for lamps, *gandhe* for perfume, *naivedye* for food, and *śabda* for music.
5. This no doubt refers to the praise in the Kangyur, *Śrī-śavarapāda-stotra-ratna*, Toh. 1176, by Vanaratna.
6. *nag po spyod pa*. He is also known as Kṛiṣhṇāchārya.
7. Lūyipa is addressed in this section, and in the mantra, by a variation on his name: Lūhipa.
8. Lvavapa is also known as Kambala, as reflected below for the name mantra.
9. Kāṇṭaka is the name of a medicinal wild rose. It is not certain whether this refers to a crown of flowers or a crown of thorns.
10. Tillipa appears to be another name for Tilopa.
11. Ratnākarashānti's alternative name is Shāntipa.

## 5. A Precious Necklace

1. *Grub thob brgyad cu rtsa bzhi'i rdzogs rim rin chen 'phreng ba rtsa 'grel*, in DNZ, vol. 16 (*ma*), pp. 149–200; DNZ-K, vol. 11 (*ta*), pp. 92–143. Second source (root text): *Ratnamāla, Rin chen phreng ba zhes bya ba*, in Narthang Tengyur, vol. 88 (*lu*), ff. 111a–112b (N3875).
2. *spro ba bsdud sgo*. The version in the Narthang Tengyur, vol. 88 (*lu*), ff. 112b2, reads *sna yi sgo* ("the nostrils").
3. This last part of the root text on the practice of transference is not explained in the commentary and, moreover, appears in different versions in the Tengyur with a wide variety of spellings. Our translation, therefore, can only be taken as provisional.

4. Lord of Speech (*ngag gi dbang phyug*) is a common epithet of Mañjushrī. However, the commentary makes no reference to this.
5. The demon child of the gods, or devaputra demon, represents laziness and attachment to pleasure and distraction.
6. *Tantra of the Vajra King, dPal rdo rje rgyal po chen po'i rgyud* (Toh. 403), Dg.K., rgyud 'bum, *ga*, f. 238a, ll. 6-7.
7. *dngos po*, a term that can be translated as "reality, matter, thing, substance, essence," etc., depending on the context. In this context, there is a play on words (not easily conveyed in English) with the term *dngos med* ("insubstantiality") at the beginning of the verse.
8. *sad pa*. This should probably read *gsad pa*.
9. The Tibetan New Year occurs toward the end of winter, its exact date, based on the lunar calendar, falling in February or March, depending on the year.
10. *gang zhig ni rten gyi gang zag gang zhig* ("'Whoever' refers to any individual who is a support").
11. *dran pa*. Although this term is defined in *The Great Tibetan Dictionary* as "to turn something over in the mind again and again and not forget it" and can be translated as "memory," "mindfulness," and so on, the implication here is that what we say simply corresponds to thought processes.
12. The translation follows DNZ-K *rang rgyud pa* instead of DNZ *rang rgyud la*.
13. *rjes kyi shes pa*, the understanding or knowledge that comes subsequent to meditation.
14. *kha garbha*. This name, normally used for the bodhisattva Ākāshagarbha, does not appear to correspond to any name variants associated with the eighty-four mahāsiddhas.
15. *bde gshegs snying po*, the buddha nature or sugatagarbha (Skt.).
16. The implication here is that the clouds and the reflections symbolize the body of form, which includes the body of perfect enjoyment and the body of manifestation.
17. *rTog pa dang po'i rgyud*. It has not been possible to identify this tantra or its contents precisely.
18. The Tibetan term *'khrul 'khor* ("machinery") is used to denote the yogic exercises in the practices of the channels and winds. The phrase *sgyu ma'i 'khrul 'khor* here covers the analogy of the magician's wizardry and the illusory yogic exercises.
19. A literal translation of the Tibetan words for the different parts of a coconut would be "flesh" for the fibrous husk, "bone" for the hard shell, and "marrow" for the white coconut flesh.
20. It has not proved possible to find a source for this quotation.
21. The other two kinds of body are the body of habitual tendencies and the mental body mentioned below in the context of the other two intermediate states.
22. The translation follows DNZ-K *nub pa* instead of DNZ *nus pa*.
23. *gdams ngag log pa* should read *gdams ngag logs pa*.
24. *li ri ltar bsgrim pa* ("tightened like *liri*"). An explanation of this expression is

given in the instructions on the Six Dharmas from the oral lineage of Rechungpa, DNZ, vol. 7, p. 507. When rope is made with *liri* grass, the grass must be twisted tight, otherwise the rope will break. Similarly, if body and mind are too relaxed, one will never make any progress in the practice.

25. Bending the neck (or throat) in this context means drawing the chin in slightly.
26. *mar la brder* (DNZ) should read *mar la brdeg* (DNZ-K).
27. *khams g.yon gnyis* should read *g.yas g.yon gnyis.*
28. *ching ste ring na* (DNZ) should read *ring ste ring na* (DNZ-K).
29. The posture the Buddha adopted at the parinirvāṇa, lying on his right side with his right hand under his cheek and his left arm stretched along his body.
30. The translation follows DNZ-K *yang ba spang ba* instead of DNZ *yang bslang ba.*
31. "Becoming" (*srid pa*) is the tenth link of interdependent origination, which precedes birth in samsara. Advanced practitioners as mentioned here are no longer subject to the cycle of twelve links.
32. *dran pa* should read *ran pa.*
33. Although the text speaks of "three errors" here, the explanation below clearly mentions four.

### 6. A River of Great Compassion

1. *'Phags pa spyan ras gzigs dbang phyug gi lam gyi rim pa'i mngon rtogs dbang bskur thugs rje chen po'i chu rgyun*, in DNZ, vol. 16 (*ma*), pp. 201–28; DNZ-K, vol. 11 (*ta*), pp. 144–71.
2. The stopper on the top of the vase (*bum pa*) ornamented with kusha grass and peacock feathers, whose elongated lower part is used to sprinkle the vase's contents.
3. Although this first section is presented as including the bodhichitta section, in the text that follows, the latter appears to form part of the second section.
4. *Ḍākinīvajrapañjaratantra, rDo rje gur gyi rgyud* (Toh. 419), Dg.K., rgyud, *nga*, f. 53b4–6.
5. See Appendix, four boundless attitudes.
6. *visarga*, the final aspiration *ḥ* (in Sanskrit), indicated by a colon-like pair of circles in the Tibetan syllable.
7. *spyan ras gzigs*, the name by which Avalokiteshvara is commonly known in Tibetan.
8. See Appendix, common vows.
9. DNZ appears to read *de na sangs*; DNZ-K is clearer with *de nas ngas.*
10. The "vajra space" (*nam mkha'i rdo rje*) here refers to ultimate gnosis (*don gyi ye shes*).
11. For the four mandalas referred to in this and the next three empowerments, see Jamgön Kongtrul, *The Treasury of Knowledge, Book 6, Part 4: Systems of Buddhist Tantra*, pp. 210–11.

12. *khyod rang yang ni de yi thabs.* A more common form of this quotation reads *khyod rang yang ni de yi pha* ("You are your own father").
13. It is concentration, clear visualization, and so on, and not the implements and substances, that are the most important thing in an empowerment.

## 7. The Glowing Jewel

1. *'Phags pa spyan ras gzigs dbang phyug gi dbang chog rin chen 'od 'phro'i mchod bsgrig dkyil 'khor ston pa bcas*, in DNZ, vol. 16 (*ma*), pp. 229–35; DNZ-K, vol. 11 (*ta*), pp. 172–78.
2. This line, which is absent from the Tibetan text here, has been inserted from an identical passage in the Avalokiteshvara sādhana. See p. 331.

## 8. Authorization Ritual for Lord Mañjughoṣha

1. *mGon po 'Jam dpal dbyangs kyi rjes gnang*, in DNZ, vol. 16 (*ma*), pp. 237–47; DNZ-K, vol. 11 (*ta*), pp. 179–89.
2. In this and the other authorization rituals, we have followed the formatting of this sentence in the Amitāyus authorization ritual (ch. 10) as nonrecited text (*yig chung*).
3. This implies not only clearing everything up but also not continuing to think about the authorization ritual afterward.
4. *rus pa.* This could be a scribal error and should probably read "jewel ornaments."

## 9. A Mine of Blessings

1. *bCom ldan 'das phyag na rdo rje'i rjes gnang byin rlabs kyi 'byung gnas*, in DNZ, vol. 16 (*ma*), pp. 249–57; DNZ-K, vol. 11 (*ta*), pp. 190–98.
2. The prayer contained in the text at this point translates as "Lord, bestow the knowledge mantra on this [person], Impregnate this person [with it], I pray." However, an identical prayer is given below for the Speech authorization, and it seems more logical to maintain consistency with the Mañjushrī and Amitāyus authorizations in this series. We have therefore taken the liberty of assuming that a scribal error has been made here and have modified the translation accordingly.
3. See Appendix, offering oneself.

## 10. Authorization Ritual for Lord Amitāyus

1. *bCom ldan 'das tshe dpag med kyi rjes gnang*, in DNZ, vol. 16 (*ma*), pp. 259–68; DNZ-K, vol. 11 (*ta*), pp. 199–208.
2. The translation follows DNZ-K *bla mas* instead of DNZ *bla ma la*.

3. This passage has been formatted in the Tibetan text to be recited aloud, but we have formatted as in the other authorization rituals.
4. See note 3 in ch. 8.

## 11. Authorization Ritual for Tārā

1. *sGrol ma 'jigs pa brgyad skyob 'khor ba 'phrang sgrol gyi rjes gnang*, in DNZ, vol. 16 (*ma*), pp. 269–74; DNZ-K, vol. 11 (*ta*), pp. 209–14.
2. *slob ma rjes gnang*. Although this might be translated literally as "authorizing the disciples," it appears to refer to their receiving the vows of refuge and bodhichitta and performing the seven branches, as distinct from the actual authorization rituals with regard to body, speech, mind, qualities, and activities.
3. This refers to the self-empowerment (*bdag 'jug*).
4. This fifth section is the Body authorization.
5. These three lines are a condensed rendering of the more detailed instructions for the Body authorization given in the previous authorization rituals.
6. The rest of this prayer is the same as the request in the Mañjughoṣha authorization in ch. 8. See p. 260.
7. This request (for the Body authorization) would apply to the previous section.

## 12. Authorization Ritual for Noble Jambhala

1. *Ārya dzam bha la'i rjes gnang*, in DNZ, vol. 16 (*ma*), pp. 275–83; DNZ-K, vol. 11 (*ta*), pp. 215–23.
2. While DNZ reads *sa gsum*, DNZ-K and DzLL both clearly have *sku gsum*.
3. Pañcapuraka could be a scribal error or an alternative name for the medicinal fruit bījapūra, which is most often associated with Jambhala.
4. See Appendix, offering oneself.
5. See Mañjushrī authorization, note 3 in ch. 8.

## 13. Routing the Hordes of Obstacle Makers

1. *Chos skyong brag lha mgon po'i rjes gnang bgegs dpung 'joms byed*, in DNZ, vol. 16 (*ma*), pp. 285–91; DNZ-K, vol. 11 (*ta*), pp. 224–30.
2. The translation follows DNZ-K *de'i khar* instead of DNZ *de'i khang*.
3. DNZ *bskyed pa gsum* appears to be erroneous. DNZ-K and DzLL read *bskyed par bya ba*.
4. *bgegs mthar byed*, the wrathful deity who "puts an end to obstacle makers."
5. Although this section is numbered "second" in the Tibetan, we have assumed that this is a scribal error.
6. "With the most exquisite scents / That perfume a thousand million worlds, / As if polishing pure refined gold, / I anoint the blazing, brilliant forms of all the

buddhas." Shāntideva, *Bodhicaryāvatāra*, *Byang chub sems dpa'i spyod pa la 'jug pa*, ch. 2, v. 14 (Toh. 3871), Dg.T., mdo 'grel (dbu ma), *la*, f. 4a7.

7. See Appendix, bathing offering.
8. See Appendix, common vows.
9. DNZ *stirti ratna* should read *ghirti ratna* as in DNZ-K.

## 14. Vajra Verses on the Graded Path of Avalokiteshvara

1. *sPyan ras gzigs kyi lam gyi rim pa rdo rje'i tshig rkang*, in DNZ, vol. 16 (*ma*), pp. 293–96; DNZ-K, vol. 11 (*ta*), pp. 231–34.
2. Although all versions have *sdug bsngal gyis gzigs rnams*, it would make better sense in this context to read this as *sdug bsngal la 'jigs rnams*.
3. "Purity" (*tshangs pa*) here appears to refer to the four pure states mentioned in the instruction manual. See note 13 in ch. 16.

## 15. A Stream of Nectar

1. *'Phags pa spyan ras gzigs dbang phyug gi bsnyen sgrub bdud rtsi'i chu rgyun*, in DNZ, vol. 16 (*ma*), pp. 297–320; DNZ-K, vol. 11 (*ta*), pp. 235–58.
2. For *sgrub* in DNZ read *sbrul* in DNZ-K and DzLL.
3. See Appendix, vows of the five families.
4. For *thogs pa* in DNZ read *thog mar* in DNZ-K and DzLL.
5. The coil of white hair between the eyebrows is one of the thirty-two major marks of a great being.
6. *bka' brgyud*. Here and below, this term has been translated literally to avoid its being confused with the Kagyu lineages featured in the earlier volumes.
7. For *ring lus* in DNZ read *rang lus* in DNZ-K.
8. See ch. 24, p. 491.
9. DNZ *chu che ba* should read *rgya che ba* as in DNZ-K.
10. *rjes chog*. This would appear to correspond to the thanksgiving offering (*gtong rag gi mchod*) listed above as the second part of the conclusion section.
11. This possibly refers to the torma-offering text called *mGon po'i gtor rdzongs gtsang sbyar ma*, currently in the eleventh volume of the Shangpa Kagyu collection (*dPal ldan shangs pa'i chos skor rnam lnga'i rgya gzhung*). Its name derives from its opening line, *gtsang zhing gtsang mar sbyar ba'i mchod sbyin gyi gtor ma* . . . ("This pure and purely prepared offering torma . . .").
12. *stong nyid kyid rang la* in DNZ reads *stong nyid kyi ngang la* in DNZ-K.
13. The elements in parentheses in this colophon are indicated as marginal notes in DNZ.

## 16. A Banquet of Nectar

1. *'Phags pa spyan ras gzigs dbang phyug gi byang chub lam gyi rim pa'i khrid yongs su sdud pa bdud rtsi'i dga' ston*, in DNZ, vol. 16 (*ma*), pp. 321–62; DNZ-K, vol. 11 (*ta*), pp. 259–300.
2. These instructions constitute a practice guide or commentary on the *Vajra Verses on the Graded Path of Avalokiteshvara* (ch. 14).
3. For *byang tshul* in DNZ read *byung tshul* as in DNZ-K.
4. A fifth section, not listed here but to which the number 5 is attributed below, is a short conclusion to the text.
5. *rdzu 'phrul ya ma zung* ("paired up-and-down miracle"), for example, blazing with fire from the upper part of the body and showering out water from the lower part.
6. *yum chen mo*, i.e., Prajñāpāramitā, Transcendent Wisdom.
7. *grang sil sel song ba* in DNZ reads *grang sil sil song ba* in DNZ-K.
8. *rata*, the slightly curved horizontal stroke below the body of the syllable indicating the subjoined letter *r*.
9. *gigu*, the hook-shaped vowel *i* located above the body of the syllable.
10. *sgra can dus me*, Skt. Rāhu and Ketū, two figures in Indian mythology representing the ascending and descending lunar nodes that give rise to eclipses.
11. *gdan*, i.e., the wheel, lotus, vajra, and fire mentioned in the empowerment of rays of light.
12. This section covering the main practice (*dngos gzhi*) is introduced as second (*gnyis pa*), presumably counting the preliminary practice as first. This does not agree with the numbering of the sections at the beginning of the text. For this translation, the original numbering of the generation stage as the third section and the perfection stage as the fourth section has been retained.
13. The four pure states (*tshangs pa'i gnas*, Skt. *brahmavihāra*) are attitudes in which Brahmā is said to constantly dwell: loving-kindness, compassion, joy, and impartiality. These attitudes, when cultivated without bodhichitta, result in rebirth in the celestial realms of the first dhyāna, such as the Pure.
14. Although the Tibetan here numbers this as the second part of the main practice, the numbering outlined at the beginning of the text has been retained.
15. *tha mal gyi shes pa*. This refers not to the deluded minds of ordinary beings but to pure awareness, which is "ordinary" in that it is the original, simple, unfabricated state of mind, free of duality.
16. *skye 'gag 'jig gsum* ("birth, cessation, and destruction"). This expression appears only once in the available searchable literature and could possibly be a scribal error for the more usual *skye 'gag gnas gsum* ("birth, cessation, and dwelling") or *skye gnas 'jig gsum* ("birth, dwelling, and destruction").
17. *thugs rjes chen po'i spyan*. This can also be read as "the eyes of the Great Compassionate One," referring to another name for Avalokiteshvara.

18. In the Tibetan text at this point, there appears a triple circle sign. Its meaning is not clear, but it might be pointing out the omission of a sentence on the extreme of eternalism, which one would expect, to form a pair with this sentence on the extreme of nihilism.
19. *snang ba'i mtha'*. Logic would suggest that this might be a scribal error for *chad pa'i mtha'*, the extreme of nihilism.
20. *bdag dang bdag gir 'dzin pa* ("grasping at 'I' and 'mine'").
21. *'jig rten chos brgyad*. See note 37 in ch. 3.
22. There appears to be an additional fifth section below.
23. For *su thams cad* in DNZ read *sa thams cad* as in DNZ-K.
24. DNZ *nyid yog pa* should read *nyid log pa* as in DNZ-K.
25. For *'dab ma brgyas pa* in DNZ read *'dab ma brgyad pa* as in DNZ-K.
26. The four excessive mental states are described in the text of pith instructions on p. 398.
27. There appears to be an error in the Tibetan numbering of this section, which is introduced as "third" (*gsum pa*) instead of "fifth" as mentioned at the beginning of the perfection stage section.
28. *rgod na sna rtse*. In both DNZ and DNZ-K there is a blank space. The missing word *rgod* is present in DzLL.
29. The Tibetan here reads *gsum* (three), which either is erroneous or refers only to the three subsections in the first of the two parts related to transference.
30. The term *bardo* is now accepted in the English language, but its dictionary definition is limited to the state between death and rebirth. It is important to understand that the Tibetan meaning of *bardo* also applies to other states such as dream and meditation. For this reason, we prefer to translate it as "intermediate state." Nevertheless, to avoid certain phrases becoming unnecessarily cumbersome, we have used *bardo* in its wider sense in the sections on the intermediate state.
31. DNZ-K and DzLL read *'char ba* for *'chang ba* in DNZ.
32. A person receiving this teaching should make appropriate offerings of a feast and a mandala of gold.

## 17. The Luminous Golden Wand

1. *'Phags pa spyan ras gzigs kyi byang chub lam gyi rim pa'i khrid kyi cha lag man ngag gser gyi thur ma rin po che'i sgron me*, in DNZ, vol. 16 (*ma*), pp. 363–76; DNZ-K, vol. 11 (*ta*), pp. 301–14.
2. A kapāla made from a skull with no sutures, so that it appears to be a single bone.
3. The lords of the three buddha families (*rigs gsum mgon po*) are Mañjushrī, Avalokiteshvara, and Vajrapāṇi.
4. *mgon pa* in DNZ should read *mgo na ba* as in DNZ-K.
5. *'beb*. An exercise whose purpose and technique are explained by the master to disciples beginning the yogic exercises (*'khrul 'khor*) related to the practice on the channels and winds.

6. *'jig rten chos brgyad*. See note 37 in ch. 3.
7. The translation follows DzLL *slar yang* for DNZ *spar yang*.
8. The translation follows DzLL, which reads *dpe lung* as opposed to *dge lung* ("virtuous transmission") in DNZ and DNZ-K.

## 18. The Wheel of Ornaments of Gnosis

1. *'Jam dpal dbyangs sku'i khrid shes rab 'phel byed ye shes rgyan gyi 'khor lo*, in DNZ, vol. 16 (*ma*), pp. 377–97; DNZ-K, vol. 11 (*ta*), pp. 315–35.
2. *tshangs pa'i rgyu bzhi*, the four causes of purity or of Brahmā, i.e., the four boundless attitudes. See note 13 in ch. 16.
3. *yan lag brgyad ldan*. The purest water is cool, sweet, light, soft, clear, and unpolluted and does not upset the stomach or irritate the throat.
4. *ngag gi dbang phyug*, another name for Mañjushrī.
5. *tha mal gyi shes pa*. The natural, original, uncontrived state of mind free of duality, which has nothing to do with the state of mind of ordinary, deluded beings.
6. *yul med du*. The corresponding passages in chs. 16 and 20 have *dbyer med du* ("inseparable").
7. *skye med*. The corresponding passage in ch. 16 has *dbyer med* ("inseparability").
8. "Gentle and Glorious" translates the name Mañjushrī in Tibetan (*'jam dpal*).
9. For *'dun la* in DNZ read *'dun pa* as in DNZ-K.
10. The Tibetan lacks the relevant outline head as presented at the beginning of the text. Its insertion here follows the layout in some of the other instruction texts.
11. The Tibetan title given (*Shes rab 'phel byed ye shes snang ba rgyan gyi 'khor lo*) differs slightly from the title at the beginning of this text.

## 19. The Spreading Rays of Light

1. *bCom ldan 'das phyag na rdo rje thugs kyi khrid bdud dpung 'joms byed 'od zer rgyas pa*, in DNZ, vol. 16 (*ma*), pp. 399–425; DNZ-K, vol. 11 (*ta*), pp. 336–62.
2. The one thousand two buddhas predicted to appear in this Fortunate Kalpa, of whom Buddha Shākyamuni is the fourth.
3. Great Mother, another name for Prajñāpāramitā, Transcendent Wisdom or the Perfection of Wisdom, the mother of all the buddhas.
4. *gdan* ("seats"), the wheel, lotus, and vajra on which the syllables repose. See note 11 in ch. 16.
5. The headings here appear to follow the numberings in ch. 16, in conflict with the structural outline presented at the beginning of this text. For the sake of consistency, the section titles here have been rearranged.
6. For DNZ *lnga'i ma par 'phros* read *lnga rim par 'phros* as in DNZ-K.
7. This section is numbered fourth in the Tibetan, but we have followed the logic of the structural outline presented at the beginning of the text.

8. *yul med du*. The corresponding passages in chs. 16 and 20 have *dbyer med du* ("inseparable").
9. The two elements of the Tibetan word for "buddha," *sangs* and *rgyas*, mean "purified" and "developed" respectively.
10. For DNZ *stong ngar* read *stong rar* as in DNZ-K.
11. For DNZ *zur du phab pa* read *thur du phab pa* as in DzLL.
12. "And so on" (*la sogs pa*) here should perhaps be interpreted as covering the signs mentioned in chs. 16 and in particular the second sign mentioned in the instructions of Mañjushrī, the appearance of a mirage, which has been omitted here.

## 20. Accomplishing the Immortal Vajra Body

1. *bCom ldan 'das mgon po tshe dpag med yon tan gyi khrid 'chi med rdo rje'i sku sgrub par byed pa*, in DNZ, vol. 16 (*ma*), pp. 427–45; DNZ-K, vol. 11 (*ta*), pp. 363–81.
2. *bdo ba'i rang bzhin can*. In DzLL this reads *bde ba'i rang bzhin can* ("blissful in nature"), as it does in the corresponding passage in the Avalokiteshvara instructions, p. 355.
3. The four occasions (*gnas skabs bzhi*) are waking, dreaming, deep sleep, and absorption.
4. See note 4 in ch. 19.
5. *stong ra* ("fence of emptiness").
6. *dmar na rang byung ba* in DNZ should read *dmar na ra ra byung ba* as in DNZ-K.
7. The two elements of the Tibetan word for "buddha," *sangs* and *rgyas*, mean "purified" and "developed" respectively.
8. For *stong rang* in DNZ read *stong rar* as in DNZ-K.

## 21. Liberation from the Perilous Path of Samsara

1. *sGrol ma 'jigs pa brgyad skyob phrin las kyi khrid 'khor ba'i 'phrang sgrol*, in DNZ, vol. 16 (*ma*), pp. 447–65; DNZ-K, vol. 11 (*ta*), pp. 382–400. In chs. 16 and 18, the title of these instructions is given as *'Khor ba'i 'phrang sgrol phrin las lhun grub* (*Spontaneous Activities That Free One from the Perilous Path of Samsara*).
2. For *sgo la ma* in DNZ read *sgrol ma* as in DNZ-K.
3. These two sentences explain the two elements in Tārā's name in Tibetan: *sgrol* ("to liberate or save") and *ma* (denoting the female gender and also meaning "mother").
4. For *stong rang* in DNZ read *stong rar* as in DNZ-K.

## 22. A Shower of Accomplishments

1. *Dzam bha la ser po'i khrid dngos grub char 'bebs*, in DNZ, vol. 16 (*ma*), pp. 467–83; DNZ-K, vol. 11 (*ta*), pp. 401–17.
2. The story goes that Jambhala was injured protecting the Buddha from the rocks

Devadatta threw at him. The Buddha healed Jambhala with nectar and asked him to grant anyone who poured water over his head every kind of wealth, both material and spiritual.

3. The third section, the instructions on the mandala practice, is absent in both DNZ and DNZ-K.
4. *nor bdag*, defined as a yakṣha or a wealth deity.
5. Bījapūra (Skt.) is the fruit of the wish-fulfilling tree.
6. "Pañcapuraka" could be a scribal error or an alternative name for the medicinal fruit bījapūra, which is most often associated with Jambhala.
7. *mkha' la spyod pa* ("those who enjoy or travel to the celestial lands"), a state achieved by many siddhas. The term may also refer to ḍākas and ḍākinīs. We have retained the Sanskrit term here to avoid its being confused with the gods (devas) of the so-called celestial realms.
8. *lte ba* (navel center) here is undoubtedly a scribal error.

## 23. Ocean of Blessings

1. *sPyan ras gzigs lam rim bla ma rgyud pa la gsol 'debs byin rlabs kyi chu gter*, in DNZ, vol. 16 (*ma*), pp. 485–88; DNZ-K, vol. 11 (*ta*), pp. 418–21.

## 24. Sādhana of Draklha Gönpo

1. *Chos skyong brag lha mgon po'i mngon rtogs*, in DNZ, vol. 16 (*ma*), pp. 489–95; DNZ-K, vol. 11 (*ta*), pp. 422–28.
2. *rlung nag dgu klong*. The translation as "dust devil" is used in the English sense of the term, meaning a localized, spiraling dust storm, rather than necessarily referring to a particular kind of evil spirit.
3. *rtsad gcod*. The other printings are not very clear, but they could read *rtsar gcod* ("annihilating") or alternatively *rtsang gcod* ("cutting the briars" of birth and death).

## 25. Resting in the Nature of One's Own Mind

1. *'Phags pa spyan ras gzigs kyis grub chen mi tra dzo ki la gsungs pa'i rang gi sems nyi ngal gso ba'i man ngag*, in DNZ, vol. 16 (*ma*), pp. 497–501; DNZ-K, vol. 11 (*ta*), pp. 429–33. Second source: *rang gi sems ngal so ba'i man ngag tshigs su bcad pa nyi shu rtsa lnga pa, Svacittavicramopadecapancavimcatikagatha*, in Dg.T. rgyud, *tshi* 175b3–176b4 (Toh. 2129).
2. The Tibetan here, which reads *gsum pa la dbu las*, makes no sense. *gsum pa la* might be a misprint for *gzhung la* ("in the main text"); DzLL appears to read *dgu las* ("of the nine [or many] parts"). Since there are in fact only eight parts, we have rendered this phrase "The main text has several parts."
3. Although this name is spelled "Ampari" here and "Ambhari" and "Ambara" in

ch. 26, for the sake of consistency we have adopted the name given in the Derge Tengyur version: Ambara.

## 26. The Quintessence

1. *'Phags pa spyan ras gzigs kyis grub chen mi tra dzo ki la gsungs pa'i phyag rgya chen po sems nyi ngal gso'i gzhung 'grel snying po bsdus pa*, in DNZ, vol. 16 (*ma*), pp. 525–52; DNZ-K, vol. 11 (*ta*), pp. 456–83.
2. These stories largely follow the account of Mitrayogin's life in the *Blue Annals*.
3. *rdo rje'i shing stan* ("a vajra wooden support"), explained in the text as *shing gi maṇḍala*, a wooden mandala.
4. A giant statue of Maitreya was subsequently erected at Tropu but destroyed in the eighteenth century during a Mongol invasion.
5. I.e., Tropu Lotsawa.
6. For *phyar med* in DNZ read *byar med* as in DNZ-K.
7. *khrid yig.* Jamyang Khyentse Wangpo is probably referring here to Jamyang Khyentse Wangchuk's *Notes* (see ch. 28).
8. The Tibetan speaks of feet and hands, but given the nāgas' serpentine nature, we have translated these as lower and upper bodies, while keeping "feet" and "hands" in the root text as the analogy for the meditator.
9. *ma bcos par btsa' ba* ("watch without contriving").
10. *rdzings thog nas*: this should read *gzings thog nas*, as below on DNZ, p. 579.
11. These three analogies are explained in Khyentse Wangchuk's *Notes*. See ch. 28, pp. 562–64.
12. The translation follows DNZ-K *yul can shes pa la bden med* rather than DNZ *yul can shes pas bden med.*
13. For DNZ *sdang ba* read *snang ba* (DNZ-K and DzLL).
14. *sems*, the mind in general, including all its various functions.
15. *yid*, in this context the thinking, deluded mind.
16. *mi mnyam pa* ("not the same").
17. The white kuṇḍa flower is a metaphor for the bodhichitta essence.
18. The name Avalokiteshvara literally means "lord who watches with his eyes."
19. *brGyad stong pa'i chos 'phags kyi le'u.* As demonstrated in ch. 27, the source sutra for this text is the final section of the thirty-first chapter of the *Perfection of Wisdom in Eight Thousand Lines*, *Aṣṭasāhasrikāprajñāpāramitā* (Toh. 12), Dg.K., sher phyin, *ka*.

## 27. Correlations with the Sutras and Tantras

1. *Phyag rgya chen po sems nyid ngal gso'i rtsa ba mdo yi lung dang sbyar ba*, in DNZ, vol. 16 (*ma*), pp. 553–58; DNZ-K, vol. 11 (*ta*), pp. 484–89.
2. In this section the lines from the Dharmodgata chapter (ch. 31 of *Aṣṭasāhasrikā-*

*prajñāpāramitā* [Toh. 12]) are quoted in sequence, Dg.K,, sher phyin, *ka* (vol. 33), ff. 283a6–284a2.

3. *rdo rje lta bu'i chos*, probably referring to the vajra-like concentration (*rdo rje lta bu'i ting nge 'dzin*).
4. *gSang ba 'dus pa'i rgyud phyi ma* (Toh. 443), Dg.K., rgyud, *ca*, f. 148b1–2.
5. Although attributed to the *Guhyasamāja*, this and all but one of the other quotations so presented here appear to come from *The Beginning Chapter of the Supremely Great Vajra, Vajraśrīvaramahākalpādi, rDo rje dpal mchog chen po brtag pa dang po* (Toh. 453), Dg.K., rgyud, *cha*, f. 116a7–116b1.
6. *Saṃputa Tantra, Yang dag par sbyor ba* (Toh. 381), Dg.K., rgyud, *ga*, f. 86b2–3. The first line of this quotation (*sdug bsngal phung po du ma'i mtshan gyur pa*), which is identical to that of the next quotation below, appears to have been misplaced here. It seemed preferable to omit it.
7. *Saṃpuṭa*, Dg.K., rgyud, *ga*, f. 86b3–6. The translation of the last two lines of this quotation is speculative and has followed other versions of the source text in reading *yan lag 'gro ba blta* for *gang dag 'gro ba lta* in DNZ.
8. *Saṃpuṭa*, Dg.K., rgyud, *ga*, f. 80a4.
9. This is again a quotation from the *Saṃpuṭa Tantra*, Dg.K., rgyud, *ga*, f. 80a2–3.
10. *Vajrahṛdayālaṃkāratantra, rDo rje snying po rgyan gyi rgyud* (Toh. 451), Dg.K., rgyud, *cha*, f. 56a4–5.
11. *Vajraśrīvaramahākalpādi*, Dg.K., rgyud, *cha*, f. 116b2.
12. *Vajraśrīvaramahākalpādi*, Dg.K., rgyud, *cha*, f. 116b7.
13. *Saṃpuṭa*, Dg.K., rgyud, *ga*, f. 85b7–86a1.
14. *Saṃdhivyākaraṇatantra, dGongs pa lung bstan pa'i rgyud* (Toh. 444), Dg.K., rgyud, *ca*, f. 164b1–2.
15. *Saṃpuṭa*, Dg.K., rgyud, *ga*, f. 86a5–6.
16. *Saṃpuṭa*, Dg.K., rgyud, *ga*, f. 85b6–7.
17. *Guhyasamāja, gSang ba 'dus pa* (Toh. 442), Dg.K., rgyud, *ca*, 94a7–b1.
18. *Guhyasamāja*, Dg.K., rgyud, *ca*, 130b1.
19. *Saṃdhivyākaraṇatantra*, Dg.K., rgyud, *ca*, f. 185b6–7.
20. *Vajrahṛdayālaṃkāratantra*, Dg.K., rgyud, *cha*, f. 56b2–3.
21. *Vajrahṛdayālaṃkāratantra*, Dg.K., rgyud, *cha*, f. 56b3–6.
22. *Saṃdhivyākaraṇatantra*, Dg.K., rgyud, *ca*, f. 185b5–6.
23. These lines refer to the primitive method of producing fire by twirling a pointed stick (called a hand drill or fire drill) between one's hands while pressing the point down onto a wooden base board (called a hearth board or fireboard). The resulting friction eventually produces a tiny ember that can then be used to ignite tinder.
24. *Saṃdhivyākaraṇatantra*, Dg.K., rgyud, *ca*, f. 185b4–5.
25. *Vārāhyabhibodhana, Phag mo mngon par byang chub pa* (Toh. 377), Dg.K., rgyud, *ga*, f. 59b2–3.
26. *Saṃpuṭa*, Dg.K., rgyud, *ga*, f. 79b7–80a1.

27. We have not been able to trace this quotation either in the *Saṃdhivyākaraṇa-tantra* or any other tantra.
28. *Vajrahṛdayālaṃkāratantra*, Dg.K., rgyud, *cha*, f. 45a1–2.
29. Although attributed to *The Supreme* (*dPal mchog dang po*), this quotation is taken from *A Section of the Chapter on Mantras of "The Supreme," dPal mchog dang po'i sngags kyi rtog pa'i dum bu* (Toh. 488), Dg.K., rgyud, *ta*, f. 234a7–b1.
30. Although this quotation appears to be commented in Śrīsaṃvarodayamahātant rarājasyapadminī-nāma-pañjikā, *dPal sdom pa 'byung ba'i rgyud kyi rgyal po chen po'i dka' 'grel padma can zhes bya ba* (Toh. 1420), we have not been able to find it in any source tantras.
31. *Saṃpuṭa*, Dg.K., rgyud, *ga*, f.158a3.
32. *Vajraḍākatantra*, *rDo rje mkha' 'gro* (Toh. 370), Dg.K., rgyud, *kha*, f.96a4–6.
33. *rnal 'byor bdag* ("owner of the yoga" or "yogi"). The source text reads *rnal 'byor ma* (yoginī). The feminine gender here seems logical.
34. *Saṃpuṭa*, Dg.K., rgyud, *ga*, f.84b4.
35. *Saṃpuṭa*, Dg.K., rgyud, *ga*, f.83b1–3.
36. *Saṃpuṭa*, Dg.K., rgyud, *ga*, f.86a2–3.

## 28. Notes on *Resting in the Nature of Mind*

1. *Sems nyid ngal gso'i khrid kyi zin bris 'jam dbyangs mkhyen brtse'i dbang phyug gis mdzad pa*, in DNZ, vol. 16 (*ma*), pp. 565–84; DNZ-K, vol. 11 (*ta*), pp. 496–515.
2. Doringpa Kunzang Chökyi Nyima (rDo ring pa kun bzang chos kyi nyi ma) (1449–1524), the teacher of Losal Gyatso, Khyentse Wangchuk's teacher.
3. This verse is specifically mentioned in Jamyang Khyentse Wangpo's teaching guide. See ch. 30, p. 578.
4. This four-line prayer is to be found in the teaching guide. See ch. 30, p. 579.
5. The four-line prayer that concludes and summarizes the seven branches in the *Prayer of Good Conduct* (*bZang spyod smon lam*) and begins: *phyag 'tshal ba dang mchod cing bshags pa dang* . . . ("What little merit I have accumulated by / Obeisance, offering, purification, / Rejoicing, exhortation, and prayer— / All of it I dedicate to enlightenment)."
6. See Appendix, mandala offering.
7. *mthe bong gi sor tshigs*, the size of the last bone or distal phalanx of the thumb.
8. *zhabs kyu*, the hook-shaped element at the bottom of the Tibetan syllable ཧཱུྃ (*hūṃ*) representing the vowel sound *u*.
9. *tshar chen rdo rje 'chang*, referring to Tsarchen Losal Gyatso (1502–1566), Khyentse Wangchuk's teacher.
10. This suggests a wrathful expression.
11. The omniscient Butön Rinchen Drup (1290–1364).
12. For *svāhā* in DNZ read *satva* as in DNZ-K and DzLL.
13. See ch. 25, pp. 501–502.
14. *gnyug mar gnas pa*. This term is defined in the *Great Dictionary* (*Tshig mdzod*

*chen mo*) as *rgyun du sdod pa'am gtan du gnas pa* ("continuously present or permanently dwelling"). This analogy for the natural state of the mind (*sems nyid gnyug ma*) works better in the original Tibetan than in English translation.

15. See note 15 in ch. 16.
16. *Hevajra Tantra in Two Segments* (*brTag gnyis*).
17. Khyentse Wangchuk is here commenting on the line in the *Hevajra Tantra in Two Segments* that follows the above quotation: "Rid of those stains, they are truly buddhas."
18. Note that the term "continuum" translates *rgyud*, the Tibetan translation of the Sanskrit *tantra*. The very basis of the tantric path is this continuum, the fact that the buddha nature remains unchanged from the beginning of the path to the end.
19. The two purities are primordial purity and the purity that results from being rid of adventitious obscurations.
20. This second subsection on getting rid of hindrances appears to be dealt with later than indicated here, after the section on meditation.
21. This section, introduced above as the second part of "A. Decisively Establishing the View with Wisdom," appears to have been placed after "B. Practicing Skillful Means by Meditation," and although numbered "2." in the Tibetan, we have renumbered it as a third section ("C.") of the Main Practice.
22. Although all printings read *dbang bstod*, this should probably read *dpang bstod*.
23. Although the text says "the skillful means of clarity" (*gsal ba'i thabs*), this is probably a misprint for "the skillful means of bliss" (*bde ba'i thabs*).
24. Khyentse Wangchuk's use here of the term *gsungs* ("it was said") and elsewhere in the text attests to his notes being a record of the teachings he received from his own teacher and not simply his own comments.

## 29. Nectarous Moonbeams

1. *Phyag rgya chen po sems nyid ngal gso'i khrid kyi nyams glu dran pas snying gi gdung sel zla ba'i zil ngar*, in DNZ, vol. 16 (*ma*), pp. 584–85; DNZ-K, vol. 11 (*ta*), pp. 515–16.

## 30. The Nectarous Light of the Words of the Teacher

1. *Phyag rgya chen po sems nyid ngal gso'i 'khrid kyi 'chad thabs bla ma'i zhal lung bdud rtsi'i snang ba*, in DNZ, vol. 16 (*ma*), pp. 585–99; DNZ-K, vol. 11 (*ta*), pp. 516–30.
2. Āryashūra, *Jātakamāla*, *sKyes pa'i rabs kyi rgyud* (Toh. 4150), in Dg.T., mdo 'grel (skyes rabs), *hu*, f. 125a1–2.
3. Vasubandhu, *Vyākhyāyukti*, *rNam bshad rig pa* (Toh. 4061), in Dg.T., mdo 'grel (sems tsam), *shi*, f. 65b4.
4. *phyag na padmo*, the Holder of the Lotus, another name for Avalokiteshvara.

5. I.e., Buddha Shākyamuni.
6. The three trainings (*bslab pa gsum*) are the trainings in discipline, concentration, and wisdom.
7. The three scriptural collections (*sde snod gsum*) are the Vinaya, the Sutra collection, and the Abhidharma.
8. The seven distinguishing features of the Great Vehicle, as described in the *Ornament of the Mahayana Sutras* (*Sūtralāṁkāra*), are its great reference, great accomplishment, great gnosis, great application, great skill in means, great consummation, and great buddha activities.
9. *bCom ldan 'das dpal bde chen ral pa gcig pa'i skor*, probably referring to *Śrībhagavadekajaṭamahātantrarāja*, *dPal bcom ldan 'das ral pa gcig pa'i brtag pa'i rgyud kyi rgyal po chen po*, Toh. 476.
10. *bLo gros rin chen*, "Jewel of Intelligence." Matiratna is a possible Sanskrit reconstruction of his name.
11. The translation follows DNZ-K and DzLL *bu ci 'dod* rather than DNZ *da ci 'dod*.
12. The full list of the teachers in this lineage is provided by Jamgön Kongtrul in the Catalog, pp. 166–67.
13. Although Jamyang Khyentse Wangpo speaks of "the instruction manual" (*khrid yig*), he appears to be referring to Khyentse Wangchuk's *Notes* (*zin bris*), the latter's record of the teachings he received from Tsarchen Losal Gyatso (ch. 28 in this volume).
14. For *'byams pa* in DNZ read *'khyams pa* as in DNZ-K.
15. For *dbang* in DNZ read *dpang* as in DNZ-K.
16. See Appendix, mandala offering.
17. There is no corresponding heading for this third section in what follows. It may refer to the Conclusion in ch. 28.
18. Getting rid of hindrances does not appear to be explicitly presented below.

## 31. A Prayer to the Lineage Teachers

1. *Sems nyid ngal gso'i brgyud 'debs gnas sbyar ma*, in DNZ, vol. 16 (*ma*), pp. 601–2; DNZ-K, vol. 11 (*ta*), pp. 531–32.
2. DNZ has *'ja' phu*, but *'jang phu* (DNZ-K and DzLL) seems more likely.

## 32. A Supplement to the Guru Yoga

1. *bLa ma'i rnal 'byor skabs bla ma brgyud pa'i kha skong*, in DNZ, vol. 16 (*ma*), pp. 603–4; DNZ-K, vol. 11 (*ta*), pp. 533–34.
2. See ch. 28, p. 555.

## 33. Thirty Verses Expressing Realization

1. *rTogs pa brjod pa sum bcu pa*, in DNZ, vol. 16 (*ma*), pp. 509–12. DNZ-K, vol. 11 (*ta*), pp. 441–44. Second source: Dg.T. rgyud, *tshi* 175b3–176b4 (Toh. 2129).
2. *rtog* ("thought") in all the Tibetan editions is clearly a mistake for *rtogs* ("realization"). This error is not repeated in the title given in the colophon.
3. For *'bas* in DNZ read *'bab* as in DNZ-K.
4. For *de ni* in DNZ read *da ni* as in DNZ-K.
5. Although DNZ, DNZ-K, and DzLL all have *'dod*, the translation follows Dg.K's *'od*, which also fits the commentary.
6. For *btsam* in DNZ read *bcom* as in DNZ-K and Dg.K.

## 34. An Explanation of *Thirty Verses Expressing Realization*

1. *rTogs pa brjod pa sum bcu pa'i do ha rdo rje'i tshig 'bru rnam par bshad pa*, in DNZ, vol. 16 (*ma*), pp. 512–23; DNZ-K, vol. 11 (*ta*), pp. 441–55.
2. The Hindu god (*khyab 'jug*), literally "the one who pervades."
3. *thab mgal gyi phyag rgya*, the posture for practicing the tummo.
4. *chos thams cad mi gnas pa'i yul mad pa* (DNZ). The other printings are not very clear, but we believe this should read *chos thams cad ni gnas pa'i yul med pa* and have translated it accordingly.
5. *sgra can 'dzin*, the name of the demon Rāhula, whose decapitated head, according to Indian mythology, swallows the sun or moon, thereby causing an eclipse, which ends when the sun or moon emerges from his throat.
6. *thabs ldan* ("those who possess the skillful methods").
7. Although DNZ reads *Pa pa ra mārtha* it would seem that this should logically begin with *sa*. DNZ-K is unclear, but DzLL's *pa* is too distorted to be a *pa* and is more likely a smudged *sa*.
8. *dpal*, undoubtedly referring to Tropu Lotsawa Jampa Pal.

## 35. Three Essential Introductions

1. *gNad kyi ngo sprod gsum pa bdud rtsi'i nying khu lta bu'i man ngag*, in DNZ, vol. 16 (*ma*), pp. 501–4; DNZ-K, vol. 11 (*ta*), pp. 433–36.
2. These three analogies are explained in ch. 28. See pp. 562–64
3. DNZ-K and DzLL both read *stong pas* rather than DNZ's *stong par*, which would render this line "The poison of appearances is banished by emptiness."

## 36. Cherished Essence

1. *gSum tshan gsum gyi man ngag ces kyang bya gces pa'i snying po zhes bya ba snying dang 'dra ba'i man ngag*, in DNZ, vol. 16 (*ma*), pp. 504–9; DNZ-K, vol. 11 (*ta*), pp. 436–41.

2. For *rtog pa* in DNZ read *rtogs pa* as in DNZ-K and DzLL.
3. Whereas DNZ has *tshogs chud pa*, both DNZ-K and DzLL read *tshegs chung ba*.
4. The suppport (*rten*) in this case is the buddha to whom one is praying.
5. For *dgong* in DNZ read *dgod* as in DNZ-K and DzLL.
6. For *rje'u* in DNZ read *rnge'u* (a baby camel) as in DNZ-K.
7. For *'jigs par* in DNZ read *'jigs sar* as in DNZ-K and DzLL.
8. For *ci dkar zhog* in DNZ read *ci dgar zhog* as in DNZ-K and DzLL.
9. The poison is transformed into medicine.
10. The rejection of defilements involves the duality that itself gives rise to further defilements.
11. *rang snang*, appearances that manifest as one's own experience.
12. These three analogies are explained in full in ch. 28. See pp. 562–64.
13. For *phyis snyigs* in DNZ read *phyis snyegs* as in DNZ-K.
14. *snying dang 'dra ba* ("like my heart").

## 37. Three Quintessential Points

1. *Grub chen mi tra dzo kis mdzad pa'i snying po don gsum gyi man ngag gi rtsa ba rdo rje'i tshig rkang*, in DNZ, vol. 16 (*ma*), pp. 605–7; DNZ-K, vol. 11 (*ta*), pp. 535–37.
2. For *rang spangs* in DNZ read *rab spangs* as in DNZ-K.

## 38. Bestowal of the Supreme Blessings

1. *sNying po don gsum gyi brgyud 'debs byin rlabs mchog stsol*, in DNZ, vol. 16 (*ma*), pp. 607–9; DNZ-K, vol. 11 (*ta*), pp. 537–39.
2. *Khyab bdag zhva lus pa*. This refers to Rinchen Sönam Chokdrup, the twenty-second Zhalu Khenchen.
3. *mchod sbyin*, an offering to sublime beings such as the buddhas and a gift to sentient beings.

## 39. The Chariot of Supreme Accomplishment

1. *'Phags mchog thugs rje chen po'i dmar khrid snying po don gsum gyi nyams len mdor bsdus pa grub pa mchog gi shing rta*, in DNZ, vol. 16 (*ma*), pp. 609–16; DNZ-K, vol. 11 (*ta*), pp. 539–46.
2. For *'di 'phras* in DNZ read *'od 'phros* as in DNZ-K.
3. See ch. 38.
4. I.e., the determined wish (*'dun pa*), the aspiration (*smon lam*), and the prayer (*gsol 'debs*).
5. For *spar ba* in DNZ read *sbyar ba* as in DNZ-K.

## 40. An Essential Recitation Text

1. *Thugs rje chen po'i dmar khrid mi tra lugs kyi rgyun gyi rnal 'byor ngag 'don snying po*, in DNZ, vol. 16 (*ma*), pp. 616–18; DNZ-K, vol. 11 (*ta*), pp. 546–48.
2. See ch. 38.
3. See ch. 39, *The Chariot of Supreme Accomplishment*, pp. 647–49.

# Bibliography

The bibliography comprises three main sections, each separately alphabetized: (1) the texts translated in this volume; (2) works cited in the texts (subdivided into scriptures and treatises); and (3) a reference bibliography (subdivided into Tibetan works and English-language translations and other works).

## 1. The Present Texts

### *The Source Volume*

Jamgön Kongtrul Lodrö Taye, compiler. *The Treasury of Precious Instructions. gDams ngag rin po che'i mdzod.* Vol. 16 (*ma*). Delhi: Shechen Publications, 1999. dnz.tsadra.org

### *The Translated Texts*

Abhayaśrī. *A Precious Necklace: Perfection Stage Teachings of the Eighty-Four Siddhas, the Root Text and a Commentary. Grub thob brgyad cu rtsa bzhi'i rdzogs rim rin chen 'phreng ba rtsa 'grel.* In DNZ. Vol. 16 (*ma*), pp. 149–200. In DNZ-K. Vol. 11 (*ta*), pp. 92–143. Second source (root text): *Ratnamāla. Rin chen phreng ba zhes bya ba.* Narthang Tengyur. Vol. 88 (*lu*), ff. 111a–112b (N3875).

*Authorization Ritual for Tārā, Who Protects Us from the Eight Fears and Frees Us from the Perilous Passage of Samsara. sGrol ma 'jigs pa brgyad skyob 'khor ba 'phrang sgrol gyi rjes gnang.* In DNZ. Vol. 16 (*ma*), pp. 269–74. In DNZ-K. Vol. 11 (*ta*), pp. 209–14.

Drakpa Rinchen (Grags pa rin chen) (aka Girti Ratna). *Routing the Hordes of Obstacle Makers: An Authorization Ritual for the Protector of the Teachings, Draklha Gönpo. Chos skyong brag lha mgon po'i rjes gnang bgegs dpung 'joms byed.* In DNZ. Vol. 16 (*ma*), pp. 285–91. In DNZ-K. Vol. 11 (*ta*), pp. 224–30.

———. *Sādhana of the Dharma Protector Draklha Gönpo. Chos skyong brag lha mgon po'i mngon rtogs.* In DNZ. Vol. 16 (*ma*), pp. 489–95. In DNZ-K. Vol. 11 (*ta*), pp. 422–28.

Jagatamitrānanda (Mitrayogin). *Vajra Verses on the Graded Path of Avalokiteśvara.*

*sPyan ras gzigs kyi lam gyi rim pa rdo rje'i tshig rkang.* In DNZ. Vol. 16 (*ma*), pp. 293–96. In DNZ-K. Vol. 11 (*ta*), pp. 231–34.

Jamgön Kongtrul Lodrö Taye ('Jam mgon kong sprul blo gros mtha' yas). *The Source of All Blessings, Accomplishments, and Qualities: A Ritual for Venerating the Teachers Who Embody the Eight Great Chariots of the Practice Lineage. sGrub brgyud shing rta chen po brgyad kun 'dus kyi bla ma mchod pa'i cho ga byin rlabs dngos grub yon tan kun gyi 'byung gnas.* In DNZ. Vol. 16 (*ma*), pp. 1–55. Also in GKZ. Vol. 1 (*kha*) pp. 949–1003.

Jamyang Khyentse Wangchuk ('Jam dbyangs mkhyen brtse'i dbang phyug). *Notes on "Resting in the Nature of Mind" by Jamyang Khyentse Wangchuk. Sems nyid gnal gso'i khrid kyi zin bris 'jam dbyangs mkhyen brtse'i dbang phyug gis mdzad pa.* In DNZ. Vol. 16 (*ma*), pp. 565–84. In DNZ-K. Vol. 11 (*ta*), pp. 496–515.

Jamyang Khyentse Wangpo ('Jam dbyangs mkhyen brtse'i dbang po). *Bestowal of the Supreme Blessings: A Prayer to the Lineage Teachers of the Three Quintessential Points. sNying po don gsum gyi brgyud 'debs byin rlabs mchog stsol.* In DNZ. Vol. 16 (*ma*), pp. 607–9. In DNZ-K. Vol. 11 (*ta*), pp. 537–39.

———. *The Chariot of Supreme Accomplishment: A Concise Practice on the Three Quintessential Points, the Direct Instructions of the Highest of Noble Beings, the Great Compassionate One. 'Phags mchog thugs rje chen po'i dmar khrid snying po don gsum gyi nyams len mdor bsdus pa grub pa mchog gi shing rta.* In DNZ. Vol. 16 (*ma*), pp. 609–16. In DNZ-K. Vol. 11 (*ta*), pp. 539–46.

———. *An Essential Recitation Text for the Daily Practice of Mitrayogin's Tradition of the Great Compassionate One's Direct Instructions. Thugs rje chen po'i dmar khrid mi tra lugs kyi rgyun gyi rnal 'byor ngag 'don snying po.* In DNZ. Vol. 16 (*ma*), pp. 616–18. In DNZ-K. Vol. 11 (*ta*), pp. 546–48.

———. *The Nectarous Light of the Words of the Teacher: A Guide for Teaching the Great Seal Text "Resting in the Nature of Mind." Phyag rgya chen po sems nyid ngal gso'i 'khrid kyi 'chad thabs bla ma'i zhal lung bdud rtsi'i snang ba.* In DNZ. Vol. 16 (*ma*), pp. 585–99. In DNZ-K. Vol. 11 (*ta*), pp. 516–30.

———. *The Quintessence: A Commentary on the Root Text of the Great Seal "Resting in the Nature of Mind" That Noble Avalokiteśvara Taught the Mahāsiddha Mitrayogin. 'Phags pa spyan ras gzigs kyis grub chen mi tra dzo ki la gsungs pa'i phyag rgya chen po sems nyid ngal gso'i gzhung 'grel snying po bsdus pa.* In DNZ. Vol. 16 (*ma*), pp. 525–52. In DNZ-K. Vol. 11 (*ta*), pp. 456–83.

Karma Ngawang Yönten Gyatso (Karma ngag dbang yon tan rgya mtsho) (aka Jamgön Kongtrul Lodrö Taye). *The Source of Accomplishments: An Offering and Prayer Ritual to the Eighty-Four Mahāsiddhas of India. 'Phags yul gyi grub chen brgyad cu rtsa bzhi la mchod cing gsol ba gdabs pa'i cho ga dngos grub kun 'byung.* In DNZ. Vol. 16 (*ma*), pp. 101–31. In DNZ-K. Vol. 11 (*ta*), pp. 45–75.

———. *The Stream of Accomplishment: A Method for Combining the Blessings of the Teacher Vajradhara and the Eighty-Four Siddhas. bLa ma rdo rje 'chang grub thob brgyad cu rtsa bzhi'i byin rlabs lhan cig tu bya ba'i tshul dngos grub chu rgyun.* In DNZ. Vol. 16 (*ma*), pp. 57–100. In DNZ-K. Vol. 11 (*ta*), pp. 1–44.

Lineage of Mitrayogin (Mi tra dzo ki). *Cherished Essence: The Most Precious Pith Instruction, Also Called "The Three-by-Three Pith Instruction." gSum tshan gsum gyi man ngag ces kyang bya gces pa'i snying po zhes bya ba snying dang 'dra ba'i man gnag.* In DNZ. Vol. 16 (*ma*), pp. 504–9. In DNZ-K. Vol. 11 (*ta*), pp. 436–41.

———. *Three Essential Introductions: A Pith Instruction That Is Like Distilled Ambrosia. gNad kyi ngo sprod gsum pa bdud rtsi'i nying khu lta bu'i man ngag.* In DNZ. Vol. 16 (*ma*), pp. 501–4. In DNZ-K. Vol. 11 (*ta*), pp. 433–36.

Mitrayogin (Mi tra dzo ki). *Resting in the Nature of One's Own Mind: A Pith Instruction Given to the Mahāsiddha Mitrayogin by Noble Avalokiteśvara. 'Phags pa spyan ras gzigs kyis grub chen mi tra dzo ki la gsungs pa'i rang gi sems nyid ngal gso ba'i man ngag.* In DNZ. Vol. 16 (*ma*), pp. 497–501. In DNZ-K. Vol. 11 (*ta*), pp. 429–33. Second source: *Rang gi sems ngal so ba'i man ngag tshigs su bcad pa nyi shu rtsa lnga pa, svacittavicramopadecapancavimcatikagatha.* In Dg.T. rgyud, *tshi* 175b3–176b4 (Toh. 2129).

———. *Thirty Verses Expressing Realization. rTogs pa brjod pa sum bcu pa. triṃśatyavadāna.* In DNZ. Vol. 16 (*ma*), pp. 509–12. In DNZ-K. Vol. 11 (*ta*), pp. 441–44. Second source: Dg.T. rgyud, *tshi* 175b3–176b4 (Toh. 2129).

Mitrayogin (Mi tra dzo ki)/Öpak Dorje ('Od dpag rdo rje). *Accomplishing the Immortal Vajra Body: The Instructions of the Lord Protector Amitāyus, the Deity Related to Enlightened Qualities. bCom ldan 'das mgon po tshe dpag med yon tan gyi khrid 'chi med rdo rje'i sku sgrub par byed pa.* In DNZ. Vol. 16 (*ma*), pp. 427–45. In DNZ-K. Vol. 11 (*ta*), pp. 363–81.

———. *Liberation from the Perilous Path of Samsara: The Instructions of Tārā, the Deity Related to Enlightened Activities Who Protects from the Eight Fears. sGrol ma 'jigs pa brgyad skyob phrin las kyi khrid 'khor ba'i 'phrang sgrol.* In DNZ. Vol. 16 (*ma*), pp. 447–65. In DNZ-K. Vol. 11 (*ta*), pp. 382–400.

———. *A Shower of Accomplishments: Instructions of the Yellow Jambhala. Dzam bha la ser po'i khrid dngos grub char 'bebs.* In DNZ. Vol. 16 (*ma*), pp. 467–83. In DNZ-K. Vol. 11 (*ta*), pp. 401–17.

———. *The Spreading Rays of Light That Vanquish the Hordes of Demons: The Instructions of Lord Vajrapāṇi, the Deity Related to Enlightened Mind. bCom ldan 'das phyag na rdo rje thugs kyi khrid bdud dpung 'joms byed 'od zer rgyas pa.* In DNZ. Vol. 16 (*ma*), pp. 399–425. In DNZ-K. Vol. 11 (*ta*), pp. 336–62.

———. *The Wheel of Ornaments of Gnosis That Makes Wisdom Grow: The Instructions of Mañjuśrī, the Deity Related to the Enlightened Body. 'Jam dpal dbyangs sku'i khrid shes rab 'phel byed ye shes rgyan gyi 'khor lo.* In DNZ. Vol. 16 (*ma*), pp. 377–97. In DNZ-K. Vol. 11 (*ta*), pp. 315–35.

Mitrayogin (Mi tra dzo ki) and Tropu Lotsawa Jampa Pal (Khro phu lo tsā ba byams pa'i dpal). *The Root Vajra Verses of the Pith Instruction on the Three Quintessential Points Composed by the Great Siddha Mitrayogin. Grub chen mi tra dzo kis mdzad pa'i snying po don gsum gyi man ngag gi rtsa ba rdo rje'i tshig rkang.* In DNZ. Vol. 16 (*ma*), pp. 605–7. In DNZ-K. Vol. 11 (*ta*), pp. 535–37.

*An Offering Arrangement for the Empowerment Ritual of Noble Avalokiteśvara, "The*

*Glowing Jewel," Together with the Revelation of the Mandala. 'Phags pa spyan ras gzigs dbang phyug gi dbang chog rin chen 'od 'phro'i mchod bsgrig dkyil 'khor ston pa bcas*. In DNZ. Vol. 16 (*ma*), pp. 229–35. In DNZ-K. Vol. 11 (*ta*), pp. 172–78.

Öpak Dorje ('Od dpag rdo rje). *Authorization Ritual for Lord Amitāyus. bCom ldan 'das tshe dpag med kyi rjes gnang*. In DNZ. Vol. 16 (*ma*), pp. 259–68. In DNZ-K. Vol. 11 (*ta*), pp. 199–208.

———. *Authorization Ritual for Lord Mañjughoṣa. mGon po 'jam dpal dbyangs kyi rjes gnang*. In DNZ. Vol. 16 (*ma*), pp. 237–47. In DNZ-K. Vol. 11 (*ta*), pp. 179–89.

———. *Authorization Ritual for Noble Jambhala. Ārya dzam bha la'i rjes gnang*. In DNZ. Vol. 16 (*ma*), pp. 275–83. In DNZ-K. Vol. 11 (*ta*), pp. 215–23.

———. *A Banquet of Nectar: A Complete Instruction on Noble Avalokiteśvara's Graded Path to Enlightenment. 'Phags pa spyan ras gzigs dbang phyug gi byang chub lam gyi rim pa'i khrid yongs su sdud pa bdud rtsi'i dga' ston*. In DNZ. Vol. 16 (*ma*), pp. 321–62. In DNZ-K. Vol. 11 (*ta*), pp. 259–300.

———. *The Luminous Golden Wand of Pith Instructions: An Appendix to the Instructions on Noble Avalokiteśvara's Graded Path to Enlightenment. 'Phags pa spyan ras gzigs kyi byang chub lam gyi rim pa'i khrid kyi cha lag man ngag gser gyi thur ma rin po che'i sgron me*. In DNZ. Vol. 16 (*ma*), pp. 363–76. In DNZ-K. Vol. 11 (*ta*), pp. 301–14.

———. *A Mine of Blessings: Authorization Ritual for Lord Vajrapāṇi. bCom ldan 'das phyag na rdo rje'i rjes gnang byin rlabs kyi 'byung gnas*. In DNZ. Vol. 16 (*ma*), pp. 249–57. In DNZ-K. Vol. 11 (*ta*), pp. 190–98.

———. *Ocean of Blessings: A Prayer to the Lineage of the Teachers of the Graduated Path of Avalokiteśvara. sPyan ras gzigs lam rim bla ma rgyud pa la gsol 'debs byin rlabs kyi chu gter*. In DNZ. Vol. 16 (*ma*), pp. 485–88. In DNZ-K. Vol. 11 (*ta*), pp. 418–21.

———. *A River of Great Compassion: The Empowerment for the Sādhana in the Stages of the Path of Noble Avalokiteśvara. 'Phags pa spyan ras gzigs dbang phyug gi lam gyi rim pa'i mngon rtogs dbang bskur thugs rje chen po'i chu rgyun*. In DNZ. Vol. 16 (*ma*), pp. 201–28. In DNZ-K. Vol. 11 (*ta*), pp. 144–71.

———. *A Stream of Nectar: The Approach and Accomplishment of Noble Avalokiteśvara. 'Phags pa spyan ras gzigs dbang phyug gi bsnyen sgrub bdud rtsi'i chu rgyun*. In DNZ. Vol. 16 (*ma*), pp. 297–320. In DNZ-K. Vol. 11 (*ta*), pp. 235–58.

Rinchen Drup (Bu ston rin chen grub). *Correlations between the Root Verses of the Great Seal Text "Resting in the Nature of Mind" and the Scriptural Sources in the Sutras. Phyag rgya chen po sems nyid ngal gso'i rtsa ba mdo yi lung dang sbyar ba*. In DNZ. Vol. 16 (*ma*), pp. 553–58. In DNZ-K. Vol. 11 (*ta*), pp. 484–89.

———. *Correlations between the Root Verses of the Great Seal Text "Resting in the Nature of Mind" and the Scriptural Sources in the Tantras. Phyag rgya chen po sems nyid ngal gso'i rtsa ba rgyud kyi lung dang sbyar ba*. In DNZ. Vol. 16 (*ma*), pp. 558–65. In DNZ-K. Vol. 11 (*ta*), pp. 489–96.

Rinchen Losal Tenkyong (Rin chen blo gsal bstan skyong). *Nectarous Moonbeams: A Song of Experience of the Great Seal Instructions "Resting in the Nature of Mind," the Thought of Which Dispels the Anguish of the Heart. Phyag rgya chen po sems nyid ngal gso'i khrid kyi nyams glu dran pas snying gi gdung sel zla ba'i zil ngar.* In DNZ. Vol. 16 (*ma*), pp. 584–85. In DNZ-K. Vol. 11 (*ta*), pp. 515–16.

———, et al. *A Prayer to the Lineage Teachers of "Resting in the Nature of Mind" in the Places Associated with Them. Sems nyid ngal gso'i brgyud 'debs gnas sbyar ma.* In DNZ. Vol. 16 (*ma*), pp. 601–2. In DNZ-K. Vol. 11 (*ta*), pp. 531–32.

———, et al. *A Supplement for the [Visualization of the] Lineage Teachers in the Guru Yoga. bLa ma'i rnal 'byor skabs bla ma brgyud pa'i kha skong.* In DNZ. Vol. 16 (*ma*), pp. 603–4. In DNZ-K. Vol. 11 (*ta*), pp. 533–34.

Tāranātha/Jamgön Kongtrul Lodrö Taye. *Collecting the Essence Drops of Accomplishment: A Universally Applicable Guru Yoga on the Supreme Siddhas, according to the Indian Tradition. Grub mchog spyi la brten pa'i bla ma'i rnal 'byor rgya gar lugs dngos grub thig le 'khyil ba.* In DNZ. Vol. 16 (*ma*), pp. 133–48. In DNZ-K. Vol. 11 (*ta*), pp. 76–91.

Tropu Lotsawa Jampa Pal (Khro phu lo tsā ba byams pa'i dpal). *An Explanation of the Words of the Vajra Song "Thirty Verses Expressing Realization." rTogs pa brjod pa sum bcu pa'i do ha rdo rje'i tshig 'bru rnam par bshad pa.* In DNZ. Vol. 16 (*ma*), pp. 512–23. In DNZ-K. Vol. 11 (*ta*), pp. 441–55.

## 2. Works Cited in the Texts

### *Scriptures (Kangyur)*

*The Awakening of Varahi. Vārāhyabhibodhana. Phag mo mngon par byang chub pa.* Dg.K. rgyud, *ga* (Toh. 377).

*The Beginning Chapter of the Supremely Great Vajra. Vajraśrīvaramahākalpādi. rDo rje dpal mchog chen po brtag pa dang po.* Dg.K. rgyud, *cha* (Toh. 453).

*Dharmodgata Chapter in The Perfection of Wisdom in Eight Thousand Lines. brGyad stong pa'i chos 'phags kyi le'u.* Ch. 31 of *Aṣṭasāhasrikā-prajñāpāramitā.* Dg.K. sher phyin, *ka* (Toh. 12).

*Guhyasamāja. gSang ba 'dus pa.* Dg.K. rgyud, *ca* (Toh. 442).

*Hevajra Tantra. Hevajratantra. Kye'i rdo rje'i rgyud.* Dg.K. rgyud, *nga* (Toh. 417).

*Later Guhyasamāja. gSang ba 'dus pa'i rgyud phyi ma.* Dg.K. rgyud, *ca* (Toh. 443).

*Prophecy of the Intent. Saṃdhivyākaraṇatantra. dGongs pa lung bstan pa'i rgyud.* Dg.K. rgyud, *ca* (Toh. 444).

*Saṃputa Tantra. Yang dag par sbyor ba.* Dg.K. rgyud, ga (Toh. 381).

*A Section of the Chapter on Mantras of "The Supreme." dPal mchog dang po'i sngags kyi rtog pa'i dum bu.* Dg.K. rgyud, *ta* (Toh. 488).

*Tantra of Ekajaṭa. Śrībhagavadekajaṭamahātantrarāja. dPal bcom ldan 'das ral pa gcig pa'i brtag pa'i rgyud kyi rgyal po chen po.* Dg. K. rgyud, *ja* (Toh. 476).

*Tantra of the Arising of Śaṃvara. Śaṃvarodayatantra. bDe mchog 'byung ba'i rgyud.* Dg.K. rgyud, *kha* (Toh. 373).

*Tantra of the Ornament of the Vajra Essence. Vajrahṛdayālaṃkāratantra. rDo rje snying po rgyan gyi rgyud.* Dg.K. rgyud, *cha* (Toh. 451).

*Vajraḍāka. Vajraḍākatantra. rDo rje mkha' 'gro.* Dg.K. rgyud, *kha* (Toh. 370).

*Vajrapañjara Tantra. Ḍākinīvajrapañjaratantra. rDo rje gur gyi rgyud.* Dg.K. rgyud, *nga* (Toh. 419).

*Verses That Summarize the Perfection of Wisdom. Prajñāpāramitāsaṃcayagāthā. Shes rab kyi pha rol tu phyin pa sdud pa tshigs su bcad pa.* Dg.K. sher phyin, *ka* (Toh. 13).

### *Treatises (Tengyur and Other Texts)*

Āryaśūra. *The Series of Lives. Jātakamāla. sKyes pa'i rabs kyi rgyud.* Dg.T. mdo 'grel (skyes rabs), *hu* (Toh. 4150).

Jamgön Kongtrul Lodrö Taye. *dPal ldan bla ma dam par mnyes pa tshul bzhin 'grub pa'i smon lam bla ma lnga bcu pa'i bsdus don dang 'brel ba mdo sngags kun gyi yang snying. A Prayer Summarizing the Gurupañcāśikā by Aśvaghoṣa.* In *rGya chen bka' mdzod*, vol. 9 (*ta*). Paro: 1975-6. BDRC 23723.

Shāntideva. *Bodhicaryāvatāra. Byang chub sems dpa'i spyod pa la 'jug pa.* Dg.T. mdo 'grel (dbu ma), *la* (Toh. 3871).

Vasubandhu. *The Well-Explained Reasoning. Vyākhyāyukti. rNam bshad rig pa.* Dg.T. mdo 'grel (sems tsam), *shi* (Toh. 4061).

## 3. Reference Bibliography

### *Tibetan Texts*

Abhayadatta. *The Lives of the Eighty-Four Siddhas. Grub thob brgyad cu rtsa bzhi'i rnam mthar.* Reprinted from *Grub thob brgyad cu rtsa bzhi'i chos skor.* New Delhi: Chophel Legdan, 1973. In Abhayadatta. *Buddha's Lions: The Lives of the Eighty-Four Siddhas.* Translated by James B. Robinson. Berkeley, CA: Dharma Publishing, 1979.

*Collection of Texts from Dzongsar Lama Lhakhang in Derge. Khams sde dge rdzong sar bla ma lha khang du bzhugs pa'i dpe rnying.* Vol. 209. A printing of vol. 11 (*ta*) of the Palpung woodblocks, identical in most respects to DNZ-K. BDRC W3PD988.

Great Dictionary. *Bod rgya tshig mdzod chen mo.* Beijing: Mi rigs dpe skrun khang, 1986.

Jonang Lotsawa (jo nang lo tsA ba blo gros dpal). *Veneration of the Teacher* (*bLa ma mchod pa'i cho ga mchod pa'i gter*). In *Jo nang lo tsA'i gsung mthor*, pp. 177–89. Beijing: Mi rigs dpe skrun khang, 2008.

Rechungpa, oral lineage of. *bDe mchog snyan brgyud kyi rdzogs rim steng sgo rnam par grol ba'i chos drug gi khrid yig.* DNZ. Vol. 7 (*ja*), pp. 501–53. Delhi: Shechen Publications, 1999.

Vīraprabhāsvara. *The Essence of the Eighty-Four Siddhas' Realization. Caturaśītisiddhasambodhihṛdaya. Grub thob brgyad cu rtsa bzhi'i rtogs pa'i snying po.* Dg.T. rgyud 'grel, *zhi* (Toh. 2292).

***Translations and Other Works in English***

Abhayadatta. *Buddha's Lions: The Lives of the Eighty-Four Siddhas.* Translated by James B. Robinson. Berkeley, CA: Dharma Publishing, 1979.

Conze, Edward, trans. *Aṣṭasāhasrikā Prajñāpāramitā (The Perfection of Wisdom in Eight Thousand Lines).* Bibliotheca Indica. Calcutta: Asiatic Society, 1958.

Deroche, Marc-Henri. "'Phreng po gter ston Shes rab 'od zer (1518–1584) on the Eight Lineages of Attainment: Research on a Ris med Paradigm." In *Contemporary Visions in Tibetan Studies: Proceedings of the First International Seminar of Young Tibetologists.* Chicago: Serindia Publications, 2009.

Dharmachakra Translation Committee, trans. *The Play in Full.* 84000: Translating the Words of the Buddha, 2016. https://read.84000.co/translation/UT22084-046-001.html.

Dowman, Keith. *Masters of Mahamudra: Songs and Histories of the Eighty-Four Buddhist Siddhas.* Albany: State University of New York Press, 1985.

Jamgön Kongtrul Lodrö Taye. *The Catalog of The Treasury of Precious Instructions.* Translated by Richard Barron (Chökyi Nyima). New York: Tsadra Foundation, 2013.

———. *The Treasury of Knowledge, Book 4: Buddhism's Journey to Tibet.* Translated by the Kalu Rinpoché Translation Group (Ngawang Zangpo). Ithaca, NY: Snow Lion Publications, 2010.

———. *The Treasury of Knowledge, Book 6, Part 4: Systems of Buddhist Tantra.* Translated by the Kalu Rinpoché Translation Group (Elio Guarisco and Ingrid McLeod). Ithaca, NY: Snow Lion Publications, 2005.

———. *The Treasury of Knowledge, Book 8, Part 3: The Elements of Tantric Practice.* Translated by the Kalu Rinpoché Translation Group (Elio Guarisco and Ingrid McLeod). Ithaca, NY: Snow Lion Publications, 2008.

———. *The Treasury of Knowledge, Book 8, Part 4: Esoteric Instructions.* Translated by the Kalu Rinpoché Translation Group (Sarah Harding). Ithaca, NY: Snow Lion Publications, 2007.

———. *The Treasury of Knowledge, Books 9 & 10: Journey and Goal.* Translated by the Kalu Rinpoché Translation Group (Richard Barron). Ithaca, NY: Snow Lion Publications, 2011.

Jigme Lingpa. *Treasury of Precious Qualities, Book Two: Vajrayana and the Great Perfection.* With a commentary by Longchen Yeshe Dorje, Kangyur Rinpoche. Translated by the Padmakara Translation Group. Boston: Shambhala Publications, 2013.

Kapstein, Matthew I. "King Kungji's Banquet." In *Tantra in Practice.* Edited by David Gordon White. Princeton, NJ: Princeton University Press, 2000.

Maitreya/Asaṅga/Jamgön Mipham. *A Feast of the Nectar of the Supreme Vehicle: An Explanation of the Ornament of the Mahāyāna Sūtras.* Translated by the Padmakara Translation Group. Boulder: Shambhala Publications, 2018.

Ringu Tulku. *The Ri-me Philosophy of Jamgön Kongtrul the Great: A Study of the Buddhist Lineages of Tibet.* Boston: Shambhala Publications, 2012.

Roberts, Peter Alan. *Mahāmudrā and Related Instructions: Core Teachings of the Kagyü Schools.* Institute of Tibetan Classics. Somerville, MA: Wisdom Publications, 2011.

Roerich, George N., trans. *The Blue Annals.* 1949. 2nd ed. Delhi: Motilal Banarsidass, 1976.

Smith, E. Gene. *Among Tibetan Texts: History and Literature of the Himalayan Plateau.* Somerville, MA: Wisdom Publications, 2001.

Stearns, Cyrus. *Luminous Lives: The Story of the Early Masters of the Lam 'bras in Tibet.* Somerville, MA: Wisdom Publications, 2001.

Tsongkhapa. *A Lamp to Illuminate the Five Stages.* Translated by Gavin Kilty. Institute of Tibetan Classics. Somerville, MA: Wisdom Publications, 2013.

### *Online Reference Sources*

84000: Translating the Words of the Buddha. 84000.co

Buddhist Canons Research Database. http://databases.aibs.columbia.edu/

Buddhist Digital Resource Center. https://www.tbrc.org/

Himalayan Art Resources. https://www.himalayanart.org/

Resources for Kanjur & Tanjur Studies. https://www.istb.univie.ac.at/kanjur/rktsneu/

Treasury of Lives. https://treasuryoflives.org/

# Index